A SISTER'S STORY.

BY

MRS. AUGUSTUS CRAVEN.

TRANSLATED FROM THE FRENCH

BY

EMILY BOWLES.

"Fundamenta æterna super petram solidam, et mandata Dei in corde mulieris sanctæ."
Ecclus. xxvi. 24.

NEW YORK:
THE CATHOLIC PUBLICATION SOCIETY,
126 NASSAU STREET.

1868.

John A. Gray & Green, Printers, 16 and 18 Jacob Street, New York.

A SISTER'S STORY.

PART I.

> "Give me the pleasure with the pain,
> So would I live and love again."

SUCH are the words in which a modern poet embodied the feeling which leads us to cherish the most sorrowful memories, rather than bury in oblivion the joys and the griefs of the past. This has always been my own feeling, and I never could admit as a truth of general application, the assertion contained in Dante's famous lines:

> "Nessun maggior dolore,
> Che ricordarsi del tempo felice
> Nella miseria."

No. I do not wish to forget either the joys or the sorrows I have known. I bless God for both, and I bless Him also that He has made me love to dwell constantly on the remembrance of those with whom it was so delightful to live. The thought of those happy days spent with them has ever been a joy, not a sorrow to me; and far from wishing to lose the recollection of the past, my most fervent desire is to preserve it faithfully impressed on my mind, and to succeed in making others know and appreciate the beloved ones whose society imparted so great a charm to bygone days. I delight in thinking of them and speaking of them since their deaths, just as I used to delight in talking to them, and being with them, when they were on earth. My chief occupation has been to collect and arrange whatever papers and letters I could obtain, that bore the stamp of their thoughts and minds; and I must plead guilty to a feeling of affectionate pride in seeing even comparative strangers struck and interested by portions of these manuscripts which I have, as I said, undertaken to put together in a consecutive form. It will please me, I own, to extend the sweet influence of their examples and of their memory beyond their domestic circle, and to make many acquainted with them who may have met them in the world without knowing, though it may be, not without noticing them. If any of these should be ignorant of the love of God, this work may perhaps inspire them with a desire to learn more of the Divine principle which pervades every line of it, and mixes with every thought. I cannot but hope that they would find in it some interest, and would not close the book without questioning whether it can be really true that the pious habits of a Catholic life "impede the development of the mind, enslave the soul,"* or harden the heart; and if it is not, on the contrary, evident that those beings so devoted to God, would have lost, even in the eyes of men, their greatest charm, had they lacked that piety which was the mainspring of their lives.

I should be glad, indeed, if certain writers of our own day, who draw such repulsive pictures of women, would study this record in which all the feelings of youth are faithfully portrayed. Could they assert, in the face of it, that a heart, habitually under the influence of the Divine Presence, must necessarily be wanting in tenderness towards relatives and friends, or lack enthusiasm for whatever is beautiful in nature and art? Could they maintain that the habitual remembrance of the world to come, must fill the mind with sadness and with affected solemnity, or suppose that the subjects of this memoir, whose manners and conversation delighted even strangers, were ever considered stiff and morose because of their piety? It is precisely because they lived in the world and followed its ordinary customs, and were not recluses and inmates of the cloister, that I hope the history of their lives will prove useful to many who turn away dismayed and discouraged from examples of more austere sanctity.

My chief difficulty has risen from the abundance of materials which the death of my beloved ones has placed in my hands; from the perplexity of deciding what to select and what to suppress. Amongst these treasures there exists one so complete and interesting that in itself it would furnish materials for a separate work. I mean the story of Alexandrine, who, by her

* Lord Russell's Letter to the Bishop of Durham.

marriage with my brother Albert, became my sister; a sister so dear and so intimately united to me, that the tie of blood could scarcely have bound us more closely together. When we first met in Russia, in the early days of our girlhood, and again in Italy, in the brightest period of our youth, Alexandrine was endeared to me by similarity of age, of tastes, and by all that inspires mutual affection between young people, as well as by sympathy in higher and holier joys. Our friendship remained one of those which nothing in life can change, and which death itself cannot weaken. When this beloved friend married into our family, she became so entirely one of us, that I do not think my mother could have felt differently toward her had she been her own daughter. Since that time Providence has allotted us some of the sweetest and darkest hours life can present. After sharing joys and sorrows such as are not often met with, our friendship was cemented by the strongest and most sacred of all ties. United as we had been by common tastes, feelings, and inclinations, we were at last bound together by the highest of all sympathies, that of a common faith. From that time forward, amidst our many and severe trials, we experienced consolations so deep and so Divine, that we both reckoned those years of our lives, without comparison, the most precious.

Alexandrine's life was divided into two periods: one filled with varied incidents and strong emotions; the other by God alone, sought and found in the perfect surrender and sacrifice of self; a surrender so entire, and a sacrifice so sweet, that the word happiness can properly be applied only to this part of her existence. The first dawn of that new happiness arose at the very time when it seemed to her that she was parting for ever with everything to which she had till then given that name. But before this consummation was arrived at, at a time when the world, with all that love, youth, and pleasure could add of attraction, had vanished from her light, and the future presented nothing but a gloomy prospect of bitter sufferings, unsustained by any consolation, Alexandrine found her greatest solace in noting down all she could recollect of her life from the first moment that she had met with Albert till the day of his death. She called this memoir, "Our Love and our Life," and filled it with such copious and minute details, that, though covering only the space of four years, it furnishes three thick volumes of manuscript. The first is entitled "Love;" the second, "Love and Marriage;" the third, "Love, Marriage, and Death." These three divisions comprise so much that is at once simple and sublime, passionate and romantic, pious and heart-rending, all written in a charming, affecting, natural manner, that it seems almost a pity not to give it to the world in its fulness. Still there is no doubt that a narrative extending over a number of years, and filled in hour by hour, presents a photographic biography which can be uninterruptedly interesting only to intimate friends. Besides which, the almost morbid truthfulness which was Alexandrine's peculiar characteristic, her anxiety to note down every action, word, and even thought, with scrupulous exactness, her horror of exaggeration, her desire to relate the evil as well as the good with equal sincerity, made her indulge in an abundance of superfluous details, which prolong her narrative to a tedious extent. Many a time when, leaning over her shoulder, I read what she had been writing, I used to entreat her to shorten and compress those pages in which we were equally interested. Little did I then think that I should survive all the principal actors in that sorrowful drama, and that it would be one day my task to present it, not only to sorrowing friends, but to that awful unknown world, the Public!

I intend, therefore, to give ample extracts from Alexandrine's manuscript, not only because it accurately relates what took place, but because the characters of those whose history it gives are best learned from its pages. Besides Albert's portrait, which none could have drawn as she did, there appears that of Eugénie, the charming beloved sister, whose image is always the dearest and brightest in my heart. Eugénie, whose love was my greatest treasure, and whose death, after so many years, still remains the keenest, most distinct, and ineffaceable of all my sorrows. She filled as great a part in Alexandrine's life as in mine, and her manuscript makes frequent mention of her. With Albert's death the record comes to an end, and I should have been greatly at a loss how to complete Alexandrine's history if the thread of the narrative had not been carried on by her own and Eugénie's correspondence, together with the letters of my young sister Olga, who rapidly trod the same upward path, and at the age of twenty gave up her soul like a young saint into the Hands of God.

I have only to add that when, from time to time, I have introduced into these volumes what I had myself written in former days, it has been for the sole purpose of filling up interruptions, in the narrative, or connecting together what would have been otherwise a series of fragments. If I am blamed for it, or if the style of these insertions should be found inferior to the rest of the book, I shall not be surprised or disappointed, provided that this work soothes the sorrows and touches the feelings of pious and gentle hearts, for whom alone it is intended. God forbid that any literary vanity or desire of praise should mingle with the motives which have influenced this publication.

My brother Charles was not born until my parents had been married several years, and he was for a considerable time their only child. Later on they had as many as ten children, four of whom died young. The remaining seven grew up and attained a mature age.*

In 1819 my father was appointed French Ambassador at St. Petersburgh, and it was in that city that the early years of my childhood were spent. But, however pleasant, I do not care to dwell upon them, for at that time Eugénie, who was some years younger than myself, was almost a stranger to me. At that age the difference of studies, hours, and occupations, creates a real separation between sisters, and Eugénie, in after life, used to laugh and say that she had *made my acquaintance* only in 1829. It was in Italy that this acquaintanceship began, and I find it alluded to in some notes of my own, written at the time when I was first obliged to learn to live without her. I will make some extracts from these notes.

"Having left Paris in 1829, I proceeded to Italy with my father, then seriously ill, and after my mother and Eugénie had joined us, we established ourselves at the Villa Civitella, near Lucca, intending to spend the rest of the summer there. In the same place, but in another house, thirteen years later, my father and Eugénie spent the last summer of their lives; but now, in

* This was the case at the time the above lines were written. Since then the two brothers who had survived Albert, whose life and death form the principal subject of the ensuing memoir, have been taken from us. Charles died in 1863 after a long illness, endured with Christian fortitude. Fernand, the youngest, expired suddenly this very year, whilst driving in the carriage with the Prince (the Comte de Chambord) to whom he had devoted his life.

1829, long years of happiness seemed to be in store for us, and this one in particular, the first we passed in Italy, as I look back to it, appears to me radiant with enjoyment and delight. Eugénie's governess had remained in Paris, and it seemed to us as if for the first time in our lives we were really together. We had indeed a third companion in our cousin, Elizabeth de Bellevue, but she was not only no obstacle to our intimacy, but added a charm to it by the holy and good thoughts with which her mind was always stored. Eugénie had always loved me, but until the time I am speaking of she had never felt perfectly at her ease with me. Then began a strict friendship, and one that can never cease. I had already been introduced into society, and amused myself very much in that new world I had become acquainted with. Now I wanted Eugénie to share that amusement with me, but she shrank from going out, and wished neither to see nor to be seen. She had contrived to hurt her foot about the time that the Grand Duke was about to give a ball, and wanted to make this an excuse for staying at home. Her foot, however, became well enough to permit of her going to this ball. She found it less formidable than she had imagined, and we both amused ourselves extremely. From that night forward there were no parties worth anything to either of us unless we enjoyed them together.

"I began to read to her out loud, and I made her acquainted with some of my favorite English poets. She had always declared that she was not clever enough to take pleasure in literature, and when she discovered how thoroughly she liked and appreciated everything beautiful, she confessed her surprise with the utmost naïveté, maintaining with her characteristic humility that it was I who made her enjoy what—without me—she would neither have understood, appreciated, nor cared for. This fancy, which arose from her affection for me, and her very low opinion of herself, is often reverted to in her letters, in the sweetest and most endearing manner, and that time spoken of as one of the most intense happiness.

"We remained at the Villa Civitella until September, and then set out with our excellent friends M. and Madame de Marcellus on an expedition through the north of Italy. We visited Venice, Milan, Como, and Lecco, and returning by Bellaggio to Lugano and the Lago Maggiore, went to Arona and Baveno, where we met the courier, who was bringing my father the news of his appointment as ambassador at Rome. This circumstance hastened our return to France, which we reached by way of the Simplon. We crossed the magnificent pass for the first time, full of the joyous sense of present happiness, and the glowing anticipations of future delights. We did not go directly to Paris, but to Montigny, not far from Vendôme, on the banks of the Loire, an estate belonging to our parents, but which had been to us a home more in name than in reality. It had never seemed to us so attractive as during the last months of that year. In January my father started for Rome, with my brother Charles and our young sister-in-law, and I returned to Paris with our mother and Eugénie for the winter. It was not until the month of April, 1830, that we joined my father at Rome. To return to Italy was a greater pleasure than even to see it for the first time, and the delight of this journey accordingly surpassed that of the previous one. Besides, we were now for the first time on our way to Rome, the object of my longing dreams since my earliest childhood. It was the loveliest season of the year. I had my sister with me, to sympathize in all my feelings, and we were looking forward to being once more with my father, who was to take us into society, and to make us spend our time in the pleasantest manner possible. In short, not a cloud darkened the bright aspect of the present or of the future, and of all the happy periods of my life, this always remains in my mind as the very sunniest.

"On the first or second of May we drove into Rome, in a thick fog, which the feeble light of the moon could scarcely struggle through. By this fitful gleam, however, I first beheld Rome, and as we passed the Porta del Popolo, I felt deeply impressed. The French embassy was then at the Palazzo Simonetti, in the Corso, and there we soon arrived. My father and my sister-in-law greeted us with the warmest welcome, and we were led up along the broad staircase to the apartments, which he had arranged in the most perfect manner for our comfort. During the short time of our stay at the Simonetti Palace, we were thoroughly happy, and often in after life our thoughts flew wistfully back to that too brief residence in Rome. We little imagined that those charming three months would be the last we should ever spend in the enjoyment of that degree of position and fortune.

"In July we left Rome for Naples, for my father was beginning to suffer from the heat, and was ordered a change of air. It had been at first settled that he was to go alone, in which case our subsequent life would probably have turned out a very different one, for if the news of the events of July had reached us at Rome, we should probably have left Italy immediately, and never seen Naples at all. As it was, we had all been settled there three weeks, when the tidings of the revolution of 'the three days,' the 28th, 29th, and 30th of July, burst upon us like a thunder-clap.

"My father instantly sent in his resignation, and we were all going back to Rome in order to pack up our things and leave Italy altogether, when suddenly my two sisters, Olga and Albertine, fell so ill, that my mother was not able to leave them. Thus no plans could be made for the future, and everything that had been arranged was unsettled. My sister-in-law, Emma (my brother Charles's wife), and I, accompanied my father to Rome. Again, after that short interval of three weeks, we beheld our dear home in the Palazzo Simonetti, now half unfurnished and dismantled, and filled with packages lying about in sad confusion. A pair of beautiful horses and a calèche, which had been sent from Vienna for my father, were to be sold on the morrow. We took our single and last drive in it round the walls of Rome. That evening was melancholy enough. I regretted Rome exceedingly, and I regretted also the loss of the delightful position we had occupied there. But I did not allow myself to indulge in these feelings, for my father had always carefully prepared us for an impending change of circumstances, and thus strengthened us against the evil day. I quickly recovered my spirits, and determined not to be cast down by any change of fortune, nor to add one feather's weight to the sorrow my dear father felt on our account, and also for France.

"I returned to Naples in September, and was heartily glad to find myself once more with my mother and Eugénie. They had established themselves in a little villa at Castellamare, which seemed to us very ugly and desolate after the charming houses we had left. The little room in particular where I slept, with Eugénie and Emma, appeared more dismal and shabby than even the rest of the house; but the view from it was so magnificent, that we gradually became reconciled to its defects.

There was one great saloon, bare and empty, the windows of which looked full on the Bay of Naples and the heights of Castellamare. Into this room we brought our tables and chairs, and Eugénie, Emma, Albert, and I, spent our mornings there, reading, writing, talking, and laughing, though in utter ignorance of what was to become of us for the future. We fancied our fate might resemble that of our parents during the first emigration; that we might be reduced to a state approaching to destitution, and on this prevision we formed our plans. Eugénie was to give music lessons, and I determined on taking a situation as nursery governess. Despite these castles in the air, the beginning of the year 1831 found us established once more in a very pretty house on the Chiaia, next door to Sir Richard Acton's palace, where his mother, Lady Acton, used to receive. Instead of the lowly destiny we had been forecasting, we spent the winter in the most brilliant and agreeable society. Lady Acton gathered round her all the young people of her acquaintance, with whom we danced, sang, represented tableaux, and acted plays. Indeed, our evenings were spent in such incessant gaiety, that the retrospect gave Eugénie many fits of remorse, and later in life she used often to say that she did not like to look back to that time. But I, who am less scrupulous, must own that I do so with unalloyed pleasure. We were so happy together! And then her humility was so genuine, her simplicity of heart so unspoilt, her gaiety so childlike and contagious, that I am sure she could have no occasion for self-reproach, even during what she called her worldly life. Compliments addressed to herself never gave her the least pleasure, whereas, if something flattering was said about her darling Pauline, she was delighted. It offended her mortally to be told that anybody liked her better than me, or even that her eyes or teeth were prettier than mine. She could not endure to be asked to dance if I had not a partner, and what annoyed her particularly was, that the young king always danced with her, and never with me. During all that time I do not remember to have seen her in any instance vain, frivolous, or occupied with herself, but was the same humble, devoted, unselfish being as ever. I therefore think and believe, that God passed a less severe judgment upon those days than she did herself. There were bright moments when we especially enjoyed the delight of being together. For instance, when at about five o'clock in the morning we went into the garden of the Acton Palace to gather flowers for our evening banquets. We then conversed more intimately than ever, and very seldom did it happen that we did not say, over and over again, at those times, 'Oh, how nice it is to be together!' We often spoke, too, of God and of Heaven, for we were never long without interchanging thoughts of this kind. I have often remembered it since with pleasure, but I must honestly admit, that we talked also of the party of the preceding night, and of the friends we hoped to meet again in the evening. The perfume of the nosegays we made during those morning strolls, remained associated with memories still sweeter than themselves. Neither of us in after days could smell the peculiar scent of those Neapolitan flowers, without being carried back to that palace garden; without beholding again—in imagination—that southern sea, that cloudless sky, all the bright dreams and visions of our youth, which a sudden whiff of the familiar fragrance would still conjure up, after the lapse of many sadder years.

"In May, 1831, we made a delightful expedition to the Villa Sora, to stay with M. Lefebvre,* whose eldest daughter Flavie (Marquise de Raigecourt) was Eugénie's greatest friend. Often separated during life, they were singularly brought together towards its close, and dying nearly at the same time, are now doubtless united in their eternal home. Charles and Emma had left us before this visit, after which we went again to Castellamare, and remained there till the end of the summer. Fernand was away, and Albert, the only one of my brothers who stayed on with us, sympathised so entirely in all my tastes, that I was scarcely more attached to Eugénie than to him. I need not describe Albert, for the work I have undertaken will, as it goes on, amply make known his character. But though I had always loved him as the kindest and gentlest of brothers, I did not at first discern how much there was to be admired in his mind and character. He had enjoyed, perhaps, even more than we did, our stay at Naples, but it had been a more dangerous visit to him than to us. Several times during the course of that winter, he had said that it was not good for him to remain in a place where a serious kind of life was impossible, and that he would soon leave us for a while, to fortify his soul in some

* The Comte de Balsorano.

solitude. This he actually did in the course of the following autumn. I found him one day walking alone, and sad, on the terrace before the house. We paced up and down together for a long time, and he told me he was very much out of spirits, and dissatisfied with himself; for that he really wanted to be good, and to fill his mind with great and noble desires, but that at Naples it was too easy to lose sight of all thoughts of this kind; that he had not strength enough to keep his resolutions, and that he had been saying the same thing to his father, who had consented to his leaving us, so that he was really going away for a time.

"I felt very sorry to hear this; I liked to be with him better than with any one else in the world, and his absence would make, I thought, a sad blank in our home circle. He did go about a week afterwards to Florence, to join his friend M. Rio, with whom he made an expedition into Tuscany, visiting every place of religious or historical note in that part of Italy. The interest these scenes inspired and the amount of reading requisite in order to make this tour a profitable one, speedily restored to Albert the energy which Naples had weakened. When he returned to Florence he made a sort of retreat, at the close of which he approached the sacraments, and fixed on a rule of life which he never ceased to observe till the day of his death. These resolutions, and the desire to regulate his future life, were confirmed by the acquaintance he made that year with Count Charles de Montalembert.* From that time forward a strict friendship united them. With his two excellent companions [Montalembert and Rio], Albert made some further stay in Florence, and went with them to Rome in January, 1832, where, as if to reward him for his good resolutions, he found in Alexandrine, whom he there saw for the first time, the true love, the object and the happiness of his life."

And here begins the actual story of Alexandrine; not hers alone, indeed, but that of many others, especially in the first part of her narrative. Her memoir is somewhat desultory, consisting as it does of all the papers she could collect connected with the four years over which it extends; of her journal and

* M. de Montalembert was then about to meet Messieurs de Lamennais and Lacordaire, in order to submit to the Holy See certain opinions advocated in the *Avenir*.

Albert's, of their letters to each other, and those they wrote to intimate friends, connected more or less by remarks suggested by her husband, or by the thoughts which occurred to herself as she wrote.

It may be as well to mention here, that Alexandrine was the daughter of a German mother and a Swedish father,* and never lived in France before her marriage. This fact will account for her having been brought up in habits of greater independence than is allowed to French girls. If the expediency of previous acquaintance and the existence of mutual affection before marriage could be decided by the strength of a single instance, I cannot but think that the story of Albert and Alexandrine would throw a preponderating weight in the scale of that side of the question; and that a marriage such as theirs, preceded by a love as noble as it was pure, is of all others the most likely to create a tender and lasting union, ending in the more sacred and indissoluble ties of an eternal home.

ALEXANDRINE'S STORY.

"On one particular Friday (sacred to the Guardian Angels), while I was still in deep mourning for my father, at Rome, in 1832, I saw Albert for the first time. He came to pay a visit to my mother. I was in another apartment engaged in conversation with a friend who lodged in the same house with us (Casa Margherita). I did not go up to our salon for some time, though I had been told that Pauline de la Ferronnays' brother was there. I had a great wish to know him, however, and fancied we had seen him at Church the evening before. At last I went into our drawing-room and met him with indifference. He did not strike me as handsome, though I liked the expression of his eyes, and he left me altogether with rather a pleasant impression. I heard from him since that he fell in love with me that first day, and had told his friends how much I had captivated him; but they had made a joke of it, and he never mentioned me to them again.

"February 5th.—I went with my young friend, Mary M——,

* Count d'Alopeus, Russian Minister at Berlin, and Jeanne de Wenkstern, who afterwards married Prince Paul Lapoukhyn. Alexandrine's godfather being the Emperor Alexander, she was immersed at baptism according to the rite of the Greek Church. It was in consequence not considered necessary to give her conditional baptism when she was received into the Church.

to hear the nuns sing at the Trinità da Monte. There I saw M. de la Ferronays (as I called Albert in those days), on his knees. Something about him interested me in a way I could not account for; and I must have felt some confidence in him, for, finding myself near him as we went out of the Church, I said I should have liked to kneel down as he had done, and that if his sisters had been there I should have done so. 'Then why not have done it now?' he replied. 'Why give way to human respect?' This straightforward way of speaking in a young man of twenty pleased me. No one before had made me that sort of sensible answer. As he was going down the steps of the Trinità with us, I looked more attentively at his face and countenance. I wanted him to come to us in the evening, and he did so.

"February 9th.—I had been spitting blood a little. My throat was still weak in consequence of an illness I had at Berlin. I saw that Albert was very uneasy about me, and I began to feel rather shy with him. He came to us oftener, and M. Rio also. By degrees I summoned up courage to sing to them. They were both absurdly pleased—especially with 'Moëris.' This song pleased them all three, for it was not long before M. de Montalembert began to like it as much as the others did. I sang with Albert, and liked his deep, sweet, full-toned bass voice, which somehow or other went to my heart, though at that time I did not yet think I cared for him, and indeed I did not. But I found, nevertheless, great pleasure in singing with him. He used to laugh at his own singing, and thought very little of it; but when did he ever think much of anything he did? Still he always sang when I asked him, without making any stupid fuss about it.

"February 24th.—Albert and I, with my mother and M. Rio, took a walk this day, which I shall never forget. We went first to the Villa Mattei, and then to the Villa Pamphili. I was very much pleased with the conversation I had with Albert at the Villa Mattei, and when we got to the Pamphili we fell back a little to talk together without being heard. There is a great sympathy in our views and our tastes, and under those grand pines, and looking at that wonderful view, we spoke quite freely of religion, of eternity, and of the sweetness that might attend death itself amidst scenes such as those we were then gazing on. This conversation, so unlike the frivolous talk which wearied me in ordinary society, sank deeply in my heart.

"March 1st.—In the midst of the Carnival follies with which the Corso was then filled, Albert threw me one day an enormous bunch of violets. This gave me great pleasure, and renewed my enjoyment of the Corso. Albert was so clever in throwing bouquets, and catching everything I threw in return. Mamma plaited a watch chain for him, which I threw him one day tied round a nosegay.

"Shrove Tuesday.—M. de Montalembert came to us this evening, which he had seldom done during his stay in Rome. Albert told me he was very jealous of him; his excessive modesty made him think everybody pleasanter than himself. For my part, even at that time, I would rather have seen him come into the room than either of his friends.

"March 19th.—I went to a concert given by Princess Zénaïde Wolkonsky, which I enjoyed because Albert was there. I did not know it, however, till he came to put us into the carriage. As we were going downstairs he begged us to drive to the Coliseum, where he was going with some friends to see it by moonlight. How I longed to go with him!

"March 31st.—Catiche* came to wake me early, and said that M. Rio was come to beg me to write to Albert, who was very ill, and would not see a doctor. I got up quite frightened, and with Mamma's consent, I wrote a few hasty lines to Albert, entreating him to be prudent, and to take care of himself for his family's sake, *and for ours.* The next day he was worse, and M. Rio came in the evening and gave me a little note from Albert, with an air of mystery which put me a little out of countenance. However, I took it from him and read it immediately, in order that my mother might see it at once, though I would much rather have had my note and the pleasure of it to myself. It contained these words: 'It is not a dream, then! I have read your note a hundred times since yesterday, and I shall read it again every day after my morning prayers. You will find that I am obedient now, for what I refused my best friends, I have done at a word from you. How come you to have such influence over me? Can no one influence *you* on the one point which makes you now so often sad and restless? Let us at

* A niece of Madame d'Alopeus, who lived with them.

least unite in begging of God the grace which brings happiness with it. It is very good of you to pray for one so undeserving as I am, and I must ask you to continue to do so, for indeed I need prayers.—ALBERT.'

"O my God, Thou art witness that in these his first written words to me, he spoke more of his desire for my conversion than of his own love, and revealed the intensity of that greater desire before he showed me the strength of his affection. Reward him, O my God, with Thy best blessing, for this singleness of heart, or rather let the blessing fall on me, for I have more need of it in Thy sight than he has now!

"M. Rio left me rather embarrassed, and then M. de Montalembert came to tell us that Albert was worse, and that he was going to be bled. I suffered very much that evening. I felt confused, and anxious about Albert; but so touched that he had written to me when he was so ill. And then I was a little doubtful how my mother would take that allusion to religion. I dreaded showing her the note, though delay made it only worse, and the longer I put it off the more difficult it seemed to be. I was glad that I had to go out the next day as soon as I was up to see Cardinal Fesch's gallery. But my mother expressed some surprise that I had not yet shown her the note, and I went to my room to fetch it; but, as I again felt great misgivings as to the religious part of it, I tried to cut it out. In my hurry I ran the scissors into my finger, and some drops of blood stained the paper, which gave me a sad feeling of superstitious fear. I went out altogether upset, and could not enjoy a single picture in the gallery. When I gave the note to my mother, I remember praying that she might be more struck with its beginning than the end, which really did happen, for all she said was, that it was rather too affectionate.

"March 27th.—Albert came to see us quite well, and in such spirits he could hardly contain himself. Neither have I forgotten how he kissed my mother's hand and mine. I only found out long afterwards that about that time he went out very early in the morning, and barefooted, in the Roman pilgrim's garb, made the round of the Seven Churches to obtain my conversion.*

* He also offered his life for the same intention. Alexandrine, herself, when confirmed in the Lutheran Church at the age of fifteen, had made a solemn offering of the happiness of life, that she might obtain in return a clear knowledge of Divine truth.

"My room had a delightful view. On one side it looked on all Rome and St. Peter's, which is rather below us. Above, on the other side, stands the Trinità da Monte and its obelisk. A group of rose-trees under my window completed the charm of this prospect. Albert often walked on the Pincio that he might see my window, and sometimes complained that I was myself so seldom to be seen there.

"April 5th.—A grand picnic at Princess Wolkonsky's. Albert came to take me downstairs to Miss M——, my English friend's room, with whom I was to go. I think it was then, as we were going down the stairs, that he said to me, 'We are now like a brother and sister.' We all met at the Porta Maggiore, and the fête was at Terra Nuova. Far away between the trees stretched the mountain line of Albano, touched with its own magical hues. At dinner Albert sat by me, and his other neighbour was Louise Vernet, who was so beautiful that I quite envied her. He was rather attentive to her, but it did not make me at all jealous or anxious. I was not then in love with him, though now I can scarcely think there was ever a time when I did not care for him.

"We played at all sorts of games, and then walked to look at the view, and on one of the hills where we are all standing—I do not exactly know how it came about—but he asked me to call him my brother. I did so with great pleasure, and it made him very happy. We did not get into the carriage again till it was nearly dark. Albert was sitting opposite me, and, looking up to the glorious starry sky, he said, 'Let us for a moment both thank God for the happiness you have given me to-day.' I was surprised, for until then, I had been accustomed only to the conversation of worldly people. But I liked this feeling in him, and we raised our hearts together to God. Only I thought Albert estimated my friendship for him too highly.

"I had been collecting for a long time all our visiting cards, and pasting them into a book. Albert sometimes helped me. Under his own, he wrote—'It is like the sweet beginning of an eternal existence, to live in the hearts of those who regret us.' They seemed to me strange and solemn words to write in an album full of nonsense. A few days afterwards, M. de G——, while turning over the pages of this album, saw this card. He read the words under it, and said to me, laughing, 'That youth is quite mad!" A long time afterwards, Albert tore out that card (but I kept it), and stuck a blank one in its place.

"About that time I began to think that even if Albert were not Pauline's brother, I should like him very much; but I still maintained that what I felt for him was only friendship.

"Wednesday in Holy week, April 18th.—I went with the M——'s to hear the *Miserere*, in the Sixtine Chapel. Albert was with us. Hiding behind Miss M——, I knelt down, so that her aunt—whose remarks I dreaded—could not see me, and it pleased me to think that perhaps Albert would.

"Thursday, April 19th.—I went again with the M——s and Albert to hear the beautiful *Miserere*, in the Choir Chapel at St. Peter's. I felt so much more intimate with him than with my friends, though I talked most to them. We saw many of the ceremonies at St. Peter's that evening, so that we did not get home till nine o'clock. Albert and I dined together on what had been put aside for me. It so happened, that the pedantry and severity of —— were talked of. He was quite surprised at the impatient and irritable manner in which I spoke, and said that his sister would make me gentle, she was so gentle herself. I am always touched by the way in which he speaks of his sisters.

"Whilst Albert's society pleased me every day more, that of my English friends grew less and less agreeable to me. I went, however, to St. Peter's with them. M. de G—— gave me his arm in the Church. I was vexed not to be taken care of by Albert, especially in so sacred a place, and I thought that it annoyed him also. As we were coming out of the Church, he told me how painful it had been to him, and a long time afterwards, when we had been married several months, he told me that he had never forgotten that disagreeable feeling. That evening, on the steps of St. Peter's, in the lovely twilight which was shedding its soft beauty on all that glorious scene, he said to me: 'Even in friendship there is jealousy.' It was on those same steps of St Peter's on the next or the previous day—I am not certain which—that he said to me: 'Oh, I am very happy, for I have been to Communion this morning, and I love you!' This startled me a little, though it was said as if he meant only that brotherly love, of which he was always talking.

"April 25th.—On that day we set out for Naples. Albert had started two days before. Though I was sorry to leave some of our friends at Rome, I felt great joy at the idea that I was going to live with Albert's sisters and near him. That charming road —especially beyond Terracina—was scented with orange blossoms. The weather was beautiful, and the glorious approach to Naples, which delights the most indifferent eyes, has always filled me with ecstacy. We drove to the Casa Paretti, on the Chiaja, and before the carriage stopped, I saw Albert close to the door, which made me very joyful. He looked beaming, and came up stairs with us, and then went to fetch Pauline, with whom he soon afterwards returned. That evening I wrote in my journal: 'I thank thee, O my God! I am at Naples, and I have seen Pauline de la Ferronays again.' The next day I saw all the family. Eugénie, whom I had left a girl of thirteen, is very handsome now. Every day we took long rambles together, and then they all went and established themselves at the Vomero, in the charming Villa Trecase, and after much hesitation my mother engaged a villa close to theirs, for the remainder of the summer. It was not a pretty house, and the garden was rather gloomy, for the magnificent view from the crest of the Vomero was only visible from the terrace which formed the roof of the house. But we spent such happy days there, that we ended by thinking it charming, and have always looked back to it with the same feeling.

"May 9th.—Spent some delicious hours with Pauline, on the terrace of the Villa Trecase. The day was perfect, and we looked upon a view which has no parallel on earth. Albert had gone to Amalfi with M. de Montalembert and M. Rio, who had just arrived. Pauline had found a little book, in which Albert wrote some of his own thoughts, as well as extracts from books. She brought it, and read what follows: 'A day like the one which has just ended, fills my heart with gratitude to God. Pauline and I spent some moments together, and I felt that the most complete sympathy existed between us. I had never before so thoroughly realized the sweetness of the tie between a brother and sister. I understood exactly what she felt, by what I felt myself. Why, then, did I sigh? Why do I crave after something more? I begin to see that friendship is in a certain sense more selfish, more exacting than that other kind of affection which makes us forget ourselves, and think of nothing but the object of our love. Under the influence of this last mentioned feeling, we are capable of making the most incredible sacrifice; that of life, if it were called for. . . . I felt, when I had left Pauline, that what seemed almost to satisfy my heart had done nothing but prepare the way for stronger emotions. But the end of that day did not correspond with the beginning . . . . I saw *her*, however, and was happy. But when I went away I was sad, and she seemed so cheerful.' Under this passage the following verses of Tasso were written and underlined:

"'Brama assai—poco spera—nulla chiede
Ne sa scopirsi o no ardisce: ed ella
O lo sprezza, o nol vede, o non s'accorde.
Cosi finora, il misero ha servito
O non visto—o mal noto, o mal gradito.' *

St. Augustine's exclamation, 'Everything that ends is so short,' is also written a little further on, and repeated four times. Pauline, who was thus letting me into the secrets of her brother's heart, thought she was making up for her indiscretion by not allowing me to have the book in my own hands, but I got hold of it, and found fastened to one of the pages the little nosegay, tied with a red ribbon, that I had thrown to Albert in the Corso, at Rome. Alas! it is lying there before me. Poor nosegay! it still remains where he placed it.

"On the same page there were also some verses of Victor Hugo's; this one which was underlined, struck me:

"'*Je m'en irai bientôt au milieu de la Fête.*' †

And further on, 'We fear death less when we are not afraid of what will follow death.'—*Massillon.* And again, 'I die young, and this is what I always wished. I die young, and yet I seem to have lived a long time. I would not disturb the peace of her sleep, or of her heart. No, no; I only ask for a few tears, and one of those remembrances that last as long as life, but do not embitter it.'

"Besides these sentences, he had written—'A terrible fit of

* "Sophronia, she, Olindo hight the youth,
Both of one town, both in one faith were taught;
She fair; he full of bashfulness and truth,
Loved much, hoped little, and desired nought.
He dared not speak by suit to purchase ruth;
She saw not, marked not, wist not what he sought.
Thus loved, thus served he long but not regarded,
Unseen, unmarked, unpitied, unrewarded."

WRIGHT'S TASSO.

† "I shall soon depart, in the midst of the festival."

spleen. I feel as if I lived through centuries instead of days. Nothing rouses me, not even the thought of *her.* I feel like a dead person, though I breathe and walk about. What is this deadly languor that sometimes makes me imagine I am no longer susceptible of any passion, nor even of any strong excitement, and which makes me envy commonplace people, because they seem to attach importance to the most trifling things.'

"On the following page I found these words :—'Rome, March 30th, 1832.—Ah! my dear father, people are called romantic by men of the world, when they choose to live only for what makes life honorable; and enthusiasm, according to their notions, is only a dangerous kind of fever. Fools! they dare not seek happiness from God. They ask only for the pleasures of the world, and end by being rejected both by God and the world.'

"He had written on the 5th of April, 1832 :—'Walked in the Campagna with ——.' It was the day I had called him *brother*, and he had added: 'There is something so pure and sweet in the name of sister, that it seems to sanction the feeling, tender beyond that of friendship, which takes shelter beneath it. Everything strengthens her increasing affection for me; everything feeds my passion for her. But to her the world remains unaltered, whilst for me *everything is changed.*'

"'*A Portrait*,' is written in very small letters, followed by these sentences :—

"'She possesses everything combined which inspires strong passion; grace, timidity, modesty, and one of those souls whose life is love; a mind enthusiastically devoted to everything good; a delicate frame, a disposition to lean on others, but a spirit so courageous and generous, that it would face death for virtue's sake.'

"There was not a passage in which, directly or indirectly, I did not find something that had reference to myself. The last one I read was this:

"'Vomero, May 3rd, 1832.—It gives me a particular pleasure to find in prose, or in verse, anything that expresses my own feelings, for lately I have been quite unable to do so myself. I am in such a disturbed and anxious state, that I cannot fix in my mind any of the numerous thoughts which come into it. Wishes, anxiety, regret, joy, are all mixed together in a confused manner, and agitate me so much, that I am afraid of going out of my mind.'

"Oh, what great pleasure this little book gave me! I did not disguise it from Pauline. I went away much happier than I had come, and I thought the view, and the matchless blue sea and sky, more lovely than ever. I felt a great interior delight in the sense of existence, and in being where I was, and yet if any one had asked me if I was happy, I should perhaps have said *no*. I did not yet acknowledge it to myself, but I felt as if the dawn of a glorious day was about to break upon me.

"Long afterwards I read what Albert was writing at that very time in his journal at Amalfi.

"'What blasphemy it is to say that we are doomed by God to nothing but misery in this world, Who most certainly created man to be happy, and how can such an absurd idea enter the minds of those who love Him? How ungrateful it is, also; and how often have I myself sinned in this way. Oh, thou whom I name only in the secret of my heart, I see thee everywhere, and I behold God, as it were, through thee!

"'Amalfi, the 11th of May.—How I should have liked to spend many days here, at the foot of these magnificent mountains. I admired their immeasurable height, and wondered that I could still soar above them, and rising higher than their golden summits, find them little, compared with my own thoughts, for my enraptured heart was entirely filled with the Presence of God. Those enchanting scenes seemed to me made on purpose for her and myself. Oh, delusive visions, doomed to premature destruction! To-morrow I return to Naples, and when I see her again, my happiness and dreams will vanish like smoke. I shall see her gentle, charming as ever, and treating me as a friend and a brother; but as to a mutual understanding, without the aid of speech, or a union of hearts felt and not expressed; these are blessings I cannot hope for. And when tremblingly I address her in a few agitated words, her indifferent manner will freeze me at once, and tell me that I have been cheating myself with vain fancies.'

"A few days after their return from Amalfi, Albert's two friends left him, and on the 18th of May he wrote the following letter to M. de Montalembert, who had gone to join M. de Lamennais at Rome.

"'My Dear Friend,—How I long to hear of you or from you. I cannot say how sorry I was not to go with you, for I am now so used to your society, that I do not feel able to do without it. There is a remarkable sympathy between us. We understand one another perfectly, and love one another dearly; your manner to me is never cold or sneering. Since you went, I feel to want you so much, for my unfortunate attachment is increasing terribly. Yes, my dear friend, I did not know how much I loved her. What can I do? Perhaps I ought to go away, but even if it was not for other reasons impossible, I do not think I could bring myself to do so. My life is here. But write and say you understand me; that you do not think me quite mad. I have just made a resolution, but I do not know if I shall have courage to keep it. I will not see her for a few days. I shall perhaps find out that the affection which appears to me so deeply rooted in my heart, has only slightly touched it. And now I am really afraid that you will think me childish and absurd. You will laugh, I am afraid, at what may very well appear ridiculous, but which nevertheless makes me suffer. Farewell. I am feverish and miserable. I cannot describe how much I miss you. Give me some hope of seeing you soon again, for I *really* want you. I leave my letter open that I may tell you if I have had the courage to do what I intended. Do not laugh at me, for I am unhappy.'

"On the 26th of May, he writes again to M. de Montalembert: 'I have received your welcome letter.* It has done me more good than I can describe. Write to me often. Give me strength and courage. If you were with me, how many thoughtless acts you would save me from committing. Oh, if she could

* This was the letter he speaks of:

M. le Comte de Montalembert to Albert.

"Albano, May 19th, 1832.

"My Dear Friend,—You cannot imagine how I have suffered during the last two days at the total overthrow of all our plans. I see that the whole of my journey—supposing I do not give it up—will be spoilt by it. I wanted to write to you at length on this subject, and to give you some idea of the emotions which swell my heart to bursting. But there is no time for it; the courier is just starting. I can only tell you, and over and over again repeat it, that my affection for you is as strong as possible. I did not think I could have attached myself so warmly to a new friend. I hope that you will not forget me, and that under the seductive sky of Naples, you will not lose those strong religious and political convictions which, to my great joy, I saw increasing in your mind. Good-bye. I will write to you more amply from Rome and Frascati. I repeat my old injunctions. Take care of yourself and of your health, for the sake of your family, of your sisters, of one whose happiness will one day be in your keeping, and also a little out of regard for me, who have already lost so many of those I loved. A thousand affectionate remembrances to Alexandrine and her mother.

"Charles de Montalembert."

know what I feel when she speaks, when she sings. She is so charming! That shyness, that fragile look, those childlike manners, that apparent helplessness, at the same time that passionate ardour for everything good, and so great a leaning to our religion, that I regret you had not time to become better acquainted with her. I really feel this is insanity, but when a man is in love, hope dies in his heart only when love itself decays. After all, I have obtained what I have always prayed for—to love as ardently and devotedly as it is possible to love, even if that love was never to meet with the least return. Hitherto I have been able to repress all outward expression of what I feel, but I am sure that if I were alone with her, I never could help telling her everything, even at the risk of foregoing all my hopes.'

"A few days after this letter was written, I had been to see Pauline, on a Sunday, the 3rd of June, and had been talking with her a long time in the garden. Madame de la Ferronnays called her daughters to go to the Benediction. I walked with them, and Albert joined us. The church was half way between their villa and ours. As I was obliged to go home, I took leave of them at the church door, and went on, accompanied by Albert. In the little lane which begins at the Villa Belvidera, and before arriving at the Floridiana, Albert, after a long silence, said to me: 'I am desperately in love with you!' This was the way in which he first told me of his love, whilst his mother and sisters were praying at Church, and perhaps praying for us.

"Albert wrote in his journal the following day:—'June 4th, 1832.—How this state of tepidity fatigues and irritates me. The heart longs to feel those emotions which it can so seldom enjoy, and it does not know how to overcome the secret obstacle which stands in their way. For some time past I have lost all those delightful feelings which the love of God, and nothing but that love, used to give me. I should like to be alone for some days. I feel that my soul requires to be strengthened. I really think that habits are more powerful than principles. At Rome I was certainly a better man than here. I took so much pleasure in fulfilling all my duties. I used to feel such devotion when I entered a Church, and such a living faith filled my soul. Now everything in me seems weakened. And what a difference, too, in my love! Then I should never have dreamt of doing what I did yesterday. I found happiness then in silently admiring her. It was an enjoyment to study her soul, and a pure, unselfish, delightful feeling filled my heart with enthusiastic devotion. Why did I disclose my love to her? Has the nature of it changed? Why did I want her to read my heart? How could I act such an insane part in my own interest, as to cease to look upon her as on a paradise never to be obtained? I am ashamed of myself. How she must have despised me, and how surprised she must have been!'

"The 5th of June:—* 'It is in vain to try to school myself. I cannot succeed when I speak to her, or when she shakes hands with me, I altogether forget what I am doing. I am afraid that there must be exaggeration in these feelings, and that they cannot prove lasting; and yet I do think I never saw anybody in the world to be compared with her, unless, perhaps, my sister Pauline. But Pauline is if anything a little too reasonable. It is perhaps wrong to say so. But what I find so captivating in Alexandrine is precisely her *naïveté;* and that she is a little unreasonable, a little exaggerated sometimes, but so charming. She really wants a friend—a protector—she is so delicate. What a picture I am drawing! and what a fool I am!'

"'June 6th.—Give me back, I beseech Thee, my God, the fervor I have lost. It is such happiness when one can pray well, and *that* is the happiness which I have lost. All the vague and impetuous feelings of youth find something in religion which calms and satisfies the soul. O, my God! I have forgotten that language of the soul which those only understand who love none but Thee—that language which is only used in a Church or in solitude. It was familiar to me once, and I thought it so sweet. Grant me, my God, to speak it again, as in those happy days which now seem to me so far distant, when I was going every moment into a Church to pray for her, and felt as if I must be heard. O, my God, when I asked for her conver-

* On the same day M. de Montalembert wrote from Rome to Albert:—"I can never tell you enough how grateful I feel for your confidence, and for the proofs of it which your last letters afford. If it was a comfort to you to open your heart to me, and to speak of your sufferings, it was a real satisfaction to read what you wrote to me. Only do not make so many apologies—do not keep on repeating that I shall think you insane. Speak to me always with openness and simplicity, and be sure that I can both understand and feel for your sorrows. You know how particularly well I understand *you*, and nobody, I think, can better estimate the character of your present attachment. I can only regret that it should not have been God's will that our intended journey should take place. I think it would have done us both good. CH. DE M."

sion, offering in exchange my own life and all my happiness, was the joy of loving Thee included in the sacrifice? Save her, O my God! save her: but save me also. Take away from me, if it be Thy will, every enjoyment which enthusiasm can give, but leave me the love of holiness; let me never lose it again.'

"The 8th of June, 1832:—'There was a time when the words "our country," used to set the hearts of men on fire; but now that the coldest selfishness, as a general rule, prevails in the world, we find our true country wherever we can feel and practise what is good and great; and our fellow citizens are those who understand and desire to lead this sort of life.'

"On the same day Albert wrote to M. de Montalembert:—'I hardly dare speak of myself. Yet I greatly need it. My dear Charles, do try and animate me again with that ardent love of goodness which I used to feel when I was with you. I now fulfil my religious duties with much less pleasure. I cannot account for the change, and am inclined to ascribe it to the air of Naples. I have been haunted lately by horrible recollections, and I am afraid of the future. But there is comfort in thinking that an angel is watching near me. Oh, no, I need not fear as long as I can gaze on that pure and lovely vision. Why, then, has my soul lost its poetic fervor? Does God sometimes withdraw His grace in order to try us? I am inclined to think so, for yesterday evening when I came into the drawing-room I found my sister Pauline in tears. We went on the terrace, where the moonlight was most beautiful. She soon recovered her accustomed cheerfulness, and assured me that the depression I experience is only a transient feeling, and even whilst she was speaking to me the fervor that doubles the value of life seemed to return. She talked to me of Alexandrine. I was quite happy then. I told her that I had been suffering for some time past, and after having spent an hour conversing together, we returned to the house quite cheered and comforted.'

"Again a few days later:—'My dearest friend, I received your delightful letter this morning, and had I not been breakfasting out, I should have answered it immediately. I wish you knew all the good you have done me. I thank you a thousand times for your confidence, which touches me all the more because I have no right to it but that which my devoted affection for you can give, whereas it is only natural that I should conceal nothing from you who are so very, very good, so necessary to me, and to whom I owe such pure, such inexpressible enjoyment. I wish I could show you my innermost soul. I am so indifferent now to all I cared about when I was with you. I do not know why this should be, for I love her. But I see her before me like some luminous object on the horizon which it is impossible to reach, but from which one cannot detach one's eyes because it is so beautiful, and that it appears linked with one's fate. You will not, I am afraid, understand me. What I feel is almost as confused as what I write. There is no doubt of one thing, which is that I love her.'

"'Thursday Morning, 4 o'clock.

"'I have been studying all night. I could not sleep, and I wanted to kill the time, and to drive away the thought of Alexandrine. I want to learn to study. This is one of those moments in which we feel that lost time can be redeemed. If you will help me, I will work as hard as I can. If you will guide me, no amount of labor shall frighten me. There is nothing I will not attempt. I must have occupation to keep me from going out of my mind. I am so in love! I am not very well. I have not slept for two nights, and last night I did not even go to bed. The weather was perfectly beautiful, and I sat at my window studying till five o'clock in the morning. Dear friend, when shall we enjoy again our pleasant merry days of Amalfi?'

"It was during one of those sleepless nights that Albert wrote me the following note:—

"'Wednesday, 2 o'clock in the morning.

"'What will you say when you see my handwriting? I know I ought not to write to you, and that you have reason to be displeased. But all I can say is, that you have revealed to me the knowledge that I possess a living heart. You have filled me with enthusiasm for everything great, and inspired me with a fervent admiration for goodness. But when I am with you, I find I cannot express my thoughts. I believe I am afraid of you; and yet you were so kind to-night. You tried to make me happy. Do not think me too presumptuous. Keep for those more worthy of them, those light words which you utter without thought. Let me enjoy in silence the happiness of seeing you, and draw from your soul the life of mine. If I could only be with you for a few minutes, what good it would do me. Here they laugh at what they call my absence of mind, but I assure you that I am not happy. I reproach myself for daring to love you, and still more for having told you so; but I was carried away by a resistless impulse. Do tell me you forgive me. I have been on the point of going to Amalfi for a fortnight, not to try and forget you, for I should have neither the strength nor the will to do so, but only to relieve you a little from my presence. But I remembered that on Friday there would be nobody to take care of you when you came out of the theatre. I do not know Madame K——, but I shall be standing at the door in case you should want any one, only let me know if you mean to stay till the end.

"'I have said scarcely anything, and am still afraid I may have displeased you. Be a little indulgent. I am alone; it is a beautiful night, and you are so present to me that I cannot sleep. I declare to you that when we are together it seems to me like the foretaste of a happier life. It is impossible that such feelings as these should not outlive the grave. No, I am sure that one cannot love deeply, purely, innocently—that one cannot love *you*—without being filled with thoughts of God and Eternity. And now I must leave you. I can ill express what I feel. You may call it folly, delusion, delirium, if you will, but I fancy I hear the singing of Angels. You are amongst them, and oh, how lovely you are!'

"He had written on the cover: '*For you. Do not be angry.*' And he gave me this letter with several other things he brought with him.

"On the Friday, of which he speaks, I was to dine at Naples with the Countess K——, and to go with her to hear Anne Boleyn. My mother did not like to appear yet at the Opera. For the first time since my father's death I put on a white gown. I had not been to a theatre for two years. The opera house was illuminated in honour of the queen-mother, and I wrote that night in my journal:—'This day has seemed to me like a long dream.'

"Ivanhoff's charming voice in the part of Percy, that magnificent theatre brilliantly lighted, the joy of loving and being loved, all combined to make that evening one of perfect enchantment to me. Count Lebzeltern* came to fetch me to his box, which he had lent to Madame de la Ferronnays. I thought myself in good looks, and was glad that Albert should see me, and Pauline too, that she might compliment me on my dress. It was one o'clock before I got back to my mother, who was waiting for me at the Comtesse de Maistre's. Little did I think as we were driving back to the Vomero, and I was lying back in the carriage, tired, indeed, but happy, and delighted with my evening, that Albert was walking by our side on the rough road up to the Vomero, pushing the carriage wheels up the steep places, and hiding himself when our servant got down from the box, and all for the sake of catching one more glimpse of my white gown in our courtyard, where he ensconced himself to see us get out of the carriage, very much afraid all the time of being himself seen. It hurt his chest very much. He acknowledged it to Pauline, who told me so afterwards.

"The next day, Saturday, he wrote me the following note:—'Whether you read this letter or not, I must talk to you a little. It is a happiness I can never enjoy when I go to see you, and if you do not allow me to write, I shall be undone. Even at the time when I had most religious fervor, there was still something imperfect in my devotion. I was not good enough to pray without any other thought but God; and on Sundays at Rome, when I was near you I felt that your prayers helped me. I wish you could have read my heart, and seen how my love for you made me love God, and filled me with enthusiasm. I loved you intensely, and you did not know it. There was something I liked in this secret attachment. Here I have been less good and less happy. I seem to have forfeited everything by disclosing my affection to you. I thought—no, I did not think at all—I did not know what I was doing. I have lost that peace and tranquillity I used to have. You accuse me of exaggeration. My words may sound like it, but if you could see my heart, you would find in it something more real than I can describe. I do not know how to express myself. Do not attend to what I say, but understand what I mean. What will you say when you read this letter? Perhaps you will only laugh. Well, laugh if you like. I am a child, a fool perhaps, but I am not absurd, for *I*

* Austrian Minister at Naples.

love you. Adieu. Above all things I want you to be happy. It is three o'clock. I am not the least inclined to sleep. Why should I sleep, when my waking dreams are so delightful!'

"I have not yet mentioned that my mother was very fond of Albert; 'as fond of him as of a son,' she used to say, and also that 'Heaven was in his eyes.' One evening that we had been saying good-bye to him from the balcony, he walked down the avenue, humming a ballad by the Duc (afterwards Cardinal) de Rohan, which he had sung to me for the first time a few days before.

"'Ton souvenir est toujours là,
Oh! toi qui ne peut plus m'entendre!'*

"I remember that a shade of sadness stole over my soul as I heard his voice dying away in the distance. Alas! four years afterwards when at my request Fernand sang to me that same ballad at Boury, with what bitter sobs I heard it once more! . . . . Albert began to reproach himself for not having positively acknowledged to my mother that he was attached to me. He delayed it from the fear of meeting with a repulse. I was a little afraid of this also. On the 1st of August, 1832, he wrote to M. de Montalembert on this subject.

"'I left Castellamare at five o'clock, and at eight I was at the Vomero. I dressed, stayed a little while at home, and then hastened to Alexandrine. My heart was beating very fast. I found her alone. Her mother was on the terrace with Prince L——.† I was a few minutes alone with her, and could not say one word. She gave me her hand. I saw by the expression of her eyes that she knew what I was feeling. My silence said more than all I could have uttered. I stayed there till twelve o'clock, quite wild with joy, for I am sure she loves me a little.

"'Dear friend! how will all this end? Shall I ever be able to exist without her? I pass from the most enchanting dreams to the most terrible misgivings. Her mother's kindness to me seems to increase every day, and I feel almost a filial affection for her. Yesterday Alexandrine was playing on the pianoforte. Madame d'Alopeus was at the window admiring the beauty of the night. I went up to her and said, "I am haunted by the

* "Ever present to me is the thought of you, who can no longer hear me."

† The Countess d'Alopeus had been at that time a widow for more than a year. Prince Lapoukhyn had travelled to Italy to offer her his hand, and she married him the following year.

fear of appearing deceitful." "You!" she answered, "with those large eyes of yours it would be difficult to deceive, and I read into the very depths of your heart." I was very much affected, and begged her to tell me what it was she saw there. "Oh! not yet," she said. "These sort of things cannot be talked about in an off-hand manner. Another time we will speak of it."

"'I must tell you about Prince L——. He is a striking looking man, with a frank, honest countenance. He is immensely rich, and would, I think, be very glad to marry Madame d'Alopeus. I must tell you what he said the other day, but promise me you will not say a word to anybody. Madame d'Alopeus was playing at patience, and in her way telling fortunes with the cards. The word "Fiançailles" (Betrothal) turned up. The Prince said, "O! that does not mean *my* betrothal; it relates to another marriage I have in view," and he looked towards us. Moreover, I know he said to the countess: "Albert is in love with your daughter, and why not?"'

"Oh, how well I remember the day he describes at the beginning of this letter. Pauline had been sitting for a long time with me in my room, till it grew quite dark. Then she went away, and I returned to the drawing-room. I had a vague hope of finding Albert there, but he was not come. It was ten o'clock, and I would not give up hoping. Mamma proposed to the Prince to go out on the terrace. I let them go on before me, and delayed following them, for I kept thinking, 'He will perhaps arrive in a minute,' and so he did. I was so happy to see him that I could not speak. I was the first, however, to break that long silence, which told more than I felt I could venture to say. All that evening was so full of happiness. O! God of boundless love! is not this pure bliss, this ecstatic joy, this love which sees nothing but perfection in the object of its love, a foretaste of the endless affection which we shall feel for those already so immensely dear to us on earth?

"Our life was becoming every day more enjoyable. Albert, once secure that his love was returned, began to show that attractive gaiety which Pauline told me was natural to him. Our dull, ill-furnished house, which had not even a view except from the terrace, seemed adorned with a bewitching brightness. We liked it better than his parents' lovely villa, where it was not so easy for us to talk together. What I liked were the walks home from it. He used to accompany me, and sometimes we came back by the avenue instead of the lane, which was the shortest road; but I did not do this very often, because I was afraid people would take notice of it, and guess why I chose the longest way. We spent the greatest part of our evenings on the terrace upstairs. How enchanting it was! Those two bays, the lovely coasts, Vesuvius with its rivulets of fire, the sky always spangled with stars, the ever balmy air, and to crown all, our love! And that a love we were not afraid to feel, even when we spake of God!

"I did not want Albert to be deceived about my character, even if in showing myself to him as I was, I lessened his attachment. 'He must either be cured of his love,' I thought, 'or if it stands the test, I can trust him *for ever*.' I therefore gave him a certain little green book, the earliest depository of all my thoughts. He read it, and this is what he wrote immediately afterwards in his journal:

"'6 o'clock in the morning.

"'I am in a perfect fever. I have passed the whole night reading this little book, which has driven me almost wild. I cannot attempt to describe the various feelings with which it has filled my soul. Sadness when it speaks of her sufferings, an overflowing tenderness, a tormenting jealousy, and above all a passionate love! A love which kills me . . . . It is six o'clock, and I have not gone to bed yet. I cannot sleep. I only want to see her, to speak to her, to tell her all I suffer . . . .' And I was suffering too. I dreaded the effect the little book might have upon him. Albert did not come early that evening, which increased my anxiety. We were going to the opera to see the 'Gazza Ladra.' I felt like a guilty person when he came into the box. He looked gloomy and out of spirits. He asked me to allow him to give me a note, because he said he was going the next day to Castellamare. He put it in the case of my opera-glass. A thousand fears disturbed me. I scarcely knew what I was about, and I must have derived less pleasure from the opera than any of the audience. Madame Malibran was drawing tears from every one, and certainly the music was in harmony with our feelings; but though I was very sorry to part with Albert for several days, I was longing to get home to read his note. Perhaps it contained a last farewell. I knew I should at once see when I opened it if his love was diminished. At last alone in my room I read as follows:

"'I shall not have an opportunity of speaking to you to-day, and as I am going to Castellamare, I am sure you will forgive this breach of our agreement. I did not go to bed till past six o'clock this morning, for, as you may suppose, your little book took away from me all inclination to sleep. I cannot tell you all the various feelings which agitated me throughout the night. I grieved over your sufferings, your scruples, your tormenting misgivings about your own character, till I worked myself into a perfect fever. Oh, every page of your book added to my affection for you! I found myself several times reasoning with you, consoling you as if you had been present. It seemed as if you were by my side and speaking to me as to your dearest friend. I felt to love you more than I have ever done before. The prayers you address to God, your feelings of devotion when you enter our Churches, your dread of doing wrong, the sacrifice of your own happiness, which you so often offer up for the sake of others —yourself, in short—revealed to me by yourself! I assure you that it was too much for my poor head, and I was obliged to throw open the window and breathe the fresh morning air, for it was broad daylight. How far off this evening still seems! I am afraid of seeing you. Shall I be able to control myself? Oh, always tell me what you think, what you do! Speak to me of everything that is good, and above all of yourself. Let me see your other book. Make me your best and greatest friend. I know *he* was clever, and I am not. That he was pleasing, and that there is nothing pleasing about me. But when he said, "I love you," tell me, did he seem to feel it as I do?'*

"On the morning of the 31st of August I gave Albert my second book, having taken care to paste a sheet of paper over the last pages, in which he was mentioned, and trusting to him not to tear it off. Alas! there were many foolish things in that book which ought to have estranged him from me; but though I did not wish it to have that effect, I was resolved to be honest, and, as we can never quite answer for our motives, I will not be

* This alludes to an attachment which had been formed for Alexandrine the preceding year at Berlin, and which at the time seemed sincere. She had not been quite indifferent to it, and this gave her misgivings as to the strength and reality of her present feelings. For she whom the sequel proved to be the most constant, tender, and devoted person in the world, originally had, or thought she had, the most changeable, uncertain disposition possible.

quite sure that I did not like him to read some passages which I was certain would please him. The agitation which the little green book had caused him, made me somewhat uneasy about the effect of the blue one.

"The day before, or the same day, he had written in his journal the following sentences, and then the *Memorare*, that prayer to the Blessed Virgin which we have since so often said together: 'O! my God, do not forsake me! Forgive me all my faults and give me an energy which I have never yet possessed. Restore to me those fervent feelings of devotion which were wont to fill my soul, and to be its safeguard against the enemy on the watch to destroy me. I dread the coming winter. It will be so different from the last. Oh, Mary, my Blessed Mother, pray for me; do not abandon me! Give me courage to conquer human respect, to make my enemies blush, not to give them occasion of triumph. I am ashamed to say it, but I dread the sneers of worldly people. I should like to act nobly and independently. To be indulgent towards others, and severe towards myself. Not to allow of any jests on my own line of conduct, but on the other hand, not to set myself up as a judge. To go a good deal into society, since I can do so without committing sin. To love Alexandrine without giving way to folly, and compromising her by childish absurdities; and, above all, grant me, my God, to love virtue. Give me back that warmth of zeal I used to feel for everything good. Make my heart burn again with the fire of Divine love. Purify more and more that passion which is now the life of my soul. Give me, I beseech thee, self-control, and never permit me, in the agitation of my feelings, to utter a single word which could wound or offend her ears. Let me hold her in the deepest reverence, and strive to become worthy of loving her without ever aspiring to a greater happiness. O! my God, give me tenderness of heart, zeal, enthusiasm, and love.'

ALBERT TO M. DE MONTALEMBERT.

"'29th of July, 1832.

"'Each day seems fraught with danger. I see an abyss before me. Dear friend, if you could know what I suffer! And yet I ought to be happy, for I am no longer indifferent to her. She has read my heart, and has been touched by my affection. And yet my depression increases! Sometimes I think she cares for me only out of gratitude, and I feel humbled. If for a moment I indulge in some sweet illusion and believe myself truly loved, a sort of anguish takes possession of me. She was so beautiful that evening! After having sung she came up to me and said: "Do not be sad!" "How can I be otherwise?" I replied. "Life is a burden to me. I can never be happy. Your kindness only depresses me, for I know you cannot love me. Spare me your pity. I should like better to be hated. It would not wound me so deeply; for I cannot tell you what I was suffering;" and to add to it, she answered: "You do so exaggerate! I know you will forget. You will return not . . ." Her way of saying this cut me to the heart. I could not answer. "Have I vexed you?" she asked; adding, "Well, no; I believe you are in earnest; but you have so often changed, and then people always forget me."

"'Oh, my dear Charles, I felt as if I should die. And when I think I can never marry her because I have no fortune! You can imagine all I endure. I have got so into the habit of seeing and being with her that it feels as if she belonged to me, as if she could not be taken away from me! When I hear her praised, I am so proud, so happy! She often speaks of you, and in a way which I assure you might almost make me jealous. When we meet I will tell you about it. I wish you knew how much I love you, how much I miss you. I used to be unfortunately open with everybody, and now you are the only person to whom I speak unreservedly.'

FROM THE SAME TO THE SAME.

"'Shall I own it? I am a little anxious as to the nature of our intimacy. There exists at present but one subject of discourse between us, and all seems to rest on a foundation which might at any moment give way. Our mutual confidence should be the result of a strong and tender friendship which would stand any test, and not simply an affection dependent on a common interest and a temporary sympathy. I do not think that we can any of us have more than one real friend, one person to whom every thought can be imparted. I have found such a friend in you. To you alone I reveal the inmost secrets of my soul. I am nevertheless quite aware of my inferiority. You are engrossed by great and important questions, and my life is very useless. But as regards the deep and intimate feelings of the heart, I hope and think that God has given me the gift of understanding and entering into them. It is this kind of sympathy between two persons which makes their friendship unalterable. A slight difference in political opinion cannot surely affect such an attachment as that!

"'You say that the warmth and vehemence of my affections prevent their being as deep as they might otherwise be. Those words pain me. No, I assure you, it is not a dream; it is no exaggerated light fancy which fills my heart. She has given me her journal. I read in it the most secret thoughts of her mind. Writing in that book is to her like going to confession. She records in it every action of her life. At the end of it there are sealed pages in which I am mentioned. She has begged me not to try and read them, and trusts implicitly to my honor. There they are. I could at any moment look at them. But she trusts me, and I will not betray her confidence.

"'Is it possible, my dear friend, that you can suppose my love not to be *deep?* After I have opened my heart so fully to you, is it thus you judge it? I will not try any more to describe what I feel. If you think I exaggerate, well, time will decide if you are right. Asseverations are absurd on such a subject. Time, again I say, will show if nothing in this life can last, if nothing is certain; if we are to care for nothing, and believe in nothing.

"'Good-bye, my dear Charles. I look upon you as my dearest friend. Remember that it is your friendship, your complete friendship that I want, and that I am not satisfied "with a great amount of affection and gratitude for my sympathy in the present chief interest of your life." I felt hurt by that sentence. You speak as if your regard for me was to be a sort of reward for what you call my kindness to you.'

"Albert was gone to Castellamare. His parents and sisters were there also, and we were soon to join them and remain there a little while. Prince Lapoukhyn wrote to my mother from Castellamare, and Albert also, and I had a letter from Pauline.

"This is Albert's letter:—'What abominable treachery! We could not make up our minds to do without you till Friday, and now you threaten to prolong our misery for four or five days longer. Do not flatter yourselves that we shall submit to this cruelty, or be surprised if one of these days we suddenly appear in your salon. I cannot tell you what a comfort it is to me to meet the prince. I look upon him as a fellow sufferer, banished like myself. Positively, without any joking, life is not endurable without you. If it is not presuming on your kindness, may I beg you to send me a line by the bearer of this stupid note. I kiss your hands, and I throw myself at the feet of Mademoiselle Alexandrine. Do say, even if it should not be true, that you feel a little regret for your poor *habitués*. And come soon, very soon, for it is absurd to suppose that we can live without you. I want very much to speak to you about something, but I have not courage. I do not know what to call you. "Madame" sounds so cold. "Dear Comtesse?" That will not quite do. I should like to find some impossible *mezzo termine*. I end my letter, for if I were to tell you all my heart is full of, you would perhaps pretend to be angry, and I should be alarmed.'

"My mother sat down instantly to answer this note, and I wrote on the same sheet:—'How do you do, Albert? I quite wonder at our solitude, and yet I dread the thoughts of plunging into that world of Castellamare. I have tried to occupy myself, but have done nothing except finish the book you lent me. The pianoforte has remained in a most untidy state, and has not even been opened for two days. Ever since your departure, the wind has been whistling in the woods about us, in a way which might suggest the plot of a novel à la Radcliffe. But I am not in the mood for composition. What is my little Pauline about? Why don't you mention her? I am going to write her a line. To-morrow we dine with the Stockelbergs; the day after to-morrow we pack up, and on Monday we shall meet again.'

"I wrote this, and went into my room a moment afterwards. I heard the servant announce M. de Pietracatella and M. de Sass, and then exclamations of surprise, and well known voices. It was Albert and the prince, who had stolen away from Castellamare to take us by surprise in that way. Oh, how pleasant it was to have so unexpectedly one of our charming evenings! It put me into such spirits. Whilst I was singing the air of *La Muette*,—'Oh, moment enchanter!'—Albert, who was standing opposite to the pianoforte, suddenly asked me what I should think if he had read in the little book what I had so carefully pasted over. I was frightened, but answered that I was quite sure he never could have done it. 'But if I *had* done it?' 'It is impossible. I can never believe it.' 'But I *have* done it.' 'No!' My confusion was increasing, but I still absolutely refused to admit that he could have done such a thing. 'Shall I quote a sentence in it to convince you?' 'No, you cannot; you would be only inventing it.' '"I think I love Albert,"'—he said, gazing at me as if from the depths of his eyes. I looked at him, and turned my eyes away with such an altered expression, that he was very sad all the evening. Indeed, I did not feel for a little while as if I had any love for him at all, but it came back again when I saw he was quite unhappy.

"On the 18th of September we left the Vomero to go to Castellamare. Albert met us, and went with us to our apartments at the Albergo Reale. He was looking as sad as when we had parted at the Vomero. I could not hold out, and said a few words to him, which made us again as happy as ever. Indeed, happier, for there was now no longer any disguise between us. Pauline came to see me, and said that Albert had acknowledged his fault to her, and that he had used such strong terms of self-reproach before mentioning the fact, that she had been frightened, and had asked him if he had had the audacity to kiss me! Albert was *quite* horrified at this question, and at her even imagining he could have ventured to do such a thing.

"Our evenings at Castellamare were generally spent at the Countess K——'s house. There were always a great many people there, and we danced on a large and beautiful terrace, arranged as a drawing-room. On the first night I went there, I was dancing the Mazurka with the Count d'A——. Albert, in one of the figures, brushed by my partner, who was of a particularly quarrelsome disposition, and who looked offended. I heard some words said which made me very uneasy, and was not satisfied with Albert's answers when I questioned him about it as we were going home. On the following day there was to be a great breakfast at Pompeii, to which we were all invited.

"In the morning (Wednesday, the 19th of September), after a very anxious night, I was delighted to hear Albert's voice in the drawing-room. At first I thought they had perhaps been fighting that morning, but I soon felt convinced that it was not all right yet. The carriages were to meet at the Café Nuovo. Pauline went with us. Albert was on horseback. She looked at me and said, 'What is the matter? You look as if you had seen a ghost.' I said nothing, as I would not frighten her without necessity. When we arrived at Pompeii, I saw Albert and the Count d'A—— walking together in a solitary road. Then I heard his father say, as I thought in an anxious manner, 'Where is Albert?' I could not restrain my tears. Only Pauline observed them. I would not tell her the cause, but kept thinking how I could save Albert. I saw Fernand standing near me. I had never spoken to him before,* but I went up to him all in tears, and could only say, 'Where is Albert? Where is Albert?' Fernand perceiving I knew all about it, told me how matters stood, and assured me they were talking together to make up their quarrel. We were just then summoned to breakfast, a great breakfast of fifty persons, in the centre of the ruins. I was dreadfully ashamed of being seen with my tearful face, but there was no help for it. I placed myself between Pauline and Hedwige Lubomirska, who I thought would feel for me. Fernand often came to tell me that it was all going on well. At last I saw Albert. Mamma was watching me. The report of what had passed was beginning to spread, and I felt more and more distressed. At last we left the table, and went to look at an excavation. While it was going on, Albert whispered to me, 'Oh, I love you more than my life.' Afterwards we danced in the Forum. I danced the cotillon with Albert. At his request, I chose in one of the figures, that terrible enemy who had given me so great a fright. I cannot describe my feelings as I leant on that arm—which might have killed my Albert.†

ALBERT TO THE COMTE DE MONTALEMBERT.

"'I have put off a long time the pleasure of writing to you, for my head is so confused that I find it difficult to put two ideas together. I read this morning your *submission*.‡ How admirable it is! My father is quite enraptured with it. Let me know as soon as you can what you are going to do. Do you return to Italy, or do you remain at Paris? Have I any hope of meeting you anywhere? I am thinking of going to Rome in the

* He was only just arrived.

† The person who had called out Albert that day, perished himself three years afterwards in a dreadful duel.

‡ He speaks of the submission of M. M. de Lamennais, Lacordaire, and Montalembert, to the decree of the Holy See, respecting the *Avenir*.

month of December, in the first place to study a little, and then to test my feelings by absenting myself awhile from Alexandrine.

"'Dear Charles, you will be provoked with me, but I must tell you about myself. Since I wrote to you last, so many things have happened! So much happiness has seemed almost too much for me. I mentioned to you the journal which she gave me to read. After having read it over and over again, and by knowing her better—having learnt to love her more and more—I came to those pages which she had fastened together with a sheet of paper, those pages which contained what is more important to me than life itself. You will exclaim at the bare thought of such a breach of confidence. What would you have done in my place? I resisted for several days, but at last, in a moment of frenzy, I tore away the slip of paper. I will not attempt to tell you what I felt. I really do not know it myself. She loves me, my dear Charles. She is actually in love with me. The moment I acknowledged my breach of trust was terrible. There was something contemptuous in her countenance. It made me think of the torments of hell. It was a long time before I could recover myself. But now my fault is forgotten, and she does not mind my knowing her secret.*

"'The other day I was on the point of having to fight a duel for the greatest nonsense in the world. On the day after the quarrel I met my adversary at Pompeii, where there was a great breakfast. We had a final interview, and the matter was made up. During all that time Alexandrine did not lose sight of me. She was weeping, sobbing. I can't tell if it was joy or pain I was feeling. You can imagine the state I am in. Is this agitation a terrible foreboding, or only the fear, the terror of losing her? Of losing her, my soul, my life, my all. My dear Charles, I can hardly be said to live. I am afraid of each coming day. I should like to stop the progress of time. Each day is so full of bliss. I have never feared or understood sorrow as much as now, when happiness fills my soul. Are these fair blossoms of joy doomed to fade and perish? Oh! no, they are a foretaste of Heaven. Heaven beginning on earth!

* It does not appear that M. de Montalembert's indignation at that breach of trust proved as great as Albert supposed it would be. This was his answer: "As to the journal, I do not blame you at all, and I am sure her anger was neither very great nor very deep; nor can there have been, as you suppose, contempt in her eyes. When you do not want a man to know his happiness, you do not put a mere slip of paper between him and the knowledge of it."

"'You will again say that I exaggerate, but no, my dear friend, the delightful calm which fills my soul is a token of the depth and reality of my happiness. To-morrow she will give me a lock of her hair. I shall carry it in a locket round my neck, as a charm against all evil. I am in a fever. Joy fills my soul with too intense a life. Her mother knows it all. She is so good, so loving. You did not know her much, and yet you were beginning to love her. When shall I see you again? I do want you so much! I have a pining for home. It vexes me to be doing nothing useful. I should like to become worthy of the great happiness in store for me. Your friend for life, ALBERT.'

"We left Castellamare on the 29th of September. I do not know why, but as we were going away, I began to cry a little. Nobody saw it but Albert, and his gentle pity soothed me. But I could not tell him what made me shed tears, for I was to see him again next day. Perhaps I grieved because a beautiful chapter of my life was closing, or because we were leaving a place where we had for the first time spoken to each other without disguise. One evening whilst at Castellamare, we were sitting together on a balcony, looking at the sunset sky and the blue sea. Mamma, even, was not in the room. We seemed to be left alone with God. Albert's eyes were fixed with an enraptured gaze on the setting sun, and he said, 'Oh, if we could go where the sun is going! It would be so delightful to follow it, to see a new world.' I think he would have liked to die at that moment. I admired his enthusiasm, but did not quite share his feelings. I was thinking of him, whilst he was thinking of Heaven. It was through him I approached God, but he went straight to Him. Such moments as these seemed to sanctify the whole of the ensuing evening. I dressed with a feeling of quiet joy in my heart, liking to adorn myself, in order to give pleasure to him, who was teaching me to be good."

The story of Albert and Alexandrine has abounded, up to this time, in expressions of feeling, which some may consider too romantic and impassioned. I could not think, however, of suppressing any of these passages. I felt it expedient to show what that love was which afterwards became so sacred and so holy. Let those who are inclined to say that the very attractiveness of the picture makes it dangerous, only suspend their judgment and read on. If they will finish the narrative, they will see how the love of God grew stronger than human affection; how faith overcame and sorrow hallowed earthly passion; above all, in what way those who had loved so well bore suffering and met death.

I must now myself most reluctantly resume the thread of the story, and, passing over some of the details carefully noted by Alexandrine, relate that after our stay at Castellamare, we went back to the Vomero, and remained there till the end of October; and then returning to Naples, we found, by a singular piece of good luck, that we could secure two sets of apartments in the same house in the Chiaia, and we all established ourselves there for the winter; Madame d'Alopeus and Alexandrine on the first floor, and we all on the second. Fernand had now been with us for two months, and since the day of the breakfast at Pompeii had formed an intimate and brotherly friendship with Alexandrine which never altered in the least. He was devotedly attached to Albert, and was inclined to approve everything he either did or wished; so that Alexandrine could not have had a more sympathising or discreet friend.

Ever since that scene at Pompeii, my father and mother, Madame d'Alopeus, and even Prince Lapoukhyn—who was now engaged to Alexandrine's mother, and had, therefore, a right to be interested in her daughter's affairs—had been discussing the question of their marriage and the means of facilitating it. And though, later on, difficulties occurred which were so many trials for the lovers, no one ever really contemplated any other eventual lot for them. But my father wished the strength of Albert's attachment to be tested by a temporary absence, and it was agreed that he should spend in Rome part of that winter which we had begun so joyfully under the same roof at Naples. We scarcely knew at that time what real sorrow is, and thought the slightest disappointments trials. We accordingly considered this decision a very rigorous one, and were all, except Albert himself, inclined to grumble a little. He was eager to prove the strength of his attachment, and wished in every way to please his father. He thought he had occasioned some anxiety to his parents on this subject, and this grieved him, at the same time that he felt deeply grateful for their kindness in lending themselves to his wishes in a matter which could not be arranged without much difficulty and even sacrifices on their part.

I ought to mention that even before the day of the breakfast at Pompeii, he had opened his heart to his father. The following note was written at the Vomero, probably after the evening when at the Floridiana he had said, "I love you," to Alexandrine.

"My Dearest Father—I have been thinking for some time past that I ought to be open with you, and tell you honestly and simply what are my present feelings. But the fear that you will laugh at what is perhaps ridiculous, but nevertheless makes me unhappy, has prevented my speaking when you have asked me if I had anything on my mind. I tried to look unconcerned. Anything on my mind, why I am sometimes almost out of my mind! But you know all about it. Why should I not own to you that I am in love? I cannot say whether the feverish excitement from which I suffer is the cause or the result of this feeling. For three months I have tried to subdue it by hard work. But far from succeeding, the very means I employ for that end only seem to stimulate what I am endeavoring to conquer. I am like the Roman race-horses; the more efforts I make to get away from the spur, the deeper it seems to gall me.

"I had thought of going to join my two friends, but in my present state of mind they would drive me mad. If you had anything for me to do at Paris, the stir and excitement there would perhaps be of use to me, and I could come back with Charles [his brother]. In short, my dear father, you see I must try to get out of this state of mind. I have endeavored to reason with myself, and Pauline has striven, too, to help me. I know that I do wrong to indulge this passion, and particularly wrong to let Alexandrine see it. She knows now what I feel. I have told her of it, and I am frightened at what I have done. And yet I cannot control myself. What will you say to this confession? Will you be vexed with me, or sorry for me? I don't know what you ought to feel, but I know that I am very unhappy. I would have told you all this, but I cannot yet speak about it. I have many things I long to say, and if we talk together, I hope to open my heart entirely to you. I am glad to have written. I could not exist without perfect confidence in you, my dearest father. If you feel inclined to laugh, spare me, for my heart is very sore just now."

Albert, as I have already said, was so happy at being allowed to hope for the eventual accomplishment of his most ardent wishes, that he accepted his exile and submitted to the trial of absence with greater resignation, perhaps, than Alexandrine. He was to leave Naples on the 4th of November. I leave her to describe the eve of her departure.

"Albert was to have gone away in the evening. I was scarcely to see him at all, for we were going to the opera. Whilst I was dining alone with Mamma, I burst into tears. She was most dear and kind. She said she understood my feelings, and gave me hopes. Still when I arrived at San Carlo, sorrow completely transformed the whole aspect of the house, the stage, the lights, and everything. Instead of the bright, fête-like look I used to think it had when I was quietly enjoying Albert's society, it seemed to me now like an illuminated sepulchre. But this impression was soon dispelled when Albert came and said to me: 'I do not set off this evening. I am going to-morrow night. I have obtained one day's reprieve.' This delay gave us strength and resignation. We were even tolerably cheerful the following evening. He started at five o'clock in the morning."

During his absence there was only one exception to the resolution they had both taken, not to communicate directly with each other. Fernand, who had no scruples where there was question of giving pleasure to Albert, obtained a few lines one day from Alexandrine to enclose in one of his own letters. This is the note:—"Fernand, after trying in vain to persuade me to write to you, told me at last that you wished it, and thus induced me to do so. For God's sake, and if you love me, try at any cost, even at my expense, in any way you can think of, to be happy, provided you do not offend God. You must not vex your father; you must do all he wishes, and as he wishes. I care not if you love another so that you are happy. I assure you I should like it better than that you should love me and be unhappy. Your happiness will always constitute mine. I hope you will not object to my making a confidential friend of Fernand. He loves you so much; even more so than your sisters, I think. It makes me very fond of him, and it is the greatest comfort to me to talk to him about you. I am vexed not to be able to tell Pauline what I am doing, for if she questions me, I shall be obliged to say what is not true, that you may not be placed in the same difficulty. I do entreat you not to write to me at all. You can tell Fernand anything you wish me to know. Your father told Pauline that he should not believe in the strength of our attachment until we had been two years without meeting or writing a line to one another. We must not be deceitful ; this is the last time I shall ever write to you in secret. Adieu ! My best prayers are those I put up for you. I hope God will hear me, and that you will be happy. Do not be afraid of unsettling me. If you forget me and yet are happy, I shall be content. I cannot seal this note, but it does not signify, Fernand will not read it."

Fernand was writing at the same time :—"You will be furious, but remember that I am the only guilty person. I send you a note from Alexandrine. I induced her to write by pretending that it would give you pleasure and that you had told me so. My dear good Albert, do not be too angry. I thought it would be such a comfort to you. I am so dull and sad since you went. I have just seen Alexandrine. She says my father has written to tell you not to come back at present ; but, upon my word, if you had seen her you never could have helped coming. The post is going out, and I can only send these few words. I promised Alexandrine to write to you, and I was bent on keeping my promise, and telling you at the same time how earnestly I desire your happiness and hers. Write to me, I beseech you. Alex begs you will do so very often. She likes to see me. I talk about you, which has made us confidential friends, of which I am not a little proud. Adieu. I love you with all my heart. Come back soon.—FERNAND.

"I need not say that I have not read the enclosed."

To this letter Albert wrote the following reply:—

"MY OWN DEAR BROTHER—It is very wrong indeed, but I love you more than ever. You can hardly know the good you did to a poor solitary fellow, far from those he cares about. That beloved note was like a drop of cold water to a wretch dying of fever. But for all that *she must not write to me again.* I try to cheat my thoughts, but if I succeed in the day, when I come home in the evening I feel that I love her, that I am not in the least changed, and as I lie down to sleep I pray for her and for myself. Not that I have slept yet. I am, however, quite satisfied. I can bear any suffering God chooses to send me. I have had more than my share of happiness. I can defy future misfortunes, for I have lived, and my life has been blessed by her love. One thing only could break my heart, which would be to know she was unhappy. I would even rather lose the recollection of those rapturous days, the only happy ones I have known, than see her grieve. I had written her a long letter, but I tore it up. She charges me not to answer her note, and it is better I should not do so. We shall one day meet again, and then she will learn all the sufferings of a heart for ever devoted to her. As she says herself: '*We must not be deceitful.*' Therefore, my best Fernand, great as is the sacrifice, do not extort from her any more letters for me. We must try to do without this consolation. If she should forget me, it will be better for her. I shall then be as one dead to the world, and living only on the remembrance of the happy past.

"Be very affectionate to Alexandrine. Win her confidence, and speak to her often of me. You will be surprised, perhaps, at what I am going to say, but I do not intend myself to act in the same way. This is the last letter in which I shall make such frequent mention of her. But tell me, what is the matter with you? Your last letter was quite a sad one. Try, my dear brother, not to give way to low spirits, especially before our dear father and mother. It increases their sorrow to see us unhappy, and they have enough of it as it is. Set to work in some way or other. The weariness which an idle life creates is a great source of dejection. I am preaching to you, and I ought rather to preach to myself. I try all I can, but find it impossible to fix my attention for one hour together on the same thing."

Our life returned to be much the same as during the preceding winters; less gay perhaps, but more enjoyable, because of Alexandrine's companionship. I find in my journal, from which I have already quoted, that at the hour when Eugénie and I used in former years to gather our bouquets, we now went up to the terrace at the top of the house, and, looking over the lovely view and the blue sky, said our Rosary together. When the day was closing, we generally met in Madame d'Alopeus' salon. To the number of her daily visitors were now added the Count Maurice Putbus, an excellent and devoted friend of Alexandrine and her mother, and the Count Malte Putbus, his nephew. The former will often appear in this narrative. The latter, like so many of the younger members of that family circle, was carried off by a severe illness, soon after Albert's death, to whom he was much attached, although very unlike him in every respect.

In one of Albert's letters to Eugénie, he says:—"You give me a charming account of the way in which you all live together. You seem so happy, so intimate! Do not talk to me so much about it, for it makes me envious." Madame d'Alopeus, who was often ill, entrusted Alexandrine to my mother, and we used to go out together like three sisters. At last, about a month before the time which had been fixed for Albert's absence, our dear parents relented and agreed that he should return. To our great joy, on the 7th of January, 1833, he came amongst us again.

I now have recourse to Alexandrine's manuscript, which carries on the narrative up to the time of our separation, three months afterwards.

SEQUEL TO ALEXANDRINE'S STORY.

"This is what I find in my journal at the date of the 7th of January, 1833. I was sitting upstairs with Pauline, when all of a sudden the door opened, and Albert rushed in. Yes, there he was, kissing Pauline affectionately with all his warmth of manner, and looking so delightfully happy! I had not seen him for two whole months! We had no secrets from Pauline, still we did not, before her, show more than a very little bit of the joy we felt at being once more together. And indeed we could hardly at first realize our happiness. It required time to take in the idea that those pleasant days were actually going to begin again, after such a long separation. Two whole months! I felt that first day a kind of embarrassment with Albert, on account of his knowing now so well how much I loved him. But it was all very pleasant. We went to a ball in the evening. I felt full of life and spirits, and everything I saw seemed transformed as if by magic. When I was waltzing with Albert it made me indeed a little shy to think that people were looking at us, and perhaps joking and saying with a smile: 'Ah! they are quite happy now!' But nothing could spoil my enjoyment. I did not care the least what was said, and was too happy to give it even a thought. During the cotillon, which I also danced with Albert, I went up to Pauline and whispered to her, in a kind of ecstacy: 'O Pauline, I am so happy.' She was quite touched.

"I went home at three o'clock in the morning with the La Ferronnays. Eugénie sent up some tea to my room. It made me feel like one of the family. I had before me the prospect of a most delightful time, and not looking beyond it, I went to bed enraptured. I was very happy for several days, though we led a worldly, unsettled life; but for me it was filled with Albert. There were several balls, and one in particular, a fancy ball, to which I went dressed in black and gold, with pearls and a veil. This costume was taken from a print of Francesca da Rimini. This is a note which I wrote a few days before that ball from our drawing-room, where I was alone, to my friends upstairs. It amused them all, and Albert kept it; I found it afterwards amongst his letters:

"'DEAR PEOPLE—When you have done your dinner, you will give me great pleasure if you will come down in a body, but the body must be as quiet as if it was only one person, for the door of Mamma's room is wide open. Be so kind, Eugénie, as to bring me the gold lace, and everything of gold you possess. If you have time, Pauline, I want you to come and see me, and to say how well I should have looked at Lady Drummond's ball.* Mind all of you, if you come, not to make more noise than one.'

"Oh, what a pleasant, home-like life we were already leading then! To live in the same house with Albert's parents, to see him from morning to night, and to know, though we did not speak of it to each other, that arrangements were in progress for our marriage. I used to awake with the thought that in a few hours I should see him, and those few hours were spent in pleasant musings, in my interminable toilette,† and in talking a little at breakfast with Mamma. Even to hear the voices or the footsteps of the dear people upstairs was a pleasure. And then at last came the moment when I could expect to see Albert. Sometimes he was present at my singing lesson; at other moments I found him in his sisters' room. I almost always saw him once in the course of the morning, and then again at that delightful twilight hour when our intimate friends assembled round our fire. We parted for a short time for dinner, and

* She was to have gone to this ball with us, but had given it up on account of her mother's indisposition.

† Alexandrine, neither then nor later, ever cared for dress. But she had nevertheless a habit of spending a very long time about it; and at a different period of her life, in spite of all her efforts, and even when her dress had become more than simple, she never could arrive at getting through the process quickly.

then met again to spend a long evening together. When we had only friends with us, I used to work at my cross stitch, or sing, or copy out favorite passages from the books I was reading. I have those passages now before me, and some words are underlined that express the feelings which were then, and have since been, my own. 'Methinks it is Heaven only to gaze upon him . . to set down as food for memory every look and every movement.' Ah! I was right in thinking that it was well for me to treasure up all Albert's looks and words! I see that the date of Saturday, the 9th of February, is underlined, which means that something of consequence happened that day, and I remember what it was. My mother and Albert's parents were dining with Count Stackelberg, and I was allowed to dine upstairs with Albert, Fernand, and their four sisters. This we thought great fun. After dinner Pauline and Eugénie had to go and dress for a party before I went down stairs. Their two little sisters were playing a duet on the pianoforte. Fernand, finding himself *en trio* with Albert and me, declared it was very awkward, and, joking about it, pretended to go to sleep, and covered his face with his pocket handkerchief. Albert and I stood conversing near the chimney-piece. After a little while I wanted to go away, for it did not seem to me quite proper to remain there alone with my friends' brothers and the two little girls. While I was lingering Albert just touched my forehead with his lips; so suddenly that I was taken by surprise. I felt very angry, and without saying a word took my shawl and left the room. When I was alone in mine, I kept thinking over what had passed, and I was really much annoyed. It seemed to me as if our pleasant existence had undergone a change, and that a disagreeable one. At that moment I did not feel quite certain that I loved him as much as I did before, and I hoped he would not come down till Mamma was at home, or some other visitor had called. Malte Putbus came, and soon afterwards Albert, looking very much out of spirits. As soon as he could do so, he told me that he had been deeply grieved by my reproachful glance. He seemed very penitent, and did not attempt to excuse himself; but he spoke so well and feelingly, that before the evening was over my resentment had vanished.

"Saturday, February 11th.—I went with Albert's parents to the ball at the Academy. When we came home I went up stairs with them to have some tea. Pauline and Eugénie ran to their rooms to take off their cloaks, and I remained alone with Albert in the drawing-room, drinking my tea in haste, for I wanted to go down again. He was admiring, I think, my long curls. He took one of them in his hands, and pressed it gently to his lips. I was displeased, but not so much as that other time. It did not seem to me quite so bad.

"Shrove Tuesday.—We spent the morning in the Corso, where the noise, the crowd, and the wild frolic raised my spirits to the highest pitch. Prince Lapoukhyn had engaged a balcony whence we could throw sugar plums. We had been ourselves deluged with them during a drive with Pauline and her father. We stood there to see the king pass in his illuminated car. At last, tired with waiting, I sat down to rest in the little room to which the balcony belonged. The king did not go by till seven o'clock, and we had then to hurry home for dinner, and to dress for the ball. I can remember so well the glad feeling in my heart whilst I was in that little room, half dozing and half watching for the passage of those pretty illuminated cars. Albert was there, and I was to meet him again in the evening at the ball. Though I was not at all sorry that Lent was coming, yet I liked that all that appearance of gaiety and those numerous festivities should mark, as it were, the hours I spent with him. My overflowing happiness made me enjoy these amusements, and I took a sort of triumphant delight in multiplying them. Oh, poor human weakness! When once Lent had begun, I felt happier every day. We conversed much more seriously than whilst the balls were going on. He talked to me a great deal about God, of the Angels, and of his dear religion, for which I felt an increasing attraction. I enjoyed a happiness so complete, so unexpected, so much beyond what I had ever even dreamt of, that it filled my heart with gratitude towards God, and made me more kind and indulgent to every one. I used to thank God that Albert was so much better than other people, and I thought myself far more fortunate than so many women who are loved in a frivolous manner, and who, I dare say, never thought of envying me.

"Holy Tuesday, April 2nd.—I felt to-day a great love for God, and for Albert also; and I wrote in my journal the first letters of the words 'For ever,' and 'May God be always with us.'

"Holy Thursday.—My mother gave me leave to go with my friends to the *Tenebræ* in the royal Chapel. The music was beautiful. Notwithstanding my frivolity, there was something in that lovely Chapel, the singing, and above all, perhaps, in the feeling that I was kneeling by my Albert's side, which made me pray with devotion. I was glad to look like a Catholic. Long before my conversion this used to please me. M. de la Ferronnays came to fetch us away. The walk home was perfect; the moon shining brightly, and the Neapolitan spring beginning to embalm the air. We stopped at several Churches on our way, to pray before the sepulchres. It is the custom in Naples to visit seven Churches on that day. Albert and I knelt down side by side on the pavement. There was in this something inexpressibly sweet to me. I do not know exactly what I prayed for, but I know we both raised our hearts to God with a full reliance on His goodness. I walked with him and his sisters; M. and Madame de la Ferronnays following us. Thus we went down the whole length of the Villa Reale, by the light of the moon and the stars, our hearts full of adoring love for God, and affection for one another."

"About that time Albert wrote a letter to the Abbé Martin de Noirlieu, a great friend of his, and received the following answer, which he showed me.

THE ABBE MARTIN DE NOIRLIEU* TO ALBERT.

"'MY DEAR FRIEND—I have received the books you returned to me. And so you copied out yourself the whole of the little volume! This is indeed a proof of the zeal which true affection inspires. And it inclines me to believe that the lady for whom you accomplished this work of love is intended by Providence to become the partner of your life. God's ways are so wonderful and merciful that we should never be discouraged by earthly obstacles. Persevere, my dear Albert, in your solicitude for that soul which is so dear to you. If you bring it to the knowledge of the truth, you will have made a conquest for God, and she will be yours not for time only but for eternity. It is especially to prayer that you must have recourse in this important matter, for light comes down from above, and thence must also proceed

* The Abbé Martin de Noirlieu, who was the first priest Alexandrine ever knew, is now Curé of Saint Louis d'Antin, Paris. It was this excellent and venerable friend of Albert's who, a few years later, received Alexandrine into the Church.

that courage which is so necessary when we have to overcome early prejudices and impressions imbibed in infancy. I am not surprised at what you tell me of the agitation which Mademoiselle —— feels at the idea of a change of religion. It seems to her as if in taking this step she had to cross an abyss, and, however courageous a person may be, it is natural to draw back on the brink of an unfathomable abyss. Protestants erroneously suppose that in renouncing heresy they are compelled to trample under foot and anathematize those they leave behind. God forbid that this should be the case! We condemn error, but we feel only love and pity for those whom it enthrals. By the fact of her reception into the Church she will simply declare that she returns to the faith which her ancestors held for fifteen centuries, and renounces the errors which separated from Catholic unity those amongst them who lived three hundred years ago. She will leave it to God to decide on individual cases, for He alone can judge who are and who are not in good faith in their heretical or schismatical position. In short, my dear friend, tell her that there is no salvation except for those who are in Catholic unity, or else for those who having been born in heresy are entirely in good faith, and would be ready to become Catholics at once if they thought that in so doing they would please God. But as to those who have doubts and will not seek instruction, or, which is still worse, who maintain that their forefathers sinned in breaking the unity of the Church, and yet persevere in remaining themselves out of its pale, they are fearfully guilty.

"'That soul interests me deeply, my dear Albert. I have already prayed for her this morning at Mass. I sincerely compassionate her mental sufferings. Tell her to hope, and, above all, to pray much. Ask her what she would do if she knew that the Mother of Our Lord was on earth and living near her. I have no doubt she would go at once and ask for her prayers. Let her, then, have recourse to this good Mother in Heaven. If she invokes her with confidence she is sure to be heard.'

"The book which the Abbé Martin speaks of, formed a thick manuscript in Albert's handwriting. He wished me to read it during the time of our approaching separation. It was to be his parting present. I received it with great pleasure and interest. It was my first book of instruction in Catholicism.

"On the 11th of April our friends made an excursion to Pæstum. Albert went with them, though he was suffering from a bad ear-ache, to which he did not pay any attention. Nobody was ever more courageous about bearing pain than Albert. His health was not good even at that time, but I felt no anxiety on the subject. I sometimes think that pitying Angels drove away from me all sad forebodings, for even up to the last months of his life, I was strangely unconscious of his danger. I now remember that at this very time, at Naples, he used often to tell me that he had fever at night; but as he was fretting very much about our approaching separation, I thought this sufficiently accounted for it. How we should ever be able to live apart we could not imagine. But we generally tried to comfort each other by hopes for the future, and by looking forward to the time when we should meet again, and then never to part any more!

"During these last days, when every moment was precious, my mother, who was a little unwell, used to have the door of her room open, and until she went to bed, Albert was allowed to remain with me in the drawing-room. I was anxious not to annoy her, and I was afraid she would be displeased if he stayed too long; so I used sometimes to urge him to go away. I had done so one evening, and then when he had left I found that Mamma was not nearly ready to go to bed, and I was vexed to have lost a few minutes of his society. I wrote on a little bit of paper: 'Dear friend, I have lost a few minutes. Mamma is not gone to bed yet. God bless you;' and I threw it from the balcony to Albert. A carriage was passing at that moment, and I was afraid he would be hurt as he threw himself forward to pick up the paper; but with his quick eyes and usual dexterity, he saw the note and secured it. This romantic little scene amused us, and the other day, more than a year after his death, I found that little scrap of paper in one of his books. I did not even know that he had preserved it.

"April 28th.—I wrote in my journal: 'I cannot realize the fact that we are actually to start to-morrow. I have always found it difficult to believe in any happy time of my life coming to an end. Surely this is a token that there is a life, and that a happy life, to come.' Pauline wrote that same day in my journal: 'May God take us all under His care,' and 'Grant us the blessing soon to meet again, all happier than in this parting hour.' On the last evening Albert stayed with me a long time. At first with Fernand, Eugénie, and Malte, and this was almost as good as being alone together. Afterwards we were by ourselves. I hardly can tell whether we felt most at that moment the sorrow of parting, or the joy which it gave us to know that we loved each other so tenderly. His sisters came down again. We four sat a little while together, talking rather sadly, and then they went away. That night was such a wretched one, that though it has been followed by many joyous ones, and by others a thousand times more terrible and sad, I cannot yet think of it without pain. It was, in fact, our last earthly separation. We met once more, and never parted again until death came; a more awful, but perhaps less bitter, separation, than earthly farewells. I said good-bye to him from the balcony, and when towards morning I went to bed, I most fervently begged of God to take pity on us; and I think that prayer gave me strength.

"On the following morning—Tuesday, April 30th, 1833, the day of parting—we were determined to be courageous and hopeful. We felt it would never do to look on this separation in its worse light. At eight o'clock in the morning Albert's sisters were in my room. Afterwards I went up with them to see their mother, who gave me a turquoise ring, which made me burst into tears. At two o'clock we all went together to the Crocelle, an hotel at Chiatamone, where Prince Lapoukhyn had invited us to dinner. But what a sad dinner it was! I could not any longer restrain my tears and sobs. I was sitting by Eugénie, who entreated me to control myself, for she was afraid my mother would be displeased by this excessive grief. At last, at a quarter to four, we had taken leave of everybody, and were seated in our travelling carriage. As we were going downstairs Albert asked me to give him full permission to hope. I looked at him quite surprised that he should still need such an assurance, and answered affirmatively. Those were our last words before that long separation. Albert and Fernand followed us for a long time in an open calèche in the pouring rain, which must have drenched them to the skin. I saw them a little longer in this way, but we could not speak to one another. At last, after a great waving of hands, their carriage stopped, and we lost sight of it. This rain, which did Albert so much harm, delayed the departure of the *Sully*, in which he was to have sailed that night for France, with his mother and Pauline and Eugénie. M. de la Ferronnays was to travel with them only as far as Civita Vecchia, and from thence proceed to Rome with his two youngest daughters."

As Alexandrine said, our departure was delayed till the next day, the 1st of May. We were all very low, first on account of the parting with Alexandrine, also from the fear that our absence from Naples might prove longer than we wished, and chiefly because we were to lose our dearest father and our little sisters at Civita Vecchia. My mother was going with us to France, on business. My father was taking my sisters to the Convent of the Trinità da Monte, at Rome, where they were to spend three months, and Olga to make her First Communion. As we were all to meet again in Rome on that occasion, we were not looking forward to a long separation; but in those days we were so used to happiness, that it made us exacting. And now this state of things was about to be interrupted, and we were for the first time to experience serious anxiety. Albert had not been strong for some time, and the wetting he had had on the evening of Alexandrine's departure, had done him far more harm than we were aware of. During the first part of our passage he looked ill, but we attributed it to the sorrow he felt in parting with her. When the evening closed in, the sea grew rough, and we all went to lie down. On arriving at Civita Vecchia, Albert asked my mother to let him remain there for a couple of days, as he wished to be bled. He would then follow us to Paris, he said, and arrive there as soon as we did. He had, unfortunately, lately adopted that common and injurious Italian practice of having recourse to bleeding, on the most trifling occasions, and whenever his head or his chest felt uncomfortable, he insisted on being bled, without even taking medical advice. Though my mother had not the slightest idea how ill he felt, she would on no account have left him alone; but as his father and his little sisters were to land at Civita Vecchia, this seemed the safest and most prudent course. Indeed, there was no time for discussion, for the boat was about to start. My father decided that Albert should remain with him, and that we should continue our journey. So at three o'clock in the morning we went on board again, with heavier hearts than on the preceding day, but still without any idea of the sorrow which was hanging over us. Our boat was not out of sight, when Albert was seized with so violent a fever and inflammation of the lungs, that the physician pronounced his life to be in imminent danger. I have often thought that my mother, who was to go through so many subsequent trials, was in mercy spared the sight of this illness. Though she felt the parting with Albert, and was uneasy about him, she did not know the urgency of the danger till it was in a great measure past. It may be easily imagined with what feelings she received the following letter two days after our arrival in Paris.

FROM M. DE LA FERRONNAYS TO HIS WIFE.

"In order to give you the account which I know you are impatiently expecting, I ought to put my own thoughts into some kind of arrangement, which is not easy. First of all, do not be uneasy. The danger is past. We might have been indeed wretched at this moment. Thank God! for He it is who puts wise thoughts into our minds, that I decided on keeping our child here. He would not have arrived alive at Leghorn. And thank Him also that Miss McCarthy* was on board the same steamer, and that there was a man-of-war in the harbor. But for all these circumstances, God knows what would have happened! You remember that just before starting, the little doctor came in to say that Albert had only caught a chill. After putting you on board, I asked him to go back with me to see him again. We had been away barely twenty minutes. Imagine what I felt at seeing the little man, after only just glancing at him, throw off his coat, take out his lancet, and at once bleed him in the arm. All aghast, I asked him what was the matter. 'The matter!' he said, 'only just feel his legs, and you will see.' They were as cold as ice. A few moments more and our son would have been dead. That bleeding saved his life. The blood began to circulate again, and he fell asleep. We owe his safety to that little doctor.

"Since that moment, good excellent Miss McCarthy became my teacher and my guardian angel. You know what a skilful nurse she is, but you can hardly picture to yourself what has been her devotedness, her tender care of Albert. I did my best under her direction, and you can imagine the night we

* Eugénie's former governess.

spent by his bedside, or in the room of our poor little girls, who were frequently startled out of their sleep by their brother's moanings. But I will not enlarge upon it now. More than once I thanked God that you were spared this suffering. In the morning the fever had abated, and being somewhat reassured by the doctor, and at the same time anxious as to the effect of this agitation upon the children, I thought it best to take them at once to Rome, and leave them at the convent. Lapoukhyn came to me there, and most kindly proposed just what I most wished, that is, to send his own physician to Albert. I will tell you another time about that dear, sweet Alexandrine. She loves him too well to have been able to conceal her distress. Her secret is no longer a secret now; but what does it signify? If, as the Abbé Martin thinks, this marriage is made in Heaven, it will take place, and prove a blessing. They both deserve to be happy.

"In the afternoon I left Rome, carrying off with me that good, skilful physician, Sauvan. We found Albert less well than when I left him, in a high fever, and with a dry hacking cough. Sauvan immediately bled him, and applied mustard poultices to his feet. My dearest love, I cannot tell you what I went through in seeing the sufferings of our beloved and patient child. At eight o'clock this morning, Sauvan found it necessary to bleed him once more, and now, as I am sitting writing by his bedside, he seems nearly himself again. I did not write by yesterday's post, for I had nothing but anxious fears to impart. I was almost out of my mind with grief, and should have talked nonsense. I am miserable when I think that it will be a whole fortnight before you receive this letter, and that during all that time you will be fearing and suffering. Oh, it has been indeed a trial! I can never be grateful enough to that dear, old Miss McCarthy. All the money I can give her, and all the affection I can show her, will never repay one half of our debt of gratitude. How we feel to love one who is helping us to save a beloved child from the jaws of death. How charming and clever we think them. I think I should have quite lost my head but for this good woman. Even as it was, I could hardly control myself. Poor dear woman, she has never taken off her clothes since she was lying on the deck of the steamer. She has scarcely eaten or drunk, or slept for more than half-an-hour, for four days, all for the sake of our child. Our poor boy's changed face looks sadly wan and pale. He is dreadfully thin, and his eyes so large and sunken. Still, he is better; he feels so, he says, and he wishes me to tell you, and to add that he dotes upon you and on his sisters. His only grief is not to be with you. He can speak now; he coughs less, and breathes more easily, and I hardly know whether to grieve or rejoice. He is, I think, out of danger, but it is terrible to see him looking so dreadfully ill. I see now there is nothing one would not go through for one's children. How glad I should be to take our Albert's place on that bed of suffering! Well, I trust Almighty God will not try us any further. He will hear our prayers, and yours especially, who have always received with resignation and sweetness every cross He has laid upon you. Ah, this has been a great trial, my dearest wife, and a great escape! I promise to bless God for it with all my heart.

"I will tell you another day what I felt when the boat took you all away. How my heart ached whilst I stood gazing on it with hot, dry, tearless eyes, until it lessened and then disappeared. For a long time I could still discern the faint trail of the smoke, then that too, passed away, and I found myself alone; alone with my dying boy. Oh, my dear Albertine, when I see you and my girls again, I may perhaps forget what I have suffered, and what I am still going through; but till then! . . . Well, on the whole, Albert is better. I would not tell you so if it were otherwise. The doctor made me very happy just now by giving me full directions about his mode of life during his recovery, and our journey to Rome. This shows he is sincere, when he says he is out of danger. I fully believe it, and so will you.

"I have agreed with Madame Barat* that Olga should commence at once to prepare for her First Communion, but not to make it till the time when we hope all to be with her, at that important moment of her life. You would have been pleased to see me watching over our little girls, and looking at them in their beds. Farewell, my dearest wife. You must forgive this incoherent letter, for my head, my heart, and my body, are almost worn out. I am nearly in a fever myself. The next

* Madame Barat was the foundress of the Order of the Sacred Heart, and who died lately a holy death, at Paris, at the advanced age of eighty-seven.

time I write, I hope to do so in a more rational manner. Farewell, my dear love. Kiss, for me, my darling girls, my dear, good Charles, and all our dear ones. Love me always, and above all pray for me and for Albert. Poor dear Albert, how much he has suffered! Once more, adieu."

FROM THE SAME TO THE SAME.

"Civita Vecchia, May 10th.

"MY DEAR WIFE—Albert is out of danger. Be happy, and thank God! He was much worse again on Monday, the 6th, and we had no medical men but those of Civita Vecchia, who showed, however, more skill than I expected. The crisis came on about the middle of the day. It was terrible while it lasted, and had it continued a few hours longer, I should have been obliged to send you to-day nothing but the heart-breaking announcement of the loss of the dearest and best child ever given to any parents. But God has had mercy on us. In less than two hours Albert's pulse rose to 170, with a dreadful difficulty in breathing. I sent for the two doctors, who immediately bled him. This produced some relief, but there still seemed reason to apprehend another crisis, which our poor child could not have lived through. We remained in agonizing suspense from three to seven o'clock. At that time an abundant perspiration came on, which till then the physician had vainly endeavored to bring about. This was the one thing to be desired, and oh, with what ardor I poured forth thanksgivings from the very depths of my soul! You will understand it, for you love our children as much as I do. How everything seems to change about us when we see an improvement in a beloved patient! As the favorable symptoms increased, Albert's countenance resumed a more natural expression; his sufferings diminished; he looked serene and almost cheerful. The perspiration lasted till one o'clock in the morning. When it began to abate, preparations were made to remove him into another bed, and he had scarcely been placed in it, before he fell into a refreshing sleep, which lasted till morning.

"I had written to Fernand at the outset of Albert's illness, leaving it to him to come or not, as he wished, and this morning he arrived at full speed. I was very glad to have him, and Albert was pleased. I dare not dwell for the present on the difficulties that may arise. Good Miss McCarthy goes away to-morrow, quite knocked up, and we shall feel her loss sadly, though she has pretty well taught me to be a good nurse. And *I have got a servant!* Why should I not indulge myself whilst fortune smiles upon us?* This expense was necessary, and therefore not unreasonable. I must send Albert to Ems, where he will find friends. We shall have to spend plenty of money, and be too happy to have only that to complain of. But meanwhile some other plans may come into my head, and in that case I will act upon them, presuming on your approval.

"Dear Albertine, these cares and trials oppress and disturb me, but at the same time they call forth an energy which I thought I had lost, and I feel I shall have strength to bear a great deal more yet without giving way. Do not be anxious about my health. I fancied myself enfeebled in body and depressed in mind, but on the contrary, though I have led a trying life since we parted, I have not for a long time felt so well. Happiness dulled my powers, but suffering revives me.

"Let me hear about the girls. I am pining for news about them. Tell me if they are looking well and blooming. Oh, do beg of them not to be ill. It is so dreadful to see one's children suffer! It is only then that we feel how much we love them. Would that I could always suffer every pain instead of them, and guard them from every sorrow. You will remind me that we may soon not have a place where to lay our heads. I can only reply, 'God will provide.' He knows it is not through any fault of mine that we are so situated. He is able and willing to assist us, and will no doubt do so when we have no other help to turn to. Good-bye, my dear and most beloved wife. Get back to me as soon as possible, for without you I am not worth a straw. Kiss, not once, but a thousand times, my darling Pauline, and my Jane,† Charlie, his pretty Emma, and all our dear ones, and love me, if you can, as much as I love you."

THE SAME TO THE SAME.

"Civita Vecchia, May 12th, 1833.

"Albert is going on well. His recovery must be slow, but there are no bad symptoms, and the fever has quite subsided.

* The reader will recollect that it was barely three years since M. de la Ferronnays was French ambassador at Rome, and accustomed to every luxury of an affluent position.

† Eugénie.

He will not be allowed to get up for some days. We cannot be too careful. It is delightful to see Fernand's devotion to his brother. If I can possibly send Albert to Ems, I will do so, not only for the sake of his health, but also to make him happy, and to turn his mind from the gloomy thoughts he indulges when away from Alexandrine. I know what comments this will give rise to, but after all, what does it signify? Having gone so far in this matter, it will be hard that it should not end as they both wish. We must make up our minds to it. They will be poor, of course, but they will also enjoy some years of happiness, and I do not think you will take a sterner view of the subject than I do. It is quite certain that as long as they are both free, neither one nor the other will marry any one else. Why, then, should they be condemned to wither apart, spending life in endless regrets? I have therefore resolved, if you do not object to it, to enable Albert to go and take the waters at Ems.*

"I have only just received your letter from Leghorn. Poor darlings, how ignorant you were of our anxieties, when you spoke of sending back Albert to me from Paris! The doctors say, and I am inclined to believe it, that so sharp an illness at the age of one-and-twenty, will serve to establish his health, and that he will be a great deal stronger than before. Poor dear boy! It would grieve you to see him looking so tall, thin, and pale; nevertheless, I rejoice to see him pale. He was anything but pale three days ago. I shall never forget his crimson face and sparkling eyes. Oh, dearest, I feel nothing but happiness to-day! Do you, who know so well how, return thanks to God for yourself and for me, and implore Him to afflict me in any other way, rather than through my children's sufferings. Our little girls' letters brought tears into my eyes. I like to hear them say they cannot do without me, and yet it saddens me too, for by this time they ought to have had other protectors than their father. Give them a thousand kisses. I shall write to them as soon as I can. Their letters do me a world of good, but do not tell them to write. Let them do so when they are inclined. Good-bye, my beloved wife. Best love to all."

* This plan was unfortunately given up, the doctors having subsequently decided that the waters were not necessary for Albert.

FROM THE SAME TO THE SAME.

"Civita Vecchia, May 14th.

"MY DEAR WIFE—I am just come back from Rome, where I have been spending a day and a night. This is the best proof I can give you of Albert's improved condition. The doctors are quite surprised at his rapid recovery. During my absence he was left in Fernand's charge, who is a stricter gaoler than myself, and obeys orders with scrupulous exactness. He is a capital nurse. It is charming to see him with his brother. He amuses him, makes him laugh, and pets him like a child. He has had his bed put alongside Albert's, and when I came back to-night, I found them both fast asleep.

"You must have had an enchanting passage from Genoa, with the view of the Riviera, and the mountains in the background in sight the whole of the day. All that bright, grand, luxuriant country forms a marked contrast to the barren and desolate coast of Provence, with its dull grey coloring, and ugly mountain line. This is by no means pleasant to our French feelings, and we have need to call to mind the poet's words—

'A tous les cœurs bien nés, que la patrie est chère !'

not to experience something like disappointment in approaching the coast of France. For the next four months the past days will be the only ones which will enable me to get through the others. My only interest will be your letters. Now that my fears about Albert are at an end, I begin to be a little alarmed at the heavy expenses I have incurred, and still have to meet. My little fund at Naples will be well-nigh exhausted in a month. But when I think of the escape we have had, I can do nothing but thank and bless God, who has spared me the greatest of sorrows, and only tries me with regard to money matters. *He will provide.* Kiss my beloved darlings for me."

CONTINUATION OF ALEXANDRINE'S JOURNAL.

"After travelling all night, we arrived on Wednesday evening, the 1st of May, in Rome, through that enchanting Lateran Gate. My affection for my good and pious Albert made me look upon Rome in a new light, and it was pleasant to be once more in the holy city which he loved so well, and where our love had begun.

We drove to Serny's Hotel. From our windows I could see our old abode, the Casa Margherita, and the French Academy brilliantly lighted up. All these places had now a peculiar charm for me, and what I cared little about before now became precious in my eyes. The next day (the 2nd of May) I went to see the M——s. When I found myself in their room a strange sense of the changes that happen in life seized me. Everything concerning myself had so altered since I was last with them. I was very glad to hear from M—— that I was looking younger, and that my complexion was much improved. She spoke of Albert, but this embarrassed me. I liked better to talk of him with Malte Putbus, who knew all about our affairs, and took an interest in them.

"In the night of May the 3rd, I had so fearful a dream that as soon as I was up I went to Mamma, who was in bed, to tell her of it. It had seemed to me that I was with Albert and Mamma on the edge of a deep hollow, which was filled with a number of graves with Crosses upon them. Albert said to me, 'Have you the courage to walk amongst all those Crosses?' I felt strangely frightened, but answered interiorly, 'Since he asks me to do so, I will.' Then I took Mamma's hand and went down with her amongst the graves, from whence I could see Albert standing above us. I felt glad to have had the courage to do in my dream what I had shrunk from till Albert proposed it. I said to Mamma that I was afraid this dream was a bad omen, and this led us to speak of Albert. She told me that in her opinion the state of his health would be a sufficient objection to our marriage, even if no other hindrances existed. But this I would never allow. On the same day I went to the Villa Pamphili with the M——s. How many pleasant thoughts of the past, and at that moment of the future also, it brought to my mind! A few hours later, after dinner at the M——s, I remarked that Count Maurice Putbus had left the room, and some one told me he had been fetched out. He came back and spoke to Mamma, who looked agitated, and I suspected that something had happened which they were keeping from me. I heard, or thought I heard, the words 'French vessel.' Immediately the thought of an accident at sea crossed my mind. My mother got up, and we went away. She would not say anything till we were alone, but in the carriage she told me that Albert was ill at

Civita Vecchia, and that his father had come to Rome to fetch a physician. At first I felt a sort of relief, for I had dreaded something worse. But shortly afterwards a terror seized me that my mother had not told me the whole truth. I knew that M. de la Ferronnays was in the same hotel with us, and I was dying to see him; but by a series of misunderstandings the evening passed without our meeting. When I was left alone, quite in despair, I wrote to Pauline the following lines, not that I thought of sending them, but only because I had no one else to speak to.

"'Pauline, I am too wretched. I write to you because I have no one here to whom I can pour out my anguish. Oh, why are you not here? And only imagine that in this moment of dreadful anxiety, Mamma has just told me that she may perhaps feel herself bound in duty not to let me marry a man whose health is so failing; when I know that it is grief that kills him, and that nothing but happiness can do him good. O! my God, I do not ask Thee to take my life, for that would make him miserable, but in any other way let me suffer everything Thou wilt, in soul and body, and let him be happy for a very long time on earth, for the sake of our Lord Jesus Christ. Pauline, I shall go out of my mind! May God help me, and not punish me for my too great love for Albert!'

"Every time that my mother tried to convince me how terrible it would be to see my husband ill, and that it would be worse then than now, I answered: 'Oh! no, if I were his wife, I could nurse him myself, and that would lessen the suffering!' I said this so earnestly that it made Mamma for the first time understand the strength of my feelings for Albert, and from that moment she resolved to do all she could to forward our marriage. She told us this afterwards. Albert's father, also, during his illness, became convinced of the depth of our attachment, and we have often said to each other that to this illness we were indebted for our marriage and all our happiness. This was true, but, alas! we were not aware at that time of the fatal results it left behind it, and which only manifested themselves long afterwards. I had news that same day of Eugénie and Pauline from their father, and he gave me also my little book of thoughts which I had left with Albert. At the time when his breathing was so oppressed that he could hardly speak, he said to Eugénie: 'Look in the vessel for Alex's little book. You will find it on my bed, and also the cushion she worked for me. Take care of them both.' Eugénie gave the book to her father, who was seeing them off, under the idea that it would be immediately returned to Albert; but when M. de la Ferronnays got back to the hotel he found his son almost at death's door. From the window that poor father happened to catch sight of the vanishing steamer, and he felt as if he would have liked to cry out: 'Albert is dying! Come back! come back!' The sight of my little book filled me with sorrowful surprise. Albert was to have kept it till we met again. Had he been conscious he would never have parted with it.

"The Abbé Martin came to see us. Mamma told him of Albert's illness, and he was so grieved that I felt a greater regard for him than ever, although even before I knew him I had looked upon him as a friend. If I could have spoken to him alone that day, I think I should have opened my heart to him, and told him how much I loved Albert and Albert's religion. If, indeed, he did not know it already. He must have seen my eyes full of tears, for I had no wish to hide them from him. I was gifted at that time with extraordinary calmness, and a firmness and courage which had not hitherto belonged to my character, so that I did not care for the remarks and opposition of the world. I felt sure of Albert's love, and of mine for him; and certain that ours was a right kind of love. When M. de la Ferronnays returned to Civita Vecchia, taking with him M. Sauvan, Prince Lapoukhyn's physician, Mamma and I went with him to the top of the staircase to bid him good-bye. What a parting it was. Would Albert be alive the next time we should meet! Not knowing how to express what I felt, I kissed his hand. In the afternoon I went to the Trinità da Monte with Mamma, to see Olga and Albertine. That was also a spot full of sweet, sad recollections. Olga came to us in tears. Whilst Mamma was trying to comfort her about Albert, I took one of the nuns aside, and gave her an alms for the poor, begging her to get prayers for the brother of these poor children.

"Prince Lapoukhyn was in the same hotel with us. His room was near mine, and he told me never to scruple sending for him if I felt too anxious. I did not do that, but sometimes very late, before I went to bed, I used to speak to him through the door, and say, 'What do you think of him? He was better, you know? Sauvan will do him good.' I wanted to hear from somebody words of hope. Oh, those nights! If there is one thing more terrible than the sickness and death of those we love, it is to be absent from them at the time. Sometimes the thought would flash across me that at that very moment Albert was dying. Nevertheless the hours of anguish which I spent on my knees at the open window were more bearable than those which I dragged out in the company of others, and obliged to exercise self-control. Yet on those nights the very splendor of the stars seemed to me ominous; those gleaming orbs, the sight of which used always to soothe me, now appeared to threaten evil. The whole world would be so dreadful if Albert were to die! Once again, in my after life, one terrible night, the moon had the same ghastly effect upon me. I do not know if my heart quite acquiesced in the prayer my lips uttered, but I know I kept repeating, with all the strength of my will: 'My God, Thy will be done!' Once when I was thus praying in one of those moments of bitterest grief, I was suddenly filled with an irrepressible joy. I felt certain I should see Albert alive, and that we should once more be glad. Then the stars shone again as brightly as of old, and everything spoke of delightful happiness to come. Fearing to lose this joyful feeling, I went at once to bed, that my last thoughts might be impressed with it.

"We went to the Trinità again to see the two children. It was the time I liked best in the day. As we went in I heard at a distance the singing of hymns to the Blessed Virgin. When we came home we found better news from Civita Vecchia. They told us that the Princess Zénaïde Wolkonsky had called whilst we were out, and had waited some time for us. I found a bit of paper on which she had been scribbling these words, written over and over again: '*La speranza non si deve mai abbandonare.*'* I felt glad, for at that moment the least trifle seemed to influence me.

"May 6th.—We dined with Princess Wolkonsky at her villa near the Lateran. How sadly I gazed on the beautiful Roman Campagna! Yet I was not without hope. When we returned in the evening we found M. Sauvan, who brought us a better account. But Albert has been so dreadfully ill that he can-

* "We must never give up hoping."

not be brought to Rome in less than a week's time at the soonest, and so the small hopes I had of seeing him vanished. I wrote the same evening to Pauline and Eugénie, but without letting them know the whole extent of what I had feared and suffered.

"'My dear Friends—May the joy I felt last night continue and increase! Till this morning I had some little hope of remaining here until after Albert's arrival, but it now seems decided that we leave the day after to-morrow. If he is but well, I do not care. I have learnt to endure absence. God's will be done! All He does is well done. I should indeed be ungrateful if I were to murmur now, when, notwithstanding all I have gone through, He has made me a hundred times, nay a thousand times happier than I deserve.'

"That same day Fernand unexpectedly walked in. He had ridden the whole way from Naples, and was on his way to Civita Vecchia, to help nurse his brother. Soon after his arrival I went with him to the Trinità to see his sisters. Whilst waiting for them we went into the Church, where I had often been with Albert to hear the exquisite singing. It was a great comfort to pray with Fernand for Albert, and to pray on my knees. It pained me so much not to be always able to do this. When Olga came to us she looked quite surprised at seeing Fernand, and said: 'Oh, is it you, Fernand? I thought it must be Charles and Emma, for they told us that *M. and Madame de la Ferronnays* were here.' This made us smile, and I thought it a good omen. After dinner Fernand sat down on the sofa by my side, to arrange about a letter to Albert, which he was to give him as soon as he was well enough to read it. This was my note:

"'It is hardly necessary that I should write to you! but it will give you pleasure to see my handwriting, and perhaps what I shall tell you may be a comfort. I am sure I need not say that I love you, my beloved Albert, and that I think I have never loved, and certainly never will love, any but you. I can endure our separation when I am certain you are well, but for God's sake try as much as you can to recover. Do try to spare me such terrible anxiety. Take care of yourself, as you would wish to take care of me. If you love me, follow the advice of your friends. It is better to be too prudent than not to be prudent enough. Thank God a thousand times that you are really better! To-morrow evening Fernand will send us an account of you to Viterbo. God grant it may be a good one. Have you heard that the waters of Ems are prescribed for you? You must not make any objection to this plan, indeed you must try to promote it, for Ems is only one day's distance from Kissingen, where we are going, and in this way we might meet in about seven weeks. Only think, dearest Albert, how pleasant that would be! Oh, yes; I think God loves us. I feel a little distressed at writing to you before everybody. Well, never mind. What I meant to say is this; if you wish me to do anything in the world for you which I can do, be sure I will do it; of course I do not mean anything wrong. If this promise can give you pleasure, bear it always in mind. Farewell, beloved friend. Let us beg of God to look on us with mercy, and promise Him to be as good as possible. May we soon meet again with His help who orders all things for the best. Al—.'

"I found this note, and all those I have ever written to Albert, in a little pocket-book which he always carried about him. Together with these were his First Communion ribbon, a prayer his mother had sewed in the lining, and a relic of St. Alphonsus Liguori. At eleven o'clock in the morning of the 7th of May, Fernand went to Civita Vecchia. He took leave of me with the most brotherly affection, and I felt myself thoroughly his sister. He understood all we felt so well, and in a few hours he was to see Albert! And when should I see him again? I kept saying this to myself as I took leave of Fernand. What a separation it was! and not a creature to whom I could tell my thoughts! I was a little comforted, however, by Fernand's visit, and at thinking he was with him, and that he would give him my letter. The next day we left Rome, and slept at Viterbo. There I heard of a young man who had died, and was lying in the church close to the Inn. It made me sorrowful. I could not bear anything which suggested the idea that Albert might die. Such was my folly at that time. I believed indeed in Heaven, but cared only for earthly joys. Our letters were brought to us early the next morning, and the accounts, thanks to God, were good."

Albert recovered rapidly. A fortnight after Alexandrine's departure he was at home, almost quite well again, and wrote thence the following letter to his mother:

ALBERT TO HIS MOTHER.

"At last, my dearest mother, I am allowed to write a few words to you. I can hardly believe yet in all that has happened. You are at Dangu, and I am here in Rome again! It is certainly very strange! The sad part of the affair is the anxiety I have given my dear father. One half hour more of that fever, I am told, would have prevented my ever seeing you again. Does it not seem incredible, dearest mother? For my own part, I had not the least notion of it. The minutes went by, and I took no notice of them. That week when I was so ill I felt strangely without pain. I may have forgotten my sufferings, but I certainly am not conscious of them when I look back, and I was on the point of departing from this life with little previous expectation of it. God has mercifully delayed a departure for which I was ill-prepared. But He has shown me that we ought be ready at any moment to obey His summons. I thank Him with all my heart for this knowledge. I am going to spend the summer quite quietly with my dearest father and my good Fernand, but longing, pining for you to come back. Do not keep us waiting too long. Do all come very soon, Emma and Charles included. Tell them that although I am bad about writing, I love them nevertheless, with all my heart. Good-bye, my darling mother. I love you more than I can express. Oh, why am I not with you and my dear sisters! Write to me as often as you can, and love me always. Your ALBERT."

FROM MY FATHER TO MY MOTHER.

"Absurd as it may seem, I have not time to write to you to-day more than a few words. Albert has borne perfectly well our journey of eight hours. He has not coughed once, and does not seem at all tired. I have given him leave to write you a short letter. I think he is going on very well. There could not have been a more rapid and satisfactory recovery. Now what we have to avoid is imprudence, and this is no easy matter. It is on this account I do not leave him. I hope he will continue to be as good and tractable as at present. He is as excellent a creature as ever lived. The children are charming, and getting on beautifully. Good-bye, my dearest wife. I will write you a real letter the day after to-morrow."

ALBERT TO M. DE MONTALEMBERT.

"Rome, May 30th, 1833.

"Well, my dear kind friend, we make plans, and God overrules them. I expected that by this time we should have met and spent many happy days together. Instead of which, I am at Rome for a short time, and then I go to Castellamare with my father and Fernand. I have been neither more or less than dying. A few more minutes, and it would have been all over with me. God has ordained it otherwise. So much the better. But when shall we meet again? Do write often. I fear our friendship will have to stand the test of a prolonged absence. I have not heard from you for ages. I am allowed to write very little at a time. Is it true, as M. Bunsen tells us, that dear Rio is about to marry a wealthy and amiable English lady? I hope it is so, and that he will be as happy as he deserves to be.

"And you, dear friend, what are you doing with yourself? If only you would not keep so much aloof, and control your imagination, which makes you see things differently from what they are, and aim at impossible results. Do not suppose that when I accuse you of exaggeration, I allude at all to your affections and feelings. No, I mean politics, which wear your life out. For my own part, I honestly confess that I have no decided political opinions, for I nowhere see perfect prosperity or perfect tranquillity. The worst of it is that we live in a period of transition, and have by no means emptied our cup to the dregs. I comfort myself with the thought that religion, the foundation of all happiness, can never perish, and that in these trying times it alone seems fated to triumph over all its enemies. With regard to political parties, I look with sorrow and something of contempt on their virulent animosities, and the insults and anathemas which they hurl at each other. To what results do those loud vociferations, those miserable intrigues tend? The Revolution in the midst of which we live will run its course if left to itself. There is but one line I can take; but I will own to you that even in that quarter also the future seems to me pregnant with storms. A dynasty which has been three times overthrown has, I fear, served its time. I acknowledge that there alone exists the rightful claim; but will a child brought up out of France, and with ideas opposed to those of the present century, secure to us what we want? I have misgivings on that point. We must be patient; we cannot see into futurity. Possibly that last remaining vestige of the old principle of authority is destined to raise us from our present state of anarchy. In the meantime, religion flourishes, and if we are fated to see a new restoration, God grant that our clergy may not make themselves subservient to the Government. The people with us are always apt to mistrust those in power, and to look upon priests with suspicion, if they unite themselves too closely with them. I hope our clergy will give up politics. They have surely a higher mission.

"I dare say I have written many foolish things, for which you will perhaps severely condemn me. Well, I can only wait, and hope that God will guide me. Of one thing I am certain, and that is, that I will never go against my conscience. So come what may, I am prepared.

"Good-bye. Write to me at Naples. Tell me about Rio; we have both been negligent about writing, but he knows my friendship for him is unchanged. As to you, I love you more dearly than ever. Let me know your plans for the winter.

"ALBERT."

ALBERT TO OLGA.

"MY DARLING SISTER—My father is too busy to write to you before the post goes out, and has asked me to send you not only a letter, but also a kiss, and I execute his orders on my own account as well as his. This . . . . Do not puzzle over that word. I had begun a sentence; my father came in to speak to me, and I have forgotten what I was going to write. It does not matter. My father desires me to say that a M. Guillet or Guillot will call on you one of these days to look at your eyes.* He

* Olga's eyes had been weak since the age of eight years. This trial proved very profitable to her soul, for on every occasion she offered up to God without a murmur the privations it entailed. She delighted in reading and study, and was peculiarly gifted with the tastes which make a person enjoy the beauties of nature and art. In these respects she had to make daily and hourly sacrifices. I do not know how oculists describe the visual defect she suffered from. Too much light deprived her of sight. When in a room moderately lighted, or out of doors on a dull day, she saw very tolerably; but the moment the sun began to shine it dazzled her, and she could discern nothing. It is incredible to how many disappointments this infirmity subjected her. Sometimes in a picture gallery a ray of light would fall on some of the best paintings, and hide them completely from her sight. Or in a walk taken for the express purpose of enjoying some beautiful view, the sudden brightening of the sky would bring on the inability to see it. In Church sometimes we used to see her quietly shut her book without a shadow of impatience, and begin to think, as she used to say, instead of reading. No doubt it was partly owing to this circumstance that she possessed a more reflective mind, and a greater depth of thought and feeling at the age of sixteen, than are often found in girls of that age. Amongst a hundred other occasions when I was struck by her gentleness and resignation, I particularly remember one day in 1840, at Naples (she was then seventeen years of age), when we went together to look at the procession of Corpus Christi, which was passing through the Strada di Toledo. Whilst we walked in the shade in the Chiaja she saw perfectly, and we were conversing gaily. We stopped at the corner of the street, and after we had waited a few minutes the procession went by; but Olga only heard the singing, for the reflection of the light

will examine them, and then will write to my father what ought to be done. Show this letter to Madame de Coriolis, that the person may be permitted to see you. And now I must tell you about ourselves at Castellamare. My father and I live like hermits. Fernand goes out a little more. He is, however, often at home, and then we talk of nothing but our absent friends, and very often of our little Olga. 'When shall we see them again? What a day that will be! How we shall hug one another! How delightful it will be to meet after four months' absence,' and so on. My dearest sister, do not forget your poor old Albert in your prayers. The happiest day in your life is drawing near; all you petitions will then be heard. Pray for us all. God will grant you whatever you ask. This is a very short letter, but I cannot write long without fatigue. I shall often write to you, but send your answers to my father, for your letters do him good, and add a little word for me. In a very short time we shall all meet and be happy together.

"Your loving brother, ALBERT."

ALBERT TO ALEXANDRINE.

(ENCLOSED IN A LETTER FROM FERNAND.)

"DEAR DEAREST LOVE—One word only to tell you how much good your letter did me. If I were not afraid of talking nonsense, I should say it had cured me. I am so surprised at not feeling unhappy; on the contrary, I am in good spirits and full of hope. You seem to be near me; it is almost as if you were speaking. You and I after all are one. No, I am not going to join you. We must be patient. Time flies only too fast, and next winter we shall meet. But I pray every day that if you could be really happier with any one else, you should give me up. I have had joy enough to last me my whole life, if only I can be certain you are happy. I do not mean to say, however, that there is not something I should like better than that. Well, let us hope. God is so good! And I am sure it cannot have been for nothing that I did not die at Civita Vecchia. I take every care of myself, for indeed I wish to see you again. Would your mother object to these few lines? I do not think she would.

on the banners and the arms of the soldiers entirely prevented her from seeing. She was silent for a few minutes, and then turning to me said: "I have seen nothing, but it does not make me sad. On the contrary, I thought just now quite with joy, how many beautiful sights God would let me see in Paradise, to make up for the pleasure I lose on earth." Dear sweet little sister, what great examples she gave us, and how many wise words fell from her young lips!

However, do just as you think best. Tell me if I may continue to describe everything I think and feel. My next letter will be for your dear mother. It was only natural that I should begin with you. Don't you think so? I shall spend the summer with my dear father and with Fernand. I can never feel any *ennui*, for you are constantly present to me. Good-bye. This letter is short, but you know well all that is in my heart. I love you, and God is very good! Let us hope. A."

EUGÉNIE TO ALEXANDRINE.

"I do pray so much for you: for you and for Pauline, for Pauline and you, and so it goes on. I don't say anything about Albert, because Albert and you mean the same thing. God loves him: God has saved him: God will bless him and you also. I have taken again to my old favorite prayer, in which I beseech God to give Pauline and you all my share of happiness in this world. This is not praying to be unhappy, for if my prayer was granted, I should be perfectly content."

Alexandrine answered:—"May God reward and bless you, sweetest and dearest little friend! You are indeed asking for your own happiness when you pray so fervently that Pauline and I may be happy, for certainly what kind of joy could we find in life if you had not an equal share of it?"

ALBERT TO PAULINE.

"DEAREST SISTER—I have received your dear letter, and between ourselves, I must tell you how much it touched me. It would have made me vain if my heart had not been full of other thoughts. I deeply feel the happiness of being so beloved by my family, but I cannot understand it. Without any affectation of modesty, I really do not see how I deserve it. Nevertheless, by all means cherish your illusions. I am very glad you have them! I am sorry not to be with you. I am so calm, so hopeful, and in such good spirits. Study, my dear ones, to acquire this sort of tranquillity. Do not be afraid if the road is sometimes rough, a brighter future lies before you. The last part of your letter gave me pain, my dear Pauline. So my poor darling is again in a state of agitation. Why should they torment her on that subject now? Did not her mother tell her one day that she could understand a woman's changing her religion for her husband's sake? Was she thinking of becoming a Greek? Not a bit of it. But that is the sort of way in which people speak who mistake opinion for faith. In matters of opinion, early associations, and a thousand minor considerations, may and should influence one, but where religion is concerned, we are accountable to God alone for our thoughts and actions, and He will not hold us guiltless if we resist the voice of conscience, which He makes use of to discover to us our errors, as well as our faults. Poor child! While I am leading a tranquil life, she is a prey to trouble. That is the worst of it, for otherwise I feel confident of the result. God watches over her, and if she did not suffer, I should smile at her troubles. Tell her not to torment herself, and to conquer all those fears, scruples, misgivings, and miseries, which only serve to waste time. God does not require us to make ourselves miserable, and nothing is more injurious to the soul than agitation. Inward peace is what we must seek. Tell her also that I love her as much as ever, and perhaps still more than ever. I do not write because I should not like my letters to be opened by others. Adieu. I love both you and dear Eugénie with all my heart. When you write to my poor darling, try to calm her as much as possible. Tell her to trust and hope."

Whilst this entire trust gave Albert perfect tranquillity, and that we on our side were enjoying ourselves in France, poor Alexandrine was undergoing many heartaches in Germany. As long as they were at Naples, her good and gentle mother had been charmed with Albert's love for her daughter. She liked him very much herself; she was touched by his ardent affection, and had done nothing to prevent matters coming to a crisis, when she could have done so without making them really unhappy. But no sooner did she find herself away from Italy, separated from us, surrounded by her own relatives, and transported as it were, into another atmosphere, than other influences began to tell upon her, and for a time she seemed to see nothing but the disadvantages of a marriage to which she had all but formally given her consent. She continually dwelt upon these disadvantages, in a manner which gave Alexandrine exquisite pain. Sometimes she objected to Albert's age; sometimes to his state of health; sometimes to his want of fortune, and his having no profession; or else to his being French, the French not being in good odor at that time with the Russian Emperor, whose consent, notwithstanding his former kindness to my father, would therefore be difficult to obtain; and as Alexandrine was one of the Empress's Maids of Honor, she could not marry without applying for it. Her friends all seemed impressed with these objections, and none of them took into consideration her feelings, which were looked upon as the result of a mere transient fancy. Added to all the other difficulties, arose the crowning one of difference of religion, which disturbed Madame d'Alopeus far more in Germany than it had done in Italy. On this subject, regarding which her friends and relatives most strongly upheld her, she had the most painful discussions with Alexandrine. Amongst these friends, the most adverse on this subject was Mademoiselle Catiche de B——, who has already been mentioned, a very good person, and quite devoted to Alexandrine and her mother, but whose views were entirely founded on the positive and material value of things. Considered in this light, Albert appeared to her quite unworthy of the prize to which he aspired, and Catiche used dreadfully to provoke Alexandrine by seeming to think that it would be a great condescension on her part to marry him. One day that she was mournfully enumerating the long array of general officers, ambassadors, and Russian and German princes, whom in her own mind she had fixed upon as suitable candidates for Alexandrine's hand, she pathetically exclaimed, "Ah, Sacha!* You, who were my pride!" This exclamation had amused Alexandrine, who told us of it in one of her letters. We answered that if Albert made her happy, we hoped Catiche would get over Alexandrine not being her pride. Eugénie wrote to her also about that time: "Oh, Alexandrine, do love my dearest father, and own that it is pleasant to have for one's friend, a parent who understands and takes an interest even in the most romantic feelings of youth. I love him more dearly than ever. Love him also, dear Alexandrine, trust him, and take comfort, for you will find that all will end well."

Catiche was not an able controversialist, but she had a wonderful knack of hitting on the worldly disadvantages Alexandrine would incur if she became a Catholic. She especially dwelt on the Emperor's certain displeasure, expatiating on the many ways

* Russian diminutive for Alexandrine.

in which it would exhibit itself, and blaming the infatuation which made her dream of adding this second offence to that of marrying a Frenchman. These sort of remarks had little effect upon Alexandrine, but a stronger and more powerful obstacle than any arguments influenced her on this point. This was her mother's opposition, and her intense fear of grieving her. This dread continued so long to influence her, that she gave up on that account the happiness which would have made her union with Albert perfect, and she only received Communion with him once, for the first and the last time.

It may have been the mysterious will of God that thus ordained it. Perhaps, also, Alexandrine would have found courage earlier to gladden her husband's heart, even at the cost of causing pain to her mother, had it not been for her scrupulous rectitude, which evinced itself in a conspicuous manner on this important subject, and induced her to examine and weigh every point at great length, and as long as she could to resist the attraction she had always felt for the Catholic religion; fearing that it might be the result of fancy, or of her attachment to Albert, both insufficient motives, she rightly judged, for changing her religion. To these very excellent reasons was probably joined—unconsciously to herself—a wish to delay the moment when an entire conviction would irresistibly impel conscience to take the final step, and when she would be obliged to choose between grieving her mother and offending God. Be that as it may, her deliberation on that point was prolonged to a point which seemed inexplicable to those who knew how she had inclined to Catholicism—Albert's religion, and who subsequently witnessed the overflowing joy and fervor of her conversion.

During her stay at Berlin, and while these discussions were going on, she was therefore far from being a Catholic, but at the same time nothing would induce her to promise never to become one. This was indeed a promise which she would not have made at any time of her life. These discussions were, however, most trying to her, and she had few pleasant days during their travels. Her journal at that time is filled with reminiscences of these little troubles, cheered only by the prospect of a return to Italy in the autumn, when we were all to meet again. The place she liked best that summer was Boklet, which she thus describes: "It is a quiet place, shut in by wooded hills, and from my window I see beyond a pretty meadow, the road which we shall travel—the road which is to me *the road to Naples.*" There also she wrote as follows:—"I can do nothing but repeat the words, 'My God! My God!' My mind is confused; I am unable to collect my thoughts. There are moments when I seem to doubt of everything I have most firmly believed. I have suffered very much since I left you, my dear friends. First there was the parting with you; then all the anguish at Rome and Florence; then the long journey without a word of news of Albert; latterly all the heart-aches at Berlin, and now the probability that after all I shall not spend the winter with him. I have, however, the consolation of feeling that our love is always the same, and God is my witness that I am willing to bear everything so that Albert is but happy; only it must not be at the expense of those I love so dearly. If God ordains that we are never to be married, I pray that he may forget me, and by a blameless inconsistency transfer his affections to another with whom he could be happy; only let her be worthy of him. For myself, I ask courage, that I may not weary others with my grief, and perfect resignation to the Divine will, so that when I die I may hope to meet in Heaven those I have loved so much on earth. There is only one thing certain as regards my future fate. I shall never marry any one but Albert, nor can I imagine that he can ever forget me, or love another as he has loved me. We have that in our natures which must, I think, unite us for time and eternity. It is worth while to suffer in this world, if we are to spend all eternity with those we love. And, thank God, that blessed thought never leaves me. I want no joy which does not come from God. If He sees that I deceive myself in this, may He render this desire sincere, for His power is infinite. My God, reward my mother, I beseech thee, for all she has done for me. I shall not open this book again till we are settled for the winter at—I dare not say—Naples."

At Stuttgard, where they went next, the painful discussions respecting Alexandrine's marriage were again renewed, and the friends they met there laid the greatest stress on the fact that Albert was not following any profession. Catiche, of course, re-echoed all their objections, and whenever she was alone with Alexandrine harped on that point. Weary and provoked with these continual remonstrances, Alexandrine vented her annoyances in the following effusion, which she scribbled in the carriage on the day they left Stuttgard :

"I should like very much to know whether there will be professions in Heaven ! and if general officers and cabinet ministers will rank higher there than nameless people. After all, what does earthly glory and dignity amount to ? Why do not people seek to win a high post in Heaven ? They seem quite to forget that in Heaven alone are to be found everlasting distinctions. A profession, indeed ! I hate the very sound of the word ! To defend one's country in case of need, I admit to be right ; but this is a remote contingency, and where is the good of wearing out one's life in a round of mechanical duties, instead of devoting it to the service of God ? It is all very well to say to a girl, 'Do not marry before you can be secure (if one can be secure of anything on earth) that you will have enough to live upon.' This is all rational, prudent and kind, but that our respect and our contempt should turn upon the possession of a little more or a little less money is really an enormity which cries to Heaven for vengeance.

"My dear young lady (this is the language of the world) when you meet with any one whom you are inclined to like, do not take the trouble of ascertaining if he is good and high-principled. Oh, dear no ! Provided he be not a thief, or has not committed some great crime, that is enough. Do not indulge in high-flown and ridiculous ideas of perfection. But be sure you inquire if he has money enough to give you and your children the means of indulging in all, and more than all, the superfluous luxuries of life. If you can make sure that this is the case, do not hesitate to marry him ; you are sure to be happy. But if, on the contrary, he has only a competency, then, although romantic people tell you that his wife will be an enviable woman ; that his character is the best safeguard for her happiness, that his religious principles are excellent, and his habits so moderate that he is never likely to run into foolish expenses, be sure you turn a deaf ear to these absurd speeches, which betray an utter want of sense and of the commonest knowledge of the world."*

* Alexandrine wrote on the margin of that page : "This is only a paraphrase of a favorite passage of mine in La Bruyère."

Alexandrine adds: "After having thus vented my spleen, I felt quite relieved. All discomfort between my mother and myself vanished, and I felt in a mood to enjoy our journey, and the delightful thought which from Frankfort onward had never left me, that every step on the road was bringing me nearer to Albert."

ALEXANDRINE TO PAULINE AND EUGÉNIE.

"Milan, Sept. 10th.

"My dear Friends—Thank God, I am once more in Italy! I have crossed those terrible Alps, which separated me from you. I feel myself so close to you all, and more than ever I adore Italy. We arrived here the day before yesterday. I asked if you had stayed at this hotel, and learnt to my great satisfaction that you had only left it three days ago. I hope, Pauline, that you will admit I have learnt to be easily pleased, since it was pleasure enough to me to hear that I had missed you by three days! I could fill four pages with the account of what I felt on being told that the Comtesse de la Ferronnays and her two daughters had stayed in this very same house so lately, and that Monsieur le Vicomte and his wife had lodged in the opposite house, because there was no room for them here."

"Wednesday, September 11th.

"The *marionettes* of Tiano, which we went to see, prevented my finishing this letter yesterday, and to-day I went with Catiche to the top of the cathedral. I will now try to explain to you why the knowledge that you had been here gave me so much pleasure. First, it was clear that you had safely crossed the Simplon. Secondly, that you were in Italy, and that we should soon meet. Lastly, you can understand that having been so long separated from you, it was like a foretaste of your dear presence. It was as if I had seen your shadow on the road before me. Do you think me very absurd, or do you admire how cleverly I account for not having been vexed at missing you when we could so easily have met? Oh, Pauline! Oh, Eugénie! I begin to feel such delight, something so sunny in my heart, when I think I am going to see you again, that I try to calm myself by the consideration that some weeks must still elapse before we actually see each other again. But I do not care about that now. God is really too good to me. There is no chance of our being at Naples before the first of November. I shall be only too happy if we reach it by that time. Well, we must be patient. What a budget of trifling and important things we shall have to discuss, and you, dear Pauline, shall condemn or acquit me, just as you used to do. I am so curious to see Emma. My dear friends, in spite of my good spirits my heart is very anxious, and my head full of disquieting thoughts. Will my ideas ever be *settled?* Some day, in Heaven, I hope. Let Albert know about us. Oh, how I love you all!"

We had, as she says, passed through Milan a few days before, with my brother Charles and his wife, who were that year returning with us to Naples. I do not remember why we changed our route, but I know we went by Genoa and the Simplon, instead of through Lyons and Mount Cenis as we intended, and on account of our doing so, my mother missed all the letters which had been sent her on the road, and thus we reached Florence without the least idea of what had occurred in the meantime, and expecting to meet my father in Rome. It was the Princesse de Bouffremont who had told us, as soon as we had arrived at the Hotel de l'Europe at Florence, that the Duchesse de Berry was there, that she had sent for my father a fortnight ago, and that three days afterwards he had gone to Prague on a mission she had entrusted him with. On hearing this news my mother determined to await his return at Florence. We saw the Duchesse de Berry several times. She had just left Blaye, and had with her Mademoiselle de Fauveau, whom I there saw for the first time. We were much struck by her strange way of dressing, her animated descriptions of the Vendée, her genius, eloquence, and passionate admiration of mediæval Italy. The charms of her conversation whiled away the tedium of delay.

I left a letter at Florence for Alexandrine, who I knew would arrive there, as at Milan, a few days after our departure, and with it a bracelet and locket containing a piece of my hair. I told her she might add anything to it she pleased. She did afterwards mix some of Albert's hair with mine, and as it was exactly of the same color she was able to wear it openly without challenging remark. In the same letter, I said to her: "While you are here go for my sake to the Church of Santa Maria Novella. In the first place, it is a curious and interesting Church. But do not go to it only as others do, to *look*, but to think of Albert and me, and to *pray*. It is his favourite Church." At last my father returned. I have no occasion to speak here of his mission, except so far as to say that it succeeded, and that when he took leave of the Duchesse de Berry, she expressed in the most lively manner her warm thanks and grateful regard.

On the 20th of September we arrived at Rome, and the next day Eugénie wrote as follows to Alexandrine: "Guess where we went this morning at six o'clock with my mother? To the Scala Santa! which we ascended *on our knees* for *you*. We prayed very earnestly. May our prayers be granted, beloved friend. It gave us pleasure really to perform the part of pilgrims. I tried hard to imitate their humility."

Alexandrine, after copying this passage, added these words: "Oh, what sisters were waiting for me at Rome! And what fervent prayers have been offered up for me there! First, my Albert's most disinterested petitions. He had then no thought of himself, and only offered up everything he could think of to obtain my conversion. Then his mother and his sister's prayers; and, again, Olga's on the day of her First Communion. Well, thank God, these prayers have been granted! God gave me to Albert, and Albert gave me to God!" Olga made her First Communion on the 23rd of September, and I will transcribe from my journal two or three passages I wrote on that occasion. "It was a rare privilege for Olga to make her First Communion at Rome, but never did God's graces descend on a soul more worthy to receive them. Religion expands her mind and governs her imagination. Her most habitual thoughts are spiritual ones, yet she is young, and child-like for her age. And is not this precisely what God loves? After Benediction on the eve of the great day, one of the nuns fetched us from the Church, and we went and kissed our dear little sister, who was looking as calm and fair as an angel. We passed through the beautiful cloisters, which were illuminated by the most brilliant moonlight, and at home that evening we prepared Olga's white veil and dress, and her crown of white roses. It was a sweet employment, and on the morrow of that day the angels, our darling loves and invokes so often, will have looked with pleasure on the fair child; for it was for God alone she was adorned, and her beauty was holy as her young heart. She and Albertine were to be confirmed before Mass, and as I was Olga's god-mother I knelt by her side all the time, which I felt to be a great privilege. Cardinal Lambruschini officiated. Nobody could have witnessed without emotion the scene in that Chapel, and I hope God will give me grace to be always faithful to the resolutions I made that day at the foot of the altar, and to bear in mind the touching words addressed to us, and the moment when with Olga we all received Communion. The complete union which existed between us, the quiet, silent thanksgiving after Mass, and the peaceful, intense joy with which our little sister embraced us as we came out of the Church, must ever live in my remembrance.

"At three o'clock we went again to the Church. Olga renewed her baptismal vows with her hand on the Gospels, and afterwards, in a clear, distinct, and calm voice, recited an act of consecration in the Chapel of the Blessed Virgin. At half-past five solemn Benediction was given, with the most melodious singing, and all the accompaniments which help to raise our weak souls to the highest pitch of devotion. A Catholic may well challenge the world to produce sights equal in beauty to those his religion affords, or anything that surpasses the feelings it inspires. Oh, how I blessed God that day that I was born in His Church! Thus ended this happy day.

"On the following morning I prayed some time in the convent Chapel, and then went into the garden, where I conversed some time with the dear gentle Mère Olympe. The sun was setting behind St. Peter's, the sky was bright, hot, and cloudless. It was all very beautiful, and we talked of things which gladden the upward glancing of the eye and heart. In the evening we returned to the Trinità to bring away my sisters, who, though happy to come home again, were taking a sorrowful and affectionate leave of the convent where they had passed three happy months, and which to Olga especially was endeared by holy recollections. The brightest moonlight lighted up the cloisters as I went to give a last look at the Church. When the doors of the convent closed behind us, it seemed to me as if we were plunging once more into a sad and restless world, whilst peace, joy, and everything which makes life sweet, were to be found within those walls. I am convinced that a true religious vocation is the greatest grace God can bestow on a soul: a foretaste on earth of the blessedness of Heaven."

When I wrote these words in my journal, I had not the slightest vocation for the religious life, but then and ever since I have always thought that those whom God calls to live for Him alone must be of all His creatures the happiest and most blest.

A few days after Olga's First Communion we left Rome for Naples, where we found Albert looking so well that it seemed as if his health was completely re-established. We went back to the same apartments we had lived in before, but that year it was Charles and Emma, with their new-born baby, who occupied the rooms Madame d'Alopeus had inhabited the preceding winter. Now that she was married to Prince Lapoukhyn she required a larger suite of rooms, and had therefore taken the house next to ours. This was all we could desire, for Alexandrine was almost as near to us as if we had been under the same roof. We hoped they would have followed us to Naples as closely as had been the case at Milan and at Florence, but as the following letter will show, we had to go through further anxieties and sorrows before that long wished-for meeting actually took place.

"Florence, October 10th, 1833.

"Dear Friends—The famous papers have at last arrived, and Mamma will be married on Sunday week, the 20th of October. Pray very much for her. I am now so bewildered and hurried that I feel as if I had scarcely anything else to say. Thank Heaven, Mamma and the Prince seem very happy. O! my God, bless their marriage!

"I must say a word about myself, even in the midst of these important solicitudes. My mother's letter to your father increases my anxiety.* Will you be grieved and disappointed at its contents? Will you wish now to draw back? For God's sake, dearest sisters, quiet my fears, if you can, and see if there will not be time to write to me before the 20th. We shall certainly not leave Florence till that day. Oh, do feel for me, and tell me the real truth. I have a terrible weight on my heart. People find me so altered in five months; they say I am grown thin and pale. You must expect to see me looking ugly. I am so sorry! I was in very low spirits a few days ago, but Sauvan has done

* Madame d'Alopeus had written to M. de la Ferronnays to say that she had not succeeded in making arrangements by which she had hoped to facilitate Alexandrine's marriage. M. de Montalembert, who was travelling in Germany, saw the letter at Frankfort, where it had been detained because the proper postage had not been paid. Under the impression that it contained something important to Albert, he paid what was necessary, and sent it on.

me good. You will see when I can speak to you that my complaints are not exaggerated. Oh, dear! oh, dear! am I wrong? am I to blame? Nothing but the conviction that it was God's will would alter my feelings towards you all. Good-bye, my dear friends. When *shall* we meet again? If you were my own sisters, I could not love you more than I do. Do not show this letter to Albert. It is too sad, too anxious. Do not fret about me, but always love me. *Au revoir*, by God's help."

Alexandrine then writes in her journal:—"On the evening of that day, as Catiche and I were standing at the window opposite to the church of San Gaetano, which had struck me as gloomy the first time I had been at Florence, she said to my great surprise that she should like to go into it for a moment. I wished it more than she did, and we slipped quietly out of the house. Catiche wanted, I think, to pray for Mamma, the last obstacle to whose marriage was removed by the arrival of the papers from Russia. I joined to that prayer another intention of my own. When our eyes became accustomed to the darkness, and we could discern anything in that gloomy Church, a coffin met our sight. This pained me, for my thoughts being occupied with my mother's marriage and my own anxious wishes about my future, I could not forbear asking myself whether this was an omen, and to which of us it applied. Still it was something to pray there on my knees, for I did not mind Catiche, and, indeed, was glad to see that she knelt also."

ALBERT TO COUNT DE MONTALEMBERT.

"My dear Friend—Here is a letter for Rio, who must be with you, I think. If not, will you forward it to him? I shall not enter upon the question of which of us has been most to blame. I like better to put off explanations until we meet, if indeed they should be necessary. Letters are apt to create misunderstandings, for an ill-worded sentence can easily convey a different meaning from the one intended. At this moment let us dwell only on our friendship, which nothing must change. We live at a time when every one should rally round their standard, and never let us forget that you and Rio and I fight under the same banner. If union does not exist between those who meet at the foot of the Cross, how will it fare with those who are not bound by the same sacred tie?"

"October 16th.

"MY DEAR FRIEND—I began this letter a week ago. Do not accuse me of idleness, I never felt a greater desire to write. Oh, why are you not here? The moment is drawing near when uncertainty must cease, and I could almost wish to put off the decisive hour; for two years of unmixed happiness are perhaps to be followed by a lifetime of suffering. My father has received a letter from Madame d'Alopeus.—[He relates the contents.]—And I do not know what to expect. My confidence in the future had been so great that I find it difficult to realise the probable consequences of this blow; and hope is so deeply rooted in my heart that it can hardly entertain misgivings, much less despair. I only feel anxious and harassed with thoughts which succeed one another without any definite result. How could she live in Russia? You who know her can judge if that could ever be. In a few days we shall have met and measured the strength of the obstacles which threaten to separate us. I have not yet taken in the idea of a final parting. I put down the thought whenever it presents itself. Still, I shall be probably obliged to leave Naples, and in that case shall join you somewhere. Let me know your plans, but do not alter them on my account. I am not afraid of a cold climate. I might suffer less in the north than I do here. Study will furnish me with the change of thought I need. The life we shall lead will be very quiet. The greatest support to me under such a trial would be your society. My poor darling would find the same comfort in my sisters; but it is impossible that the fair days of our happiness are thus to end. To you I am not afraid of saying it: I do not think that God intends to inflict this blow upon us. He is only trying us.

"I am weary, and I do not know what to think, what to hope. I could joyfully endure her absence, if I foresaw the end of it, or if I only knew that she would be surrounded with loving friends. But alone, and in Russia! O! God forbid!—My head is splitting, and I feel that I am writing a most absurd letter. What will have happened by the time it reaches you? I had so longed for something decisive, and now my heart sinks within me at the beginning of each day. Farewell, my dear friend. I can, at all events, look forward to the joy of seeing you again."

Whilst Albert was thus pouring forth his feelings to his friend, Alexandrine was writing in her journal these sorrowful lines:—

"Florence, October 7th, 1833.—My mind is oppressed by an intolerable weight. I cannot imagine how things will turn out, how difficulties can vanish, and malicious tongues be silenced. I feel in a perfect labyrinth. I have strength enough to go against the opinion of the world and act in defiance of it, but not that of despising its remarks. They throw me into a fever, they destroy my peace, and I sometimes almost wish to die, for I fear these incessant heart-aches will deprive me of all energy, and then I shall not make Albert happy."

About this time I was writing from Naples the following letter to Alexandrine:

"Naples, October 7th, 1833.

"Albert and I spend our days together; we have never before conversed so much, and I love him more than ever. God gave me a great blessing in such a brother. We talk of his sacred, his holy love. He was saying to me the other day that when he recapitulates the events of his life, he cannot but recognise such special mercies towards him in the dealings of Providence, that he can never be grateful enough. First he spoke of his leaving Naples two years ago, and his retreat with M. Rio, in Tuscany; of his repentance, regret, and resolutions. Of all that time of improvement and sanctification which preceded his arrival at Rome, where he found his reward. Of the emotion and agitation which ensued, and then of his happiness at the Vomero last winter; and lastly, of the calm and peace which now make him ready to bear whatever God ordains. He is not afraid now of your marrying any one else, and is satisfied to leave himself and you in the hands of God. He has improved in every respect, and with all his goodness and high principles, he finds means of pleasing persons totally different from himself. He is so amiable and unaffected, that everybody esteems and likes him. Albert has not as much talent or information as his friend Charles de Montalembert, but he is quite as intelligent, quite as enthusiastic in his love for all that is good and beautiful, and possesses at the same time greater gentleness of character, and of language and manners. In short, seeing what he is, you would be wrong to take to heart the wretched criticisms which can touch neither him nor you. Every day, moreover, his intellect acquires greater vigour and scope, and I have no doubt that before many years have elapsed, you will be as proud of the estimation in which he will then be held by indifferent persons, as you now are pleased at what his friends think of him. You live in a state of terrible agitation, dearest Alex., but I am sure that in your heart there ought to be peace. If only we could meet and talk! However, God will order all things, small and great, in our lives."

This letter, which would perhaps have a little consoled Alexandrine, found her in bed, and not in a condition to read it. Whether her previous state of agitation had been caused by latent illness, or whether her illness was the result of all she had gone through, it so happened that she fell dangerously ill. Her mother's wedding was postponed, and of course their departure also. For some days her friends were much alarmed about her, and we at a distance shared their painful anxieties. The eve of the day when she became ill, Alexandrine wrote in her journal that Prince Lapoukhyn had given a dinner-party, where they had met Count Malte Putbus, who was passing through Florence, and who came to take leave of them, and to wish all kinds of happiness to her and her mother. They never saw him again.

Alexandrine speaks thus of her illness:—"On the following day my internal agitation had reached its utmost limits. I told Catiche that there were moments in which I felt as if I was going out of my mind. I was in this state when I answered Lady D——'s letter, who had spoken in a somewhat offensive manner of my marriage, and I replied in a way which seemed to set my head on fire. Immediately afterwards I went to dinner, trying all the time to conceal my agitation. I suppose this helped to make me ill. I could not open my journal again till the 27th. I had not written in it since the 15th. I was suffering terribly in my mind, and felt increasing uneasiness in my body. A dentist had given me some opium to put into a tooth, without telling me what it was. I used it too freely, and had been swallowing some of it for several days. This, together with my mental troubles, threw me into a high fever, with dreadful headaches, and for seven days I was in bed, making my poor mother, and all those about me, terribly anxious. I was nursed and coaxed, and spoilt in every possible way. From my bed I could see that gloomy church of San Gaetano, which always makes me melancholy. But what I cared most about, was the thought that my illness was delaying our return to Naples."

Alexandrine was recovering from this illness when she received the following letter; my answer to the one in which she spoke of new difficulties having arisen, and said her mother had written to my father a discouraging letter. Singularly enough, this letter did not reach her till a fortnight after I sent it:—

"I will pray for your mother, dearest, on the day of her marriage, and also for you, whom God will never forsake, however long He may see fit to try you. My father and mother love you exactly as they do their own children, and I am sure that their anxiety and solicitude about you are such as they would feel under the same circumstances for me. Your mother's letter was rather the occasion than the cause of my father's saying what he did on the subject. We all spent an unpleasant hour talking over those prosaic, matter-of-fact, and hatefully indispensable matters. My father said, 'In their case we are not obliged to make provision for luxuries, they are both so prudent.' But even taking this into account, dear Alex., he thought you would have greater difficulties than you fancy. As to Albert, you know how he shrinks from the idea of inflicting privations upon you. But neither my father nor mother, nor any of us, despair of better prospects: on the contrary, we have a sort of confidence that all will end, as we wish. For my part, I am convinced it will. Indeed, when prudent thoughts are uppermost, my father never looks to anything worse for you than *waiting*. The idea of breaking off your engagement never entered into anybody's head. It has not occurred to your mother, I trust. Tell me, dearest, if I have grieved you. I write in fear, and almost in tears. The short of the matter is, that there *are* difficulties, but at the same time, hopes which no difficulties can destroy.

"God will help us, dearest sister. Leave everything in His Hands, and remember that as long as the certainty of mutual affection exists, there is no real cause, or at least any great cause, for sorrow. Albert thinks so, too. Religion, poetry, and love, are sweetening your lives, and if God chooses by a few more trials to make you earn the joy of an endless union, take courage, dear friends, and believe and hope. We shall soon meet and talk this over. Oh, when will this month come to an end! Let us fix our eyes on Heaven, God will not lose sight of us. Our struggles, anxieties, and sorrows, nothing we can do or suffer are lost. Do not for a minute doubt that we shall one day be sisters, and pray together in the same Churches."

CONTINUATION OF ALEXANDRINE'S STORY.

"I have sometimes thought that God did not permit this letter to reach me whilst I was ill. (By some strange accident it remained lying at the post office.) It would probably have made me worse. I could not help showing it to my mother, who was rather anxious to know what effect her letter had produced, but I was terribly afraid of her seeing those dear words: 'we shall pray in the same Churches.' She did not take any notice of them at the time, but she reminded me of them three years afterwards. I read them again with Pauline also at Paris, in June, 1836.

"It was on the 29th of October, the eve of my mother's wedding day, that I received Pauline's letter. I had been allowed for the first time to go out in an open carriage. It gave me a thrill of pleasure, and I wrote in my journal, 'When we are young and looking forward to a bright future, there is a peculiar charm in the feeling of recovering from illness. A rosy hue seems spread over the earth. When we recover from the malady of life; when we rise from the bed of our grave, how young we shall feel! And before us we shall see — not an uncertain and transient happiness, but cloudless and eternal joys. Oh, my God, give me faith here and Heaven hereafter!' The next day (the 30th of October) my mother was married to Prince Lapoukhyn, first at the Greek Church and then at the Protestant Chapel. I was still very weak, and hardly conscious of my own thoughts. My lips quivered, and I could with difficulty stand. I remember, however, that it crossed my mind during the ceremony, that there would never be bridal joys or bridal flowers for me; and yet it seemed to me that they would suit me better than my mother. My weakness made me melancholy. Still I must confess that I was very selfishly glad that that important event which my illness had delayed, was at last accomplished.

"On the 31st of October we left Florence. Whilst the horses were being put to, Mamma and Catiche slipped into the Church of San Gaetano. They had not told me what they were about to do, for fear of my wanting to go with them, and catching cold. I travelled in the large carriage with my mother's maid, and they covered me with furs, though it was as hot as in summer at home. I was so glad to be off to be getting nearer to Albert! All I wanted was to see him; that he should not be gone before I arrived, and then I cared but little for all the rest; I felt as if all other obstacles would vanish! The journey revived my strength. On Saturday, which was All Souls Day, we arrived at Viterbo. My mother was so unwell, that we thought we must have stayed there; but the doctor finding it difficult to procure the proper medicine, advised our pushing on to Rome, where we accordingly arrived on the 3rd of November. It was a great joy to cross the Ponte Molle; a great joy to be once more in Rome! My mother was ill there, which delayed our departure. Then I was again not well, which was a fresh anxiety. But at last, on Saturday the 9th, I had the happiness of starting for Naples, which we were to reach the following day; but at Velletri, new uncertainties ensued. It was proposed that on account of our health, and the brigands, we should sleep there. There was nothing I would not have done to arrive at the end of our journey—that end so long sighed for, and so often postponed. They saw I was dying to proceed, and we went on and travelled through the night. I was enjoying the foretaste, if not the actual possession of happiness, and every step brought me nearer to it. There was something charming to me even in the darkness! It seemed to shroud me and my joyful thoughts. At last the sun rose, and shone on Mola di Gaeta in all its enchanting beauty. Mola di Gaeta, washed by the waves of the Bay of Naples; Mola di Gaeta, whence I could see Vesuvius and Ischia; Mola di Gaeta, where in 1829 I had knelt in a grove of orange trees, and gazing with enraptured eyes on the blue sky and sea, had prayed to see Naples once again, and to enjoy a little of this world's bliss! We breakfasted there, horribly impatient for the post horses. At one moment I thought we should have to stay the night. But when the horses were forthcoming! When they actually came! . . . . Alas! there is now no place on earth towards which I long to rush; no possible moment of life so rich in joy, as that little space of time when I had not yet seen, but when I was expecting to see, Albert. That little moment of impatient expectation which seemed almost painful, when I looked back to it from my aftertaste of joy!

"At nightfall we arrived at Capua, and from there they drove us dreadfully badly till Aversa. At last—at last, we reached Naples, but at a foot's pace. At Chiaja they were mending the pavement. I could not help wondering at the sort of fate which seemed even at the last moment to multiply delays, for the heavy carriage in which I was, had to turn into the Vicofreddo, and I, the only one of the party who was dying to arrive, was the last to reach our house. I waved my handkerchief as I passed the adjoining one, thinking some of them would be at the window, but they were already at our house. I was almost wild with joy. The first person I saw was Eugénie, who was opening the carriage door and letting down the steps. I sprang out, and at one glance saw Albert on the stairs—Albert's own self! Albert alive! for I was always thinking of Civita Vecchia. He was very calm, and that immediately calmed me. I saw Pauline, Fernand, every one of them. It was ecstacy to go up the stairs thus surrounded. In such moments there is an instinctive but intense consciousness of happiness, which makes us feel as if it must be eternal. We cannot conceive that it should end. Poor creatures that we are! But, oh, beloved Father in Heaven! if Thy Paradise is the endless continuation of such bliss as that, unspeakable, indeed, must be its joys!

"Madame de la Ferronnays was in the drawing-room, and M. de la Ferronnays came in afterwards. I thought Albert much better than when we had parted, and I could feel nothing but gladness. Our apartments were charming. I had a pretty room on the side of the house nearest to the La Ferronnays', and we could talk from one balcony to the other. It was delightful to wake the next morning. I enjoyed a sort of happiness I had never expected to feel. Before I was dressed, Pauline and Eugénie walked in just as they used to do. Albert came later to the drawing-room. I made acquaintance that day with Charles and Emma, and kissed little Alfred for the first time. A few days afterwards Albert's parents and mine began to talk over the possibilities of our marriage. I was afraid this might give rise to painful discussions, and wished they had let us enjoy for a little while in quiet the happiness of being once more together.

"On Sunday, the 17th of November, I was not at all well, and when M. Sauvan asked me, in a somewhat inquisitive manner, if my indisposition was not perhaps attributable to some mental cause, I burst into tears, and simply assented, without entering further into the subject. My tears of course were very significant. An exaggerated report of this little scene reached M. de la Ferronnays' ears, and he spoke to Pauline of the desperation with which I had rolled my head on the pillow while M. Sauvan was speaking to me. As it happened, I was not in bed, but standing at the time. I was glad to be able to tell Pauline, who thought that sort of thing would not have been like me, what had really passed, and given rise to this bit of gossip which wounded my pride. I had no objection to be thought anxious and unhappy, as long as it remained doubtful whether Albert and I were to spend our lives together, but it annoyed me to be represented as giving way to that sort of passionate despair.

"In the evening of that day I was lying on the sofa rather sad, when Eugénie came in. I shall never forget that moment of my life. The day was closing in, and the room getting dark. Eugénie began by pitying me because I was ill, but did not at first make any reply to my complaints that our happiness was still so uncertain. At last she said : 'Then you don't know?' Oh, those words, they stillseem to ring in my ears ! She told me as much as she knew of what had been settled. Pauline came in afterwards, and from her I learnt that I might look upon Albert as my future husband."

ALBERT TO COUNT DE MONTALEMBERT.

"Naples, December 10th, 1833.

"Now, my dear friend, let me try if I can achieve writing a few words to you. For a fortnight I have tried to do so, but never could finish a letter. That you may understand this, I must tell you that Easter is to be the final term of our trial. You may imagine, for I cannot describe it, the happiness which fills my heart to overflowing. I know you will not think that my silence on that point proceeds from a want of confidence. I would give anything to see you. What are your new plans? Is there no chance of their bringing you this way, and of your being present at the happiest moment of my life? I want to know what you are thinking of, and where you are. Oh, I wish I could give you a share of my happiness! I am unworthy of so many blessings, of that life of joy and gladness which began two years ago, and will never end!

"This letter will be very confused, for I am in a most unsettled condition of mind. But these are our plans. I am to be married after Easter, and we set off the same day for Frankfort, where we shall part with my mother-in-law, and then go on to establish ourselves at Montigny. My family will meet us there. I am telling you all this as if it were the most natural, simple thing in the world, and all the time I hardly know if I am on earth or in Heaven! Forgive the incoherence of this letter. I do so want to talk to you. Pray for us, dear friend, and bless God for His goodness to me. As I look back, I feel you so closely connected with my past life. You have been associated with all this happiness, and it began when I was with you. What is to happen to us? Are we to meet again, and to spend delightful hours in each other's society? I sometimes fear that the life of agitation and excitement which you have hitherto led, will not harmonise with the calm existence I am looking forward to. We tread such different paths; and yet I cannot do without you. The star which I have followed side by side with you will guide me as long as I live, and your name and the thought of you are for ever linked with it. I love you more dearly than a brother. Adieu, write to me. Alexandrine sends you her kindest remembrances; she must be included in your friendship for me. If you write to M. de Lamennais, beg him to pray for us."

ALBERT TO COUNT DE MONTALEMBERT.*

"Naples, December 20th, 1833.

"My dear unhappy friend, I have just received your letter from Frankfort. It has thrown me into the greatest agitation. What would not I give to be with you. It is perhaps presumptuous to think I should be of any use, or could give you any comfort. I should like to answer the first part of your letter, but the end of it haunts me like a painful dream. Dearest friend, for God's sake do not go back to France at this moment. Measure the depths of the abyss into which you are about to cast yourself, and remember that if once you take that step, it may become impossible to turn back. There was but one voice in praise of the Abbé de Lamennais when he made his submission. Some evil-minded persons were wicked enough to throw doubts on the sincerity of that act, but their insinuations were treated with contempt, and the sacred authority of the Church was vindicated by its means. It may be that the words which you have scattered over the world have been inspired by God, but everything com-

* This and the following letters allude to decisions in regard to the *Avenir* and other publications of Montalembert and De Lamennais.—[TRANSLATOR.]

bines to show you that *enough* has been said. If they are really of Divine birth they will bear fruit, and shine out one day in all the splendor of truth. The time is not yet come, perhaps, when we can reap the blessings they promise. We must shudder at the sight of the calamities which an excess of zeal might bring about, and shrink with horror from the idea of a schism. Let us gather round the Cross, the foundation-stone of the Church, to cherish and defend, not to undermine her. I implore you, my dear friend, *compel* yourself not to yield to M. de Lamennais' persuasions. May God bless and save you! Do keep out of the way, and travel for a year or two as you intended. I would give anything, as I have already said, to be with you just now. I dread your being alone, and have wearied my brains to hit upon some plan that would enable me to go to you. But it is so difficult.

"If you have received my last letter, you now know the happiness that awaits me this spring; but I assure you, my dear friend, I would willingly defer it in order to hasten to you. But I fear it cannot be. The princess leaves Naples in April. If she took away her daughter with her, it is impossible to tell what might happen. The happiness which even now I dare not make sure of, though the difficulties seem at present smoothed away, might in that case be for ever forfeited. I am going, however, to speak about it to my father, and by the next post I will tell you what I can do. With what impatience I shall look for your letters. I do not know what will become of me if I hear you are gone to Paris. In the name of our friendship, and of all who love you, and in His sacred Name in Whom we are for ever united, let *duty* overcome every argument urged against it. All my belongings, who love you as one of our own selves, are alarmed at seeing such an alternative before you. My father speaks of you with a paternal solicitude. As to me, my beloved friend, I cannot tell you the anguish I felt on receiving your letter. On Monday I shall be calmer, and able to write to you at greater length. Between this and then I shall ascertain if it would be possible for me to go to you. Adieu, my dearest friend. I love you far more than ever. My sisters and Alexandrine wish me to say everything affectionate and kind. They are all terrified at the idea of your going to Paris. Your friend for life."

ALEXANDRINE'S STORY (CONTINUED).

"Is it not evident that Albert's love for me must have been very great, if a friendship such as his for M. de Montalembert, which he never disguised from me, did not make me at all jealous? If he had left me at that time to go to him, it might have grieved me perhaps, but not made me to doubt his affection. There was so much devotedness in his character, that his first impulse was to sacrifice his love as a happiness exclusively his own. This generosity of spirit pleased me. Albert's numerous friends were always satisfied and felt no jealousy, because that gentle heart of his, so rich in tenderness, could afford to love them all, and opened to a new and wholesome affection, without taking anything from those already dear to it. Oh, my beloved one, you loved even on earth as the Blessed love in Heaven! There was something infinite in that love."

ALBERT TO COUNT DE MONTALEMBERT.

"December 24th, 1833.

"MY DEAR FRIEND—You must have received a letter I wrote you immediately on getting yours. It was, I am sure, very confused and incoherent, for I was very much agitated, and would have given anything to go to you at once. Indeed, I think I half promised I would. Since then I have seen it was a vain hope. I cannot leave Naples, and I very much fear we shall only meet for a moment in the spring. I feel often so sorry to have spent these two years at a distance from you, but then the thought of my great happiness checks this transient, though real regret. I am not afraid to own it, for you know well how ardently and deeply I am attached to you. Would we were together, so that you might read in my eyes all the affectionate sympathy with which I would fain soften the bitterness of your disappointment. I feel your suffering all the more acutely because my own heart is steeped in joy. God has showered His blessings on my worthless self, and you, dear friend, have hitherto known nothing but sorrow!

"I tremble to think of you so alone. Do write soon and often, and tell me M. de Lamennais' plans. I scarcely venture to fix my thoughts on that subject. Everybody's eyes are upon him. What will he do in this decisive moment? Why does he urge you to return to Paris? If Rome decides against you, surely you will submit. You could not do otherwise! I must, I am sure, have mistaken your meaning. But why does that idea haunt me like a dream? Why is it that I see watchful heresy preparing to applaud a new desertion from the Church? You speak of the incompatibility of liberty with religion, which is, you say, dividing a soul asunder. Could this be possible? Oh no; believe me these are groundless fears. Liberty means the Cross of Christ, and God has planted it in the world as the rallying-point of the human race.

"Mark the gradual progress of true liberty from the hour of its first descent from Heaven. It has grown and spread, slowly indeed, for men must have faith before they receive it into their hearts; but we must not deem it extinct because its advance does not keep pace with our wishes. Shall we despair of the future when it appears so much brighter than ever? If all is hopeless, whence comes the wide-spread sympathy among nations, this universal craving for new life and for religion? No, my dear friend, let us cast from us such unworthy fears; let joy, on the contrary, fill our hearts. God's Hand is visible in this check from Rome. It will give time to younger men to overtake you, and later you will resume your onward march. They are but feebly enlightened yet by the fire which burns in your heart. My knowledge of politics is very limited. It is only to you that I impart my opinions, or rather my feelings on the subject; for I simply utter what I feel, and nothing more. Each one has his vocation; mine is quiet and obscurity. Yet in its higher flights my soul sees life under another aspect, and understands happiness of a different kind. With anxious eyes I watch your course, and seek to penetrate your thoughts. It seems as if I were walking after you along your toilsome road, ready, should you grow weary, to catch you in my arms . . . .
I had left this letter on my table, and when I came back I found these few lines from Pauline.* Enclosed in mine is also one from Alexandrine. She asked me immediately if she might write to you. You see you have many friends here. It makes me happy to think so. For God's sake do not despond. There are good days in store for you.

"Write to me often, for I cannot bear to be long without hearing from you, now that you are alone and out of spirits. My

* Not given.

father is very sorry that you are not doing something to divert your thoughts. He dreads your going to Paris, where you might not be master of your own actions. My dear Charles, do have mercy on your friends. I have always believed that you will be one day as happy as you deserve, and I hold to that belief in spite of the clouds which beset us. Never let me lose your friendship, for I cannot do without it. Your devoted friend,

"ALBERT."

ALEXANDRINE TO COUNT DE MONTALEMBERT.

"DEAR M. DE MONTALEMBERT—I must tell you myself how deeply I feel for you at this painful moment. I am sure you will not be annoyed at Albert's speaking to me of what concerns you. I should not believe he had confidence in me if he tried to conceal the pain which your trials give him. They make him so unhappy that I venture to implore you not to do anything likely to increase your present troubles; and so, strange as it may seem, I join my entreaties to Albert's, and beg of you to stay quietly at Munich, or else to come and see us in Italy. I hope I am not presumptuous in thinking that you will be a little influenced by my advice, for you had the kindness to say that you loved me because I love Albert. I often repeat those words to myself, for that is the way in which I now like people to love me. Though I am abundantly happy as it is, I should consider your friendship as a great additional blessing, and I hope, thanks to Albert, I may one day enjoy it. Even now I feel for you as for a brother. And, oh! I wish I could do something to comfort you! But please, please, never give way to hopelessness. God has happiness in store for all, and you deserve more than any one to be happy. I trust He will hear our prayers. I say *our* prayers, because I too will pray for you. You do not, I suppose, object to it, in spite of your severity towards us poor Protestants, which is my only quarrel with you. Excuse my having said so much, and believe me to be your true, though very useless friend, whom I trust you will not disown. Farewell, and promise us to come in a few months. Above all things, never doubt of the boundless goodness of God. I have such strong faith in it.

"ALEXANDRINE."*

* On the 3rd of January, 1834, Albert received an answer from M. de Montalembert to these letters, which contained the following passage: "I am lost in amazement at the effect

ALBERT TO COUNT DE MONTALEMBERT.

"I begin not to mistrust the future, the bright beautiful future; my earthly Heaven, in which I can discern no possible cloud. Still it somewhat saddens me to reflect that my fate will necessarily be henceforward less closely connected with yours. This gives me at times a heart-ache, which I am not sorry to find you also feel. Yes; I cannot but regret our old habits of intimacy, but I get over this regret by hoping that my marriage will only increase our friendship, which will grow stronger by the addition of Alexandrine's, who is already so much attached to you. Our home will always be yours, dearest friend, and whatever affection can give of peace and happiness, you will find treasured up for you in our hearts. I can quite understand that you were surprised at our letters, for we ought to have known you too well to have had a doubt as to your conduct, under these circumstances. Nevertheless, I must confess I was anxious. You were pushed to such extremities, so exasperated, so without consolation, that I felt afraid you might become desperate. It is quite true that you told me of your resolution to avoid Paris, and to spend the winter at Munich, but you added that M. de Lamennais was pressing you to come back, and though I had no misgivings as to your own sentiments, I could not divest myself of fancies and fears. You must forgive them, for they were the result of excessive affection.

"Do not be cast down, my dear Charles. Do not give way to discouragement. If you were deceived then, let us thank God that He has enlightened you, and do not reproach yourself for what was only an excess of zeal—a too fervent passion for good.

which my letter from Frankfort has produced on you all. I must certainly have expressed myself very ill if I can have led you for an instant to suppose that I should not act precisely as you advise. I cannot but think, however, that I told you in so many words that I was going to Munich, and that if it had ever crossed my mind to go to Paris, it was only to use whatever little influence I may possess with M. de Lamennais to dissuade him from all idea of resistance to the Holy See. All that you say with so much affection, good sense, and heartfelt eloquence, I have likewise felt, and there is not a sentence of your letter which does not perfectly agree with what I have thought and resolved since I read the decisive brief of the 5th of October. Moreover, there is not a word in it which I have not said or written to M. de Lamennais, in order to induce him to act as I have done, that is, to withdraw from the field, to bow down before God's severe decrees, and patiently and humbly await the accomplishment of his designs. But what is incredible (and I almost hesitate about mentioning it), is, that M. de Lamennais has been offended by my advice, though I gave it with more gentleness, affection, and openheartedness, than I have ever used towards anyone on earth. His answer shows me but too plainly, that this difference of opinion has pained and estranged him from me. I could not have believed it, and my conscience absolves me. He has, however, followed the line of conduct I recommended, and even gone beyond it, for he has not only forsworn all political action, but has purely and simply accepted the Encyclical letter, without excepting anything, and bound himself—according to the form prescribed by the Holy Father, 'neither to write nor to approve of anything contrary to it.'"

But for Heaven's sake try to feel calm. In spite of all the joy I have been accustomed to in hearing your praise, in witnessing the renown which attaches to your name, I am unspeakably glad to find you determined to withdraw from the lists, and remain awhile aloof. I know your ardent soul. I know your fiery zeal; I know that you are inclined to despise even the semblance of prudence, and that you dearly love danger. On the other hand, I saw envy, and perhaps hatred, gaining strength. I cannot tell you the fears I entertained, and gladly would I have given my life to ward off the storm gathering above your head. How gladly I should see you leave the mountain top, always most exposed to the rage of the elements, and take refuge in our vale of peace and love. Soon you will feel joy stealing into your bruised heart. I have a sweet foreboding that the moment is approaching, when God will shower His blessings upon you, as the reward of constancy and faith. Oh, my dearest friend, may God for ever bless you!"

ALEXANDRINE'S STORY (CONTINUATION).

"On January 1st, 1834, I wrote these words in my journal: 'Oh, my God, bless this year to us all. I ask it in the Name of Our Lord Jesus Christ.' On the eve of that day I copied this passage into my book: 'Slight joys are followed by slight sufferings, but to extraordinary happiness succeeds extraordinary sorrows.' What a sentence! If this is true, we, who are so happy, ought to tremble.

"On Friday, March 7th, 1834,* I happened to go to my mother's room at a somewhat unusual time, whilst she was dressing. She had on her knees a number of old-fashioned trinkets. Prince Lapoukhyn was very fond of these sort of things, and people often brought some to the house, in hopes that he would buy them. I looked at them in an indifferent manner — I was very careless in those days — and I said to my mother, little thinking how important the remark would prove, 'That little trinket is exactly like the one which Madame de Marcellus had on her forehead at supper, on Easter day.' These words instantly

* On the 18th of December of the preceding year, as we were coming out of the house of Count Stackelberg, on the night of a ball, we were told that a considerable robbery had taken place that evening at the Comte and Comtesse Marcellus'. Money, jewels, and all sorts of other things had been carried off. This crime was unanimously attributed to one of their servants, a Neapolitan of the name of Carminello, who was immediately thrown into prison, in spite of all his protestations of innocence.

struck her, and recalled to her mind the robbery at that lady's house, on the 18th of December. Doubts were at first expressed as to the correctness of my impression, but on examining it closely, I declared and maintained this trinket to be the same I had seen Madame de Marcellus wear. It was a miniature shrine in enamel, containing the figures of a king and a queen with their crowns on, and its style and workmanship were so peculiar, that it was very unlikely that an exactly similar one should exist. We sent it to Madame de Marcellus, who recognised it at once. This discovery gave a clue to the real authors of the robbery, and poor Carminello, who had been wrongfully accused, was acquitted and set at liberty. He came on the 15th of June to thank me as his deliverer. He had been absolutely tortured: hung with his head downwards, had a wound in his leg, had been flogged, and drenched with cold water, and besides, was threatened with twenty-five years of the galleys, where the actual thief now is. I took it as a good omen, that just before my marriage, I had been, under God, the means of saving an innocent person, for no one else had noticed the trinket. Whenever afterwards poor Carminello saw me, he always renewed his expressions of gratitude, and included Albert in the blessings he showered upon me.

"On March 9th, I opened for the first time since Boklet, my locked journal. The last words in it were these: 'When shall I open this book again? Oh, if I dared to say "At Naples!"'

"And *here* I am, at Naples,—at Naples! Oh, my good God! was it not ungrateful never to open this book for eight months? Not even to record that all my wishes were fulfilled. I am happy, rapturously happy, and I believe I shall continue to be so. Still, there is a mixture of feelings in this joy. Sometimes I fear that I love Albert too much, and I am humbled by this thought. At another moment I fancy I do not love him enough, that I am not capable of a deep love. I am not satisfied with myself, and often not with others. I think myself very worthless, and yet I am vexed that others do not think more highly of me. If I better deserved to be happy, I should not feel these misgivings. One thing at least I ask of Thee, my God! Let me not be a cause of sorrow to any one. Grant me this for Our Lord Jesus Christ's sake! And so I shall be married in a few weeks. Oh! may I never grieve Albert. I wish I were worthy of him. I am so afraid of displeasing him, that there is nothing I would not do to be in every respect what he would wish. And yet I am sometimes careless. Nothing, not even his love, seems perfectly to satisfy me, and yet I am not good enough to care for Heaven alone. At least, I must change very much before that happens. I am such a strange being, suspicious, proud, irritable, and apathetic at the same time. What will become of me? Shall I fail to please Albert, or shall I be unhappy myself? On March 18th (I think), I wrote the following note to Albert:—'My darling, why did you go away? My mother left me almost immediately afterwards, and I am sore of heart and must write, for we should have spent an hour-and-a-half together. Oh, dear! I hope God will not punish me for feeling so acutely what after all, is unimportant, seeing that we are to spend all the days of our life together.* I am unreasonable, I know, but what a vexatious evening it has been, and I am so afraid the same thing may happen again to-morrow. Let us try to manage better. Oh, how I love you, and how sweet it is to feel that I may tell you so! You are perhaps just going to say your prayers! Oh! may I not rest assured that everything which has befallen us has been God's will, and that He has chosen that our lives should be linked together? Farewell till to-morrow. God be always with you.'

"Albert always kept this note in the little pocket-book I have mentioned, and two years afterwards, beside his coffin, I read it again.

"That same day I received M. de Montalembert's answer to my note. He spoke in it of the strong and deep attachment he had felt for Albert ever since he had known him, and said that my affection was the reward God had bestowed on 'that heart so full of love and devotedness to his fellow-creatures; the most affectionate and the most faithful heart he had ever met with in this world.' Delicious praise, and well-deserved by my Albert!"

In the midst of the press of his own affairs, Albert found leisure at this time to write the following letter to a young Englishman, with whom he had made acquaintance the year before at Rome. It is too interesting not to insert here.

* Later on, Alexandrine wrote on the margin of this page: "O life—life! What, alas! are *all our days?*"

ALBERT TO MR. A. S. C.

"My dear Friend—I did not expect, when we touched upon so important a subject, that we were to go deeper into it. I said to you one day that my religion was in perfect keeping with the feelings which beautiful scenery inspires. We started, I think, from that point. As we have, however, arrived at considering the subject in a closer manner, I am well satisfied to discuss it with you. I have never much read the Bible, as I told you, but I will set before you, in the best way I can, the grounds of my attachment to our religion. I look upon it as a mark of God's infinite goodness to have given us a belief which preserves us from falling into error in matters of dogma. If it were true that we all had the mission and right to determine our faith for ourselves, and to trust to our own light alone to do so, only tell me, my dear friend, what opinion or conviction would be the same in any two individuals? Would not each man's belief be influenced by the extent of his capacity, or the comparative goodness of his heart? What confusion would ensue! You must see, on the one side, to what excesses imagination might lead us, and on the other, how much at a loss uneducated or incapable men would find themselves. Where would justice be if knowledge and research alone could guide us to the truth? Instead of this, God in His goodness has given us a light to protect us from error. The Church is the visible form of faith, the foundation on which we are to build by a constant increase in holiness. Were we obliged to spend our lives in seeking this starting point, death would overtake us before we had begun our most important work.

"You say that you cannot understand confession. I will not speak of the happiness it affords, for we must have practised it to appreciate its value. But, my dear friend, do you think that because every man knows, as you say, that he ought to be good, it is useless that he should be reminded of it; and that his own reflections always suffice? There is in words directly addressed to ourselves by a living person a power and fulness which we should seek in vain in books and in our own thoughts. The man whose life is a perpetual struggle against his passions knows by experience all our miseries and sufferings. He is acquainted with the malady and the means to overcome it, he rouses us from apathy, comforts us in affliction, and restores to us hope and trust when we are cast down.

"You say again that it will not excuse me before God to plead that I have learnt my errors from a priest; but this is exactly the danger from which we are quite safe. The priest can neither deceive nor be deceived, for his doctrine is not his own; he gives us that of which the Church is the keeper, in which we have all one and the same faith, and form one and the same body.

"You are alarmed, you say, at the enormous objections to the celibacy of the clergy. In the first place, this is only a simple matter of discipline; but I should like to point out to you what wisdom and beauty is contained in this institution. 'Men who have desired to attain by thought to the heights of religion or philosophy have always abstained from human contact. The first Christians held this virtue in such esteem that in their opinion no other could spring up or attain perfection in a soul where it did not exist. Do not ask me to explain how this can be, for to understand it we must also believe that when the sanctuary is prepared God does not disdain to enter into it; that there is intense happiness in such a life when this virtue is fully practised, that He grants to those who thus give themselves up to His absolute influence unspeakable joys, which amply make amends for the miserable pleasures of the world. The visions of the desert, the inspirations of holy recluses, and the contemplations of saints forbid us to doubt it. There are not wanting authentic revelations to establish the fact in the face of the most suspicious scepticism, and certainly it is not incredible that a soul raised above the wants and hopes of our gross flesh, should attain at last to that sublime devotion which is called by this world folly, but the highest wisdom in the world to come.' *

"My dear friend, I am far from having exhausted all that could be said on this subject. I am sorry to have done it so little justice, and I wish with all my heart you could meet with some one fitter than myself to carry on this interesting discussion.

"Yours most sincerely,

"ALBERT."

ALBERT'S JOURNAL (BEGUN MARCH, 1834).

"Naples.—I have resolved to write a journal, but why to-day and not yesterday I cannot tell, unless it is that I thought that

* The inverted commas which mark this fine passage seem to show that it is a quotation, but no reference is given.

the obligation of giving an account of each day compels one to spend it better.

"Read Byron. Got up late; wrote a few lines to Montalembert; translated some of Moore, and since two o'clock spent the time as usual in a quiet, happy manner. I talked and thought a great deal of our journey to Jerusalem, which I do not believe in; but what would I not give to go, supposing, of course, it were with her!

"Naples, March 22nd.—Got up late, having slept badly. Read English with Miss McCarthy. Went out riding, and enjoyed a gallop along the shore. I feel often a wish to plunge into the sea, to be in the midst of something boundless. This is, perhaps, the reason why I so like to be alone. When I went in I made my usual visit to Alexandrine. It is in those worldly salons that one loses so much time. I should not often honor them with my presence, if an angel were not to be found there who makes up for all their emptiness. *** is a strange man. I like him, and he interests me. His life has been a failure, but I do not know what else would have suited him. A long habit of independence makes the slightest chain galling. Thank God! I have known early in life the blessing of restraint.

"March 23rd.—Got up early. Read. Found in Moore a woman's portrait, which I thought very like Pauline. Went to Mass, and at two o'clock to see Alexandrine. Poor darling! I found her very sad. She torments herself with the idea that it would have been better for me that we should never have been engaged. And I too feel it at times, but only as far as she is concerned. But, on the whole, I do believe that it has been a happy thing for both of us to have met, and that God blesses our love. I speak very coldly, for I cannot disclose the deep and intense feelings of my heart. I have the most perfect faith in the fulfilment of my dream. O! my God, let Thy love descend upon us like the dew!*

"March 24th.—I got up early, and went to Monsignor Porta. I do not deserve so much mercy. Received absolution and heard Mass. Came in and breakfasted. I should like to follow

* Alexandrine wrote by the side of this passage: "O! my God, my Albert's prayer was heard. It was the kind of prayer which pierces the clouds and reaches Thy throne. I had been that day to a Protestant confirmation, and it was when I came home, I think, that in the course of conversation with my brother and my mother, I refused to promise never to become a Catholic; and I spoke in the evening to Albert in a way which made him write, 'that he had a firm belief in the accomplishment of his dream.'"

a sort of rule of life, not for my health, but because I think it good for the mind. Rode out. Wrote a little to Montalembert, for whom my friendship seems to increase every day. Went to Alexandrine, but we did not talk much. She went to dress for dinner at Count Stackelberg's. Her dress was pretty, and she was looking lovely. In the evening I sat a little while in Emma's drawing-room, and enjoyed it; but I seem to have entirely lost the habits of the world, for when I go into society everything seems strange, and I do not feel myself at home. I like so much my evenings alone with Alexandrine, and those dear conversations to which nothing else can be compared. When the Princess came home I went there. We talked of all kinds of things. I had a dispute with * * *, who is possessed with the spirit of contradiction. He would have taken my side of the argument had he been talking to one who held a different opinion from me, for I am sure that in reality he thinks as I do. At eleven o'clock, thank God! everybody went away, and then came our own delightful hour, which passed too quickly. Oh, I do love her beyond all power of words to express, more than she knows herself. It is always so difficult to leave her. I have to tear myself away.* I walked on the shore in the moonlight. The sea was rough and there was wind, a kind of weather that I like. Wrote my journal, and went on with my letter to Montalembert. Went to bed at one o'clock. I have not finished my letter, but I am sleepy. Good night.

"March 26th.—I got up at eight o'clock, under the impression that I had a number of things to do, which I found to be quite a mistake. I heard Mass, and received from the parish priest the attestation of our banns. It is done, then! I can hardly believe it! Life is very strange, and it frightens me when I think how unworthy I am of this great blessing. Easter is very near. I am not prepared, or rather I am ill-prepared for it. O! my God, have mercy on me. Have mercy on us! Had a delightful ride. I never feel happier or more free than when alone on horseback. At nine o'clock I went to my mother-in-law's house. The evening was, as usual, tiresome at the beginning, and we were not left alone till eleven o'clock. It is midnight, and I am going to bed. O! God, have mercy upon us, and fill our lives with the love of Thee and of each other!

* Alexandrine wrote on the margin: "Ah! yes. That short absence was always a suffering. Our hearts are insatiable. We desire happiness to be perfect and eternal."

"Naples, March 27th, Holy Thursday.—Got up early. Went to Church. Came back at twelve. We did not breakfast till about one o'clock. At two went to Alexandrine. We were not in good spirits. She cried, sweet angel, and big, beautiful tears ran down her cheeks. How I felt to love her! At four o'clock I came away, and went to Tenebræ, visiting several Churches on my way. I like the custom of forbidding carriages in the streets on Holy Thursday and Good Friday. The troops trail their arms as a sign of mourning, which is a beautiful and touching idea. There is so much poetry in these southern customs. Dined at seven o'clock, and at eight went to Alexandrine. Had a pleasant little bit of time with her, standing by the fire-place in the prince's room. I have always a greater abundance of thoughts and of power to express them, when I am alone with her than at any other time. I am scared by a third person, and altogether extinguished by a room full of people. Is it possible that it is a quarter to one? I must go to bed. O! my God, bless us both!

"March 28th, Good Friday.—A beautiful service at the Chapel of the Fortress. Breakfasted at about one, and at two went to the princess. Alexandrine was at her Church, and did not come in for an hour. Half-an-hour after that I left her to go to Tenebræ, and came back at eight o'clock. Company again. We were only one minute alone, at the tea-table. Alexandrine asked me not to go to Mola di Gaëta, but only to Castellamare. I like that as much, or perhaps better, and we shall talk of it again. What happy days are at hand! My father and I came away about midnight. Said my prayers, and to bed at past twelve o'clock.

"March 29th.—Got up at eight o'clock, intending to go to Communion, though very unworthy. I went to Monsignor Porta, who was officiating at an ordination. A most touching ceremony. What life there is in our worship! how it affects the soul, and how striking was the patriarchal beauty and piety of that venerable countenance, and the fervor of the assistants, a Franciscan and a Benedictine. I did well to go to that Church. My heart was cold, but life and fervor have now returned. Monsignor Porta was too tired to hear me in confession, and put me off till to-morrow. I went to Emma's room, where I found Alexandrine. I took her home, and remained till their dinner-time. Went back in the evening, and we spoke of the devotion to the

Blessed Virgin, about which she has doubts. This grieves me, and I wish I could convince her. O! my God, give her faith and simplicity of heart! When I came in, I looked out for certain passages upon this devotion, and found one which I shall copy and translate for her. We had a pleasant evening, and I left early. May God watch over my angel! On coming home I found some people still with Emma. I withdrew and sat by the fire to think and read."

That same evening Alexandrine wrote in her book:—"To-morrow I am going to Communion, and my heart is so cold. Even about earthly things I feel nothing, and for those of God I have little faith, and no fervor. Yet I wish to believe. O! my God, give me Thy help at every step I take, so that I may not commit sins which I should have been less exposed to when my soul was in a better state. O! my God, I beseech Thee, in the name of Thy Divine Son to let me die rather than communicate unworthily—rather than sin grievously against Thee. As to those who have sinned and will communicate with me without thinking themselves in danger, I feel confident Thou wilt not betray their hope, for Thou hast promised that those who trust in Thee shall not be put to shame. Thine only begotten Son hath asked of Thee to forgive those who know not what they do. O! God most pitiful, Whom I fear, and yet whom I love for Thy infinite sweetness and mercy, my Father Who art in Heaven, forsake me not when my heart is dead and dry, but give me faith, hope, and love, and enlighten me as to all I ought to believe. *I beseech Thee in the name of Jesus Christ teach me the true faith!*"*

ALBERT'S JOURNAL.

"March 24th, 1834.—I went out riding with my father at eight o'clock in the morning. To the Camoldoli, where we heard Mass. It was charming. New life seems to fill the soul in prayer, and the lot of these monks is a blessed one. There is something so majestic in that place, so suggestive of high and noble thoughts. Far from cities and the world, they are unconscious of its evils, and you read, in the serenity of their countenances, that real happiness which has its source in God. Yet the world, sectarians, and the enemy of mankind

* Alexandrine afterwards wrote under this: "This prayer has never yet been uttered in vain."

all strive, though in vain, to discredit the purity of these angels in human form! What am I by the side of these men, who have made sacrifice the only joy of their lives? I who am cast down at the least trouble or contradiction, at the least obstacle that opposes my passions. I reverence mortification, for there is nothing so beautiful as purity. This evening I talked to Alexandrine. I want her to have more faith. God loves little children for their simplicity, their openness, and their love. Faith is beautiful as Heaven is beautiful. Oh, for words! for words to convey to her these thoughts!

"April 1st.—Got up late. Had my English lesson. In the afternoon went to see Alexandrine, and talked over plans for the future. Our wedding-day is fixed for the 17th, and we go that day to Castellamare, where, after a few days, my mother-in-law will join us. After some excursions in the neighborhood we shall return with her to Naples, and see her off. I live in dread of never actually arriving at such happiness, and that something or other must happen to disturb it. O! God of goodness, guard and bless us! This evening there was company at the Princess's, which was tiresome, and I had only half-an-hour with my angel. I asked her to give me a ring on which was engraved 'For Life;' but she refused, for our love, she said, is not to end with life. From Heaven it came, and to Heaven it must tend.* Came home, wrote in my journal, read some of Byron's poetry, and the Imitation of Christ. I am sleepy, and my last chapter of the Imitation suffered from it.

"April 2nd.—Went out with Ventignano. To-morrow the witnesses are to meet at Count Stackelberg's to attest Alexandrine's baptism. In the afternoon to the Princess's. Had a nice time with Alexandrine, and dined with them, but stupidly outstaid everybody. I thought the evening would never come to an end, thanks to the * * *, who tired me to death. I got into such a nervous state that I very nearly made a scene. Twenty times I was coming away, which would have been the best thing I could have done; for after they and my father left I was so out of sorts that even a *tête-à-tête* with Alexandrine could not soothe my irritation, and I came home. I am sorry, and I

* Alexandrine made this note: "How well I remember that evening, Albert was looking at my rings, wishing to have one that had belonged to my father, but I refused, saying, with a smile, 'For life! No, life is too short!'"

would put off my marriage two days not to have had it happen. I am an idiot. I must read a chapter of the Imitation, and the Confessions of St. Augustine, and go to bed. I wish it were to-morrow, and that I had seen her again.

"April 3rd.—Up at eight o'clock. First to Ventignano, and then to the jeweller. At three in the afternoon a grand function. Seven witnesses, nearly all ministers, counsellors, and generals, met and forswore themselves, or something very like it, about Alexandrine's baptism.* A horrid solicitor contrived to make up four pages out of a matter of four lines. I thanked the grandees, and saw the judge into his carriage—which I had to pay for. The rogue! Came back to Lapoukhyn's, dined; the evening began stupidly, but afterwards I had half-an-hour alone with Alexandrine, which was pleasant. Dear love! She must take me as I am, two different men in one. She loves them both. So much the better, or perhaps so much the worse. All I know is that I adore her. Twelve days more! God be with us!"

ALBERT TO COUNT DE MONTALEMBERT.

"Naples, April 5th, 1834.

"I am behind hand with you, my dear friend, but you can hardly imagine to what a degree my approaching marriage engrosses me, which is natural enough. It is impossible to describe to you my happiness, or the agitation it causes me; and yet, as I must always mix up a little sadness with everything, I am often out of spirits, which is not only foolish, but I am afraid ungrateful too. You must, alas! take me as I am. I really dread the responsibility of drawing that angelic being into all the sufferings which life is perhaps preparing for us. I am afraid of my own character, of my fickleness, my inexperience, and above all of the want of real merit in myself. I love all that is noble, and shrink from all base and vile things, but I am wholly deficient in the merits which result from education, character, or power of mind. You would hardly believe how this thought pursues and grieves me. I feel my own inferiority,

* An absurd formality made it necessary for seven persons to affirm that Alexandrine had been baptised. This was to supply the place of a certificate, which could not be obtained. None of those witnesses, as they were called, had been present at her baptism, which made Albert say they forswore themselves, or something like it. They only took her mother's word for the fact, and her testimony alone ought to have been sufficient.

and my natural shyness diminishes even the small capability I may possess. Your letters are the only things that encourage me a little, for you have the gift of making me think better of myself than I should naturally do. If I were not speaking of you, I should say this was flattery, and Alexandrine was right when she said the other day: 'I wish all those who do not know you could read your friend's letters.' No doubt they represent me in the most favorable light. While on this matter I may as well mention how pleased I was at what you said about my style of writing. It flattered me very much, and my pleasure was not diminished by what you added as to the want of method in my ideas. I admit the perfect justice of your friendly advice, and do not think that I am unconscious of my defects. I know but too well the inordinate tendencies of my restless imagination. Will this ever be cured? Ah! my dear friend, examine the cause, and acknowledge the existence of the evil, and instead of deceiving yourself about me, lament as I do my deplorable barrenness. I have reaped nothing from an education which, what with bad teachers, what with weak health, and still more, perhaps, from the want of real desire to do well, proved a complete failure. This is a state of mind which you have never known, and an intolerable one it is. I want to make up for lost time, and notwithstanding the continual distractions which do and will beset me, the leisure I enjoy at present gives me an opportunity of filling up the void which a want of knowledge creates. But, my dear friend, to know *how* to study is half the battle, and this is just what I require. I long to undertake everything, which is the very way of doing nothing. A dreamy habit of thought, which I know is most pernicious, makes me deplorably absent. In short, I am thirsty, and do not know how to drink.

"I have already told you what made my marriage for some time doubtful, and gave me fears that my hopes might be suddenly deceived. But God has willed it otherwise, and all difficulties are smoothed away. I shall owe all my happiness to my mother-in-law, upon whom everything depended, and Prince Lapoukhyn has been also very kind to Alexandrine. My brother-in-law is the member of the family who likes me the least; he is, however, gentlemanlike, well informed, and high minded, but a captious, irritable disposition prevents his good qualities from having free play. There is another brother, who is said to be better tempered, and a good fellow, but I have not seen him. There is one other person whom you know by sight, but whom I have never mentioned to you—Count Putbus; you may remember him at Rome. This good man had no other home than Madame d'Alopeus's house; he has travelled about with them for twenty years, and has always been considered like one of the family. When Madame d'Alopeus married at Florence, he fell into a state of terrible despondency, and during the wedding this cold man of the world was deeply affected. However, he was very brave about it, and followed them all here. I cannot quite tell what he feels about Alexandrine. If, as I think, it is only friendship, it is so strong a friendship, that to see her give her heart to another is more than he can bear, and he is going away in a few days. Nothing will induce him to stay. Every now and then I see tears in his eyes, though he tries to hide them from me. This shows how unlike his cold exterior is to his true nature. I have no doubt he will come back to us after a while. He is trying to persuade us to go to Egypt. That is a beautiful dream! In that case you must join our caravan. What do you say to it?

"I intended to have begun by answering what you tell me of M. de Lamennais. Remember me to him, I beg of you; tell him about us, and entreat him to draw down upon us the blessing of God by his prayers. If I were not afraid of being troublesome, I would write to him myself. Ask him also to continue his kindness to me, and to let me entertain for him those feelings of admiration which he always inspires, and that silent attachment which his goodness gives me a right to feel. Remember me also to M. Lacordaire. I can never lose the recollection of our stay at Rome.

"You speak of Montigny, and alas! Montigny is sold.* You cannot think how it grieves me, for without some fixed home in one's own country, now that political changes have unsettled everything, there is a great chance of being condemned to wander about without end in a foreign land. How many castles in the air I had built! When the mind has fed for a while on the beauties of this Italian earth and sky, our happiness is not com-

* To the Duke de Laval Montmorency. It now belongs to his grandson, Count de Levis Mirepoix.

plete until we can go and live on them at home. I own that I often get a fit of home-sickness.

"Tell me about Rio, and talk to me at great length about yourself. Oh, my dear friend, I know you will one day be happy. Believe me, I am right. ALBERT.

"P.S.—Pierre de Brézé* said his first Mass the other day, to the edification of every one."

ALBERT'S JOURNAL.

"Naples, April 6th.—Went out at eight o'clock to buy a present for Catiche, and ordered my own and *my wife's* cards, which seems a wonderful point to have reached. Dined at Count Stackelberg's, stayed till ten o'clock with Emma, and then went to Alexandrine. They were not yet returned from the play. At last they came in. I talked some time to Putbus, and then everybody went away. Nothing can be compared to my pleasant life for the last two years, and now my happiness seems complete. Such a tie can never be severed. Came in at midnight. Found Emma's room still full of people; when they were gone I had a good talk with *her*. And now I am in my own room, not sleepy, but I have no fire, and the cold is driving me to bed. I like sitting up in my room; I like its silence and its solitude. Nobody sees me, and if Alexandrine is asleep, no one even thinks of me. I like that sometimes. I have found a little poem by Campagna, on *Buondelmonti*, which I am going to finish. It is pretty and interesting. How important at that time were the events of private life! Now everything is more commonplace; the nobler kind of passions seem asleep or dead. Selfishness creeps into everything. Every one shifts for himself. Society would fall to pieces but for an approaching regeneration, the tokens of which we can discern, though confusedly. We experience the first shock of the coming earthquake, but men's minds are gradually preparing for it, and I incline to think that the new era will take possession of a soil made to its hand, on which it can establish itself without violence or commotion. The best pledge of its stability will be Religion, and I believe it will become the soul of our future, the last form of social transformation. The end we shall reach as we grow more perfect, will

* Now Bishop of Moulins.

bring us back to our original destiny, light and innocence, happiness and Heaven.

"April 8th.—Bought something for Catiche at last; something ugly, I am afraid, but it relieves me from suspense on the subject, which is all that signifies. Ordered a Scotch cap, which is very becoming: I am glad of it. I should like to look well. Lost nearly the whole day. Went out riding. Felt in a detestable mood. Finished *Buondelmonti.* He perishes by the hand of an assassin on the day he is married to the woman he loves. An enviable death, perhaps, for then no cloud can ever sully the paradise of his happiness.

"April 10th.—At this hour a week hence I shall have been already married eleven hours. Spent the evening at the Lapoukhyns'. Alexandrine was sad at the idea of leaving her mother, and shed tears. This will not last, I hope. But what if I should find that I do not fill up the blank which her mother's departure will cause? I must either die or go and live in Russia, which would be a kind of moral, intellectual, and possibly physical suicide. I am stupid, or mad, or something of the sort. I am haunted by the fear that I shall make Alexandrine anything but happy. I almost wish I were a monk. This is folly. I am writing nonsense. I will bury my head in the pillow till I have recovered a little common sense.

"April 11th.—To the podestà. Then to Monsignor Porta, with whom I conversed a long time. He wishes to repurchase the convent at Amalfi.* I quite enter into his wishes, for never was there a more appropriate spot for such a purpose. Oh, what has the world to offer in comparison with the pure and holy joys of those blessed vocations, with that boundless love which loses itself in God, and therefore can never end.

"April 12th.—Started at eight o'clock for Castellamare to arrange about our apartments, which will be very nice. Ah, what happy days are in store for me! Came back to Naples. A dinner at Temple's† of a most intolerable length. After dinner to the Lapoukhyns', where there was a long melodramatic scene. Putbus insisted on going away. Everybody tried to detain him. He was obstinate; he was absurd. I love him dearly, and I wish

* The Capuchin convent at Amalfi had been turned into an inn. Monsignor Porta was superior of the order.

† Sir William Temple, brother of Lord Palmerston, who was then, and for a long time afterwards, English minister at Naples.

him with all my heart to look upon our house as his own. He either will not or pretends not to believe that people care for him, which is unjust and ridiculous. I wanted to stay with Alexandrine, who was crying bitterly, but it was half-past twelve o'clock. Nobody would go away, so I went home."

ALEXANDRINE'S STORY.

"Maurice Putbus actually left us that night. For a few days I had been rather sad. I had not the least uneasiness as to my future happiness, and Albert was dearer to me than all the world besides. But the near approach of the greatest event in one's life naturally suggests grave thoughts, and then the idea of parting with my mother haunted me like a spectre. Even Putbus's departure grieved me. To lose what I would fain have kept, even though I thus obtained what was still more precious, produced a kind of vague depression, which was, however, always dispelled by him who was the cause of these changes. Perhaps it sprang also in part from the fact that in this life of uncertainties, when one is very happy, any kind of change is looked upon with dread. I had been so happy in my mother's drawing-room, and afterwards in my own little room, thinking of *what he had said*, of *what he would say to me*. Nevertheless, I did long for the solemn moment when before God and man I should vow to love him for ever.

"On the 14th Albert dined with us, his mother and sisters, and M. Valetti, the Protestant minister, of whom he makes the following mention in his journal:—'He has quite the look of a Protestant. Why did they cut themselves off from the Church, tearing and rending Christendom to pieces by their divisions? Unity is so glorious. Oh! why have they marred that cry of love which ought to rise as if with one voice from earth to Heaven?'

"April 16th.—Albert took me to his father's house, and before Monsignor Porta I promised that all my children should be Catholics. I remember that when I had to answer *yes*, Madame de la Ferronnays looked at me, as if she was afraid it would give me pain, and she said gently: 'You wish it to be so, do you not?' She little knew what pleasure it gave me to make this promise, or with how great a joy it filled me. Strange to say, at no time of my life would I have wished to have had Protestant children.

Rather than that I should have preferred their being Greeks, but always, and above all, wished them to be Catholics. It was about that time, perhaps that very day, that in talking to Pauline I told her that one birth, or any one of three deaths would at once decide me to become a Catholic. That meant my own death (for I felt even then that I would not die in another religion), or my mother's, which would free me from the pain of grieving her, or Albert's. I thought, too, that if once I had a child, I should feel courage to bear my mother's grief. The most sorrowful of all these conditions was the one which came to pass.

"On the 16th of April, the eve of our marriage, Albert dined with us. In the evening I was some time with him alone, and he spoke to me in a way that filled me with love and admiration. Everything that he said and did, increased my affection and reverence. I thought him more like an Angel than a man. I had often been struck with this before, but never so deeply as on that evening before our wedding day. It was not a mere earthly happiness I felt, and not even my mother's sorrow, when I went afterwards to give her a kiss in bed, could disturb it. When I returned to my room, I wrote in my locked book these lines: 'Oh! my God, to-morrow I am to be Albert's wife, and I grieve that I am so unworthy of him in all respects. I beseech Thee, in the name of Thy Son, Our Lord, to end this marriage-tie by my death, if ever it should be burthensome to Albert. I also commend to Thee my poor mother's, Albert's, and my brothers' happiness,—in this world, if possible, but above all in Heaven. For myself I desire light, and that Albert and I may abide in Thy love. Grant me my father's blessing—my father who is gone to Heaven, and who loved me so much in this world. Oh! my God, I would that all men might attain one day to perfect innocence and love!' Then I packed up this book, which was to be sent to Pauline, with a note:

"'Dear Pauline—I leave this book with you; I prefer doing so, and you will give it me back by-and-bye. It is now past midnight. I feel sad on Mamma's account, but otherwise I enjoy a delicious peace, thanks to Albert, who is an angel of whom I am not worthy. You will be glad to hear I am in a frame of mind which promises tranquillity, and even an immense happiness for to-morrow. How can I be thankful enough to God? Good-night, my darling sisters. Good-bye till to-morrow. Love me very much. Both of you pray for Mamma.

"'ALEXANDRINE D'ALOPEUS.'

"The last words in my journal, at this period of my life, were, 'Bless us, oh, my God! for Jesus Christ's sake!' And as I wished the last passage in my book of extracts to be also something holy, I chose this text: 'Let every one give as he hath determined in his heart, not with sadness or necessity, for God loveth a cheerful giver.'—2 Corinthians ix. 7. Yet how far I was from leading a Christian life. Sometimes I am afraid that it was to punish me for my forgetfulness and negligence in thanking Him for my happiness, that God took it from me.

"The morning of our wedding-day, April 17th, Catiche woke me at seven o'clock. I asked her immediately what kind of weather it was. It did not rain, but the sky was cloudy. I was superstitiously anxious that it should not rain on that day. I got up, went to my mother, breakfasted with her, and then returned to my room to dress. Before I had finished, Pauline and Eugénie came in. They were both in sky blue; my mother had on a white cashmere gown, trimmed with red; mine was white satin, trimmed with lace, and a wreath of white roses and myrtle* fastened my veil. My mother would not let me put on the pearl necklace she had given me, on account of the German proverb: '*Perlen deuten Thränen*' (Pearls betoken tears), but I wore a fine diamond cross, Albert's present. I prized it as his gift, and because it is the sign of our salvation. Oh Cross! token and emblem of love and suffering, how full of meaning you have seemed to me ever since! During the long process of dressing, my mother was very much upset, but I felt calm and happy. Pauline still remembers little things, I said, which made her laugh. She thought it so odd I should be exactly like myself on that momentous day. Albert came just as I was ready, and I went to my mother's room, where I asked her blessing on my knees, and begged her to bless me also in the name of my departed father. Then the marriage contract was signed, and afterwards we all went to the Palazzo Acton, where the Catholic ceremony was to take place. Just then the sun came out, which I was glad of, but it was only a gleam, which did not last long.

* Myrtle is in Germany the proper wreath for brides, and the Princess Lapoukhyn had insisted on it for that reason.

"Monsignor Porta married us in the Chapel. He wore splendid vestments, and his fine white beard gave him a venerable appearance. I knelt beside Albert, and did as I was told. I was quite ignorant of the Catholic liturgy, and, as in all important moments of my life, I felt bewildered, and hardly understood what was going on. When the ceremony was over, I was surrounded and embraced by everybody, and then we proceeded to the Protestant Chapel, where M. Valetti gave an excellent discourse, which, to Mamma's great delight, touched all the Catholics present. As we were driving to M. de la Ferronnays' house, Mamma made Albert and me sit together on the back seat of the carriage, and placed herself in front of us. There was a great breakfast, and afterwards I went in my wedding gown to see the Countess Stackelberg, who through some mistake had not been invited. Then I came back to my mother's house, and to the room which I was about to leave for ever. There I took off my white gown, and put on a grey silk dress, and a straw bonnet trimmed with pink, for our journey to Castellamare. Once ready to go, I gave a sorrowful look at the people and places I was leaving behind. I felt deeply moved, and asked to go once more into all the rooms. I kissed my mother, and then everybody else. At last, getting into the calèche with Albert, we drove away. It felt to both of us like a dream!"

PART II.

"What doth he know who hath not been tried?"—Eccles. xxxiv. 9.

If this story were a novel, or if it were only meant to preserve the remembrance of happy days, it would now be drawing to a close; but those whose lives are here related are not imaginary persons, they were Christian men and women, who were accounted worthy to suffer, and the memory of whose earthly happiness is only fraught with blessings, because it was received with thankfulness of heart, and surrendered without a murmur. Therefore, the story proceeds—I might almost say now begins, so much does the importance of the sequel exceed what has already been told. We had not, however, arrived at the time of trial, when a few days after the marriage of Albert and Alexandrine, we joined them at Castellamare, where they were established in a charming house. Indeed, that summer was one of the most joyful times we ever spent, but though we did not know it, our happiness had then reached its meridian, and never did we *all* meet again in this world.

A flight of steps, overarched by a trellice of vines and roses, led from the road to that pretty house. The ground floor was inhabited by Albert and Alexandrine; Charles and Emma occupied the first floor, my parents, Fernand, my sisters, and I, the second. Each set of apartments had a balcony, and we could pass from one to another by means of an out-of-door staircase. We all assembled for meals, and often also read together, for we were always delighted at any opportunity of meeting. Never, I believe, were there brothers, sisters, brothers-in-law, and sisters-in-law, so gladly and cordially united as we were. It was in the course of that summer that I was married, and the event interested the dear people about me very nearly as much as it did myself. Happy days followed the one in which my marriage was finally decided upon. One of them I particularly remember as having been as calm and blissful as any I ever spent. I have already said that Albert and Alexandrine occupied the ground floor of our house. Their windows opened on a short flight of steps, which led to the garden. On that evening, which I so well recollect, their room was full of light, flowers, and music. Eugénie was singing, and as we sat on the steps outside, we listened whilst chatting to her wonderfully beautiful voice. We enjoyed the perfume of the orange flowers and roses, and gazed on the matchless view, then illuminated by the moon and stars, and also by the flames of Vesuvius, from whose crater a broad stream of fire was descending towards the plain, in the direction of Ottegano. Ah, we were all indeed perfectly happy at that moment! The joy of Albert and Alexandrine seemed a foretaste and a pledge of our own, while ours heightened what they felt. Dear Eugénie, with her overflowing affection and sympathy, was as gay as a bird and as bright as a sunbeam. Fernand, also, enlivened by his merriment the graver thoughts which important events might have induced. We generally spent the evenings in Charles' and Emma's room, whose cordial sympathy was all we could wish. They had the largest of our three balconies, and there we all used to sit, and remained often far into the night—those Italian nights which never pall upon one, and which are more glorious even than the days. I think my father and mother had never been so fully satisfied, or so entirely enjoyed seeing their children gathered around them. But, alas! we were on the mountain top. We had attained the highest point of earthly happiness, and it must be owned, that never was summit gilded with a brighter light. If it can be said of happiness that it is too great and perfect to last, it might indeed be asserted of ours at that time. But the cloud which was soon to darken our horizon, was already casting its shadow upon us.

We had had already one alarm about Albert, but anxiety, the destroyer of human joys, had not yet taken possession of our hearts, and we soon resumed the careless security which belongs to inexperience. It was only when Alexandrine's trial had reached its final term, that mounting, as it were, from one anguish to another, to the first uneasiness that had troubled her peace, she traced it to the day when, for the first time, she had seen Albert put his handkerchief to his mouth, and take it away stained with blood. *And that had been ten days after her marriage.* Ten untroubled, peaceful, cloudless days. Ten days of actual and full enjoyment of the most perfect earthly happiness, thus much and no more was given to Alexandrine. And yet her life may be called, even in that respect, a blessed and privileged one, for are there many who obtain on earth, even for a single moment, the perfect accomplishment of their hopes and desires? In her case this did happen. She possessed for one instant all she had ever coveted. Not only did she find in her husband the qualities she most esteemed, and had nearly despaired to meet with in any one person; not only did they feel for each other the most deep and ardent love; but in other comparatively unimportant respects, yet to a certain degree essential to perfect happiness, her wishes were fully gratified. Having never had any sisters, and seen little of her brothers, living always alone with her parents, she had painfully felt this isolation, and had always wished to form one of a large and united family. She had been attracted towards us from the first time she and I had met, long before she knew Albert, and afterwards Eugénie became as great a friend as myself. She had also learned to love and admire my father, and was tenderly and reverently attached to my mother. It is certain that the happiness of being their daughter and our sister, added to that of being Albert's wife. And then he belonged to the country she preferred to all others, for to marry a Frenchman, had been her favorite wish; and lastly, her new name pleased her fancy. So that it may be said her lot was exactly what she would have chosen for herself, if she could have planned her life as she pleased. As to wealth, which she certainly did not possess, she had never coveted it, and in after life she gave ample proof that this contempt of money, common enough among young girls, but which is hardly to be taken into account as long as it remains a mere theory, and a theory maintained in the midst of the actual enjoyment of all the luxuries of life,—this contempt of money, I say, was in her case sincere and real. Though brought up in a house abounding in all the magnificence and profusion habitual to the Russians, she never departed for an instant from her simple habits, and from her marriage-day to the hour of her death, by dint of method and economy, always managed to make their moderate income meet their expenses. She knew how to join elegance and good taste with a perfect simplicity of life; and, moreover, always exhibited a noble generosity. Later on, indeed, she gave up everything she possessed, but it was charity and not necessity that caused the sacrifice of means which her wise economy had ever husbanded.

The symptoms in Albert which I have mentioned, and which at first had no serious results, were soon followed by others, which led to the decision that the air of Castellamare did not suit him, and he was advised to spend some time at Sorrento. This separation broke up — in a great measure — our delightful life, and it was therefore with keen regret that, on the 27th of July, we accompanied them to the port of Castellamare, where they were to embark. The magnificent road which now runs from Castellamare to Sorrento, did not then exist, and it was necessary to travel, if by land, on horses or mules, but most people generally preferred the sea, as being the least fatiguing. That evening the weather was stormy, with a cloudy sky, and when we saw the little barque tossing on the rough and gloomy sea, it looked so melancholy, that Eugénie burst into tears. This feeling on her part was overstrained, for we were to see them again the next day but one. But if her sadness was a foreboding, it was assuredly justified, for this parting was but the prelude to many others more sad, and that day brought to a close for Albert and Alexandrine, the sweet family life she had so pined for, and which both of them delighted in. Not many hours later, the boatman brought back the following note from Alexandrine:

"TO MY SISTERS.

"Sorrento, Villa Cesari.

"My three dear sisters, Pauline, Eugénie, and Emma, if I did not love you so much, I certainly should not write to you, for I am quite 'used up.'* Just fancy my being sea-sick! But my enchantment with this house and a delicious tea have revived me so much, that I can write you a few lines. You cannot think how exactly I am lodged to my taste — *mio genio.* Were you a little frightened for us? It certainly looked very adventurous, but I was too sea-sick to enjoy the romantic situation in the least. I hope our boatman took back the note which Albert

* The English words are in the original.

scribbled by the lightning flashes, to say we arrived safe and sound. It takes an hour-and-a-half to get to the shore of Cassano, and at least another half-hour to our Villa Cesari. To-morrow I expect to see Alexander, and the day after my little Eugénie and her father. It is charming to think of these sort of meetings every day. I have been pining already for them, in spite of the delights of this place. My dear little Eugénie, be so good as to find out to-morrow if there are any letters from Mamma for me. Having no news of her spoils my pleasure. May God bless you all! I hope soon to see you again. Do not give our direction to tiresome people, for we are now delightfully secreted. Do you think we do not miss you? Ah! ah! Your

"ALEXANDRINE."

It is evident that she had not felt the same depression that day as we had. But later on, on inserting this letter in her story, she added these words: "I never, perhaps, after that day, wrote anything with such gaiety of heart as this note." We all went to see them two days afterwards, and found them quite settled in their house, and the whole time of their stay at Sorrento, either Eugénie, Fernand, or I, and sometimes all three of us together, went with my father and mother to see them, so that there was no real separation between us, and the month passed rapidly away. But during that whole time Albert was ailing; once he spit blood again, and the doctors gave it as their opinion, that instead of staying with us for the winter, he must leave Naples and settle at Pisa. This was anything but cheering news, but we were so steeped, as it were, in happiness, that anxiety for him could not easily take possession of our minds.

During their stay at Sorrento, Alexandrine's journal, as well as Albert's letters, were gay, but that cheerfulness was now and then dimmed by painful thoughts, which could scarcely be called forebodings, for the evil threatened was but too evident, and when fear took possession of Alexandrine's mind, it was the sad reality which impressed her, in spite of all her efforts to believe that her present bright life would last. It was this terror, these melancholy forebodings, which made her shrink from the sight of a funeral. She thus describes this feeling:

"Living as we do close to a Church, funerals often pass under our window. It is the custom here to leave the face of the dead uncovered, and to place a flower between their lips. I had seen several go by in this way without being particularly affected; but now," (after Albert had been ill, she meant), "when I went to look at them, I had a vague, dreadful feeling, which I dared not own to myself, and I remember that it used to give me a kind of superstitious satisfaction when the corpse proved to be that of an old man, a woman, or a little child. I was so afraid of its being a young man."

In the same month, her anxiety, and what she expressively calls the "prose" which sickness casts upon love and life, caused her to "breathe one sigh after eternity," and to utter the mournful cry: "Oh! my God! Is there then only the shadow of happiness on this earth? Can nothing be delightful but what is seen from a distance? and must all we lay hold of lose its beauty and rich coloring? Is the love of God, then, the only true poetry, and are we so miserable that it cannot suffice us? Must we always thirst after earthly idols and ideal objects? Oh, are we not often consumed with the desire for a country where we can be sure of what we see, certain of loving for ever, have no vain fears, and may cherish without misgivings a heart like unto our own? Heaven—if we ever reach it—will be such a country as this. We long intensely for it, and yet, through weakness and sloth, we do nothing to make it our own!" The following letter, without date, was written from Sorrento:—

ALBERT TO M. MARTIN DE NOIRLIEU.

"Sorrento.

"How glad I was to see your handwriting again! I never entertained a doubt of your friendship, but your long silence made me afraid I had offended you. I did not know your direction, and already two or three of my letters have remained unanswered.

"I must tell you that I am happier than I can express. Dear sir, and most excellent friend, I regretted exceedingly that you were not present at my marriage, and I much wish you were with us now, for I should then eagerly treasure up your words, to instill them afterwards into a soul which I have not wisdom enough myself to cultivate. Alexandrine is not the woman to yield merely to influence, or to be led only by her tastes, and however much she may be drawn towards our faith, her conscience requires some other warrant than the impulse of her heart. Your words would have thrown so much light on our minds. I think often with emotion of our conversations, which, alas! I made but little use of at the time, for we are apt to neglect the treasures within our reach, and it is only when they are taken from us that we discern their full value. I often look back to the time I spent with you, and feel deeply the good effects it ought to have produced upon my life. Now, I would beg of you, as we cannot meet and converse, to supply in some degree for this, by writing to us. God only knows when my angelic wife will be actually a Catholic. Meanwhile, I am glad to see her frequent our Churches of her own accord, and take delight in doing so. On Sunday, she seems to reckon it a duty to hear Mass. But even if she were fully convinced, there would still be the difficulty of leaving the religion professed by her mother, whom she tenderly loves, and who has hitherto strongly opposed her doing so. We must trust in God for this, and hope.

"We are now reading a book which came out some time ago, and which perhaps you know, called 'Travels of an Irish Gentleman in Search of a Religion,' with notes, by Thomas Moore. It goes back to the primitive Christian times, and demonstrates by authoritative testimony, which he quotes, that Catholicism is the *constitution*, so to speak, of Christianity, and that what we believe at this day was the faith of the Apostles. It proves that Fasting, Transubstantiation, the Supremacy of the Pope, Mass, Oral Tradition, Reverence for Images, Prayers for the Dead, Purgatory, and Confession, made part of the faith and practice of primitive times. He also dwells on the discipline of the Secret observed among the early Christians, which has no doubt often led to false interpretations, and furnished Protestants with arguments which it is, however, easy enough to confute.

"I hope you have received a letter from my sister Pauline; but in case it has not reached you, I will repeat the news it contained. She told you in it of her approaching marriage, with which we are all very much pleased. It may perhaps appear strange that such strict Catholics as we all are should be marrying Protestants; but we have good reason to be thankful if God makes use of us to bring others to the love of the Church and the true faith. There is no vanity in saying this, for our share in these conversions is a very indirect one, and they would have taken place even without our co-operation. My future brother-in-law is a Catholic in heart, and he will be received into the Church soon after his marriage. It is only on account of the false interpretations which might be given to this act that he delays it awhile. I wish the same blessing were as near at hand for my wife, but I fear that happy day is still distant. If you had spent this winter in Italy, how happy it would have made my sister and myself, to receive the nuptial blessing at your hands. Monsignor Acton* will take your place, and is coming from Rome for the occasion. He has known Pauline since she was a child.

"We have seen M. de Lamennais' work,† which, as you may believe, has made some noise; but, thanks to the frivolity of a thoroughly worldly society, this publication, which has caused so intense an excitement in other countries, was forgotten here in three days. Although I shared the general surprise which this book created, it pained me to see such a man judged by such opponents. What a strange mixture of fury and tenderness reigns in every page of it. Does not the poetry of this work a little excuse the stormy bursts of a fiery zeal and ardent imagination? I must own to you that I listen with some pleasure to these anticipations of a new era. Will not selfishness at last disappear from the world? And are we not right to thirst after the refreshing dew which will soften our hearts? Efface from M. de Lamennais' pages their angry violence, and then tell me if his hopes are not yours? A work by Silvio Pellico has also just appeared, which forms a striking contrast by its angelic sweetness to that we are speaking of. The whole life of man is indeed contained in these words:—'Dei doveri degl' uomini.'‡ The peace of the author's soul seems to pass into our own, while his overflowing tenderness draws from us purifying tears. How I wish, dear M. l'Abbé, I could get *your* book, for you too are one of the men whose purity of mind and peace of heart lift us above this world. I long to read it, for if you remember I witnessed its beginnings.

"Farewell, and forgive this long rambling letter. I can no longer enjoy those conversations by moonlight in a room on the

* Afterwards Cardinal. † *Paroles d'un Croyant.*
‡ Of the Duties of Man.

third floor of a Roman palace ;* nor do I now hear that voice which used to fill me sometimes for hours with peace and holy joy."

Albert and his wife returned to Castellamare a little before the end of the month, and on the 19th of August Eugénie wrote in her journal: — "Dined at Lady Mary Paget's,† at Boccapiano," (the next villa to ours, taken by the Marquis of Anglesea and his family.) "After dinner we sat on the terrace looking at Albert and Alexandrine, Pauline and Augustus, and conversed with Lady Mary about French and English marriages. Those two pairs of lovers came back to the house, walking slowly like old people, and stopping now and then to converse more at their ease." Alexandrine, after quoting these words of Eugénie, adds:—"Oh, I well remember that *promenade à quatre!* I sat a long time that day gazing on the most beautiful view in the world with Albert, who was often obliged to stop and rest." The other two were to be married in a week. We were all thoroughly happy and comfortable together, talking and making plans, the pleasure of which was only in my case a little spoilt by anxiety about the future. She goes on to relate that two days afterwards Albert was a little provoked with her because she would not interest herself in a book he was reading, her attention being at that moment engrossed by the gown she was to wear at my marriage, and was just trying on. She had gone out into the balcony in her pink attire, in order that my two other brothers on the terrace below might judge of the effect. She very quickly, however, went back to Albert, and began reading with him again, that he might not suppose she was indifferent to what pleased him.

I was married on the 28th of August, and my father and mother returned to Castellamare from Naples a few hours after we left for Rome, on the same day. My poor Eugénie felt in going back into the room we had so long shared together something of the same grief I experienced later, when visiting old scenes from which she had for ever departed. She wrote to me immediately. This letter is the first of a correspondence which long subsequent absences swelled to a considerable size. It must

* Palazzo Pamfili, in the Piazza Navona, where M. Martin de Noirlieu lodged.
† Afterwards Lady Sandwich, who died young and much regretted.

find, as well as many others, a place in this record, but I own that if there is a moment when I feel unequal to the task I have undertaken, it is when I approach this too dear, too tender, too precious memory. I have known other and as deep sorrows, but this particular grief is accompanied by an amount of emotion which I can neither master nor give way to without suffering. It seems to take entire possession of me, and I can do nothing but weep. It is not speaking of her which so deeply affects me. I delight in describing Eugénie, in painting her such as she was. No; what moves me is to recall her tenderness, her passionate affection, too excessive indeed, but so true and deep that I can never think of it as long as I live without the fondest regrets and the most poignant reminiscences of a past happiness, which I shall never regain except in Heaven.

EUGENIE TO PAULINE.

"Castellamare, August 28th, 1834. Midnight and quite alone.

"My Pauline, can it be possible? They tell me to go to bed, but I cannot. I thought I had grown used to the thought of this separation, and that I should not miss you so very much, but how could I fancy such a thing? The house is dreadful without you, and as to this room—ah! Pauline, this room without you—I cannot bear it! But it is very wrong of me to tell you all this. After your departure (the word sounds so strange to me!), my father, Emma, Alexandrine, everybody except Mamma and I, went out. I began to feel very lonely, and went about kissing every single thing I could find of yours—your dear little gloves, your nosegay—weeping, weeping all the time tears enough to make me blind! Then Mamma and I took your dresses to the Palazzo Serra Capriola. It was dark, but as far as I could see, the rooms looked pretty. When we left we went round by Monsignor Porta's to thank him.* Ah! my Pauline, there again I began to cry. He talked a long time about you both, and sent you his blessing again, promising to pray for you every day. Then we left him and came home. Dinner was ready, and upstairs the drawing-room was lit up, which did so remind me of the first part of the time we were here. How quickly it has passed!

"Pauline, I hear such strange noises; I am afraid of being

* Monsignor Porta married them, in place of Monsignor Acton.

alone. As soon as I came back to this room I knew that I should hate the sight of it. . . . I can hardly tell you how I feel. I keep walking up and down, and calling out your name, without the least attempt at self-control. It is very wrong; and then I reproach myself for saying all this to you. But never mind it, darling, you know this is the first day. I really am frightened. . . . I think I shall go to Mamma, . . . but all the doors are shut! . . . Pauline, my own Pauline! . . . no, I will *not* say what I was going to say; and, indeed, it was not true, for I should have been very sorry if you had not gone away. I wonder where you are now? They said you would be at Mola by midnight, and it is midnight now. I do hope this month will pass very quickly! I think I will go to bed, but I am afraid; Vesuvius is making such a strange mournful noise. Good night, for I believe I am going to begin to cry again, I feel so miserable, and it is so bad of me! But it is only just the coming back to this house—to this room—without you. Good night, Pauline. Good night, Augustus. Oh, I do love you both! My dear love, I have read what you have written in my journal. You are a darling a thousand times over!"

"August 29th. Seven o'clock in the morning.

"I am much better. I am not going to cry any more, and am getting all right again. When I think of the day when I shall see you, my heart beats so fast. I could not have believed that this separation would have made me so wretched. Vesuvius goes on burning up everything. We are going to-night as far as the lava. It is a long way off."

"Same Day.

"My dear love, I am better. I have not cried for some time. I wonder if I ought to love you so much. It almost amounts to idolatry. Alexandrine has just brought me your picture, which made me begin again, and I have not yet recovered myself. Ah, your sweet face! your dear eyes! Please come back soon! Let me see them again. Dear Augustus, it will be in three weeks, will it not? Not one day later?"

"Friday Evening.

"Emma, Charles, and Fernand are gone to Vesuvius, but I said I was tired. The real truth was that I should not have had time to write to you, and I do not care for anything else. I am not yet as I should be. Just now, at the thought of getting a letter from you, and of seeing your handwriting again, my eyes filled with tears. My father bids me tell you that he kisses your picture twenty times a-day, that he loves you, and sends you his blessing. My mother is very sad, but she loves you, ah, so much! She is so gentle, so good. I see no apparent reason why this letter should ever come to an end. Last night I felt dreadfully lonely, and then the strange face of the new lady's-maid annoyed me. I like Saunois* better. I was glad to see her this morning, she is so fond of you. I have found all your dear little shoes, and was sorry to part with them. My dear brother, do, *do* come back soon!"

"Same Day, midnight.

"Good night. I am pretty well to-night, not too sad. My horrid fit of selfishness is over. I have left off crying, I am glad that you are happy, and sometimes the thought of it makes me wild with joy. I spent a long time on the terrace, thinking of the time when we used to be chaperoning you there. I suppose you do not regret those days? Emma has just come in, and says that the stream of lava was magnificent, but that it was terrible to see the immense crowd of poor people who were driven out of their houses. Thank God! the eruption is subsiding. It is two o'clock, and I cannot manage to feel sleepy. Mamma told me when she went away to kiss you for her. My own Pauline, I have been praying, and they were good prayers, for they were for you. God bless you!"

"Saturday, August 30th.

"How do you do, Pauline? I slept well, and only feel a little remaining sadness, which I try to shake off, and wish to get rid of. I have already been praying for you and for your husband, for you are now always together in my mind. I am very sorry Alexandrine is going away.† She is so kind and so affectionate to me, and particularly so since you are gone. They go to Naples this evening, and I with them, but I return to-morrow by sea. On Monday at two o'clock in the morning, I am to go with Marie de Mortemart‡ to Capri, and home by Sorrento. I do not much fancy it, for I am afraid of being sea-sick. It seems so strange to make all these plans, or to go anywhere without you. I cannot get used to it. I shall go on with my letter at

* Madame de la Ferronnays' maid had gone with Mrs. Craven.—(TRANSLATOR.)
† To Pisa.
‡ A daughter of the late Prince Borghese, married to the Vicomte de Mortemart.

Naples. I love you, my own Pauline. I feel a real pining to see you again."

"Naples, Sunday.

"Here we are at the Vittoria. Albert was a little unwell before they started, which made us anxious. I shall be glad to hear of their arrival at Pisa. I am writing as closely as I can to save space, and perhaps you will not be able to read it. I had your little note from Aversa. Ah! my dear Paule, what happiness to see your handwriting! Well, I must leave off, but it will not be for long. My dearest love, I love you almost too much. Good-bye, my dear brother. Good-bye, my two dear ones. My father says that at the bottom of each page I am to put, as the burden of my song, that he loves you; and as for my mother, poor dearest mother, she thinks of nothing but you. Good-bye."

Eugénie was right about my mother. She loved us all dearly, but if there was the least preference in her heart for one above another of her children, it was for me, and it seemed to me, too, that I loved her more entirely than the rest, with a keener appreciation, and above all a more unbounded confidence. Even in childhood it was so complete that I never could conceal from her a single thought, even for an hour; and I remember that when I was about fifteen or sixteen years old, and she went out without me in the evening, I often wrote down all that I had been thinking of while she was away, and pinned this kind of examination of conscience on the pincushion of her dressing-table, that she might find and read it as soon as she came in. I could not have gone to sleep in peace with the thought that she did not know everything in my mind. This will show at once what she was, for there are not many mothers, even amongst the best, who inspire their children with a desire to disclose their feelings to them with such entire openness. No ordinary share of kindness, judgment, or sympathy will suffice to establish this perfect trust, which was the blessing and safeguard of my own youth. However loving and submissive a daughter may be, it is not always in her power to feel a confidence which depends on the character of the mother far more than that of the child. Oh, my own mother! when I think that you are now where your humility can no longer shield you from praise, nor your self-denial sacrifice your own happiness, where every virtue is rewarded, and even suffering compensated, there are moments when I am filled with an intense joy, and I feel reconciled to your loss, nay, almost glad to live without you.

We came back from Rome at the beginning of October, and going first to Castellamare, where my parents still were, returned afterwards to Naples with the whole family. They lived that year at the Palazzo Gallo, and we at the Palazzo Serra Capriola, where for the first time I took possession of an apartment of my own. Eugénie spent several hours every day with us; it was almost like living under the same roof, and that winter would have been as pleasant as the preceding one, but for the absence of Albert and Alexandrine, whom we sadly missed. They had arrived at Pisa on the 9th of September, and established themselves in the Casa Soldaïni on the Lung'Arno. At first Alexandrine was rather depressed by this banishment from the family circle which she so delighted in. She mentions this transient feeling with something like self-reproach. "I do not think it was any want of love for Albert that made me feel a little melancholy on our first settling at Pisa, after the very gay and pleasant family life we had been leading, for he felt it also during our first days in this house, which, although the most cheerful in Pisa, is not to be compared in that respect with the one we had at Naples. But I remember with pleasure that this did not last long, and that at the end of a few days we were charmed with our little rooms, and did not wish for other company than our two selves. This was better, I think, than if we had been amused at the beginning by the novelty of living alone together, and had ended by being bored with it. Indeed, I never reproach myself for having liked to live with my husband in the midst of his family, even better than alone with him. The hours spent all together heightened the enjoyment of our occasional *têtes-à-têtes.* The meals, too, were merrier. In short, I have always delighted in a numerous family and a set of intimate friends, and so did Albert. One kind of affection does not interfere with another. Our souls are made in the image of God, and there is something even Divinely infinite in our capacity for loving."

Some time after their arrival in Pisa, Alexandrine was somewhat ailing. Her indisposition was ascribed to a cause which did not unfortunately exist, for she never enjoyed the happiness of being a mother. It was at that time that Albert wrote to his mother-in-law as follows: — "My head is full of *that* thought, and yet it may prove, after all, to be a groundless hope. Almighty God seems, as it were, to try my feelings. May his blessed will be done! He knows what is best, what is most desirable for us. So if this blessing is vouchsafed to me, I shall indeed be overjoyed; but if it be denied, I shall still be grateful that my dearest wife is spared sufferings which perhaps might be too much for her, and in any case shall say: 'Thy will be done.'"

In the same letter, speaking of his brother-in-law's conversion, he says: "He has changed his religion, but not the least from the motives which the world ascribes. Neither my father, my mother, nor Pauline would have approved of this step if such unworthy motives had prompted it. Such an act would be exceedingly impious if it were not the result of a thorough conviction. While I feel that the dictates of conscience must be imperious when once we perceive the truth to be on one side and not on the other, so I blame and earnestly deprecate conversions arising from human considerations, whether of interest or affection."

Alexandrine's mother, who had been up to that time so tolerant, so indulgent, and who had gone so far during Albert's illness as to pray in our Churches, and burn tapers before our images, kneeling with a devotion very similar to that of Catholics, had entirely changed in that respect since her daughter's marriage; and far from seeming to admit that she might one day wish to embrace her husband's religion, she wrote to Alexandrine that if she should ever take such a step, it would "*nail her up in her coffin.*" Sad words, which contributed not a little to make Alexandrine struggle with the conviction which was gradually making its way into her soul. Alas! poor unhappy mother, never was a prophecy less justified by the event! Not only did she live to see this dreaded conversion, not only did she witness during several years the holy and pious life which Alexandrine led after her reception into the Church; but the most unforeseen dispensation doomed her to survive this beloved daughter. If after her death any human consolation was capable of assuaging her grief, it was the remembrance of those virtues and good works which under the influence of the true faith threw a halo round her memory approaching that of sanctity.

But at the time of which we are speaking, Alexandrine had

not arrived at the sort of conviction which triumphs over every obstacle. It seemed, on the contrary, as if, since she had been surrounded by Catholics, a sort of antagonism was roused in her which she had never before felt or shown. She wrote to me in this spirit a number of letters full of objections and attacks, which I answered as well as I could, and with all the freedom which had ever existed between us on this subject. She appeared on the whole to sympathise less with us about religion since she had become one of us. And yet, as she herself mentions in her journal, it would never have entered into her head at Pisa to inquire for a Protestant church, and she delighted in going to Mass with Albert. "A singular state of religious independence," she remarks, "consistent enough, however, with the belief I then possessed." I find on this point the following passage from one of my letters copied into her story: "I managed at last to decipher the part of your letter which referred to your religious difficulties. As to the primary one, that terrible separation from your mother, which you are always talking of, there is only one answer to make. Of course, nothing could be more dreadful than such a thought, but you always lose sight of what is our belief on that point. We hold that our religion is the *true* one, and consequently the *only* one, for you must admit that God cannot have revealed *two* different truths. We therefore think that to be safe we must be Catholics, unless *in perfect good faith* we remain in error without ever having had the least doubt on the subject. Well, I thoroughly believe your mother to be in that state of mind, and I am equally persuaded that you are not. I do not think a serious doubt with regard to Protestantism has ever crossed her mind. Can you say the same of yourself? And may not God excuse her for remaining in a religion she believes, and condemn you for persevering in doing so when you have not the same excuse? In one word, would you not be taking the surest means of meeting her in the next world by obeying the dictates of conscience in becoming a Catholic, as she apparently does by remaining a Protestant? I have already submitted to you this argument, but you forget it, and always repeat your objections, and also the story of your Pagan king,* which does not apply to the case;

* Alexandrine had found somewhere the story of a Pagan king, who, though convinced of the truth of Christianity, would not be baptised, because he preferred, so he said, to be condemned with his parents than saved without them. She thought this very generous, and was inclined to agree with him!

since, according to what I just said, his parents, supposing them to have been Pagans in good faith, might, strictly speaking, have been saved, whereas he himself, for persevering in a worship he knew to be false, would justly have been lost."

In another letter I said again:—"I see with regret that a Protestant atmosphere seemed to incline you more favorably towards us than a Catholic one. But when do you mean to make up your mind? I want to know if you really think that it is not necessary to decide, and that you can go through life without being positively Catholic or Protestant. I should be better satisfied to see you one or the other, so that you were really in good faith."

Alexandrine expatiates thus on this point:—"Pauline was right in saying that a Protestant atmosphere inclined me more favorably towards their side, and that after my marriage I became more disposed to argue against their faith. Alas! this is human nature. Being the only one of my religion in their family, I felt as if it was looked down upon, and that I ought to stand up for it. I had never, however, this feeling with Albert. I had the deepest reverence for his faith and piety, and he never seemed as if he wished to attack my religion. He only showed a constant and affectionate desire that we might one day have the same faith. I shared this hope without any very definite ideas on the subject, for at that time I should not have ventured to take any step in that direction on my mother's account."

At the end of October Albert had the unexpected pleasure of hearing that M. de Montalembert was in Italy, and about to pay them a visit at Pisa.

ALBERT TO COUNT DE MONTALEMBERT.

"Pisa, October 29th, 1834.

"I am enchanted at your plan of spending two months with us here. This will make up a little for our long separation. We shall have plenty of time for castle-building, an amusement which does not cause any heavy disappointments. Alexandrine and I often build one of living in France with all we love best. I am tired of Italy, and, shocked as you will be at the confession, I assure you, that if you had spent four years, as I have done, with Italians, you would begin to feel a little home-sick. It would be a perfect enjoyment to me to be in France among my friends, and in the midst of the interests which must one day or other be everything to me. I hope my health will allow of it. I think it improves, thanks to the tender care my darling takes of me. I know that you will not tire of the sight of my happiness. I had never imagined it could be so complete."

THE SAME TO THE SAME.

"Dear friend, before you leave Florence make a pilgrimage for me to Santa Maria Novella, and say a little prayer to the Blessed Virgin in the first or second chapel, near a black marble tomb, with a statue of Our Lady, surrounded with Angels, which stands behind the altar. Three years ago I used to pray there very often, and I have always thought I owed my happiness to those prayers, for it was immediately afterwards that I met Alexandrine at Rome. I am superstitiously inclined, perhaps, because I am so happy. Pray there yourself, and ask for happiness. Who knows? Everything is possible with God, and so much is promised to faith. Ask also health for me. Is it wrong to wish for it? With so much happiness, should I not be satisfied to suffer a little? Well, God's will be done! I hope my petition will not displease Him. So, then, pray earnestly for me. Then also before you come away, gò and see Mademoiselle de Fauveau. She is a sculptor, and does beautiful things, I hear, in the Florentine style. I was looking in the dictionary to see if there was a feminine to the word sculptor, and I happened to read this sentence: 'It is the worshipper, not the sculptor, that makes the gods.' Well, this applies to her. For I am told her works breathe the devout spirit of a Perugino, and moreover, she is a Vendean, and when at her ease with those about her, talks of La Vendée in a most interesting manner. I tell you all this from hearsay, for I am not myself acquainted with her.

"Dear friend, try not to leave Lucca till twelve, for I should like so much to drive and meet you, and I am not allowed to go out till two o'clock. If, however, you could start early in the morning and arrive here before that time, then, of course, it would be all the better. I am dying to see you."

FROM ALEXANDRINE'S STORY.

"November 10th, Monday.—Montal arrived at seven o'clock in the evening. Albert was so happy! We met him on the stairs. He has told me several times that the warmth of my welcome made him feel quite at his ease; he had been a little alarmed at the idea of finding himself *en tiers* between Albert and me. I could not have been otherwise than delighted to see him, for there never was a more devoted friendship than Albert's for him.

"Tuesday, November 18th.—I went with Montalembert to see the Campo Santo by moonlight, and thought it so beautiful, so solemn! Albert, who would be so keenly alive to these sort of enjoyments, was obliged to give it up on account of his health. We take long walks on foot, and Albert follows us in the carriage. Montalembert was speaking one day of Albert's extraordinary tenderness of heart, and he said *he did not think he could survive the loss of any one he very much loved.* How often I have recalled those words to mind! Albert never knew that anguish. Alas! it was himself—himself who taught us what it is!

"Wednesday, December 26th.—This morning my beloved Albert went to Communion in the Church of St. Francis, at the altar of St. Philomena, where a Novena had been made for him. Yesterday he confessed, with touching humility, to a Franciscan. All this has been good for his soul, but a little fatiguing for him. Dr. Betti, however, saw him yesterday, and finds him better. The day before yesterday I went to midnight Mass at the Cathedral with Montal. I shall never forget that sight. I do not know any Church I admire so much. All those fine columns, with innumerable lights, but not a great many people, had a magnificent effect. I was very sorry to go there without Albert, who would have enjoyed it so much. He was unwell that day, and had been obliged to lie down, but when we came home we found him sitting up, and tea ready for us. He is so admirably patient, so cheerful, so charming! I had told Eugénie of Albert's going to Communion, but I did not tell her, and perhaps I liked better not to tell her, that it made me burst into tears when I saw him kneeling at the altar. Partly, I think, from sorrow that I was separated from him at such a moment, and partly because I was beginning to feel convinced of the truth which I was still struggling to resist.*

* In 1841, five years after Albert's death, Alexandrine was again at Pisa with my parents, and she then wrote these words in her journal, at the edge of the preceding passage:—" A few days ago I had also in the same chapel the same happiness as Albert, and was more closely united to him then than when he was alive. I did not this time shed any tears. My whole heart was filled with gratitude to God, who permitted me to receive Communion in that very same spot.'

"On the evening of the 28th of December Montal began to read aloud to us the manuscript of his life of St. Elizabeth of Hungary, with which we were both delighted. Albert took a fancy to the names of 'brother' and 'sister' which St. Elizabeth and her husband gave each other, and since that time, when we were alone, he used often to call me 'sister;' and I remember the beautiful angelic expression of his countenance at those times. I told Montal that in the Campagna at Rome, in 1831, I had once called Albert 'brother.' We read and converse alternately in this way.*

"Tuesday, January 13th, 1835.—We went to the Cascine, and then, which amused us all very much, to order a new bonnet for me. At dinner Albert suddenly announced that he intended to go to a ball that evening where we had all been invited, but had sent an excuse. I objected, for I was so afraid it would hurt him, but he persisted, and ended by saying, '*I will go.*' He sent for my maid, and desired her to get everything ready. At last I submitted to the not very disagreeable command of making myself as smart as possible. I was certainly two hours about it. To make the thing perfect, we forced Montal to come with us. He required a great deal of pressing, and declared he had nothing to wear. Albert lent him almost everything, but we had to send for a shoemaker, and for a hairdresser to cut his hair. All this amused us immensely, and as we had at that time no man-servant, we got the shoemaker's boy to escort us to the ball, which made us all die of laughing."

Albert wrote the next day in a letter to Eugénie:—"My health improves daily. Yesterday I compelled my wife to go to a ball, and we dragged Montalembert *ditto.* After an hour of moderate pleasure we came home to tea. My little Alex looked lovely in her blue gown and her diamonds." And then he adds:—"I am

* Alexandrine, in a letter to Eugénie, speaks thus of the books they read:—"I read Dante, and Montalembert reads to us legends. Some charming ones just now about St. Francis of Assisi, a very good saint, who called all God's creatures his brothers and sisters. He says '*Brother wolf*,' and talks to him a long time, and calls the doves his sisters, &c., &c. Montal is writing the life of St. Elizabeth, a queen and a German. He has travelled in Germany a great deal about this book. He will read it to us when it is finished. I am sure it will be delightful, but pray do not mention it to anybody but Pauline. I am sure he would dislike very much that it should be talked of before hand. So please let it go no further. He is so fond of that St. Elizabeth, and has collected every sort of detail about her. He told us the story of a knight who wore the colors of a Saint who had appeared to him in a vision. The history does not end here, but it is too long for a letter. What do you think of the life we lead? I like it. Our tables are covered with newspapers and reviews (those are for Montal),—Sir Walter Scott's novels for Albert, and all sorts of books for him and me, from the circulating library at Leghorn. Albert is learning German, but he does not work at it with your laudable zeal. I am sure you will know it very soon."

learning German, but like a sulky individual who will never let you know him, it repels all my attempts at better acquaintance. It would seem as if the world in general was not worthy of that honor, and that it is only vouchsafed to the chosen few. Montal has made a charming collection of German airs during his stay in that country. He has been hunting up legends and every sort of popular tradition about the saints. It has been a very pleasant occupation to him, and softened the sorrows of the last years. You may well imagine that he adds not a little to the enjoyment of our life. It is so pleasant, so strange, so much what we all like, to spend our days without any of the obligations of society, in perfect intimacy, and without any other ties than those of affection. Were it never to occur again I should still be thankful to have known so satisfactory and so agreeable an existence for a while."

ALEXANDRINE'S STORY.

"On the evening of the 15th of January I went up with Albert to Montal's room. He was packing up his things, having to start the next day. It was the first time I had been there. Albert used to sit with him every morning. During that time I dressed, or read, or wrote, all the while thinking with delight of the pleasant moments to come. I remember one afternoon that I was sitting by the fire-place reading a review, whilst Albert was upstairs. When he came back with Montal I hastened to tell them that there was an abominable infidel article in that review (by Heine, I think), ending with infamous jokes about the bell which gives notice of the approach of the Blessed Sacrament. I told Albert that when I read that passage I was so horrified that I had fallen on my knees. When I said this I saw in his face joy, emotion, and a little surprise. Oh, I shall never forget his look, nor the feeling with which he uttered some words of tenderness. I can, indeed, say that we never loved each other so much as when we saw how we both loved God. But to return to that last evening in Montal's room. He was bewildered in the midst of his parcels, books, and papers. I looked at his books a little. They were all more or less religious. There were amongst them legends and stories. I helped him to pack up, and we talked meanwhile a little about religion. He read to me in a triumphant manner a fine passage of Alphonsus Liguori on the devotion to the Blessed Virgin, which I had still some difficulty in admitting, and he recommended me to burn '*Father Clement*,' a book lent to me by my Protestant friends as an antidote against Catholicism, but had rather had the contrary effect. Then we went down again to our sitting-room, and spent a merry evening. Montal made me sing a number of ballads and national airs which he had collected during his travels. There was among them a beautiful German hymn. The words were translated from St. Bernard ('*Jesu, wie süss wer Dein gedenkt*'), saying that there is nothing so sweet as to think of Jesus, nothing so sweet as to feel His Presence. Montal was always getting me to sing it, though at first he thought it almost a scandal to let me do so. He was surprised afterwards to find that I sang it with almost as much expression as the pious young girls at Ratisbon, who used to sing it at their work."

ALEXANDRINE TO EUGÉNIE.

"DEAR LOVE—Our dear Montalembert is gone. We could not get him to stay longer. We sat up with him last night till half-past two, and then he started with tears in his eyes. He regrets so much this comfortable family life, as he calls it, which we lead, and which he had become quite accustomed to. There is one comfort, and that is, that we are friends with him for life. Tell Pauline that I have received her letter, and am going to write to her, but we have not got a man-servant yet, and we are quite at a loss, now Montalembert is gone, who used, in a friendly and good-humored way, to do all sorts of little things for us, such as carrying all our letters to the post, buying us chestnuts, &c. Our little maid servant will not go to the post after dark, and at any time I am afraid of her making mistakes about prepaying or not prepaying letters, so that this want of a servant prevents my writing."

ALBERT TO THE COMTE DE MONTALEMBERT.

"'*Derision and contempt!*' DEAR FRIEND—What horrible weather you must have had! It has not left off raining since you went. '*It is disgusting to think of*.'* We are longing to hear from you, and to know whether the journey did not increase the pain in your face. We are feeling quite unsettled since your departure. Our life was so comfortable. When shall we enjoy

* Two expressions Albert had heard at some play, and afterwards continually quoted.

the like again? Even in France will the evenings of Pisa be ever renewed? Alexandrine has been ailing these two days. It is nothing to signify. The greatest inconvenience this indisposition entailed was three visits in two days from Punta (the doctor). We have heard nothing, as yet, of the conjectures which our mysterious mode of life during your stay must have excited. Our plan of a journey to Odessa seems likely to be carried out. I have received a letter from Naples, and I see my parents are beginning to look upon it as a simple and even natural idea. Your suggestion of taking Fernand with us meets with great success. Dear good friend, would you, could you, come too? How pleasant it would be! But if, after all, this journey does not take place, I shall try to go to the Pyrenees. There you would be obliged to come, for you must really do something for your health. You can hardly imagine how much we miss you in our little house. We want you every moment of the day. My morning visits to you, our walks, your errands to the post-office, and, above all, our treasured evenings! Every instant of the day was sweetened by the pleasure of the most thorough friendship. Alexandrine's indisposition, which prevents her from singing, makes the contrast still more striking. She insists, however, on finishing this letter, and has already bespoken the last page. So I leave you together, and shall fancy I am following you in one of your walks to the Argini. Good-bye, my best friend. Write to me often, though your letters are but a poor compensation for the loss of your society."

Alexandrine wrote in the same letter:—

"DEAR GOOD FRIEND—Albert has written to you a great deal about our regret, but I must also tell you how very much we miss you. We shall scarcely be able to be so merry again as before your visit, for both at dinner and tea there is that melancholy empty place which puts us so sadly in mind of the dear friend who filled it so pleasantly. Punta has been drinking tea with us these two days instead of you — an agreeable exchange! Only think, I have been stupid enough to fall ill, which made matters worse, for two poor invalids want a third person sadly. It was nothing of consequence, and I am quite well again. How I long to hear about your journey and your face-ache, and whether you have met with any of these misadventures which you say always fall to your lot. Do not be angry with me; I want you so much to believe that you are one day to be very prosperous. When life begins without happiness it comes later. Did you ever know of a whole life spent in sorrow? Think that you have two devoted friends who pray for you every day, and that the prayers we offer up for others are the most sure to be heard. Let us hear constantly how our dear St. Elizabeth is going on — you know how very much it interests us—and give us every kind of detail about yourself. You may write as fast and as illegibly as you please, we shall manage to make it out. I have only sung your favorite airs once, for since that day I have been too unwell. By the way, do not be uneasy about a little manuscript-book you left on Albert's writing table — the one which contains the pretty passage out of 'Corinne,' and another by the Comte de Maistre. It is in safe hands—in ours, I mean—and we will take some opportunity of sending it back to you, unless you will let us keep it. I wish you had left the little black book behind.

"Madame de C—— called the day after you left, and was most gracious. Modesty will not allow me to repeat all she said about my apparition at the ball. Our servant has not yet arrived. I care less about it now, for what I had looked forward to was the fun of laughing at his installation with you. Maria carries the letters to the post now. The day after you left we took the same drive as we all did the last day you were here; that is, by the Florence road and the Capuchins; and on our way back we left one of your cards, with 'P.P.C.' on it, at the Countess Mastiani's. We met Therèse* as we came home, who made a mournful gesture in speaking of you. She raised her arm and struck her forehead in quite a despairing manner. These are all the little souvenirs of Pisa, dear Montal, which you wished us to write. They are still present to your mind, but you will not be long in Paris before your great interests throw them into the shade. You know the state of our writing-table, so I will not make any apologies for this scrawl. How I do hope we shall meet again this year. I shall never forget the kindness of your last words. May God bless you! Pray for us, and remember me to the Rios."

The 21st of January had been Albert's twenty-third birthday.

* A servant who had waited on M. de Montalembert while he was at Pisa.

My mother had written a letter to him that day, in which I find these words:—"It is twenty-three years ago that I gave you my first kiss. It seems to me as if it was only yesterday; and since that day there has not been a single one in which my heart has not been full of you. You have always been so good that not the shadow of a cloud has saddened that tenderness, or the least irritation existed between us. I cannot, therefore, express, my beloved child, how dear you are to me, and how intensely anxious I am to know you well and happy."

Albert wrote in answer:—

"January 30th.

"I begin on this large sheet of paper without knowing whether I shall fill it. At this moment it seems to me too small to hold all the love and tenderness my heart pours out to you, my dearest mother. You did not forget the 21st of January, and I never felt on my part such deep affection for you, and the happiness of being so loved by you and my dear father. Is it because I so wish to have a child myself that I feel deeply touched by what you say about the twenty-three years which have elapsed since I received your first kiss, or is it only the remembrance of your uninterrupted tenderness which so moves me? This last reason would be enough to account for it, and that other feeling would only be its natural consequence. I must long to bestow on a child of my own all that tender affection which you have lavished on me. You say that never has the least irritation existed between us. Oh, I thank God for it! Nothing, my beloved mother, could have made me happier than to hear this. I have often been afraid that I had, on the contrary, been guilty of ingratitude by my want of gentleness and docility to your and my dear father's advice."

It was in the month of February of that year that Albert began to keep a regular journal, in the form of letters addressed to (I think) the Abbé Martin de Noirlieu, but without any intention of sending them.

ALBERT'S JOURNAL.

"Pisa, February, 1835.

"You know, my dear friend, that you have often accused me of trying to appear worse than I am. If you knew the whole of my life you would, I am sure, view the matter differently, and come to the contrary conclusion that my good reputation is sadly undeserved. So much so that I am sometimes tormented by the fear that there must be something false in my character. It is no doubt true that I have never been really wicked, or altogether stifled the bright but transient lights which have flashed through my soul. But perhaps this only increases my blame. Dante describes these hesitating souls as shut out from both Heaven and hell. I take up everything at first with ardor, and almost immediately afterwards I feel indifferent and disgusted with the very thing I had been most keenly anxious for. Often before my marriage, even when at the height of my passionate love, I felt a sort of despondency come over me, I could almost have wished to put off the moment which I yet felt was the only one which could secure my happiness. I did not know what I wished except to get away. The only thing that seemed to do me good, was to ride very fast on the sea-shore. It gave me a sense of relief and freedom. Once I went alone to Amalfi for some days, and felt almost unwilling to return to Naples. I ascribe this waywardness in a great measure to the weakness of my health and the irritability which it produces, and also partly to a desultory kind of education. My father made every possible sacrifice for my advantage in that respect, but the people with whom he placed me did not fulfil their trust. I was naturally gentle and diligent, and if I had been treated differently I might perhaps have committed more faults, but I should have grown up with greater energy of character. When I left their care I had lost that youthfulness of soul which some happy natures retain long after their entrance into the world, and yet I was as shy as a child. Then I came to Italy, which on the whole has done me more harm than good, for its climate increased the irritability of my constitution, and over-excited my imagination. Ever since I have been a prey to the inward strife of the two natures we carry within us; sometimes feeling good and aiming at the highest degree of virtue I could hope to reach, and at others letting myself go wherever the inferior part of my nature chooses to lead me. I cannot master these conflicting influences so as to make them minister to my physical and moral improvement. This prolonged struggle brought on the inflammatory illness which carried me to the brink of the grave. Ought I to regret that it did not do so?

"I need not dwell on the three past years of that love which has secured my happiness, for you know God has blessed it. Henceforward I have only to speak of the present and the future, and day by day I intend to do so, not so much for the sake of conversing with you as to see whether by analysing them I can succeed in mastering my contradictory impulses."

"Monday, February 9th.

"Though I had resolved to write in this book how every day had been spent, the thoughts which occurred to me, and the resolutions made, I have not done so for three days. I do not know if it is the fault of the weather or of my weakness, but I have been in a state of nervous irritation which precluded all regular thinking. To-day I am better, and I have scarcely coughed at all. My poor Alexandrine has been ill also for two days. She is very delicate, and I get frightened when the least thing is the matter with her. She so easily looks ill. I have sent for the doctor, and I hope it will be nothing. I have little to record. Nearly the whole day has been spent in struggling against that unaccountable, indescribable nervous suffering. It is twelve o'clock. God be with us!"

"Thursday, February 12th.

"I make fresh strides every day towards health and strength, and trust by God's mercy to be soon delivered from the need of taking these tiresome precautions. I think it is the coming of spring, which gives me such a desire for fresh air, movement and life. You know, I am sure, the feeling which causes both body and soul to long for activity, the heart to spring up, as it were, with faith and hope, which makes us hunger and thirst after God, and cry out—prostrate in adoration—for the Bread of life. Our plans for a sea-voyage are being matured, but we shall meet with some difficulties in bringing them to bear. This evening I finished '*Les Souvenirs*,' by Nodier. They have interested me very much. I admire the youthful enthusiasm and boldness of this writer. His earnestness reconciles us with mankind, and we feel the need of it after wading through all the miseries described in his journal. It has renewed my regret that during his best years my father should be obliged to give up public service in France; for Nodier truly says in his epilogue, 'It is indispensable to society that honest men should coalesce, whatever be the political creed which chance or circumstances have assigned them.' But the oath of allegiance is an insuperable barrier for sensitive consciences. If once that mockery of an oath were abolished, my father could resume his place in the Chambers."

"Friday, February 13th.

"I am quite proud of being able to read and understand Shakespeare. I am reading *Hamlet*, and thrill with delight as I read. I had no idea of this sort of writing, and I look forward to much enjoyment from it. My quiet life alone with my angelic wife is indeed enviable. Last night the thought of Sorrento brought tears into my eyes. What a charm clings to all the reminiscences of the last three years! I am not *blasé*. My heart is still alive to all the beauty and value of life and poetry. Yes, you may envy me, for I fully feel the value of all that God has given me. I am reading '*Ayesha*,' which interests me; and then it is the East again, and I do love the East."

"Saturday, February 14th.

"My passion for travelling increases daily. There are moments when the soul seems to pant after unknown lands, where it appears as if everything must be more beautiful than what we see about us. Is not this desire of change, of progress, the wish —so to speak—of getting rid of one's self, this yearning after boundless space and freedom, a sort of indication of our eternal destiny? Byron says:—*

"'Though sluggards deem it but a foolish chase,
And marvel men should quit their easy chair,
The toilsome way, and long, long league to trace;
Oh! there is sweetness in the mountain air,
And life that bloated ease can never hope to share!'

"You blame, I know, these sort of fits of enthusiasm, my dear friend, and you have told me more than once that the soul is indeed called to an immortal destiny and the knowledge of the infinite, but only when stripped of its earthly shroud. But can we hinder the soul, unable to cast off at will this miserable body, from sometimes striving to drag it upwards towards its Heavenly home? It is very long since I have been in so steady a state of activity and fervor, as at present. My weak and slothful nature has been more thoroughly mastered than usual, and I suppose this comes from my improved health. My friends used to find fault with my taste for solitude. But how will it now be increased? How shall I ever endure the noise of crowded draw-

* Childe Harold, Canto I.

ing-rooms, after learning by experience the unspeakable sweetness and fulness of life's best joys? Is there anything in the world to be compared to Alexandrine's beloved face, seen by the dim light of our dear old lamp?"

"Monday, February 16th.

"A melancholy sight met my eyes this morning. Eight galley slaves were sweeping the street before our door. They were fastened to each other by a heavy chain, and dressed in red, a sign that they are condemned for a limited number of years. Two only were in yellow, which means that they were sentenced to the galleys for life. These wore a badge on the breast, on which was written: '*Robbery with violence.*' Judging from the newness of their clothes, they must have been recently condemned, and are probably the same men who were publicly exposed and sentenced the other day for that crime. It is a dreadful thing to look at these men, banished from society, and never more to meet with anything at its hands, but contempt and dread, or, at the best, pity. What bitter feelings must fill their souls. O! most just and merciful God, grant them submission and the hope of another life! May the example of our Lord Jesus Christ, and the thought of His passion, His patience, His strength, and His love, make them accept their bitter chalice. O! my Lord Jesus, when Thou wert forsaken by men, Angels came to strengthen Thee, their Divine Master, and to shed tears over Thy sufferings. Unworthy as these poor creatures are, let them also be comforted by Angels now they are scorned by men. They have none to help them but Thyself. Have mercy on them, Blessed Lord. Soften their hearts before they die! It is not the severity of the sentence, awarded either justly or unjustly by society, which I most apprehend, in their cases, but the misery entailed by the ill-usage of the gaolers, who are too often themselves the refuse of society. In such an office the most sublime charity ought to be exercised, and hope, patience, and love infused into hearts which have nothing to look to on earth, but the hatred and execration of their fellow-men. O! God, increase the number of Thy sacred ministers, the true shepherds of Thy poor sheep!"

"Tuesday, 17th.

"I found an article yesterday in a number of the *Presse Britannique* on railways. How remarkable it is, that just at the time when vague but new and important ideas of fusion are occupying the minds of men, industry and fresh discoveries second them so admirably. It would be presumptuous, I think, not to recognise a Divine agency in this coincidence. Experience has already shown how much prejudice and national animosity disappears, in consequence of the increased modern facilities for travelling, and how many bonds of union have thus been formed between nations once bitterly antagonistic. The spirit of nationality, and even patriotism, in itself a noble feeling, but still too narrow and selfish if considered from the highest point of view, will by degrees give way, I am convinced, to a spirit of union which will embrace all Christian nations. But this immense change will be more certain and immediate, if the material interests of men find in it such advantages as are undoubtedly obtained by that inconceivable rapidity of communication which has not by any means reached the perfection to which steam will bring it. But can many nations be formed into one? No, I do not look forward to the existence of a single nation, or a single kingdom. The unity I contemplate would consist of such an intimate association between different nations, as should satisfy their moral and material wants. Men's interests will soon make them understand this truth. Yet I look back, I own, with a sort of regret to those distinct nationalities, which are gradually about to disappear; and the total change I have spoken of can of course only succeed some period of confusion, through which we dimly discern its probable results. We live in an age of transition. We seem to belong neither to the past, nor the future. We stand, as it were, at a point, whence on the one hand we look wistfully at the bright hues of the setting sun, and on the other at the dawning beauty of a new day. I sometimes feel quite lost in thought, absorbed in the contemplation of this strange vision, and a melancholy feeling comes over me as I meditate on our inevitable farewell to that poetic past, whose monuments bear such glorious witness of generosity, enthusiasm, and faith; —that past whose treasures are about to vanish, and give place to a new society, over which union, simplicity, and equality, will reign."

"Wednesday, February 18th.

"Do you happen to remember that poor child whom I once

mentioned to you? Alexandrine and I went this morning to buy some string of his mother, and found the boy dying. He was almost speechless. I sent our physician to see him. The poor parents are miserable; their little home is in confusion, their work is interrupted, and all their happiness at an end."

"Friday, February 20th.

"The poor child was still alive this morning; he was even a shade better. I am afraid he is not well cared for, and his poor parents keep talking incessantly before him of their fears. They were to have fetched Maria (Alexandrine's maid) this morning, but nobody came. I shall send the first thing in the morning to inquire. May God spare him to his parents. My Alexandrine was looking too beautiful this evening. She little knew it, or what I feel when I look at her. She is always lovely, but there are moments when the expression of her face and countenance quite astonishes me. Dear angel! how gentle and patient she is! And yet you would not believe it, but even from her I cannot bear the least opposition, the least contradiction. If this irritability does not altogether proceed from ill-health, and does not disappear when I get well, I shall be a perfect brute.

"The chapter we read to-night, in the '*Imitation of Christ*,' was *on the test of real love*. It is admirable, but describes too exactly our misery and weakness. 'O! my Lord, without Thee, without the Holy Spirit, we can do nothing. Strong as we may be, when Thy grace sustains us, we are utterly undone and helpless when Thou dost withdraw it. Strengthen our poor weak nature, my Lord and my God, and let me hope to receive Thee into my soul. For without Thee, what am I? And with Thee I can do all things.'"

"Sunday, February 22nd.

"That poor child died last night. At ten o'clock they came to tell us he was still alive. About midnight his soul went to God. The father left the house with a little girl they have, to get away from the sight of the corpse. The mother remained with it. We went there after Mass. The funeral will take place this evening. Poor little angel, his face was looking quite calm again. He was dressed in white, covered with pink ribbons, and surrounded by a garland of flowers."

"Monday, February 23rd.

"We have been to the cemetery to see the poor child's grave.

Part of the burial-place is set apart for children. The *custode* said to us: 'Here, they are all Angels.' How many little Angels have thus flown away, leaving their mortal remains behind them. There seemed to me something especially holy in that spot. In another part of the enclosure, separated by a low wall from the children's burial-place, is the portion set apart for persons who have died without the Sacraments. I can scarcely say why this touched me. Perhaps it was the thought that all those innocent souls might possibly be pleading for the guilty or wretched ones, whose remains lie so near their own."

Albert received, about this time, a letter from my father, which must have expressed some uneasiness on a subject which often made him anxious. Albert answered it in these words:—

"MY BELOVED FATHER—I am quite grieved at your uneasiness about the smallness of our fortune. I know we are not immensely rich—neither Alex nor I thought of marrying for the sake of wealth; but I must say I have not found out that we are so very badly off. There are not many young people, I fancy, who manage to put by a little, as we have done, during the first year of our marriage. Whatever be the amount of fortune they start with, is it not generally the case that the income of the second year goes to make up the deficiencies of the first? You, my dearest father, who know how simple our tastes and habits are, should not be so anxious on this subject. Even here we lead a kind of life which does not at all look like poor. There are very few people, for instance, who have a carriage every day, and we have no difficulty in meeting the expense of two doctors, one of them a first-rate physician. . . . Good-bye, my dear father. Love always your Albert, and rely upon it that nothing can exceed our happiness."

On the same day, Alexandrine wrote to Eugénie:—"Fancy your dear father writing to Albert, that *he really sheds tears when he thinks how badly off we are!* . . . And that when we shall actually have saved 4000 or 5000 francs at the end of this first year.* And yet we have had a great deal of outlay,—physicians, travelling expenses for ourselves and the servants we have sent for. Indeed, I am very glad that I have seen your father get into these fidgets about others, without reason, for I should

* £160 or £200.

otherwise be so vexed that he should torment himself about us. Montalembert positively thought us rich, and, indeed, we have everything we can possibly want, especially for two people on a journey."

It is touching to see how perfectly satisfied they were with an income which would have been considered very insufficient by most persons in their condition of life. This shows with what method and economy they regulated their little household affairs, and proves that matter-of-fact people, who have no imagination and are incapable of enthusiasm, do not possess that monopoly of good sense which they are so ready to claim, as a set-off, probably, against all their other deficiencies!

ALBERT'S JOURNAL (CONTINUED).

"Wednesday, February 25th.

"We have quite a spring morning to-day. What a climate it is! We went out in the open carriage, and drove through the woods and fields. There is nothing to be compared to one of these first days of spring. We could hardly bring ourselves to come in. We pine more than ever to travel, and soon, I hope, shall leave Pisa. I shall, however, always preserve a grateful recollection of this place, where I have spent so many pleasant hours and enjoyed such unmixed happiness. But I carry away with me the source of all this enjoyment, and you know what a perfect delight it is when two people who sympathise in the most complete manner travel together. You will not, therefore, look upon my passion for travelling as a proof of inconstancy. How often, in former days, I used to envy a young couple travelling in a comfortable calèche, and lost in a paradise of youth, hope, and love! Well, I now possess that happiness, and I find I was not mistaken, and that the joy I used to see in the countenances of those I so much envied, was but a feeble expression of the ecstacy which filled their hearts! The father and mother of the poor child came to see us this evening; but just imagine how superficial and transient are the feelings of these Italians! When they left us, they were actually going to the play!"

Alexandrine relates that Albert had reproached his servant Julien, because he seemed to doubt the extent of these poor parents' grief. She also mentions their having had a visit from

Father Luigi Galligani, Albert's Confessor, who in the course of conversation spoke of a young Englishwoman who had become a Catholic, and who said she felt in Paradise. Alexandrine remarks :—" I was very much surprised at this, for I was so earthly that it seemed to me a great stretch of imagination to find one's happiness in invisible things. I could not at all understand it, and it used to astonish me also when Albert said, 'Oh, if you only knew what happiness it is to receive absolution !' But the expression of his countenance when he said it, is still imprinted on my mind !" A few days afterwards they went to the Franciscan Convent at Santa Croce, Albert wanting to speak to Father Luigi. Whilst he was inside the house, a good lay brother, Fra Clementino, brought Alexandrine some coffee, who swallowed it with mingled feelings of gratitude and disgust. The good brother was advising her all the time to become a Catholic, and promised to give her his Jerusalem beads, if ever he saw her one.*

ALBERT'S JOURNAL (CONTINUED).

"We may, perhaps, go to Russia by Vienna, and in that case we shall possibly see ——, whom Alexandrine has never met since she gave me her love, the joy of my life. This evening we talked of him, and these reminiscences seemed to interest her. Dear angel! she did not know how eagerly I listened. It is not, however, the first time she has thus revealed her inmost soul to me. It is so with her father's death. The least word which reminds her of that great trial leads her to describe the various emotions which she went through at that time. Oh, how I feel with and for her! She need not be afraid of tiring me. The tears which rush to her eyes will always be sure to call forth mine. Nor need she fear to dwell on that other period of her life which she remembers so well, for in it I find that same heart which has so entirely given and opened itself to me for time and for eternity. God bless her for never thinking I could be troubled at her saying that she once thought she had loved that man. Oh,

* "Five years afterwards," Alexandrine says, "alone, and in a widow's weeds, I went to the same convent. Meeting a brother carrying his bag, I asked him if Father Luigi Galligani was at home. He told me he was absent. I then inquired after Fra Clementino. I was speaking to himself! He recognised me, and his joy at seeing me again, was as great, he said, '*as if his mother had risen from the dead.*' He hastened to fetch his Jerusalem beads, and gave them to me as he had promised. He too had grieved for Albert, and tears of compassion and tenderness fell from his eyes as we spoke of him. Joy was, however, the prevailing feeling in our hearts during this interview, for our beloved faith makes up for every sorrow, and only destroys sin." And yet five years before, Alexandrine could not even understand that it was possible to find happiness in invisible things!

no! I feel at those moments a sort of fatherly protecting tenderness which makes me only love her the more, and I also have a few little cherished tears lying at the bottom of my heart. And she, too, listens when I tell her all that has occupied my thoughts before I knew her. She knows there are recollections which one would not for the world discard, by rubbing out, as she says herself, the landmarks of the past, and thus forestalling the work of death. Oh, she is right! As long as the heart is full of love, let us believe and hope in God."

ALEXANDRINE TO COUNT DE MONTALEMBERT.

"DEAR MONTAL—It is several days since Albert received your dear letter from Alessandria and Geneva, and we wanted to answer it much sooner. We are impatient to hear of your having arrived in Paris. (Oh, what dreadful paper, pen, and ink!) I write to you to-night instead of to-morrow, because to-morrow I must work. You cannot imagine what a passion I have taken for needlework. I am very sorry it did not begin when you were here; first, because there is nothing so pleasant as to work while somebody reads to you; and then because you would have admired the really enchanting things I make; and finally, because you would have conceived a more favorable opinion of me had you seen me so *femininely* employed, and it would have convinced you that it was not out of pedantry that I used to read instead of sewing. You think of me, however, only too favorably. I suppose you did not expect I should read your letters to Albert. I did read every word of the last, and felt pleasantly ashamed of the praise you give me. Still, whether out of vanity or only from a real knowledge of my own character, I do maintain that though I am not nearly so good as you think, I reflect a great deal more than you suppose. Then, I must add, that I was a little shocked at the words *dissipated and dangerous* which you use in reference to the life I led before my marriage. I feel it on account of my parents. My dear friend, I always think you too severe on the poor world. It has many dangers, I grant, but also more virtues than you seem inclined to think; and when this is the case, is not the merit greater than when they are practised in a quiet life? Mine has been the usual existence of all the young girls of our time. You will perhaps reply that this is no excuse, but, after all, many a one far better than I am has led it. And to return to my parents. They are not responsible for the three hundred and seventy-nine admirers, or any other name you may choose to give them, which you suppose me to have had. If it were anybody's fault it was my own; but that *simplicity of affection* which you say belongs to my character, that I inherit from my parents. It has often and often touched and delighted me in my father, who up to the very end of his life liked what children like, and enjoyed all that children enjoy. And my mother! what tenderness of heart she possesses, what a sweet, open, unaffected character! Oh! I assure you that if there is any tenderness, any gentleness, any simplicity of heart in my disposition, it is to them I owe it.

"Dear friend, I like to think you pray for me. I have great need of it; but do at the same time pray for my father's departed soul, and for those I love on earth. Those are the prayers I like the best, and as I have a great reliance on yours, I earnestly beg for them, and I am sure you will grant my request. You are too true a friend not to do so.

"Albert has given me the beautiful *Spina* in alabaster. I should like to leave it with you whilst I travel. I must work something for you whilst I am in the humor, but you are so hard to please that I am sure you will think it ugly. Write to us as often and as much at length as possible. By-the-way, our *Jocrisse* has arrived. His name is Julien. He is tolerably civilized. He certainly says, 'M'sieu,' as you predicted; but then he says, 'Madame's dinner is served,' which is rather *elegant*, and 'Madame' is still an amusing novelty to my ears. He cannot read or write, but he gets on pretty well without it. He is very ugly. Albert says he is humpbacked. It is your own fault that I send you all these particulars. You would have them. Adieu. I have no more room. May God give you all the happiness I wish you."

The journey to Odessa, which had been for some time contemplated, was at last resolved upon. Alexandrine was by this means to visit her mother, and spend a part of the summer with her at Prince Lapoukhyn's magnificent estate, between Odessa and Kiev. The doctors approved of this plan for Albert, because of the long sea voyage, and after some discussion it was settled that they should come to us at Naples, and embark thence for Malta, then go on to Constantinople, and so on to Odessa. It was a great undertaking, and involved a long separation from us, but hopes were entertained that it would greatly benefit Albert's health, and Alexandrine was of course delighted to pay a visit to her mother. They neither of them the least dreaded the length of the journey. Count Putbus, with that devoted friendship which he on every occasion evinced, as soon as he heard of their plan, offered himself as their companion and protector for the journey. He was to meet them at Naples, where we were all looking forward with joy to their arrival, and with sadness to the parting which was so soon to follow it.

A day or two before leaving Pisa, Albert wrote a long letter in Italian to Father Luigi Galligani, who kept it, and five years afterwards gave it back into Alexandrine's hands. The first part of it was lost, but here is what remains: "I feel it impossible to doubt that God looks on my beloved wife with those eyes of mercy and love which He fixes on all upright and sincere souls really seeking the truth. You have seen enough of Alexandrine, my dear Father, to be convinced that such is the case with her, and you notice how full she is of tenderness and charity. It is God's infinite goodness which has made her what she is, and granted me the blessing of meeting with her and making her my wife, the treasure and joy of my existence. I shall never cease to thank Our Blessed Lord, and to hope everything from His mercy. I shall carry away from Pisa very precious recollections, and can never forget your affectionate and fatherly kindness to us. I beg your blessing, my dear Father; I assure you that we are both your grateful children, and that as long as we live we shall preserve that respectful attachment which on so many accounts we owe to you. ALBERT DE LA FERRONNAYS."

Alexandrine, on reading this letter five years afterwards, exclaimed: "Oh, my Albert, with what partial eyes you looked upon me! but your faith and that certainty you felt that God would have mercy upon me have met with their reward. O! my God, my God! Finish the work Thou hast begun. I am not yet safe. My angel, plead for me!" No, she was not yet safe, for she was still on earth. But now that I am copying her words, I feel a joyful confidence that she has attained the final, unalterable blessedness of endless peace and light.

On the 23rd of March they embarked on board the *Sully* for Leghorn; and on the 26th Eugénie wrote in large letters in the "*Journal of Family Events*," which she began to keep on the day of Alexandrine's marriage:—"Arrival of the Alberts! At eight o'clock my father gave us notice that the ship was in sight, and that they were coming. Emma, Mamma, my father, and I rushed to the port. Great joy at meeting, and bringing them home with us. Albert is much better!"

ALEXANDRINE TO COUNT DE MONTALEMBERT.

"Naples, March 28th.

"MY DEAR MONTAL—Here we are happily arrived at Naples. The *Sully* brought us from Leghorn, and Albert is well, thank God! We are neither of us sick, and it evidently agrees with him. We shall probably make our great start from Malta, but we wait for Putbus, who has given up his Paris journey. You may imagine how delighted I am at seeing my sisters again. I have just time enough to think of you, but not enough to write. I am very *élégante*; it is a pity you cannot see me. I have not made any blunders yet. Good bye, my dear good friend. I have, and always shall have, a great affection for you. Your friend, ALEX."

Albert wrote in the same letter—

"MY DEAR FRIEND—We have been so unsettled lately that I could not answer your last letter, and indeed I cannot do so now, so near the time when the boat leaves. I am afraid that I shall be ordered to spend next winter also in Italy. My father is, however, going to France at the end of this month, to see about a place in the country, which will, I hope, hold us all. I long to get there, for my home-sickness increases every day. Remember me to the Abbé Lacordaire. What would I not give to hear his conferences, and to find myself in the midst of those wholesome excitements of the heart and mind which are so little known in Italy! Dear, good friend, we are going to be again a long time parted, but you must always look on Alex and me as your most devoted friends. Write to us often. In my next letter I will tell you where to direct to us. Shake hands with Rio for me, and remember me to his wife. If you see the Abbé Martin, speak to him of my unalterable attachment."

ALBERT'S JOURNAL (CONTINUED).

"Naples, March 29th, 1835.

"The last days of our stay at Pisa were so full of bustle and business, that it is only now I have resumed my journal. We had a most excellent passage, and very few passengers on board. My wife was alone in the ladies' cabin. Neither of us were ill. It was the first time we had travelled quite alone together. We stopped at Civita Vecchia. How full of recollections are all these places! When we reached Naples I could scarcely believe my eyes. The sight of that coast, where every spot is associated with the most vivid remembrances, that perfume which is like the soul of Naples, and exists nowhere else, all those charming outward impressions tallied with those equally charming reminiscences which seemed to meet and welcome me, as if seeking to efface the recent emotions awakened amidst other scenes. You know my weakness; I gave myself up at once to those dear delights. Oh, Naples! Naples! no place on earth has ever made my heart beat with such joy as thou!

"How many different shades there are in enjoyment. I enjoyed Pisa, and that sort of pleasure must have been more grateful to God than what I feel here. The thought of God was mingled there with all I saw, and I was not so feverishly excited. Why did everything at Pisa make me think of God? I enjoyed nothing without Him. At Naples the natural beauties which surround me, bewitch the senses, and my soul seems lost in the loveliness of creation. Still, I do not think that God condemns this sort of enjoyment. It is more earthly, no doubt, but after many a struggle, after wading through many obstacles, the cry of the soul is still directed to Him; and may He not make it pure, in spite of all it has passed through? This too fair, too bewitching scenery, is a stumbling block here. The poor weak heart loses itself amidst all this ecstatic beauty. It ceases to seek God, for it seems already to have found Him."

ALEXANDRINE'S STORY (CONTINUED).

"Friday, April 3rd.

"I went out with Albert. We found that good, excellent Monsignor Porta in bed, and ill. He thanked me so much for my visit, and repeated very often his favorite saying about Albert's family: '*Son tutti Santi*' (they are all Saints), and he told me that I too am to be a Saint. Then we went to M. Valetti, the Protestant clergyman. He received us very civilly, and talked of some poor Trappists whom he assists.

"Sunday, April 5th.—Albert and I went to see a doctor who is staying at the Comtesse de Maistre's; then I breakfasted with Pauline, and the conversation turned on the difference between various kinds of affection. It soon became an argument. Albert called for me just when the dispute was at its height, and carried me off to the Villa Reale, where we took a little walk. He scolded me, said that he hated disputes, and in everything loved peace. In the evening we had music and company. I liked then to be well-dressed, and to move about from one corner to another of that great drawing-room of the Palazzo Gallo. Albert, on the contrary, used to go to his room when people came, and often regretted Pisa.

"Monday, April 6th.—I was with Pauline at a party at the Duchess of San Teodoro's, and that was the last time we went out together. This made Pauline always remember the dress I wore that night; she has often reminded me of it. I had on a black velvet gown, and in my hair, round my neck, and on the front of my dress, pink rubies set in black enamel. I am not sure which day it was, but about that time Albert complained once quite seriously, that I had left him for five hours. I had been out on some necessary business, and I exclaimed, 'How could I help it? Was it to amuse myself?' And provoked at Albert's injustice, I scratched his finger, as a little cat might have done. He laughed, and looked at his finger in such a funny manner, that I saw the quarrel was made up. But I was very much ashamed of my bad temper, and I went and accused myself of it to Pauline, who burst out laughing.

"Saturday, April 11th.—I was very sad on account of a letter Albert wrote to Montal. This is it:—

ALBERT TO COUNT DE MONTALEMBERT.

"'Dear Good Friend—You say in your last letter that you are ashamed not to have answered ours of the 8th of February. How much more ought I to reproach myself for my unpardonable silence. How is your brother? What is he going to do? And you? Are you still so out of spirits? When shall we lead again our dear Pisa life? I am threatened with the necessity of spending another winter in Italy, but I do not allow myself to think of it, for I have an intense desire to go back to France. The longer this sort of exile lasts, the more I fear it will prove fatal to me. There is at this moment a spirit stirring among the young men in France, which I am always regretting does not influence me. This new life; this craving for faith; this bright dawn of awakening religion, which infidelity had for a while obscured. Nothing can equal the beauty of all this, and in contrast with it, Italy resembles some fair corpse! In the meantime, we sail for Constantinople the end of the month. It is a beautiful journey, and I shall long for you at every step. We shall put in at Palermo, Girgente, Malta, Smyrna, &c., and towards the end of August we shall return the same way, and then God knows where we shall spend the winter! Do pray that this journey may prevent the necessity of my being longer away from France. Dear friend, you can understand better than any one how intensely I desire to return, for it can only be at the close of our interminable wanderings that I can hope to see that act accomplished, without which my happiness can never be complete. At this Easter time I suffer in a way which you, to whom alone I say it, will well understand, in seeing my Alex unite herself in spirit only with the feelings which fill every heart, in these blessed days. That state of mind which is neither one thing nor the other, that feeling of uncertainty, doubt, and transition, is dreadful. She ought to see one of such priests as are to be found in France, but are not to be met with here. What I suffer from the thought of spending another year in this state, you can easily fancy; and again I say it, I look to France alone for the person who will make her feel the necessity of a fixed belief, the absence of which, if prolonged, must exercise a disastrous effect in the long run, upon her religious feelings.

"'Remember me to the Abbé Lacordaire. Tell him how I envy all who are present at his conferences. There is no place like Paris for satisfying those inner wants of the soul, without which it vegetates, but cannot be said to live. The strong emotion which lifts it up to God, can only be felt, ordinarily speaking, where love is an active principle. Here, indolence and dreaminess prevail on every side. Italy certainly suggests loving thoughts, but it is love of an enervating kind. Even in the intercourse of the soul with God, there is something weak, cowardly, and vague. Nothing is clear or positive. How is it possible that this general tendency should not affect the very ground-work of all ideas? The whole country exhales a perfume which none but vigorous souls can resist, and even these must be soon overcome by it, if they breathed it too long, and did not at times renerve their energy amidst the labors of more active charity, and in the atmosphere of a sterner love. What you tell me of the Abbé de Lamennais must break the hearts of his friends. But what really are his ideas at this moment? Every one construes the state of his mind according to his own fancy, and his enemies, availing themselves of the uncertainty in which he leaves us as to the exact form he would give his Utopia, ascribe to him the most disastrous views. Tell me also what is the work Rio is engaged in. You can easily suppose that I take the greatest interest in it. I must bid you good-bye, my very dear friend. Pray for my Alex—pray for us! ALBERT.'

"This letter made me very sorrowful. I could not think of it without tears. As I had never even thought of going to a Protestant Church at Pisa, Albert naturally enough could not understand why I acted differently at Naples. I knew very well that I went because I was afraid my mother might hear I had not done so, and out of human respect on account of M. Valetti and the Protestants at Naples. I felt restless and miserable, and sat up till three o'clock with Eugénie, who kept comforting me to the best of her power, and assuring me, in spite of my tears, that it would all end well. We opened together a little volume of texts, which my mother had given me when I married, and I was glad when my eyes fell upon this passage: '*Surely Ephraim is an honorable son to me; surely he is a tender child; for since I spoke of him, I will still remember him. Therefore are my bones troubled for him; pitying, I will pity him, saith the Lord.*'

"Monday, April 13th.—I went to the Protestant Chapel; Albert walked there with me, and left me at the door. It pained me very much to part, as it were, with my husband, in order to draw near to God, and it seemed quite a relief when I found myself with him again. That was the last time of my life, thank God, that I attended any Protestant service.

"Thursday, 16th.—Albert went to Communion with all his family. I was not well, and the pain which our religious separation gave me, increased my discomfort."

ALBERT TO COUNT DE MONTALEMBERT.

"April 17th.

"DEAR FRIEND—We start on Monday, and to-day is Friday. My father, who is going to Paris, will take you this letter. We shall return from Odessa in August, and settle again for the winter in poor old Pisa. I pine for France, and am in despair at being obliged to spend another year away from home. The reaction which is now going on is so important and interesting. I only hope that enthusiasm will not carry anybody too far, and also that those to whom it belongs to keep us in check, will understand the greatness of the move we are making, and that instead of arresting it, they will become our leaders in the paths of faith, hope, and charity. I am reading at this moment the Abbé Beautain's work, 'The Philosophy of Christianity.' It interests me very much. I think he exhibits admirably the history of true religion; the plain series of promises and their accomplishment. What is the fault found with him? All I have read of his writings seemed to me strictly orthodox; yet my brother Fernand, who is a great admirer of his, writes to us that the Bishop of Strasburg has forbidden him to preach. The most painful thing now-a-days, is the opposition of the heads of the Church. Well! Providence never permits anything to happen but for some wise end, and it may be that these checks from the rulers of the Church are ordained by a still higher power, in order to moderate the impetuosity of so many young and fervent souls, who, with their thirst for changes, and passionate desire for improvement, might easily press forward beyond the proper limits. Be this as it may, I am thankful to have been born at this time, for we shall witness many wonderful changes."

On the 30th of April, 1835, at about three o'clock in the afternoon, Albert and Alexandrine went on board the English vessel which was to take them to Malta. At the same moment my father and Albertine, who were going to France, embarked in the *Sully* for Marseilles, and we who remained behind were going in a little boat from one vessel to another, taking a sorrowful leave of the travellers, and particularly of those who were to go furthest, and to stay away the longest. It was that day, and on board the English ship from which he spoke to us for awhile, that I saw Albert for the last time up and in health. I seem to see him still, looking at us with his animated countenance, and the tender, sad expression of his beautiful eyes. The next time we met was when I went to bid him another and final farewell. But no such fear crossed my mind at the period I am speaking of. This may appear strange, and the state of blindness in which we lived on this point, will perhaps surprise those who are happy or callous enough never to have known what it is to fear for a dear and precious life. Those who have experienced this anguish, can tell how both hopes and fears conspire to deceive us; and I believe that God often allows this illusion, that our peace may be prolonged up to the day when we find ourselves face to face with the trial, which His powerful grace enables us then to meet with a courage hitherto unknown. The doctors besides, had considered that this voyage would prove an efficacious remedy for Albert. Their opinion justified our hopes, and indeed, as will be seen, they seemed at first likely to be realized. Therefore, our chief sorrow in parting with them, was the great distance about to separate us, and the difficulty and uncertainty as to tidings during their long absence. But now, thanks to their letters and the journals they both kept during the long voyage, we can easily follow them sailing to the East, and relating as they go, the incidents and impressions of each successive day. This kind of narrative is necessarily brief and incomplete, but it would be a pity to substitute any other account.

ALEXANDRINE'S JOURNAL.

"At three o'clock we all went on board the *Sully* to take leave of my father-in-law and Albertine. The rest of the family then accompanied us to our vessel. Hector de Béarn came to wish us good-bye. They all stayed a few minutes, and then left us. O! my God, protect and bless every one of us, and all those we both love. My mother-in-law, Pauline, Eugénie, and Olga stayed for a long while in their little boat between the two vessels, one of which was carrying away M. de la Ferronnays and Albertine, and the other Albert and me. There was a band on board our ship, and the sea was calm."

ALBERT'S JOURNAL.

"Here I am writing in the cabin of the ship which is taking us to the East. All things considered, this is rather an absurd expedition, and to make it at all reasonable, I ought to be as strong as a Turk when I come back. We sailed from Naples three hours ago. There is nothing so sad as leave-takings. It would be better to have the courage to do without them. The beginning of our voyage has been very promising. Nothing can exceed the good-nature of the officers. The captain does not speak French. I speak to him in English, so I leave you to imagine how fluently we get on. . . . We coasted the much loved shores of Sorrento, discerned Amalfi, doubled Capri, and have since seen nothing at all."

"Malta, May 2, 1835.—The day after the last noted, we passed Stromboli at daybreak. It was smoking as usual, but as it was broad daylight we did not see any fire. The weather was very cloudy when we went through the Straits of Messina. The coast of Calabria must be beautiful, as well as Sicily, but to travel by land must be exceedingly difficult, on account of the ravines which intersect the shore, and along which the mountain torrents come rushing down. When we came in sight of Etna the clouds which veiled its summit disappeared, and we saw it quite plainly. The following morning we neared Malta, and landed there at about twelve o'clock. We had some trouble to find apartments; at last, late in the afternoon, we took possession of a very nice set of rooms. Yesterday, Sunday, we went to high Mass at the Cathedral, which is a very fine and interesting Church. The pavement is covered with the tombs of the knights, incrusted with their shields. I shall have to leave this place, I expect, without seeing much of it, for the heat is intense, and my cough very troublesome, which does not serve to raise my spirits. Nobody enjoys travelling more than I do, but to leave one hotel for another, and have no pleasure but that of saying to myself, 'I am at Malta, Smyrna, or Constantinople,' and know them all only by hearsay, is, you will admit, a way of travelling, hardly preferable to a quiet and monotonous, but comfortable home life. We are making our preparations for the voyage to Smyrna; that is to say, dear Count Putbus bustles about for us, for I do not leave the house. He has engaged a vessel for ourselves alone. It takes us to Smyrna for one hundred piastres. We have to buy beds, linen, plates, candlesticks, blankets, glasses, &c., and then also to lay in provisions. There is a shop here well provided with every kind of portable food, and we take with us besides a good number of live chickens and plenty of macaroni, &c. This town seems to me charming, but if I cannot walk about more than I have hitherto done, I shall carry away a very vague idea of it. The houses are handsome—the streets clean—everybody speaks English. As to the native dialect, it is a mixture of Arabic and incomprehensible Italian."

ALBERT TO HIS MOTHER.

"Malta, May 11th.

"MY BELOVED MOTHER—I will not leave Malta without once more begging for your dear blessing. Write to us often, I beseech you, and send us every little detail. Remember how we pine for the sight of your handwriting. We are well, and leave Malta to-morrow. May God watch over us! The most interesting part of our journey is to come, and I look forward to the great enjoyment of coasting the islands of Greece, and of seeing Smyrna, Gallipoli, the Dardanelles, and Constantinople. But I have so great a yearning for France and for all of you, that my eyes are too often turned homeward, and what lies before them loses a part of its charm. Malta has interested me very much. We have been twice to the beautiful Cathedral and the tombs of the old knights. The women here are lovely. Good-bye, my dearest mother. With God's blessing we shall spend in a year's time happy days together in France. Kiss for me our Jane, Paule, Olgette, and Augustus. It is twelve o'clock. We sail to-morrow at eleven. Your affectionate ALBERT."

Alexandrine adds:

"MY DEAR MOTHER—Your Alexandrine kisses you most fondly. Do all be happy, as happy as we ask God every day to make you; and let us hope to be one day together again, and that soon."

ALBERT TO HIS FATHER.

"Malta, May 11th.

"We are still very near Naples, and we hear nothing of those we left there, whereas you who are so much further off have already had tidings of them. May we all soon meet again. What is dear Fernand about? What a pleasant travelling companion he would have made! On the other hand, how I envy him and you also being in France. If you see our dear Montal, tell him about us, and how many affectionate remembrances we send him. I regret so much that he is not travelling with us.

"It is an Austrian steamboat—the *Mary Dorothea*—which will take us from Smyrna to Constantinople. So far from you! I do declare my home sickness grows worse than ever. Well, God bless us all. At the end of August we shall steer towards you. My Alex is quite well, and I love her if it is possible a thousand times more than at home. Putbus begs to be remembered to you. He is kindness itself, and arranges everything for us in the most perfect manner. Like an idiot, I managed to let myself be robbed of a purse containing fifteen of the *louis* you gave me. You know I did not wish you to be so generous, my dearest father. May God bless you a thousand times for this and all your other kindnesses. The further I go, the more I think of the beauty and charm of France. Bless us also from the far end of our own dear country."

ALEXANDRINE TO PAULINE AND EUGENIE.

"Malta, May 10th.

"DEAR SISTERS—One little hurried line for you both. Do not be vexed with me if I do not write all the little details of our voyage. It bewilders me too much. We are charmingly lodged here. Large, lofty, pretty, cheerful rooms, with every kind of comfort in them. I hope you like your new home. You are not many there just now, but it is the best of a large family that there are always some of them together. Fernand is the only one alone at this moment. Your father is going to be with Charles and Emma, I suppose? What is my little Eugénie doing? Oh! pray very much for us. I wonder where we shall be when you receive this letter. Oh! that Albert may be the better for this long voyage!

"My dearest sisters—my little Eugénie, my little Paule, I kiss you most affectionately."

ALBERT'S JOURNAL.

"Monday, May 8th, 1 o'clock.

"I write from the port of Malta. We are on board the English ship, which takes us to Smyrna, and are waiting for the papers without which we cannot start. The French party who were to have sailed with us are going in a man-of-war, but we have plenty of fellow passengers—the deck is crowded with extraordinary looking women, Turks, and all sorts of individuals, not of the most cleanly description. Fortunately we are below and alone. Three deaf and two blind men are making dreadful music, or rather noise, alongside the ship in honor of our departure. Edwardes* is here. His yacht, which is lying alongside of us, came in eighty hours from Marseilles. The thought that I was only at that distance from France renewed my home sickness, but I shook off the feeling, and here I am making for other shores with all the eagerness and curiosity of an enthusiastic traveller.

"We are out of port, and a fine breeze, which we have been partly wasting by these delays, is filling our sails. An hour after our departure the deck began gradually to clear, and we are now almost alone, making our five knots an hour, and fast losing sight of Malta.

"Tuesday 12th.—We are going on slowly this morning, and if the wind does not favor us our voyage may last us twelve days, during which time I shall not write, for there is nothing on earth so monotonous as this ship life, unless we happen to encounter pirates or tempests."

ALEXANDRINE'S JOURNAL.

"Thomas (Count Putbus's servant) brought two rose trees into our cabin. Last night I went on deck with Putbus to look at the moon. It was beautiful seen through the sails, and so was its light reflected in the sea. I enjoyed it immensely, for I have never seen anything like it. My dearest Albert, who would have been so worthy of the sight, could not venture out in the night air. But he is better, thank God! He coughs much less than at Malta, and his pulse is good.

"Wednesday, May 13th.—Julian cooks for us, and a goat we have on board helps to feed us, Albert especially. Ah, I wonder what all those who love us are thinking about now!

"Thursday, May 14th.—To-day the ship rolled very much. Everything was crashing and rolling about. Albert was seasick. I was very glad of it, for consumptive people are not considered to be liable to that suffering. They say a dove is following the boat. To-night, whilst I was lying down in my horrid cabin, some of the women near me and one of their husbands said and sang some prayers for a long time.

"Friday, May 15th.—I felt keenly at the sight of the shores

* The Hon. Richard Edwardes, younger son of Lord Kensington.

of Greece. I was glad, too, to see land again. I was a little frightened last night. A dove, perhaps the same which was following us yesterday, was caught this morning. I have been on deck. There is lightning, and I saw luminous fishes (palamidæ) in the sea. It was very pretty."

ALBERT'S JOURNAL.

"Saturday, May 16th.—Yesterday, for the first time since Tuesday, we saw land. The coasts of Greece have been growing more visible, and towards evening we were opposite the shores of Laconia. Cape Matapan rose in beautiful relief against the sky, gorgeously shining at that moment with the last rays of the setting sun. There was a fresh breeze, and the Captain, afraid of nearing the island of Cerigo (Cythera), hemmed in as it is with low rocks, kept clear of the coast; but this morning, going on deck, I saw Cerigo behind us. We had just sailed past it. Now the wind has fallen. We are becalmed.

"Sunday, May 17th.—Not much more wind than yesterday. After dinner a little breeze sprang up, and we passed the islands of Falionara and Caravi. The sun sank magnificently behind the mountains of Napoli. Its last rays threw over all these coasts a hue of burnished gold, still more beautiful perhaps than the color of the mountains of Italy in July. The heat has been oppressive to-day, and although I feel infinitely better than at Naples, I cannot overcome a sort of impatience at the precautions which shackle all my actions, and may perhaps continue to do so for years to come. This prospect depresses me. I feel a burthen to myself and to others. If I get accustomed to this mode of life, shall I ever be able to lead another? My temper is soured by these thoughts, and I get irritable. My poor Alex, whom the least thing makes anxious, takes it into her head that I am worse than I seem. Poor dear love, I am afraid she will have many a sad day to go through on my account! Putbus is an excellent man, and a real friend, whom I sincerely regard; but the entire want of sympathy in our feelings and hopes will always stand in the way of a close intimacy. Oh, I like to find myself with those who abound in faith and love! I long then to pour forth all I think and feel. But in presence of anything like scepticism, I shrink into silence and reserve, like a snail who comes forth when the sun shines, and withdraws into its shell when the sky is overcast."

ALEXANDRINE'S JOURNAL.

"Syra, Wednesday, May 20th.

"So dreadfully noisy that I was quite frightened last night. The weather was really stormy, and I have not been able to get up. Albert was sick. But he is really getting quite well now. There is a balmy air blowing from the land which does one good.

"Thursday, May 21st.—There was a terrible storm last night, but I did not hear it. Albert and Putbus went on deck. Another anchor had to be cast. I slept part of the day. At one o'clock Albert woke me to give me some flowers which had been brought from the town. Ah! dear Mamma, would not you have been frightened about us last night! And Alexander and Fédor, and the Naples people too! What are they all about, I wonder?

"Friday, May 22nd.—I have been very cross. It is this violent wind which irritates me; but I am ashamed to be so ungrateful. What would it be if we had had an accident at sea, or if Albert had been ill? and I might have been sea-sick, and poor Putbus too. Oh dear! How ungrateful one is!"

ALBERT'S JOURNAL.

"Friday, May 22nd. Ten o'clock at night.

"The hurricane blowing incessantly since Tuesday has at last subsided. We hoped to sail yesterday, but the wind was still too strong. To-day it has changed, but fallen also, and we are now delayed by a calm. It is very unlucky, for now it would be favorable. What shall I say of Syra? I only went on shore once in four days, and felt no inclination to repeat the visit. There is but one principal street full of shops—provision dealers, bakers, tailors, linendrapers, and cap-makers. Alexandrine brought me a Greek cap. We looked into a Church, rather a pretty one, but wonderfully fragile; like a sort of lantern covered with pictures, with benches below for the men, and circular seats upstairs for the women. I did not see the Catholic Church, which is at the entrance of the town. A very well-dressed Greek came up to us, who said he was a prince, and ended by begging. We gave him a five-franc piece, and he went away highly delighted. The scent of land reaches our vessel, and we inhale it with delight.

It is reported here that King Otho's coronation is put off till August. I saw a specimen of the new gens-d'armes in the streets of Syra, and they look strange figures. I think it is the Bavarian uniform they wear, with the Greek colors, white and blue. They have little caps like the German students', blue coats, with white facings, and white metal buttons. The uniform is hideous beside the picturesque Greek costume. You see I have nothing to say, and therefore am dreadfully prosy. The sailors are working on deck. I trust this is a sign that we are going to start; that to-morrow we shall coast Tino and Myconi, and the day after to-morrow be at Smyrna."

ALEXANDRINE'S JOURNAL (SAME DAY).

"To-day, while reading in St. Augustine's *Confessions*, how his conversion was brought about by the words: 'Take up and read,' [*Tolle, lege*] which he thought he heard, and which made him open the Epistles of St. Paul, I resolved to do the same thing, and after a short prayer I opened at this verse: 'Do not therefore lose your confidence, which hath a great reward.'* This struck me very much, and when I showed it to Albert he was quite pleased."

ALBERT'S JOURNAL.

"Sunday, May 24th, 6 o'clock in the morning.—We left Syra. The wind did not cease to be contrary. We tacked all day between Delos and Tino, and came near enough to the latter to discern the town, which has a marvellously beautiful appearance from the sea. We could perfectly well distinguish a magnificent Church, built in the Saracenic-Pointed style. I wish we had been there instead of losing our time at that horrible Syra! After sailing all day backwards and forwards between Tino and Myconi, we passed between the two islands during the night.

"Wednesday, May 27th.—God be praised! Here we are at last at Smyrna! We arrived just at half-past four. Sixteen long days and nights at sea!

"Smyrna, May 27th, 1835.—The nearer we drew to the shore this morning the higher our spirits rose. A favorable wind filled the sails, and drove us with rapidity along the coast, so rich in its abundant vegetation. We shot quickly past the fortress with its white walls. A Turk rowed up to our vessel, and inquired if

* Hebrews x. 35.

we were from Alexandria, whence no passengers are allowed to land, owing to the plague raging there. We soon discovered Smyrna; the lofty citadel of Mount Pagus, the minarets, the cypresses of the cemeteries, and the Mahometans' town. There are a great many vessels in the harbor. Two French ships of war, an English brig, and a little Austrian schooner enlivened the view. The consuls inhabit the lower part of the city, and their different flags, together with the minarets which are everywhere to be seen, break the sameness of aspect which would otherwise belong to the streets of Smyrna. The town is divided into two parts, upper and lower. The former is inhabited by the Turks and Jews; the latter by Greeks, Armenians, and Franks. Our hotel is on the sea-shore, and our vessel has cast anchor at a short distance from the port. The inns at Smyrna are anything but good, but we were very glad to get in here. Think of our surprise when, as we were looking at the rooms, I saw, in a little drawing-room I coveted, M. de M——. I did not know him again at first, but when he heard my name he introduced himself. He was just come from Aleppo, and was going to Constantinople. He insisted on giving up the drawing-room to me, which he had very naturally taken possession of. I had scruples in depriving him, tired as he was, of the best sitting-room, but at last I agreed to accept the offer, on condition that he shared it with us.

"May 28th, Ascension Day.—Alexandrine and I went to the Catholic Church. I had a feeling of being at home when I entered it. In a country where one sees so many divisions on the point which ought of all others to unite men together, it is a real comfort to find one's self amongst brethren in the faith."

ALEXANDRINE'S JOURNAL.

"May 28th.—We have been in the street of roses, and we saw, sitting at their doors or on their balconies, a number of really lovely women. Their faces are uncovered, and they have very delicate, regular features, and a sweet expression. They wear the most charming Greek caps (sactikos), surrounded by beautiful plaits of hair, with flowers on one side, and generally on the other a long blue tassel. After dinner we went on the sea, and enjoyed the beautiful sunset. M. de M—— amuses me, for he is very droll. He pays me compliments, which is perhaps what amuses me; and I like to be called '*Madame*' and '*Madame de la Ferronnays.*' I am not quite used to it yet, though I have been married more than a year.

"Friday, May 29th.—I read the *Confessions* of St. Augustine with Albert, and admired it so much. Then we went to see M. de V——, the Dutch consul, who is our banker, and afterwards into a caïque to Bournabat, the fashionable promenade at Smyrna. The view from it is charming. We also visited M. Tricon's country house. He is the French physician here. We awoke him from his siesta, but he received us nevertheless very politely, offered us coffee, and gave me some lovely flowers.

"Sunday, May 31st.—Albert and I went to the Austrian Catholic Church. I read there the Epistle of St. John, in which Smyrna is mentioned. We saw afterwards the exterior of the Pacha's seraglio and the barracks, and had a glimpse of a Turkish cemetery, and then of the slave market, where some black women were waiting to be sold, dressed in rags, but with such pretty little feet. This painful sight made my heart ache. There was a lovely young Jewess with waving golden hair looking at them. There are immense numbers of pretty women here. Many of them wear enormous gauze turbans, which match strangely with their linen gowns.

"Monday, June 1st.—On board the *Mary Dorothea.* I was delighted this morning to think we were going away, particularly after M. V——, who came to see us, had said that a man had just been seized with the plague, as he opened a trunk which happened to be overlooked at Syra, where he had performed quarantine on his way from Alexandria. This increased my impatience to leave Smyrna. We started at half-past two. The heat was intense. Our crew of the *New Fame* made us no end of farewell signals.

"Tuesday, June 2nd.—They awoke me this morning to see the plain of Troy, and the Island of Tenedos. I looked with great interest at these places of ancient fame. We sailed all day between Europe and Asia. At half-past eleven we stopped before Gallipoli to take up passengers. We had already done the same at the Dardanelles. Some of them were women. I found it amusing to talk with them through an interpreter. There was a darling little girl, the niece of a slave merchant, who thought me pretty, and said I should fetch a high price! The merchant was talkative and jocose, which is not at all like the Turks. They were wonderfully quiet and motionless on board. It is said that they are frightened at sea, but they never give any signs of fear. Last night at sunset I saw them spread their carpets on the deck, and take off their slippers. They prayed a long time, and with great earnestness. We have also a Greek priest in the patriarchal dress. The other passengers are Jews, Armenians, Turks, Negroes, Greeks, Abyssinians, English, French, Russians and Italians. I was glad to find that I was not so afraid of the plague as I had supposed. I sat with these women, to whom I lent my spy-glass, and stood near the Abyssinian merchant, without a thought on the subject, till the Abyssinian who travels with M. de M—— came to warn him not to touch those people, who were just come out of the bath. After that I was more careful. Most of the Turkish women I have hitherto seen are covered with a veil, much in the same way as nuns; only their white veils hide their faces more completely, and a kind of black mantle is worn over the veil. Some of those we have on board come from Mecca. Their black mantles are made of silk, and are such as the Italian women wear. Their noses and mouths are concealed by a white band. I saw this evening that they were taking off their veils for a short time to breathe a little fresh air. Among the Turks there is the handsomest man I ever saw. Most of the Turks and Greeks are fine looking men.

"Constantinople, June 3rd, 1835.—We are arriving, but the day is only beginning to break, and it is too soon to form a definite idea of the city. We can, however, discern the Seven Towers, the suburbs, the peak of the Seraglio at the entrance of the Bosphorus, and the barracks at Scutari just opposite (in Asia). We can well imagine that when the sun shines on this spectacle it must be most beautiful. We discern St. Sophia and the Mosque of Sultan Achmet. Now we are going into port, and are casting anchor at half-past four o'clock."

ALBERT TO HIS MOTHER.

"Constantinople, June 3rd.

"We arrived here this morning in excellent health, and delighted with our journey. The best steamer I ever knew brought us from Smyrna. The Dardanelles exceeded all my expectations; nothing I have seen can be compared to that lovely shore on the left side of us, Europe and Asia on the right. We were surrounded by the most picturesque figures; Greeks, Turks, and Arabs, and at last the Eastern element prevails. Unfortunately we steamed in so swiftly that we did not see Constantinople for the first time by broad daylight. But afterwards the sun illuminated for us the wonders of the Bosphorus. It is beautiful, very beautiful indeed. I cannot compare it with Naples, for the two scenes are totally unlike. Naples is lovely, this is magnificent. How thankful we ought to be for this prosperous voyage. We found here a letter from my mother-in-law of the 25th, very anxious about our voyage. As the boat sailed four days ago we cannot write to her, and she will not hear of us till she sees us arrive. Good-bye, my own beloved mother. Your Alexandrine sends you a thousand affectionate kisses. When shall we meet again?"

ALBERT TO HIS FATHER.

"I was greatly delighted with Smyrna, but since I have seen the Dardanelles and Constantinople, all my admiration for other places has vanished. . . . M. de Boutenieff has been most kind; although he is at Therapia, he has written to offer us his house at Pera. I have declined with a thousand grateful thanks. I shall call on Admiral Roussin. I have made his acquaintance since Fernand sailed under his orders. Good-bye, my dear father. Love your children and pray for them. God grant that you may come and join us at Pisa in the autumn! If you see Montal, tell him I shall very soon write to him, and that we talk of him continually. Putbus begs to be remembered to you. He is so kind, and the pleasantest travelling companion in the world. My Alexandrine is in great beauty, in excellent health, and she loves you with all her heart."

ALEXANDRINE'S JOURNAL.

"Thursday, June 4th.—M. de Sabouroff arrived here this morning, looking exactly like a Turk. Soon afterwards the Prussian minister, the Comte de Koenigsmark, came to fetch us, and we went out accompanied by his dragoman and ours, by a janissary in a semi-European dress, whose business it was to walk before us, stick in hand, driving away the Greeks, with whom contact might be dangerous, and then by the chasseur of the Comte de Koenigsmark. We embarked in the smart caïque of the Prussian Legation, visited several bazaars, bought perfumes and bargained for shawls, which I handled rather imprudently, according to what M. de Boutanieff told me. There are always cases of plague at Constantinople, but fortunately not at Pera. We saw the Hippodrome, the magnificent Mosque of Sultan Achmet, and had a distant glimpse of the interior, which looked like the nave of a Christian Church. They showed us afterward the serpent (in olden days the tripod of Delphi), whose three heads have been cut off by the Turks, and then the lovely Court of the Sultan Bajazet, and the tower of Seraskier, to the top of which we ascended. I had implored Albert to remain below, but no sooner had I reached the top than I saw him standing by me. It was so imprudent, the wind was very high up there. I trust it may not have hurt him. The view was perfect from that height, and had it not been for my anxiety I should have enjoyed it very much."

"Friday, June 5th.—To-day being Friday, the Mussulman's Sunday, we started at eleven o'clock to see the Sultan going to a Mosque. We were close to his pretty palace in Asia, whence we saw him sally forth, and we followed him at some distance. He was saluted by the ships, and the cannons along the shore fired. The Bosphorus was looking more beautiful than ever. The palace is large, richly gilt, and well situated. We had glimpses of the most delicious gardens beyond it. As the Sultan was coming out, there were sounds of music, and at his return we were near enough to enjoy the perfume of the pastilles which are burnt before him. Three horses with embroidered saddles, studded with emeralds, rubies, and pearls, were standing in the court. The Sultan rode one of them. He had a handsome face, grave, sad, and striking-looking, in spite of the hideous red fez he wears. We saw him go by, and then went round to the Sweet Waters of Asia, where we found the most magnificent trees, the loveliest verdure, and a variety of people strolling about in every kind of costume, amusing themselves and swallowing all sorts of refreshments, in which we also indulged. I saw at a little distance a young Turkish lady sitting on cushions, with some other women. I went towards her, and with a graceful cordiality she made me a sign to sit down. Our interpreter helped us a little, and then withdrew with Albert. She lifted up the lower part of her veil, and showed me her whole face; one of the loveliest I have ever seen. She is eighteen years of age. After she had shown me her dress she examined mine with curiosity. My waist seemed to surprise her. These lådies have no figure at all. A cashmere shawl was wrapt round her form. After a little time she called my dragoman, and with much courtesy and graceful eagerness of manner, told him she invited me to go to her home the next day before twelve o'clock, or if later, to one of her friends at Bujukdéré. The way in which the Turks bow is very graceful. They touch the breast, the lips and then the forehead."

"Saturday, June 6th.—At half-past eleven we set off with our dragoman in search of my pretty little Turkish lady. We found her already gone to Bujukdéré. Then we drove to Therapia, where Albert wanted to call on Admiral Roussin. We paid a visit there to a relative of our dragoman, which interested me very much, and then went on to the Russian embassy, at Bujukdéré, where they said that nobody was at home until the evening. It was four o'clock, and I determined to make another trial to find my Turkish friend. We were close to the house she had mentioned, when a servant of the Russian Minister came running after us, to say we were expected at dinner. Putbus advised me, nevertheless, to pay a short visit to those women whom I felt very curious to see. I resolved to do so, fancying the house was two steps from where we were, but instead of that, I had to climb a steep hill, and arrived at the door breathless and in a flurry, thinking I should be too late for dinner. I saw a most beautiful view, but was in too great a hurry to enjoy it. At last I was conducted to a kiosk (summer house), where my Turkish friend was sitting with her friend and some other women, all with their faces uncovered, and roses in their hair. Some European sugar plums were brought in, which I meant to give them in return for the preserves I knew they would offer me. But I did not leave them time to do so. I was so agitated by the hurry I was in, and also by the embarrassment of not being able to speak, that I did not do much more than sit down and rise up again. My little beauty, looking more lovely than ever, rose also, and accompanied me to the door, where she kept me a little while longer, whilst she was talking to my dragoman (without thinking of drawing down her veil again), and giving him all sorts of civil messages for me. At last we both arrived at the Boutenieffs', who received us with the greatest kindness. They sent for Putbus, who was hiding, but was found at last, and dined with us. After dinner we had coffee in the garden, and M. de Fahrmann, the Secretary of Legation, showed us a charming kiosk, which belonged to him, and which he had offered us. It gave me pleasure to meet young Grégoire Gagarin again. It was late before we came away. The moon had risen by that time, the weather was beautiful, and that evening ended a very enjoyable day in an agreeable manner."

"Sunday, June 7th.—At ten o'clock Albert and I heard Mass at St. Mary's (of the Franks). They took me to a gallery set apart for women. The sound of the organ, the High Mass, and the thought of Christians assembling to pray in the Sultan's dominions, affected me more than I can quite account for.* At one o'clock we went with the Count de Koenigsmark to the Sweet Waters of Asia, where, thanks to his diplomatic privileges, I saw the Sultan's palace, which is well situated, built of wood like all the houses here, fancifully painted, and not in good taste; still on the whole, picturesque, and out of the innumerable windows there are most lovely views. We saw in the distance a magnificent large green tent, and numbers of people who come there to amuse themselves. We stopped to look at some Greeks, who were performing the most inconceivably ridiculous dance. We also visited Ayoub and the Coronation Mosque, which it is absolutely forbidden to enter. But the court, with its two beautiful plane trees, is charming, and so are the tombs around the mosque. They are surrounded with gilt railings, which enclose magnificent trees, and rose bushes in flower. The mortuary chapel of the Sultan is particularly beautiful. The tombs were ornamented with mother-of-pearl, and over some of them were thrown cashmere shawls."

"Tuesday, June 9th.—To-day we began our sight-seeing with M. Texier, by visiting the Jenigané Mosque, built by the Sultana Validè. I was charmed with the interior, as well as with the grand and solemn Saracenic architecture of the exterior. The pavement was covered with matting, which serves for carpets in the winter. I had taken off my galoshes, and some of

* Alex wrote here on the margin of her manuscript: "I received on that day one of those invisible impressions of grace which leave behind them a deeper remembrance than any material things. I suppose that Mass at that time had the kind of effect upon me, which the sun might produce on blind people."

our companions took off their shoes. All that the Turks require is, that no one should enter their temples with soiled feet. A number of strange shaped colored glasses are hung around the mosque. There were Turks there chanting the Koran in a half-speaking, half-singing tone. Between them they have to read the whole of the Koran every day, each, of course, a different part. We went up to a gallery to obtain a general view of the place. The large cupolas of the mosques have a wonderful effect. Thence we proceeded to the mosque built by the great Solyman, and began by visiting the mortuary chapel. The coffin which holds his remains is immense, for the size of a tomb indicates the rank of the person it contains. Other coffins surround it, and are covered with the usual quantity of mother-of-pearl and shawls. The roof of this chapel is gorgeous, and studded with real diamonds, which gradually disappear as the repairs of this immense building necessitate an increased outlay. We examined the inside of this mosque, which is, if possible, still more beautiful than the other, went to some bazaars, and then came home, tired to death. As I was lying on a sofa, very cross, the third dragoman of the French embassy, M. de Tranequeville, came and begged me to come and look at some shawls. He and the merchant began by conversing together for a quarter of an hour, and then the handsome majestic-looking Persian asked me in a solemn manner, if I would accept flowers, fruits, or preserves. It is the custom not to begin to talk of buying at first, but to behave as if it were an ordinary visit. Some delicious cakes and excellent coffee were set before me, and at last M. de Tranequeville began gently to speak about shawls, and the Persian showed us some beautiful ones—black, green, and red. Afterwards we drove round the walls, that is to say, we went as far as the Seven Towers. The walls, which are as old as the time of Constantine, are well preserved, and covered with ivy and creepers. From one of the towers there is a still finer view than the one from Seraskier, which made me at last exclaim that Constantinople was really the most beautiful place in the world. I had never said so before, for up to that moment I had given the preference to Naples.

"Thursday, June 11th.—M. Texier took us to St. Sophia. On the way to it, we admired the fountains, which are very numerous and beautiful at Constantinople; and we stopped a moment before the 'Sublime Porte.' When we arrived at St. Sophia, that dear, excellent M. Texier had a long conference with a softa, to try and obtain entrance for us. We were anxiously waiting the result. At last the softa came and said that two persons, Albert and I, could go in. They allowed us, indeed, to enter, but we could only just get a glimpse through one of the three doors which lead to the interior of this celebrated Church and mosque. I could not, therefore, see the famous cupola, but I did obtain a sight of one of the four Angels which are painted in it, and which the Turks have allowed to remain, destroying, however, the faces, in consequence of their horror of all likenesses of living things. At the seraglio, thanks to M. Texier, we were more fortunate, and we saw the greatest part of those lovely porticoes and gardens, the verdure of which is beautiful, though they have no flowers, and thence ascended the long enchanting terrace, which overlooks the sea. We got into a boat, and went to Scutari, in Asia, and rode to the burial-place, which is filled with a multitude of tombs, surrounded by cypresses of the most incomparable beauty. The view all the way was lovely beyond description. The sea was rough when we returned. In the evening we rested, and several people came to see us, amongst others M. de Tranequeville and Doctor Maroncelli, the brother of Silvio Pellico's famous fellow prisoner.

"Friday, June 12th.—We left Constantinople this morning. M. de Boutenieff, M. de Fahrmann, and Prince Gagarin, saw us on board the steamer, the *Newa*, and gave us flowers and fruit. Then, immediately on entering the Black Sea, we began to roll dreadfully, and to be sea-sick.

"Saturday, June 13th.—I awoke, crying bitterly. This day four years my father died. All to-day we have seen nothing but sea and sky.

"Odessa, Sunday, June 14th.—Oh, what a happy moment it was when I saw Odessa, and a letter from Mamma, written on the very same day it was brought me! Oh! my God, how good art Thou! I got into a boat with Albert and M. Sabouroff. We approached the shore, and then they both exclaimed that they could see Mamma. My short sight prevented me from doing so, but soon afterwards I saw her—actually saw her coming towards us. Oh, that blessed moment! How happy I was! I did not even care for not being able to kiss her. My heart overflowed with gratitude and joy! After such a long separation, to see her, to hear her, to look at that dear beautiful face looking at me, and speaking to me, was it not immense happiness? They threw me some flowers and a ring, which Mamma had brought me. We were near enough to look and talk, but an agent of the board of health was watching to prevent our touching one another. At sunset we parted, for we have to sleep on board to-night."

ALBERT TO HIS MOTHER.

"MY MOST BELOVED MOTHER—Here we are in quarantine, our journey as good as ended, and in perfect health. We arrived at Odessa yesterday morning. My mother-in-law was already there. An hour after our arrival she came to the Lazaretto, with Lapoukhyn and Catiche. They were only four steps from us, we could talk together, but not approach any nearer. As soon as Alex and her mother caught sight of each other, both of them burst into tears (you know Alex's big beautiful tears), and the daughter cried out: '*Liebe, liebe Mama!*'* and the mother, '*Sacha, Sacha!*' but at last they became more composed, and for an hour we conversed quietly together. This morning we have begun our quarantine, and are established in the Lazaretto, which is a magnificent building. We have a house to ourselves, another for Putbus, and a large space to walk in." (The rest of this letter is illegible, on account of the fumigations it went through.)

ALEXANDRINE'S JOURNAL.

"Odessa, Monday, June 15th.—We are to stay here a fortnight, and during that time we can see my mother for a great part of the day.

Tuesday, 16th.—To-day Count Woronzoff, the governor of Odessa, came to see us.

"June 20th.—The days are slipping by, and meanwhile we lead a pleasant sort of life. What an agreeable quarantine! Not only do my mother and Prince Lapoukhyn spend the day with us, but quantities of friends and acquaintances pay us visits. Count Opraxin and Count Woronzoff to-day; then Madame Narishkin, Madame de Choiseul, and many others. Yesterday we kept Mamma waiting whilst we were preparing a funny surprise for her, which Sabouroff had planned. He had dressed

* Dear, dear Mamma.

himself in a magnificent Turkish dress, and lent Albert an equally splendid one. I arranged my hair as the Smyrna women wear it, and putting on a sort of dressing-gown, I tied a shawl round my waist, and stuck a dagger into it. Thus equipped, I sat down by Sabouroff in a fine tent he has; the carpet M. de Boutenieff had given me serving as a seat. Albert stood near us, the little negro boy* behind, Mr. Tchefhine as a Circassian, and Putbus as a Bedouin, at the entrance of the tent. We then sent for Mamma and the Prince, who laughed very much, and enjoyed the joke."

ALBERT TO HIS FATHER.

"Odessa, at the Lazaretto, June 22nd, 1835.

"You can hardly imagine, my dear Father, how kind everybody has been to us at Constantinople. It is impossible to be more obliging and gracious than all those with whom we have had to do have been. To begin with, M. de Boutenieff, the Russian Minister, showed us every kindness. He had known Alexandrine since her childhood, and the affection he seemed to feel for her touched me very much. Admiral Roussin was also very kind, and spoke to me of Fernand with great interest. And the good, excellent M. d'Eyragues, who is devotedly attached to you and to all our family, was more hospitable and amiable than I can describe. He speaks of you with the deepest gratitude. M. de Tranqueville's interpreter, a particularly pleasing young man, attached to the Legation, did everything in his power to be of use to us. In short, I shall never forget the reception we met with at Constantinople. Perhaps the better to account for this unanimous good-will, I may as well mention that my Alex has something about her which wins everybody's heart. I know, by experience, the irresistible power of this attraction. We are here in the Lazaretto, exactly as in a pretty country house. My mother-in-law comes and spends the morning with us, goes home to dine, and returns in the evening. We spend the time in chatting together, and after a few more days' patience we shall rush into one another's arms. Lapoukhyn had thought beforehand of engaging for us an excellent cook, who is shut up with us. So you see we are by no means to be pitied. We meet with all sorts of attention, and Count Woronzoff provides us with every comfort, even with French newspapers, which he sends us every day. But for the confinement, it is like being at home."

* Belonging to M. Sabouroff.

ALBERT TO M. DE MONTALEMBERT.

"The Lazaretto of Odessa, June 25th.

[This letter describes their journey, their residence at Constantinople, and their life in the Lazaretto, and then Albert goes on to say]—

"In four days we shall be released, and after spending two days at Odessa, we start for Warsaw. In the early part of September we shall direct our steps towards Italy, and next summer, I trust, join my father in France. My longing for home quite oppresses me. I read in the 'Journal of Frankfort,' that M. de Lamennais had arrived in Paris to defend the accused in the April business. Good Heavens! what a strange idea! how did it ever come into his head? Thank M. Lacordaire for his kind message. I hope his conferences will be published, for a poor exile like me cannot forego his interest in what so powerfully excites the youth of Paris. Alex is very grateful, dear friend, for your constant friendship, and I am sure she will be very angry with me for leaving her so little space in this letter. I must confide to you, as to a friend who takes a lively interest in my fate, that she makes conquests wherever she goes. At Smyrna one; at Constantinople three; one of them reciprocal! Here in quarantine, declarations come in showers. I am obliged to implore her to encourage only her amusing admirers."

Alexandrine in the same letter:—"He has, indeed, left me very little space. I must add, that the four individuals he alludes to are all French, which supports Pauline's assertion that I have a special power of pleasing them. What will become of poor France when I live *there?* I have too many things to tell you, so I will not write at all, and, moreover, there is no room. Do let us hear from you. Dear friend—dear brother—I have always prayed for you, in Asia as well as in Europe, and I hope God will make you happy, and that we shall all meet again. We have got hold here of one of Swedenborg's books, which has puzzled and interested us. What do you think of that man? What a singular life! always conversing with spirits, and talking of them as we do of people. And then all he relates about the Angels! His life seems to have been very virtuous and peaceful. But for all that, I have no doubt you anathematize him in the most unsparing fashion, or perhaps for the sake of contradicting me, and because I had said so, you will take his part! I do not speak of the ecstatic happiness of seeing my mother again. I have found her, thank God! better than I expected. My Albert is also well. Dear, good friend, come and spend the winter with us. What could you do better?"

ALEXANDRINE'S JOURNAL.

"Monday, June 29th.—At last I was able to-day to kiss my dearest mother. It was like meeting her again a second time, and a most delightful moment. And my good Catiche and the dear Prince too. What a nice day it has been! When we arrived at the Hotel de Richelieu, it was so pleasant to look at all the things which spoke of Mamma's being there. Then our good Kruger came to kiss me, and made acquaintance with two little maids (and slaves) of Mamma's. We dined all together. Everything seemed to me so strange and so pleasant. Dear Catiche made tea. I am sailing back into my old laziness, and letting everybody help me.

"Thursday, July 2nd.—At seven o'clock we left Odessa, Mamma, Putbus, Albert, and I. The Prince had gone the day before. The heat was terrible. The steppes are regular deserts without trees, fields, or inhabitants. Nicolaieff, where we slept, is well situated. The Churches even in the smallest villages are handsome. Their architecture reminds one of the Turkish Mosques."

ALBERT TO HIS MOTHER AND SISTERS.

"Korsen, July 9th, 1835.

"One hurried line to tell you that we arrived this evening at this enchanting Korsen. I am so bewildered with wonder that I shall never be able to describe it. A beautiful situation, a magnificent house, comforts of every sort and kind. An apartment for Alex and me such as I should desire for the rest of my life. Alex's room is lovely. Our drawing-room a perfect gem. My room charming, and furnished with a huge silver toilet service; and never saw anything like my mother-in-law and the Prince's apartments. The drawing-rooms and immense ballroom are full of copies of the most famous statues in the Italian galleries. All this is magnificent. I am forgetting to mention the orangery through which we pass to our room. The house is on a rocky eminence, with several waterfalls running from it, and from the windows we see boats with floating pennons.

Everything is perfect, and so is our health, barring a little fatigue. Oh, if I could but transport you here if only for one day! When shall we hear from you? I pine for letters. What are you doing? What have you decided? Where shall you spend the winter? No news at all, and we have been gone so long! You never knew anything so kind as my mother-in-law. If I were her own son she could not take greater care of me, and the good Prince does not know how to do enough to make us comfortable. They both beg to be remembered to you. My mother-in-law says you are to depend upon her to watch over my health, for she loves me as a son, and I can assure you that this is true. Nothing can exceed her goodness. Oh, if we only had you here! What a happy country-house life we should then lead! By the way, tell us when you write if my father has bought or rented a country house? Kiss my dearest sisters, and let me, dearest mother, kiss you with all my heart."

Alexandrine in the same letter:—"Here we are, thank God! and everything surpasses our expectations. It is all so bright, so comfortable, and in such perfect taste! Only fancy, darling sisters, that my room is all pink, the bed, the curtains, the blinds, all rose-colored silk; a lovely folding-screen, which surrounds the bed, is of the same silk; and the rest of the furniture of pink velvet. In our sitting-room there are two beautiful statues of white marble; the hangings, chairs, and sofas are of red silk, and from the charming table where I am writing, I see from each window the most lovely views. Parterres of flowers surround the house on all sides. It is impossible to describe it all to-night, and this is only to give you a little idea of the place, and make you enjoy it with me. The best news of all is that Albert has perfectly well borne all the fatigue. I am quite astonished at it, and am now convinced that travelling, whether by sea or otherwise, is good for him.

"I feel the want of rest, and I must perform long ablutions before lying down in my luxurious bed, so good night. Dearest mother, I will write to you soon, and more sensibly. May God bless us all!"

For a fortnight nothing interfered with the pleasure and repose of their residence at Korsen. It was a rapturous delight to Alexandrine to be with her mother in that beautiful spot, and Albert, better in health than he had been for a long time, was able to share all her enjoyments. They were satisfied with the success of their long journey, and were already planning future ones. These days were among the happiest of their brief union. But they proved brief indeed, for on the 14th of July, a slight spitting of blood obliged Albert to resume his life of privation and restrictions, and proved a fresh signal of the sorrows which awaited them. Alexandrine relates that about that time, as she was writing one evening in her pretty sitting-room, she was frightened by a bat which flew across it into her bed-room, and, sitting on the top of her bed, begun to scream in a way which made her shudder. Not wishing to wake any one, she found it difficult to get rid of the ill-omened visitor, and this circumstance, in spite of herself, left on her mind a painful superstitious fear. A few days afterwards, Albert received from his mother a letter which gave him the greatest pleasure. It contained the news that his father had just purchased the Château de Boury. He was overjoyed at this, for thus his ardent wish to have some home in France, a meeting-place for the whole family, was carried out. He laughed, sang, and was in wild spirits the whole morning, Alexandrine said, but she was surprised to see that in the evening he suddenly became very grave. When they were alone in their room, he told her that he did not feel so well, and that he was afraid he was going to spit blood again. He did not choose to tell her yet that it had already begun. He walked about part of the night in a state of nervous agitation he could not control. At last, at his wife's entreaty, he went to bed, and was much quieter for some hours. But the next day, in the afternoon, the spitting of blood returned and increased. He was bled, and the doctor thought the danger over for that time. Towards evening Alexandrine had gone to her room to undress, but soon after, as she was going up to his bed thinking he was asleep, she heard him cough, hurried to his side, and arrived just in time to find him in the midst of a fresh bleeding from the lungs, and that so violent, that she was struck with a terrible fear of seeing him die in her arms, yet dared not leave him to call for help. She did rush to the door for one minute, and cried out, "Julian! Cleophile!" Albert told her not to make a noise, and Alexandrine, knowing that to speak at such a moment might be fatal, ran hurriedly back to him. But this terrible bleeding going on, and nobody coming, she rushed out a second time quite distracted into the orangery, and meeting Cleophile, cried, "Ice! bring some ice, and a doctor!" Albert's bed was soon surrounded with people, and ice and bleeding in the arm at last stopped the frightful hemorrhage, but during three days the doctor declared that he could not answer for his life, and insisted on his remaining perfectly silent and motionless.

Alexandrine writes: "On one of those days I had got up very early and had just been with him, going back into my own room in a state of silent anguish, and scarcely daring to glance in thought at the future; I looked about me, and my pretty room seemed to have lost all its rosy beauty. I stood at the window, and the hues of the morning sky had no brightness in them. It suddenly occurred to me to open the New Testament, and to seek in its pages a solace of my lot. I did so, and my eyes fell on these words, '*Honor widows that are widows indeed.*' I felt as if some spectre had risen up before me and uttered its cry. Even in thought that horrible word '*widow*,' had never yet presented itself to my mind."

Albert rallied quickly from this severe attack, and Alexandrine was beginning to feel a little more secure, when on the 13th of August, Catiche told her she thought there was blood in the silver basin by his side, but that it was, perhaps, some of the juice of the fruit which had been his only sustenance since the morning. Alexandrine was perfectly aware that so prompt a recurrence of the fatal symptom would leave no hope of his life, and the excess of her love and her anxiety, led her to perform one of those actions which might disgust certain minds, but which I record in this story as a proof of self-forgetfulness and affection equal to any that have been given by those who sucked a poisoned wound to save the life of one they loved. As soon as she was alone, she took up the basin and raised it to her lips, to prove whether or not it was Albert's blood, and if the fatal inward wound had opened again. A month of nursing and medical treatment ensued, and was followed by a decided improvement; so that the usual habits of life were gradually resumed, and the last weeks of their residence at Korsen were spent in a still anxious, but, on the whole, happy manner. As soon as he was at all better, Albert's character recovered all its sweet cheerfulness. He thought so little about himself, that there is scarcely any mention made in his Journal of the dangerous illness he had gone through, and nothing appears in it but his natural gaiety and devoted affection for his family. One day, when he was still very unwell, he wrote as follows :—

"In the night from the 15th to 16th of August, I dreamed that my beloved brother Charles had fought a duel, had fired first and from a distance, and that his adversary had advanced four paces and shot him dead! Fortunately that adversary was poor C——, who was killed himself in a duel three months ago. Still, I cannot help feeling that I shall be glad to receive a letter from France dated on or after the 16th of August, 1835." And then, after writing to Eugénie some grave, earnest words about them both, he goes on in another strain: "As regards matters of taste, I am quite easy about you. I know you have the sort of taste I like, and that you know exactly what I mean. That universal good taste, which belongs to all nations, but to none in particular, which is neither altogether German, French, English, Italian, or Spanish, but a little of all, which has its own style in dress, manners, and even as it were, its own special fragrance. I am sure you understand this. I want you, my dear sisters, not to be French or English, for that would only spoil you. Here I am at the fountain-head of this sort of universal refinement, of which my mother-in-law is a special instance, and I now know that it is in a great measure the secret of Alex's attractiveness. Good-bye, my dear, dear sister. You must henceforth direct your letters to Pisa, for we are soon going to Italy by a delightful route. Let me know something about Charles. I had a stupid dream about him, which worries me. How I do long to see you all!"

This letter shows that Albert had recovered his spirits; but it was not so with Alexandrine. In spite of the undefined anxiety which had more or less disturbed her since their marriage, she had never till now, really looked forward to the future with serious misgivings. She had always expected that Albert would grow strong some day, and that all the privations he was undergoing must insure him long years of health and happiness. But after his illness at Korsen, though she did not give up hope, all her confidence had vanished. Her eyes were opened to the future which awaited her; and though she resolutely closed them again, as far as possible, she never again recovered her child-like gaiety. The following letter will show what deep sadness had taken possession of her, in spite of the efforts she made to believe herself mistaken.

ALEXANDRINE TO PAULINE.

"Korsen, August 26th, 1835.

"MY DEAR PAULINE—I must write you a long letter, to ease my heart a little. It is full to bursting, and my nerves are in a sad state. I could shed such bitter tears when I think of Albert's illness, and of what he has already gone through. I left off here, for I was tired to death. I am now a little quieter and less unhappy, because, God be praised! Albert is better, and (which we think a very good sign) not much pulled down or changed by his last attack. I will not talk about that now; the very thought of it frightens me. Oh, Pauline. I am a little comforted now, but what an anxious life I lead, and how many terrors I go through. Even when I hope for the best, and think of the time when Albert will reach the blessed age of thirty, which I look forward to with such intense impatience, as they do not allow me to hope for his complete cure till then, I cannot help remembering that in that case he will be strong, handsome, charming, full of life and spirits, and that I shall have grown old, aged by care even more than by years, and my health destroyed by incessant anxiety. Even that is the very best I can look for, and would to God we had reached the moment when my only sorrow would be that I was not young and pretty enough for him! Well, let it all be as God wills. I unload my heart of these painful thoughts by imparting them to you. It is a relief sometimes to complain, but God forbid I should murmur. I acknowledge that I am not patient, but I hope I am not envious when I compare, for instance, your lot with mine. You married, as I did, the husband of your choice, and you have never had one day's anxiety about him. You are of the same religion, and to obtain your wishes you had only to encounter a transient opposition. You had not to break a mother's heart. Oh, my Pauline, make the most of your happiness, and do not, through discouragement, create imaginary sorrows for yourself. Excuse this sermon from your poor old sister, but remember at the same time, that I would not for the world change places with any one on earth. It is because I feel this that I venture to speak as I do. You can guess what I felt when I read those words of your letter :—'This is the reward for all your troubles of the past year! Who would have thought, when you were so anxious at Sant' Aniello, that this year you would be enjoying such a charming and successful expedition?' Oh, Pauline! you thought and wrote this, and yet in spite of this charming journey, in spite of the happiness of seeing my mother again, I am more sad than at Sant' Aniello; not that Albert is worse (I hope he is really better), but I am now conscious of the danger which then I was not aware of."

This letter was written just before they left Korsen. It was essential for them not to be overtaken by the winter season, and on the 1st of September, 1835, they began their long journey.*

ALEXANDRINE'S JOURNAL.

"Korsen, Tuesday, September 1st.

"This morning my dearest mother came to my room before I was ready. We were to start at eight o'clock. I went down to have tea with her for the last time in her dear little drawing-room. And then came the terrible good-byes. Mamma and I remained clapsed in each other's arms, and so absorbed that we did not hear the clamor that was going on outside. Putbus's calèche had been overturned, and it was at first thought that the coachman was dead. It turned out, however, that he was not even hurt. We waited a little while to make sure of this, and then after my poor mother had kissed and blessed me a thousand times over, I had the courage to get into the carriage and leave her behind, crying as if my heart would break."

ALBERT'S JOURNAL.

"Bielotzerkoff, September 1st.

"We left that dear Korsen this morning. How sad these partings are; they set one against travelling. My poor mother-in-law was in a terrible state at our going away. These two months have passed too quickly away. I cannot describe to you with what affectionate kindness the good prince and Alex's mother treated me. If I had been their own son it could not have been greater, and I love them as I do my own parents. Oh! why is not that place on the banks of the Rhine, or in Italy?

* At about the same time, we all left Naples for the Château de Boury in France, where my father had preceded us.

How different it would be then, and what happiness we should find in dividing our time between our two families. That good excellent Catiche ; she too was quite like a sister to us. There are persons whose lot seems self-devotion, and she is one of them. At the moment of starting a terrible accident happened to Putbus's carriage. I can scarcely conceive how the coachman escaped. The calèche was broken to pieces, and we started without him. He will overtake us to-morrow, we hope, by travelling all night. We are going to bed immediately after supper. The day has been beautiful, and I do not feel the least tired. I think travelling, as usual, does me good. I have just driven away a whole flight of Jews, who are the pest of this country. Just as I was going to bed, who should arrive but Putbus ! He must have half killed his horses. He brought us a letter from Korsen, written an hour after we left."

"Berditscheff, (Podolia), September 3rd.

"After a lovely day and journey through a pretty country, we arrived last night at Berditscheff, a small town swarming with Jews. They positively assault one, and are the most infamous set of people imaginable. They carry on all the chief business here. When we drove in, the town was full of carriages, horses, people, Polish noblemen, &c. We lodged in a private house, kept by a good German, but destitute of all accommodation. We shall start in a moment, but not with post horses, as before. We trust ourselves to the Jews, which shortens the distance by a hundred versts, but I fancy we shall go dreadfully slow."

"Novogorod, September 4th.

"Those Jews, wretched robbers that they are, made so many difficulties at the moment of starting, that we sent them about their business, and had post horses. We travelled all yesterday through a well wooded country, and slept at Novogorod, which seems rather a large town. But what miserable inns ! There is nothing of any sort to be got, and of course nothing fit to eat. Fortunately, our provisions are not yet exhausted. The abominable Jews who kept this inn, sent out last night for some plates for our supper, though they had some at home, because forsooth they could not eat off plates which had been used by Christians. It is bitterly cold. At ten o'clock we start."

"Ostrag, September 5th.

"We arrived here yesterday at four o'clock. A dreadful inn kept by Jews. However, one gets accustomed to everything, and we made ourselves tolerably comfortable in this kennel. Ostrag is a small town, with old walls in ruins, and in the principal square a large dilapidated Church, which used to belong to the Jesuits, who were expelled under the Emperor Alexander. The architecture of the Church and cloisters is Italian. The Jewish country women all wear caps embroidered with pearls; sometimes very beautiful ones. The mistress of the house here has even diamonds in her head dress. We shall start in an hour, and cross the frontier to-day, unless they detain us at Radziviloff for our passports, and there we part with our good doctor (Heinrich Trütschel, of Westphalia), who returns to Korsen."

"Radziviloff, Wednesday, September 9th.

"We are just on the point of quitting Russia. We arrived here yesterday rather early; but what a place! In two hours we shall start for Brody, which is about one hour's distance from here, and where we shall probably have to remain two or three days for our passports. The Russian and Austrian frontiers meet here. After having gone through at great length all the required formalities of the former, we stepped over to the latter, and the Austrians tried our patience a little also. They did not, however, retain us long at the custom-house. Soon afterwards we arrived at Brody, where we are at length in something like a European town. The postboys wanted to carry us to an inn which they patronize, but we insisted on coming to the Hotel de Russie, which is really comfortable. I am afraid we shall have to stay here some time waiting for our passports, which were sent on to Lemberg. The country we have travelled through for some days past is almost wholly Catholic. It is the predominant religion in Podolia, and here almost the only one."*

"Lemberg, Monday, September 9th.

"After a very tiresome sojourn of a day and a half at Brody, we came on to Lemberg. The country seemed pretty; the hills well wooded, the villages clean, the roads good. We arrived here late, the Hotel de Russie was full, and we were obliged to

* It must not be lost sight of that these notes were written in 1835. Everything has since changed for the worse in these unhappy provinces.

put up at a miserable inn. A bad supper, but I went to bed immediately, feeling tired and ill. After a good night I awoke much refreshed. I heard Mass in a fine Church, a little spoilt by a multiplicity of ornaments in wretched taste, with which the devotion of the inhabitants has encumbered the altars and walls. A great number of men, almost all of them young, were hearing Mass or praying without any affectation or human respect at the different altars. I was struck with the expression of all their faces, both of the men and women. Most of them were good-looking, especially the young girls. Their eyes, here and there, reminded me of Hedwig, but there were quantities of hideous old women in the style of good Madame ——. I was so happy to be in a Catholic Church again, and to hear Mass. I have been in a sadly tepid state for some time past. What has become of that fervor I used to feel? Have I lost it by my carelessness? Has God withdrawn from me, because I no longer thought of Him, still less felt devotion in His service? Oh, how the soul loses all its light when it no longer draws it from Him! How it creeps when it does not lift itself up to God! Oh, shame, shame upon me! But yet have mercy upon me, O! my God! Return again to Thy servant, who has so often and so basely forsaken Thee!"

"Landçhut, Friday, September 11th.

"We arrived here yesterday after a pouring wet day. The rain did not cease for a single instant. This whole country is in the hands of Polish noblemen. Yesterday we passed by Przeworsk, the property of Prince Henri Lubomirsky. How wonderfully things turn out! Who could have imagined when I saw so much of them at Naples two years ago, that this year I should see their home in this distant country? The house seemed charming, and prettily situated in the midst of a beautiful park. But they told us that the family were not at home, and indeed they are all at Prague. This place belongs to Count Alfred Potocki. It is a pity that our way of travelling does not allow us the pleasure of seeing something of these fine country houses, and of enjoying that Polish hospitality which has so great a reputation."

"Tarnow, Saturday, September 12th.

"Tarnow belongs to the Sangusko family. It is a tolerably large town, and the Hotel de Cracovie, where we are staying, is kept by a valet of Prince Lubomirsky's who was with him at Naples two years before. I heard here that Prince Henri was after all at home when we passed through his estates. I am very sorry not to have seen him. It was his wife and daughter who were absent. We may perhaps meet them at Vienna. The papers say that the cholera is decidedly at Leghorn. What shall we do in that case, and where shall we go?"

"Cracow, Monday, September 14th.

"We have been here since the day before yesterday, and lodged in a dog-kennel, for all the good hotels were full. Yesterday morning, Baron Sternberg came in, and there was a most affectionate meeting between him and Alex. He is an old friend of Count d'Alopeus; and she looks upon him and all them whom she knew at the time of her father's death as real friends. He took my fancy at once, and seems an excellent man. We drove with him to see the town, and were deeply interested with the Castle, the ancient residence of the kings of Poland, the Cathedral, a beautiful Church dedicated to our Blessed Lady, containing the tombs of many of the kings and princes of Poland. The town is charming; it abounds in magnificent Churches, and on every side extend the most varied and lovely views. The Crapach Mountains separate us from Hungary. This city, sole remnant of the kingdom of Poland, is curious enough. It is a free town, and has its own president, senate, and little army. It is surrounded on every side by Austria, Prussia, and Russia. The Austrian territory comes up actually to the city-gates. It is really a curious thing this little remnant of the poor kingdom of Poland, which has been suffered to exist by the three powers lately, because none of them would consent to cede it to the others. It is perhaps destined to form the nucleus of a new Poland, or will more probably fall a prey before long to the rapacity of one or the other of its great and jealous neighbors. The famous salt mines, which are one of the wonders of the world, are two miles from here. . . . Alex is gone to see them with Putbus and M. de Sternberg. I could not venture on this expedition on account of the cold and damp of the mines. Another of the privations inflicted upon me by my precious health! Yesterday, we dined with M. de Sternberg, who showed me a charming portrait of Alexandrine, which I should like to steal.

The eyes and mantle are perfect. Nothing can be uglier to be sure, than the arrangement of the dress and hair; but if I had it, those defects should be quickly removed. We are to dine with Putbus when they come back, and to-morrow we start for Vienna."

ALEXANDRINE'S JOURNAL.

"Monday, September 14th.

"This morning before nine o'clock, I left my poor Albert, and drove to Williczka with Putbus and Sternberg. We were taken into a large shed; when some planks were removed, and then we plunged into the bowels of the earth. At the sight of the depths, and the ropes by which we were to descend, I felt frightened, but made up my mind to sit down on one of the five seats upon which sight-seers descend into the abyss. They made each of us put on a kind of white dressing gown, to prevent our clothes from being spoiled. The descent lasted about five minutes. It was a very new and strange sensation. Fortunately we did not go down fast. Other lifts below ours, were filled with men carrying lighted torches. At first the earth was very damp, but as we went lower, it became quite dry. The first thing we saw on reaching the bottom was a vast space closed in with walls of salt. There were several machines worked by horses, but no human beings remain long in this part of the mine. We went and got a little further down, and all at once found ourselves in the midst of a fantastically beautiful scene. An immense lustre of salt illuminated the wide sparkling roof in every direction, and lit up numberless grottoes and caves of the same material. Oh, what wonders exist under the earth as well as on it and above it! The further we advanced the more picturesque and dazzling became the effects of light produced by the light of our guide's torches. After walking for some time we came to the brink of a lake, the water of which was as black as ink. We crossed this lake in a boat, and on the other side came upon the gigantic salt statue of St. John Nepomucene, which is placed here, and in all parts of this country, by the waterside, to commemorate his heroism in submitting to be drowned, rather than reveal the confession of his murderer's wife. Further on we descended by torchlight into marvellous depths, at the further extremity of which is a beautiful Chapel, excavated in the salt, and full of statues of the same material. The effect is singularly fine. Afterwards we saw a ball-room illuminated with lustres also of salt. They told us that Souwaroff had given a ball here, and that a Russian officer had been married in the same place. After spending at least two hours in the midst of these splendid marvels, we returned to the surface in the same way as we had gone down. I had grown more bold, and could bear then to look below and about me. The whole time it seems as if one must be dashed against the walls, but thanks to the skill of the guides, who direct the machine with a small hatchet, no collision took place. Sternberg made us eat something at Williczka, and then I returned to my dear Albert. After I had slept a little while we both dined with Putbus, and they came to tea with us in our room.

"September 15th.—Slept comfortably at Wadowice.

"16th.—At Teschen, where we heard a military band, which enchanted me.

"17th.—We passed through Friedeck, a place delightfully situated in a picturesque, pretty, cheerful country. I hope Boury will be like it. We slept at Weisskirch.

"September 18th.—I had a painful dream last night, that Albert was spitting blood again. Our calèche broke down to-day, and we were obliged to get out in the most dreadful wind, and to get into Putbus's carriage. This accident forced us also to sleep at Rosnitz, and to stay there the whole day.

"September 20th. Vienna.—We got up at 4 o'clock A.M. It was a beautiful morning. To-day the most trying part of our journey is ended, which nevertheless has had its pleasant moments. At last we saw Vienna, (the Church of St. Stephen is discernible from a distance), and soon we were driving through that most beautiful approach to the Archduke Charles's hotel, where we shall stay some days."

ALBERT TO HIS MOTHER.

"My beloved Mother—Here we are at Vienna, after a journey of twenty days, which I have borne very well. On the whole, travelling seems to do me more good than anything else. We had the pleasure of finding your letter of the 1st of September here, and like yourselves we are in the greatest uncertainty as to our plans. The terrible cholera is in Italy; very bad at Leghorn, and two cases already at Pisa. What are we to do? What

I should most like would be to follow your suggestion, and at once join you. We are thinking very much of this, but the doctors must be consulted before we decide. This morning I went to see the celebrated physician, Malfati, who asked me if I was the son of the Ambassador and Minister, M. le Comte de la Ferronnays, for whom he had the greatest regard? 'Exactly so,' I answered. He is to come to-morrow. Alex will shew him all the prescriptions for my case, make all the explanations, and after having read, listened, thought, and considered, he will feel my pulse, and give his opinion as to where we are to spend the winter.

"September 23rd.—I end this horrid scrawl with Malfati's decision as to our winter quarters. He sends us to Venice, which, as he says, being nothing but one great ship, will suit me better than any other place, as the sea is just what I want. It seems to me rather absurd to go to Italy when every body else is flying from it, but Malfati insists that the cholera will not touch Venice, and if it does, that we can take refuge either in Trieste or Ancona, if it does not break out in the Roman States. I think with him that it is not likely to spread all over Italy at the same time, and that if it advances from Leghorn towards poor Naples, *Venice will be preserved*, at least for some time. Do not be uneasy, and rely upon my caution in this matter. I need not tell you anything about Vienna, for you know it well. The life we lead here makes us long to get to our winter quarters. All day long we are running about, as there are so many people and things to see. Princess Lubomirska is here, and Count Zichy. You complain of the cold, while here everybody is wondering at the beauty of the weather. It is now like Italy—but this will not in all probability last long."

ALBERT TO HIS MOTHER.

"Vienna, September 29th.

"MY DEAREST MOTHER—We positively start to-morrow for Vienna, where we establish ourselves for the winter, provided the cholera does not drive us away; but before I go on to tell you about that, I must speak of a provoking thing that has happened to us here. Some days after our arrival, it suddenly occurred to me that as Louis de Blacas was in the Austrian service, he might very well happen to be here. I enquired, and found that he generally stays at the Hotel de Londres. I rushed to the said hotel, and was told that the duke, the duchess, and the *little dukes*, had been there for the last six days! We made great exclamations, and desired to be at once shown up to my aunt's room,* but every body was out. In the evening we called again, and were sent away by a goose of a porter, though my aunt was at home and expecting us. At last, this morning, at nine o'clock, she came with three of her sons to our hotel, and found Alexandrine only just out of bed. A quarter of an hour afterwards, my uncle arrived, and then hurried back again, for they were to start at eleven o'clock. Alex dressed as quickly as possible (wonderful to relate, in half-an-hour!) and we went off, post haste to the Hotel de Londres, to spend a few minutes more with them. At eleven they left for Prague, and we went with Louis to his barracks. He dines with us to-day. We find him very much grown, drill and military carriage have greatly improved his figure. My aunt was as usual most perfect and kind; my uncle as amiable and gracious as possible to Alexandrine. I hope they were pleased with her. You will tell me what they say. But was it not strange and provoking to be for seven days in the same place without meeting? Stanislaus is like Fernand; Xavier still keeps his pretty childish face. Malfati prophesies wonders from the climate of Venice. He has prescribed a course of gold dust, which he says will work a perfect cure. I am to swallow every morning a few particles of it. This sounds like a joke—but we shall see. We found —— here, who is very kind to us. He dines with us to-day, and, without thinking of it, I also asked Louis de Blacas! What would M. de —— have said of this acquaintanceship, and of our intimacy with Mr. O'Sullivan, the Belgian minister? For the life of me I cannot manage to trouble myself about these little political squabbles; and, if some of my relations are to disown me for associating with such people, I must e'en resign myself to it."

On the 1st of October, 1835, Alexandrine appeared in evening dress *for the last time of her life.* It was the eve of their departure from Vienna, at a dinner given by the Comte de la Rochefoucauld, the French chargé d'affaires. She was in white, with a set of mediæval jewels, which she was fond of wearing. Little did she think that it was for the last time. After dinner they

* The Duchesse de Blaças was Mm. de la Ferronnays' sister.

went to the opera, which was "*Norma*," and this was also the last time she ever entered a theatre or went to a public amusement. The following day, the 2nd of October, they left Vienna, and, travelling slowly, reached, on the 8th, the Italian frontier. Count Putbus had left for Paris on the same day they started for Venice ; he was to join them there afterwards.

At Ponteba Alexandrine wrote :—"This entrance to Italy is like all the others, very beautiful and grand, but to my mind not so striking. As we advance, however, we see fig-trees again, and all the rich vegetation of the South. Oh ! beloved Italy, this is the fifth time I approach thee, and always with fresh delights ! Oh ! may Albert find health in thee ! It does one good to feel the climate softening, and it is a pleasure to look at the houses, so unlike those of Germany. Yet when I wished Albert good-night at Ospedaletto, he told me he had a foreboding that Italy would work him woe. . . . O ! my God, my God !"

As Alexandrine was copying this part of her journal in 1843, seven years afterwards, at Brussels, she broke off her narrative, and wrote the following words :—"And now, after so many afflictions, my passion for Italy still remains the same, or rather it has strengthened, for I know now why I love it. I know the secret of that fragrance which exhales from Italy. Ah, yes, I love, and shall always love it, for its people believe in an eternal Home, and possess unseen friends whom they invoke in their joys and sorrows. I love it because in all its cities an ever-present God is worshipped on His altars by adoring crowds ; because it has been foremost in every thing which exalts mankind, and has laid its renown at the feet of God ; because its people have excelled in every form of beauty, yet have not sought ambition and their own glory.

"I love this country, where both hearts and flowers give out a sweeter perfume than elsewhere ; which gave birth to St. Francis of Assisi, and to that other meek saint bearing the same name, and to so many men and women saints, with ardent, loving hearts, where, at every step, we meet the sons of St. Benedict, St. Dominic, St. Francis, and St. Ignatius, and many whose names are written beside theirs in the Book of Life. Where in the depths of the cloister, and the obscurity of many a poor village, holy and hidden lives are closed by saintly deaths. I love this country, for in it is the city of the Vicar of Christ, the holy city Rome, where so much virtue has been practised through all ages, and where all the great benefactors of humanity have come to gather strength and light. Ah! yes, I love this land of corn and wine, which spring up and overflow as if they hastened to abound for the great Mysteries of the Altar. This land so dear to the heart, so fair to the eye, that it seems as if one's last dying thoughts might be :—'Now, I am about to see something more glorious than Italy!'"

After this out-pouring, Alexandrine went on with her record, inserting the passages and letters she had written at the time.

ALEXANDRINE TO PAULINE.

"Pordenore, October 9th, 1835.

"MY DEAR LITTLE SISTER—Since yesterday we are in Italy. I bless God for it, and I do hope it will be the means of restoring Albert's health. I feel more passionately fond of this country than ever. I am always so enchanted to return to it. There is music in the street at this moment; such fine voices, singing familiar airs! Albert is as delighted to be here as I am. I like to be writing to you whilst listening to this singing. There is a charm, a perfume, an indescribable attraction about Italy, all the more remarkable because there is so much that one hears continually found fault with. Do you not also feel this *smania* for Italy? All other countries seem to me so cold and common-place in comparison. It is only the East and Spain I fancy, which possess the same kind of poetical charm. What will you say to this burst of enthusiasm? My letters have been more than common-place lately. Well, you see we have come safely so far, and to-morrow, please God, we shall be at Venice. Only think, those singers—to whom we sent down a *zwanziger*—came up-stairs, and have been singing and acting for us, '*Un Segreto d'Importanza*,' whilst I was writing all this. They act admirably, and I wish that you and Eugénie could have heard the *prima donna* sing '*Le Romeo*.'" They did arrive at Venice the next day, Saturday, the 10th of October, and the following letter from Alexandrine to M. de Montalembert, is dated the 15th October, 1835. At the top of the first page of this letter, these words were written: ("Albert does not like the first page of my letter, but I do hope, my dear friend, that you will not be angry with me for what I say, nor think it comes from any bad feeling.")

"My dear Montal—I am going to write you a volume, though I have not much time, because ever since Albert received at Vienna your letter of the 31st, I have been composing the said volume in my head. Whether you have time to read it or not, write it I must. . . . If you knew Albert's life better, you would not think him so much happier than yourself. What man of his age would not feel it a great trial to be shackled during his best years, by a multiplicity of restraints, and to be condemned with a singularly quiet and active disposition, to complete quiescence; to suffer more or less every day, causing anxiety to a wife that he loves? For my own part, I do not believe in any great inequality of happiness. I believe in compensation. They seem to me to consist with our ideas of God's justice, and I have so often had opportunities of observing the erroneous nature of men's judgments with regard to the happiness or the unhappiness of others, that I am inclined to think—generally speaking—that the beggar is no worse off than the person from whom he begs, and if the latter has troubles of conscience, then without doubt he is the most miserable of the two.

"I have been married eighteen months, and without any exaggeration, there have not been fifteen days in which I have been free from anxiety about Albert's health. Ever since I have known him, how much suffering and trouble have always been mixed up with my happiness! What did not I go through when I thought he was dying at Civita Vecchia, and I was not allowed to see him! Do you not think that these continual terrors, and that obstinate disease, are, to say the least of it, as great a trial to me as is for you the one you speak of? . . .

"October 23rd.—I have left this letter unfinished for the last week, but I will go on with it now, for I feel I must unburden myself thoroughly. Let me speak to you with the greatest openness. I should deal as freely as a sister with you, for a sister could not love you better than I. I have also a sorrow akin to yours, which is continually on my mind. There is nothing that would make me so happy as to be of the same religion as Albert; but besides the doubts I still have, I am kept back by the feelings that I should break my beloved mother's heart; that mother to whom I owe the happiness of being Albert's wife. I should break her heart *inwardly*, and perhaps *bodily*, too. I know she will never believe that Catholics think it possible that those of another faith can be saved. And how could a mother bear such a thought? Indeed, if I should be obliged to believe that my poor father was excluded from salvation, and that by making my choice between two religions, I was separating myself from him for ever, I believe I should forsake Albert, who is sure of Heaven, and cleave to my poor father, like the Pagan prince." (Here she relates at length, the story already quoted, of which she was so fond, of an unbaptized heathen king.) "I fear that with your usual severity you will stigmatise this as weakness. But I remember that you were very much touched by what is said of the mother of Tobias, who *would not be comforted* for her son's departure, though it was Almighty God who commanded him to go. Well, it was weakness, but nobody thinks of blaming her. My position is a painful one, and I cannot help *rejoicing* that I have not yet *made up my mind*, and I do not wish for instruction, or to be convinced that it would be my duty to go against my mother on this point. Dear friend, if you have any charity you will pity, and not condemn me. I try as much as I can to cast this, my heavy burthen, on Our Blessed Lord. I also ask the Virgin and Saints to pray for me, for I believe in their intercession in some sort of way, more than I do in some others of your doctrines. It is your Pope whom I cannot yet believe in." (Alexandrine wrote afterwards on the margin of this page, "And now if I did not believe in the Pope, I should not feel that I was a Christian.") "Well, I hope God's goodness will deliver me from this torture and difficulty which embitter my life. *I hope*, for I have that blessing which the Divine Mercy has made a virtue. Who is it that said: '*That must be a Divine religion which makes a virtue of hope.*' Dear friend, I wanted to say it. You do not hope enough. It is a fault as well as a misfortune. You see that Albert and I, whom you envy, have also sorrows, though God forbid we should not gratefully acknowledge our happiness too. And do you think that there are not many people who envy you? You have religion, learning, and poetry, for your friends, and good friends they are. Then, how many interests there are in your life; and does our friendship go quite for nothing? You always forget us, Albert and me! When I remember that after the first days of awe and reverence you inspired me with, I grew so bold as to throw eau-de-Cologne and orris powder at you, and got you to order me a bonnet, I feel you must forgive everything! . . . . But, dear friend, I must really now leave off, for you must be bored to death with this long scribble. Who knows if you will even read it? Please write to me very soon. We have heard of your speech in the Chamber of Peers; how I should like to read it; and how I wish we may see you soon! Were you ever at Venice? It is so interesting. Always your sister and friend,

"ALEX."

ALEXANDRINE TO PAULINE AND EUGENIE.

"Venice, October 27th, 1835.

"Good-night, my dear sisters, I am not the least inclined to write. The sirocco is dreadful. It is quite as oppressive at Venice as at Naples, and I feel for the first time that nervous effect of it which my mother and Albert used to complain of, viz., a difficulty in forming the letters in writing, so read this letter if you can. I have a great *smania* to see you again, my darling sisters. We certainly see very little of each other since we have been sisters, and were much oftener together when we were only friends. Have you—any of you—I want to know, had the shadow of a doubt as to what we should have chosen, had it been a matter of *pleasure*, between spending the winter here, or at Boury, with that dear family party where we are the only missing ones? I must say, it would vex me to think that your father had such a doubt, and for his own satisfaction I should like him to be convinced that Boury could not be so good for Albert's health as Venice or Pisa. As to the *moral* good and comfort it would have given him to spend this winter with you all, there can be no two opinions about it; and you know well enough how I like and enjoy our large gatherings. But as I am quite aware that this place is far better for his health, I am glad we are here. It is also impossible not to love Italy; and Venice is in the highest degree interesting, so I cheerfully make up my mind to what the doctors, not ourselves, decided. And now, Madame, and Mademoiselle, how comes it that you do not write a line to your poor sister-in-law Alex, who sends you whole volumes, to which you do not vouchsafe the least bit of an answer? And she who holds so much to getting answers to what she says. Mademoiselle Eugénie, on the day of her arrival at Paris, scribbles very deceitfully to that poor Alexandrine, 'How can I like Paris when I have not time to write to you?' Oh, what an untruth! and now that she has left Paris not one line does she send me; not one poor little description of Boury, which I am dying to be able to picture to myself. As to Madame Pauline, she writes a letter certainly on the 12th of September, which perfectly satisfies me (I beg to say this is not always the case); but in that letter she promises another, which was to follow immediately, and now a month has passed, and no such letter has appeared! Your parents write much oftener than you; you ought to be ashamed of yourselves, young ladies! Another family defect is to write without answering, and to repeat questions which have already been answered. Still, on the whole, you are not a bad set of correspondents. My father-in-law in his last letter praises our dear Eugénie immensely; and Albert (rather uncivil to his wife, I think!) says that she is more delightful and captivating than either you, Pauline, or I! Good-bye, Eugénie; love me, and write to me. I love you dearly. God bless you! Tell Fernand, when he comes, to bring me some songs, and all the music he can steal from the pianoforte at Boury, without creating too much notice; I have left all mine at Leghorn, and do not want to send for it."

EUGENIE TO ALEXANDRINE.

"Boury, November 5th, 1835.

"Did anybody ever write that it had entered into anybody's head to imagine that you were spending the winter out of choice at Venice instead of with us? When we talk of nothing else here than of your taste for family parties and a country life, and that we are all longing for your return, because we know how you will make us enjoy our home! It is true that we had for a moment been foolish enough to think you might have spent the winter at Boury, and our heads being full of that notion, we were a little disappointed when we heard of Venice. But now, if you only knew how sorry we should be that you were here! It is only November yet, and we are suffering so much from the cold, that we do not know where to sit, or how to light fires enough. The wind is piercing, and the idea of Albert crossing these cold passages, and going up and down these icy staircases, makes one quite shiver. Oh, no, dear friends, God keep you safely in Italy, for if we feel the difference of climate so much, what would it be for him? Oh, Alex, how often I long to be with you, and to begin again at Venice, not the anxieties, but the Sorrento sort of life, and to help you, dear, dearest sister, in all your minute daily cares. You are so loveable in that sort of intimacy."

Fernand in the same letter: "How do you do, dear little friends? Whilst Eugénie writes a note to Emma, which I am to take, I have seized on a pen, and beg to announce that you will soon see me. Dear people, I wish I could write something that would amuse you, but I am afraid I cannot; I have no funny ideas. Eugénie's note is finished, and I must go. Good-bye, dear little people. Tell dear old Albert, with my love, that I shall bring with me lots of music, novels, plays, scraps, and chit-chat to amuse you with this winter. Good-bye."

Eugénie goes on: "What a man that Fernand is! he writes such a large hand, and wastes no end of paper. I must tell you that my throat is in a very bad state since my return to France. It has been so painful lately that I am not allowed to sing or to read aloud, and I may soon be forbidden even to speak! My voice is almost gone, and if I sing for a minute, I am quite exhausted. I am taking a sort of syrup, which is to do me good, I am told, but hitherto it seems rather to hurt me. My poor singing is what I most regret. The doctor says that if I want to get well I must be a whole year without using my voice. It is the sharp, sudden cold which has seized me by the throat like a robber. Olga's eyes are worse too; the cold does not suit her either. Think, then, how happy I must be that your dear husband is not exposed to it. Albertine is at the convent, very well, very good, gaining prizes, and preparing for her First Communion. My dear friends, here is another letter from you! Dear Alex, it is like yourself to be always doing everything to keep up your own spirits and those of others. I am sure you dote on that Englishman who has been worse than Albert, and who is now quite well again, thanks to Venice air! Well, now I must have done. I hope my letter is long enough, and that I have made up for past deficiencies. I did not lose sight of you a minute, and henceforward I shall always write with your last letter open before me. I shall in that way be certain to answer exactly. Good-bye, my dear friend, whom I love with all my heart, and admire with all my mind. God bless you both, for two such little people are not easily found on earth!"

ALBERT TO HIS PARENTS.

"Venice, November 17th.

"My dear Father and sweet Mother — I answer your dear letters of the 30th and 31st at the same time. I see you have evidently given up for the present all idea of coming to Italy. We are very sorry for it, but understand all the difficulties in the way. Yet all you say about your health, my dear father, makes me afraid of the winter for you either at Paris or Boury.

"Dearest mother, perhaps you don't know that you have written me the most enchanting letter. But I cannot yet answer all your questions, for I have only been twice to St. Mark's, and am, indeed, delighted with its wonderful and mysterious architecture, which far exceeds my expectations. Venice cannot be understood in our day; but the more I see that magnificent Piazza, the dome of St. Mark, and the Campanile, the more I am in love with them. Our apartment is charming, and the view from it lovely, which, besides all the other reasons, make us prefer Venice a thousand times to Pisa. You ask me how we came into Italy this time; we passed, as you did, through Ponteba. Though this entrance is less beautiful than any of the others, we had a feeling like that of love for one's native land when we heard the '*Si Signore,*' instead of the tongue of our heavy, tiresome, German post boys. We passed through Klagenfurth, and thought, dearest Father and Mother, of your having been married there. We can form no plans as yet, but towards the spring we fully intend to make our way to France. I am dying to get there. We love you with our whole hearts. We live with you in thought, and long for the time when we shall share your dear family life. Fernand's arrival is what we are now impatiently looking forward to, and we talk of nothing but what we shall do when he comes. According to my usual habit, I do not mention my health, for the good reason that *it is capital.* . . . ."

In spite of the confidence these letters seem to imply, the following passage in one of Alexandrine's, shows the sad anxiety she was feeling. She used to conquer it, and to force herself to trust. Nevertheless, that time was one of deeper melancholy to her, than any other of her life. Earthly joys were vanishing from her grasp, and she had not yet found the happiness which God alone can give. "Oh, if in the grave there is a sense of being asleep, a quiet awaiting of God's judgment, with a conscience unburthened with any great crime, a repose not without thought, but free from the puzzling troubles of earth, then there may be something sweeter in the feeling that one's lot is fulfilled, than all in this world can offer: for whatever joys are to be found in it, they are always mingled with anxiety or shame—both intolerable drawbacks. I do not, perhaps, express what I mean, but the real truth is that I pine for repose, and if old age or death itself can give it me, I shall welcome them both. If this seems to you very sad, do not attach importance to it. I have a headache; but I am in good spirits in spite of these thoughts." Seven years afterwards, by the side of those words, "*I pine for repose; if old age or death can give it me, I shall welcome them both,*" she wrote on the margin, "*Before old age and death, Faith has given me this repose.*"

EUGENIE TO ALEXANDRINE.

"Boury, November 13th.—Friday evening in my room, by such a good fire! Only I wish it was not Friday, and the 13th! My poor dear Fernand is sitting talking to me for the last time. He starts to-morrow, and though I am very glad he goes to you, it makes me not a little sad to part with him. We are so happy, and get on so beautifully together! I had a quarrel with Pauline the other day. It arose from a sentence in her letter to you, which I chanced to read. We both cried, and then we kissed each other, and finally we agreed to tell you all about it, and said that you were a charming judge, before whom everything may be laid. But do you not know what we said besides? We agreed that nothing can be compared to the time between fifteen and twenty, and that however happy one may be later, those years are the most perfect in life, it may be, because one is less conscious of it. There is then an instinctive want of joy, affection, and amusement, and not the least misgiving as to attaining them. The path which leads to them seems so bright and fair. The scent of flowers is ecstacy in those days, and fine weather makes one jump for joy. The mind is full of everything and nothing. I have entered upon a wide subject. I have not time to go on with it. Here is poor Fernand wishing me good-bye. He goes at five o'clock in the morning. Oh, I am very sorry for it. Poor dear brother! So there must be always partings!"

The quarrel of which Eugénie speaks in this letter arose from my having fancied that in a circumstance which had lately occurred, she had not spoken to me with her usual frankness, and I had expressed this doubt and fear in a letter which happened to fall into her hands. This grieved her, for it was the first time I had said anything to our sister-in-law which I had not said to her. We agreed to refer the matter to Alexandrine, who decided that I was quite in the wrong. I received her letter at Paris, where I was spending a few days, and sent it on to Eugénie, at Boury. But dear Eugénie was never inclined to assent to a judgment favorable to herself, and unfavorable to me; and she was very ill-pleased with Alexandrine's verdict. She wrote me a dear letter on the occasion.

EUGENIE TO PAULINE.

"Boury, Tuesday.

"My dear little Darling Pauline—You are quite right to forbid my writing to Alex, for I am very angry with her. You need not be afraid of my accusing you. I accuse *you!* Why the very thought of it makes me cry! especially when I was the one really to blame! Did I not go and complain to her, and was not all this trouble my own fault? It was wrong, wrong, and all my fault. Forgive me, for it was my doing. Nothing, nothing on earth can create the least coldness between us—our souls are linked together like the bodies of the Siamese twins. What hurts one hurts the other. We may live and act separately, but we must always feel and love alike. My darling Pauline, forgive me for having been the cause of the harsh words which our mutual friend has written. Would I had been there to kiss away the tears from your dear eyes! Promise me that you will write to Alexandrine, and tell her what I say. All this only serves to show how impossible it would be for anything to alter our friendship in the least."

ALBERT TO HIS FATHER.

"My dearest Father—I have received your dear letter of the 30th of October; such a kind and delightful one. Oh! my dear father, how very much I love, and how touched Alexandrine is by all you say! I am so afraid of your suffering from this winter in France. Do come as soon as possible, and warm yourself in Italy, where the sun is never long without shining. Poor Fernand will be frozen on the road. It is very good of him to come to us. I feel it very much, but have almost a scruple about his doing it. I shall keep him in exercise by getting him to walk with Alexandrine, who, if left alone, would very willingly stay in the house the whole winter. She thinks moving about the room sufficient exercise, and she certainly takes a great deal in that way. I wish you could see her busy about her household affairs; with her provisions of rice, candles, coffee, sugar, &c., and giving out these things every day. We have a kitchen-maid, whom she directs, and all goes on with order, regularity, and economy. Is not that creditable for a person who was considered capable of everything except the management of a house? Are you afraid that the poetry of life may suffer? Well, perhaps a little at the moments of actual overlooking and work, but in the salon you will find her again the same charming, refined, captivating Alexandrine of other days. In short, my dear father, God seems to have created my home on purpose to make me happy, for a mere housewife would have destroyed me, and I should also have been bored with a fine lady who would have been good for nothing in one's home. We have already made a number of acquaintances here. As nobody expects me to return visits, I am much pleased with their civilities. Good-bye, my dear father. Alex and I love you more than we can express."

At the end of one of my letters, at this time, Eugénie wrote to Alexandrine as follows:—"When I pray to become good, I see you far, far in advance of me on the long road of perfection. I admire your character so much; it has so much force, so much sweetness, courage, tenderness, and fidelity. You do not give way to discouragement; you rise so quickly again. Oh! God has been very good to our Albert, and He will complete his happiness. I have no fear about the one great thought. God will lead you. You are His own gentle sheep, which He calls, without frightening. He will grant us a peaceful consent, and will bring it all about without wounding your mother's heart. My Alex, I shall pray so ardently for you!"

ALBERT TO PAULINE.

"Venice, November 28th.

"DEAR PAULINE—Alex has received your letter, which, on account of the postage not being paid, did not reach here for so long. You are great darlings, both you and Eugénie, and all the pretty things you say to Alex make me love you ten times more than ever, if that were possible. She deserves all your love, for there are not many women like her. One ought to be, as I am, the object of her solicitude, to understand the sweetness and tenderness of her incessant self-devotion. God bless and reward her! You give us an immense wish to read Montal's speech, and I am certain beforehand that I shall like it, for whether it is enthusiastic or not, it comes at any rate from the heart of my dear friend, and nothing but what is good can flow from such a source. You say that —— thinks it a singular speech. What does he mean by that? It is a mean term which expresses nothing, praise or blame. Others, you tell me, are of opinion that religion and politics should be kept apart. Those good people do not perceive that, in these days, everything turns on religious questions, and that religion, which they affect to speak of in a patronizing or contemptuous manner, is in fact the tone of everything, and even of those politics which they would fain separate from it, poor freethinkers that they are!"

ALEXANDRINE TO M. DE MONTALEMBERT.

"Venice, December 3rd, 1835.

"Do you recognise this paper? You bought it for me yourself at Leghorn! How comes it that I have delayed, not for a week, but for a single day, answering your letter, which has given me so much pleasure? I was afraid of what you might say in reply to mine, and now you write more kindly to me than ever. I am so grateful, and you have made me so happy! Dear friend, when I spoke of your sensitiveness, it was not from our experience of it; on the contrary, we always think and say that few friends, even the most intimate ones, would be so unceremonious and so like a brother in every way, as you are with us; but it is your austerity of character in other cases which makes us a little afraid for ourselves. You would pity and laugh at me at the same time, my dear Montal, if you knew how I am given up body and soul to household cares. There is not a trace left of 'the *poetical* Alexandrine.' The present one is surrounded with stores of oil, potatoes, rice, candles, &c., and is perfectly well acquainted, as I beg you to believe, with the prices of everything, *eggs included*. You would be charmed with our lodging. It is ten times as comfortable as the house at Pisa, in the best situation, and with the best view in Venice. I am quite engrossed by domestic duties, seeing that I have a kitchen-maid seventy-four years old, and that our poor Julian has been ill for the last four weeks. Oh! what absurd things I write to you. My pen, as usual, draws me on to chatter away most unwarrantably. The immense time I waste with my kitchen-maid has proved to me that our Antonini (at Pisa), in spite of the apparent moderation of his prices, used to take me in a little. But if our purse suffered, *poetry* fared better. We are living in the same house as Mr. Rawdon Brown, an Englishman, who lends us books, amongst others the Koran, which interests us very much, and Byron, and numbers of others about Venice. But he hates Moore, and will not admit that he has written a single good line of poetry.

"Dear friend, my mother writes that she hopes to receive the Sacrament with me next year, and entreats me to remain always firm in our faith. Oh, when shall I be calm and at peace? I have had all through life less of that blessing than of any other! Venice continues, thank God, to agree with Albert, though the weather has been too cold and damp for him to go out. Are you yourself quite well? Please answer this question. Albert thinks the first sheet of my letter savors dreadfully of the kitchen. It is quite true. I am ashamed of it, and beg your pardon; but the fact is that our poor little old woman has so little knowledge of cooking, that it is *I who teach her*, and this is such a new talent, that I cannot help boasting of it. And then I was encouraged by your kind request for household details.

"There is a sentence in your letter to Albert which made us laugh the whole of the day. Who would ever fancy that you wrote such things to us from a convent? Dear friend, with all your gravity you manage to be very amusing. You will never have so affectionate a friend as Albert. Even I see some defects in you, but in his eyes you are perfection, and he would take any treatment from you without a complaint. Farewell. May God bless and make you happy. Your Sister (I may say that; you do not object to it?) Pray for me, and write to me."

ALBERT IN THE SAME LETTER.

"DEAR FRIEND—I am not in the mood for writing to-day, and as Alex has answered at length your kind letter of the 10th of November, I shall put off doing so till another day. I want to say only that as time goes on, I find more and more comfort in your friendship, and that I thank God with all my heart for our intimacy. It is inexpressibly sweet to me that my wife is included in it. Be always her friend.* Affections of this sort only increase as time goes on. Your letters are looked forward to and welcomed as if they were a brother's! Write to us often, but to her rather than me. You can do her so much good. There is a subject which cannot be touched upon except by a friend, and a friend whose heart and mind are as well known to us as yours, and who is more likely than others to succeed in broaching it. Such subjects of conversation will be moreover very useful to me, for I am in a sad state of tepidity. What pains me most is the fear that this apathy which has taken hold of me must arise from self-indulgence and neglect. This invalid existence and minute precautions take all energy out of me. I never had much, but now there is none. If my body could recover strength and elasticity, perhaps my tone would get stronger. You can therefore understand how little I am likely to influence the mind of my angel wife beneficially. Far from being her guide in anything, I owe it to her that I am not utterly prostrate."

ALEXANDRINE TO PAULINE AND EUGENIE.

"Venice, December 8th.

"It is foolish of me, dear little sisters, to sit down at past twelve o'clock at night to write to you; but I have a strange passion for writing at night, and the post goes out at two in the day time. My household duties, which increase every day, the journeys backwards and forwards, the time spent in Albert's room, all this (and not my poor toilet, as I dare say you think) fill up a good part of the morning. Alas! I am much less well got up than I used to be. I have given up not only many of the things which you considered exaggerated, but some which you thought essential. I am becoming matter-of-fact, common-place, unrefined, a regular house-wife, a cook, anything you please to ima-

* Alex justly remarks on the margin:—"This expression '*her* friend,' instead of '*our* friend,' in this his last letter to Montalembert, does it not read like a farewell?"

gine, and it is terrible to think how it suits me! Not that I am pleased with myself. The way in which I nurse Albert, which you praise me for, has no merit in it whatever. If you ask Putbus, he will tell you, as he has told me, that I have a natural taste for all the little details of a sick-room; that I shall miss this sort of thing when Albert gets well; that there is nothing which amuses me more than to measure, arrange, contrive, &c. What have you to answer to that, and when I know it myself to be the truth? No, I have no merit, but perhaps I am blessed with a happy disposition, for when I have it to do, I like attending to household matters, and when it is otherwise, I like just as much having nothing whatever to do with them. I like travelling, and I like staying in the same place. I am glad both of excitement and repose. I like to be idle and to be busy, to nurse the sick, finding all sorts of little pleasures in the occupation, and when my sick people get well, I think it is pleasanter still. My dear friends, how foolish you are to apologise for talking of yourselves, for here am I, writing a whole letter about myself, for which I suppose I ought to beg your pardon. Oh! my dear sisters, what a blessing it is for you to have no worries about religion. When shall I see my way out of my present state? My poor mother writes me such touching letters. Oh! may God never forsake me, and make Albert well again! I cannot break my mother's heart. She has been the happiness of my life; she has allowed me to marry a Catholic; and I am all that she has. If I could act truly, I would examine, *study*—and TRY to become a Catholic. The Pope is my difficulty. I think I am convinced, *quasi all the rest.*

[Alexandrine wrote afterwards on the margin:—"God has been very patient with me."]

"Thanks, my dear little Eugénie, for your comforting words on this subject. Farewell. May we soon meet again. If you knew how I love you!"

ALEXANDRINE TO PAULINE AND EUGENIE.

"The same day

"DEAR SISTERS—I wish you could see us with Fernand. We lead such a pleasant kind of dawdling life—doing nothing at all; not that that is the beauty of it, but we are so happy, so snug. We chat so comfortably together. It is charming, and dear Fernand is in such spirits. He does not seem at all sorry to be shut up with us here."

ALBERT TO HIS MOTHER.

"Venice, December 23rd.

"My Poor dear beloved Mother—How I do long to clasp you to my breast! The spring is still so far off. Seeing dear Fernand, increases if possible my *smania* to be with you. His arrival has been a great joy to us. He was fresh from home—coming straight to us from you all. It seemed as if seeing him we saw you all again. And then, you know, dearest mother, I have always had a peculiar fondness for Fernand, the brother of my childhood, the companion of its sorrows and joys. We have grown up together, and there is a great deal in that. He is in very good looks, and I feel quite proud every time I introduce him to a new acquaintance. You know how fond Alex is of him. He was the great protector of our love affairs, and we can never be too grateful to him. In those sort of things adverse acts and friendly ones remain deeply engraved in the mind, but especially the latter. I therefore hope we shall spend a pleasant winter, full of affection and comfort in each other; and in the spring I shall at last see every one of you again. I am charmed with what he tells me of Boury. We never tire of hearing him talk of it, and describe the place and the country about it. What a charming summer we shall spend with you! I do so enjoy the life of a château, and so does Alex. We make all kinds of plans about the furnishing of our rooms. As we have now a *home*, and a most comfortable one, and that our own particular one consists of two rooms, we think it will be easy to make it pretty, and we intend to make it so. Our present idea is to bring back with us from Italy enough pieces of old silk, if our means allow, for hanging the whole walls. What do you say to this? If it was only for the curtains, would not it set us off? Alexandrine and Fernand are hurrying me to send the letters to the post. I have written nothing but nonsense, but this is not to count for a regular letter. Let us hear from you by each courier. Good-bye, beloved mother. Alex loves you like your own children.

"Your Albert."

ALBERT TO PAULINE.

"Venice, December 19th, 1835.

"My Dearest—You must see Constantinople! It is more

beautiful than anything you have yet beheld. My love for the East is as strong as ever, and we have serious thoughts of spending some part of next winter in the Holy Land. Jerusalem is my dream. I cannot imagine anything equal to the interest of following our Lord Jesus Christ's footsteps, with the Gospels as one's guide. Every Christian ought, I think, once in his life to enliven his faith by resorting to its fountain-head. I feel as if mine, tepid as it is, would be for ever kindled into fervor. For where are there interests comparable to those bound up with religion? How dry and cold all others seem by the side of that one which is unchangeable, inexhaustible and Divine. There is to me something very peculiar about Constantinople. It strikes one as a place of passage, an encampment where all is pretty and brilliant; but nothing gives the idea of a people firmly established, with a future to look to, and a work of self-improvement to fulfil and hand down to posterity. It looks as if each individual had built for himself a tent for the momentary enjoyment of that beautiful sight. Does this arise from a natural apathy, or are they under the influence of an inevitable fatality which hides the Russian fleet from them, ready to rush in through the narrow gateways of the Black Sea? It was thus that Mahomet the Second was attacking the walls of Constantinople, whilst Priests and learned men were absorbed in vain theological controversies. When a people reaches the last stage of dissolution, Providence, perhaps, permits this sort of apathy to mitigate the sufferings of the final moments. . . . I begin this letter again at the end of two days. Our dear Count Putbus is arrived, and has brought Alex and me all sorts of pretty things; but not, as we had hoped, letters from you. It is one of those beautiful Italian days, which make one forget all the previous bad weather. Venice is in all its glory. The air so pure—the palaces, the sea, the gondolas, and everything gay as for a festival. Dear Pauline, do you not delight in Venice? After Rome, it is the thing I like best in Italy, and it has the advantage over Rome of not being inundated by crowds of foreigners. My wife is becoming every day more captivating. She is the only woman who could have made me happy. Everything is charming about Alex; her simplicity, her tenderness, which you know so well; her unutterable sweetness. No happiness on earth can equal mine. With my dislike of the world, it would have driven me wild to have had a wife who did not like her home better than anything else. Oh, my dearest, how real life becomes when everything is concentrated in the same circle of interests, affections, tastes, and sympathies! There is something so genuine in all Alex's feelings—not a grain of affectation about her. I do not know if my sufferings increase her attachment; all I am sure of is that nothing can exceed the sweetness of our mutual love. It really seems as if this letter could never get itself done. This is the third time I have left it unfinished. I continue what I was writing on the last page; and say that for my part I cannot ununderstand marriages without affection, or conceive that married happiness can exist without that precious attachment which guarantees a real union of heart and mind. I own I admire those who marry from prudential reasons, without inclination. It would require less courage, in my opinion, to stand by a mine about to explode. I should never have been able to undertake it; and had I not met my Alex amidst those enchanting scenes at Rome, and the secluded, almost cloistered life she was leading there, I should, perhaps, never have fallen in love, and then certainly never married. The word marriage alone is to my mind an alarming one. Good-bye, my dear sister, my best love to my dearest father, my beloved mother, Eugénie, (God bless her!) Olgette, Charlot, Emmy, and her dear little Alfred."

ALBERT TO THE PRINCESS LAPOUKHYN.

"Venice, January 1st, 1836.

"My Dear Mother—Let me begin this year by speaking to you of Alex, and of all the happiness which I owe to you. Time as it goes on, only increases its amount and intensity. How can I ever thank you enough for having entrusted to me the happiness of your daughter? You who knew what an angel she is! God grant that I may never disappoint you in that respect. But if I do make her happy, it is not owing to anything in myself, but to her own sweet disposition. Besides being the only woman who could make me happy, she is the only woman, I believe, who could be happy with me. She has serenity of temper, indispensable to my peace. A capricious and uncertain person would have driven me wild. Her greatest charm of all, perhaps, is her perfect simplicity, and entire freedom from affectation. If you could only see her busying herself with household matters, and all their wearisome details, with such gaiety, and such perseverance! Where did the *élégante* Mademoiselle d'Alopeus acquire this patent? How has she learnt to be a perfect housekeeper in her kitchen, and at the same time to retain all the captivation and charms which makes everybody fall in love with her? And these are the smallest of her merits. Everything about her is admirable. Perhaps the whole of her qualities would have been less conspicuous in another kind of marriage, but in such a tie as the one that binds us, the daily monotony of life increases rather than lessens its strength. I have the consciousness that ours is an everlasting happiness, and have always dreaded the disenchanting effect of habits; having been so often carried away by enthusiasm and then saddened by disappointment. And shall I confess it? at the very moment of my marriage, I had for a few days a sort of uneasy feeling which might have made you anxious for your daughter's happiness. I felt a kind of longing to escape. I thank God I did not, but the longer I live the better I can understand in others the vague dread I then felt, and I am more convinced that it requires courage to marry in the way most people do. For my own part, when I see how perfect Alexandrine is, it makes me shudder to think how easily I might have missed having her for my wife; and I feel to love you—you to whom I owe this blessing, more than ever. And that good Count Putbus too, to whom I am also so indebted. What a charming character that man has, so modest and unaffected, and so simple! But do you know that I never venture to speak to him of my attachment and my gratitude, from a feeling that it would put him out, besides not liking to make speeches, so I say nothing. But I do hope he knows how I like him, that is, if he has ever given it a thought. This dear friend arrived here five days ago, and will spend the rest of the winter with us, and so will our good Fernand, who has given up Paris and its delights to give us his company here, and I assure you that our life is really quite a merry one. I only wish you were here too, my dear mother. We should enjoy it all then twice as much. But you will come, shall you not, to Paris next summer? It will be so pleasant to meet you there. Alex looked into her accounts yesterday with Putbus, and they were delighted to find her so well off. This is fortunate for our journey to Paris, where I am bent on her being very well-dressed. She is always charming, if ever so simply dressed. She inherits this from you, dear mother. There is a special perfume of refinement, if I may so speak, which I have never known in anybody but you and your daughter. It is that which at once struck me at Rome; that and a kind of mysterious charm belonging to yourselves, your rooms, and everything about you. How I must have bored you with my long disquisitions, but I will stop now. High time I should, you will say, but I wished so much to talk to you a little, and more even than I have done. I converse more easily by letter than *vivâ voce*, for I am absurdly shy, and particularly so with you, dear mother, who have always been so good and kind to me. But this does not prevent me from loving you beyond measure, and I entreat you to continue your kindness to me.

"Your devoted and respectful son, A. F."

This letter, dated the first day of the year, the close of which he was not to see, was the last he ever wrote to his mother-in-law. Would it not seem as if both it and the preceding one were a sort of farewell to his vanishing happiness, an acknowledgment of affectionate gratitude for all he had been permitted to enjoy, and was now about to leave?

The 17th of January, a date which was afterwards a very sad one for us all,* was also a painfully memorable one to Albert and Alexandrine. On that day, in 1836, they took a walk together on the Lido, and for the last time in this world, tasted one of those happy hours—never to return again—which up till now had flashed across their sweet though chequered life, like gleams from a better world. Albert had seemed better than usual, and Alexandrine thus writes:—

"When we landed on the Lido, I said that my poor Albert was like a bird escaped from a cage, and I was also in the highest spirits at finding ourselves once more together in the open air. The weather was very beautiful, and the island gay and bright, in spite of being covered with tombstones. Ah! that was my last walk on earth gilded with earthly joy. Since then there have been others, bright with golden and rosy hues, but their brightness came from another world. Albert and I came back in a gondola by ourselves. He was afraid that Putbus would not like to be alone with Fernand in the other, but I

* M. de la Ferronnays died on the 17th of January, 1842.

could not trouble myself about that, for a whole hour seemed to me too long a time to be away from him. We had that delicious hour together, and that lovely sea, turning over the pages of a book Putbus had lent us, and applying to our own love the beautiful passages we found in it, amongst others, this sentence which delighted us: 'Would there not be suffering in loving only for a life-time? Have you not felt the desire of an eternal affection?' Ah!—one of us was soon to become acquainted with that kind of love! The only thing which disturbed the perfect enjoyment of that hour was the anxiety I felt because Albert had wetted his feet on the sands of the Lido. I should have liked to dry them with my hands."

Alexandrine's anxiety proved not to be without foundation. On the following day Albert was worse, and by degrees all the symptoms of his fatal malady returned and increased. The end of January and all February passed without any improvement, but at the same time, without any attack which could open Alexandrine's eyes to the extent of the impending danger. During the latter melancholy month, she still cherished delusive hopes. I do not like to interrupt the course of this painful narrative, but the following passages of the letters they both wrote, and some extracts from Alexandrine's writings, are too indicative of her state of mind during the days, which preceded the great trial of her life, to be omitted.

ALBERT'S LAST LETTER TO HIS FATHER.

"Venice, January 31st, 1836.

"I have narrowly escaped an attack of inflammation. Had it not been warded off, it might have fallen on the lungs, or been a brain fever. Thank God, it was taken in time, and all is right for the present. *Fiat voluntas Dei!* But it is not cheering at twenty-four years of age, and when, but for health, life would be unspeakably happy. Forgive my grumbling, but illness make me feel so *old*, I lose patience and courage, and should give way entirely if it were not for my sweet angel Alex, who keeps up my spirits and makes me feel ashamed of my cowardice. Love her very, very dearly. There is no one like her in the world."

A few days afterwards, Alexandrine wrote these words in her locked book:—"My God, Thou hast granted me some keen enjoyment during my life, but Thou hast denied me *repose*. . . .

I hope that I do not murmur at this. Thy will be done. Oh! yes, *I hope that I am convinced* that all I have done is well done. But Almighty Father (for Thou hast permitted us to ask), I ask in the name of Thy Son Jesus Christ, to whom Thou hast promised to grant all things, I ask Thee that I may live and die and rise again with my cherished Albert. I love him, O! my God, I love him much in Thee. I love him much because he loves Thee. Oh! keep us ever together in Thy love; never separate us! Pray for me, ye saints, and love me, dear Jesus; let my voice reach Thee as that of the poor woman reached Thee, as of the centurion, and so many others! Like one of them I cry, 'Lord, I believe, help Thou mine unbelief.' Deign Thyself to enlighten me; make Thyself Thy truth to shine in my heart. But let me, sweet Jesus—Thou who hadst pity on Thy mother—let me deal tenderly with the heart of mine. My soul was very sad and troubled yesterday. The sky was beautiful, the sea so fair and calm. Such sights have often of themselves led me to believe in an eternal happiness extended to each and every one. Well, yesterday I felt nothing but the sorrow and the danger which grow up side by side with all that is sweet and joyful. I thought that the glorious sun often causes many deaths and great sufferings; and the sea, so calm, so unbroken, and so deeply blue, are not multitudes drowned in it for all its beauty? Danger and suffering are all around us. Our life, the life of all those we love, hangs on a thread, and even that thread is not broken without frightful sufferings. Oh, is not one sometimes tempted to ponder upon the truth that God, immense, incomprehensible, and almighty, has certainly the right to make His creatures for different uses; some for misery, others for happiness; and what can we do in the matter? As to murmuring—it would be absurd, for compared with God we are less than the clay which the potter fashions into different vessels, or the wax which the artist moulds at will. I am less before God than the grain of dust which whirls before me. May I not then be as indifferent to Him? . . . I had some such thoughts yesterday as I sat in the window looking at the lovely view, and then, wafted to me perhaps by one of the Angels who care for me, there came into my mind those words so full of comfort, '*The very hairs of your head are numbered.*' Thus, then, our troubles have all a purpose. Oh, I know it is good for me to be tried. It makes me think of God; it makes me, I hope, somewhat better. And then another Heavenly word came into my mind: '*Blessed are they that mourn, for they shall be comforted.*'"

ALEXANDRINE TO PAULINE.

"February 25th.

"MY BELOVED PAULINE—Does it not seem very strange to you all that I have been so many weeks without writing? It would have been a torture to me, and you can look upon it as a good sign that to-day I feel able to write. Yesterday Albert got up for the first time. But I am still terribly afraid that this violent attack must have done his poor chest a great harm. Oh! Pauline, how the roses that bloomed in my future are turned into thorns; my flowers are withered or drooping. Will the dew of a brighter day never revive them again? I was surprised at something Eugénie wrote, but it was a *listless* sort of surprise, and perhaps in my present state of mind I was not sorry to hear her say, '*Why should I wish to find anything sweeter than death?*' Oh! *happy*, happy are those who can love that terrible thing *death*, and whose faith is so strong that it makes them look upon it as the greatest of blessings! All the joys of earth could not give Eugénie as much happiness as these foretastes of Heaven."

ALEXANDRINE TO PAULINE.

"March 1st.

"DEAREST PAULINE—He is better, still better, I venture to trust than when I wrote to you a few days ago. I am very grateful, but still very anxious. These poor human hearts of ours! I hope I have never dared to think that God need not have created sufferings; but I own that I have often asked myself how it could do good to the soul to be so tortured; and why God with all His power and love, can look on at such agonies and allow them to exist. And yet, even as I write the words, I feel that, if such questions did cross my mind, they were most absurd. For I myself find that it is good for my soul thus to suffer, that it weans it from the earth which it loves so much, and makes it pray with greater fervor to that merciful God whom in the midst of happiness I forget. Oh, we are base and ungrateful beings, to be so much more occupied with God when we feel our great need of Him than when He showers upon us blessings! I rely on your prayers, my dear sisters. I feel for the anguish which you and your parents are enduring, while we, comparatively speaking, are more easy. But dearest, I too want pity. I want comfort; and to be folded in the arms of some one I love, and weep and sob there without restraint. My too full heart needs the relief of tears to calm the agitation which I am perpetually concealing. Fernand and Putbus are both most kind, but they are not enough for me now. I want to feel my mother's arms about my neck, and yours, beloved sisters. I am sitting writing to you lonely and sad in my Albert's room. He is asleep. I should like to have somebody watching with me. You will understand this. Fernand is writing in the drawing-room, a good way off. It would be a comfort to me to have him here. But he is not quite as noiseless as I am, and for our dear patient it is better that everything should be perfectly quiet. Oh, I hate being alone! During this terrible month, when Fernand and I have been together nursing our beloved one, we sometimes have laughed. It was to be sure only a transient gleam of merriment, but my poor weak soul requires sympathy and companionship. Well, it does not signify whether I suffer more or less, so that he is better; and he *is* better. I trust it is God who allows me to think so."

FROM ALEXANDRINE'S JOURNAL AND NOTES.

"On the 3rd or 4th of March Albert saw that I was in tears. He called me and said softly a few words. I could only catch this sentence: '*Well, dear love, and suppose it pleased God to call me to Himself?*' Another time I forgot what I wanted to say, but I made a slip of the tongue, and said by mistake, 'I shall feed on the good God,' and stopped and smiled at my own mistake; but he said with a grave sweetness, and an expression in his countenance which I shall never forget, 'And when will you *feed* on the good God?' I remained speechless."

"March 5th.—Oh, my God! that sharp pain, that stitch in his side, has returned. It is three o'clock. He is gone to bed again. What a miserable thing is life, and men dress it up in luxury and pleasure! Such were the words (words of despondency) which ended one phase of my life, for from that time forward a new existence began for me. Out of the very midst of the shadows of death, light was about to dawn!" I had not courage to resume my journal till the 28th of March, but this was what happened. On the 5th, Albert's cruel pains in the chest terribly increased. What would have become of me if he had died then, ignorant and undisciplined as I was then, I tremble to think, and it might so easily have happened!"

"March the 6th.—Albert slept during the night, but on waking, he began to cough, and toward morning his pains had passed from the shoulder to the centre of the chest, and he sometimes felt as if he should be choked to death. At half-past five I went to wake Fernand, who went to fetch Brera" (the physician.) I sat anxiously watching by Albert's side, waiting for Fernand's return. He came back with his lips white, and scarcely able to speak. He said: 'We must get a confessor.'—'Have we come to that? Have we, indeed, come to that?' I cried to myself. Then I added, almost instantaneously, 'Now I AM A CATHOLIC!' When these words had been uttered, courage at least, if not joy, came back to my soul. I asked with a sort of impatience what this dreadful malady was called: '*Pulmonary consumption*,' replied Fernand at last. Then I lost all hope. This passed in another room, close to Albert's, and we had to go back to his. Fernand opened the shutters, and I looked out on the morning. I saw the palaces gilded by the sun just as usual, but I no longer seemed to take note of what I saw. The light fell on Albert's face, and it looked perfectly white. I fell into a kind of stupor, but controlled myself, for I had now been for many days practising how to conceal my fears. My dear Albert, looking on this new day, whose importance he was unconscious of, began to say sadly and sweetly, '*Oh, I wish they were all here! I am afraid I shall never see them again! France—if I could but reach France, I would bow my head!*' Some nuns of the Visitation, to whom he had a letter of introduction, which Fernand had delivered, sent him a relic of St. Francis of Sales, by Padre Catullo, their confessor. When Albert saw the good Father, he was very glad; he asked him at once to hear his confession. He then turned to me with a sweet expression, and bade me leave the room. I gave the good Father a host of injunctions to be careful before I left, and I remained outside near the door, full of anxiety, and trying to hear what passed, without thinking it the least harm. Padre Catullo remained a long time with us. He told me with great earnestness that Albert was 'a most Christian man.' He did both him and myself the greatest possible good; and notwithstanding the misery of that day, there was a germ of joy in the irredeemable resolution I had taken, which I felt by anticipation to be good. Soon after Fernand had uttered those terrible words, I opened the little book of texts I have already mentioned with a superstitious feeling, and I found these words for the 6th of March: '*He hath not despised or contemned the affliction of the afflicted.*' Fernand went off on horseback in the afternoon to fetch his parents and Eugénie. After his departure, which agitated me, I felt a surprising peace. To be sure, Albert began then to amend a little. Since that day I left off reading novels, and did not even finish the one we had before. To occupy my thoughts I read the Bible, or some spiritual book. Albert made me dine in his room, and what a dinner it was! The evening was, however, calmer than I could have ventured to hope. I said to Albert that Brera's medicine was doing him good. With a beautiful smile he kissed the relic of St. Francis, and replied, 'No, it is *this* which has done me good.'"

ALEXANDRINE TO PAULINE.

"Venice, March 17th, 1836.

"He lives, Pauline! Mother, sisters, all of you, he lives, and there is fresh hope; much more hope, perhaps, if I can venture to believe it, but I have been so often disappointed. Fernand will have arrived, I think, before you receive this letter, and I am afraid you will be much alarmed. And then, if anything has delayed him on the road, what terror this letter will cause you! My own Eugénie, I wonder if you will have set out before you get it. Oh! if only you were all here! My heart feels so sore, yet it is wonderful how God supports one when no human help is at hand; and last night, after that dreadful day, I felt an extraordinary peace. Our dear, kind Putbus did me good also, for it is extraordinary what a need I have of some one to share my cruel anxiety. We spent the evening in Albert's room, who was only too much inclined to be sociable and to talk. I am sure you could not but hope, if you saw him so cheerful. But, alas! in his disease, this does not show anything. I am obliged to repeat this to myself, that I may not be too hopeful, which has always been my disposition; still I must add, that yesterday evening, and again this morning, the doctor said it was a miracle to see him as well as he is. Oh, if this were indeed from God's will! Fernand will tell you about the relic of St. Francis of Sales, which the nuns of the Visitation sent him. He holds it constantly in his hand, and I believe I have as much faith in it as he has. Ah! what will happen to us! Oh, Eugénie, my dear father and mother, come quickly to us, and I need not say 'pray for us.'" The next letter was also written during that time of painful suspense. Tears had blotted it so as to make it almost illegible. Many years and other saddest days have passed away since I received it, but nothing can ever efface the remembrance of the place, or the hour when it came, or the feelings with which it was read.

ALEXANDRINE TO PAULINE.

"Venice, March 9th, 1836, twelve o'clock at night.

"He is alive, dearest Pauline, but I can hope no more. It is very hard quite to lose it, and it is only to-night that I give it up, though I have been told innumerable times that he may die from one moment to another. . . . . It is so hard, even when one has gone through it once, really to believe that our beloved ones can die. I am here alone in his room, he sleeping and I watching him—knowing that he is dying, but without father, mother, sisters, or brothers into whose arms I could for a while give way to my dreadful anguish, and who all through my life have felt such intense need of sympathy. I must write to relieve this intolerable burthen.

"This, then, is the end of our love. Ten days of happiness out of less than two years of married life, and this for us who love one another as much as it is possible to love. Ten days! for it was not longer that I was entirely free from anxiety about his health. God in His mercy slowly, almost imperceptibly, prepared me for my lot; yet, in mercy, for I have always chosen some long sorrow to any sudden shock. I am then *calmly* looking my future in the face. First, O Lord! grant me that this blessed angel may not suffer again as he has done, and that all the joys of Heaven may be his for ever. As to me, whose life will, as I feel, be prolonged, I shall have no other happiness on earth but the love of my God. May I only have courage to give myself up entirely to this! It ought to be the strongest of all love, but I have always been so weak. I have always felt such need of tenderness, that it frightens me to think that at my age, I must give up every help of this kind for ever. And yet my only rest will be in knowing that nothing on earth can ever comfort me; for I should detest myself if I could set my foot again in any worldly scene, or take the least interest in worldly things. But still I shall crave to see those I love. For one moment I thought I might be a nun, but I felt again that I should not have courage for it, and that the desire to see my mother, and all of you, and my brothers, would disturb me; and if I could, I should seek to be calm and at peace with God. I must therefore lead a lonely life, but with some one I love and who will love me as much as my mother. Perhaps I may go to her. But in that case, or in any case, I must profess Albert's faith, I will not and cannot believe anything he does not believe. . . . Do you remember, Pauline, my telling you that nothing but a *birth* or *one of three deaths* would make me a Catholic? This was a foreboding which it has been God's will soon to realize, and alas! not in the one only happy way in which it could be fulfilled. Then, who knows, perhaps after some years, I might have the courage to return to France, and to become a Sister of Charity; to look upon suffering, sorrow and death; perhaps to save by careful nursing some consumptive patient, and bless God that others were happier than myself. . . . I should like that! But, no, I am not good enough—I shall never practise any great virtues. That I may not commit too great sins, it would be well for me soon to die. O! God, grant that I may soon be with Albert, and my father! Does not the certainty of seeing those we love again prove that we shall do so? It is impossible to imagine anything greater, more beautiful, or sweeter than what must really exist somewhere, in a better life than this earthly one, from which I do not look for one single day of happiness again. God help my weakness, and keep me from doubts or murmurs. May He give me a taste for heavenly joys! I hate this world and its deceitful happiness, and yet my soul does not rise towards Heaven. I wish I had Eugénie's feeling about death, both for myself and every one I love. But I could not bear to be alone at last, when I shall have to close his eyes. I cannot reckon on my own courage. Those beautiful—always so beautiful eyes, with their loving, sweet, beaming expression! The brightness of that glance I have not seen for a long time, but its sweetness and beauty still remain, and sometimes with it a look of sorrow which breaks my heart. And yet I must be cheerful before him. . . . Ah!

that reserve between us kills me, and heart-rending as it would be, I often think I would rather speak to him of his death, and endeavor to comfort ourselves by thoughts of faith, hope, and love. The doctor was tolerably well satisfied to-day, but this does not raise my hopes, and ten days must yet elapse before they can all be here.

"O! God, Thou God of love and mercy, if to such anguish as this eternal happiness and re-union succeed, we shall bless Thee for these sufferings, the remembrance of which will but add to the blessedness of everlasting joy! Pray for me more than ever, my dearest Pauline, for indeed I pray very badly for myself. Do you know a very sad thought mingles with my grief? I sometimes think that I did Albert harm by vexing and contradicting him; for the least irritation increased the agony of his chest. Perhaps I brought on this terrible crisis—perhaps he would have recovered if I had been more what I ought to have been. O! my God, is there any happiness to be found?"

"Thursday, March 10th.—I send you this letter, dear Pauline, just as it is. I have seen a new doctor this morning, who does not think the danger is immediate, though he does not hide from me how serious it is. This was, alas! no news to me. The day after to-morrow, Albert will receive the Last Sacraments. He said to me; 'If they knew it at Boury how finely frightened they would be!' May God comfort you all, and make everybody happy some day! Since I have been so miserable, I want more than ever to think that suffering will at last end for everybody.

"ALEX."

ALEXANDRINE'S JOURNAL.

"March 12th.—To-day Albert got up at six o'clock, partly dressed, and then lay down. At eight o'clock his confessor came, and at nine the curé brought him the Viaticum. In the afternoon we got a number of *L'Université Catholique*, which contains Montalembert's *Introduction to the Life of St. Elizabeth*, and to satisfy Albert's impatience, I read it aloud to him. We admired it very much, and even Putbus was struck with its beauty. That same day he called me to his bed-side. I knelt down as I used so often to do by that beloved one. He spoke to me. I cannot remember exactly the words he used about my marrying again after his death; and as I began to weep bitterly, and to assure him I never should do so, he said, in a gentle, melancholy way, '*Oh! you are too young. . . . You will marry again.*' He also added, '*If I die, be a Frenchwoman still. Do not forsake my people. Do not go back to your mother.*'

"Since the moment when I said, '*Now I am a Catholic,*' I never for a single second had the idea that any other religion can be the true one. On the 14th of March I wrote in my journal, '*A moment of inspiration,*' and I marked the day in that way because as I was writing to my mother for the first time since Albert's danger, I made up my mind to tell her the whole truth. I knelt down, therefore, before I began my letter, and asked all my Catholic ancestors in Heaven to help me. I felt delightfully encouraged by a bright sunbeam which just then shone out across the room, and was quite in keeping with the state of my mind. As Albert lay in bed he had no idea of what was to make both him and me so happy."

This is the letter which Alexandrine wrote in that solemn moment to her mother. She was not mistaken when she called it "*a moment of inspiration.*"

ALEXANDRINE TO HER MOTHER.

"Venice, March 13th.

"Thank God he is alive! Dearest Mamma, I can now begin to write to you again. What a wonderful feeling it is, and how you would pity me if you were here! . . . I cannot express what I have gone through, or what I still suffer. It is extraordinary how I can keep up, and in the midst of it be calm. Putbus has no doubt written to you. I always begged him to do so, that you need have no fears about my health. I am not at all ill. But, oh! through what anguish has the mind to pass! For the moment Albert is better. The doctor says it is a *miracle.* I venture to hope that danger is less imminent, but it always more or less exists. What becomes of me is still uncertain, but everything seems to indicate that it will soon be determined by the sorrow hanging over us. . . . It is not for us to question the ways of God, or to murmur at them. There is no real happiness in this world, and I am convinced that nobody is really happy."

"March 14th.

"Every morning calls for gratitude when I can say, 'He is alive. God be praised!' I have suffered so much. When Fernand left us the anguish was terrible, and afterwards, too, when it came to praying that he might live just long enough to see his father again. Oh! how hard it is to accustom oneself to think that love, happiness, youth, and all hope for this world, are at an end; that all one's dreams of earthly joy are vanished for ever! In one of your last letters you say, 'I have now to go through life without you.' You little thought that Providence was about, perhaps, to bring us together again by a terrible sorrow. But now, my own beloved mother, I must open my whole heart to you. I will not conceal from you a single thought, a single wish. I have an irresistible desire to belong to the same church as my poor Albert, and I give you my word of honor that it is only during these last dreadful days that I have felt this wish take complete possession of my mind. But I must also add, that up to this moment it is my love and respect for you which has prevented my seeking instruction upon the Catholic faith, dreading to find out that it was the true one, and of being then obliged to embrace it. For when we find out something to be more evidently true than what we have hitherto believed, it is certain that we are bound in duty to receive it. If people were never to change their faith merely because they happen to be born in a particular religion, neither Jews nor Pagans could ever become Christians. My love and respect for you are in no way diminished, but I now feel myself irresistibly impelled towards a decisive step, and also fully persuaded that you will forgive me, and even feel that in my position you would think and act as I wish to do. You would never, dearest mother, I am sure, refuse to make a dying husband—who may possibly linger a few months, but whose days are numbered—exceedingly happy by receiving Communion for the first and perhaps for the last time together! . . . You would never, I repeat, refuse him this, provided always that conscience did not forbid it; for on no account, not even to gladden the dying hours of my husband, would I act unfaithfully towards God, and it would be acting unfaithfully to embrace a religion without being convinced of its truth, and for the sake of human affection. You need not fear that, for I assure you I shall only act from conviction; but let me examine, learn, and then resolve. You know me well enough, my dearest mother, to be certain that I could not think of becoming a Catholic, if I were in consequence obliged to believe that the souls of my Protestant parents, brothers, and friends, can never be saved. But

I have taken great pains to read and convince myself that Catholics do not hold this belief. They do not believe that those who are in good faith in their creed will be condemned; but they consider their own to be the best religion of all,* and this, I must confess is what I have been, ever since my childhood, inclined to think too. It is the oldest faith; it seems to me the most likely to have handed down the doctrines of the Apostles, and from the Catholic Church we have received the gospels themselves. I can never admit that my change of religion could grieve my father, for where he is all things must appear in a different light than here on earth. He now sees more clearly than any living person, be he Protestant or Catholic, and if in the light of that Heavenly wisdom he perceives the Catholic Church to be the true Church, will he not rejoice to see his daughter received into it on earth? Besides, dearest Mamma, I am embracing no new faith. On the contrary, it is the ancient creed, the creed of our ancestors, to which I return. My father's grandfather was a Catholic, and your family, which is so old, must have had a far greater number of Catholic than Protestant ancestors. These might, indeed, more justly grieve in another world to behold their descendants professing a new and different religion, and not their own ancient faith!

"Ah! my sweet mother! permit me then to be instructed in the Catholic religion; and if your poor child returns to you a widow, you will not mind, will you, if she comes to you a Catholic? You will not banish her from your heart? She will love you and cherish you more than ever. Her religion will never be a source of annoyance to you. That little Chapel which Lapoukhyn so kindly arranged for Albert, will be the sanctuary of my grief, where I shall pray for my beloved one, and all those who are dear to me. O! dearest mother, if the Catholic religion had but that one advantage over ours, of prayers for the dead, I should choose it, and in so many other ways it is so full of consolation. Henceforth I will devote my life to you. If you wish it, we will live and die together at Korsen, for I shall need quiet and repose."

While this great change was taking place in Alexandrine's mind, Fernand had reached Boury (on the 17th of March), and left it again on the evening of the same day with my parents and

* This was understating the truth, but Alexandrine was not a Catholic at that time.

Eugénie. The following letter from Eugénie to myself, gives the account of all that took place from the day when Alexandrine wrote the preceding letter:—

EUGENIE TO PAULINE.

"Venice, March 24th, 1836.

"We got here yesterday morning, but how shall I collect my senses to tell you all about it? My dearest Pauline, I hardly know where I am, or how I feel! There are emotions too strong to be contained either by the heart or brain. They bring about a kind of dulness which looks like indifference, and all the time the poor heart is bursting, and cannot express what it feels. Well, yesterday at two o'clock we arrived at Mestre. What anguish it was, for at that decisive moment all our fears seemed to return! With beating hearts we asked at the post office whether there is a letter for us. None. Then was it a good or bad sign? Without speaking a word, trembling, but trying to hope, we got into the boat, and drew near that sorrowful Venice.

"Pauline, how good God is! We were soon released from our cruel suspense. Half way up the canal, at the place where the passports are given up, it occurred to us to ask if by any chance there was a letter for us: '*Si Signore c'è una lettera.*' ['Yes, sir, there is a letter.'] What worlds one has time to think and feel in one single second! It can never be described. There it was, that dear letter, and in the twinkling of an eye was opened and read! He was better, he was getting better every day. We might even find him out on the balcony. Pauline, my dearest, I write incoherently, just what I felt and thought at the moment, and even describing it renews my agitation. I almost wished to make you share the anguish, in order that you might enter into the joy and surprise that succeeded. Alexandrine insisted in her letter on the extraordinary precautions which were to be observed, for Albert could not bear the least excitement, or even to see us, till he had been gradually prepared for it. After many comings and goings from their lodging to the hotel, and calculations between us, he was told of the arrival of a party of travellers, and then Alex came in and said we were the travellers, and upon that my father went to him, and afterwards each of us in turn. And God blessed it all, so that he was quite composed, and the terrible danger of any shock was got over. O! Pauline, had we not great reason to be grateful? At the end of the evening Papa and Mamma returned to the hotel. I helped Mamma to undress, and then went back to sleep at Alex's house. Then, dear Pauline, I heard the details of that unspeakable grief, and then I thought how God must love our Alex, for He alone could give such strength and sweetness, and mix such immense consolation with such bitter trials. She has spent hours of agony by his side, but always remained calm and tearless, that he might not be troubled. She used sometimes to feel her hand growing cold and her knees trembling, as the thought came into her mind: "*Perhaps he will die now—perhaps this is the moment!*' For two days, having given up hope, she made no prayer but this: '*O! my God, let him not die without Communion!*' and when that prayer had been heard came another: '*O! my God, grant that he may not die without seeing his father and mother once more!*'

"When these two hopes had been realised, she felt resigned. But how strange it is, dear Pauline, to be able to scan everything, speak of everything, and look sorrow so closely in the face. I believe it is the thought of another world which makes it possible; the conviction that there alone will be happiness, and that this life is only a journey, the end of which we long for, because then the weary will be at rest, darkness will vanish, and the great yearning for love and happiness be for ever filled. Alex and I were talking quietly yesterday of the great sorrow which is hanging over us, and supposing it to have happened, we could understand, not indeed the possibility of being in one sense comforted, but that of living so entirely in sight of a future happiness already enjoyed by some one beloved, that earthly sorrow would be lightened. It is not very difficult to detach oneself from this world, and when that is once effected, death is no longer terrible. Poor Alex! I must speak to you now of the important step she is about to take. It is not yet done, but it is, thank God! as good as done. During those terrible days, when Albert was so ill, her great anxiety was that he should not die without the consolation of receiving Communion with her; she has written to her mother. I do not know whether her letter will strike you as it did me. I think there is something about it that shows her mind to be irrevocably made up. She is so Catholic! It is easy to see that she thirsts for our religion. In her letter to-day to M. de Montalembert, there is this strange expression: '*I should be happier as a widow and a Catholic, than as I am now, a Protestant.*' What do you say to that? It seems to me as if nothing could go beyond it. But now having given you a little hope, which I myself cherished, I am going to discourage you again. It is perhaps cruel; and forgive me, but I want you to go through all the alternations we ourselves experience. Albert's terrible illness keeps us continually fluctuating between hope and fear. Sometimes we hope—sometimes we despair. It is thought that he may be able to travel in a fortnight or three weeks. But, dearest Pauline, what a journey it will be! For it is easy to perceive, from the doctor's anxiety for it to be over, how much he dreads the possibility of a fresh attack on the way, and he does not conceal from us that such an attack would be fatal. He speaks without the least reserve. Yesterday he said to my father: 'Sir, I have nothing more to say; I have seen one miracle, and God may work a second. It is a miracle that your son is still living, and another miracle may still cure him. Humanly speaking, I can give no opinion, but God can do all things.'

"Pauline, this seems so sad! So sad that it would make one giddy and sick, if one looked upon it from an earthly point of view. I can only bear it by thinking continually of God, and of that life where at last there will be rest. Alexandrine and I were talking just now of this to one another. It is this only which prevents her from going out of her mind, and will save her from it, if she is to lose him.

"Good-bye, my beloved Pauline. When shall I have a letter from you, and when shall we get back again? Oh, that we had wings and could fly with him to France. Whenever we start you must pray, and get everybody to pray for us. God's will be done in all things!"

FROM ALEXANDRINE'S JOURNAL.

"Long and cruel suspense is often followed by great joys. Through the God of goodness, of love, I have had the happiness of seeing Albert in the arms of his parents once more. I knelt down in silence behind them to thank God for this great mercy. Eugénie spent the night in my room. Oh, what sweet hours we spent in talking and weeping together! She brought me a rosary and a letter from Montal, which at first she did not like to give me, because he had written it under the impression that Albert was at the worst. I guessed, however, that he had not sent me the rosary without writing, and she saw that it was useless to hide anything from me. So she gave me the letter, and this is it:—

(COUNT DE MONTALEMBERT TO ALEXANDRINE.)

"'MY DEAR UNHAPPY FRIEND—I have no idea what state these few lines will find you in, and which I send by your mother-in-law; but I know too well that you are suffering from the most cruel anxiety, if not from the most heartrending grief. I know also that you have often called me your brother, and have been a true sister to me, and this gives me a right to approach you at this terrible moment, and to unite my sufferings with yours. Not having heard from you at all since the 3rd of December, I knew nothing of our dearest Albert's relapse, of your fresh anxiety, and the danger he was in, and had remained under the favorable impression produced by your letters from Venice. And now I suddenly hear of that dreadful attack and its alarming results. And, alas! in what state are you now, whilst I write? Is he still with you? and are you still in possession of that noble energy and admirable courage which I have observed in your character? This mournful uncertainty—this terrible doubt paralyses me; I have not courage to write; still less to speak to you of that ray of hope which I cherish in spite of the most hopeless evidence. I am afraid of each of my words sounding like an involuntary mockery, a cruel contradiction of what you may be feeling at this moment. I know them well, those horrible fluctuations, those sudden transitions from trust to despair, those instinctive clingings to hope, that belief that the Divine mercy will intervene, which nothing can root out of our hearts, till the moment when it has no longer any place! I, too, have watched for six months by the side of a beloved one wrestling as it were with death, that she might remain with me—my poor sister, whose lot was so sad. I have therefore recollections which help me to enter into all your sufferings, besides that powerful sympathy which affection produces. Even at this sad moment I cannot refrain from saying what comfort it gave me to hear that you had made up your mind to complete your union with Albert, by that only tie which was still wanting to make it perfect. My dear sister—for so you are indeed become by this important act, inspired by Divine grace—what a consolation there is in this, not only for you but also for him, as it has been doubtless through his means that you have become a child of the Eternal Truth, and that your soul will be the rich prize he can present to his merciful Judge.

" 'You, too, dear Alexandrine, will now quench your thirst for consolation at that inexhaustible source; you will be nourished with the Bread of the strong, and God will reward you for the sacrifice you have had to make, a hundredfold in this world, and for ever in the next. He will show you the immense, the unspeakable difference between suffering as a Catholic, with all the sweet and abundant riches of the Church imparted to you, and suffering with no other support than the cold and barren faith poor Protestants profess.

" 'Farewell. I have not courage to go on. I dare not speak of Albert. You will understand this terrible silence. Pray accept this poor little rosary. May it often suggest to you the thought of abandoning yourself wholly to the tender compassion of the Mother of sorrows, the Comforter of the afflicted, the Health of the sick. It is a humble token of sympathy and affection. When you feel able to do so, write a line to one who is not afraid to call himself your brother, and who will ever be so by the tie of a common faith, as well as by the most sincere attachment.—M. March 15th, 1836.'

(ALEXANDRINE'S ANSWER TO COUNT DE MONTALEMBERT.)

"Venice, March 24th.

"MY DEAR FRIEND—I hardly know how to begin this letter. My thoughts of late have been so confused! I must, however, begin by thanking God. His goodness to me has been, as it always is, *infinite*. You have heard everything; all that has been dreadful to us, and all that has been comforting. It would be ungrateful in me not to say that there have been moments of consolation, but always mingled with cruel fears, and daily wearisome apprehensions. But, however, Albert gets up now; he walks about, and is able to sit and enjoy the fresh air on the balcony. He can talk a good while without coughing, and since yesterday has had the happiness he so ardently desired of seeing his parents and Eugénie once more. For many days my only prayer was that he might not die without

Communion, and that petition was heard. Then I implored that he might live to see his father once more, and this too was granted. I obtained these favors and still went on asking for others, for I was sure God in His mercy would pardon my importunity. Eugénie gave me your little rosary last night. It touched me more deeply than I can say. As a token of sympathy and affection, it did not surprise me, but the sort of regard it implied astonished me very much. Afterwards I understood it better, for having pressed Eugénie to tell me all you had said, I found out that there was also a letter for me, but that you had told her it would be cruel to let me have it, if the worst grief had not befallen us. You may suppose that I insisted on her giving it to me, and sorry I should indeed have been not to have possessed it! Alas! dear friend, you may judge of what I have been obliged to hear and say, and of the words I have become forcibly accustomed to, when I tell you that your letter did not startle me, and that the friendship and sympathy it expresses, did me good. May God reward you for your compassionate feelings! I am almost glad, however, that you still have misgivings as to my courage, and that your *cruel* zeal makes you say: 'If happily as regards Albert, but *unhappily* for her, he got better, she would draw back.' Dear friend, ten days after he was in such imminent danger, I wrote my mother a letter which you must let me copy for you. German is as familiar to you as to me, and therefore I send it just as it is. I must beg you beforehand to remember that mine is the best of mothers, and that it will certainly be better if I can do my duty towards God without breaking her heart. The letter is so long that I am afraid it will tire you to read it; but it was written with a good purpose, and before I began I begged all my Catholic ancestors who are in Heaven to pray for me.

"Dear friend, I long to be a Catholic. You think me inclined to be weak, indifferent, and cold, yet I believe I have felt that *I should probably be happier as a widow and a Catholic, than as I am and a Protestant, or neither the one nor the other.* . . . Oh, my God!* Yes, my dear friend, unless God strikes me dead I will receive Communion with Albert, whether he is to live or die. This is my firm resolution, and may God enable me to fulfil it!

* When, long after, she read over this letter, Alexandrine wrote on the margin:—"How wonderful is the attraction of Divine truth, since one single ray of it falling on my soul was enough to make me prefer it to my husband, before even I had embraced it."

Either I believe in nothing or I believe in the Holy Eucharist as much as in the Blessed Trinity. Then I see in my Protestant New Testament that St. Paul's garments and handkerchiefs had power to heal the sick, and why should God altogether discontinue such manifestations of His grace? My faith is not very keen, but I should be afraid of uttering a blasphemy if I said it was impossible that a particle of the bones of a Saint should, through God's mercy, heal the sick. Oh! how many things I shall have to say to you! Pray that my beloved one, with whose life God has linked my own, may live, die, and live again in Heaven with me . . . . and do not you judge any body, my dear, good, sweet brother, you whose heart is made to love. Do not judge my mother, with whose pious motto you were so pleased. '*Wie, was, und wann Gott will.*'* You are quite right: from a *loving weakness* for her I delayed my conversion, and from another loving weakness I hasten it now. But I trust God will forgive it all."

"March 25th, Feast of the Annunciation.

"My dear friend, I prayed very much for you at Mass. I took your rosary with me. You will some day teach me to say it, and I shall ask you too, for another present, for I want my first Catholic Prayer-book to be your gift. You can choose it at leisure, for it will be some time yet before I really want it. If it is possible, let it be in German, the language that is so full of feeling and power, which we are both so fond of; the language of my childhood and my parents, which will seem to form a link between them and my new religion. I hope we shall meet soon. Pray for me every day. Albert continues well, all things considered. Thank God." ALEX."

The same day, March 25th, in her journal:—"Eugénie dined with me, and afterwards we went to Benediction at St. Moses's Church, where we heard Mass in the morning. One evening during Benediction, I had one of those sudden impressions of faith, those beams of light which made me realize the existence of God, religion, the Blessed Virgin, and the Saints, with the same certainty as we have when we look upon external and material objects; I say the same certainty, because in our gross manner of considering things, we are always tempted to think

* How, what, and when God wills.

that there is nothing so certain as what we see and what we touch. This pleased me very much, and I told Eugénie of it as we walked home through the narrow alley."

FROM A LETTER OF ALEXANDRINE'S TO PAULINE.

"March 26th.

"You are quite right. We must be like Eugénie, and try to love death. It is the only love which cannot deceive us. As regards myself, Pauline, I ought never to complain of anything, for after my father's death, I asked with all the fervor and earnestness in my power, not to have a single happy moment on earth, if only God would make him eternally happy, and yet how many happy hours I have known since then! My daily prayer used to be: '*My God, let me suffer in his stead!*' During the last dreadful months I changed it to, '*Accept what I have suffered, and do suffer, but spare my father suffering.*' My weakness shrank from asking for more sorrow."

EUGENIE TO PAULINE.

"Venice, April 2nd, 1836.

"MY DARLING PAULINE!—How sad it is for you, but thank God you know how to pray. There is after all no sorrow without comfort, for we can always pray, and in prayer there is endless solace. I have felt this so deeply during this last, truly *Holy Week.* Its *holiness* had never struck me so much before. If the weather improves, we shall start on Thursday, and begin our long, tedious, and anxious journey. I shall write to you continually on the road, for our letters will precede us up to the last moment. My beloved Pauline, how I bless God that He permits me to retain that same strong, religious feeling with which I started. I have had moments of thorough happiness, in which I felt one absorbing and intense love of God. I think I am not deceived. It was love, joyful, earnest love, filling the heart so fully, so enviably, and at the same time a general charity for all mankind. It seemed to me as if there were not a single being on earth against whom I had the least animosity, or for whom, moreover, I would not have been willing to pray, and even to suffer. It was a Divine feeling, for it came from God, and so was, of course, full of peace."

ALEXANDRINE'S JOURNAL.

Easter Monday, April 4th.—Fernand brought me two little manuscripts which he had stolen from Eugénie. Albert was asleep, and as I was alone till late that evening, I read them from beginning to end.* What feelings rose up in my poor untamed heart as I devoured those pages in Albert's silent room! I tore a page out of an account book, and began to write upon it to Eugénie:

"'Twelve o'clock.—EUGENIE, MY DEAREST SISTER—I owe it to you, that twice while reading your written thoughts, I knelt down and prayed most fervently. My good angel, I feel such faith in you, that if you tell me you hope, I shall not despair. It is thought praiseworthy in me because I am careful of Albert, and give him his medicines at the proper times, and because I did not lose my head when he was in danger. But *you—you* offer yourself up for him,† and God knows with what ardor and singleness of heart, while you think nothing of it yourself, and no one praises you! Oh, my angelic sister, I implore you to plead for us. Ah! where will you be in a few years' time? Happy? Yes, happy in a way which can never know any change. So be it. Continue to give your heart to God as you have hitherto done, but stay with us awhile, to make us happy and good also. You help me to realize Heaven, and if any one could teach me to despise this life it would be you. I really believe that to know you would have been enough to make me embrace the Catholic religion. Your modesty must not take offence at this. It is impossible that it should not give you pleasure to hear it, and God does not condemn that pleasure. Reflect a little, and you will see that you ought to rejoice at it. Do not be afraid that the admiration I feel for you will ever blind me. We shall live together a great deal, I hope, and rely upon it I will watch your conduct very narrowly. It is not presumption which makes me engage to perform this task. Those who have a beam in their own eye see very clearly the mote in another's eyes, and I shall look very carefully to see that nothing tarnishes the purity of God's beautiful little pearl. Oh! what happiness undreamt of by the world it is to have a sister like you, and to love her as I do.'

* The pages from Eugénie's journal here alluded to will be found in the appendix. The deep impression they made on Alexandrine will be easily understood by those who read them.

† See Appendix.

. . . In the morning I sent this note to Eugénie, and she came to me quite ashamed and blushing. . . . But it was only much later that I read the whole of her manuscripts."

EUGENIE TO PAULINE.*

"Venice, April 9th.

"We are still here, and have spent the morning in such uncertainty! When we got up it was fine, and we were to go. Albert had had a good night. He was calm, and glad to be moving. Then it began to rain. The doctor advised us to put off the journey, and this excited Albert so much, that we did not know what to do. Alex and I did nothing but wander about like restless spirits. On the whole, we both wished to start; she, because she has a superstitious idea that it is unlucky to delay anything which has been settled, and I because of the words a good Priest had said to me at Church that morning, '*Andate, andate! non importa la piove; fidatevi a Dio; partite. Iddio vi benedica, fidatevi, partite!*'† Well, I regretted that we did not go, but what could I say? Who could have ventured to incur the responsibility of giving an opinion on the subject? My father has just decided to stay. Alex and I are alone with Albert, who repeats over and over again, 'I had always a foreboding that I should never leave Venice.' You may imagine how this depresses us; and you will feel for a little vexation we have just had. Whilst Albert was speaking to us in that way, and getting more and more out of spirits, I opened my desk, and found my poor cornelian ring, which was not at all a brittle one, with the stone broken, and the anchor split in two! (It was a red cornelian, with an anchor cut upon it). This gave Alex and me a kind of shock. Our poor shattered hope! Tears came into our eyes. I cannot guess when and how it can have happened, but we are quite out of sorts. *Pazienza!* to-morrow will come, please God, and happier hours with it. Our forebodings and our *broken hope* will prove fallacious omens.

"Five o'clock.

"Dearest, as we complained this morning, we must hasten to tell you that things are looking better. Albert slept very well after his fit of despondency. He seems well now, and in good

* We had left Paris after hearing of their safe arrival at Venice, and I received this letter in England.

† "Go—go—never mind the rain. Trust in God—go. God bless you. Have confidence, and go."

spirits, and he declares that the broken ring, which he, too, had thought an ominous token, means the anchor which fastens us to Venice, and that it breaks to let us go free!"

"Sunday, April 10th.

"Nothing so lucky as forebodings, omens, and broken anchors! The weather is beautiful. We are off. Albert is better, and very happy. Good-bye, dear little sister. May God be with us. Pray for us all."*

EUGENIE TO PAULINE.

"Padua.

"We are here. Can it be really true? We are actually here with Albert, and bringing him home."

"April 10th, 1836.

"My darling, we are at Padua! If I had written immediately my letter would have gone to-day, but it was right before we thought of you, to think of God, and to thank Him, for we have started, and we are here, and Albert is not very tired; indeed, scarcely tired at all. As soon as we had seen him comfortably in bed, we went to the Cathedral. Oh, it was just what we wanted, to kneel there and unburthen our hearts by repeating a thousand times: 'My God, I thank Thee! my God, I bless Thee!' That beautiful Church was lighted up, filled with people, and the organ playing. We had Benediction, and it was, indeed, a good token, this holy ending of a day in which we had been so mercifully protected.

"Do you really believe it, Pauline? Do you think we shall get home? Well, let us hope and trust in God. Come what may, God can never ordain anything but what is good. I am so pleased to think that we shall be able to hear Mass every day before we start. How Heavenly sweet is the thought of God; and when it rules the soul, how easy everything becomes; nothing is then really sad. Mass every morning; every evening a blessed moment in Church, in which to thank God, if the day has been a good one, or to implore His aid if it has been trying. This journey is a real pilgrimage of prayer. Dear Pauline, we shall see you again, I *hope*, I *hope*. You who, like ourselves, have a kind of faith in opening upon passages of books by chance, should see what we read in our volume of texts as we were leav-

*That broken anchor sealed two months later the letter which told me that all our hopes for Albert were at an end. Six years afterwards it also sealed the one which announced to me my father's death; and by a really singular coincidence, the saddest letter I ever received, the one which was sent to me from Palermo after Eugénie's own death, was stamped with the same seal.

ing Venice: '*Before they cry out to me, I will hear them; and whilst they are yet speaking, I have heard them.*' (Isaiah.) And then, '*Let us draw near to Him with a sincere heart, with a full and perfect confidence.*' (Hebrews xi.) What do you say to that? Good night, dearest."

EUGENIE TO PAULINE.

"Verona, April 13th, 1836.

"DEAR LOVE—It is wonderful how well Albert is at present. We are quite astonished, and so grateful to our good and merciful God. Oh, if only this improvement might last! He is so well and cheerful, and enjoys feeling himself so much better than he had done for a long time. Pauline, surely God protects and hears us . . . but come what may, we must always be grateful. Let us always pray, always love, even if this unexpected improvement is only a reprieve and comfort under the terrible sorrow which is hanging over us. Amidst such trying circumstances, if God chooses to send us this grief, let us not murmur at His will, and always gratefully call to mind the happiness of these present hours.

ALEXANDRINE TO COUNT DE MONTALEMBERT.

"Genoa, April 22nd, 1836.

"DEAR FRIEND—Through the mercy of God we are so far safe on our journey . . . . . but I dare not look beyond the present moment, and I dread to think even of the next day. I pass from one anguish to another, and when a little ray of hope comes athwart me, I feel comparatively happy. Nothing can be more fatiguing than this existence, and yet it does not affect my health. It is all so strange. Everything seems reversed. I feel at times a singular insensibility, and at others such wonderful impressions. The coloring of my mind seems reflected in all I see in this sad life. What are God's intentions for me? I am often afraid that he punishes me for refusing to give Him my whole heart, for clinging as I do to earthly joy. Alas! it is on these I had fixed my desires, and now I see there is nothing but a semblance of happiness here below. I ought to seek it elsewhere, but I cannot lift up my soul as I would . . . . I do not understand the bliss of Heaven, and yet I see that others have a foretaste of it which detaches them quite from the world. But, dear friend, notwithstanding this thick mist which encompasses my soul, I have the deepest reverence for Heavenly things, and I hope this reverence will gradually lead me to love them. I admired so much in your *Introduction* the picture you draw of the ties which unite the Saints in Heaven with men on earth. I have not, or at least I have lost the pride of *private judgment;* for I have often thought that it would be enough to think that Albert and his sisters and you are Catholics, to make me one. My feeble intellect may therefore very well accept what the Saints have believed, who no doubt are a little better still than you! Thank you for your dear letter, which I found here, and the counsel and advice it contains. I should have so many things to say to you, but I am overcome with drowsiness. . . I showed Albert your rosary; of course not your letter; but he does not wonder at your silence. He is too affectionate, too full of trust to do so. He looks up to you as much as ever . . . Oh! shall I soon be able to talk to you? Do not be afraid that I shall keep from you any of my doubts and religious difficulties. You will always know, if you wish it, everything I think. The best part of my character is perhaps its sincerity and openness. Pray every day for me, for I pray badly myself; yet I feel to love God. Eugénie is very grateful for your message. I am delighted that you were so struck with her goodness. I do not think there is anywhere on earth another woman so like an angel.

"Dear Montal, will God allow us to get to Paris? I will write to you again on the road. May we *all, all, all* meet again!"

EUGENIE TO PAULINE.

"Paris. We are here! May 13th.

"MY PAULINE—Here we are, and thank God! But what an excitement it has been, for only think of our being here since the day before yesterday, and of my not having had a moment to write to you! I am so excited, so bewildered, and only wish you here. I have so many things to say, and wish you could see and judge for yourself. Now I must try and collect my thoughts. On Wednesday at six o'clock in the evening we arrived at Villejuif, where we found Madame de Lagrange, Charles, and Emma. This, to begin with, was exciting for Albert. Then Montal came, and in the evening a number of people . . . Hahnemann, the discoverer of homœopathy, came yesterday at five o'clock.

He is a kind, excellent little old man. He was so much touched at the sight of Alexandrine, that he took her by the hand when he went away, and said :—'During the sixty years I have been a physician, I have never seen a woman so fond of her husband.' He wishes us to leave this house where the rooms are too small. We are going to look out for some apartments near the Luxembourg."

ALEXANDRINE'S JOURNAL.

"May 19th.

"Yesterday, while I was dining with Eugénie, she told me that the idea of death made her heart beat with joy. It astonished me, but these things strengthen my faith."

"May 22nd, Whit Sunday.

"My God, Thou hast sought in so many ways to detach me from this world, and still I cling to it. Oh! why cannot I love and long for Heaven? Since yesterday (the 21st) we have been settled in the Rue de Madame, No. 13. I shall be a Catholic before Corpus Christi! The Abbé Gerbet* will be my confessor, but the Abbé Martin de Noirlieu, the first Catholic priest I ever made acquaintance with, will receive me into the Church. Our apartment is pretty and spacious, and our windows look on the fine trees of the Luxembourg. As I was coming back from Mass on Sunday I saw Albert at the window smiling at me, and when I came into his room, I saw a charming little table and a carved chair. His father, who was there, told me this was a present from Albert to me, and that he had wished them both to be covered with blue cloth, because he knew it was my favorite color.

"This afternoon I went with Eugénie to the service for the month of May at St. Etienne du Mont. Before going out we wished Albert good-bye, and we saw that he was writing in the green velvet book I had embroidered for him at Venice. Before we went to bed, Eugenie and I, who were together in the drawing-room, took up the book and looked into it. I do not know what I felt when I read as follows :—'My God, formerly I was wont to make to Thee this prayer: "Let her be mine, O! my

* She had never seen him there. But one day at Venice, she had read an article by him in the "*Université Catholique*," and was so impressed with it, that she resolved if ever she became a Catholic to choose him for her confessor. The Abbé Gerbet was not at Paris when she arrived, but she nevertheless persisted in the resolution formed before she heard him, and so great was the consolation she derived from his ministry, that it would seem as if Alexandrine's choice had been directed by a special Providence.

God, grant me that happiness, if but for one single day!" Thou didst grant it, O! Lord, and why should I now complain to Thee? My joy has been short but intense, and now my other prayer is about to be fulfilled. Thy divine goodness has granted also that my angel wife should be received into Thy Church, and I can look forward with hope and trust to our meeting before long, where we shall both be lost in the immensity of Thy Divine love.'* Albert had offered his life to obtain his wife's conversion. Oh, with what deep emotion I read these lines, containing such deep love of God, such great tenderness to me, and so calm an acceptance of death; when it still seemed to me so horrible that he should have to look it in the face! and afterwards, how often I kissed those words '*before long*.'"

EUGENIE TO PAULINE.

"Paris, May 28th.

"I begin my letter this evening, and shall finish it to-morrow. Pauline, to-morrow Alexandrine will be a Catholic, and you, alas! will not be with us! Shall we ever quite get over this? If, at least, you could come in time for Thursday, of which I have still some hopes, and write this letter reckoning a little on your not receiving it. On Thursday she will make her First Communion. These are great joys, dearest, in the midst of our sorrow. How can we murmur with such real reasons for thanksgiving? I shall not write any more now, for I look forward to seeing you before you get the letter. But in case you receive it, good-bye. I love you more, even more, than in the happiest days of our loving childhood. May God bless our Alexandrine to-morrow!"

ALEXANDRINE'S JOURNAL.

"May 29th, Trinity Sunday.

"This morning I went early to Mass, came home and dressed. I put on a white gown and a broad blue ribbon across my chest, the colors of the Blessed Virgin, which have always been my own favorites. This is her special month, too, and I owe this grace to her intercession, which the good Franciscan at Pisa told me to ask, and to Albert who offered himself up as a sacrifice for me, *who offered everything to God, even the joy of sensible devotion*,

* These were the last words Albert ever wrote. The Abbé Gerbet described them later as the most sublime bequest of tender love and heroic resignation which the spirit of Christianity ever enabled a husband to make.

for my conversion, only asking always to love good things. The Abbé Martin de Noirlieu said Mass at an altar prepared in Albert's room. When Mass was over he beckoned to me to come and kneel down before him, and told me to make the sign of the Cross, and then I read the following profession of faith:—

"'In the name of the Father, of the Son, and of the Holy Ghost:

"'I, with a firm faith, believe and profess all and every one of those things which are contained in that Creed which the Holy Roman Church maketh use of, viz.: I believe in one God, the Father Almighty, Creator of Heaven and earth, and of all things, visible and invisible; and in one Lord Jesus Christ, the only begotten Son of God; born of the Father before all ages; God of God; Light of Light; true God of true God; begotten not made; consubstantial to the Father, by Whom all things were made. Who, for us men, and for our salvation, came down from Heaven, and was incarnate by the Holy Ghost of the Virgin Mary, and was made Man. Was crucified also for us under Pontius Pilate; He suffered and was buried; and the third day He rose again according to the Scriptures; He ascended into Heaven; sits at the right Hand of the Father, and is to come again with glory to judge the living and the dead; of Whose kingdom there shall be no end. And in the Holy Ghost, the Lord and Life-giver, Who proceeds from the Father and the Son, Who, together with the Father and the Son, is adored and glorified, Who spoke by the prophets. And I believe one holy, Catholic, and apostolic Church; I confess one baptism for the remission of sins; and I look for the resurrection of the dead, and the life of the world to come. Amen.

"'I most steadfastly admit and embrace apostolical and ecclesiastical tradition, and all other observances and constitutions of the same Church.

"'I also admit the holy Scriptures according to that sense which our holy mother, the Church, has held, and does hold; to whom it belongs to judge of the true sense and interpretation of the Scriptures; neither will I ever take and interpret them otherwise than according to the unanimous consent of the Fathers.

"'I also profess that there are truly and properly seven Sacraments of the new law, instituted by Jesus Christ our Lord, and necessary for the salvation of mankind, though not all for every one: to wit, baptism, confirmation, holy Eucharist, penance, extreme unction, orders, and matrimony; and that they confer grace; and that of these, baptism, confirmation, and order, cannot be reiterated without sacrilege. I also receive and admit the received and approved ceremonies of the Catholic Church, used in the solemn administration of all the aforesaid sacraments.

"'I embrace and receive all and every one of the things which have been defined and declared in the holy Council of Trent, concerning original sin and justification.

"'I profess, likewise, that in the Mass there is offered to God a true, proper, and propitiatory sacrifice for the living and the dead. And that in the most holy Sacrament of the Eucharist there is truly, really, and substantially, the Body and Blood, together with the Soul and Divinity of our Lord Jesus Christ; and that there is made a conversion of the whole substance of the bread into the Body, and of the whole substance of the wine into the Blood; which conversion the Catholic Church calls Transubstantiation. I also confess that under either kind alone Christ is received whole and entire, and a true Sacrament.

"'I constantly hold that there is a purgatory, and that the souls therein detained are helped by the suffrages of the faithful.

"'Likewise that the Saints reigning together with Christ, are to be honored and invocated, and that they offer prayers to God for us, and that their relics are to be had in veneration.

"'I most firmly assert that the images of Christ, of the Mother of God, ever Virgin, and also of the other Saints, ought to be had and retained, and that due honor and veneration is to be given to them.

"'I also affirm that the power of indulgences was left by Christ in the Church, and that the use of them is most wholesome to Christian people.

"'I acknowledge the holy, Catholic, apostolic Roman Church for the mother and mistress of all Churches; and I promise true obedience to the Bishop of Rome, successor to St. Peter, Prince of the Apostles, and Vicar of Jesus Christ.

"'I likewise undoubtedly receive and profess all other things delivered, defined, and declared by the sacred canons and general councils, and particularly by the holy Council of Trent. And I condemn, reject, and anathematise all things contrary thereto, and all heresies which the Church has condemned, rejected and anathematised.

"'I do at this present freely profess and sincerely hold this true Catholic faith, without which no one can be saved; and I promise most constantly to retain and confess the same entire and unviolated, with God's assistance, to the end of my life.

(*Signed*)

"'Paris, May 29th, 1836, Feast of the Holy Trinity.

"'Martin de Noirlieu.
"'Alexandrine d'Alopeus de la Ferronnays.

"'In the presence of:—

"'Albert de la Ferronnays.
"'Comte de la Ferronnays.
"'Montsoreau, Comtesse de la Ferronnays.
"'Eugénie de la Ferronnays.
"'Fernand de la Ferronnays.'

"Montalembert was present, but I forgot to make him sign.

"When all was over I kissed Albert and all our other dear ones. The Abbé Martin came up to me and said: 'Madam, you have now brethren in every part of the world.' I felt as if a new existence had begun for me; and I was so happy, so happy! I was quite surprised at it myself, and was almost afraid to have been in too high spirits the rest of the day with my poor Albert. Eugénie wrote the following sentences that evening in her book, and I read them:—'Oh! my Lord, what can we say? or how can we thank Thee, for the mercies of this day? Thy little lamb has been gathered into the fold. She is now a Catholic! Fill her gentle soul with joy, my God; bless and comfort her for these long years of banishment from Thee; let this return to her true home be full of happiness. Pour down Thy gifts upon her, and if out of Thy great love for her soul Thou sendest her trials, give her that immense love for Thee alone which will make her bear and love all things Thy Almighty Hand may inflict. Ye blessed Angels, watch over her, that her peace may be great, and her soul untroubled.' I have since heard that in that night, of the 29th, my mother dreamed that she saw me sitting in a white garment, looking like a little child again, with a crown of flowers on my head like rays; and that all this apparel displeased her. But I continually offered her some of the large flowers with which I was crowned, and she refused them. Ah! how long will she refuse?

"May 30th.—Montal came and brought the Abbé Gerbet

with him. Albert was in the drawing-room when they arrived, and many years afterwards the Abbé Gerbet told me that he could never forget the gleam of intense joy in Albert's eyes, when he saw him who was to administer God's grace to his own Alex. He was the more struck with that expression because Albert's glorious eyes were the only feature lit up with life in his altered face.

"May 31st.—I went with Eugénie on foot to the Chapel of St. Stanislaus' College. When I got there and saw the Abbé Gerbet in the confessional, I felt frightened, and it was some time before I could summon up courage to approach it. Eugénie had told me how to calm myself by prayer.

"June 1st.—O! my good, good God, I dare to think Thy Hand has guided me, notwithstanding my unworthiness! I now discern so many threads woven together and in one strand, so many prayers heard and granted. Sweetly and gently hast Thou guided my footsteps, even when lightning-strokes seem to have levelled my way. Heavenly Father, give me faith, then, if Thou wilt, take from me earthly joy. Or rather, give me faith, and then I shall find unfailing joys both here and in Heaven. Faith, which I have so intensely longed for, I now possess, and shall possess it more and more, for I have prayed for it, and he that asketh receiveth. I do trust my faith will be bright and strong next Sunday. I am so glad to be a Catholic; so glad, that it seems to me almost miraculous, and persuades me more and more of the truth of this dear religion. How I thank God, and how I thank all who have helped me. I like confession so much, though it causes me great pain. My sweet Jesus, grant me a new heart, but let me keep all my deep affections. Let all I love be saved, and let all whom I and Albert love be happy for ever!

"*I have believed.* I believed so wholly to-day. And I felt so profoundly happy in spite of my deep humiliation and of the suffering which awaits me on Saturday, in confessing the rest of my sins. What a Priest has my Heavenly Father sent me! He surpasses everything I had ever hoped to find in a confessor. My God! even in Thee let me not forget my mother, my dear brothers, my departed father, and my duties to my husband. Let me ever remain by the side of that beloved one whom Thou Thyself didst give me to be my husband; let me follow him in the midst of the shadows of death, even as in the strength of life, and beside his sick bed to the gates of the grave. Let me ever be close beside him, and let a well-known and beloved face be before his eyes, a familiar cheering sound in his ears, and give him to the last a friend and a familiar companion. Let this be my only desire. Amen. Sweet Virgin Mary, dear Saints of God, pray for me!

"During the following night, June 1st, I was in Eugénie's room at one o'clock in the morning, and I thought Albert was asleep. Suddenly we heard somebody softly playing chords on the pianoforte, which affected us painfully. I felt sure it was Albert, and that he was playing for the last time. It was he. I sat down beside him, but he seemed absorbed in a sad but soothing reverie. His faithful nurse, the sister of Bon Secours, was there with him. Montalembert was much delighted with Albert's love of music during his illness. He told me that sick persons generally take a dislike to it. But this was in keeping with Albert's gentle and loving character. He always loved it; but just at last it wearied him too much, unless the piano was played very softly. On the following night, between one and two, Albert got up and spent many hours in his armchair; I gave him my confession to read, and his rectitude and clear-headedness were of great assistance to me in examining my conscience. But in the morning he went to bed again, and suffered terribly. I could not fail to see that he was getting worse. Despair then gave me courage, and I desired Eugénie to go to Hahnemann and ask him to let me know the truth. Whilst she was away, I took a prayer-book which my mother-in-law had given me, and wrote in it the following passages:—'But the things that were gain to me, the same I have counted loss for Christ: furthermore I count all things to be but loss for the excellent knowledge of Jesus Christ my Lord; for Whom I have suffered the loss of all things, and count them but as dung, that I may gain Christ.' (Philippians iii. 7, 8.) 'I have learnt, in whatever state I am, to be content therewith.' 'I can do all things in Him who strengtheneth me.' (Philippians iv.) Eugénie came back, and quietly answered my pressing questions, but was alarmed by the shock I felt at what she told me. Till then I was not aware that I had still so much hope to lose. When she added that Hahnemann said I was running a great risk by sleeping in Albert's room, I smiled, and felt strangely glad."*

EUGENIE TO PAULINE.

"Paris, June 3rd, 1836.

"God showers down His graces on Alexandrine—He treats her like a favorite child. Since she has been a Catholic, her calmness, peace, and fortitude are wonderful. In the midst of her terrible grief she has a peace of the soul, which God only can give. She, dear child, has been twice to confession, and to-morrow she will receive absolution. You can picture to yourself what a general confession must be to her with her merciless memory, which tracks out minutely the occurrences of years and years with the most scrupulous accuracy. I went twice with her to the Chapel of St. Stanislaus College. She stayed so long that I fell fast asleep, which made us laugh, for we laugh sometimes in spite of everything and ourselves. But we feel there is no harm in it, for that kind of gaiety is not like the world's. It springs from the peace of prayer. The Abbé Gerbet thinks so too. Ah! Pauline, what an immense grace it is that Alex should have met with him just now. She says so herself, and constantly declares that he is everything she could wish. His exceeding gentleness, and the boundless charity which belongs to his character are perceptible in his words, and very looks, as well as in his writings. Alexandrine is to make her First Communion on Sunday, if Albert can go there; it will be in the chapel of the Infant Jesus, where you received absolution before your First Communion. Oh, do come if you can, beloved Pauline! Come and see her in the strength of her faith, hope, and love. She is very calm. She speaks of their approaching separation as she would if Albert was only going to leave her for a long journey. Let us pray and love more and more. I will write to you every day, if only a line. Good-bye, dear angel. May God be in our hearts, and fashion them according to His will!"

"June 3rd, 12 o'clock at night.

"DEAR LOVE—My letter went this morning, and to-night I am

*At that time Alexandrine was possessed by the absurd idea that she had not loved Albert with sufficient tenderness and devotion. And it was a sort of relief to her when she could hit upon some tangible proofs, as it were, of the intensity of her affection. This was the reason of that strange gladness she speaks of at perceiving how indifferent she was to her own danger. It seems wonderful that she could ever have such doubts, but the absurd torments which imagination conjures up in times of sorrow are well known to those who have really loved and suffered.

beginning again. The Archbishop has given leave for Mass to be said at twelve o'clock at night, in Albert's room, so that he may go to Communion fasting; otherwise, in order to communicate at the same Mass as Alexandrine, he would have had to receive as *Viaticum*, as he could not remain without food till morning, and this would have been too sad for them. But can you picture to yourself anything sweeter, more solemn, and more sad, than this Communion in his room at midnight, with the little Altar dressed with lights and flowers? Alexandrine will then make her First Communion, and Albert—perhaps his last!"

"June 4th.—We are expecting the Abbé Gerbet. Alexandrine will confess, and receive absolution. The Abbé Dupanloup* is coming to hear Albert's confession, and we are all going to Church for that intention. Then this evening, my father and mother, Albert, Alexandrine, Olga, and I, shall all communicate together. Ah! dearest Pauline, we shall miss you too much! Oh, if I could make certain of never being separated from Alexandrine! People are so foolish, they will say that it was not a sufficient object for life. I should be told that I must have something more definite to live for. Is it not, then, a sufficient object to devote one's self, one's time, one's care, and one's whole life, to a friend, to a beloved sister? It is done every day for a husband, for whom in very many cases much less love is felt."

ALEXANDRINE'S JOURNAL.

"June 4th (same day).—Before going to confession to the Abbé Gerbet, I had been reading to Albert, and in one of the reflections added to each chapter of the '*Imitation of Christ*,' I found these words: '*Love is stronger than Death*.' Those words raised my courage. '*Love is stronger than Death*'—I thank Thee, my God, for that word! It is a great gift, and how can I be wanting in faith, when Thou hast answered my prayer, by showing me the strength of my love? Those dreadful misgivings were mere temptations, and now filled with a sweet and triumphant joy, I am ready to go down with him into the valley of death, which till now I have ever feared. O! my God, let me never be divided from him! Never! never! He has need of me, and I can bear to leave everything on earth.

"My gentle husband, who loved me so much before thy suffer-

* Now the Bishop of Orleans.

ings began, do not be afraid of my leaving you when your last sufferings approach. God will not refuse me the grace to be with you in that hour, and then your agony will be a little softened by my presence. Oh, do not fear that I shall move from your side. Do not look at me with your beautiful eyes, as if you thought I was going away. I will hold you in my arms, even if my heart should break with the anguish of seeing you die. My arms shall clasp you, my eyes will follow you, and yours to the very last shall behold me there. And now, my God, as Thou wilt, whatever Thou willest, and when Thou willest, I am ready to die, ready to live, so that I am with him. But if I must live on earth without him, I will not refuse to be comforted. Let it be as Thou willest, my God, but save me from sin and remorse. My God! my Jesus! give me but faith—a true, living faith. I ask for nothing, and I ask for all things. Amen . . . . When I left Albert to go to confession, I begged him to forgive me for all I had ever done to displease him. He answered me so tenderly, so humbly! In the evening the doctor came; I was putting on a white dress for my First Communion, and I told Eugénie to follow him down stairs, and ask if Albert was in danger of dying that very night. He answered 'Yes.' But at that moment I did not feel anything as usual, for I seemed to be lifted up above this world, and Eugénie the same. I quietly put on a white muslin gown, and on my head a veil—even my wedding veil! I had for the first time, a true feeling of contrition, as I sat all in white in Albert's room, reading aloud to him and Eugénie, a chapter of the '*Imitation*;' I told her what I felt. She bade me to have no fears, and that my soul was really pure and white, as I had just received absolution. Albert was in bed—he had not been able to sit up at all. I knelt down by him, and held his hand, whilst the Abbé Gerbet began his Mass. I did not know where I was, or what was passing, but soon Albert made me let go his hand—that hand which I had looked upon as something so sacred, that even at the most solemn moment of my life, I could not be offending God to hold him. But he made me let him go, and said, 'Go, go; think now only of God.' The Abbé Gerbet addressed a few words to me before giving me Communion, and afterwards he gave it to Albert. I then took his beloved hand once more, for I almost thought he was going to die that night."

The next day Alexandrine wrote in her journal—"I was at High Mass at St. Sulpice. It was Corpus Christi. Everything was lovely; the hymns, the swinging thuribles of incense, the flowers scattered before the B. Sacrament. Eugénie whispered to me to look round the Church, but I bent down my head, and felt again that deep contrition and sorrow for my sins which I had had the day before. Before my conversion, I had so often earnestly prayed in that Church: 'O! grant me one moment of faith, hope and love, and then welcome death!' For I had not faith at that time, I only longed for it.

"June 5th.—For the first and last time to receive Communion with Albert—he for the last, I for the first time! Our union made perfect only then to be broken. O! my God, it matters not in what way Thou givest us what we both asked. We can only thank Thee for what Thou didst vouchsafe to bestow. What does the world, that condemns religious enthusiasm, and looks upon it as a misfortune, give as comfort to the suffering, and does not prudence alone suggest the wisdom of making some little provision against the innumerable sorrows of life? Foolish, beyond measure foolish world! It finds fault with those who love God too much, and, alas! it is easy to understand why He is loved too little, but to say He can be loved too much is a folly bordering on madness.

"June 8th.—Albert seemed to think for one moment that I was not quite so much occupied about him as usual, and when he saw that this had made me shed tears, he was so grieved that he asked me most tenderly to forgive him, and then said to Eugénie and me: 'I have been very wicked—I was jealous of God!' O my God—my God! just now I thought I should like to yield up life in one deep sigh, a sigh as deep as my sorrow. Poor wretched me! I did not ask to be happy. All I prayed for was freedom from remorse, never to give pain to any one, and now my husband causes me again these two tortures, which I have not courage to endure. I have grieved Albert, and I reproach myself for it. Alas! it is utterly true, I am not a good nurse—not to be compared to Eugénie. When he saw my tears it gave him pain, and, dearest love, he asked me to forgive him! He said he had been 'jealous of God.' Yes, I have indeed neglected him, I have left him too much to Eugénie. Oh, to atone for this neglect let him behold me when in Heaven dying of grief at his loss! May he never either here or hereafter have cause to be jealous, no, not even of Thee, my God! My head has been very weary of late, worn out with thoughts, and now it positively aches with them. O! for light and peace!"

That day Alexandrine sold her pearl necklace* and then wrote the following lines—

"Perles! symbole de larmes!
Perles! larmes de la mer.
Recueillies avec larmes au fond de ses abimes.
Portées souvent avec larmes au milieu des plaisirs du monde.
Quittées aujourd'hui avec larmes dans la plus grande des douleurs terrestres:
Allez enfin sécher des larmes, en vous changeant en pain."†

ALEXANDRINE'S JOURNAL.

["In the night] the 8th of June.

"Am I deceiving myself? Do I really wish to have nothing more to do with earthly joys and delights? Do I care for nothing but faith and peace of conscience? Shall I be able quite to forget that such a thing exists as love and all its delightful visions? After all, is not the perfection of love to be found in God, and that without any fear of change or disappointment? And have I not been thinking for a long time past that all earthly love is but a ray diverging from its true centre? Will not the best and highest of all love suffice me? I sometimes hope so, for though my heart is not on fire with that love like Eugénie's, I see signs of it in myself, of its beginning. I cannot endure to see God insulted, or even neglected. And then I do not care now for any books but such as speak of Him. I was writing this when Pauline, whom I had not seen since we parted at Naples in the Palazzo Gallo, arrived."

* The sale of this beautiful pearl necklace was the beginning of that complete surrender she eventually made of all she possessed to the poor.

† The following beautiful free translation of Alexandrine's lines, appeared in the *Month*, and has been kindly allowed by the Editor to be inserted here.

"Pearls by nature wrought to be
Symbols of the tears we shed—
Tear drops of the moaning sea
Rain'd upon his rocky bed.
Snatch'd with tears from ocean's treasures,
Worn with tears 'mid worldly pleasures.

Darkest depths of human woe,
Close around my shattered heart,
Tears have flow'd, and tears must flow—
So in tears I bid you part:
That some fewer tears be shed,
Go and change yourselves to bread!"

The Month, November, 1866.

I shall never forget the suffering of that moment of our waiting in the street for the gate to be opened, and then for the answer to my husband's question, which I did not dare to utter myself. Twelve o'clock struck at that moment; I counted the strokes almost unconsciously. "Are we in time?" I gasped. "Yes, and he is a little better since the morning," was the reply. I rushed upstairs, and almost immediately into his room, for he was not asleep. Falling on his neck I heard the sound of his sweet, feeble voice, saying: "my own Pauline!" And yet—and yet—I was not present at his death! One of those sudden treacherous gleams of recovery which occur in consumption, took place just at the time of our arrival, and lasted during the few days we remained in Paris. It did not of course lead us to hope for his eventual recovery, but it held out a possibility of removing him to Boury, where he earnestly wished to go. When the time had elapsed therefore, which my husband could spend in France, we went away. It is only now, as I am looking over these letters and papers, that I am able to discern the consolation, and, if I may so speak, the hidden meaning of that absence which at the time materially added to my sorrow. But owing to my not being there, my sisters regularly wrote a full account of all that followed, as they had already done before my arrival. Had I been present, neither those letters would have been written, nor the daily journal have been so carefully kept; for it was for my sake that everything was so minutely recorded. The effect produced upon me by all I saw and heard at that time, by the change which grief and faith had wrought in Alexandrine, by the manner in which Eugénie shared that grief and strengthened that faith, was to me strange and unlooked for. It was the first time I had ever been brought into close contact with sorrow and death; and though, humanly speaking, it was impossible to witness anything more heart-breaking, yet, strange as it may seem, these things left upon me an impression of happiness to which earthly joys seemed the vainest dreams.

Eugénie and Alexandrine were lifted above the world during those sorrowful days, and, as the Abbé Gerbet said, "It seemed as if the veil which separates the visible from the invisible world was withdrawn, and they were given a momentary foretaste of the realities which no human happiness can afford." And now, in transcribing Alexandrine's touching soliloquies and prayers, where memory conjures up her image as I beheld her at that time, on the eve of her final trial, when she was already beginning to practise that entire detachment which in the end became so fulfilled; when I think that this dream of earthly sorrow is past, that as truly as I yet live, she has reached the long wished-for haven, that she is with Albert, never to part again; that they are in the full enjoyment of that bliss of which she speaks, where all life's sufferings, seen from the heights of Eternal Blessedness, are as nothing—now I deeply feel how selfish it would be not to bear their loss, and all other sorrows of this life, with the patience which such examples and lessons more enforce upon me than upon those never so marvellously blessed. But I must now return to the battle she had yet to wage, and which, although lightened by Divine grace, was one of the hardest ever fought on earth.

ALEXANDRINE'S JOURNAL.

"June 16th.

"MY OWN ALBERT! my dearest love! I now may no longer say to you, 'Do you remember our happy days?' Happy days! No, rather those few joyous *hours*, when I used to dress and strive to look well in order to please you; when, in the middle of a crowd, we felt so intimately united; or those other more precious hours when we were alone, far from the world. Light of heart, and forgetting sorrow, we have sometimes even danced together; and now, overwhelmed with sufferings, you lie on your deathbed. God be praised that I am here too; and that as I have shared your joys, I share your anguish as well. And if I had had to choose between them, it is the anguish I should have claimed. The great love of my life has proved a virtue, O! my God, for it has led me to Thee; and if it has also been the source of sorrow, how can I complain? for perhaps it has opened to me the way to Heaven. And then, how do I know what is worked in the secret councils of God? How can I be sure that the earnest prayer to suffer instead of my father, which I have constantly made since his death, has not been heard, and that he may be the happier for all I have endured. Oh! that my sufferings may have availed him! . . . It was after writing this, I think, that with a full heart I bent over Albert and murmured, '*Do you remember*'—I was going to say '*our happy days:*' he stopped me, and said gently, '*Those were other times.*' Ah!

nothing less than this affliction would have sunk deeply into my heart, and given a mortal blow to my inveterate frivolity."

THE ABBÉ GERBET TO ALEXANDRINE.

"Thieux, June 16th.

"I am struck with the two-fold mark with which God has stamped this epoch of your life. Suffering and faith—two of the most important circumstances of life—have influenced you at the same moment. With the Cross in your hand, you have made your first Communion; and there is a holy and a Providential mystery in this, of whose meaning and end you will fully discern by and bye. Meantime, continue to correspond with God's grace in studying the lesson set before you, which is how to sanctify your sufferings. Do not disturb yourself, by aiming at other degrees of devotion, which will follow in due time. Do not be over-anxious to change everything in yourself which seems to need improvement, all at once. Your great perfection just now lies in suffering well. Do that, and then one day other graces will be given to you. L'ABBÉ PH.-GERBET."

ALEXANDRINE'S JOURNAL.

"June 17th.

"Oh! Eternal Beauty, Youth and Love; Thee only will I love; by Thee alone will I seek to be loved; for in Thee is neither decay nor anything wanting. Thee then, will I serve, for Thou alone art worthy of my service. Alas! I *think* these things, but my heart does not feed on them. One part of my soul utters them, and another disowns them again. There is a voice within me crying out that it is folly and baseness to seek anything but God; and another voice whispers, 'No matter; I do not care for holiness; I do not wish to be a Saint, for these things would weary me. Perfection and eternity are too high, too far away, too incomprehensible for me; I have no thirst for them. Give me what is wanting still—feed me with change and decay.' O! ye holy inhabitants of Heaven, pray that I may not be guilty of the inconceivable folly of choosing evil, knowing it to be evil, and casting away what is good, acknowledging it to be such! What should we think of a man who, seeing poison before him, and dreading its baneful effects, should nevertheless swallow it?"

EUGENIE TO PAULINE.

"June 20th.

"*Pace sia con noi* [Peace be with us]. Poor, dear, beloved darling, so you are gone; everything passes away so quickly! It was so nice to have you. We both miss you very much, and when we are here together, it makes us feel only the more deeply how indispensable and precious is the third member of our sisterhood. Nothing has happened since your departure. Albert said to me just now, 'If you are writing to Pauline, send her a kiss for me.'"

Amongst their visitors at that sad time, was one person who, little aware of the wonderful strength which religion afforded to Eugénie and Alexandrine, deemed their piety an excess of religious enthusiasm, which ought to be combated. This was repeated to them, and Alexandrine immediately wrote a letter, which contained the following passage:—

ALEXANDRINE TO ———.

"June 24th.

"Allow me to defend what is now my only source of happiness, for although I cannot compare my feelings with Eugénie's angelic ones, nevertheless I have enough of that religious enthusiasm which you condemn, to support me in my grief. What is religious enthusiasm? It is something that raises one above this earth; lifts us up to Heaven, and helps us to realize true blessedness, and eternity itself. My dear friend, can that support which makes me bear such a sorrow as mine, and would make me bear anything, which, as you know, has helped men to endure the most dreadful torments, not only with courage, but with joy; can this be looked upon as a pitiable thing? And can we feel afraid to see them we love armed with so strong a shield against every kind of evil! Really, those who take such a view must be very strange people, and when any external evil falls upon those who so judge, or perhaps at the hour of death, I am sure they will feel a vague, perhaps unacknowledged regret, that they do not possess this *religious enthusiasm*, which makes all blows light, and fills every circumstance with hope. To condemn religious enthusiasm, is, in other words, to condemn a too great love of God. And now only tell me if you really think one can love God too much? All I can say is, that if it is a kind of insanity, it is a beautiful and wise one."

ALEXANDRINE'S JOURNAL.

"One of these latter days, Albert suddenly threw his arm round me, and exclaimed: '*I am going to die, and we might have been so happy!*' O! my God, I felt then as if my heart would really break."

"June 26th.—Before Mass, which was again said at twelve o'clock at night in his room, Albert looked at me a long time, and then said with deep feeling, 'God bless you!' Then he made the sign of the Cross on my forehead, and added, 'And God bless your mother, too.' After a while he said: 'Good-bye.' I seemed surprised, and perhaps frightened, and then he said: 'Good-night,' as if to change the sad meaning of the word he had used. And all the while I wished so much to speak openly to him of his death. It was I, perhaps, who prevented it, by my fear of exciting him. During that last Mass, every time that I looked at him, he made me a sign to look at the Altar. The window was open, but the night was quite dark. At the moment of Communion the Abbé Martin de Noirlieu and Albert's father, who was serving Mass, came up to him. The Abbé gave one half of the Sacred Host to him, and the other to me. Even in this solemn moment there was something very sweet to me in this. Albert could not open his lips without much suffering—it was for this reason that the Abbé Martin had divided the Host, but even so, he had some difficulty in swallowing, and they were obliged to give him some water. This disturbed him, but the Abbé Gerbet—who was present—assured him it did not signify. Then Albert exclaimed: 'My God! Thy will be done!' O! my God, this thanksgiving of his must, I think, have been pleasing to Thee!

"Before Mass he had said to the Abbé Martin, who was speaking to him of his sufferings, 'The only thing I ask of God now, is strength to fulfil my sacrifice.' 'You are nailed to the Cross with Our Lord Jesus Christ,' the Abbé said, and Albert answered in a very sweet and humble way: 'Ah! but I am such a miserable sinner!' The Altar had a blue silk frontal, and was dressed with flowers. It was Eugénie who had arranged it. The blue silk was one of my trousseau dresses that had never been made up, and now was applied to this use."

"June 27th.—Albert was light-headed; was continually talking of going into the country, and pointing to me, cried, 'She is coming with me! She is coming with me!' [I was in the habit of writing down every word he said on these latter days of his life, and these words—'she is coming with me'—were the last I wrote.] After dinner that same day, we were sitting by his side, without speaking. Eugénie bent over him, and gently suggested his receiving Extreme Unction. His countenance did not change in the least. He said gently and quite quietly, 'Will it not be taking advantage of the graces the Church bestows to receive it yet?' He was anointed, however, that same evening, and during the whole time I was standing near him, with my hand on his right shoulder. Eugénie was on the other side of me. An explanation of this sacrament, which we had read together in our happy days, made me understand all that was going on. The thought flashed through me with a wild feeling of grief: 'What, must his soul be purified even of its ardent love for me? Must that, too, be destroyed?' But I did not shed a single tear. His own wonderful calm was so holy. When it was over, Albert made a little sign of the Cross on the Abbé Dupanloup's forehead, who received it with respect, and affectionately embraced him. Then I approached, feeling that it was my turn to receive that dear sign of the Cross, which was a sweet habit of happier days. He kissed me, his parents, Eugénie, Fernand, Montal, and then Julian (his servant), who was weeping bitterly. When it came to that, Albert burst into tears, and that was more than I could bear, but he quickly recovered fortitude when I kissed him again, and beckoned to the Sister, whom he would not leave out in this tender and general leave-taking, but with his delicate sense of what was befitting, and in token of gratitude, he kissed the hand which had ministered to him, in spite of her resistance. M. l'Abbé Dupanloup, who gave him Extreme Unction, had prepared him for his First Communion, and never forgot the edification it had given him at that time to find Albert on his knees praying in the same place where he had left him three hours before in the Church of St. Sulpice—that church in which his beloved remains were so soon to be deposited. I sat down by his side. He was asleep, and I held his hand in mine, while Eugénie was writing the following lines to Pauline:

"'Oh! Pauline, what a night has this been! and yet not terrible,—no, a most blessed night. Albert has just received Extreme Unction. What wonderful graces God bestows; but why were you not here to receive that dear angel's blessing, who, fitter for Heaven than ourselves, is going before us there . . . .' After relating all that has been mentioned, she adds: 'Pauline, I could not have conceived anything more touching, more holy, more soothing, or a more Heavenly peace. I bless God that nothing in all this time has troubled my notions of happiness in death.'"

ALEXANDRINE TO THE ABBÉ GERBET.

"The same day.

"I should feel it a great mercy if you could come, but I am, however, perfectly composed. I entreat you continue your prayers for me, for I can no longer pray for myself. I can only think of God, and remind Him that I asked for faith in exchange for happiness. ALEXANDRINE."

ALEXANDRINE'S JOURNAL.

"June 28th.—To-night I called Albert's attention to the rising moon. I thought it had the lurid aspect which once before I saw at Rome, when I thought he was dying at Civita Vecchia. The window was open. We looked on the fine trees of the Luxembourg, and the perfume of the honeysuckles and many flowers was sometimes almost too powerful on the night air. Montal came in later, and brought me Albert's letters to him, which I had asked for. It was as if a dagger had been driven into my heart. Still I immediately began to read those pages, which though heart-rending were very sweet. The Abbé Martin gave Albert absolution and the plenary indulgence for the night. I was kneeling by his side, and said to him afterwards, 'Do kiss me.' He raised his feeble head, put up his lips, and kissed me. Then I asked him to let me kiss his eyes. He shut them, in token of assent. Later still, feeling unable any longer to forbear pouring my whole heart into his, and longing to take advantage of the few moments yet remaining to us of life, I said to him: 'Albert, Montal has brought me your letters. They comfort me very much . . .' 'Stop!' he cried feebly. 'Stop! I cannot bear it—it troubles me!'—'Oh! Albert! I *worship* you!'—The cry burst forth in the anguish of not being able to speak to him, for the fear of troubling his soul forced me to be silent; but those were the last words of my love for him that my lips ever uttered, and he heard them, as he had asked—even as he lay dying. O! my God! Whom alone I now worship, Thou hast forgiven me for that rash word which I never again shall use but to Thee, but which I cannot help being glad—and Thou wilt pardon my weakness—to have said to my poor dying Love. I wanted to sit up, but from grief and want of sleep, my head was confused and wandered so much that I thought I was speaking to Fernand at the window, when he was not even there. Then I became afraid of losing my senses, and Eugénie forced me to lie down on the bed. I trusted more to her than any one else to waken me in time. Already, once or twice, I had experienced that terrible feeling when roused from sleep, of thinking that the dreadful moment was come. I was resolved at any cost to be there.

"At about three o'clock in the morning, the 29th of June, I saw Eugénie at my bedside, and was terrified, but she calmed me, and said that Albert had asked 'Where is Alex?' 'Do you want her?' Eugénie had said. 'Of course I want her,' he replied, and then began to wander again. I behaved as if I had lost my senses. I passed twice before Albert's bed, and then went into the next room, not the least knowing what I was about. Eugénie came in holding clasped in her hands the Crucifix indulgenced for the hour of death, which the Abbé Dupanloup had lent her. She appeared then as a meek angel of death, for that Crucifix was a sign that the end drew near. Albert saw it, seized it himself, kissed it fervently, and exclaimed: 'I thank Thee, my God!' After that he became quite calm. They changed his position, and turned his head towards the rising sun. He had fallen into a kind of sleep, with his beloved head resting on my left arm. I was standing and afraid of slipping from my place. The Sister wanted to relieve me, but Eugénie told her not to do so, and that I was glad to be there. When Albert awoke, he spake in his usual voice, and in quite a natural way, to Fernand. . . . .

"At six o'clock he was then lying in an arm-chair near the window—I saw and knew that the moment was come . . . Then I felt so great a strength pass into me, that nothing could have driven me from my place as I knelt by his side. My sister Eugénie was close to me. His father was kneeling on the other side. His poor mother stood leaning over him; the Abbé Martin by her side. O! my God! No one spoke except his father, and each one of his words were words of blessing, the worthiest that could accompany the dying agony of a son. 'My child, who hast never caused us pain—the very best of sons, we bless you. Do you hear me still, my child? You are looking at your Alexandrine'—his dying eyes had turned towards me,—'and you bless her also.' The Sister began to say the Litany for the Agonizing. And I—his wife—felt what I could never have conceived; I felt that death was blessed, and I said in my heart: '*Now, O! Lord Jesus, he is in Paradise!*' The Abbé Martin began to give the last absolution, and Albert's soul took flight before it was over."

Alexandrine's story is ended, that is to say, the period she thus designated, and of which she wished to keep a record. From that day she no longer cared to preserve the memory of the events of her life. And I, too, must pause awhile, for the recollections awakened by the last pages are too harrowing to allow me to continue this narrative now. But before I conclude this portion of my task, I will add to it the following letter, for it was a few hours after the fulfilment of her sacrifice that Alexandrine had the strength to write it.

ALEXANDRINE TO THE ABBÉ GERBET.

"Monsieur, a few hours ago Albert left me. His end was very sweet, and he died leaning upon me. One of my greatest desires has been fulfilled, the greatest of all is not yet accomplished. Faith such as I covet it, is at present no more than as a vast hope in my soul, but I have a very sweet hope for my Albert, who offended God very little whilst he lived, and loved Him above all things. During that last Mass you said for him, whenever I looked at him, he made a sign to me to look at the Altar. He would not have loved me as he did, if he had not loved God a great deal more. But certainly, after God, that beloved one loved me best of all, and this was my greatest happiness on earth. And now help me to be united with him in the happiness of Heaven. My loss is immense—but not so my grief—for hope is at the bottom of that, and rises ever more and more in my soul. Would it not be great ingratitude in me to question God's boundless love, since in the midst of all these earthly sufferings, the necessity of which I do not yet understand, He has granted me what I most desired. For it was not Albert's life I most desired, but to be united with him for eternity; to love God, and in the same way as he did; to have been loved by him, and to have loved him as much as it is possible to love in this imperfect world; and also that his death should be sweet, his last glance rest on me, and that he should discern in his last moments that I was beholding him die without any fears about his eternal state. It would indeed have been sweet to spend my life with him; but when once we believe in Heaven we cannot grieve so much to see those we love, sooner happy than ourselves. I need not say how much I long to see you; I am sure you pray, and will continue to pray for me. I believe it is to those prayers I partly owe the strength I have been blest with. May God reward you for all the good you have done to me."

In the night which followed that day of sorrow and of mercy, Alexandrine also wrote these lines:—"Albert, my Albert! beloved one, you have left me. My friend, my brother, my husband, I must now learn to live without you. I bless God that I feel the full extent of my loss, and that I now know how I love and have always loved you! Yes, I feel deeply that you were everything to me on earth. I know well my own unworthiness, but still I did love and appreciate you well, and more than ever do I love you now. Your noble character, your charming qualities, your loyal, tender heart. O my own dear and modest Albert, at last in the Home of the Blessed, you will know your own worth and the intensity of my love. If I had not been with you when you died—always my terrible fear—I should have thought God had forsaken me. But He mercifully granted that the sleep which leads to endless happiness should overtake you whilst resting upon me, with your hand clasped in mine, and with the last look of your dear eyes fixed upon me. As long as a shade of consciousness remained, you felt a sort of sweetness in knowing that I was there, and feeling that my arms were bearing you up.

"Oh, blessed and eternal union! My God, I thank Thee that Thou hast given me to enjoy such exceeding happiness; and that my life has been thus blessed. Oh, my sweet Jesus! I have given up to Thee my happiness. Give me instead Thy gift of faith."

Alexandrine did not leave off writing in her Journal during the heart-breaking days which ensued, but for the present I shall close the record with the following words, which seem to sum up, as it were, both the love and sorrow of this portion of her life, together with the immortal hope with which both were crowned. They were written a week after Albert died.

"July 6th, 1836.

"O, my God! Do not put asunder what Thou Thyself hast joined together. Pardon my boldness, and do Thou, O, my Father! who art in Heaven, let me bring before Thee that we never ceased to bear Thee in mind. That we never wrote to each other even a little love-letter without naming Thy Name and invoking Thy blessing upon us. Remember that we continually prayed to Thee together, and that we always besought Thee that our love might be eternal in Heaven."

PART III.

"Farò come colui che piange e dice."—DANTE.

THOSE who have read the preceding part of this story, will scarcely wonder that I could not for a while summon up courage to continue my sweet but painful task. In fact, its last pages awoke such poignant recollections, that it was a long time before I could get over their effects. And then Alexandrine's manuscript had come to an end, and I felt disinclined to carry on a record which had borrowed both light and coloring from it. Energy and talent seemed equally wanting for the work, and for some years it remained untouched. Yet Alexandrine's story was far from being ended. She had herself related the details of her earthly happiness from the day of her first meeting with Albert up to his death. But from this time forward, a new life began for her, fruitful in merit as well as in happiness. It was useful and desirable to reveal the mystery of this supernatural happiness, and the latter part of her life was therefore necessary to complete the first.

There were also two other characters in this *Sister's Story*, which live in my remembrance side by side with those of Albert and Alexandrine. The record of their brief lives remained also unfinished, and therefore, sooner or later, it was incumbent upon me to set to work again, and at the end of four years I made the attempt, but it was only to find that the effort was beyond my power, and my health broke down under it. I was forced to lay down my pen and interrupt an occupation which affected me too deeply, and which, though soothing in one sense, was too trying to a sore heart. Six years have now elapsed, and though the feelings I have described are but little altered, I will nevertheless, with God's help, endeavor to overcome them, and pursue my labor to the end. But some will ask why the effort should be made. Is this record so important to complete? I have often asked myself the same question, and I will humbly and simply reply that I *do* think it important to finish what I have begun. I am sure that many of those who have followed Alexandrine up to the time when her life was so sadly blighted, will like to know what God did with that blighted life. I think that the glimpses which have been given of Eugénie and of Olga, will excite in some of my readers a wish to hear more about them. Above all, I believe that the latter part of this story, though possessing none of the romantic interest and varied incidents of the former, will contain even more useful lessons, deeper solace, and examples such as are good for every one of us to study.

I therefore take up the thread of the narrative at the time immediately succeeding the days which followed Albert's death, and I carry my readers with me to the Château de Boury, where Alexandrine spent the autumn of 1836, with the relations and friends who surrounded her during the early days of her sorrow. It was in that depressing place, in that château, gloomy at all times, that almost everything took place which I am about to relate, for, by a singular coincidence, being purchased by my family the year of Alexandrine's marriage, it passed into other hands the year of her death, my mother dying also about the same time. Indeed, so many sad events were crowded into the short space of time when this property belonged to us, that I have often thought the term applied in Italy to places and persons deemed unlucky—(*Jettato, Jettatura*)*—might have been used with regard to Boury. Long before half of these sorrows had befallen, we find Eugénie employing this word in one of her letters. And later on, when, on returning to France, I missed another beloved face from the home circle, and found one more tomb in the churchyard, I could not help thinking and saying that the place was fatal to us. But this was an unreasonable and ungrateful thought, for if that period was marked by many unhappy days, there were others whose remembrance must always be most dear to me. Since 1836, sorrow had become inseparably united with the lives of those who retired to Boury as to a refuge, but from the earliest moment this deep sorrow was allied with peace, charity, and hours of absorbing study. It was

* Doomed, having an evil-eye cast upon them.

sweetened by the mutual affection of hearts devoted to God and to one another, and hallowed by calm resignation, and joyful anticipations. Nothing harsh or austere met the eyes of those who visited this retreat; that unaffected gaiety which proceeds from purity of heart and innocence of life, the true sunshine of the peaceful soul, survived every storm, and was always to be found there. For my own part, I can never forget the inexpressible comfort of arriving there, from those other lands and the busy world in which I habitually lived, and of getting back into that pure atmosphere of loving-kindness and religion; of resting in a place where life was so regular and active, though quiet, and at the same time where the subjects and the questions which agitated the world, were freely admitted and discussed as far as they were really of interest. Even now, as I write, the shadow of the past rises before me; the pain I felt in returning to my tale vanishes before the gentle vision, and the bitterness of regret gives way to the more soothing feelings with which I formerly began this record. I hope to finish it, therefore, with a peaceful heart, aided, it may be, by those dear ones, who, from their home in Heaven, would not that I should darken by gloomy thoughts the light of their past lives, or the brightness of their present joys.

Per Crucem ad lucem.

When her long-dreaded sorrow came upon Alexandrine she was strengthened to bear it in a way which seemed almost supernatural, and which lasted during the first hours which followed Albert's death. What she wrote on that day has been already seen. She had courage to stay beside her husband's coffin, and to follow his beloved remains to the Church, and the grave. A powerful and Divine energy sustained her beyond what could have been hoped or expected beforehand. But it would be a delusion to suppose that we can fly from suffering even under the mighty influence of faith and the love of God. Sorrow is, indeed, tempered by these feelings, but they do not destroy it; and it often happens that the grace which in any great affliction raises the soul at first above itself, seems to be afterwards purposely withdrawn, and we are left to struggle alone against the trial. Thus, the very day of a great trouble is not generally so painful as those that follow afterwards. It was so with Alexandrine. We have seen her accept her cross with wonderful courage. Later on we shall find her carrying it with yet more wonderful joy and love. But between these two phases nature resumed for a while her sway, and agonizing indeed was the struggle in that warm and tender heart. Overwhelmed by loneliness and grief she tells us: "That her strength fails her, and that each day finds her more beaten down than the last." We shall then see by what efforts of resignation, by what self-surrender she obtained peace, and entered upon that other period of her life which she speaks of in her story, and of which she once said: "*Even before old age and death, faith gave me rest.*" This rest, which went beyond resignation, even beyond peace, which Alexandrine had soon recovered; that rest which marked the latter part of her life by a joyousness unknown to her young days, she did not attain till she had gone through many fresh sorrows. It was God's will that she should outlive most of those who had proved her firmest friends and most tender comforters in her widowhood. Almost at one time she lost her own brother, my father, Eugénie, and Olga. It may be that this was allowed, that when after such repeated blows she was still able to say she was happy, no one might mistake the source whence that happiness sprang.

At the opening of this third part of my narrative I have still Alexandrine's journal as a reference, for, as I have already said, she continued to keep it during the days which immediately followed her husband's death. At that time writing was a consolation and a relief. This was not always the case, and a time will arrive when this resource will fail me, and I can then only depend on God's assistance to help me to convey to others the lessons which Alexandrine unconsciously gave us. And after having been so often delighted with the talent she possessed of describing what took place in her own soul, may it be given to me to feel and to make known that yet rarer and higher gift which ended by destroying every desire to speak of herself, and even that craving to live over again her past life, which at first so entirely engrossed her. At this moment her often-quoted journal lies before me. The following pages, which I had not courage to add before, must now be given, as well as Alexandrine's and Eugénie's letters, so that at present the narrative can be carried on without any labor of my own. I resume the journal at the point where I broke off, that is, the 30th of June, 1836, the day after Albert's death.

ALEXANDRINE'S JOURNAL.

"June 30th.

"Albert, I am writing to you leaning against your coffin. I am writing, for it is like speaking to you. Albert, do you see me now? Do you know what I am feeling? Oh! this dreadful uncertainty! Angel of my life, who hast now left me to go on my way alone, my greatest virtue, the best thing in me, was my love for you. It is a sweet thought, that my love for you, and yours for me, have made me better, and that I must not lose you for ever, I will now strive to be as good as possible. Our Lord will forgive me if I go to Him through you, my Albert, who went so straight to Him. I felt to-day that I should like to suffer as much as Albert did; that true love wishes to suffer as much as the object of its affection; and then I thought that this is the sort of love which the Saints have for Jesus Christ, and that I have no right to that sweet feeling.

"But O! my compassionate Lord Jesus, Jesus Who wept over the dead, Jesus Who felt all our sorrows, Thou knowest that the more I loved him the more I loved Thee, therefore forbid me not to love him, and that with an immense love! It is only now that my love has become perfect, for now I love, I am sure of it, a perfect soul. My angel, Albert, pray for me, that I may now doubt no more about my faith; pray for me that I may not sorrow as those unhappy ones who have no hope. Sweet Jesus, I pine more than ever in this sorrowful hour for the day when there will be nothing but sinlessness and joy! How often, O, my God! I was wont to pray that Thou wouldst unite both Albert and me in Thy love. But for some time past I ceased to make this petition. I foresaw, it may be, that we must be separated by that Divine love, which he being far purer would attain much sooner. How he loved me! Is it possible, such a one as I?"

EUGENIE TO PAULINE.

"July 1st, 1836.

"On the 29th, the day before yesterday, after my letter went, Albert was laid upon his bed. His calm face seemed asleep and at rest after so much suffering and so many wakeful nights. We stayed the whole day in our own room, or else praying by his side. Yesterday the body was laid in the coffin, which we covered with flowers, and the whole room was scented with them. I send you a rose and a little bit of jessamine to put in your *Imitation of Christ.* We were praying the whole day in that room, and it was sweet to feel he was there. But at last, this morning, they carried him away. Alexandrine and I went to pray by the coffin whilst it stood under the archway, and afterwards, hidden in a corner of St. Sulpice, we were present at the service. As the day of his death recedes, so the remembrance of our beloved brother's sufferings fades away, and that of the joyous time when they were so happy together, becomes more and more vivid. At times Alexandrine feels quite broken-hearted. The feeling of solitude, the thought of a whole life spent alone, takes such strong possession of her, that I fear, my dear Pauline, her dear bereaved life will not be a long one."

ALEXANDRINE'S JOURNAL.

"July 1st, 1836.

"To-day, hidden in the Church, I was present through it all. I asked our Lord to grant me in the first place faith, because that includes all; then to feel that Albert has forgiven me everything; and lastly to be convinced that I loved him as much as it is possible to love in this earthly frame of clay. I also asked eternal happiness for all those I love and those that Albert loves, and again resumed my ardent prayer, that one day all men may be blessed. I ended by imploring to be as pure and as faithful a widow as ever lived, but without the least pride, and if I can obtain this, I accept all the torments of foolish fears and vain scruples, if only I may live without blame. My dear love, you rested in my arms during your last earthly sleep, and then afterwards in the sleep of which we know not the end! God grant that these arms, after my death, may open to you again when we meet in the Bosom of God, in the full joy of eternal union. O, my God! the day before yesterday he was still living—I still heard his voice; and yesterday I could say, '*yesterday* he was alive.' And now it is further away; and to-morrow I can no longer say, '*the day before yesterday.*'"

"July 3rd, 1836.

"Thank God! I believe, I hope, and love also! May God bless with His best blessings the Abbé Gerbet for all the good he has done me! It comes from Albert, too, I think, for I am sure he still loves me, and prays a great deal for me. When I sink again I will call to mind those sweet moments of consolation, and await their return. There is a bright light behind that dark veil. I may not lift it up, but a ray of that brightness pierces through the mournful folds, and Albert is in that light. I thank Thee, O my God! that Thou hast made him enter before me into his joy. A butterfly before his glorious change takes place, suffers, sickens, and drags painfully along his caterpillar-skin, and the nearer draws its hour of beauty and of light, the more he seems to suffer, the more painfully he languishes. But he does not complain. He knows what is before him, and then freedom comes at last. His discolored skin remains behind, a few grains of dust are left to mingle with other dust, but for him captivity is at an end. He flies where he lists in the fulness of his joy. Thus, my beloved one, is your soul freed. My God, my Jesus, unite us in Thy love!"

"July 4th, 1836.

"I wish I knew what is going on in my soul! Sometimes I positively wish to die, but this is so little natural to me, that I scarcely think the desire can be real. But what is the meaning then of those yearnings for Heaven, where I am always thinking that Albert is. And then I inwardly cry out, 'O! take me also to Thyself!' And why have I become so indifferent to everything in this world, even to the beautiful places of earth to such a degree, that to go through a lovely or an ugly country would come exactly to the same to me, which is what I never felt before. But now, the only thing I care to look at is the sky, lit by the sun, or spangled with stars. Music and perfumes give me still perhaps a little pleasure, but riches, power, jewels, travelling, and even comforts, seem to me all wearisome and stale. The only thing I still passionately care for is to have fresh water—cleanliness! I must after all die one day, all the care in the world will not prevent this. Would it not be then more charitable to wish me to die now, when I think I could go through every kind of suffering with courage, in order to attain that glorious meeting I hope for? But God is a jealous God, and He will perhaps detain me here till I wish to die for love of Him, and not for love of Albert only. But O! my compassionate Jesus, who hast known all our miseries, and how much we need a loving heart to lean upon, may I not, being much lower than Albert, look upon him now as I did while on earth—as a stepping-stone to Thee! Four years ago at Rome when he was already beginning to love me, I saw a bas-relief representing the martyrdom of a young man and woman about to be thrown to the wild beasts. His eyes were raised to Heaven, while hers were fixed upon him. He was drawing strength from God and conveying it to her. I have often thought since, that if Albert and I had been martyred, this is what we should have done. Oh! my beloved Albert, now an angel, draw me towards you, for I love you more than I ever did before. My heart is consumed with the desire to see you again. Oh! why can it not consume my body also? But no, I am quite well. There is nothing at all the matter with me."

"July 5th.

"My God! my God! I say as Albert did: '*Oh! for a little respite!*'—a little respite from my great anguish. What a day has this been of agony, trouble, hurry, and unrest throughout! Of impatience and growing regrets of all sorts, and above all of hopeless confusion of ideas. My good Jesus, help me! Sometimes I do not feel more wretched than when I have parted from him on earth for six or seven months, and at other moments it seems as if I had lost him for ever. O! my God, Thou who art all-powerful, let me have, if only in a dream, some word of comfort! There is but one thing that could make me bear never to see him again, and that is if I could think it would make him happier; but I cannot believe it; on the contrary I am sure he wishes for his poor wife, all unworthy as she is, to complete his happiness. This blessed thought remains firmly fixed in my mind through all my grief. I shall never believe that his love for me can vanish, and so I feel sure of seeing him again. O! my Jesus, grant me a word, a dream, a feeling of comfort! Come to my aid, strengthen my courage, increase my desire of death, and when this life is ended, give me to pray for my mother and brother, more effectually than I can do on earth. My Albert, who was so ill-appreciated, so often misjudged by a stupid world, I would fain honor in death even more than I did during my life. I sometimes think it may be sweet to live if only to hear what is said of him now, by the very persons who once held him cheap; and to pay him the highest tribute in my power by showing the world that there is nothing on earth I care to live for now he is gone. So be it, my Father and my God, if it be not contrary to Thy will! I like to go to sleep with the hope that I may see him in a dream, but the hope is always vain."

ALEXANDRINE TO THE ABBÉ GERBET.

"July 6th, 1836.

"It is now a week, dear Sir, since my husband died. It seems to me already a very long time, and I hate the feeling that I am getting further and further from the day on which he last spoke to me, and when I saw him for the last time, unless indeed it was to bring me nearer to the moment of meeting him again. Sometimes I hope God will show me this mercy. But I do not suffer, I am afraid, as a Christian ought to do. I have not enough faith, but if God takes pity on those who suffer, He must indeed have pity on me. You cannot but think it would be a charity to wish me to die, for when could death be a greater boon? And even when by dint of cherishing and care, those who love me have succeeded in reconciling me to life, will they then be satisfied to see me die? How can my friends desire to see me die with regret? There is but one reason in my opinion which can justify Christian people in wishing me to live, which is that they may think me unworthy to die. Ah! dear sir, in pity tell me that I shall see Albert again! If you who are so good, whom God must love so much, are convinced of this, then I too shall believe it. But oh! let me long for death. Though in truth, I am proof against everything, and often think that I have no feeling either in my soul or body! Pray for me. I am so afraid God must be displeased with me!"

EUGENIE TO PAULINE.

"July 7th, 1836.

"We started at four o'clock this afternoon for Boury. Oh! Pauline, Alexandrine breaks my heart! She looks calm and resigned, but no one sees her as I do. With me she gives way to all her misery. She looks dreadfully altered, and longs only to die. The Abbé Gerbet is the only person who can comfort her at all. I wish he could be always near her. Poor dear darling,—she never murmurs—never says 'Why was this sorrow sent?' so I hope God is not displeased with her excessive grief. And as she finds relief in indulging it, I am not of the opinion of those who try to cheer her—as they understand it—because they cannot make up their minds to see Alexandrine sad for the rest of her life. For my own part I think, provided she grieves in a Christian way, and not as those who have no hope, she may well be allowed a sadness which will become a second nature to her; for, dear Pauline, her life can only be a miserable one. Dearest, give my love to your husband, a sister's love—who loves you both more than herself. And after all that is saying very little!"

EUGENIE TO PAULINE.

"Boury, Sunday.

"We are at Boury, Pauline, at Boury with Alexandrine, and without Albert! Oh! it seems impossible—and if one loses sight for a moment of the world to come; it is absolute despair. When we arrived this evening, that poor darling made my heart ache. She looked so pale, her eyes wandered over every thing with such indifference, her deep mourning, which looks deeper on her than on any one else, her drooping figure, all her attitude betokening a person who has nothing more to do or to hope for in life, who does not care to stay anywhere, and is only pining to depart. We have this great sorrow always before our eyes. Just fancy how the thought of Albert must have been present to us when we arrived to-night. He wished so much to come to Boury! It seemed at every turn as if we heard and saw him. And there was Alexandrine, so listless, so cast down. With what shouts of laughter she would once have arrived here, while he would have made such joyful exclamations. Both of them had so much of the frank gaiety of children. Ah! Pauline, Boury is certainly a doomed place [has the *jettatura.*] Do you remember what we used to say? 'Those dear Alberts will make everything cheerful here. They will bring with them the sunshine of their own happiness!' But the place does not seem intended for happiness. It all looked very nice to-night; so clean, and well lit up, but I had no sooner put my foot into the house, than all my painful recollections came back. My mother's accident,* Fernand's arrival, our dreadful starting for Venice. I shall never be able to shake off all these painful associations. The die is cast, and Boury can smile upon me again."

* On the 17th of November of the preceding year, my mother and Olga had been thrown out of a carriage, the horses of which had run away. Both had been rather seriously hurt, and they had both scarcely recovered from this accident when Fernand arrived from Venice with the account of Albert's dangerous relapse.

ALEXANDRINE'S JOURNAL.

"Boury, July 7th.

"At Boury—at Boury, which Albert so much longed to see! Boury, about which we made so many plans. And now I am here alone, without that dear bright companion who made every place equally delightful to me. O! my God. Thou knowest how dearly we loved each other, like happy children, who cannot be happy apart, and who are amused with everything when they are together. It is very foolish to think that anything can be wanting to the happiness of Heaven, but it always seems to me that if those innocent joys of earth are not found there, that I shall miss them. Our love and our happiness are too intense for earth. His illness first troubled it, but nothing but death could destroy it. O God, my God! let me love him in Heaven as I loved him on earth, as I love him now, and let him ever be the same to me. In spite of the indescribable feeling of being here without Albert, the quiet of this house, and the idea that I am in the country, soothe me. Perhaps too much, for I dread every thing that could prolong my life, and I should be sorry to care for any place again. During our short journey, however, I looked at the world with quite a strange new feeling, as if I were bidding it farewell, as if I noticed nothing, and scarcely belonged to it. Albert was indeed the light that gilded everything for me. Did I not find pleasure when with him, in things which would once have seemed to me insurmountably difficult and tiresome? Did I not interest myself in the most minute details of housekeeping? But now all is changed. With him, pearls, jewels, pretty rooms, and lovely scenery, were all beautiful to me. Now everything is dull, and cold, and worthless. I only pine to know where he is, if he is still happy, if he still loves me, and to share everything with him, as I promised to do before God's Altar. I do nothing well; I am not really resigned; I make other people unhappy; I am cold and hard; and then I love God so little; I am doing nothing to win Heaven. O! sweet Virgin Mary, pray for me! Dear Angels, bear up my prayers to the throne of God, and bring down again into my heart purity and a meek spirit. May I grieve no one, and be firmly established in faith. O! Heavenly Father, love me, Thy poor child, with a very pitying love, for our Lord Jesus Christ's sake!"

"Boury, July 8th, 1836.

"Yes, I believe I really wish that this earthly form which Albert loved should be dissolved, in order that the immortal soul which it encloses may be joined through Thy Divine love, with that soul which God joined with it on earth. My poor darling love, how I tormented you about your health! Alas! had I known that nothing could cure you, I would have let you do everything just as you wished!"

ALEXANDRINE TO THE ABBÉ GERBET.

"Same day.

"I like this place, and in spite of the acute pain I feel in picturing to myself the happy days I might have spent here with Albert, who wished so much to come to Boury; notwithstanding the desolate feeling of being alone in this pretty apartment which we were to have shared, I find it still almost too sweet to be staying here with Eugénie, and all the dear recollections of the past! It is perhaps in mercy, and to bring my sorrows more quickly to an end, that God will have me leave this place; or it may be that I grieve for my Albert in too soothing a way here, and that I must expiate my fault by other bitter and many trials. I entreat you, dear Sir, to come here before I go,* and to give me once more absolution and your blessing. Come and strengthen my hope of seeing Albert again in Heaven. Come and inspire me with that charity which forgives and hopes all things, and at the same time allow me to wish to die, for I think I can declare with truth, I would not ask God to change the least of His decrees for me, but only I wish that my desire for death might prove in accordance with His will. Did I say that I would not change the least of His decrees? Then I was wrong, for had He ordained that I was never to see Albert again, I should wish Him to reverse that decree. Do in mercy tell me He does not will that. Tell me that He intends to join in Heaven those that were joined on earth, in spite of so many obstacles. Ah! what regrets, what sad regrets of all kinds! They are sometimes so intense, that I am afraid they border on murmuring. Let me not forfeit my place beside a husband who died so holily. O! my God, keep me from any great sin!"

* She was going to Germany.

ALEXANDRINE TO PAULINE.

"Boury, July 10th, 1836.

"My Dear Pauline—I ought to have written to you on the 29th of June. I was busy in other ways, but I could have written, for God has given me more strength than I could ever have believed. Did I not see Albert's eyes close in death? Did I not feel his hand grow cold in mine? Eugénie will have told you that I obtained the favor I had so often asked of God. That he died resting in my arms, his hand in mine, and that I did not give way the least while there, watching his last sighs, and when I saw that he was near his end, I asked the Sister if he was still suffering, and she answered '*never again!*' Then I let him go without regret, so at least it seemed to me. Only I very gently kissed his dear eyes, which were sightless, and perhaps without feeling, and I breathed in his ear his own beloved name: '*Albert!*'—the tenderest thing I could think of then, for that included everything. I did it, that through the clouds which gather about the dark valley leading to Eternal Light, he might still hear my voice, which, like my poor self, now parted from him, must linger on the shores of life; and which perchance he heard like some echo dying away in the distance, as it may be he saw me like one little by little vanishing in the gloom. Ah! Pauline, I had a great deal of strength at that moment, and it lasted for three days afterwards. Then I began to sink, and sink, and each day I feel more beaten down than the day before. I cannot live without him, and I cannot die, for nothing seems to kill me. We were but one soul—and now God has parted that one soul asunder. There was no being on earth in whom I could find such sympathy. I do not believe a more perfect union, a more thorough confidence, or a stronger desire to make one another happy was ever known in any marriage. Notwithstanding his sad state of health, its joy was indeed too sweet, too intense for earth; and two years of such a marriage, four years of such mutual love, exceeded the measure of happiness allotted to men in this world.

"Albert died on the 29th of June, the anniversary of the day when, four years ago, and for the first time, I felt conscious that I loved him. How I congratulate myself now on every proof of love I gave him, and if anything can comfort me it is the thought of the joy he had in my love. Never could such a creature be loved enough; so modest, so humble, and possessing, above all others, the qualities which make a man most like an Angel. How soon I found out this, and felt that there was something angelic in his nature. The Vomero, Pisa, and Korsen, appear to me bright with hues of Heaven in spite of the sufferings which mingle with it all. Even at Venice, during the first months, there was somewhat of Heavenly joy. Afterwards it seemed to be God's will to separate me from him in some measure, even on earth, probably that I, poor miserable creature that I am, might learn to live without him. It is, therefore, perhaps His will that I should live on still!

"Dear Pauline, Eugénie sends you the beginning of my letter, but my heart and eyes burn when I talk of Albert, and I must go on. Pauline, you have never known, never enough appreciated your brother. Do not be hurt at my saying this, for I accuse myself of the same thing. But I thank God that at least I always despised the opinions of those who wished me to give him up, and I am glad — God forgive me — that I was sometimes a little weak in yielding to him about everything. The wish was almost irresistible to try to make him happy in every way not wrong; and he was so free from conceit, and there was something so pure and holy about his happiness even in the height of his earthly passion. I am also glad that I did not hesitate risking my life, or at least my health in nursing him, or if that is going too far, at least that I know I never stopped to consider what could hurt me or not, and I felt pleasure in exposing myself to the danger of breathing the same air with him. And lastly, for his sake, I had courage — which I thought could never be done—to tell my mother that I wished to become a Catholic."

"July 14th.

"Dearest Pauline, I have let this letter drag on from day to day, and now we have received yours of the 7th. You speak so well of the reasons why God may have prolonged his life. My only consolation is to see His Providence so clearly shown in our story, for then I think He intends us to be together in Heaven. If only I am not too unworthy to be there. I have not the slightest energy now for any good work. I have even lost the keen interest I took in religious subjects before his death, and I could neither write nor keep up any conversation on points of controversy. I am, however, gladder than ever to be a Catholic. As to everything else I feel frozen and petrified. Albert has taken away my heart with him, and sometimes I am barbarously indifferent about other people, and even sometimes about my own sorrow, for I eat, sleep, go out and listen to music, with a painful sort of pleasure which breaks my heart. I like to listen to what he liked, and then music more than anything else, makes me enter into what Heaven is.

"Ah! poor, wretched me, we might have been so happy! His health during the last five months spoilt our joy, and yet it was better than nothing, that breath of life, that possibility of hearing his voice. I did not think I should ever come to feel this, I who used to say:—'*It is better for him to die than to live and suffer for months in this way*'—and who imagined I really thought so. And now, I can scarcely bring myself to feel:—'He is happy now, and it is well that it should be over!' My earthly nature, always so strong within me, cannot conceive that the joys of Heaven are better than the joys of earth. It seems to me as if *nothing* could go beyond what I have known. I think I have a sincere desire to follow Albert, it matters not by what painful ways or sharp sufferings, so that I may reach the Home where he is, and that I see him happy. But, alas! I forget God so much in him. What will He do with me? Perhaps He will keep me a long time in this world, or perhaps not let me die till I have regained my former zeal in His service. Oh! sometimes I am tempted to say that He has forsaken me! He has allowed me to fall from a height whence I could discern Heaven, and I am now in a dark abyss. The first days of my sorrow were bright in comparison with these. The first evening after his death when he had still been speaking to me in the morning, the starry sky and the moon seemed to me fair and smiling. I had a strange feeling of Albert's happiness, and did not suffer more than I used to do when he was away for a while. On one of those days, at St. Sulpice, the sound of the organ, the sight of the blue sky through the Church windows, gave me an ecstatic foretaste of Heavenly joy, and made me shed sweet tears. Now it is all darkness. Only fancy that I can never even dream of him! And yet your father's love for him was not greater than mine—he was not everything to him as he was to me.* Will you send me all Albert's letters that you have, and you must give me back all mine too, that I may dwell on the picture of our past happiness; first, because nothing can interest me so much, and then because I am writing our story."

ALEXANDRINE'S JOURNAL.

"July, 1836.

"O, my God! how is this grief to be borne? And yet I am sometimes afraid that after having longed so much for death, I should be wanting in courage were it really at hand. My greatest regret is not that I have lost Albert, but that I so little appreciated the blessing of having such a husband. I desire nothing but what God wills, for any joys which do not come from Him always frighten me. I do not pretend that I never drank from poisoned fountains, but my wish, or at least my prayer, was, that neither I nor Albert, nor those we loved, might ever quench our thirst for happiness at an unhallowed source. These were my daily prayers: '*My God, enlighten Albert and me, and all who are dear to us. Teach us the true faith, the true religion, and let nothing be joyful to us that does not come from Thee.*' Oh, my God! continue to bless me, for in spite of the darkness in which I live, I feel that Thy grace helps me still. Ah! if I might but begin over again our sweet married life, even with the knowledge that it would end the day it did. And yet poor creatures that we are, in vain the past yields its lessons; we go on failing in duty towards the living, who may at any moment be taken from us, we fall into our careless ways again, we wound others, forgetting that those wounds may one day torture our own hearts, and cause us more suffering than they could ever inflict on others. Albert, forgive me; my sweet Saviour, pardon me. Let me be with him in Heaven. Grant me to be with Thee for ever. Amen."

I can add nothing to these words. I could not better picture than Alexandrine has done that desolation which took possession of her in the spot where she had hoped to spend such happy days with Albert, and when she found herself in the rooms they were to have lived in together, and for which such joyful prepara-

* M. de la Ferronnays often saw his son in his dreams.

tions had been made. To live in France, in the country, under his father's roof; to build themselves a nest, whence they could have taken flight from time to time, but to which they would always have returned; such had been their dream, and had it been realized, they would have wished for nothing more; and in all probability this kind of existence which always enhanced the enjoyment of their married life, would have been to them as perfectly happy as anything this world can afford. Too perfect, it may be, and we must believe that they were permitted to look forward to it only to sharpen her trial, and to add to that exceeding weight of glory, which is the crown of earthly suffering. Alexandrine found, however, in the physical repose which succeeded so much fatigue, in the society of my mother and that of Eugénie, who was watching like an Angel beside her grieving sister, in the tranquillity and even sadness of the place, something which suited the state of her mind; and notwithstanding her affection for her mother, and the longing she had to be with her, it was not without a painful effort that, after spending some weeks at Boury, she prepared to go to Kreuznacht, where the Princess Lapoukhyn then was. How often, before and during that journey, she must have repeated the "*Credo* of Sorrow" which the Abbé Gerbet had sent her a few days before:

"I believe, O my God! that in suffering with submission I help to fill up the Passion of Christ. I believe, that everything created in this world groaneth and travaileth as if in the pangs of labor, waiting for the manifestation of Christ. I believe that we have no continuing city, and that we seek one to come. I believe that all things work together for good to them that love God. I believe that they who sow in tears shall reap in joy. I believe that blessed are the dead that die in the Lord. I believe that our tribulation worketh in us an exceeding weight of glory, if we look not at what is seen but what is unseen; for the things we see are earthly, but the things we see not are Heavenly. I believe that our corruptible body shall put on incorruption, that our mortality shall put on immortality, and that death will be swallowed up in victory. I believe that God shall wipe away all tears from the eyes of the just, that there shall be no more death for them, neither sighing, and that there shall be no more pain, when the first earth shall pass away."

Alexandrine left Boury on the 21st of July. My father and Eugénie accompanied her as far as Paris.

EUGENIE TO PAULINE.

"Paris, July 21st, 1836.

"MY DEAREST—We got here this morning from Boury, my father, Alexandrine, and I. On Sunday Alexandrine starts for Kreuznacht with my father. This evening M. de Montalembert, Alexandrine, and I, went to that sad but dear house.* She fell on her knees when she went into Albert's room, and for five minutes had a sort of nervous attack. As there was no one there but ourselves, we allowed her to give full vent to her grief, and this was a relief to her. Poor, dear love—she seems to me to grow more wretched every day! What a miserable existence she will lead; she is so thin, so changed; her long black gown hangs about her, her pretty figure droops, her whole attitude betokens sorrow, and her eyes wander over everything with such listless indifference. It makes me sad to look at her. St. Francis, of Sales, says, in speaking of widows: 'What does the word mean, but destitute and bereaved, that is to say, forlorn and miserable.' That is so like Alexandrine now. This other picture, which St. Francis draws, suits her exactly. It is so pretty:—'The true widow is in the Church like a little March violet, which sheds an incomparable sweetness by the perfume of her devotion, and keeps herself almost always hidden under the large leaves of her lowliness, and by her sober color shows forth mortification.' Oh! Pauline, when the idea comes into my mind that it is all over, it bewilders me! When I remember our journey, Venice, our arrival, getting there, it seems to me sometimes that I must have dreamt it all, and that Albert cannot be really dead. What a terrible blank the loss of so beloved a brother makes in a house! And then to think of Alexandrine going on as she is to the end of her life, and yet not able to die! When and where shall we meet again? Will the keen edge of all these feelings be worn away by then? What a trial we have known! and, besides its great griefs, what troubles there are in life!"

* Rue de Madame, where Albert died.

EUGENIE TO PAULINE.

"Boury, Saturday, July 30th—11 o'clock at night.

"MY DEAREST—I must write to you this evening, and my letter must be short, for I foresee a great many things to do to-morrow, besides going to High Mass and Vespers, so that I shall not have five minutes to myself. I have received a letter from Alexandrine, dated from Metz, two days after her departure. Think how this journey must have reminded her of the return from Venice. The startings, the stopping at inns, the very act of travelling, and even the motion of the carriage, must be all painful sensations to her, and she writes :—'My soul dies within me a thousand times, but my body cannot die!' Alex, Pauline—my beloved ones—I doat upon you! So much so that I really do not want any other love in this world. I should like to give to God all the most fervent feelings of my soul, and to devote my life to you and to Alexandrine. Thus my heart would be abundantly filled. My own concerns must, as a matter of course, be wearisome to me; yours interest me so much more. My only desire, my only recreation, I think, is to be always with you both, to be near *you*, and to look on at your happiness; with *her*, to share her remembrances of the past, and with you both, to speak of the eternal joys to come. Do you not agree with me, Pauline, that this is really my only work in this world? Well, God knows best! let Him direct my life! Good-night, my faithful sister, my companion, everything that is most dear and precious that I can call you. You have been everything to me in all ways, and may God reward you for all you have done for me, and ever preserve to you that happiness for which I have offered, and do gladly offer up every joy, every pleasure, of my own, and would sacrifice life itself—*my life!* The *sacrifice* would be more applicable, if I offered to live for you to be ninety years old! Oh, my own Pauline! God bless you a thousand and a thousand times!"

ALEXANDRINE TO PAULINE.

"Kreuznacht, August 1st.

"DEAREST SISTER, DARLING PAULINE—I was waked up this morning by your delightful letter. God sends me from time to time these little helps. How good of you to have copied for me those words of Albert's. You might not have thought of it, you might have lost them, and he, without loving me less, might never have written them. Everything coming from him that I recover in this way, seems to me specially sent by the Fatherly Hand of God ; nevertheless, nothing appeases the hunger of my heart. Pauline ; no one can conceive what I suffer. The blank, the gloom, the weariness, the darkness with which the whole world is filled—that world I once thought so charming, that I was afraid my love for it would outlive even Albert's loss. But he has taken away with him, thank God, all the attractions it possessed, and I see now that I only cared for him, whilst I seemed to care for other things. 'I am in love with death,' (I think it is St. Ignatius who said that,) and I hope that amidst the sufferings which will bring it on I shall enjoy the thought of being on the road which will lead me to Albert. Mine is a strange life ; I feel beforehand, and at every hour of the day, the solemn sensation of approaching death, and I watch for the least symptoms of illness with the same eagerness with which others watch for indications of good health. But do not be uneasy about me, dear Pauline. I take care of myself. I drink the waters of Ems, and only think what it must have been to speak to a doctor about myself! I feel sometimes a wish to cry out, so as almost to die in the effort, an agonizing desire to fly from myself, to try anything new, that I may get back, even for a moment, the happiness I have lost, to hear his voice, to see him smile! Oh! why has not a soul the power to break its prison when it suffers so dreadfully? Some souls have done so, even as there have been prisoners who, little by little, have succeeded in piercing a passage through their dungeon walls. My body seems too strong to be ever touched by weakness. Sometimes I detest this body, though even now I feel two quite different sensations—one of utter detachment from it, the other of great interest—so that I sometimes say to myself, as if speaking of another person: 'This then is the wife that captivating Albert loved so much.' And at such times I feel again an odd desire to look pretty, though he is no longer here, that others may praise his taste, and as it were, to make our story more interesting. *Apropos* of our story, you know I have begun to write it, and it gave me pleasure at first, but I have since lost courage about it. Still I should like to finish it before I die. All that interests me now is to copy his letters, because they are himself. I wish there were enough of them to last me to the end of my life.

"Pauline, you are, I am sure, too reasonable and too wise to wish me to become bound afresh to life, and then be satisfied that I should die? Not that I think I shall ever be attached to it again, still those about me wish that I should. And after all, I must die in the end, and how absurd it is not to wish me to do so now when it would give me so much pleasure! Yesterday I was at a delightful High Mass. Such an organ, and such music! During the Elevation I shut my eyes, and my mind seemed to be filled with a kind of delight in keeping with the sounds I heard. I fancied myself dead—mind you, this was my own doing—there was nothing extraordinary about it;—it was in the night, and in the midst of the darkness I felt the presence of an Angel shining white and shadowy, who led me to Albert, and I said to myself:—

"'It is not possible, and yet it must be he.' Our bodies, or perhaps only his—for it is difficult to remember distinctly these sort of dreams—seemed transparent and bright as gold. Poor human mind, how little it can picture things which it cannot comprehend! But it was a sweet moment, and I long for another like it. What religious people the Germans are! Fancy an immense Church quite full, and every one so profoundly attentive. And then the fine chanting in unison, with such true and solemn voices, and the devout way in which they take holy water—no levity or incredulity in any of their faces—all this makes me feel among brothers and sisters, and I believe I should have found the truest sympathy in every one of these good peasants. . . ."

Once at Kreuznacht, Alexandrine opened her locked book and wrote in it the following page:—"Kreuznacht, August 3rd, 1836. O! my God, I feel so cowardly and cast down, that I do not like to write even in this book. I hardly know how I should like to spend my days: in listening to music, I suppose—always music*—and turning over pious books—above all in reading everything that Albert wrote—and in talking of eternity and of our meeting in Heaven; and I have scarcely one of these enjoyments here. But no matter, how could I really wish for any sweetness in a life so wretched, humbled, and blighted as mine is without him? How true it is that a widow's position is a humbling one. And if she has loved her husband she would not have it other-

* This will seem strange to those who knew Alexandrine's courageous activity during the last years of her life.

wise. I should think I was forgetting him if the slightest feeling of pride rose up in my mind, for in him I have lost all. Any beggar who loves and is loved is a thousand times richer and happier than I am now. No wonder that St. Elizabeth said she should be glad to go and beg with her husband. If I were allowed to see Albert alive before me, with what joy I would put on rags and walk barefoot by his side! It would not signify to me whether the pebbles were wounding my feet, or his either, as long as we could talk together and I could enjoy the charming gaiety, the delightful tenderness with which he would say to me: 'Poor Alex, you wept for me as dead, and here I am, and now we shall never be parted as long as we live. Let us go on bravely. Are not all the privations of poverty better than parting?' I could have been so happy in that kind of life. Nature would have delighted us more than the most splendid palaces, and fresh water is to be found everywhere, so that poverty could not have prevented me from appearing cleanly bright in my husband's eyes. We loved the beauties of Nature so intensely; we have so enjoyed being together, under the clear sky, amongst the flowers and in the woods, among rivers, lakes, and mountains. He was gentle and gay at once, both grave and merry, tender and enthusiastic, kind and thoughtful, high-minded and humble, modest and pious. Yes, he was all and more than all I have said."

Towards the end of September Alexandrine returned to Boury, and not long afterwards the Abbé Gerbet arrived. At that period of gloomy sorrow—when she was still given up to such passionate regret, and looked back with such intense longing to the joyous days which had for ever fled—he seemed specially raised up by God to heal and comfort that bruised and suffering soul, and his presence at Boury was one of the things for which she felt most grateful in her after-life. His healing influence soon began to tell upon her, and the over-impetuous element in her grief calmed down. In September Eugénie wrote to me:—"Alex and I lead quite a convent life. We do not see a single soul, we neither pay nor receive a single visit. Now and again we laugh, and then are surprised at the sound, and tell each other that people must laugh sometimes as long as they live. They live on hope, I suppose." All this time I was absent from Boury. Nine months had passed away since Albert's death, and I had not yet seen any of my family. Once even there had been a question of my husband's going suddenly to Portugal, and in that case I must have made up my mind to leave England without first going home. We should not then have met before a fresh parting which was to separate us by a wider distance and an indefinite time. This sorrow, however, was spared me, and we went to Boury in October, having left it in April, when Albert was still living, and Alexandrine had never yet been there. I was now going to see her for the first time since Albert's death. We got there about eight o'clock in the evening, when no one but a servant received us at the door, and told us that my father and mother and Eugénie, who did not expect us so soon, were gone out to dinner at Dangu, and that *Madame Albert*, as Alexandrine would always be called, was alone in her room upstairs. The servant wished to let her know that we were come, which I foolishly prevented, and running up the stairs, I crossed the corridor and went into Alexandrine's room without even knocking. The room was thickly carpeted, so that the door opened without noise, and I was within a few steps of her before she saw me. The sight of my poor sister struck me to the heart. I had left her in Paris, carefully and even elegantly dressed—for during his last illness, Albert had liked to see her in the gowns and ornaments which she had worn in happier days—and I found her in that deep mourning, which, as Eugénie had so well said, *looked deeper upon her than on any one else.* She was sitting in the carved high-backed chair which was Albert's gift, and leaning on a table covered with a sky-blue carpet. The mournful widow's cap she usually wore was hanging on the back of her chair, her head was uncovered and her brown hair somewhat in disorder. One small lamp on her table was the only light in that large room, and the thick green damask hangings of her bed, which had been brought from Venice by Albert, quite concealed me from her sight. There she sat, looking exactly like the picture of her which I possess. I never shall forget that moment. I went towards her—"Alexandrine!" At the sound of my voice she looked up quickly, saw me, and sprang forward to catch me in her arms, but the surprise and emotion made her stagger, and she fell suddenly on the floor. I was very much alarmed, for I thought she had fainted, but she got up quickly, and began by begging my pardon. "You must not think I am always like this," she said; "I assure you I am not. I am much calmer than you would think, and I still enjoy a great many things." And, in fact, as soon as she had recovered from the sudden shock, she sat down beside me, and we held our first sad conversation with some kind of calmness, and in spite of all that had passed since we had met, and all she had to tell me, in spite of our sorrow and our tears, that first hour we spent together was more sweet than sad for us both. After that, my father and mother returned with Eugénie, and that was also a meeting, the sweetness of which no sorrow could destroy. And still, after the lapse of many years, I see before me the great drawing-room at Boury, just as it looked that evening when I found myself there for the first time after such great and sad changes. Death had struck one of our most beloved ones, and broken up that happy and charming family circle which made our lives so enchantingly bright. We had for ever lost that mistaken idea of youth, that happiness is the earthly reward of a good life, and that love and trust in God will guard us from every sorrow. This idea had been uppermost in our minds only a few months before, and we had all been blind to Albert's danger, because we thought it impossible that God would take him from us. And now how was it with our thoughts, our love, and our trust in God? What had been the effects of this trial, and what would be its fruits? Such were my thoughts as we gathered round the fire, and I looked at each one of the circle by turns, and it may seem surprising, but it is nevertheless certain, that I experienced once more the feeling I had at Paris, during Albert's last illness.

It seemed to me that evening that they were all endowed with a new strength; that something had been learnt, something gained; that fresh heights had been reached, new truths realised, and more wonderful than all, a sort of happiness won, which the careless days of childhood and early youth had never known. I know that such gleams as these are but transient lights; that they are quickly clouded, and often wholly vanish, but the gloom which follows is not so rayless as if that light had never been discerned. There sat Alexandrine by the fireside, much changed from what she was, her beautiful figure bent, and wrapped in the long black scarf she now always wore. Her face was very pale, and the expression of her eyes, as Eugénie had said, as calm as that of a person who no longer expects or desires anything on earth. But there was at the same time a deeper sweetness, and something so serene in her countenance, that it seemed to impart peace to all who approached her. During this time of sorrow, my mother showed her usual self-forgetfulness, and was more than ever occupied with the least joys and sorrows of others; that tender heart seemed to have enlarged, in order to take in and share every cross and every burthen. As usual, I enjoyed with her that fulness of confidence and sympathy which had been the earliest happiness of my life; she was always ready to hear everything, perfectly understood all that was said to her, and joined to the utmost sweetness of temper, the most intelligent tenderness of character. Perhaps I have already said these things of my mother, but I can never recall her dear image without giving it a token of my love, and sometimes I feel as if I received one from her in return. As to Eugénie, of whom I shall now have to make frequent mention, I found her much improved in looks. At her age, the effects of fatigue are not lasting, and she had recovered from the strain she had gone through beside Albert's dying bed. The beauty of her complexion was enhanced by her deep mourning; the open, radiant expression of her face conveyed the idea that some mystery of joy and comfort had been revealed to her by her first acquaintance with death. Olga was grown tall, and her slight figure was very graceful, her profile as regular as Eugénie's, but her countenance more serious. At fifteen she already inclined to meditate on deep subjects, which might have proved dangerous if her rare candor and simplicity had not always led her, without the slightest reserve, to disclose her inmost thoughts. She was singularly gentle and docile, and therefore easy to guide. Eugénie, especially, whom she loved above every one, could do what she pleased with her. Olga was, of all my mother's daughters, the one who most resembled her in looks and character. The word *angelic* seemed peculiarly applicable to my young sister throughout her short life, and yet more affectingly so at the moment of her death.

But it was my father who seemed to have reaped the most profound, sanctifying, and permanent benefits from Albert's death. It seemed as if the beloved son, whose departure had been attended by so many paternal blessings, had borne them up with him to Heaven, and showered them down again in abundant graces on that revered and beloved head. I shall not be contradicted, I am sure, by any of those who have known my father, when I speak of what was felt for him, even by those out of his own family and immediate circle, who knew the winning charm which he exercised on every one who approached him. These fascinating qualities, and his delightful kindness, caused him almost to be worshipped by his children. But now a new motive of affection and reverence was added to all those which had rendered him already dear to his family and friends. Perhaps that very love and respect ought to check my pen, and make me fear to speak on so delicate and sacred a subject, but I think it would not be possible, when writing the story of Albert's life and death, to suppress the fact that from the very hour he died in his father's arms, the principle of faith which had slumbered but never died in his soul, woke up to a full, fervent, and energetic life, and brought forth to the end of his life such fruits of virtue, that the world looked on amazed. The world indeed (I apply this word to what is usually called the *great* world), which had lavished upon him so much praise in other days, had none to bestow upon this new phase of his life. But a silent thanksgiving rose from that pure, humble, and fervent heart, which had so prayed, so hoped, and so patiently waited beside him, and thus at last obtained a reward beyond what she had prayed for, and sweeter than her hopes. From the moment my father had seen Albert die, that son whom four years ago, at Civita Vecchia, he had nursed with such anguish and such devoted tenderness, a sort of foretaste of the graces he was about to receive made him accept this grief with resignation, and even with a kind of joy.

My mother, whose heart was still sore with the recent wound, said to me on the first evening we met: "Oh! I do envy and admire your father. Since our dear child has gone to God, he seems to be in Heaven himself." In this way then, I saw those that are now gone to their rest. Thus I met them on that evening with Fernand, and Albertine,* and soon afterwards the Abbé

* Albertine was several years younger than Olga. She married in 1850, the Vicomte de la Panouse.

Gerbet.* We all went to the Chapel for night-prayers, and I heard there several hymns set to words composed by that kind and excellent friend. To speak of the poetical talents which the Abbé Gerbet possessed in common with the more essential gifts which the Church and the world have so long recognised in him, would be to displease and even perhaps to disobey him, but I cannot help mentioning the way in which he employed this talent in the exercise of a wise and heart-felt charity. Of all the things which had once delighted Alexandrine, music was the only one for which she retained a fondness. It seemed almost a necessity to her, and it is impossible to describe how much those pious songs, which expressed her grief, helped to soothe and raise her spirits during that sombre period of depression. It was one of the many ways in which that good Samaritan sought to heal the wounds of her poor heart. Besides the hymns which were sung in the Chapel, he was so kind as even to change the words of the favorite songs she used to sing with Albert into others applicable to her present position. And Alexandrine found a sort of painful pleasure in hearing them sung by Fernand, whose voice was rather like his brother's. Considerable pleasure was mingled with the pain of my first return home, though the contrast was very striking between the joyous party assembled at Castellamare two years before, and the family group in deep mourning in the cold melancholy country house in Normandy; but after the first agitation had subsided, I could not but feel happy to sit between Alexandrine and Eugénie, and the whole time of our visit was wonderfully enjoyable. When people are of the same heart and mind, there is no end to the subjects of conversation; but besides our pleasant talks when we three were together, there were always certain times when each of them came to me alone. Alexandrine then talked to me about Eugénie, and Eugénie about Alexandrine. They had gone through days which had increased their mutual affection, and at the same time somewhat changed its nature. Alexandrine now felt towards Eugénie much as she would have done towards some Angel had it appeared to her under the form of a child, and on her side, Eugénie looked upon Alexandrine with so much compassion and tender love that she would have thought little of devoting to her her whole life. For my part, I had a

* He died Bishop of Perpignan, in 1864.

thousand things to tell them, for neither sorrow, nor seclusion, nor the distaste of the world which both felt almost equally at that time, interfered with the tender interest they took in all the incidents of a life cast amidst distant scenes and persons wholly unknown to them. Eugénie especially insisted on the most circumstantial details, and from the most important matters down to the color of a flower or a ribbon worn at a party, nothing was to be left untold. Those who have known what it is to be loved in this way and then had to endure the loss of that happiness, know what a blank is left, not only in the places whence the visible presence of the beloved ones has departed, but also among scenes they have never visited.

It was during this stay at Boury that I became well acquainted for the first time with the Abbé Gerbet, and learned to appreciate the qualities which so particularly fitted him to be the author of the book he was then writing: "*On the Treatment of the Soul's Diseases.*" Few indeed ever possessed in a higher degree that Divine science, or better knew how to read the soul or to reveal to it its own secrets; few men have so joined compassion to firmness, or have had greater skill in imparting peace to a troubled soul, at the same time rousing it to efforts which it deemed beyond its strength. I should be tempted to say that *no one* ever excelled as he did in this sacred ministry, if I did not know and gratefully acknowledge, that most Catholics in the course of their lives have met with some such wise and good physician, whom they have had cause to bless in time of need. Long and earnest were my father's conversations at that time with his holy guest and friend. And when we all met in the evening, the Abbé Gerbet knew well how to second his efforts in promoting cheerfulness, and I retain the most delightful recollections of the talent, the kindness, the nobleness of thought, the gaiety and peculiar charm, which made those conversations so extremely enjoyable. Then came the blessed hour of night-prayers, which were always accompanied with beautiful music. Eugénie's voice, assisted by Olga's fine contralto and Alexandrine's pure and high soprano, formed a choir such as is seldom met with. My brother also often took a part, and the singing in that little Chapel long lingered in the memory of those who were then present.

The Château de Boury may be described in a few words. It

was a fine building, more like one of the hotels of the Faubourg St. Germain than a country house; with a great staircase, vast corridors, lofty and spacious rooms, and plenty of air and light, which might have rendered the dwelling bright and cheerful, if the view from every window had not been to the utmost degree dull and monotonous. A green plot in front divided from the house by a broad gravel walk and ending in a shrubbery, a few flower-beds close to the house; and in the distance some dull fields fringed with poplars ;—all this under a sky nearly always grey, and with a temperature both moist and cold, did not prove particularly attractive to people so long accustomed to Naples and Italian skies. And although it may be said that such a landscape harmonized as well with this phase of our lives as Naples had done with the previous one, it is very certain that a less dull and depressing view would have been good for Alexandrine, who so quickly regained her former intense enjoyment of beautiful scenery, and still more so for my father—always keenly alive to such influences—and who soon suffered in health from this cause even more than from the climate. It may perhaps be thought that too much space has been given to these details, but it seemed advisable to draw out fully the circumstances then bearing upon Alexandrine's life, and the story now continued through the medium of a correspondence which will supply the place of her manuscript. My short stay at Boury was drawing to a close, and we were about to separate again for a considerable time, when the last part of our visit was saddened by a bad accident which happened to my brother Charles. By a singular coincidence, on the anniversary of the day that my mother and Olga had been overturned, and nearly killed—the 17th of November—Charles met with the same disaster, and nearly at the same spot broke his leg. The fracture was so serious that at the first moment the surgeons spoke of amputation. This new anxiety painfully disturbed the sweet, sad peace of our home, and while it was still at its height, a letter from London brought my husband an order to start immediately for Lisbon. He was directed to sail from England on the 30th of November, and to do that, it was necessary to leave Boury the very same evening. My journal relates at length all the sad details of that day and those which followed; my father's grief and reluctance to part with me, his proposal that I should stay in France, in which case he would have himself taken me later to Lisbon, my husband's perplexity, my mother's fortitude in advising me to go with him, which lent me strength to resist my father's entreaties — my sister's sorrow, and the comfort afforded by the Abbé Gerbet. I find recorded our assembling together in the Chapel at eleven o'clock at night, our departure in the midst of so many depressing circumstances, and finally the storm, which after we had hurried away from Boury, kept us at Boulogne for eleven days unable to cross the Channel! I did not return to France for a year and a half, and during that time what took place at Boury is related in the following letters. It so happened therefore, that these very partings, which then seemed so cruelly long and frequent during the few years we spent on earth together, I now look back upon with thankfulness, for they were the means of accumulating that store of precious recollections which enable me to draw a faithful likeness of my departed loved ones, and moreover to allow their own words to speak for themselves.

EUGENIE TO PAULINE.

" Boury, Nov. 27th, 1836.

"You are gone then, our dear old, pretty little sister! How pleasant it was to have you! I do so love you, and should have been so glad not to have let you go. We are often separated now, Pauline, after having been so long inseparable! May God soon bring us together again! Our intimacy is so delightful, and our friendship, including as it does Alex, such a blessing! What kind of passage will you have this evening? I feel anxious about it. What a sad parting we had. There was something so mournful and strange about it. Those farewells in the Chapel and the blessing given by the Abbé Gerbet were more like what we read of in books than what happens in real life. And what is the meaning of these dreadful things we hear about several English having been assassinated in Lisbon? May God protect you! If Augustus is likely to be in any peril, we cannot regret that you went with him, for no doubt it was the duty of a "*muger de bien*" (a good wife)*. If anything had happened to him I should like to know what we should have done with you? And so once more I beg of God to keep you safe, my two dear ones, and I do so with perfect trust. There is bad news from Naples.

* Quoted from a comedy of Moratia, which we read in Spanish, at Boury.

The world is in truth a gloomy place, and there is sadness everywhere, both in countries and in families. Pauline, it is pleasant to know that in a few years we shall be out of it, for the longest life is short, and God has mercifully ordained it thus. I love you unspeakably, and I do not want any other interest but to watch your life and to help Alexandrine to be patient. If it is God's will, I should like not to be cumbered with thoughts of my own happiness and personal interests. I belong to you, my two dear sisters, and I should like to leave you only to go to God. And oh! do not be angry! *There* I would go without even regretting you."

"December 14th.—Now you are on the other side of that horrid sea! I am very glad of it, though I seemed to be with you still as long as you were on this side of the Channel. But anyhow may God's blessing follow you across every sea and through all kinds of storms, both moral and physical! I send you the *cantiques.* Are we not well off to have these flowers strewn in our path by one who knows so well how to teach us that the most fragrant of all nosegays is gathered in death? The few days of life glide sweetly by, while we think of the great Eternal Day. Farewell, my dear angel! Once again, may God hear and grant my prayer, now and until my death: namely, that my whole share of happiness may be given and added to yours; that all your days may be happy days, and if possible that you may reap in Heaven the reward of your faith and love alone, and not the fruits of suffering and trials!"

"December 27th.—I missed you, I cannot say how much, at our midnight Mass. If you had been there, my enjoyment would have been complete. The Altar was covered with candles and flowers, then Grandmamma's beautiful carpet was spread upon the Altar-steps, and up to the rails; the piano was just outside by the door, and the singing a little better than usual, for we had Alix, Constance, and Desirée* for our choir, whom I had drilled most wonderfully, while Alexandrine, Olga, and I took parts—and such parts, too!—In short, my father was perfectly amazed at the perfect music and the general effect of the flowers, candles, incense, and above all, of a new vestment from Paris, and two choir-boys in white

* Village girls.

surplices and long blue ribbons, once belonging to my father's order of the *Saint Esprit,* which Mamma had made over to us. During the three Masses we sang the *Adeste,* the *Adoremus,* and the *Magnificat* in parts—most splendidly—and then *Jesu wie süss** and *Evviva Maria* at the end; but what will quite set us up is an organ coming from Paris; there will then be nothing to wish for in the little chapel. I thought of you at midnight, my dear Paulette. Oh! may God bless you during your passage, and bless you always!"

MONS. DE LA FERRONNAYS TO PAULINE.

"Boury, January 6th, 1837.

"I owe you a good many letters, my dear Pauline, and I am afraid, though you are so accustomed to it, that my long silence may have given you pain. I own you have good reason to complain of me, and I do not know if you will blame me less when I tell you the only reason which hindered me from writing sooner. Your departure grieved me much more than you imagined, and my grief had several causes which I will not enumerate; first, because I do not wish to make you sad, and also because it might look like a reproach to you or your husband, a thing as far from my feelings as from my thoughts. You, my poor dear child, have only done your duty, as any other wife, as your dear mother, placed in the same position, would have done; if at your age I had left her free to choose, glad enough would she have been to have accompanied me in all my travels and voyages. I repeat, my dear one, that as the choice was left to you, you could only act as you have done, and your husband has not any more than you behaved unkindly to us. I hope, therefore, that you will dismiss from your minds all idea that I am annoyed at your departure. If I feel any resentment, it shows itself only by an increase of tenderness towards you both. All that I beg of you is to be indulgent to your poor old father, and bear in mind without grieving over it that at my age long separations give rise to serious reflections. We think that you must have reached the end of your long voyage yesterday, but I need not say how impatiently we look for your first letter. For ten days the weather here has been

* Sung by the girls at Ratisbon, and spoken of by Alexandrine in her letters from Pisa.

gloomy and very cold, but no wind. The papers, however, are filled with terrible accounts of the disasters on the coast, which show that the stormy weather is not over, as we hoped. You know how apt we are to be anxious, especially your mother, so you can imagine the state we shall be in till we get your first letter from Lisbon. As it is, we are uneasy at not having had one from Falmouth. It would not be like you not to have written. What can have happened that we get no tidings? You can guess how painfully anxious we are, but we trust you to the protection of God, for we hope that He watches over our dear good child, whom we pray for daily most earnestly. This trust, which our dear Abbé Gerbet enforces with his warm faith and loving eloquence, calms our fears, or at least enables us to control them. We are afraid that they might look like mistrust or murmuring. Nevertheless, I look for your first letter from Lisbon with anxious impatience. I am too much occupied about you to-day to write about ourselves, and besides, the sisters write to you so often, that they leave me nothing whatever to say. And again, you know what our life is, its perfect regularity, its pleasant monotony are just what constitute its principal charm. It has in my mind the great advantage that one day is like another. Our bright, kind, thoughtful, and comforting Abbé Gerbet introduces an unspeakable charm into our morning and evening conversations. With him science and metaphysics lose their dryness and asperity. Virtue preached by this excellent man penetrates the soul, fills the mind with light, and goes straight to the heart. X—— used to say at Naples that I was his *corkscrew*, that I was always drawing him out. This is far more the case with me and the Abbé Gerbet. My ignorance overwhelms him with questions, objections, subtleties, and sophistry, but nothing discourages or wearies him, he answers everything, and in a manner which makes me feel while he is talking—and I make him talk till his throat is quite parched—that my heart is enlarged, my mind expanded, and my thoughts elevated to a degree I should never have thought possible. Oh! if our divine religion was always taught and explained as it is by this true Apostle, it would soon be universally received! The presence of this admirable man amongst us is so great a blessing, that I look upon it as a special miracle of God's goodness, and a token that our trials will soon end. This comforting thought fills me with devout thankfulness, especially when I think of you, my precious one, whose happiness is immensely necessary to us. But for God's sake, my child, write to us soon.

"Charles goes on as well as possible, but his patience is well nigh exhausted. It will be ten days before he can get up, and ten more before he can be moved to Paris, where he is anxious to be. Farewell, darling Paulette, my dear excellent child. Forgive your old father for having allowed you to think for so long a time that he was angry. Give my best love to Augustus, that he may see I am not a bit more cross with him than with you, and be sure, so long as you are both happy, that I shall always be well satisfied. Good-bye again, my dear child. I will now close my letter and give it to Eugénie. Alexandrine has taken a new lease of life since she has had the benefit of the Abbé Gerbet's conversation and instructions. He stimulates and interests her, and I see her mind is regaining its wonted activity. Moreover, she sews and knits, whether with skill or not I cannot tell, but I know she makes an enormous quantity of caps and petticoats, visits the poor, and gives them money, visits the sick, and gives them receipts, and even has gone so far as to prescribe for them herself. The day before yesterday she rashly ordered a bread poultice, and yesterday a mustard plaster!

"Thank you, and God bless you! My dear child, we have just received together your letters from London and Falmouth. You are a good excellent daughter, whom God will love and take care of. Yesterday you must have reached Lisbon, you will write to us to-day, and ten days hence we shall get your letter."

EUGENIE TO PAULINE.

"Boury, January 7th, 1837.

"To-day, thank God! we have had your letters from Falmouth. It was indeed high time! The accounts of storms and snow-falls, and your silence, began to make us very anxious. Dear Pauline, when I read your letter, I felt to love you so much, and you seemed so very far off! I thought of our former life spent always together, and now we are always divided. If one of us were to die away from the other it would be sad indeed. Let us pray that at that time we may be together. I like to think that you are now on shore, but we shall still say the prayers for travellers till we get your first letter from Lisbon. Oh! my very dear little sister, I hope nothing will happen to you! I love you so dearly, that the tears come into my eyes while I am writing these words."

"Boury, January 27th, 1837.

"My Dearest—At last we have tidings of you, and how much good your dear long letters have done us! Dear Pauline, when I look over your letters it makes me sad to see how often we have been separated lately, but you were quite right to go with Augustus, you would have been too sorry now not to have done so. I feel everything is for the best, and this is I hope because I try more and more to will only what God wills. The letter you sent me back surprised me when I read it again. I am changed since the days when I wrote it, and most of all with regard to castle-building. For a year past, I do not think I have once sketched out a plan of life or any combination of circumstances of so-called happiness on earth. Sometimes I find that when such ideas cross my mind they seem altogether new. What I now talk over with Alexandrine is how we shall live when we are seventy or seventy-five years old, she remembering exactly the hours and minutes, and I forgetting whole months and years. We shall have a little dog, take tea, and three days in the week have no dinner. Such is our plan, and many a time we laugh over these schemes for our old age. Poor Alex! If she should really live to be sixty, what will the short time of her married life look like, seen through the vista of that length of years? However, if it is so, it will be because it is God's will, and we shall find it good, like everything else He does. Good-night."

EUGENIE TO THE MARQUISE DE RAIGECOURT.

"You ask what I am doing. I do not know much about it, except that I never find my life dull. I read, write, sing—sometimes I have a sore throat, and sometimes a headache. I have a class of little girls for catechism, I go out, and I visit the poor sick people in the village. Sometimes I feel so merry that I laugh from morning till night, and then again I am often sad, when life seems interminably long, and full of sighing and groaning. But what I most truly feel is cheerfulness and peace of mind, a blessing for which I thank God every day. Yes, Flavie,

I do feel at peace, and nobody can describe what this is to those who have at any time known the contrary. It is the greatest of gifts, for if real it certainly comes from God."

TO THE SAME A LITTLE LATER.

"What can I say, but that I am calm, and that my soul is as peaceful as my life? There is nothing to be told about me, but that I am here, that I am well, that I sing, and play admirably on the organ; read, write, think, laugh very often, have neither regrets nor wishes, and love my friends more truly and tenderly than ever. I hope this last sentence will touch you."

MADAME DE LA FERRONNAYS TO PAULINE.

"February 11th, 1837.

"After having been so anxious about your passage, and been tossing with you on those great waves, and just when I was at last resting in the thought of your being on shore, to my great grief I have to tell you of Richard's death.* You must have been very much shocked, very much affected by this sad news. Is it not difficult to realise that on that side, too, all is at an end? A poor young wife, formed, as it seemed, to be happy, and to enjoy happiness, is now thrown into the deepest of all sorrows, full of sadness, obliged to attend to the most wearisome business, and perhaps to go through difficulties of every kind. And imagine the affliction of his poor mother, who was so used to nurse her son, and had brought him through so many illnesses, and now has been away from him at the last! What can ever comfort her? I speak of comfort, but resignation is the only word. Poor Marie† writes herself to-day to Alexandrine. She says that Richard dictated a letter to his mother on Monday. He was suffering from influenza, but hoped soon to be well, when at eleven o'clock that night his poor wife had the courage to tell him of his danger. He had not the least idea of it, but immediately prepared to receive the Sacraments, and showed the utmost faith and submission to God's will. When quite cold and motionless he was still praying with fervor. Whole pages might be written about this sad event. Now that delightful house at Naples,‡ which holds so marked a place in our recollections, has

* Sir Richard Acton.
† Marie de Dalberg, Lady Acton, afterwards Countess Granville.
‡ Sir Richard Acton's, where Albert, Alexandrine, and I were married.

become a ruin which can never be restored, whose traditions will live in our memory alone. Everything that ends *for ever* is so depressing! I should never, probably, have seen that house again, but still I liked to think of it as it was. Now everything at Naples seems so gloomy, for although the remembrance of my poor Albert had already thrown a shade over those bright spots, still my heart rejoiced at the sunshine lighting up the houses of my friends, and the thought of their happiness did me good. Now the sight of misery on all sides seems to deepen the abyss which encircles ourselves. We reckon that to-day that poor mother will hear the sad news. But we will not dwell upon this mournful subject. How are you getting on, my child, who are the joy and brightness of my life? Your father is delighted with your letters, and is now satisfied that you did well to go. He sees that the difficulties are less than he imagined, and, now the dreadful passage is over, he admits that it was right. You have been justified by the event, and let nothing disturb your happiness. You cannot be too happy to please us, and I say again, you are the only bright spot in my horizon!"

THE SAME TO THE SAME.

"Boury, March 26th, 1837.

"My Precious Child—I want to tell you a little about our Easter. Then I shall leave off, to write to several other people; and afterwards return to you. How did you spend your Holy Week? I hope as happily as we did. The excellent young priest whom the Bishop of Beauvais sent us, went through everything as well as possible. He preached an excellent sermon on the Passion on Holy Thursday afternoon, and this morning again. To be sure we had no Tenebræ, but we said them in our own pretty peaceful Chapel. On Good Friday your father read us Bourdaloue's admirable discourse on the Passion, and yesterday again he read to us both in the morning and afternoon. To-day he read to everybody in the house Bossuet's sermon on the Resurrection. And then what do you think we had at Mass in the way of music? Neither more nor less than Haÿdn's *Gloria*, and admirably performed too. The effect of Eugénie's voice in the solo was beautiful. She sings as well as ever again, and has recovered the power and sweetness of her notes. This comes of her having practised a great deal lately, and I am happy to say, without being the worse for it. Alexandrine's voice also is stronger, and her high notes are sweet, true, and full. The dear children find that this beautiful music, instead of disturbing them on Communion-days, helps to raise their souls to God, and awakens holy thoughts. To-day, therefore, at Mass they sang the *Gloria,* and after Communion, at the end of the Mass, the *Magnificat,* which is to me the sublimest of all thanksgivings. Alexandrine and Eugénie had dressed their scholars in white, and the children came in to show themselves before Mass. They are doing more good than can be conceived, and of a sort that is most useful to themselves. On your birthday, I intend giving a dinner to the poorest of our neighbors, that is to say, food will be distributed to them, which they can carry to their own homes. The heart is ten times more alive to charity in the country than in towns. I have always forgotten to tell you of our carnival-amusements, which, as they were quite innocent, were prolonged through Lent. I had given Bertha,* on New-Year's-Day, an immense white dog—a toy—which she left here when she went to Paris. This dog goes from bed to bed and from room to room, and your sisters never seem to weary of the joke. They make it appear in all sorts of characters, and dress it up in all kinds of ways, and always with the same success. Two days ago, when I came to bed, I found it sitting before the fire, wrapped in a dressing-gown, a shawl on its head, a pipe in its mouth, and a newspaper in its hand. Thanks to my sharp eyes,† I thought at first it was your father! I was surprised that he did not move, and even felt frightened for a moment, but only just long enough for the joke. Yesterday evening, on going up to bed, I saw a little hump-backed fairy sitting by my curtain, which made me start. It was *Sifflotte*—the children's name for this famous dog—whom Olga had covered with a shawl, put a hood on his head, and her knitting in his paws. You see it is an endless source of fun, and poor dear Olga does not get tired of it. I do admire her for being so bright, so contented with her dull life, not even giving a thought to the amusements from which she is cut off, and which you all so enjoyed at the same age."‡

Eugénie also told me in her letters of several jokes of the same kind, and especially of some mystification she had contrived, and

* Berthe de la Ferronnays, then a year old, now Vicomtesse de Dreuse Brégé.
† Madame de la Ferronnays was extremely short sighted.
‡ Olga was seventeen at this time.

which had taken Alexandrine in, and then added :—"Dear Pauline, what will you say of these diversions from our habitual gravity? They are whimsical enough, and not in keeping with the state of poor Alexandrine's feelings. But then, you know, she does not of her own accord turn her mind to anything which would distract her from her grief. These jokes occupy her thoughts for a few minutes, and make her laugh. They do not make her less unhappy, but they take off her mind for a few minutes from the thought of her unhappiness. Often after these little fits of gaiety she has returns of gloom. The fact is, she can never be really happy again, and thus can only have moments of gaiety. Well, in sixty years we shall all be dead. Amen!"

COUNT DE MONTALEMBERT TO ALEXANDRINE.

"Venice, November 27th, 1836.

"DEAR ALEXANDRINE—You will have received, before this letter reaches you, everything you asked me for in yours of October 17th, that is to say, every letter I had in my possession of Albert's and of yours. I begged Cornudet to look for them, and then send them to you. He will also have told you why I did not write sooner, and amongst other reasons that I had been ill, and also your letter did not reach me till long after date. I do not very well remember what you took and what you left before you went away, but I told Cornudet to give you *everything* he could find in the place where I kept all his letters and yours. I hope you have found in them much which must be soothing and precious to you. I take a great interest in this work, which seems to me a direct inspiration, the accomplishing of which will have an unspeakable charm in spite of all its sadness. But while sending you everything you wish for, I protest solemnly as to my rights of property. I depend both upon your friendship and integrity for giving me back what I only lend you. I am too proud and too glad to have been so trusted, and so tenderly loved by Albert, to be willing to give up, even to you, these many and precious memorials of that trust and affection. I told you that I would make you a present of two or three of the letters, which mention you in so special and striking a way as to become sacred and peculiar treasures to you. These you may keep, but you must send me back all the rest.

"To return to your letter of October 17th. I will not conceal from you, my dear friend, that I was a little grieved and even wounded at your long silence; but I forgive you at last, chiefly on account of those admirable, sublime, and delightful words of Albert's, which, like a good sister, you copied and sent me. I do not use these expressions in any theatrical sense, for they simply express my thoughts. These are things which, if they were in a *printed book*, as poor people say, would be admired by the whole world—so, at least, it seems to me. I know of nothing finer in Réné, or in any of the great writers who have described the workings of the heart. To me there seems something wonderfully satisfactory, and even, I think, honorable to the human mind, in the knowledge that such beautiful thoughts arose quite simply and spontaneously in the pure and modest mind of a young man unknown to all literary fame, without the last idea of publication, only occupied with God and his love, and never dreaming that passages were flowing from his pen which the greatest genius in the world might have coveted. I know nothing more touching than that address to you of the 26th of August, 1832: '*Is it not true, my angel, that I love you right well?*' It is one of those bursts of feeling which, to my mind, have not their like; and then there are thoughts of another kind, which it is astonishing to find in the journal of a young lover: '*This wearisome world which offers us nothing great but its own emptiness.*' Yes, I repeat it, apart from the tender interest I feel, when I reflect that it is my friend and brother Albert who wrote these things, I am thankful to God for having given such beautiful thoughts to a young man who never went beyond the limits of his home circle, and had no other teachers than religion and love. I wish you had seen the tears running down Anna's* cheeks when I read these papers to her; you would not have thought it an unacceptable tribute. We were both reminded of our Abbé Gerbet's admirable words which apply so well to Albert: '*For my part, I listen more attentively to the utterances of a holy soul, than to the voice of genius.*'

"Armed with the directions which you gave in your last letter, we made a pilgrimage to all the places, and visited all the people you mentioned. We began with the *Casa Paolinelli.*† Those good people gave us a most cordial reception, and seemed to

* Madame de Montalembert.
† The last house in which Albert and Alexandrine lived at Venice.

take the utmost interest in your story, having heard of your conversion from Brera.* We visited Albert's room with the deepest emotion; and recited—at least, I did—in a low voice the *De profundis*, and lived over in thought those sad heart-breaking scenes which had taken place in that room. It is a pretty apartment, now occupied by the Marquis Gherardi. We should have liked, for all sorts of reasons, to inhabit it ourselves. Then we went to the *Visitandines*, saw the Superioress, and spoke at great length about you. She seemed much interested in Madame de la Ferronnays, but was very cold to us, though I had taken my wife with me, that she might see I was a respectable married man, but it did not succeed. The good lady thought, I believe, that I was not a legitimist, for her great object, during the conversation, seemed to be to make cuts at *Philippe* and the *France of July*. On the other hand, Padre Catullo received and treated us in the most friendly manner possible. We went to confession to him, and to Communion in his beautiful Church on St. Elizabeth's Day. He is a charming man to my mind, and dotes upon you all. '*E la Eugenia, il Ferdinando, e tutti quanti.*' We talked a long time about you, and especially about your conversion and former doubts. I do not remember if it was he who once said to you in reference to the salvation of Protestants in good faith: '*Per me non lo posso credere.*' (For my part, I cannot believe it.) He does not seem to me to hold any such opinions. I also saw Brera, who was touched by your message, and is very much attached to you. He told me that Caraba had become a waiter at a café. Then there was the good old Gamba, the conceited Perrucchini-Romanini, the musician, who makes out that he taught *Ferdinando* German, the English Williams, etc., etc., who all spoke of you with great interest, and desired to be remembered."

THE SAME TO THE SAME.

"Florence, March 3rd, 1837.

"My dear Little Sister—You have good reason to complain of your brother Montal. I own myself guilty, and very guilty, for not having written to you for so long—not so guilty as you were yourself during the latter months of last year, but still very guilty, and I fully admit it. However, you must remember that I was at Rome with my wife, that I had only two

* Albert's doctor.

months to spend there, and that during that time it was requisite to see everything, and moreover to *show* everything; that besides this, I had no end of important business to arrange for myself, for the Abbé Lacordaire, for a Polish religious house founded by Count Plater, and though last not least, for the Abbé Gerbet. You forgive me then, do you not, dear and good friend, on condition that I repent and do better for the future, which I promise with all my heart? Tell the Abbé Gerbet, that in spite of his stay at Boury—where he neglects, not merely his letters but his work, having published, after six months' silence, but three pages in the *Université Catholique*, and only one fragment of the complete refutations [of M. de la Mennais] which is expected from him; tell him, I say, that his article in the January number is admirable, that several persons have written to me that it excels everything he has yet written, and though he had not the politeness to send it to me, I got it before I left Rome, and took it the next day to the Pope, with whom I left it, and that His Holiness was much interested in it, and read aloud in my presence the whole of the first page. The Pope seemed specially pleased with the paragraph which so magnificently opens the article, and in which he says that all M. de la Mennais' old friends have gone over to the right hand of the Vicar of Christ. He took it away to his own rooms, read it to several persons, and gave it to Cardinal Lambruschini. Tell all this, if you please, to the silent Abbé, and if he is not turned into a tree in the park at Boury, I think it will interest him. The Pope gave us each a beautiful Crucifix and a number of rosaries for our friends, of which you shall have your share, if you behave well to me till I see you again. I did not get your letter of the 8th of December till I was in Rome, and consequently could do none of the things in Venice that you asked me. I never saw M. B. except at a distance, rowing in a gondola in bright yellow gloves and a blouse. We left Venice on the 8th, after receiving Communion and Padre Catullo's blessing, who loves you and Eugénie as he does his own two eyes. We went through a short quarantine at Rovigo, and rushed at full speed to Rome, to get there by Christmas, and to see and enjoy that wonderfully grand Pontifical Mass at St. Peter's. We looked with the most affectionate interest at the house under the Trinità da Monte, where Albert saw you for the first time, and where I everything almost with a smile, you would forgive me for looking upon the world as a grave-yard, where every one suffers, has suffered, or will suffer. I admit that these are sad ideas, but they are true, and truer than any others. Sad realities do not grow less real because we shut our eyes that we may not look them in the face; would it not be better to comfort ourselves with the idea of what lies before us beyond this gloomy life, which is merely like a dark cavern we have to pass through on our way to Paradise?

"It was not God Who made death and suffering. I always like to repeat this to our poor village people, for I am often afraid our dear, good Lord is slandered. Forgive me, my dear one, for speaking of these sad things to-day, but you know religion turns sadness into comfort and hope, whereas without it, when we come to think, everything happy and bright is sad. This is in short the real truth of the matter. But I have very little faith. Pray, my dear Pauline, ask God to give me more. My dearest, I was surprised to find that you thought me quite cured of my scruples—*circles*, as we used to call them—when just lately I have had *an attack of spiritual fever;* I lost my head, feeling sometimes elated and sometimes in despair about myself. It all comes from my stupid imagination; the Abbé Gerbet will cure me in time, by forbidding me to analyse. This reminds me that he said I was to let you have a *decade* which I made some time ago, and which I had a scruple in sending, because I knew you would praise it. Now there may be pride in telling you that I did not send it on that account, for that is boasting; and in saying that it was boasting, and that I concealed a thing in order not to be praised for it, there is pride again; and in acknowledging that there is pride in my confession of having boasted, and that I concealed a thing not to be praised—Oh! I am out of breath!—I shall go distracted! But I only wished to prove to you that I have not lost the art of conjuring up scruples, or of fabricating circles, and that on this point we are sisters still. Here, then, is my *decade*—but no, it would take up too much time; if I have any left, I will put it in at the end of the letter.* Thank you, my dear sister, for wishing so much to see me again. I, too, wish it. I think it quite natural that you would not like

* I have lost that decade, but I remember that it was made up of ten different flowers, and that to each was attached the idea of some virtue and a little prayer.

me to die, but your fright when I had the influenza, touched me very much. I dare say I shall live a long time, and with God's help, I hope patiently. I am not in such a hurry to die now, though I should still like it, and I hope the feeling will last till I reach the next world."

EUGENIE TO PAULINE.

"April 10th, 1837.

"I am sure you must have thought a great deal about us yesterday, prayed for us a great deal, grieved and hoped as we did.* Yesterday, the third anniversary of that poor marriage, so joyful at the time, so full of the promise of happiness, but from the first day so saddened by anxious care! And Alexandrine had to spend that anniversary without him, and now ten months have passed away since that happy life came to an end. We all went to Communion, and prayed and wept, but thanked God too, and it was a thanksgiving Mass, that the Abbé Gerbet said. He made Alexandrine return thanks on this day—for Albert's love, for her marriage, and for her reception into the Church. In short, he turned yesterday rather into a day of hope than one of mourning."

MADAME DE LA FERRONNAYS TO PAULINE.

"I am sure that you thought much of us and poor dear Alexandrine on the 17th. Oh! what heart-breaking recollections! What bright days seemed then to open before us all, and what an endless source of comfort we should have found in those dear children, so happy in their marriage, and so good! I cannot tell you how charming and touching Alexandrine was throughout that day. In the midst of her sadness she is so gentle and resigned. After Mass I went to your father's room, where she came to us, and kissed us both most tenderly, without uttering a word, for no words could express what filled her heart at that moment. It is impossible to be a greater darling than she is. The word *suave*† seems made for her. But oh! in spite of the certainty of our precious child's happiness, how impossible it is not to think of what his enjoyment would have been here, if a few more years had been granted him. I should have been too blessed for this world, if what seemed then to have been my lot had all been realised. To have him here with his Alexandrine, enjoying our

* The anniversary of Alexandrine's marriage.
† This word in French is generally applied to perfumes, in that case it means balmy.

O MY GOD!

THY NAME

IS THE FIRST WRITTEN AS I BEGIN THIS BOOK: I DESIRE THAT IT MAY MOVE MEN TO LOVE THOSE REMEMBERED IN IT: BUT FAR MORE EARNESTLY I DESIRE THAT IT MAY KINDLE LOVE

FOR THEE.

home and living with us. Oh! my God, this would indeed have been too great a delight. And now what gloom takes the place of all that future, so full of sunshine, and which seemed to me beforehand only a matter of course."

EUGENIE TO PAULINE.

"Boury, May 4th, 1837.

"MY DEAREST—I have received your immense letter, and shall answer it presently, but first let us speak of all those deaths which have taken place, as if to detach us from the world, and oblige us to be always ready to leave it. You must have been terribly shocked by Antonine's* death, for you heard less about her illness than we did. Even now I can scarcely believe it. I see her before me as she looked on the day she went away, so fresh and bright, and making me promise to go to Lumigny, as soon as she returned. Poor Antonine! there is now no return for her. I cannot bring myself to pity those who die, but I feel very sad when I think of her parents. I recall poor Mons. de Mun's worshipping looks at her last year, and I fear he must be in a dreadful state. I knew Antonine better than you did, and at Lumigny I quite loved her. She was so affectionate to me; she foresaw clearly that she should die young, and she regretted life. You know how well I understand the opposite feeling, it is the prevailing one with me, but still when I see any one die regretting life, I feel it so acutely for them, that my heart aches, and I think how gladly I would die in his or her place. Antonine knew well that hers was an incurable illness; she said so to my father and me, and then expressed the wish to become weaned from life. But though she expected to die young, she did not think it would be so soon. She hoped to come back, and now she is dead, and so suddenly! She had made her Easter† a few days before, so that there was nothing terrible in her sudden death; on the contrary, it may be looked upon as a mercy, for as she regretted life so much, it might have been too great a trial for her to watch the approach of death. As it is, she found herself in the presence of God before she had had time to feel the pain of quitting this world. If she has anything still to expiate in the next, let us pray earnestly for her that God may have mercy on her soul. There has been another death

* Antonine de Mun, Countess de Biron.
† Her Easter duties of Confession and Communion.

which will grieve you very much. Poor Helene* has also left this sad world. God knows well what He does, and as He has promised to reward those that weep, He surely knows that sorrow is good for the soul. It certainly draws one nearer to Him than joy. Mamma was afraid that these two deaths would affect you so much, that I ought to have made some one break the news to you, but I, who know that you heard of Albert's death by letter, feel sure that you can bear anything else."

THE SAME TO THE SAME.

"May 7th, 1837.

"Two words only this evening, for I am excessively tired, and must go to bed. We are so busy now, both out of doors and at home, that sometimes the whole day goes by without my being able to sit down. All the poor people who die want to see us, all the sick send for us, all who wish to become good come to us, and we go and seek out those who do not want to be good; which altogether keeps us actively employed and always on the move. Alas! what has become of my plan of spending part of the summer at Lumigny, and my friendship with Antonine that my father so wished me to keep up? Nothing is certain in this world except uncertainty. In a few days my father starts for Nantes. He will not be long away, but still we do not like to part with him. He is so good, and kinder to us than ever. You cannot think how much his indifference to earthly things increases. Poor dear father! this is the effect of all the sorrows of the past year. Antonine's death grieved him very much, for you know how he liked her, and if he were not now so completely resigned to everything, this new grief would perhaps have done him harm. Thanks, dear love, for thinking of me so much, for wishing to have me near you, to jog your elbow, as you say. How dear you are! What friends we were when we went out into the world together. Do you recollect how often we surprised people by liking to sit next each other, or by exchanging a word in a ball-room? There may be sisters who love each other as much as we do, but certainly not better—and I like to think that for my own part, I have loved you both as a friend and a sister, and as much as either can be loved."

* Helene de Tourzel, Comtesse de Hunolstein, grand-daughter of the Duchesse de Tourzel, gouvernante of the Dauphin and Madame Royale, and aunt of Madame de la Ferronnays.

"May 19th.

"I am convinced that the only really happy people are those who are not afraid of death. To love death is to hate everything that dies, and to long for what is really life. God has made death a punishment, but it is the means through which we attain our reward. Oh! do not mourn for me when I die; for if I thank God every day for my birth, it is because if I had not been born I could not have died. Pauline, Pauline, may our meeting in Heaven be a blessed one!"

"June 1st.

"I can well understand your sorrow at not being with Albert when he died. I thank God very much that I was with him on the journey, and in all his last sufferings. Since the anniversary of our departure from Venice, Alexandrine and I have commemorated the events of each successive day. On Monday it was a year since she was received into the church. To-day it is a year since Albert played for the last time on the pianoforte. Whenever he did so latterly there was something inexpressibly melancholy about it. He used to modulate the chords in a way which made one sad in spite of oneself. In the night of May 31st, he began to play at about two o'clock in the morning. I was awoke out of my sleep by that music, and not being able at first to imagine what it was, the effect was most painful. I cannot help breaking off writing to read his last words in Alex's book; and if I go on doing so I shall not be able to finish it in time, for it breaks my heart. Tears oblige me to lay down my pen; I forget you to dwell upon him, to speak to him, to call him, to ask him where he is, what he is doing, and I cannot help exclaiming, 'Why, why, may we not see into Heaven?' And now I am in one of my fits of the love of death."

"June 2nd.

"You are right in saying that we all seem to be rather nearer to Heaven since Albert is there, and you as much as any of us, dear Pauline. I do not like your way of leaving yourself out. We may well repeat the words Albert wrote: '*A sweet communion begins to exist between Heaven and our souls.*' This communion is the greatest happiness on earth. You may talk as you please, but, however happy life may be, nothing I am sure can equal that of leaving it. You must let me speak my mind. Perhaps I am no judge, for I do not know the happiness you describe, and if I have guessed at it, and imagined it, I have also pictured to myself the happiness of Heaven, and all other kinds of joy fade away before that, so that I feel neither curiosity about, nor desire for, nor need of, earthly joys. Now I am going over your letter of the 9th of May, line by line, as you grumble at the quantity of things I forget to answer, so now I am writing methodically. Did I really never tell you about our class of forty-four children? How stupid of me! Well, I have twenty-two scholars, and Olga as many. I teach them catechism. I explain to them that the Blessed Trinity is God, and that the Holy Ghost is not a Saint* like SS. Peter and Paul, an error to which they incline, &c., &c. I have a great ugly room with a Cross over the chimney-piece, and there I hold forth, and four times out of six it amuses me very much.† You were interested with the account of our poor savage.‡ Well, I must tell you the happy conclusion of the story; she is established here as a sort of gardener's assistant. I cannot describe her joy and surprise at this change, and the various ways in which she shows her gratitude. She takes our hands, kisses them, gets quite red and flurried, and exclaims: 'Oh! I am so comfortable!' and other remarks of the same kind. She is very nervous, and even subject to hysterics; and after coming here the great change nearly turned her head. One evening, during dinner, she was seized with one of these terrible attacks, to the infinite terror of all the maids, who were so foolish that they would not speak to the poor little thing all the rest of the evening. The fit was certainly a bad one; she rolled on the floor screaming and tearing her hair; then as usual, when she calmed down a little, she burst into a flood of tears. After which she got up suddenly, and would go to the Chapel, where she began to say all the prayers she knew by heart, and afterwards came and fell on her knees before me, saying, '*Mademoiselle Eugénie, I beg your pardon for having vexed you;*' then before Alex, '*Madame Albert, I am so sorry for all the bad things I have done.*' Poor child! it touched us very much. I played a little to her on the organ, and at the first sound of the music she became quite quiet, stroked my hand while I played, and repeated, 'Ah! how beautiful, how beautiful!' It

* "Le *Saint* Esprit" often puzzles quite young French children.

† The Curé of Boury at that time was an old man of ninety, almost superannuated, and not able to attend to the instruction of the village children.

‡ A poor beggar-girl they had rescued.

is really affecting and strange to hear her speak about young girls and children who were leading the same life as herself: 'That girl was not like me—she was not obliged to go about—she had a good mother, she had, who worked, and begged her to stay at home; but she always ran away and said, "Ah, bah, I won't work!" and then went about with the *gangs*. I met her one day when she was tired and hungry, and said to her, "So there you are again; you don't stay with your mother, you goose, you!" She had had nothing to eat for two days, and I had three bits of bread, so I gave her two of them, and I had twenty *sous*, so I gave her ten.' What do you think of that speech? Are not such acts of charity and goodness in the midst of such ignorance worth more in the sight of God than heaps of gold bestowed by the rich out of their abundance? Is it not also extraordinary that these generous instincts should take birth and continue to exist in a poor creature brought up in the midst of crime, and ignorant of the very name of God?

"But to go on to another subject. Yes, the Abbé Gerbet's verses are admirable. Ever since I have read and understood what I read, and pencilled my books in every direction, and in all manner of shapes and colors, according as I found in them things that I have sometimes thought and felt myself, I have never met with so many of my own thoughts as in the Abbé's writings; expressed, indeed, in words I could not have hit upon myself; and, again, others which never had occurred to my mind, but must have lingered about my heart, for when I see them in print the pleasure they give me is not one of surprise, but rather an agreeable sense of having heard them before.

"And now, to go on to something else. Ah, Madam, I thought so indeed! So, in the wisdom of your scruples, you think you do not fulfil the precept of hearing Mass if you are playing the organ all the time, and so help to kindle the fervor and devotion of others? Well, Madam, being better advised than you, I begin by raising my heart to God before Mass, and beg Him to accept my intention and to forgive all distractions. Then, when the Priest is at the foot of the Altar, and everybody on their knees, I seat myself at the organ, and Mass goes on, as far as I am concerned, with no other means of offering up my worship, my self-abasement, my petitions, and the thousand wants of my soul, than the changes and modulations of the chords, which, after all, are a thousand times more expressive than any language in the world. I do not deny that I have a thousand distractions, but I recall my wandering thoughts, and remind Almighty God that my heart lies before Him, and I beg Him to pardon the infirmities of my mind. And, moreover, if I go to a second Mass it is not a bit with the intention of making up for one imperfectly or not heard. And, to cut the matter short, it has been decided by the Church that those who play or sing during Mass, hear it in a proper manner, and we are not to think otherwise. The day after to-morrow we go to Paris, and thus ends a happy time of quiet, a time of peace and comfort. What will be the next phase of our life? I shall write to you from Paris, and tell you how I get on in another sphere. We had a grand procession on Corpus Christi. The organ sounded admirably out of doors before the temporary Altar. I must leave off. Good-bye. God grant we may soon meet again!"

MADAME DE LA FERRONNAYS TO PAULINE.

"June 2nd.

"I take Olga's place, who was going to write to you, but she is attending to two girls, one of whom is going to make her First Communion to-morrow, and the other to renew the act. Did Eugénie tell you about the processions? I think not, for she did not write that day. They were really charming. It was all so pretty; the girls dressed in white, the music near the altar in the garden, and the wonderful effect of Eugénie's voice in the open air. My dear child, I want you to know how much touched and pleased I was with your letter of May the 20th. It is a subject on which we have always agreed, but there are not many, I believe, who are heartily of our mind. What you say on the matter, '*chatouille de mon cœur l'orgeuilleuse faiblesse,*'* by proving that I was right; for I have maintained a hundred times that the women who plunge headlong into dissipation after their marriage, are generally those who have been kept from all enjoyment in their youth. In Paris, women *begin* their career of pleasure and dancing when they marry, whereas in my opinion they ought then to leave off caring for pleasure and dancing; but if this is to be the case it is not amiss that they should have had a little amusement beforehand; and, therefore, I have never been sorry

* "Flatters the proud weakness of my heart."

to have given you all opportunities of amusing yourselves, but you know I always told you that you must make up your minds to do without amusement at any moment, and for ever if necessary. And now, I think, I have praised myself enough. I must leave off, my dear child, for I have all my goods to pack. The last Mass the Abbé Gerbet says here—for this time at least—is just over. We all went to our duties, and I offered up my Communion in thanksgiving for the consolation granted, and the favors bestowed during these last six months. The abundance of spiritual blessings we have enjoyed has given us fresh life. This is certainly the case with Alexandrine and Eugénie, and though I may not perhaps have derived so much advantage from them as they have done, still I can testify to the comfort it has brought. I love you with all my heart."

COUNT DE MONTALEMBERT TO ALEXANDRINE.

"Paris, May 6th, 1837.

"You pay me the highest possible compliment when you tell me that I write about Albert in a way that satisfies you. Alas! my dear friend, I assure you it is not in a way that satisfies myself; on the contrary, I often accuse myself of a want of gratitude towards him and his holy memory. In the midst of my present happiness I am afraid of too often losing sight of his affectionate solicitude, who, as you justly say, obtained that blessing for me by his fervent prayers. Still, God knows that my thoughts and memory revert to Albert whenever I can withdraw them from the present scene. In Italy, indeed, it was natural that his remembrance should haunt me. The past contains no dearer one to me. I liked to feel myself as it were, under the protection of my companion and intimate friend, with whom I used to share all my feelings, and who would, I am sure, have sacrified half his own happiness to secure mine. I was obliged to give up the hope I had cherished of spending some days at Pisa to dwell upon these recollections.

"Having been detained at Florence, as I told you, by my wife's illness, we had to hurry to Genoa as soon as she had recovered, in order to reach Paris before it became unsafe for her to travel, and to avoid the snow on Mount Cenis we were forced to take the Cornice road. Thus we only just passed through Pisa, and that in such weather, that it was impossible to set foot in the streets, which were nothing but streams of melted snow. In the evening, however, I managed to paddle by moonlight from the hotel to the house in which we lived, but it was too late to try to renew acquaintance with our famous professor and poor Thérèse. The next morning we were forced to start in a violent snow-storm—this on the 25th of March! I do not know Italy again in such weather. Many regards to your father and mother-in-law. I saw Charles yesterday, who was very amiable to me and admirably patient."

THE SAME TO THE SAME.

"Villersexel (Haute Rhone), June 5th, 1837.

"MY VERY DEAR FRIEND—I came here on the 29th of May, on the anniversary of your reception into the Church. I found here your letter of May 22nd. I read first with the deepest interest what you tell me of the good the Abbé Gerbet has done you all. I rejoice at it most heartily, but in spite of it I cannot help deploring his prolonged stay at Boury, and especially his inaction while there. Everything you tell me is excellent in itself, but it is not the kind of good the Abbé Gerbet ought to be doing. I do not hesitate to say such is not *his* mission, it is the mission of a village Curé, an excellent and a high one, I grant, but not his. What should we have thought if your father-in-law, when he was minister of foreign affairs or ambassador, had taken it into his head to turn himself into an Inspector of Domains, or a Collector of Taxes, and boasted of the services he was rendering the King in that new capacity? Would not every one have cried out against him and said it was not his place—that he was wanting in his duty? Well, that is the story of the Abbé Gerbet, with the difference there must always exist between even the greatest minister and a priest, and such a priest as he is. It is not for Boury, nor for any given locality he ought to be laboring; but for *Rome* and *Paris*, and that means for the *world.* The *Catholic world*, the whole Church, requires his services, and not the little parish of Boury, or the diocese of Beauvais. The Church has a right to his services, especially at this moment when she has been assailed and violently outraged by a most dangerous enemy. When the Abbé de la Mennais' dangerous and insulting book appeared, all eyes turned towards the Abbé Gerbet and the Abbé Lacordaire, because every one felt that it belonged to them to defend their mother. This was not a question of the salvation of five or six souls, but of the salvation of thousands, perhaps of millions, for it is one of those struggles which go on reverberating through centuries, and may affect the farthest generations for good or evil. The Abbé Lacordaire nobly fulfilled his duty, and at the end of three weeks his work* was completed and sent to the Pope. Every one knows that it was the Archbishop of Paris who stopped its publication.† This should have only served to kindle the Abbé Gerbet's zeal, and urged him not to abandon the field to triumphant error. But he did not come forward, and every one regrets it, and so much the more that we can tell by the fragments published in the '*Université Catholique*' what a glorious monument he could have raised to truth and the Church. But nobody thinks he has fulfilled his obligation by these scanty pages, and there is no one who does not feel as the Pope did when I gave him the first edition: '*E peccato, non è finito.*' (It is a pity it is not finished.) This was last January, and now we are in June. You say that you despise the outcry of '*that wretched world which always cries out, and never knows or understands,*' but I am not speaking of the worldly world, but of the Catholic world, both priests and laymen. I know nothing more worthy of respect or of being listened to than that world. You quote St. James, and I quote the Gospel. Indeed you will do me no injustice at all (as you seem to think you do) by supposing that I do not like the *hidden* good the Abbé Gerbet is doing. No, certainly I do not like it, it is this very hidden life I complain of. Did not our Lord say: '*Neither do men light a candle and put it under a bushel?*' Now Boury is the bushel which covers and hides the light God has given the Abbé Gerbet to enlighten His Church. Remember that I do not find fault with him for choosing Boury as his abode, though for my own sake I should have preferred Trélon, or Villersexel; what I find fault with is, that he does not work at Boury, and I conclude from that idleness that the place is not good for him, and that the sooner he leaves it the better. I am not afraid of people saying: 'There is a friend for you!' for I do not believe that the Abbé Gerbet has a better friend than myself; but I am a still greater friend to the Church; and that is why I

* Afterwards known as the "Letter on the Holy See."
† From prudential reasons.

complain of his sinning against the Church. I am not quite certain that his silence does not amount to a *sin against the Holy Ghost!*—but as he is a better theologian than I am, he can tell you this himself. You said in your letter 'Answer me,' and now I hope you *are* answered. But in spite of my outcry against the Abbé Gerbet, I cannot forget, my very dear friend, the holy and admirable words he said to you this day year.* The recollection of that address and of all that affecting scene fills me, even now, with deep emotions; and I wished to write to you to-day and sympathise as much as in me lies, with this glorious and holy anniversary. The remembrance of that First Communion of yours which was to be Albert's last, and in which I was so happily associated with you both, will always be one of the sweetest, holiest, dearest recollections of my life, for never did that religion, which I love above all things, seem to me so sublime and beautiful. I cannot but think it was the best day of your life, for you never had made Albert so happy, or been so yourself, and in so holy a manner united to him. I found my wife perfectly well, thank God! Pray for us a great deal from the 10th to the 15th,† and beg Eugénie and the Abbé Gerbet to join in these prayers. I am not afraid of asking you all to bear this intention in mind at a time when you will be dwelling on remembrances as dear to me as to you. And now to conclude, I must say in reply to your wise sisterly remonstrances on my passion for *raising an outcry* and my *sudden extasies and furies* that you are quite right, but I am afraid this tendency will contine. It belongs to my nature, and you know the proverb: '*Chassez le naturel, il revient au galop.*' It is therefore probable that we shall both go on to the end, I going into rages and you scolding me for them; that is the likeness between us. Only you will be doing right, and I wrong; that is the difference. You see it is entirely to your advantage. Farewell!"

Notwithstanding the exaggerated expressions in some of the passages of this letter, I have not thought it desirable to suppress a single word of it, for they reflect no discredit either on the writer, who penned them in the full ardor of his youthful impetuosity, or on the venerable object of his strictures. They ex-

* The day of Alexandrine's First Communion.

† Eugénie wrote on the 22nd, "Have you heard of the arrival of *Demoiselle Marie Elizabeth Hiltrude de Montalembert*, who I am sure will not fail to do honor to her great patron Saints."

hibit M. de Montalembert's somewhat impetuous zeal, and that love for the Church of which he has given so many proofs; and they also prove how important in his eyes were his friend's labors, and how much *prestige* even at that time surrounded the name of one who afterwards occupied so high a position in the Church. For my part, I may still be allowed to question whether the Abbé Gerbet's work at Boury was as unworthy of his mission as Albert's friend considered it to be. And it seems now even more doubtful whether any additional refutation of the Abbé de la Mennais' doctrines were really an object for which that other work ought to have been given up. Time, which, alas! has overthrown all the hopes we then still cherished for that great fallen intellect, has also shown that the dangers with which his apostacy threatened the Church were far less considerable than was supposed by men who concluded that the power of the enemy would be proportionate to the champion's strength. Their alarm was natural, and when they saw the light which had guided them—and which some of them had followed with even passionate affection—transformed into the lurid flame of an incendiary, we cannot wonder that the alarm should have been excessive. But what no refutation could have done, God Himself effected by quenching the fire of genius in Mons. de la Mennais' mind, when he himself extinguished the fire of charity in his soul. I repeat of *charity*, not the light of faith, for it always seemed to me that the ruin of that great, but unhappy man, was brought about by anger and not by unbelief.

Alexandrine answered Count de Montalembert's vehement letter in the following manner:—

ALEXANDRINE TO COUNT DE MONTALEMBERT.

"June 13th.

"I see you are not cured of your despotic humor. What! you lay it upon me, *per la santa ubbedienza*—I should like to know by what right—to order the Abbé Gerbet to leave Boury? I gave him your letter, and admired the smiling placidity with which he read all your impertinent invectives. But if I must answer you, I will say, first, that his health is not good, and he is consequently obliged continually to interrupt his work; then, that he has good reasons for putting off writing to you; then, that he once wrote you a letter of six sheets, which ought to reckon for five years; then, that when you see his handwriting again it will be in a volume; then, that he has a splendid plan for a new work in his head; and lastly, that you have no business to judge him at all, though you are an eminent and even celebrated man. Apropos of this, I see how truly I feel like a sister to you, by the joy which it gives me to hear your *St. Elizabeth* praised up to the skies. In spite of frivolity and affectation, the fashionable world has been touched, whether it would or not, by the charming naïvéte, the tenderness, the love of God, and the earnestness which stamp this dear book, and which are rendered in such a simple and graceful style; and besides all this, it has a hundred other merits. You have, I am sure, heard all this said much better than I can say it. And now I end by the warning you have so often and so usefully given me:—'*Beware of pride.*' My dear friend, summon up all your faith, and make one earnest prayer that I may get rid of the spirit of subtlety, and the endless reasonings in a circle which result from it, and from scrupulosity, the source of both. But never pray for me without beseeching that God may make that poor love of ours, which was so full of trials in this world, eternally happy in the next. You are bound to do this for Albert's sake, for I think no man ever so earnestly desired a friend's happiness as he did yours. I know you admit this, my dear brother Montal, and it makes me love you very much. Oh! I should like to see you again, to tell you a thousand things, to weary you with a thousand repetitions—but you would have patience with me. I thank you for telling me about that good Princess Volkonsky. What did she say about our poor days at Sorrento? Ah! indeed our life there was sweet! I never, even in my dreams, could conceive anything more enchanting; and it must have struck others even more than ourselves, who did not know that such joys are really to be found on earth. It was his health only that prevented it from being perfect; but I looked forward to happiness with such certainty; I was so sure he would get well. Pitying Angels must, I think, have closed my eyes, for such blindness was not natural, or in accordance with my character and my continual anxiety about him. Thank you for thinking of us when you saw our house under the Trinita da Monte. Yes, we met there for the first time, and there his love, by God's grace, began to draw me towards Heaven. I like to think that you have seen Pisa too once more.

"We are very busy, and the dear Abbé, whom you so scandalously and irreverently accuse of idleness, is saving many souls at Boury. The village takes up almost all our time. Eugénie is superioress, prime minister, and head school mistress. Olga is almoner and chaplain, and I am chancellor, grave-digger and missionary. Our kind Abbé Martin de Noirlieu has been spending a fortnight here, and has done us all good. He loves and admires you, and while he was here read your *St. Elizabeth*, which he could not forgive you for not sending him, till he heard you had treated the Abbé Gerbet in the same way. And after that, you reproach him for not having sent you an article in a newspaper! Farewell, and God bless you!"

These letters were written only a few days before the Abbé Gerbet's departure. He left Boury the following week, with all the inmates of the château. They were going to Paris for the last fortnight in June, and did not return to the country till after the anniversary of Albert's death. During their stay in Paris they met several of the friends most connected with those sad recollections, and among others the Abbé Martin de Noirlieu and Mons. Rio. The Abbé Gerbet went to Juilly, but returned to spend the 29th day of June with them. But it will be seen that even at a distance he had shared all their feelings during those melancholy days. Amongst several letters written at that time by absent friends, I find one from myself which I think I should not omit.

FROM PAULINE.

"Cintra, June 1st, 1837.

"MY DEAR SISTERS—Here we are, since the day before yesterday, settled in our *cottage*. The view from it is charming, and will, I hope, do me good. Everything in this said cottage is in a style of rustic simplicity, and it is impossible to imagine anything more rural, but the view is still more lovely than from Lisbon. From my window I look on a richly-wooded hill, and a deep valley, in which picturesque villas lie embosomed in gardens. From another window in the same room, I see the Church with its arcade, one of the prettiest I have met with here. In front of it stands a great stone Cross, covered with ivy, and shaded by fine trees; and at the back of all this, the plain stretches on to the old convent of Mafra, and to the sea, which bounds the horizon, and completes the picture, though it is not visible everywhere at Cintra. Does not this make up a beautiful view, and one which adds to all its other charms, that of reminding me both of Rome and Naples? The return of this month, however, makes me very sad. Amidst the recollections which each day brings with it, what saddens me most is the thought of my absence last year. Eugénie, you said in the letter you wrote to me after Albert's death, 'Your feast will not be saddened by these associations.' Ah! that was your first impression at the moment, when it almost seemed as if you could look into that Heaven whither his soul had fled. But it was not true, alas! there is no longer any festival for us on that day. It is for ever devoted to him alone. When I was a child it was my *birthday* that was always kept. At Rome, in 1830, we began to keep my *feast*, and I spent that lovely 29th of June with Albert in greater happiness and intimacy than we had ever yet known, and everything about us was still joyous and bright, though we were so near the great reverses of July. The following year we were at Castellamare, still with him, and very happy and gay. In 1832 came the famous 29th of June at Vomero, when Alexandrine put on a white dress for the first time after her father's death, and allowed Albert to hope that she might love him some day. In 1833 we were certainly far away from them both, but we were continually thinking of them. In 1834 they were just married, and all was happiness then, and it was my own bright time also. In 1835 came Korsen, and in 1836—Heaven! You see, then, how recollections of him are mingled with all these days. Before 1830 I did not know him as I did afterwards. If the 29th had always been kept as my feast day, there would have been several years in which he would not have been connected with it, whereas now for all these six years he has always held a prominent place on that day, and henceforward it will be consecrated to his memory. I am rather glad, however, that Mass cannot be said in black on the 29th of June; it is a Feast of the Church and a Festival in Heaven, though it is no longer one for us. Farewell, my dear little sisters, may God bless you always as He does now, and keep you what you are."

THE ABBÉ GERBET TO ALEXANDRINE.

"Juilly, June 15th, 1837.

"Your welcome letters have come, and it has been a real

charity on your part not to have made them too short. They are as meritorious as some good alms bestowed upon a poor hermit. In my retreat at Juilly you may rely upon it I do not forget Boury or Paris. I keep these anniversaries with you, my dear, afflicted child, whose sad heart is broken by this terrible storm. You carry with you, however, your compass and your guiding star—God guides you. Patient suffering is pure gold, and suffering joined to charity and self-devotion a priceless diamond. Sail on, then, sail on, and with that freight make your port."

"Juilly, June 24th.

"It is just midnight, and at this moment, my poor child, your week of sorrow begins. . . . I had written these two lines when I was interrupted by a little occurrence that I am going to relate, as it suggests sweet and comforting thoughts. While I was writing, a moth that had flown in through the half-open window fell down upon the brick floor. It had probably hurt itself, and was fluttering about, making some little noise in its efforts to raise itself from the ground. The noise drew my attention to it, and it struck me that if it managed to fly about in the usual way, it would soon scorch its wings in the light of my candle and die, and that it would be better to put it out of doors in the starlight. I chased the little insect, caught it, and set it at liberty. Poor moth! we are like you. Struck down by grief, we sink and struggle in our pain, but at the same time we flutter our wings —the wings God has given us of hope and prayer, and at those moments He specially watches us. When I was pursuing you, poor little moth, you were terribly afraid of me, you thought I intended to add to your sufferings, and I was pursuing you only to save you, and it is thus that God pursues us. When I cast you out, poor moth, into the dark night, then you especially accused me of cruelty. Poor unknowing thing! The coarse light you regretted would have been your death, and instead of death to-morrow you will enjoy the fresh air and the rising sun. The dark night is an image of death, and when God casts us out into that night, it is only to set us free, and to give us life and joy at the dawn of an eternal day. This is what I said to the poor little moth, and this is what our good God says to us.

"This is all that I shall write this evening, my dear child, at the beginning of this sorrowful week, but you and your Eugénie will find in these words what God intends you to learn from them. I kneel with you at the foot of your Cross. Reckon me, my dear children, among the friends who feel most deeply for you at this moment."

ALEXANDRINE TO PAULINE.

"Paris, June 16th, 1837.

"MY DEAR PAULINE—It seems to me that in writing to you to-day, one name and date are enough to convey to you all that fills my own mind and yours too, for I am sure you are with us in spirit. I thank God for my good memory, for one of the greatest miseries of human nature is the gradual blotting out and disappearance of all that one has felt the most intensely. God preserve me from this! It is sweet to be convinced, as I am more and more, that in God our affections are best kept alive, and that He, being all love, knows how to maintain in us the recollection of every affection which He has blest. Ah, my dear sister, how well I know that you understand me! My darling old friend, if you should happen to be told of my ungracious refusal to dine out with our aunt de Damas, do pray take my part, for you have such influence in the family, and say that you enter into my feelings. I must stand out a little at first, in order that my retirement and deep mourning may be accepted as a thing of course, and then no one will think any more about it. Good-bye, I love you and do wish I could see you again."

COUNT DE MONTALEMBERT TO ALEXANDRINE.

"Villersexel, June 27th, 1837.

"MY VERY DEAR FRIEND AND SISTER—I should not like the holy anniversary of the day after to-morrow to go by without your receiving a word from me. You will allow me, I am sure, to commemorate with you those sufferings, that grief, that fruitful sorrow I once shared, and through which your soul was won to God—I believe there is no one in the world, after Pauline and Eugénie, better able than myself to understand and share all that your poor heart endured during these memorable days, so sorrowful in your remembrance, but so great and precious in the sight of God. I have sometimes reproached myself that in consequence of the sudden and excessive flow of happiness which at that moment was agitating and preoccupying me, I did not feel in that room of the Rue de Madame all the devotion with which a Christian and a friend ought to have witnessed the sublime and welcome sight of a soul purified and sanctified by suffering, preparing with such resignation to leave all things and seek God alone, where, in the flower of his age, and the height of happiness, I saw my friend die, who as you truly say loved me best, and most earnestly desired my peace and happiness ; where, I also saw a soul very dear to me, even yours, dear Alexandrine, brought to the true faith by means of sorrow and love. I have often grieved and even blushed at the recollection that I did not devote myself entirely to you, in that great crisis of your two lives. But God, who disposed of events otherwise in my life, has at least allowed me to preserve a clear, vivid and minute remembrance of those days. It would have been gratifying to me, and perhaps not unwelcome to you, could we have met at this time and interchanged our thoughts of the past. But as this is impossible, you will not deny me, my very dear Alexandrine, the favor I ask, which is to give me a place in your prayers the day after to-morrow — a very special place, as Albert's greatest friend, as to one who loved him much, and was loved by him, and who was present at the beginning and the close of your earthly union. Whether you wish it or not, you must always think of me while thinking of him, for our intimacy was a very close one, and began at the very same time as his love for you.

"I shall have Mass said for him here the day after to-morrow, but for his intention only, as no solemn service for the dead can be performed on account of the beautiful Feast of St. Peter and Paul, the Feast of Rome, where you saw and loved one another for the first time. I like continually to ascribe some of my present happiness to Albert's intercession, to his fervent and affectionate prayers during life, and protection now. This must give you an interest in my welfare, and I do not hesitate to speak of it even during this mournful time. Did you receive the parcel I sent to Boury, and the letter telling you of my daughter's birth? My wife is wonderfully well, and nothing has occurred to disturb our joy. She desires me to say a thousand kind things to you and Eugénie, and sympathises with you in every way. Farewell, my dear friend. You know whether I am your friend and brother for life."

PAULINE TO EUGENIE.

"Cintra, June 29th, 1837.

"It seems to me that I am nearer to you to-day, my precious sister, because since waking this morning our first and last thought will be the same. It is a day of union, just as if we were looking at the same star. Our eyes are more continually than usual fixed upon our Albert, and we are united in him. You must tell me how you spent this day, that I may feel as if I had been with you, even as on that solemn one, when, alas! I was absent, but which I live over again with you now. I have spent the last few days in reading all your last year's letters, in which I found so many heart-breaking things, especially those words of his when he spoke of me for the last time and said, '*Kiss her once more for me.*' Ah! I cannot tell you what a fresh pang it gave me to think that I was not there to embrace him once more. A year, it is actually a year since he died—the time when some widow's mourning is ended! How strange it would have seemed if Alexandrine had been like other people! I cannot picture her to myself otherwise than I left her, and as I shall find her again, and what is commonly said of the effects of time seem merely absurd when applied to her. All I wish is that she should be allowed to spend her years to come as this one has been spent, surrounded with such joys as God gives to those whose earthly ones are ended, and with you, my darling sister; and then that I too, may be sometimes with you both, and that what we have gained by Albert's example and his remembrance, may be strengthened in us day by day, and make us worthy to meet him again speedily on leaving this world."

ALEXANDRINE TO COUNT DE MONTALEMBERT.

"Boury, July 7th, 1837.

"My Dear Friend—It touched me to receive on the 29th your good, brotherly, and friendly letter, containing such precious words about Albert. I had just come from Communion, and had prayed that God would unite us in His love, my very frequent prayer. I need not say how pleased I should have been to have had you here, and I had also hoped that that other friend of Albert's, dear Rio, who has been with us in all these anniversaries, would also have come this morning; but his health prevented it. We received Communion from the same hand as

THE ABBÉ GERBET TO ALEXANDRINE.

"Juilly, June 6th, 1837.

"This morning I read in my Breviary a text of Scripture, which says that *In Heaven there shall be no need of lamps.* What, no tapers? not even gas lights? How will it be possible to do without tapers? I am sadly afraid that the light of Heaven will not be enough. This is what, in one way or other, we are always saying to ourselves. I say 'we,' and very sincerely, for we all do so now and then. Do not mistake this for a personal remark. It gives me great pleasure to hear that you are less troubled. Strengthen your will against sadness, strive courageously against depression of spirits, and may God's Angels ever guard you! I enclose you a passage from one of Mde. de Hautefeuille's books. I read it the other day, and it struck me very much. 'This world, then, has joys which the Angels might envy us. But to be perfect, these joys ought to be tasted by some other kind of hearts than ours, in which a sad admixture of earth's taint spoils everything. This incompleteness and uncertainty, this voice that cries at night: "*There is nothing lasting*"—this sort of incapacity to relish happiness, or must we say it, a kind of weariness in the enjoyment of it, a sort of need of tears and sorrow, teach the heart of man that the joys of Heaven are for Heaven only, and that here the extatic happiness which the Seraphim enjoy might kill us, or alas! alas! would *weary* us.' This last sentence contains a profound truth. This weariness results from a disproportion between our faculties in their present condition, and the use we make of those faculties. We are not capable on earth of bearing the highest degree of happiness. When St. Francis Xavier was overwhelmed with the weight of Divine consolations, and cried out: '*Enough, Lord, enough!*' he felt and expressed this truth. My dear child, your life is a grand preparation for future joy, and the sharper the trial, the deeper, higher, and wider will become your capacity for enjoyment. Courage! then, you are going through your noviciate for Heaven. The black veil is only ordained for the period of probation."

A few days afterwards the Abbé Gerbet wrote to Alexandrine, to recommend to her notice a young man whose poverty precluded him from entering the seminary. In it he says: "My affection, or I may say my *reverence* for him, the strength and disinterestedness of his vocation, his past misfortunes and unvaried resignation, his self-devotion, a humility which I have scarcely ever seen equalled, together with a delicacy which shines out all the more brightly because of that humility and his ardent desire to labor for the salvation of souls, have all determined me to do everything in my power to remove, by a few voluntary contributions, the obstacles which detain this angelic soul on the threshold of the temple."

Alexandrine's answer may be deduced from the following letter, written by the Abbé Gerbet a few days later:

"Juilly, July 11th, 1837.

"I have only a moment, my dear child, to thank you, not only for your good work, but for the letter which was even better than the work. Do not be afraid, I am not going to praise you. Still, I wish and ought to tell you that the feelings and emotions you speak of *are* graces for which you should thank God. There is nothing new to me in what you say, but it is none the less pleasant for that, for whenever the good qualities of those we deeply value, show themselves in any special way, it is a great pleasure. It belongs to you to be humble, but I may be a little proud of them. You must forgive me for telling your name to M. L——, for in asking him to pray for '*Albert and Albert's wife*,' as you wished, I should equally have disclosed it. Do you think Albert's name is so unknown here that I could have mentioned it without revealing yours? But I told no one but him, and have undertaken to convey to you the expression of his gratitude. It is calm and deep, such as a Saint would feel. You have a right to his prayers, and when I say you, I mean also that half of you called Eugénie. Bless that dear Eugénie, and make her bless you. My dear children, the good you do rejoices my heart. I should like to be at Boury. Meanwhile, may its air be ever sweet and fragrant to you both, its shades soothing, its poor cottages fair in your eyes, and its Chapel peace-giving and full of comfort!"

Alexandrine had kept the rooms in the Rue de Madame, not for herself, as she lived with my father and mother, but that she might go when she liked to the room where Albert died, and pray there as in a sanctuary. She gave up this satisfaction, as well as a secret wish to die there herself afterwards, that she might practise that economy which her increasing charities necessitated.

But at the moment of which we are speaking, she still kept possession of the rooms, which she liked to lend from time to time to a friend, and especially to some priest who had known Albert, and who, when living on the spot, would naturally keep him more particularly in remembrance, and pray for him. At this time the rooms were occupied by the Abbé Martin de Noirlieu, one of the dearest and most esteemed of Albert's friends, and thence he wrote the following letter to Alexandrine.

ABBE MARTIN DE NOIRLIEU TO ALEXANDRINE.

"Paris, July 16th, 1837.

"I am now in possession, Madame, of the rooms you have been so good as to lend me, and find myself most comfortable. I always live in the *room of memories*, and have already often prayed there for *unsere verewigten.** I must own, however, that the first evening here was very painful. When I found myself alone in that large room, the whole scene of June 29th so clearly rose up before me, that I was deeply moved, and I seemed to see rehearsed what we then saw and heard. I had recourse to prayer, and soon the anguish ceased. I have put a little table and a Crucifix between the windows, and there I hear confessions and say my prayers. You see, therefore, that the spot made holy by the struggles and victory of a just soul has become an oratory where your Albert's remembrance lives in the Presence of God, Who has called him to Himself. After the children's confirmation, who are also going to make their First Communion, I shall set off for Boury as quickly as I can. I will take the portraits to Mlle. Thomas. She came on Wednesday to show me her copy, which is nearly finished. I thought there was a harshness in the expression she has given to our dear Albert's countenance which did not at all belong to it, and I regret very much that the portrait does not in the least convey the beauty of his angelic smile. I wish it could be done over again by some artist who had known and loved him, but it is certain that his features are indelibly engraved in your heart and in the hearts of his friends. Say a thousand affectionate things for me, I beg of you, to Mons. le Comte and Mde. la Comtesse de la Ferronnays, to Mlle. Eugénie, and Mlle. Olga. They are all present to me before God, only to know them is a pleasure, and the very thought

* The departed; those who are ours for ever.

of them a rest to the mind. Farewell, Madame. I am your devoted servant and friend, MARTIN DE NOIRLIEU."

Up to this time, in looking over my mother's letters, I have tried to select those only which, with Eugénie's, furnish a complete account of the foregoing year, but I have been often tempted to depart from this rule, especially when I came across evidences of her affectionate tenderness to me. Who does not know that of all the painful thoughts which recur to the mind in days of grief, and which have been so well called the *invidious pangs of sorrow*, there is none so acute as the idea that we have not felt or shown enough affection to the departed ones? Yes, those who have thus suffered are well aware of the aspect the past assumes, even under the most favorable circumstances, if the memory is disturbed and faithless. They know the regret, the remorse, the self-reproaches we feel, and they can judge of the happiness it gave me to find the following letter, and which they will forgive me for not omitting.

"Boury, July 14th, 1837.

"You seek in vain amongst the daughters you know for one who can think and say of their mother what you say and think of yours. Well, my dear child, for my part I wonder if there are many daughters who love their mother as you do. I indulged myself by reading to your father and Eugénie the sentences which most deeply touched my heart. It might seem to them, perhaps, that a feeling of personal gratification induced me to do so; but I assure you this is not the case, for I fill a secondary place in the picture. It is you, my child, who appear to advantage in it, and that is what I like. No better praise can be given to a daughter than to show how she fulfils every desire of her mother's heart. And now I hope you are not going to torment yourself because you have not always been of the same opinion with me. Nothing would have been more insipid, and with regard to contradiction, and its being offensive or not, it depends entirely upon manner. You know how easy it is to bring me round to another opinion than my own, and if my feelings are easily wounded, it is not by opposition so much as by the feeling which seems to prompt it. Let nothing then on this head trouble your conscience, for God alone knows how truly I can say that you have never caused me anything but joy."

This passage evinces my mother's angelic kindness, but there is another feature in her character, which it will not be useless to touch upon, as it will serve to explain much that follows. Together with her great piety and irreproachable virtue, my mother had a strong dislike to anything like intolerance or severity towards others, and in spite of her own strict observance of the slightest practices of religion, she did not like anything approaching to exaggeration or eccentricity. Her piety was free from littleness, narrowness, or the slightest disposition to set herself up as an example to others, and to avoid even the least appearance of this, she would sometimes abstain from an act of piety. Eugénie had in reality much the same disposition, but she had never paid much attention to what others thought of her, and after the strong impression she had received at the time of Albert's death, a keen and wonderful disgust ensued for the world and its transient pleasures, together with a passionate, exclusive, and enthusiastic interest in religious subjects; so that at that time her distaste for everything not immediately connected with such thoughts, or with her daily occupations, was perhaps excessive. Prayer, the love of God and the poor, and devotion to Alexandrine, formed the sum-total of her life, and she took no pains to conceal the fact that outside of this, the requirements of the world and the people in it did not seem to her worthy of the slightest notice. My mother gently combated these notions, for she believed that not even under the highest plea is it good to become absorbed in any one line to the detriment of that consideration for others, which is one of the most excellent forms of charity. Nevertheless, with that humility which she practised, even in the exercise of her maternal authority, she was loath to condemn a feeling springing from so good and pure a cause, and in a letter written at the beginning of 1837, she thus expressed this feeling:—

"I am ready to acknowledge that I may be mistaken; but I have always thought it more perfect to make oneself all to all, and to prefer giving up some pious practice not of obligation, than to annoy or discourage those about us by going far beyond their capability. In short, never to lose sight of the great object of attracting others to the service of God, by making it appear sweet and pleasant to them. I grant that there is something very admirable in a sudden and complete renunciation of the world. Eugénie has chosen the better part, and this may be the judgment God will pass on the difference between her views and mine. I see to what heights her soul easily rises, and how far short of her I remain, and this may be the humbling reason why I do not always understand and approve of what she does. My heavy wings scarcely lift me off the ground—and indeed, instead of wings I ought to say firm and strong hooks, which rivet me to earth, and only allow me with some effort to raise my head a little, and look at Heaven and all Heavenly things."

My mother's gentle remonstrances, to which, at her request I added mine, were not made in vain, and a few months later she wrote to me as follows:—"Eugénie is much improved lately. Last winter no idea of consideration for others on certain points ever entered her head. She brought forward her religious duties full front even in the narrowest defiles, and seemed always vexed when she was advised to practise the slightest prudence. Now the dear child understands this herself, and does it of her own accord, which gives me great pleasure. She is the first to study what are the most judicious means to adopt on such occasions, and I must say that for my part I cannot but think the little efforts we make to serve God without shocking or wounding others, are a fresh means of obtaining blessings for ourselves."

EUGENIE TO PAULINE.

"Boury, July 21st.

"This afternoon the Rios arrived from England. I do love that dear excellent Madame Rio.* She is so good, and it is impossible not to feel at one's ease with so kind-hearted a person. We spoke of you, and immediately felt like old acquaintances. And to begin with, as we happen to be tickled by the same jokes, we brought the famous Sifflotte into play to-night, and so had the pleasure of frightening poor Madame Rio, who found our dear little innocent dressed in white, and sitting reading at her table. There is one thing I must ask of you, dearest, which is not to *apologise* when you find fault with me. Who has so much right to remonstrate as you, Paul-

* M. Rio had married in 1834, Miss Jones of Llanarth.

ine, who are never unjust? I only wish I had asked you to do so oftener, and wish I may now follow your advice with a perseverance as great as my present desire to improve. It is since I received your dear letters, that Mamma is better satisfied with me, and you may, therefore, take the merit of it. Ah! dear Pauline, make me everything she would like me to be, and I beg of you, on my knees, never praise me again as you sometimes do. Those praises give me a painful feeling, for I know I do not deserve them. Remember, that if on the one hand I do some few things beyond what is of obligation; on the other I neglect essential duties, and what can be so essential as to do *everything* that the best and dearest of mothers wishes? Yes, you are right, if anything separated me from my mother, what bitter grief it would be to think of the tears I have made her shed. Ah! each of those tears which I might have wiped away, which I might have turned into sweetness, but which through my own fault I allowed to flow, would then weigh like lead on my heart. Thank you, thank you, for setting before me this painful but powerful consideration—I call it powerful because I look to its working a change in me—I am now struggling courageously with my natural character, but I am still full of faults. Be sorry for them, dear Pauline, and pray that I may grow better."

ABBE GERBET TO ALEXANDRINE.

"Juilly, July 27th, 1837.

"I should be very glad, my dear child, to be able to confirm the news you have heard.* The newspapers spread the most contradictory reports on this subject, and though I have written to Paris for information, I have no answers yet. Go on praying for that soul, and commend him to Albert's prayers. For my part, I dare not yet rejoice, the uncertainty is still so great, but even the vague hope is something. Thank you for sympathizing beforehand with the happiness I should feel if the news were true, for the break-up of this long and sincere friendship is a bitter thing to me. Pray; pray that God's grace may work this conversion, which would make me so happy, both as a man and a priest. Thank Mlle. Olga for all her messages, and tell me about her. If sometimes when you are writing Mlle.

* On the return of Mons. de la Mennais to the Church.

Eugénie could, without tiring herself, write me a line on the same sheet, it would give me great pleasure. You know how much I value every letter, every line from Boury. My dear children, as you all like birds and symbols, I must copy out for you a passage about a Mexican bird, which I read lately, whose old Mexican name is *Vicicili*, and Gomara describes it thus:—'It is no bigger than a bee, its beak is long and very flexible, it feeds on dew and the fragrance of flowers, flying from one to another without ever resting on any. Its plumage is a sort of down, variegated with a number of beautiful colors. The *Vicicili* dies, or rather falls asleep, in the month of October, and remains fastened to a branch by its little claws till the month of April, the time of flowers. Then it wakes up, and thence its name, which means, "*raised to life*."' My dear children, this life is our winter. Are we not worth more than many sparrows — worth more than the *Vicicili?* Adieu. Good-morning and good-bye."

"The same night.

"The Abbé Martin, who has just come, brings word that there is unhappily no truth in the news we were hoping to hear confirmed about M. de la Mennais."

EUGENIE TO PAULINE.

"Boury, August 2nd, 1837.

"MY DEAREST DARLING — I am decidedly of opinion that you must make a heroic sacrifice of all further discussion on the chaperonage question, for I think it worries Mamma.* Your letter this morning is, however, extremely amusing, and I myself, the charming object thus fought for, certainly give you my votes, my beloved sisters, and maintain your rights. I dwell upon *your* indisputable look of dignity, and upon Alexandrine's art of putting on her shawl so as to make herself look like a woman of ninety. In short, my eloquence is all in your favor, but it falls to the ground before my mother's argument that you both look too young, which would indeed be the case with Emma, if Charles' being with her did not make the difference. I am going, therefore, and must leave my poor Alexandrine; and on the way back we are to stop at Montgermont [the Countess de Gontaut's], and then afterwards Alexandrine will be going to her mother. But all this is still a long way off, and it requires very few days, or

* Mde. de la Ferronnays was going to send Eugénie to England with her brother and his wife, after refusing to let her travel the year before alone with Alexandrine or Pauline.

even hours, to set aside many things and many plans. Did I mention to you a little book called '*L'Ame Exilée?*' A story about a holy girl who is raised from death by a Saint, and who, after languishing for a while on earth, dies again with sorrow at having left Heaven.* You may imagine how I liked it. There are words and thoughts which made my heart beat, by answering to deep, cherished ideas of my own which I found it difficult to put into words; and whole passages which made me shed tears of joy from the belief that no one could read them without admiring religion, and that among these there might be some who would be touched and return to God, when once convinced of His mercy, goodness and love. Ah! Pauline, when will men love one another and love God? I desire this sometimes so ardently that it makes me quite ill."

MONS. DE LA FERRONNAYS TO PAULINE.

"Boury, August 5th, 1837.

"Your mother assures me that her last letter to you was a real *chef-d'œuvre* of idiotcy, and that she is ashamed of having sent it. *I made believe to believe* her, and thought to myself, now is the time for me to write, for if I lose this opportunity, their wits will return, and they will leave me nothing to say to my dear child, who has been accustomed to letters full of details and interest. These three women, my wife and your two sisters, are the most inexorable of reapers, leaving nothing whatever for the gleaners; so that a poor old fellow like me, however he may wish for a long talk with you, finds himself with nothing to say, and sits before his sheet of blank paper without a single fact that has not been stolen from him beforehand. And yet *you* find means of writing to us all, to me among the rest, and of telling each one something interesting. For instance, I got this morning your capital letter of the 19th, the third I have received, without answering any one of them. This is rather too bad, and at the risk of proving myself a thousand times more idiotic than your mother, I must make some reply, and so here I am. Your letter gave me great pleasure, like everything else that comes from you; but the pleasure is a little damped for this once by uneasiness about the position of affairs at Lisbon. Mind you, I am not talking politics; I am exclusively occupied with you and Augustus, and not at all with

* "L'Ame Exilée," by Mde. de Hautefeuille.

Portugal, which I should never think of if you were not both there. I am neither *Camorrist*, *Pedrist*, nor *Miguelist*, for it is all quite uninteresting to me. What I wish and ask is, that nothing may happen in any way which can make you ever so little uncomfortable, or disturb the least in the world your peaceful retreat at Cintra. I do hope this heartfelt wish may be fulfilled, and that the quasi-revolution may be carried out, or come to nothing, without inconveniencing you or your husband. Still we shall look for news even more impatiently than usual, and we rejoice at the idea that in future we may hope to receive letters five days earlier than formerly. If I were younger or richer, I should not refuse myself the pleasure of spending some weeks with you. I know that the voyage is an easy one, and would be still easier to me, who am always well on the sea. It would not even be *very* expensive, but still at this moment, it would be above my means, and I am obliged to give up, for this year at least, the idea of coming upon you by surprise. Your sisters, Eugénie and Olga, are gone to England with Charles, and we are left alone with poor Alexandrine. It breaks my heart to see her without Eugénie. Still she must accustom herself little by little to live without this second self, for the time draws near when she will be obliged to leave us to go to her mother, who intends spending the winter in Germany or Italy. Alexandrine thinks she will set out the beginning of October. I had thought I should be obliged to go with her, but suddenly that good Putbus arrived in Paris from I know not where, and says he is coming here in a few days. He is *the* travelling companion *par excellence*, and indeed I think it is his only business in life. We shall therefore probably trust Alexandrine to his care. I need not tell you how sorry we shall be to lose her, and I hope it is now settled that she is to live with us whenever her mother goes to Russia. Boury will soon have a new sad attraction for her. We are getting the cemetery here laid out, where, if God wills it, we shall ourselves rest bye-and-bye. As soon as it is arranged, we shall have Albert brought here, and I think the transfer may be made in September. You can well understand how his dear and sainted remains will bind us to the place, and how earnestly Alexandrine will then desire to come back to it. She wishes a place to be marked out and kept for her next to him. This is at present the idea which fills our minds, the great subject of our conversations, and the future we look to; and though to so many people it might seem a sad topic, it is not sad to us. The joys hoped for at the end of our course shine out so brightly that the mind dwells calmly and fearlessly upon the circumstances which must attend their fulfilment.

"My dear good child, when your mother and I rest near your sainted brother, you will come to visit and pray for us. And some day, my child, for that day will surely come, your blessed dream will be fully realised.* You have no doubt read the Père Géramb's letter to the poor Abbé de la Mennais. For a moment, perhaps, you may have shared our hope that the appeal would be listened to, and you will grieve as we have done that words of contrition and humility find no echo in a heart overflowing with pride and anger. My heart aches whenever I think of this terrible case, but at the same time it seems to me that faith becomes more vivid and strong when we measure the abyss into which pride has cast a soul whose earlier impulses led it so near to God. Let us hope on still, for His mercy far exceeds His severity. There are in Heaven and on earth so many praying for this poor strayed sheep, that I cannot but think they will some day obtain him pity and pardon, that his long wanderings will be followed by a repentance more striking than the scandal he has given, and that his return will bring back more souls than his apostasy has led astray. I intend at the end of the month to make a journey to Gerbevillers; from there I shall go on to Montgermont, where I hope to meet your mother and sisters, and then to return to Lumigny, where I shall stay as long as I can be of any use to its poor inmates.†

"Farewell, my dear, a thousand times dear and beloved. Pauline, my most precious daughter, has your mother told you that we often shed tears when we read your letters together? I thank you both for myself and for her. Farewell, my dear child, everything kind to Augustus, and my best regards to Boislecomte.‡ Remember me to Lord Anglesea and Lord Clarence Paget."

* A kind of reverie written upon the happiness of the meeting in Heaven with all we love in this world.

† Mons. and Madame de Mun.

‡ Formerly in the Russian Embassy, then at Lisbon.

MADAME DE LA FERRONNAYS TO PAULINE.

"Boury, August 10th, 1837.

"The Blessed Sacrament has been brought back to the Chapel, which is a great joy to me. It is as if a dear and long absent friend had returned to us. The château now seems inhabited and filled, and I hope Our Lord blesses the roof under which He deigns to dwell. I confess I am glad to hear that * * * is living in a thoroughly *aristocratic* society. It will be very good for him. 'What a strange notion!' you will say. Well! but I maintain that there are good things in this sort of *entourage* which seem to grow spontaneously, and do not spring so naturally in soils where no ancient roots exist. I have too often found and felt this not to be convinced of it, which of course does not prevent people of high lineage from doing many things which shame their birth. But I speak generally. The house is much improved, and is now really charming. Your father's study is thoroughly furnished as well as the library, and now we are busy adorning Eugénie's room to surprise her on her return. I have had a pretty blue *satiné* paper put up, and Alexandrine undertakes the curtains and chair-covers. Dear 'Jane' will be very indignant, but I hope very much pleased too. They will be home to-morrow evening, and I long to see them. The poor child was so sea-sick, that she quite frightened Emma and Olga, for she actually fainted away, and yet I did not hear that the sea was at all rough. I should like you to tell me if you think she only took this little journey to please others, or if she really enjoyed it herself. I know that she has been bright and charming, and never refused to do anything that the others liked, and I was pleased to find that she made no objection to going to the play at Havre. Of course it is not that I care about her liking to go to the theatre, but I rejoice that she was willing, for the sake of others, to give in to what she would not have done of her own accord. I am sure that whatever she did in this way was to please Charles, and that is what I approve of, for I am quite certain that this amiability on her part will have a far better effect upon her brother than a more stiff and rigid line of conduct. And it is this that gives me pleasure. I do not know if I am right, but I think her repugnance to marriage is not so great as it was, and that she would not now refuse an offer from any one who pleased her."

Whilst Eugénie was in England, Alexandrine wrote to her several times in answer to letters in which she dwelt on the enjoyment of her journey, and seemed to have a scruple about it, and to be afraid lest these new impressions should weaken those which the last year had made on her mind. She was, no doubt, easily impressed by change of scene, but this is the case with all young people, and it is on the other hand somewhat rare to find a young girl calling herself to so strict an account on that score. Alexandrine's letters are full of the childlike originality which must have been already often noticed in her style of thought and writing, even in the midst of the highest flights of a naturally grave and reflective mind. This *something*, peculiar to her, was observable during the most beautiful and romantic time of her youth, the sorrows of after years could not alter it, and it existed to the very last day of her life, while practising an almost ascetic piety and heroic charity. It was that *something* which made one smile even in the most deeply-affecting moments, and made it possible to say that a person, upon whom such heavy afflictions had fallen, and who was led to adopt a line of more than ordinary Christian perfection, was also extremely amusing. The word will sound strangely to those who did not know her. It will surprise them perhaps, and they will scarcely understand it, and yet if there is one original characteristic which ought to be brought out more than another in a description of Alexandrine, it is certainly that one. Those who remember her, will I am sure agree with me, and tears will fill their eyes at the same time that a smile hovers on their lips at the recollection which my words call forth.

ALEXANDRINE TO EUGENIE.

(While Eugénie was in England.)

"Boury.

"My Darling — Is it really you to whom I am writing? How strange it is not to see and hear my Eugénie any more than if she were dead! And it seems to me I bear it very well. This is because I know your absence will be short, and that in a few days I shall enjoy the sight of your countenance again. Ah! if we could but comfort ourselves in this way for that other parting! If we had only faith enough we should be able to do this, for expectation is delightful when we are certain that it will be realised. But what weakness it is in me to feel more sure of seeing you again here than of meeting my beloved one in Heaven! I hope you will have returned by the 15th of September, and will be able to give me some of your wonderful advice, which I cannot manage without, and which I shall want then for so many things. Meanwhile I can tell you that I have managed, acted, thought, and run up and down stairs more than you can imagine, for I do not wish the nation to feel the absence of its sovereign. And now must I send Alix to Paris before you come back, and must I give her a gown? And must Olympe* go too, and is she also to have a present? You see what a prime minister you have in me, a faithful one at all events, who will be sure to answer you at once. My dear little sister, our friendship is a great blessing. It is as deep and calm as that beautiful Mediterranean sea we so often think of. Kiss my little Olga, and say kind things for me to Charles and Emma. Do not forget. I hope you regret my absence to an extraordinary degree. Are you amusing yourself? Write me everything that happens. Twice last night, and this morning at Mass, I have felt sure that our thoughts met. May God bless you, and ask Him to bless me too."

"Boury, August 9th.

"Good-morning, my dear, lovely angel! I have a letter from you and one from Mamma. You say such delightfully kind things. I knew very well you would miss me, and I do miss talking to you dreadfully, but otherwise your pretty description of your travels does not make me envious. As regards little journeys, I only want to go to Montigny, or longer ones to Italy, or very long ones to the other world; though it would indeed interest me to see all the places where I was with Albert again. But did I not tell you that it is very easy to think and meditate while travelling, and seeing God's beautiful scenery spread before our eyes, and I am sure that this thought has been in your mind, notwithstanding other ideas which you mention, and which I had not foreseen would occur to you. I had forgotten what steam-boats are like, and how immediately one looks at the people that go by.

* Alix and Olympe were village girls.

But I cannot really see the least bit of harm in that vague notion of vanity my *severe* Eugénie fancied she felt. So she would like to be ugly! Had I been you I should certainly have been vain, for formerly I could not see a cat without thinking what that cat was thinking of me. The word *vain* as applied to you seems to me stranger than I can say. And had Olga any scruples too, and how many, and did she make you count them? Tell me a great deal about her, and how her eyes are.

"My dear, dear friend, it is not that I wish you to become altogether like other people. Provided that you understand what it is to love as I have loved, I am satisfied to see you loving only God. There are different vocations, and if God receives into His Kingdom poor human beings who have loved one another, I can perfectly understand that there are in that same Kingdom souls who have loved Him only. But nevertheless you see how some things can easily find their way again into our hearts, since you yourself have begun to understand that this world and its pleasures can have some attractions.

"Thank you, dearest, for thinking of *us* in the midst of that pretty world of music and flowers which you describe. Such scenes as these would break my heart, and it is to spare myself suffering that I fly from the sight of pretty things, which show me too really how sweet is that loving life that is ended for me. Still, thank God! they have never—*could* never make me think that I could find any such life again on earth. I know this as surely as I know that I exist, and that my heart could never be, has never been, given to any one but Albert. But my folly is such that I might perhaps still be susceptible of vanity. It is not dead in me, it still watches its opportunities, and if I were not on my guard, it would perhaps draw me into what I should hate more than the cruellest sufferings. If wisdom consists in shunning danger, I shall be wise, by God's grace, and wiser than ever, now I have seen that even you have felt your moods of mind influenced by change of scene. And in fact, allowing that some change did take place in you, so that it did not go beyond a certain point, I should not see the least shadow of harm in it, but as regards myself, the slightest leaning towards the world would be odious.

"My dear sister, these little odds and ends of letters will be a record of our present feelings and dispositions which it will interest us to read over some day if we remain a long time on earth. You know how much I like written recollections of what we have felt and seen. Last year, we had our correspondence at the time I was at Kreuznacht, and every year there will be short partings —God grant they may be only short—which will give us opportunities of testing our progress on the Heavenward way. Constancy and hope are blessings enough for this valley of tears. My good angel, you say you are less fervent now you are away from me; this is flattering me too much. And on my part I have thought: 'well, now Eugénie is gone, I should not be surprised if I sink into a state of wretched tepidity. Friendship helps us on wonderfully in the narrow path of goodness.' I cried bitterly yesterday in my own room. I had been to Gisors with your parents in the morning, and as I walked silently along the street between them I thought—oh! I thought: '*How can I ever live in this way without him? Without that dear, gentle friend, so good, so amiable, so kind, who made everything bright to me and threw such a charm over my life!*' Pray for me, my good angel. Kiss all the others for me, and tell Emma her children are darlings. I am working at the little chemises, and cut out, and tack, and piece, and it amuses me more than I can describe."

"Boury, August 19th.

"I am going to write you a line, for I am just now at leisure. Why are you silent? The first day that passed without a letter from you, your father began to be uneasy, to-day he says he heard a bat screaming, which put him in mind of the German ideas about bad omens. This little bit of superstition touched me, and then I thought: 'Suppose I were to hear that Eugénie was dead!' I dare say I should faint away for the only time in my life; but I should be the first to think: 'she has now what she so much wished for!' And yet it would be your poor unhappy Alex who would miss you the most. Even your parents, who love you as much as I do, would not be so bereaved as me, for they would still have one another to turn to, and their other children to love. Still my heart would bleed for them if such a misfortune were to befal us. Thank God we can speak of these things calmly, and I hope that when that solemn time comes for any of us it will still be the same.

"I must tell you that Jeanne has succeeded Louise in the kitchen, and that after all my praises, she is found to have every kind of fault. I should also say that there has been a cabal against me in the said kitchen, but I maintain a dignified silence. Still I am a coward at heart, and look forward impatiently to your return as a protection. At prayers too, I actually have the *creeps* from shyness—I have said prayers twice instead of you, once before Mde. de Lagrange, Mde. d'Istrie, Mlle. de Classé, and the lawyer, who came that evening to make the agreeable. Whilst I was saying the prayers as loud as I could, I kept inwardly repeating: 'O! my God, forgive me for this stupid shyness, which is nothing but vanity'—for I am always dwelling upon what people will think of me. Every time I repeat the *Pater* and *Credo* I am so dreadfully afraid of making a mistake that it gives me the cramp! Yesterday Mlle. Hélène came to ask me for a straw mattrass, because she says, she is determined to remain at Boury. When I asked her what she was thinking of doing, she answered that you were going to find her a situation; and she had not sense enough to master the fact that the situation would make her leave Boury, where she declares she will stay! She is horribly stupid. I think you will like to hear all this village-news, though I have not spared my neighbor. The children's whooping cough is better, and the day before yesterday, I boldly gave the remedy used by the Superioress at the Hospital. I go on stealing butter and stripping your gooseberry-bushes. Julian has made me some excellent syrup of marsh-mallow, and I amuse myself in the best way I can. I shall leave off now. My dear little woman, how long it is since I have seen you! Our little nephews are charming. Kiss everybody for me."

THE ABBÉ GERBET TO ALEXANDRINE.

"Juilly, August 6th, 1837.

"I grieve for you, my dear child, at your dear sister's absence, and I hope it will not be long, but now that your over active mind will be left more to itself, try to restrain its self-tormenting power. I suppose by your asking for careful answers to your questions which you number like those of the famous letter to M. le Duc,* that you concluded I was not going to Boury, and that you would only see me at most for two or three days in Paris. My yesterday's scrawl, such as it was, will have unde-

* There is no explanation of this allusion. [Translator.]

ceived you, and I presume that you would now rather have vivâ-voce answers which I can give you, please God, next week. I shall then be much better able to answer your thoughts than I can in a letter, but I will nevertheless make some general remarks this evening, to quiet a little that activity of imagination which fatigues you so much. And first, my dear child, do not be always putting this kind of questions to yourself. *What should I do—what should I feel—if God chose to ordain such and such things?* This habit is at once useless and dangerous. When you imagine, for instance, something that seems to you to contradict our ideas of God's goodness, you place your understanding and will in opposition to one another, and consequently in a false position. You cannot find a satisfactory solution, and it is only by setting aside some hypothesis not admissible that you can recover peace of mind. And, moreover, even granting these suppositions not to be altogether impossible, you should not dwell upon them when they imply the existence of extraordinary circumstances, which would call upon the will to make some exceedingly difficult effort. As I have often told you, the necessary graces are given us to do what God actually asks of us, and we must remain convinced that if we should be placed in extraordinary circumstances, as, for instance, in the case of martyrdom, God would then give us the strength we should stand in need of. If you would be at peace, my dear child, look on all these tormenting thoughts in the light of noxious creepers, which a good gardener roots up because they absorb the sap of the tree. Remember me to the good people of the village, to the Prudent family, Mère Lafosse, and Mons. and Mme. Brebion. Good-night, my dear child. I must finish my office before midnight, and shall end the day by praying for you."

COUNT DE MONTALEMBERT TO ALEXANDRINE.

"Villersexel, August 8th, 1837.

"MY VERY DEAR FRIEND—You surely might have added a word to the Cravens' thick packet, though, by your idleness, you no doubt wished to remind me that I am in your debt for your July letter. Well, I consider myself so reminded, and therefore answer at once. It was a little wrong of you not to have written to me from Paris from the Rue de Madame, during the solemn and holy days you spent there, instead of waiting to go back to

Boury. But you have a right to be much forgiven. I reckoned also on hearing news of you from Rio. It must have been a real comfort to have seen him during your sad anniversaries, for he was Albert's faithful friend, and contributed more than any one else to develop in him those feelings of tenderness and enthusiasm which afterwards produced such good results.

"Alas! for our poor Roman trio, for that time when we all first knew you, and our Albert was studying so zealously, even in the midst of his love for you. He wrote volumes of notes on Italian and Tuscan history, with a little *scaldino* between his legs, in the enormous cold room he lodged in at the Palazzo Giustiniani. I may say that the pleasantest and brightest recollections of my youth are connected with Albert. After all my political agitations at Paris in 1831, he cheered me by his charming kindness, his warmth of heart, his ardent friendship, and intense admiration for everything great, beautiful and good. In the midst of my present happiness my thoughts incessantly revert with emotion to those troubles of my youth, in which Albert always took the kindest interest. Many outward things remind me of him, even here where he never was. In the first place we are reading Dante, and at every verse I come across some of those passages which were our favorites at Pisa. I think of those pleasant evenings so peaceful and so agreeably occupied, when we three were together, and we were still so full of hopes of his recovery. I include myself, though I knew long before you did, what the doctors really thought of his case. Then I have read over with my wife many of my old journals, where I find Albert's name in almost every page; and latterly I copied out again that passage of his own journal that you sent me last year to Venice, and I still maintain that I have never read anything more full of devout inspiration and enthusiasm. I must tell you an idea I have. I have thought of including in my series of works upon the Catholic ages, a special book upon Christian Love and Marriage. Albert's fragment has very much confirmed me in this plan, and has suggested the idea of embodying in it the story of your lives by way of epilogue, to show that even in our degenerate age some privileged souls know how to be faithful to the holy traditions of which the Middle Ages have left us such numerous examples. Tell me if this idea smiles upon you. But, in any case, I shall not be able to carry it out till ten years hence, when my age and position may shelter me from the animadversions of *scandal*-talking individuals! Meanwhile, keep carefully for me everything that Albert wrote, either to you or of you, and especially that little book of which I should so like to read the whole."

ALEXANDRINE TO COUNT DE MONTALEMBERT.

"Boury, August 11th, 1837.

"See what pleasure your letter, received this morning, has given me! Here I am writing to you again, though I have already done so yesterday. But yesterday it was to ask you to do me a kindness, and to-day it is because I want to talk to you. I am so pleased with your letter. Everything you say about Albert touches me greatly, though I think it quite natural, but, my dear friend, we must speak and not write. Why do you not come to Boury? I venture to say that it would interest you. You ought to see it once, this poor Boury, and Eugénie and Olga's school, who, with God's help are going to make all the inhabitants of the village good Christians; and then our Chapel, with the organ, and our night-prayers, and our village choir, and my room so full of memorials of Albert, &c., &c. Tell me quickly if at least you will not be in Paris before I go away. I come back to the pleasure your letter gave me. It was particularly welcome at a time when Eugénie and the Abbé Gerbet are both absent. To hear Albert praised as you praise him, rejoices my heart. Dear friend, the idea of your writing our story, *does* smile upon me. Only imagine that the same thought had crossed my mind. You are the only person to whom I would entrust this work, for you would write our story as it ought to be written, in a Christian manner, but at the same time, without that kind of austerity which always frightens me. I know, also, my dear friend, your love of truth, and I feel sure that, though you would make it an epilogue to your book, you would say nothing that had not really happened, and with this view, what I am now writing will be of great use to you. It is a full journal of our life, in which you will find all that Albert wrote. Unfortunately I have as yet only finished one year of it, which I showed to Rio, who thought it interesting, but for some time past I have been longing for an opportunity to show it to you. All Albert's letters to you are copied into it. Oh! yes, dear friend, it would be indeed a work worthy of you, as well as a great satisfaction to me, whom God made so happy in my marriage, if you were to show the world how good and desirable that kind of happiness is; that there is nothing so sweet on earth as a love which we are not afraid of owning before God and men, and that two human beings can never so fully enjoy their mutual affection, as when they both serve with *one mind* the God Who created them. Albert was far more advanced than I was in this Divine love, but I understood all he felt, and was glad to see him as he was. For even in my frivolous days I wished to have a husband better than myself, and I think this is one of the wishes that God often rewards.

"Oh! Montal, if you could contrive, by writing the story of your best friend, to make the cold and dull world understand all this, how glorious it would be for you, for Albert and for me! I hope I should not wish to enjoy that glory in this world, for it would make me too proud, though it was all owing to Albert. I know there are in our story a number of details which make it as interesting as some old chronicle. That first meeting at Rome, and the words we exchanged at the doors of the Church, when he rebuked me for human respect. The offering he made of his life, and of every earthly blessing, to obtain my conversion; then the little fact you remember, of the strip of paper torn off my note book; the fright I had about the duel at Pompeii, and the tears I could not conceal; Albert's exile to Rome, and Fernand's little artifice to get me to write to him; that happy life the following winter, under the same roof as his family; Mamma beginning to revolve in her mind the possibility of our marriage, and our both being aware of it, but not venturing to speak to one another on the subject, yet still feeling secure in the strength of our mutual attachment; then our departure for Germany, and his for France; our being delayed at Rome, whilst he was dying at Civita Vecchia; my despair, which made me exclaim: 'Oh! if only I were his wife!' I am sure that God heard that cry, as my mother also did, and at last—after seven months' absence—we met again at Naples, with every obstacle removed. And then I found in him an angel of whom I was not worthy, and in our marriage such peace and happiness as I never believed could exist. Then followed our brief paradise at Castellamare, and my first anxiety about his health. You know it all, and what ensued, but *no one* will ever understand the wonderful mixture of sorrow, love, and joy, of our life. You will make me out to be far better than I am, and the story will gain by it. People will believe that I made Albert as happy as he deserved to be; they will think of me as the tenderest of wives, whereas I could have been such a much better one, and have made him much happier, just as I would do now if I could have him back again. But you can never, Montal, relate all that was admirable in him, for you can never know it yourself. Even I cannot remember half the dear words by which, even in our very first conversations, he tried to draw me to God. At Venice, on the evening of his terrible attack, the first words he said to me, as soon as he could speak, were these: 'When I awoke, I felt such deep love of God, and then for you, that it took away my breath.' This he said with a smile. Was not that sentence the epitome of his life? And then add to them the last words he ever wrote, and those which he uttered from time to time, and the whole history of my conversion.

"Yes, I am sure, and I thank God for it, that all that makes up an interesting record, which may do good some day to those who will read it. Oh! Montal, tell me that I shall see him again without danger of ever losing him, and that I shall love him as much as I did on earth. Why should I fear that the presence and worship of God in Heaven should lessen our love, which never lessened our love of God on earth? On the contrary, the more we loved each other, the more I think we seemed to live in His sight. I am not afraid of having tired you with these reminiscences of a life which you are thinking of writing. I mentioned the subject to my mother-in-law, who only observed that no names should be given, but this was before she heard it was only to be *ten years hence.* We shall have time enough to consider of this later. You will not complain any more of my silence, though you have a marvellous talent for defending yourself by attacking others. Farewell, my dear brother and friend Montal. May God love you, and all whom you love."*

EUGENIE TO PAULINE.

"On Thursday the letter arrived, which informed my father that

* This letter seems to me fully to sanction the work I have undertaken. Alexandrine was indeed intrusting it to one who would have performed it with as much reverence and respect, and far more talent than myself; but thirty years instead of ten have elapsed since that time, and M. de la Montalembert's life has been devoted to other objects. I think, therefore, that the present publication is the fulfilment of the wishes expressed in the foregoing pages.

all the arrangements for the transfer of Albert's beloved remains to Boury were complete. Alex and I went to Paris with him on Friday, to bring back the body of our dearest one. The journey and the whole day were very impressive. My mother and sisters waited at the Cross at the entrance of the village, and knelt down when the carriages came in sight. Soon the Abbé Gerbet appeared at the head of the procession, the whole village following him. He blessed the coffin, Mamma and Alexandrine kissed it, and then the procession formed and passed through the garden and the court of the château on its way to the Church. This then was the way in which Albert was to arrive at Boury, which he had so longed to see, and to which he had looked forward as the scene of so much future happiness! I took Alexandrine's arm, and we walked close to the coffin. Poor Alex, how touching she looked! Her tears, her large tears, flowed fast; but in her whole figure there was a calmness, a simplicity and a resignation so deeply Christian! I cannot tell you how it affected me! The carriage stopped before the Church steps, and we all knelt down while the coffin was carried into the Church. After Vespers, we went to the Cemetery. You know the road and how pretty it is. The evening was beautiful, and during the sorrowful journey, many comforting thoughts of hope in a happy meeting again, filled our minds. Before the coffin was let down into the grave, the Abbé Gerbet said a few words, which I send you; and then that dear body which had suffered so much, was finally laid in its last resting-place, where room is prepared, when it shall please God, for her whom he loved so well. She looked with a kind of joy into that empty grave, which though now closed for a little space, shall be re-opened when all her troubles have ceased—when her submission to God's will, her constancy and her love, shall have won for her the promised reward, for she will have much suffered and much loved."

EUGENIE TO PAULINE.

"October 29th, 1837.

"Yesterday the great stone which is to cover both graves with a single opening — for there is no division between them on the inside—was brought home. There is no separation between them, and the two coffins will touch one another, as our poor dear little sister wished. Since the day the corpse was transferred, the grave had been temporarily closed in with planks, which were taken away yesterday, and Alexandrine was able to carry out a wish she had formed, but did not know how to execute. I tell it you as a secret, for she would not let it be known, lest people should think it too strange. Yesterday, with Julian's help and a little ladder, she went down into the grave, which is not very deep, that she might once more touch and kiss the coffin which holds what she best loved on earth. To do this she had to kneel in her own grave! Here is food for meditation; and indeed, since that grave was opened, we have made many reflections that the world would call sad, but which we are happy enough not to think so."

MONS. DE LA FERRONNAYS TO PAULINE.

"Boury, October 27th, 1837.

"I have spent five weeks at Gerbeviller,* and the day after returning to Boury, I went to Paris, as you already know, with Alexandrine and Eugénie, to bring back Albert's precious remains. This journey and the coming back, would have been very trying to many people. Well, I cannot tell you what unspeakable sweetness filled my mind, though I felt more keenly than ever the blank which the loss of this dear child has made in our home. But he is happy, very, very happy . . .

"Dear Pauline, how glorious faith is; how good it is to believe —to hope; and how beautiful death is when it opens the gates of eternal life. I do pity those who condemn themselves to live without faith, and to suffer, pine, and die without hope. I hear that you often have scruples and fears, but oh! my dear daughter, do not so wrong our good God or yourself. Why *I* am full of trust and hope—and if you only knew what *I* am!—if *you* are afraid, *I* ought to die in despair. Do not let us be appalled by those terrible threats which it is necessary to address to hardened and impenitent sinners. We must thank God who wills to save us all, that He thus threatens those whom His love cannot soften, and who refuse to give Him their hearts. But when we are not of the number of the wilfully rebellious, when we believe and love, we have the right—and it even becomes a duty—to hope, and expect every blessing from God, who is all love for faithful souls, and all mercy for those who offend Him. Believe me, do not listen to any teachers but such as speak of God with love,

* Belonging to the Marquise de Lambertye, *née* Rohan-Chabot.

and lead you to love Him, and avoid and fly from every one who would make you afraid of Him. But what business have I to be holding forth in this way? Forgive me, my dear child, I am like Gros-Jean preaching to his Curé.

"I was telling you how we brought Albert back to this little corner, where we all hope to rest one after the other, and where Albert has the half of a large grave, the other half of which is intended for dear Alex. You will understand all I would say without my putting it into words, and will feel as I did that that blessed spirit was hovering over those who loved him so deeply, and whom he so doated upon during his short life. This is one of the wonders of our wonderful religion. In that grave, which, to the unbeliever, presents nothing but silence and despair, faith shows us the portal of true life, and an eternity of happiness. And this is the belief of which our so called philosophers would fain deprive us! What monstrous wickedness, or, rather, what inconceivable folly! This dear cemetery will become the object of our daily pilgrimage, where we shall go to pray for him, and to ask his prayers. You, too, will come there with us, dear Pauline, for I do hope that you will not remain much longer in a country which seems to me a little too uncivilized, and you may think how delighted we should be if you could spend some months at *Boury Abbey.* Yesterday we kept your mother's fifty-fifth birthday, and on the fourth of December I shall be turned sixty. At our age it is natural to feel rather eager for a much-desired pleasure, which, if long delayed, we may not live to enjoy. Farewell, my dear, excellent child. Tell your husband that I love him for his own sake, and for yours too, which makes up, I can assure you, a very powerful mixture of affection. Do not be anxious about my political opinions, for they have nothing whatever to do with my feelings, and whether they agree with yours or not, we are neither of us so foolish as to allow them to influence our affection or disturb our comfort. Good-bye again, my precious Pauline, your old father's joy. I love you, darling, as nobody can love who has not a daughter like you. I say nothing for the others, as they write volumes themselves."

It was just at this time, when the very last duties had been performed in Albert's case, that Eugénie, Alexandrine's inseparable companion, whom we have hitherto seen setting her face resolutely towards Heaven, and turning her back on all earthly joys, was suddenly induced to pause and to deliberate whether she should accept or not a proffered happiness, different in circumstances from any she had pictured to herself, and already rejected in imagination. Under the form now presented, this lot, instead of involving any return to the world, seemed effectually to preclude it. In all respects this opening apparently bore the impress of God's will. A true, deep, and even at twenty years of age, already a long-cherished attachment; a course of self-devotion and sacrifice, with a generous confidence offered; a life spent in complete retirement; a place to be filled, instead of in the gay world, by a desolate hearth; and a sorrow as deep and far more bitter than Alexandrine's to be soothed and comforted; such was the lot offered to Eugénie. I think I shall not transgress the limits of the strictest veracity when I say that the last-mentioned circumstances were those that determined her consent. Having been led, so young, to love God ardently, and despise the world, I think she would not have been at first attracted by the mere prospect of a happy domestic life. An irresistible instinct of devotedness and self-sacrifice had, I believe, greater power over her at the outset than the feelings she had herself inspired, and also shared, but which alone, I think, would not have sufficed to induce her to change her course of life. This thought was a comfort to me when I afterwards questioned with the bitter sorrow softened by time only, why that heart, so free, so unhampered, and so joyously ready to quit this world, must again be fastened to earth, and made to undergo both the joys and pangs of a wife and mother. It helped me to answer this question, and to believe in the mercy hidden under the seeming trial. A doubt as to her real vocation, which had flitted like a shadow across my mind after Albert's decease, and which rose up again in the midst of my grief at her own death, was never entertained by my mother, whose judgment upon this point was no doubt safer and more discerning than mine. Together with a great independence of character, Eugénie possessed an impressionable nature, which no doubt formed one of her greatest charms. This disposition did not in the least interfere with her ardent piety or fervent charity, but it seemed to forbid all idea of a cloistered life. My mother had always endeavored to combat the effects of this tendency, of which Eugénie was conscious herself, and on this account dreaded the world and the world's influence. But between the two extremes, family life in the retirement of home seemed the true sphere in which to exercise all her good and attractive qualities, and thus, when this lot fell to her choice, my mother felt, with reason, that the true object of Eugénie's life was attained, and that her wishes for her were fulfilled.

Time enough has now elapsed to enable me to relate fearlessly all the facts contained in this narrative, but sometimes the question arises whether in drawing out some of the characters, I may not touch upon things too sacred and delicate to be made public. Still, is it not the inner history of the souls I have loved that I am relating, and not the mere external events of their lives? It is a *true history*, not a panegyric, that I have undertaken, and what will be its value if it is not carried out, and if stripping it of its originality I purposely bring forward only the touching, edifying, or even elevated side of the picture? These reflections decided me to quote a passage from one of my mother's letters, relative to Eugénie's character, and it will also show how deeply convinced she was that Eugénie's vocations did not tend in the direction I had supposed.

"Ah! my dear child, do not say that you think all is finished for my dear 'Jane,' and that so many gifts are to be buried out of sight and lost. Believe me, there is something in her disposition akin to that of the little boy in the story-book, who, when it was winter, and he went out sledging and making snowballs, exclaimed, '*Ah! if winter would only last for ever!*'—but when spring came with all its flowers, '*O! I wish spring would never end!*' and so on through the summer and autumn. At Paris she thought she could never live out of Paris, and that its religious advantages and interests of all kinds were as necessary to her as the air she breathed; and now she is here, she cannot think how she could ever leave her Chapel and the poor to go to Paris. If only some such circumstances should occur as I sketch out for her in my dreams, I see no reason why she should be impenetrable to a new impression; and you really grieve me by seeming to accept for her the life she has shaped for herself under the influence of the moment, and without any thought of the future. Well, God will provide, and, as you say, we have had too many proofs of His care not to leave everything to Him, and place ourselves entirely in His Hands. I ask nothing for Eugénie but that I may know His will with regard to my dear child, and that He may continue His blessings to her."

ALEXANDRINE TO PAULINE.

"Boury, November 7th, 1837.

"MY DEAR PAULE—Eugénie is writing to you in the drawing-room, where everybody is busy, so that I am giving myself the pleasure of a little gossip with you as well as the rest. It is perhaps an omen, along with several other little things, that for the first time I cannot find a sheet of black-edged paper,—which, however, is a part of my mourning I do not intend to give up. This is a parenthesis, before coming to a wonderful thing, a thing most unlooked-for, a singular instance of the strangeness of life. You must certainly have already had a hint of it from your mother, who hides nothing from you. Now for the fact—but I shall not say much, partly because I am very prudent, and do not wish to commit myself, and also because I do not yet feel sure of anything. But I must say that I am rather puzzled, and it seems to me as if Eugénie's great aversion to marriage was *slightly* shaken. Poor darling! I know she would be vexed with me if she read this, and it might even put an end to that dawning inclination. We must be careful, for the least imprudent word might nip the little flower that is just beginning to peep through the snow. So, dear Pauline, you must begin by writing *to me*, but upon a *separate* sheet, and, for Heaven's sake, not enclosed in a letter to Eugénie. Take care you make no mistake, and when you write to her, do not indulge in the smallest approach to a jest on the subject. Do not even give the slightest hint, if you wish for this marriage! I scarcely know yet what to wish myself, but I see very clearly that M. de Mun is not the least, the *least* disagreeable to Eugénie, and I think it not impossible that he may take her heart by surprise, provided he knows how to manage well, as I rather think he does. I must tell you, Paule, that I do not think it presumptuous to say that Eugénie's heart is a little in my hands. I am almost frightened to find out this, and at the great responsibility it lays upon me. I pray that every word I say to that dear angel, and to every one else about her, may be rightly guided. I did not know I had such influence over her, and thought on the contrary that it was she who governed me. In the meantime, she still goes on saying the same things as she did some months back, that she would rather be burnt alive than change her state of life, etc. Then I represent to her, that unless she is absolutely resolved never to marry, it is better to accept a good husband whom she can love, than run the risk of making some marriage without affection later on, only to please her father and mother."

"Wednesday.

"Ah! do come quickly, dear Paule, that we may plot together for Eugénie's happiness. The Abbé Gerbet thinks her vocation really is to marry, and does not at all allow that her heart is closed to earthly affections. This ought to give me confidence as to the influence I think I can exert; and yet I am sometimes tempted to feel remorse at seeking to turn a single ray which now goes straight into another direction to God. '*But are not the rays which go most directly to God as their Centre, those which follow the leadings of His Providence?*' (I underline this sentence, because I repeat after the Abbé, who said I had not written it at first correctly.) Answer me quickly, and write *only to me.*"

MADAME DE LA FERRONNAYS TO PAULINE.

"Boury, November 22nd, 1837.

"MY DEAR CHILD—I am a great deal too much agitated to write at length to-day. Everything is arranged for Eugénie's marriage, and so speedy, so sudden a conclusion has thrown me into a state of indescribable agitation. I can hardly connect two sentences together; but I send you some letters to read, which, with these hurried lines, will make you understand what I can scarcely express, the gratitude with which my poor heart is overflowing. Join me in thanking God. But, my dear child, is it possible that we must have the sorrow of your not being with us at the time? If you could possibly be here by February, we should certainly wait till then. Send me word quickly what we may hope for on this point, for I shall look for your answer most impatiently."

EUGENIE TO PAULINE.

"November 23rd, 1837.

"MY DEAR PAULE—Forgive me not writing. I reckoned on doing so at length to-day, but the day is gone by, and I have had so many things to think about—naturally enough, you will say—that I have not had time to breathe, and just as I was going to write you a long letter, things happened one after another so quickly that I have scarcely known what I was about. Dear Pauline, can it be possible that you will not be present while all this is going on? Ah! do come. Dear Augustus, do bring her, for I cannot do without her now! I hope God is guiding me, for I know nothing, and pray for nothing else. You may fancy whether I have been able to carry on a regular journal in the midst of this hurry. However, I am quite calm, and may God vouchsafe to watch over one who so much wished to belong to Him alone. Ah! life—life is short, but there is time in it for great changes, and joy and sorrow take care to save it from monotony. I have one distinct wish, and that is always to love death, and to desire to see God above all things. Yes, Heaven above all things! I certainly feel this even at this moment. I have not lost the relish for Heaven!"

THE SAME TO THE SAME.

"Boury, November 26th.

"You are right in thinking that what I am most anxious about at this moment is to place it beyond doubt that whatever may be the change in my lot, I cannot allow anything to alter my intimacy with Alexandrine. And as she is determined to spend the great part of her life in France, she shall divide it, please God, between Boury, Paris, and Lumigny. Ah! dear Paule, this is why I wish for you so much, because you can speak out so much more boldly than I can; for though where Alexandrine is concerned I am pretty bold, I have not courage enough to say all I feel on the subject, and the dread of any change in my intimate friendship with Alex has given me more than one fit of wretchedness."

"Monday, November 27th.

"I wish I could send you all the letters I have received. They have renewed my hopes of not being separated from Alex, and this is why I am writing in better spirits than yesterday. The letters from Lumigny show that it will be perfectly easy for her to stay with us whenever she wishes. So that between Boury, and Albert's grave, and Lumigny, and me, the bereaved life of our dear sister will be as happy as it ever can be. In short, I have every reason to hope that through God's mercy and Albert's prayers, Adrian will prove the earthly protector of our friendship. And so I am going to be married! Ah! Pauline, I have been very happy, very peaceful. Who knows that this will not now be changed, and oh! how I wish you were here! Will you come, will you come? When will our minds be at rest on that point?"

EUGENIE TO PAULINE.

"Boury, December 29th, 1837.

"One word to you this evening, dear Paule, as I am going to Paris to-morrow. Poor Boury! I am leaving it now, with all the recollections of the calm and happy life I have led here, and I shall return to it in the midst of excitement, and not feeling like my own self. I am still very much bewildered. Yesterday when Adrian went away, and said it was the last time he should leave Boury without me, it seemed very strange, and to-day when I thought that the next time I see the house it will be in a state of confusion, and the preparations for my marriage going on, I was very much agitated, but I go on repeating to myself 'God help us!' I have been setting to rights my dear Chapel that I had decorated with such joy for the beautiful Christmas Night. Our midnight Mass was magnificent—the organ—the singing—the number of lights—the Altar and windows covered with pink flowers—it was all very beautiful and devotional. How many thoughts that Chapel brought to my mind, and how I notice everything now that I am about to change my state of life. I only hope nothing may ever change the feelings of my heart. Good-night, we are to start very early, and I am sleepy. Your last letter touched me deeply. Ah! Pauline, if you were not to be here for my wedding, it would be a sorrow for our whole life. Let us pray that this may not be."

"Lumigny, January 4th, 1838.

"Your last letters make me afraid you will not come. The idea is so intolerable, that I have not even once admitted the possibility of such a disappointment. Oh! do let me see you again before the great change, let me have a few days with you and Alex such as we three used to spend together. Let us pray that God's goodness may bring this about, and make your passage a safe one, for indeed it is a trying journey for you, my poor dear little sister. We are, as you see, at Lumigny. My heart aches for Adrian's parents, now about to become mine. God alone can soften such grief as theirs. Joy and sadness attended my arrival; and tears were the only language on either side. God knows that this element of sorrow at a time when everything is generally full of joy, is an additional link between us; it increases my tenderness for them, and my gratitude to God. There are so many things I should like to say to you, so many particulars which it is impossible to write, especially as there is some hope of seeing and speaking to you soon. But in the meantime I must tell you that I love Adrian, not so much as he deserves, but still enough to leave me no room to doubt of my own feelings. Loving as I do the souls of every human being, think how earnestly I must love his. I pray that God will help me to be and to do everything that can ensure his peace and happiness in this world and the next.

"Dear Paule, now that I am beginning to foresee the possibility of your not being with me at my wedding, everything seems different; up to this time I would never admit this possibility, but now I dare not say one word to press you to leave your husband, and to take such a long voyage alone. But then how sorry we shall always be. Oh! I still hope that something may bring it about that I shall have you here. Let us hope in God; if He sends us this trial we will offer it up to Him, you for my happiness, and I for yours, and then later on I shall see you again when I am married. Married! How strange it sounds! Adrian's father and mother are more good to me than I can say, and they love Alexandrine very much too. They have quite settled that she is not to leave me, and her room at Lumigny is already fixed upon. They think her charming, as everybody always does, and the more they see, the more they wish to see of her. Think how happy all this makes me. Well, I do not know what God will ordain for me hereafter, for happiness is not the object of life, and I am at this moment overwhelmed with blessings."

"Lumigny, same day.

"Madame de Mun is as kind as possible. It breaks my heart to see her grief, for she does not, like Mons. de Mun, seek comfort from others; her only wish is to die, but even while expecting death from one moment to another, she does everything that is required of her, sees to every one's comfort, makes all the arrangements for the household, and in short is admirable, for it is only by exercising a wonderful self-control, that she can go through what she does. I need not tell you how attached I am to them, and how sweet I find the part of comforter which God seems to have assigned me. In a word, I am happy, Paule, happy to a degree that would even frighten me if I did not feel that it came from God; that it is His gift, and that if He chose to take it from me, I should submit without a murmur. Indeed, surrounded as I am by so many evidences of departed happiness, I could scarcely be deluded into thinking any earthly joys lasting."

My wish to be present at Eugénie's marriage equalled hers, but the way from Lisbon to Boury was very long. My husband could not possibly leave his post, and hard as it would have seemed to him to have left France without me the year before, it was even more painful to him to let me undertake such a journey as this alone. At the same time, he could not bear to deprive me of what he knew would be so great a pleasure, and after much hesitation, it was settled that I should go. It is not at all my wish to mix up personal recollections with this narrative, but I am tempted to relate some of the incidents of this journey, which have become almost a curiosity, now that increased facility of communication has smoothed much of the difficulty I then encountered. I embarked at Lisbon, in February, 1838, for Southampton, where I was to get into another steamer for Havre. There my father was to send Fernand to meet me with a carriage. My heart beat when the steamer left the Tagus, and for the first time in my life I was travelling entirely alone. Thanks to the time of the year, and also because the packet bore a bad reputation for speed, there were only three passengers on board: an old English captain, a gigantic Mr. L., also an Englishman, whom I had seen in Paris, and a young French actress of nineteen, who had played in the French theatre at Lisbon, and who shared the ladies' cabin with me. The weather was dreadful, and during the whole passage—which was seven days instead of four—I could only venture once upon deck, where I stretched myself upon a mattrass, and even that once I was suddenly carried down again by Mr. L., who seeing a huge wave coming, swept me up with my mattrass in the twinkling of an eye, and laid me down in the cabin, without uttering a word, while an enormous sea deluged the deck just where I had been. I scarcely stirred again after that, for I suffered very much from sea-sickness, and still more from exhaustion, as ever since I left the shore it had been impossible to swallow a mouthful. Once when I was nearly fainting, some one put into my mouth so powerful a stimulant, that my tongue and lips were burnt, and yet I distinctly remember how eagerly I swallowed the burning cordial. Far different was the case with my companion, who, though very ill also, never lost her appetite, and as she did not know a word of English, I had the ordering of her numerous meals. Besides this, I rendered her various little services, necessitated by her ignorance of the only language spoken on board, and her gratitude was deep and expansive.

Poor Mlle. C. interested me, and I could not help pitying her. I compared my happy and safe life with hers, and felt surprised that we should have been so brought together for a few days, where our lots were so differently cast, and could not help forming plans for her benefit, such as one forms in youth—to which, to tell the truth, though she was younger than myself, she did not seem much disposed to accede.

When we reached Southampton, and went on deck, followed by Mlle. C., Mr. L. offered me his arm to leave the ship. As I was hesitating whether to take it or not, I heard Mlle. C. exclaim: "What a pleasing face that young man in the boat has!" and glancing in the direction she pointed out, I joyfully recognised Fernand, who, tired of waiting for me at Havre, had fortunately determined to cross the Channel, to meet the steamer from Lisbon at Southampton. After a week of separation from every one I knew, I shall never forget my joy at his unexpected appearance. As soon as we were on shore, I asked when the packet would leave for Havre, as, though very tired, I wished to start immediately, but I was told—to my despair—that as the Thames was frozen, no boats had been able to leave London, and that all communication was cut off between Havre and Southampton. The boat that Fernand had crossed in was the last that had made the passage, and it had sprung a leak, which prevented it from going back. Fernand then proposed that we should start in a little sailing packet, such as were used to cross from Southampton to Havre before steamboats existed. I am now astonished that I ever agreed to this plan. The passage was to take twelve hours, but the next morning we were to be at Havre, and ten hours afterwards at Boury. Tempted by this prospect, I took his advice, and as I expected to be at home the next day, wrote to no one. After I had dressed and taken some food, of which I stood in great need, I walked with Fernand to the place where we were to embark. Half way down the street Mlle. C. joined us; she was more than ever in need of an interpreter, and having caught sight of us, she joined us, hoping to cross in our company. She, too, had changed her things, and was now smartly dressed, and I own that my impression of her then was not quite what it had been in our cabin out at sea; but nevertheless, I could well understand that she should be as anxious as myself to reach Havre, and we all embarked in the vessel which was about to start. There was only one cabin in this little cutter, and that was so heaped with luggage, that we could scarcely find room near a little stove, around which everyone was standing, for it was icy cold. The wind was rising, nothing could look less pleasant, and the night, after my week of fatigue, promised anything but rest. In fact, it was spent in struggling against a violent contrary wind, and at six in the morning we were only just off the Isle of Wight, when the captain said he should put in till the wind changed. This raised a general outcry, all the passengers insisted on being taken back to Southampton, and there, after fifteen hours of fatigue and sickness, we were put on shore. We had lost so much precious time, that though thoroughly exhausted, I had but one idea, which was to start again, for I well knew how uneasy those expecting us would be, and I still never wrote, thinking that we should see them before they could get a letter. After waiting an hour or two, therefore, and escaping for once from Mlle. C., we got into the mail and reached London at five o'clock in the morning. We only waited there time enough to have post-horses put to my own carriage, which I had left there the year before, and then once more we set forth on our way. It was so cold that Fernand, who had got on the box to leave room for my maid inside, came in a couple of hours' time to implore us to make room for him in the carriage, for he could not stand the cold any longer. My poor man-servant, who was obliged to remain outside, was nearly frozen when we got to Dover. We were all completely worn out.

I can see now, as if it were yesterday, the look of the room lit up with a bright fire, and the large bed in which I spent the night, the first night of rest since I left Lisbon. I had never in my life been so in need of sleep; but I could not help thinking that Eugénie's marriage was to have taken place on that very day, and I had come so far on purpose to be at Boury at the time. Had I really taken this long journey for nothing? What must they all be thinking at home of my non-arrival, and their receiving no letters to account for it? All this flitted through my brain, but nothing could keep me awake. I slept soundly, and never once woke till some one knocked at my door. It was broad daylight, and thinking it was the chamber-maid, I cried, "Come in!" The door opened, and in walked Mlle. C.! She had just got out of the coach, and having recognised some of my luggage, she came to express her joy at having found me out in time to cross with us from Dover to Boulogne. We did make the passage together—a long and dreary one as it proved—for six hours elapsed before we reached Boulogne, where we finally parted. She bade me good-bye, with many expressions of gratitude, and got into the diligence for Paris. Once, and but once, I saw Mlle. C. again, which was one evening, several years afterwards, at the Porte-Saint Martin, where she was acting some grand melodramatic part.

We were obliged to wait a whole hour at Boulogne for a carriage, and at last started for Boury, which we were to reach the next day at six o'clock in the evening. When we arrived at Gisors, a town at an hour's distance from the château, we sent on a man on horseback to announce our coming. He was to precede us by about twenty minutes. How sweet were those moments spent in the anticipation of so great a joy! The night was very dark, and the weather nearly as bad as it had been on the day of my departure, but everything seemed joyous and bright, and my heart throbbed with happiness and impatience. At last we were at Boury. The iron gates stood wide open, we drove in, and I expected to see all the dear people on the steps. But when we stopped, there was not a creature at the door. I sprang out of the carriage, hastened into the vestibule, and there saw Charles alone. A dreadful fear came over me, but he understood my look and said, "No, no! there is nothing the matter; come in, come!" and dragging me to the dining-room, he suddenly opened the door. Coming out of the dark night, I was dazzled by a multitude of lights, and saw confusedly my father, mother, and sisters, who instead of hastening towards me, seemed all stopped by some incomprehensible obstacle, and I even saw my father make a sign with his hand to Charles to take me away again. Charles did, in fact, draw me back, and led me, half-stupefied, into my mother's room, where I sat down and burst into tears. But before he had time to explain, father, mother, and sisters rushed into the room, followed by a number of friends, and I was in their arms, and full of happiness. In the midst of such joyful confusion it was a long time before I could take in what had happened, but at last I learned that it was on account of Mde. de Mun that I had been received in this strange manner, and to spare her the sight of the family joy at the return of a daughter of the same age as the child she had lost. It had already been a great effort to her, in the gloom of her unhealed grief, to be present at her son's marriage, and to endure the gaiety of a large family-party. Every care had been taken to avoid useless emotions, and she had herself expressed a wish to be spared witnessing my arrival. All possible precautions had been taken for the day when I was expected, but the long delay and great uneasiness consequently felt, had caused other things to be overlooked. Our courier had ridden up just as they had all sat down to dinner, when great as was the joy, the anxiety was so to manage as to get Mde. de Mun back to her room before I should reach the château. This could not be achieved, and before dinner was over the noise of the carriage-wheels was heard, and Mde. de Mun looked ready to faint. What with their fear, joy, anxiety, and flurry, all they could do was to prevent me from coming into the room, and hence that moment of strange apprehension which was well repaid by those which followed when joy could show itself without restraint. All the bed-rooms in the château were full, and I had part of Alexandrine's, which opened into Eugénie's.

Our conversations were prolonged far into the night, and peaceful was the sleep, and joyful the waking which followed.

The next day was the eve of the wedding, and the last of Eugénie's girlish life, upon which so many graces and blessings had been showered. It sped quickly by, and not without mingled feelings, for our joy in looking forward to this wedding had in it a shade of sadness, as it revived recollections which it was impossible for Alexandrine or for us, both on her account and our own, to lose sight of. Eugénie also felt deeply that her departure was about to take from that dear sister's deprived life its greatest enjoyment, and in spite of all her unselfishness, Alexandrine could not but feel it too. And so that day came to an end, and on the morrow, at dawn, I went into Eugénie's room, where a trifling matter gave me a painful feeling, wholly superstitious, but which I have never since forgotten. The furniture of the room was blue, but her writing-table was covered, as was the fashion at that time, with a thick black velvet, trimmed with gold fringe. On this oblong table, which stood in the middle of the room, I found the whole of Eugénie's wedding toilet laid out, and the appearance of the wreath, and veil, and white gown upon the black velvet, had a melancholy effect, and though the impression lasted but for an instant, it was so strong that I seized the whole array and threw it upon the blue coverlet of the bed. Eugénie saw me do this, and understood the reason, but only smiled, and we thought of it no more. Indeed a far sadder incident darkened this wedding-day with gloom. Eugénie dressed with great composure, put on her white gown covered with lace, her veil, her wreath of white roses and orange-flowers, with the same diamond cross which Alexandrine had worn on *her* wedding-day, and which she had given to Eugénie the evening before. Then we went down with her to the drawing-room where Adrian, and his father and mother, were expecting us. The weather was beautiful, but a good deal of snow had fallen, and it was very cold. Mde. de Mun on this great occasion had left off her deep mourning; she wore a large black velvet mantle over a grey dress, and kept her hands in a muff. She was very anxious for the ceremony to be over, and after having kissed Eugénie very affectionately, she wished to proceed instantly to the Church, and went out of the room with Adrian by her side. My father followed with Eugénie and my mother, and all of us after them.

On leaving the drawing-room the way was through the library, and on going into it Mde. de Mun caught her gown in the door. She slipped, and her muff preventing her from catching Adrian's arm, she fell heavily and at full length on the stone floor of the library. The confusion that ensued may be imagined; Mde. de Mun was nearly stunned, she had hurt her head, her face was covered with blood, and Eugénie's wedding-gown—she had rushed to save the fall—was stained in several places with the red drops. There was a moment of terrible anxiety. Mde. de Mun was carried to her room, but when once in bed she came completely to herself, insisted on the wedding not being put off, and that the ceremony should proceed without her; and this was agreed to as soon as the doctor had come and assured us that there was not the least danger. Eugénie and her husband spent some days at Boury, and when Mde de Mun was well enough to move, they went with her and Mons. de Mun to Lumigny, where we were to join them later on. I remained alone with Alexandrine, and could then judge of the suffering she had gone through. The effect of these festive days, followed by a separation which no amount of self-forgetfulness could quite soften, was greater than she had allowed it to appear, and I witnessed in her at that time real paroxysms of despair, and yearning after her vanished happiness, which did not seem in accordance with the tone of her own letters, or with what others had written to me about her while we were apart. But she soon recovered herself, and then I found her again such as she had been a year and a half before, calm, peaceful, active, but always dwelling on the past and divided between her energetic desire of accepting God's will without murmuring, and the bitter grief of her loss, so hard to that ardent and loving nature, which scarcely knew as yet how to give herself solely to the only love worthy to satisfy her heart. The day of that blessed and thorough surrender came at last, but its time was not yet. More sorrow, other partings, and other trials had first to be gone through. The two following letters, written by Alexandrine a few days after the wedding, show few traces of the painful feelings that reigned within.

ALEXANDRINE TO EUGENIE.

"Boury, March 5th, 1838.

"Here I am writing to you again! Your sorrow about me gives me pain. You must not grieve about me—you know that I am used to suffer—that God has compelled me to it—and that all sorrows seem light compared with that which has changed the face of the earth to me. It is a rest to know that such dear interests divert your mind from me, and I find that my days pass quickly, and that I like solitude far better than I used to do."

"Saturday, March 10th.

"This little parting reminds me of the time when you were in England, but it will be a shorter one. And then, which is pleasant to think of, you are happier now than you were then. The idea that you are happy, really happy, would enable me to bear an unknown length of parting. You have now that best friend that anyone can have on earth. One thing more. Would it be indiscreet to hint that I should like one room better than another at Lumigny? In any case I may say it to *you*. I should like best—always supposing it would be no trouble, and that it would not disturb any one else—to have that little room that you were in the last time, and that Pauline should take the blue room I had. She will perhaps like the exchange, because she will have two rooms instead of one; but I would rather have the little yellow room because it is sunny, because I like the view, because I feel sure that when the window is open I can hear your piano and your dear voice in the turret, and also because it seems more by itself than the others. What a string of reasons! And now if you have the least feeling that it would seem strange, say nothing about it, and leave everything as Mde. de Mun has arranged it. Thank God you are happy! Enjoy it and do not think it is wrong because others cannot be happy. When I was happy myself I know that I had no such idea." (She gave Eugénie several commissions, and then added) "I give you as much trouble as usual. I hope and believe that you will forgive me for this and all the other small and great clouds—storms they have sometimes been —with which I have saddened your life. I fancy you must be at Paris in such a perfect whirl of civility, business, and commissions, as can leave little time to read a letter. So I will bring mine to a close, especially as I like better to talk than to write, and I hope to have that pleasure in ten days' time. Yesterday I went into your room.* All trace of you had vanished, everything had been put back into its old place, it had become what it was before. There is another of life's dreams over!"

I spent the whole of March and part of April at Lumigny, after which I returned with my father and mother and Alexandrine to Boury, and there Alexandrine wrote the following letter to Eugénie the day before I went away.

ALEXANDRINE TO EUGENIE.

"Boury, April 21st.

"Our dear Boury! It gave me an indescribable pang to come back here for the first time without you, but nevertheless, I cannot tell you how soothing this place is to me, how full of sweet and pleasant memories, in spite of all my sadness. Pauline will write to you. Your mother hoped that before she left, you might have been able to spend a few days here with her. Let us know how Adrian's father and mother got through the sad anniversary. I wish their hearts were full of Heavenly hope. Tell them how much I feel for them. I must leave off to write to Mamma. May God be with you every moment of your life!"

I added the concluded lines.

"MY DEAR LITTLE SISTER—Farewells are indeed sad things, and blissful will be that life where they will no longer be known. After so joyful a meeting, I expected to part with you without pain, leaving you as I do so beloved, calm, and happy; but it is not so, and I feel just the same keen and sorrowful regret for that happy time when we were never divided. Now indeed we possess a new kind of happiness; but that pure and uninterrupted enjoyment of each other's society we shall never know again. May God bless you and Adrian with every blessing of Heaven and of earth, for time and for eternity. Farewell. Love me ever as you have always done."

* The room Eugénie had occupied after her marriage.

"Qui enim hæc dicunt, significant se
Patriam inquirere."
AD HEBRÆOS.

I left Boury at the end of April for England, where I was to embark on the 3rd of May for Portugal. I am not going to recount the incidents of my journey at length, but there are some particulars relating to my father, which I cannot help mentioning. Notwithstanding the favorable time of year and the fact of my having twice safely accomplished the voyage, he did not feel my departure less acutely than he had done before. I was going quite alone, my maid having preceded me that she might spend two or three weeks with her friends in England before starting with me for Lisbon. This decided my father to go with me at least as far as Boulogne, where I was to take the steamer direct to London.

We left Boury on the 28th of April, and reached Boulogne the next evening. The steamer was to start at midnight, and it was at that hour and in a pouring rain, that I kissed my poor father on the quay, and went on board the crowded vessel, weeping very bitterly. I had an excellent travelling servant named Phillips, but he could not look after me in the ladies' cabin, and when I went down alone, it was with difficulty that I could find a place among the crowd of woman and children. I had been sitting there very sorrowfully for an hour, feeling dreadfully solitary in the midst of that crowd, when suddenly I heard piercing cries followed by a general flight of passengers. Some serious accident, happily found out before we put to sea, had happened to the engine, the boat was not able to start, and the rush of passengers leaving her, led to a confusion which was likely to produce dangerous results. I looked for Phillips, who was making every effort to reach me through the frightened crowd, and at last he managed to get me out of the ship. Notwithstanding my fright, I felt great joy at the thoughts of seeing my father again. Leaving Phillips to look after the baggage, I went back to the hotel and into my father's room, but was astonished not to find him there. The fire and candles were nearly out, and it was evident that he had not come in since we had left the hotel together two hours before. Where could he be? I never remember to have felt so intensely anxious, for the only idea that occurred to me was that he had met with some accident, which the darkness of the night and the bad weather did not make at all improbable. I could not go out into the streets alone at two o'clock in the morning, so I called a waiter at the hotel and was just going to start with him, when I heard my father's voice, and felt myself in his arms. Then I learnt where he had spent the last two hours. After he had seen me disappear among the passengers, he had not courage to go back to his solitary room, and in spite of the darkness and the rain, had gone to the end of the pier to catch one more glimpse of the vessel which carried away what he called "her old father's joy." Finding that the steamer did not appear, he went back to learn the cause of the delay, and heard among the crowd what had taken place. His joy at finding and embracing me again was very great, but the fright had so taken possession of him, that he would neither let me go alone, nor allow me to undertake the long and unpleasant passage from Boulogne to London. The next morning he crossed the Channel with me as far as Dover, and there I parted from him, and in my turn sadly watched the steamboat which carried him away. Alas! what repeated farewells fell to our lot before the time came for the last parting of all! and in this one at Dover there was to me an additional pang. Not many years had elapsed since my father had held an important position, and as he had a number of friends and acquaintances in London, and as he would have been warmly welcomed there, I begged him to accompany me so far, and he was himself tempted to remain with me some days longer, and even to take another glimpse of the political and diplomatic world in which he had played a still-remembered part. But he resisted the temptation, saying, with his usual firmness and simplicity, that he could not allow himself useless expense; that it was necessary to see me safely to England, but not necessary to go farther, and the sacrifice therefore must be made. In making it my father supposed that he was doing a very simple thing, and I note it only because these words evince his utter freedom from bitterness, a state of mind not always to be found in those who have been called upon to make sacrifices for their opinions.

I left England a few days afterwards, and reached Lisbon in safety on the 10th of May, where I remained for more than a year, without seeing any of my family. I return now to their letters:—

ALEXANDRINE TO EUGENIE.

"Boury, May 4th, 1838.

"Thank you for your dear letter. It was really too kind. How can you think of reproaching yourself for your own happiness? I do entreat of you never to grieve me in that way again, though I own that I liked to read your affectionate expressions. No, I can never forget that you wished to devote your life to me, and may God reward you for it! Fernand is very well, and has been so good to poor Saint Amand,* who is dying, but happily in the best state of mind. Yesterday afternoon I went there with Fernand, and made him very happy by telling him that you had found his daughter a place. It is a great consolation to give joy to a dying person; his eyes brightened up, and he smiled when he recognised me. Then I showed him Albert's miniature, which he could still see clearly, for he said, 'Monsieur Fernand is there too beside him.† Ah! I should know them both, no matter in what manner you showed them to me!' Then, speaking of us all, he said, 'Who would not love you?' I thanked him again for having saved Albert's life. It is now two years since he came to see Albert on his death-bed, who gently lifted up his finger, and begged him to give up the habit of drinking, which has hastened his death, but I hope he has made up for that now. This morning I went to him again, with your father and mother, and Fernand, but we could not understand what he said. The Curé of Nauples, at Fernand's request, remained with him. He was delirious, but kissed the Crucifix every time it was given to him. Thank God! your father has come back safe, after taking our dear Paule to Dover, where he was better satisfied to part with her. Farewell!"

ALEXANDRINE TO EUGENIE.

"May 12th.

"What a charming letter I have had from you this morning; It touches me much, and ends with a delightful little word; 'Tell me—if you wish to comfort me for being so happy—that I am still good for something, still a little what I used to be to you.' Can you doubt that you are still, and always will be, immensely dear to me? We have talked so much of what relates to the soul, that it ought to make us, I think, better endure to

* An old servant, who had saved Albert once in Russia from being drowned.
† Both the brothers were drawn in the miniature.

be separated, for though divided, we can still be together. Ah! my dear sister, my sister for eternity, thanks for loving me; I do need it so much. You must have been surprised at my silence, but since then you have received my wretched little note, though it is nothing to the point, for you know you are always first in my thoughts and in my heart. The Abbé Gerbet came here the day before yesterday, and you know how much good he always does me. We talk over all kinds of things, and say so much about you, that we have hardly time to discuss metaphysics; still, they are always a little mixed up with those other subjects. Meanwhile, we are going away on Tuesday, and I, perhaps, on a long journey. I have not even thought of packing up, and spend my time in working at my chasuble, and listening to the Abbé. I read aloud the conversation about music which you sent me. Adrian seems to have spoken well, but the good people he was arguing with could never have read Mde. de Stael's *L'Allemagne*, in which she notices that even the most austere Saints looked forward to enjoying music in Heaven; and then, does not King David always mention singing and instruments of music? Are not beauty and the gift of speech just as appreciable by the senses as music, and yet how they affect the soul? According to their argument, it would appear as if these excellent persons had never been touched or excited by anything not entirely spiritual, which I am inclined to think is not exactly the case."

The Abbé Gerbet added these words to the foregoing letter:—

"MY DEAR CHILD—I have begged leave to fill up the blank space. I wish to ask you to express my thanks to all at Lumigny, for the kindness I have received from them; and also to say how deeply I sympathise with both their sorrow and their happiness. I must positively be in Paris, at the Church of the Assumption, on Tuesday morning, and, according to the present arrangements, we are all to start on Monday at midnight, which will be much pleasanter for me than travelling in a wretched diligence. I shall write from Paris. May God bless you, and make you a blessing to others."

While Alexandrine was waiting at Paris for letters from her mother, Eugénie wrote to me as follows:—

EUGENIE TO PAULINE.

"Lumigny, May 8th, 1838.

"I shall write to you to Lisbon, for I hope you are at least very near it now. My poor dear sister, how did you get through the long voyage? I hope you reached home without any further adventures. Thank you—thank you again and again—dear Augustus, for the sacrifice you made in parting with Pauline for my sake. Lumigny is so pretty now! The fine trees with their fresh green, the flowers springing up, and a multitude of birds singing either by day or by night;—the enjoyment of all this in peace and happiness, the thought that this earth is most beautiful—without losing sight of Heaven, and with no fear of death—is a greater amount of happiness than I had ever looked forward to. However, God has given it, and God may take it away; and as I bless Him now, so should I bless Him then, and for ever. Good-bye—tell me if there is anything you wish to know, and which I have not spoken of, for I wish my letters to be as satisfactory as possible. Good-bye, my best beloved sister; God's peace be with you!"

"Wednesday.

"Alexandrine does not yet know what she is going to do, and I think it very probable that she will not move this year. I own I shall be anxious on several accounts, if she leaves us to take so long and fatiguing a journey. She does not look the sort of person who ought to be travelling all over Europe by herself, and Constance's* appearance does not help in the matter. But God will order everything as is best for one so entirely His own. Do you know that Mons. de Talleyrand is to all appearance on his death-bed, and that he is perhaps about to give more joy in Heaven than a whole army of just men? Oh! may he indeed shed those blessed tears of repentance, tears which are a still more precious and grateful offering to God than the prayers of an unstained heart!

Dear Pauline, because of all I said formerly to you and Alex, I feel I ought to tell you now again and again, that I am happy. My road to Heaven is indeed a different one now from what it once was, but the peace I feel makes me hope that it leads equally to God. May He hearken to the cry of my heart, for I never lose sight of Him, and keep me unspotted from the

* Alexandrine's maid.

world. Now I must leave off. My father and my mother-in-law's affection for you delights me. Ah! may love and blessings and happiness be for ever your portion! This is a bold wish to frame, and how could it ever be realised but in the one way; which is to love life without being afraid of death, and to enjoy what God gives on earth, even while longing for Heaven."

"Lumigny, May 11th, 1838.

"We have received your Falmouth letters, thank God! As all was well so far, I trust the voyage is ended, and that you are once more with your husband. In my last letter I spoke of Mons. de Talleyrand's illness, who persevered in his good dispositions to the end. Mons. Dupanloup* was constantly with him. His great-niece, who had just made her First Communion, persuaded him to see a priest, and thus brought about his Christian end, for which God be praised! My mother-in-law is reading part of Alexandrine's story, and is much touched by it. She is very much surprised at some of the things in the Journal, and in Albert's letters. She says, 'Why really, this makes one believe in novels; I had no idea that such feelings existed!' I wish I had any news to tell you, but there cannot be a more monotonous life than mine. How wonderful and strange things are, and nothing more so than the force of habit! Impressions change so quickly, that the mind easily gets accustomed to what beforehand it could not even understand, and we are not the least astonished at things which would have once seemed to us impossible. I am as peaceful, which means as happy as possible. I lead a most pleasant life; but how can I hope it will last? I ask of God that happiness may not weaken my soul and make it unfit to meet the sorrows and troubles of this sad world."

THE ABBÉ GERBET TO ALEXANDRINE.

"Juilly, May 4th, 1838.

"MY DEAR CHILD—To-day is the feast of St. Monica, and I said Mass for you, for though you are often in my thoughts, I have more especially remembered you to-day. I think I can venture to say that if you could look into my mind, you would see that out of your own family you have not a more sincere friend than myself, and that no one in the world sympathises

* Now Bishop of Orleans.

more truly in your troubles—*all* your troubles without exception, from your deep trials to your least vexation. I do not think that even your mother is more anxious for your welfare than I am, and I would go through any pain to spare you suffering. Believe all this, my dear child, and believe also that this friendship is useful to me, not only because friendship is always a consoling thing in this sorrowful life, and that our devotion to others is good for ourselves, but because there is something in the tone of your mind, notwithstanding all the bad things you say of yourself, which always seemed to raise mine higher. It is not St. Monica who has suggested these thoughts to me, for I have long had them, but she has been the occasion of my writing them to you, and I thank her for it. On your account I have a special devotion to this holy widow, and I wish to make friends with her, that I may transfer to you all that I may obtain through her intercession. May St. Monica then, who suffered so much, be with you in your sufferings. Her greatest cross seems to have been the spiritual death of her son, for whom she prayed, and he was given back to her according to the words of the holy Bishop: '*It is impossible that the child of such tears should be cast away.*' Your great trouble, my dear child, is the earthly death of your husband. He will be given back to you, and I, who am not a Saint, but only a poor priest, declare to you that a union hallowed by so many pious tears, cannot be dissolved. Such tears would make even a dead branch flourish again. Yours have not, like St. Monica's, to accomplish so arduous a task, they have only to keep alive the sap which will gradually transform your soul. May God bless you, my dear child, and shed upon you the Divine balm contained in grief. May He bless you always, for all the good you do, and for the constancy with which your thoughts are fixed on the grave and on Heaven. May He bless you for your faithful mourning garb; it will one day shine with a whiteness which has no parallel on earth. May He bless your holy seclusion; may He reward your watchfulness in guarding against every danger of weakening your undying love; may He bless your faith, your hope, your thirst for all that raises the soul, your worship of the truth. I have no time to read over this, and must put off all the news about Lumigny, till we meet."

ALEXANDRINE TO EUGENIE.

"Paris, May 20th.

"MY DEAR ANGEL—I must say two words of thanks for your dear, dear letter, which I found yesterday, after the 'Month of Mary,' at the Church of the Assumption. I was to have dined with Mons. Lacordaire to-day, at Montal's, but there was some mistake, and he engaged himself elsewhere. As we stay till Friday, I shall meet him some other time, please God! I am so grateful, not to you, for that is a matter of course, but your mother-in-law, for wishing so much to keep me at Lumigny. Since yesterday I have had three letters from poor dear Mamma, but nothing is decided yet. She says, that in the course of a week she will tell me decidedly whether she leaves Korsen for Germany, or not."

"Paris, May 23rd.

"I had your little note this morning, and will give your message to the Abbé Gerbet, who is coming to me at three o'clock with Mons. Lacordaire, whom I shall see at last. He could not dine with me at Montal's, but to make up for this disappointment, I met Count Confalonieri, Silvio Pellico's friend, who was, like him, shut up in Spielburg for fourteen years, chained, and lying on straw. What interesting accounts he gives, and what wonderful resignation he had! He is very good, straightforward, and unpretending, and tells you so simply that his imprisonment turned out a great blessing to his soul; that he always had faith, but that formerly he was worldly, etc. He had been several years in prison, when a messenger came one day and told him abruptly that the Emperor had sent to let him know that *his wife was dead*, without a word more, and he quite worshipped his wife. I will tell you another time all she suffered; she died after he had been some years in that terrible captivity, 'worn out, but not conquered by suffering,' as Manzoni says in her epitaph; and he also adds: 'She died, trusting in God, the Comforter of the sorrowful, and hoping to understand in Heaven the mysteries of mercy veiled on earth by what we call the *severity* of God's decrees.' Here are two people who have gone through all these mysteries of sorrow, and never said that God was cruel. At Montal's, this good, admirable man wished to speak to me. He told me that he had read compassion so clearly in my eyes, that he saw I, too, had gone through much suffering, and having questioned the Abbé Gerbet, had asked if he might venture to allude to my loss; then he came up to me, and talked in a way which did me more good than anything I had heard for a long time; of his hope of happiness to come, of the benefit of sorrow to the soul, and the sympathy between those who suffer. He asked leave to shake hands with me, and we both said we would try to meet often again if Providence ever brought us within reach of each other. Ah! I say of him, as Manzoni says of his wife, that man has a noble, tender, and strong soul. He gets a little agitated when he speaks of his sufferings, and his eyes fill with tears, but not a harsh word escapes him about the Emperor of Austria; and yet he was never engaged in any conspiracy, and was treated in that way only for his opinions, which he says are shared by all the Milanese. When he left his prison, the first book Manzoni sent him was the Abbé Gerbet's work on the Holy Eucharist; and he speaks of the Abbé with a respect and esteem which delighted me. He is now between fifty and sixty years old, and has a very noble face. This has been an interesting and pleasant meeting to me."*

After this short stay at Paris, Alexandrine went to Lumigny for a few days previous to a general dispersion which was about to take place. She was to meet her mother at Ischl, and if the Princess Lapoukhyn did not spend the winter in Italy or Germany, she meant to go back with her to Korsen. This plan was not carried into effect, but the uncertainty as to the time of her return threw a gloom over Alexandrine's departure. Before going so far away, she wished to receive the sacrament of confirmation, and went from Lumigny to Meaux for that purpose. Eugénie was with her, and from there wrote me the following letter:—

EUGENIE TO PAULINE.

"Meaux, June 2nd, 1838

"You see we are at Meaux, and will guess that it is for Alexandrine's confirmation. I came here yesterday, leaving my father

* It will be adding another incident to the romance of real life which this volume contains, to mention that about this time Count Confalonieri met a young Danish lady in Paris, who, when a child, had taken a deep and singular interest in the fate of the prisoners of Spielburg, and especially in Confalonieri's character, simply on account of what she had read and heard of their sufferings. Notwithstanding the great difference in their age, a strong attachment sprang up between the Count and Mlle. Ferral, who were afterwards married; and during the few years the Count survived, they were both as happy as possible.—(TRANSLATOR'S NOTE.)

at Lumigny till Monday, when we shall all meet at Coulommiers, and then divide. My father, Alexandrine, and Fernand are going to Germany,* and I back to Lumigny. We are here in the Bishop's Palace, and magnificently entertained. I am lodged in Bossuet's own room, and every attention and kindness are shown us. The Bishop (Monseigneur Galard) comes back to-night from Paris, and we think he will confirm Alex to-morrow. The Cathedral is very fine, in a pure and grand style. We shall have a delightful Whit-Sunday, for they say the functions are wonderfully well done. My pretty little Pauline, I love you with my whole heart. It seems to me now that I love *so much* all those I love. The tenderness with which I am loved myself seems to influence my whole being. The Bishop is come back, and we have been dining with him and with Mde. Casimir Perier. Alex will certainly be confirmed to-morrow. The Bishop is very good, and one feels so at home with those who love God. Now we are going to bed, and through the wide-open window of our bedroom we can hear them singing and practising for to-morrow on the organ. The music sounds delightful."

Alexandrine finished this letter the next morning.

"Eugénie wishes me to write to you, and she is right, for my dear sister, you ought to have been present at my confirmation. It is done. I am so grateful, and happier than I had ventured to hope. It took place in the Bishop's pretty little private Chapel, and then the Abbé Gerbet said Mass for us, and we went to Communion. Afterwards we had a grand High Mass in the Cathedral, where I felt my heart full of gratitude for the gifts of the Holy Ghost and the blessings of our faith. The magnificent Cathedral, the music, and the *beauty* of our dear religion filled me with delight, and the tears I shed, even those for Albert, were very sweet. It is two years to-day since he looked up to the sky and said: '*Everything is beautiful in Heaven; I shall no longer suffer from my chest, but the angels must carry me up, for I have no strength to go alone.*' To-morrow it will be two years since I received my First Communion at his bedside. To-morrow, therefore, I shall go to Communion again, and hope to come away strengthened."

* Mons. de la Ferronnays and Fernand went to Prague, where the family of Charles X. then were.

EUGENIE TO PAULINE.

"Lumigny, June 8th, 1838.

"My dear Sister—My father and Fernand left us on Wednesday, and some delay about the carriage gave them time to receive the first news of you from Lisbon, which was a great comfort to my father. I can breathe freely now I know you are safe with your husband. You must never leave him again, and above all never for me, not even to come and say good-bye to me when I am dying. You would be certain, with God's help, to see me again in Heaven, and you would not be certain of seeing your husband again on earth, if you left him. Our dear travellers, then, are all gone, and now I enjoy the pleasure of having my mother and dear little sister here. Only think how dismal it would have been for them at Boury alone! Here we talk of the travellers, look forward to their letters, and pray for them in the meantime. I must leave off to-day, as it is late, but I will go on with my letter this evening, to keep up the good habit of writing a little every day, for this is the only way of telling all the little things which are interesting to those who love one another as we do. Darling, if our union is nearly perfect on earth, what will it be in Heaven?"

ALEXANDRINE TO EUGENIE.

"Strasburg, June 9th, 1838.

"My dearest Love—Here I am, all alone. There is always some new thing happening in this sad life. Since I came away I have many times felt that nothing could give me any pleasure. This life has no charms for me but when it speaks to me of another world, and I do not know how *to speak to myself* of that better world. I have often thought what this journey would be to me, if instead of Constance, I had with me that sweet friend whom God gave me for my companion, and whom He so quickly took away again. And as I am no longer to know the intense enjoyment which made me love this world better than Heaven, I should like to have you all with me, to talk to me about Albert and Heaven. But do not think that I am just now particularly sad. I am neither sad nor glad. I feel dull and stupid; in that wretched, indifferent state which Albert used always to dread so much. Even in the glorious Cathedral at Mass to-day, I could not shake off this apathy, except during the Elevation, when for a moment—too short a one, alas!—I had a feeling of joy. What a Church it is! Such architecture, such stained glass. I am sorry to say I did not find Theodore* here. He left Strasburg yesterday, after waiting for me some days. I am so sorry not to have seen him, for being a convert like myself, I should have liked to have talked over many things with him. It made me sad to part with your father and Fernand at Nancy. When and where shall I see them again?"

ALEXANDRINE TO EUGENIE.

"Stuttgard, June 10th, 1838.

"As you are no doubt taking a great interest in my fate, I conclude you will be glad to have a word from me every day, especially as I get further on. Here then I am; I have dined. It is nearly six o'clock, and I am going to start again, for I shall travel day and night, and by the day after to-morrow I hope to see Mamma. Poor Mamma. It makes my heart beat to think of it! I should like to have written more, but Mons. de Fontenay† has been here, and sat with me some time. He loves you all very much, and was very kind to me. Tell the Abbé about me. He is one of the priests who, as M. de Lacordaire says, have *a mother's heart.* Give your dear mother my very best love, and say that I am waiting to write to her till I can do so in a less hurried manner. What news have you of your father? Pray for us all. The horses are come. Oh! France, France! It is always with sorrow I leave it, and I should like never to lose sight of those who yet remain to me there."

"Ischl, June 13th.

"Arrived—arrived at last, safe and sound! I saw my mother at nine o'clock this morning, after a journey of five days and five nights. Catiche descried me from a distance, and rushed down with Mamma, who had a nervous attack in the street. Poor, poor Mamma! Her emotion was so violent, and I was so frightened! Pray for me, my darling sister, and let your mother and everybody know of my arrival. Tell the good Abbé that I have begun a long letter to him, which I shall send on Sunday. The French post goes only twice a week, and I am afraid of missing this one. God bless you, my beloved sister."

* The Vicomte de Bussières, who had lately been received into the Church, and has since devoted his pen, time, means, and whole energy, to the service of religion.

† French Minister at Wurtemburg, and formerly Secretary to the Embassy where Mons. de la Ferronnays was, at St. Petersburg.

EUGENIE TO PAULINE.

"Lumigny, June 22nd, 1838.

"Alex has written a volume to the Abbé Gerbet, which I read on its way to him. She has very little time, and what she writes she likes me to see, and then to pass it on to others. This is what I gathered from her letter, and what you will like to hear. At Pfortsheim she went to confession to a good priest in a Chapel where Mass was being said for convicts condemned to hard labor, and Alex found herself alone there in the midst of this respectable assembly. At Ischl, on Corpus Christi, having been misinformed as to the hours, she came into the Church just as the procession was coming out. She pounced upon the Canon, who was already vested, drew him into the Sacristy, gave him in a few words the history of her conversion, and her First Communion with her dying husband, of which that day was the anniversary, and of her great desire, on this account, not to be deprived of the happiness of Communion. The kind Canon, being hurried by the approaching procession, put a few questions to her, and having made sure that she had nothing of moment on her conscience, gave her absolution as she stood there, or at any rate, his blessing and leave to go to Communion. Then she goes on to give a long description of the procession—one of the most beautiful she ever saw—what with the music, the flowers, the men with their hats dressed up with flowers, the women looking so good and earnest, and the faith of the whole population on their knees, singing beautiful hymns, and singing them well. From all that she says of the faith of the country, I do not pity her for being there, nor can I look upon her as isolated in a religious point of view, though she is far from those who speak the only language she cares to hear. The Princess goes to Korsen from Prague, and then the winter plans will be decided. That will be a painful time for Alex. Painful if she goes with her mother, and painful if she leaves her—every way there is struggle and pain. Poor darling, what a sad life it is! Can he who would have gone through anything on earth to spare her a single annoyance, can he see her suffer so much and not be grieved at it even in Heaven? Well, we must believe what we are told, that the foreknowledge of the blessed, which reveals the promised reward, makes the trials and sufferings of life seem short and trifling compared with the reward of Eternity. I think I have given you a faithful abstract of Alex's letter. I am pleased to think that you cannot complain of me as a correspondent, and you must own I fulfil my promise of being exact and going into details. Olga is now remarkably pretty, and there is such simplicity, purity, and charm about her. I am so glad to have her here. I cannot end my letter without telling you that I am as happy as ever. Ah! that earthly happiness which I thought I despised so much, how could I bear to do without it now? Farewell, dear and faithful friend of my whole life. Now as always I say, may God deprive me of every joy, rather than in any way embitter yours." The second anniversary of Albert's death was drawing near, and this time Alexandrine was separated from all those who had been with her the year before. But she was not forgotten, and the best friend of her sorrow wrote to her as follows.

THE ABBÉ GERBET TO ALEXANDRINE.

"Meaux, June 29th, 1838.

"I thank you very, very much, for your good, excellent, and interesting letter, begun at Ulm, and ended at Ischl. I will come back to it bye-and-bye, but the sad anniversary of to-day must be thought of first. I hope, my poor child, you have been able to spend it in the way you wished and that your heart was at peace in its grief. It is just twelve o'clock, and you are, I hope, free to weep, to pray, and to lift up your heart and mind to God. For some days I have said Mass for you, but I should like to have seen you at least for a few minutes, and said some of those words which used to comfort you two years ago. If, besides the consolation which God alone can impart, there is any sweetness in the thought that you have on earth a friend who sympathises with your grief, who feels it in his own heart, who would fain bring you within reach, as it were, of Heavenly melodies, who thinks he is appointed by God to be to you a friend in mourning, a brother in tears, a teacher of hope, and who esteems this mission a high and a sacred one—if, I repeat, there is any comfort in the thought of such a friend, remember, my dear child, that among others who do thus feel and labor for you, I have accepted and will fulfil these dear duties to the utmost of my power. I ask Albert to obtain for me this favor, for such I consider it. I have specially prayed for him during the last few days, and I have also asked him to pray for me. The grave at

Boury, though so far from Ischl, was not deserted on the 29th; there is no solitude for a soul except when it is forgotten. Wherever you go, you carry with you that grave, and its prophetic inscription.* God gives to love and sorrow something of His own all-powerful attribute."

We shall now see in what way Alexandrine was spending the anniversary which the Abbé Gerbet was commemorating with her at a distance. Eugénie sent me the letter to Lisbon with this comment: "Has she not Heavenly joys in the midst of her sorrow?"

ALEXANDRINE TO EUGENIE.

"Ischl, July 3rd, 1838.

"My dear Sister—I have always something to tell you, and though it is fatiguing to write so much I am now going to do so at great length. This evening, in the drawing-room, I felt a silent joy, a pleasant excitement, which made me mentally exclaim as I began in thought a letter to you: 'Blessed be God for having brought me to Ischl!' The common-place evening, and the conversation of four women besides ourselves, have cooled me down a little, but still I am very happy; I have been able to assist a young man, and moreover a priest, dying of consumption, and unless I had come to Ischl, he would have died with a weight on his heart from which, thank God! I have been able to relieve him. I must relate the story at length. Yesterday it came into my head to go into the garden, where I admired the roses and the butterflies, and then having sat down in a little arbor to read Bossuet, I was surprised to hear Church-bells ringing. I thought it must be for some service, and having asked one of the maids, she told me that they were just going to take the Blessed Sacrament to the young priest who was ill. I had already heard Mamma speak of this young priest, and had been restrained by my usual shyness from saying I should like to see him. Now I could go quite naturally. I knelt down with every one else at the street door while the clergy were going by, and then I went upstairs and was present whilst he received the Last Sacraments. Every one, even the Curé, shed tears. Afterwards I asked leave to speak to the sick man, and said my husband had been ill in the same way. It affected me so much! Think

* Alexandrine had caused to be engraven upon the Cross: "Quod Deus conjunxit, homo non separet."

of a young priest only eleven months ordained, and who I knew had hastened his death by too much study, dying of consumption; there was something to me so sacred about it. A calm smile was on his face; I asked his blessing and knelt down by the bed. He seemed touched, and blessed me by laying his cold hand on my head. I thought of it with pleasure all the remainder of the day. I wanted very much to go again to-day, for he had said he should like it. Fortunately they came to tell me he was worse, and that his death might be looked for at any moment; this gave me an excuse for going there in the evening. Mamma, however, thank God! never objects to this sort of thing. He begged me to excuse his not talking to me, as he was not allowed to speak. After I had stood a little while looking at him with reverence and compassion, listening to his difficult breathing, a sound, alas! I know so well, it seemed cruel to stay there doing nothing, and I was about to go away, when it occurred to me to ask him if there was anything in which I could be of use to him. 'There might be something,' he gently answered. I quickly asked 'What?' He replied: 'If you knew all the circumstances.' I pressed him to mention them, and he said, with that strange expectation of getting well, which is one of the symptoms of consumption: 'that he would tell me about it when he was better.' Of course I urged him to speak at once. Then he said: 'I cannot speak now.' The nurse was in the room. I understood what he meant, and she also took the hint and went softly away, and I told him that we were alone. He still hesitated, and said: 'It is too bold a thing to do.' I exclaimed that he must look upon me as his sister, and speak to me as he would to a sister, for we are all members of one family. This seemed at once to decide him to speak. He said he owed what he called the *immense* sum of three hundred francs, for he was quite a poor man, he had been obliged to study very hard, and his books had ruined him. His parents had eleven other children, and he was dreadfully distressed at the idea that they would be burdened with this debt, the amount of which he had only ascertained a few days ago. I told him at once that his debts were paid, and oh! how happy I felt. He thanked me, and I thanked him for the happiness he had given me. What it was to hear him say that *an enormous load was taken off his breast.* I assure you it was a great joy! But he kept on repeating 'that he had been too bold, and that it was only his illness which had made him speak.' On the other hand, I went on saying that we all had one Father, and were all brethren; and when I told him to sleep well, he smiled at me in a way which implied he could sleep well now.

"To-morrow I shall take him the money, after my beloved seven o'clock Mass. He will not die to-night, but I do so long to give it him. I can hear him coughing now! My window is open, and I can see the light in his room from here. Oh! I think it was Albert who brought us to this lodging, to be here *exactly on the 29th of June.* This indeed has been a great blessing from God, and I had such pleasant thoughts as I sat at work this evening. After such joy as that it is impossible for several hours to be sad. I feel nothing but faith and love. How sweet is the tie of Catholic brotherhood! The whole scene in his room yesterday and to-day was so serene and peaceful. The sun's rays fell on his bed through the green blinds, and there were a piano and some flowers in the little white cheerful room. There is something particularly solemn about a priest's death. He wrote to his father and mother to-day. I do hope they will come in time."

"Wednesday, July 4th.

"I took the money to the sick man this morning. Imagine the happiness I felt when I saw the look of joy in his eyes, and heard him say *that a great weight had been taken from his mind, and that he had slept several hours during the night.* When I told him how glad I was that I happened to be here, he answered that it had indeed been a blessing to him. He had been in such great trouble, and did not know what to do, but God had sent an Angel to help him. He said it quite simply, and in this case I could acquiesce in what he said; for Angels are only the messengers of God, and I have evidently been His messenger. What good it does one! It is the second time that I have been happy enough to assist a priest just at this time. Last year it was Mons. L——, and this year this poor consumptive young man. I like so much to help consumptive people, especially on their death beds, and I had prayed so much to have some really good work sent me to do on Albert's anniversary. Send this letter to our good and holy friend [the Abbé Gerbet], for I cannot write it twice over, and I should like him to know the pleasure I have had. I get blessings whenever I can, the other day one from an old woman who was dying, from whom I heard nearly the same words which the Abbé quoted: '*To suffer is not to sin.*'"

Alexandrine left Ischl* before her mother, and took a little journey alone, which she speaks of in the following letters:

ALEXANDRINE TO EUGENIE.

"Salzburg, July 20th, 1838.

"I am trying to write to you, my darling sister, while my hair is being done, for I am so hurried. I have a thousand things *after my own heart* to see in this dear town, and I am going to set out again this evening and travel all night to rejoin Mamma on the road to Vienna. I left her yesterday at Ischl, from whence she will start to-day for Prague. I am surprised to have been able to like anything as much as I did Ischl, and to have become so attached to a new place, but this comes from that spirit of Catholic unity which makes us care as much for everything within its bounds as we do for what we have always loved. Long after I am dead, prayers will be said at Ischl for *Albert and his wife*, and the good peasants in these mountains are sure that she will never leave off her mourning for him. It often happens in this life that we seem to feel most attachment to things just as we are about to lose them, and thus the last days at Ischl were those I enjoyed the most: so much indeed as quite to surprise me. I was sorry to leave these holy poor people, and also some excellent priests I knew there. At the last moment I made acquaintance with the Archbishop of Vienna, and I was sorry not to see more of him. He is a most kind and venerable man, full of gentleness and earnest faith. He is very old, but his face is still beautiful. After some comforting words, he gave me his blessing. His voice was full of emotion, and I felt such reverence for him, that it did me good to kneel at his feet, and to feel his hands resting on my head. After writing so far, my dearest, I received your letter. You talk delightfully, my darling, and say things which give me great pleasure; but don't you know perfectly well, Eugénie, that there was nothing worth speaking of, in what I did for that young priest, except the happiness it gave me? Don't you know that it would cost me more at any time to refrain from

* The young priest died soon after Alexandrine left Ischl.

saying a hasty word than to give three hundred francs? and that I find it much easier to tire myself out by walking to see a poor person than to feel charitably towards those whom I do not like? It amuses me to hear that Mde. de Mun is amazed at timid me doing such bold things. What would she say if she knew that being here alone to-day, I asked and obtained an audience of the Archbishop,* without a letter of recommendation, or anything of the kind, and to my great delight I am going to see him. I am afraid of worldly people, because I am sorry to say I am full of vanity, and dread their criticisms, but priests do not, or at least ought not to criticise, and then it gives me so much pleasure to see a priest, or anyone living only for the next world, that it makes me overcome my shyness. I admire the virtues of this young prelate, for he owes his high dignity to his personal character. He is now only twenty-eight, and has been Archbishop for two years. You know that I am going to Kirchberg, or near it, this day week,† to see your father and your good aunt De Blacas, who has written me a very kind letter. Fortunately it is on the road from Vienna to Prague. You see I do plenty of these kind of things, in spite of those cruel attacks of shyness from which I suffer so much, and which I must overcome. I very much approve of the collection you are making. There is more merit in that effort than in giving thousands of francs of one's own. It is conquering human respect for the love of God. I shall be reduced to this kind of almsgiving myself for the present, for prudence will not allow me to give anything to the poor till next month, and I shall be in still greater straits if I do what I should like to do for those dear friends; that is, if I put out to interest eight hundred francs to accumulate for their benefit. But for several years it will be very tiresome. I shall have to call upon your purse."

"9 o'clock in the evening.

"Here I am, my dearest, just come in from innumerable expeditions, and resting myself, as I am going to start immediately to rejoin Mamma to-morrow morning. I will tell you about Salzburg, and a thousand other things from Vienna. God bless you."

* The Prince de Schwarzenburg, afterwards Cardinal-Archbishop of Prague.

† An estate not far from Vienna, belonging to the Duc de Blacas, where he received the exiled royal family of France, when they were suddenly obliged to leave Prague.

"Vienna, July 27th, 1838.

"My Darling—You praise me so much that it is quite a scandal. Still I cannot help liking to know that you think well of me, for in spite of my vanity the praises of the whole world would give me very little pleasure without your approval. I do not like this place. Large towns are not to my taste, especially before I have got into my own groove. I have none of my Ischl pleasures here; no poor people to brighten my life—no priests to speak to, and the house is always full of shopmen. That odious languor and heaviness is beginning to steal upon me."

"Prague, August 7th.

"Here I am at Prague, a most interesting city in interesting Bohemia, but it seems very odd to find myself suddenly in the midst of people speaking a language I cannot understand—I might as well be in Spain, for the Bohemians do not understand a word of German. I shall write to your mother all the details of my visit to Kirchberg, and will only tell you that I set off alone on Saturday from Vienna, and am still in amazement at all I did and saw. You can imagine how pleased I was to see your father and Fernand again, and our good aunt Blacas. And then all those I found there.* Fancy my arriving without having had time to change even my gown or stockings, or hardly to arrange my hair. It was all so sudden, that I was obliged to put my vanity in my pocket. I thought it all very interesting, and every-one was so good and kind to me, that I am still quite touched when I look back to my visit. My mother is come, and your father spent some hours with her, after which he went away, and left Fernand with me for a few days, which is pleasant, for I am very fond of him; all this time he has been writing me such nice dear letters. We are afraid my brother Alexander will not be here, as we had hoped; but Putbus is coming, and only think who else?—the Duke and Duchess de Rauzan!† Fernand professes great admiration for the Duchess, and you know the Duke is an old friend of ours. I have not a moment more. You know how I love you."

Alexandrine's visit to Kirchberg was thus described by Eugénie:—"Just fancy how our Alex made her entry into the Château de Kirchberg. Shy people are always those who take the

* The family of Charles X.
† Claire de Duras, daughter of the well-known Duchesse de Duras.

bull by the horns. You know that my aunt was to have met her five miles from the château, but when Alexandrine got there, she found no one. Upon which, without Julian or Constance, she got into a kind of cart, with a great travelling-bag in her hand, and her bonnet all crooked, as it so often is. In this way she made her appearance at the château, where she was received by my aunt with the utmost kindness, and immediately presented to all the royal family! After staying there about two hours, she started again to return to her mother. Poor darling! Cannot you see her driving up in the cart, with her hair flying about? With her shyness exposed to such a trial, how distressing it must have been. I have no fears as to the effect she produced, for she pleases everybody everywhere, no matter in what dress or under what circumstances. Nothing could exceed the cordiality of her reception. There had been indeed a great desire to see her."

It was during this stay at Prague that Alexandrine's visit to Korsen was again put off. She left her mother, therefore, about the middle of August, and as her brother, Count Alexander d'Alopeus, had not been able to go to Prague as she had hoped, she went to stay with him at the Hague, where he was secretary of the Russian Legation. From there she wrote to Eugénie:—

ALEXANDRINE TO EUGENIE.

"The Hague, August 24th, 1838.

"MY DEAR SISTER—Behold me at the Hague, and safe after the perils of the Rhine.* I have seen my dear Alexander again, who came to Rotterdam to meet me. I was waiting for post-horses at the inn, to go on to the Hague, when some one knocked at the door, and Alexander came in and embraced me with such deep feeling and affection, that I was quite touched. After we had sat down to talk, I saw that he still trembled, and tried to hide it, as if it were a great weakness. Poor dear brother, he loves me very much, and may God reward him for all his kindness! I am so glad I took this journey for his sake, and that I can stay with him the whole week. But it is painful to me to find a number of acquaintances here, whom it is impossible to avoid; while at Paris I would not even go into your mother's drawing-room. I shall, however, refuse all invitations, and must

* A violent storm had come on when she was in the steamboat.

therefore decline even a little family party at Mons. Maltitz's, my brother's first attaché, and that old friend of ours I told you of, who became a Catholic at the time of my father's death. My dearest, about that change in my dress which Mamma so urged upon me at Prague,—I promised her to wear white collars and caps, which she said looked better and were more economical; —this, however, did not seem to satisfy her, as she thought them almost as melancholy as the black ones. She wanted to persuade me to wear silk and grey things. Poor Mamma! She would like imperceptibly to draw me back into the world again. I do not like to annoy her, but she does not know what effect even that little word *grey* had upon me. Meanwhile, I shall arrive at Lumigny as I am, but please to get me some white collars, the *deepest* mourning you can find, and let them be the simplest, cheapest, and the least smart-looking possible. I hope to be there to-morrow week, that is on Saturday, the first of September; but it will be late—perhaps not till the evening. Pray for me and Mamma and my brothers. Ah! dearest, how pleasant it will be to see you again!"

Whilst Alexandrine was at the Hague with one of her brothers, she went through much suffering on account of the other. I shall briefly state the circumstances, as they are connected with an incident which occurred during this journey. Some after-dinner frolic which had taken place at an officers' mess at St. Petersburg, in which Count Féodore d'Alopeus had been concerned, had drawn down severe military punishment on all those who had taken part in it. Count Féodore was sent to the Caucasus, deprived of his rank of officer, and for several years was made to undergo in that humiliating position all the hardships of the dreadful war. In time, however, his irreproachable conduct and great bravery not only obtained his pardon, but also the Emperor's favor, which after his return from exile was evinced in a marked manner. But in 1838, when Alexandrine was in Germany, her brother was still undergoing the full rigor of his sentence, and she had thought of going to Töplitz, where the Russian Emperor then was, to solicit his pardon in person. She remembered that when at sixteen she had broken off a marriage arranged for her at St. Petersburg, and had thereby incurred the ill-will of many persons both at Court and in the town, the Emperor had lent her his fatherly support. She still bore in mind that on a certain day, in the gardens of Tsarskoe-Selo, where she had last seen the Emperor Nicholas, at the beginning of his reign, and in all the splendors of that majestic beauty which added so much to the prestige of sovereign power, he had taken her hand, kissed it, and placed it in her mother's, saying these words to Madame d'Alopeus, which Alexandrine had often thought of since, "Promise me she shall never marry any one against her inclination." * This recollection strengthened her desire to seek the Emperor and implore his mercy; she could not feel afraid of a sovereign whose image was associated in her remembrance with everything most attractive and kind. But twelve years had elapsed since then; dark clouds had obscured the brightness of that dawn, much gloomy resentment, and many a bitter prejudice had taken hold of that once noble heart, and the mournful consequences of absolute power had worked sad changes in one who at the outset of his reign had showed himself full of moderation and generosity. Alexandrine was advised by a friend not to present herself before the Emperor, who was irritated against her both on account of her marriage and her change of religion. Still, Albert was the son of a man whom he had always taken pleasure in calling his friend, and to whom he had given proofs of his friendship and interest which can never be forgotten by his children. It could not, therefore, be expected that Alexandrine's marriage could have criminated her in the Emperor's eyes, or that, as she had been brought up a Lutheran, her conversion could offend him as much as if she had left the Russo-Greek Church, of which he was the head. But the French Revolution of 1830, and that in Poland which succeeded it, had excited in this monarch the most violent antipathy to the French and to Catholicism. The two leading acts of Alexandrine's life went in direct opposition to both those feelings, and had therefore awakened in the Emperor's mind a keen resentment, which the weak part of his character led him to show as much to the helpless and obscure as to those high in power. He possessed one of the characteristics of generosity; he knew how to resist the strong, but he never thought of sparing the weak.

Alexandrine did not, therefore, execute her plan, and went on straight to the Hague; but my father, who was then at Töplitz, and had frequent occasion to see the Emperor, one day broached

* "Promettez moi que vous ne lui ferez jamais faire qu'un mariage d'inclination."

the subject which Alexandrine had so much at heart, and spoke of her great wish to have come in person to solicit her brother's pardon. But at the very first word, the Emperor frowned, and said, "*The Princess Lapoukhyn is very unfortunate in her children!*" With some quickness, my father reminded the Emperor that Alexandrine was his own daughter-in-law, and asked if he looked upon her marriage as a misfortune? "No, no," the Emperor instantly replied, "it is not that," and he added some flattering expressions about Alexandrine. "*But*," he continued, "*I detest these changes of religion. They are brought about by priests, and I cannot endure them.*" My father immediately answered, "Would the Emperor have been of the same opinion if my daughter-in-law had joined the Greek Church?" At these words, the Emperor reddened with anger, and cutting my father short, exclaimed, "Enough of this, my dear Count; do not let us have a controversial discussion." He abruptly changed the conversation, and it was never possible to allude to the subject again.*

Alexandrine remained a little while with her brother, and before leaving the Hague, she wrote me the following lines:—

"PAULINE—I have not even time to write to you. The world is like *glue*, and we like poor insects with a hundred legs, who, while they are getting one foot free, are fastened down by all the rest, and if we loosen ourselves on one side, we are caught again on the other. Being absent from our friends is one of the most tiresome imperfections of this life. Only think that I have never yet had an answer from you to my letter from Ischl, in which I told you of my finding Mamma there, and now I have parted from her again! Ah! pray for Mamma, do me this kindness, and God will reward you. You describe things so well, as usual, in your last letter, and understand exactly what suits me, and in what way I can still find pleasure in life. I shall answer your dear letters at Lumigny, where I shall have a little quiet time to myself. You know that Mamma was most kind to me, but after hesitating a long time, she would not accept my offer of going to Korsen. She dreads a Russian winter for me, but she would like me to go to Korsen in the spring, with Alexander, by sea from the Hague to Petersburg. Pray that I may not have reason to repent agreeing to her suggestion, which had

* The desired favor was, however, voluntarily granted a little time afterwards.

enabled me to return to France as I wished. I parted with her at Prague on the 12th of August, with a sorrow as great, or rather greater than ever. We both started at the same time, and I came to Dresden with Putbus. I left Dresden alone on the evening of the Assumption, after being present at the magnificent service, and hearing the famous choir. At Leipzig I had the great joy of seeing Pauline the First for some hours."*

EUGENIE TO PAULINE.

"Lumigny, September 1st, 1838.

"I am in momentary expectation of Alexandrine's arrival. Every crack of a whip, and every sound of cart-wheels, makes me jump. These are the moments that I have always thought make up for the sufferings of separation. I know few feelings so pleasant as that of expecting some one we love. When will *you* give me this pleasure, you, very dearest of all? Ah! my own Pauline, when shall I see you again? Perhaps I may be able to tell you this evening before I go to bed, that our third sister is arrived—or if not this evening, it must be to-morrow. What joy! Yes, there are great joys in this poor world; transient ones, but often very bright. I have been arranging her room—that little room you know so well; and I have put in it a quantity of flowers, a black straw bonnet I had made for her, and a little white muslin cap with a plain black ribbon; all those little preparations which are tokens that we expect a beloved friend. My darling, it ought to be your turn now. Come, do come soon! I am going to bed, and I have nothing to tell you—she is not yet come."

"Sunday.

"It is twelve o'clock, and she has not arrived. *Pazienza!* But I shall be very much vexed if she does not come this evening, as I am obliged to go to Paris to see Emma, whom I have not seen for six months, and who cannot come here just now on account of her poor sister Caroline,† who is in a hopeless state. The Abbé Gerbet has done her (Caroline) immense good. We all know what it is to hear him speak of Heaven, and can imagine what it must be to any one just about to depart from this world."‡

* Madame Wolf, also named Pauline.
† The Duchesse de Cadore.
‡ She recovered, and was restored to her family, whereas it was Eugénie who had to receive the consolations she speaks of. Thus are our apprehensions and hopes often equally deceived.

"Paris.

"I was obliged to leave home without seeing Alexandrine, and to-day I hear that she arrived about two hours after I had left, which you must allow was vexatious. I am sorry to have missed that welcome sound of the horses' bells, the rattle of the wheels, the joy of rushing into the arms of the darling traveller. I have heard from her, and now at least she is at Lumigny quite well, and to-morrow I shall see her. Dear Pauline, why are you not here to share our joy?"

"Lumigny, September 8th, 1838.

"It was impossible to send off this letter from Paris, and I was obliged to bring it here. You have heard from my mother all about Alexandrine's arrival. What joy it was to kiss her, and clasp her in my arms! She is just the same outwardly and inwardly as when she went away, with the exception of the little change in her collar and cap, which are only rather less pretty than when they were black. Good-bye. God be blest for giving us happiness in this world, without depriving us of that which will be eternal!"

ALEXANDRINE TO PAULINE.

"Lumigny, September 5th.

"I must write you a line. I still feel a kind of surprise at finding myself here. All changes I think more or less astonish me. This ought to assist our faith. If we can scarcely believe in departures and returns, it is not extraordinary that we find it difficult to realize the immense change from time to eternity. You see, dearest, that I still indulge in my favorite metaphysical disquisitions. I am always so glad that you also like to look at things in this way. Think of *my* being at *Lumigny*, expecting Eugénie. Is it not strange? How little we know, even in the smallest matters, what course things will take! How many little vexations are mixed up, too, with our joys! It was a real disappointment to poor Eugénie to miss the sound of my carriage driving up to the door, and I also was much damped when, in the height of my delight at arriving, I heard that she had left the house about an hour and a half before. And now it is I, with your mother and Olga, who am going to meet her. This disappointment reminded me of what I had felt at Boury on the night you arrived there. My heart was beating with joy, and I was dying to throw my arms round your neck, but we had to suppress our tears, kisses, and everything not to wound the feelings of Mde. de Mun."

EUGENIE TO PAULINE.

"Lumigny, September 15th, 1838.

"Adrian has been ill. I felt afraid that God was going to withdraw from me the blessing which I indeed promise every day to resign without murmuring; but, alas! when I examined myself yesterday to see how I should make the sacrifice, I found myself exceedingly weak. How wonderful that is! A year ago I held very little to this world, and though I loved you all with a great and tender love, I looked upon death as a short and insignificant evil. I neither believed in happiness nor in misery, because they are both fleeting, and six months have sufficed to revive my faith in happiness, and to teach me that the loss of it is a sacrifice worthy of God's acceptance. Ah! these two days' anxiety have shown me how changed I am, and it is altogether a new feeling to be so attached to earth."

"October 11th.

"Adrian is well again, and now a word about myself. Last Wednesday I was not allowed to write to you, they are so afraid I should tire myself. I am to be kept in cotton, for the hope of a whole kingdom is not hailed with greater joy than the expected blessing in our little home. It is the one idea in everybody's mind, within and without doors, in the château and in the village, and there is not a creature that does not tell me to take care of myself. My first thought, my darling, was to be sorry to possess any good thing which you are deprived of. Oh! how much greater would mine be if you were equally blessed, my dearest little sister, so long and fondly beloved! May all earthly joys be poured upon you, and Heavenly ones too. I am very glad you have got a pretty house, but sorry you are settled there for another whole winter. I hope, at least, that spring will bring you back again, for there seem to be so many separations before death. There are, indeed, too many of them."

"November 3rd, 1838.

"You have been uneasy about me, but the letters you have by this time received must have quite satisfied you as to my interesting health. I am, in fact, wonderfully prosperous. Will it last? Indeed, I hope so. I cannot but think God intends to give this poor father and mother the only consolation they are willing to accept. For my part, I am resigned, whatever He sends, and I pray every day to be deprived of the happiness of having a child rather than to have one who would not be really a Christian. A thousand times a day I offer that little soul to God, that He may grant it His love at the same time as He gives it life, and then after thinking of the kind of beauty I wish for the soul, I think also of the beauty I desire for the dear little face. I confess I should like it to be pretty, and to have eyes like those I often dream of. But, however, God will ordain it all, and everything He does is well done; but I keep pondering over this mystery of *birth*, which is so great that there is no equal to it but that of *death!* To think that a creature will be who now is not; that within me an immortal being will live, and that this soul, once created, can never perish. In all this there is surely cause for admiration at the wonders God works! We shall not probably stir from home till after the great event; and what happiness it would be if you could be all assembled here before the end of April! And then if *you* were here at the very time; you, whom I feel so much to want in all the important moments of my life! May God grant it, for there is no joy like the joy of meeting!"

Before this last letter had been written Alexandrine had gone back to Boury with my father, mother, and Olga. The Abbé Gerbet went there also, and stayed some time with them. He had just made up his mind to go to Rome, as he thought, for six or eight months. He ended by remaining there ten years. Three years later, those whom he left at Boury met him in Rome at a time of deeper and more painful trials than any they had yet gone through. The Château de Boury he never saw again, for when, after a long absence, he returned to France, it had passed into other hands; and there remained no longer on earth a single one of those souls which he had so wisely guided, and helped forward on their way to that eternal Home whither he has now himself followed them.

ALEXANDRINE TO EUGENIE.

"Boury, October 14th, 1838.

"Here I am again in this dear place which we both love so well. This morning I went to the cemetery, and it seemed to me as if

I had left it but the evening before. To go away from that spot is what feels strange to me, and to return to it so very natural. I am so at home there with that dear grave, my only property and my garden! Well, do you know that those tender, sweet feelings were followed by a fit of vexation when I saw the number of frightful flowers which were growing about it? Nobody will understand that it is only some particular flowers I wish to have there, and only in certain places. For instance, in a spot where I had desired them to plant nothing but roses, I found a flower that I hate, and where there ought to have been jessamine and honeysuckle, there were only ugly bushes. I shall never see it quite as I should like, for probably I shall never be here in the summer, but if I cannot have at other times of the year the flowers I like, I will not have those I dislike. I pulled up myself those hideous yellow flowers! Yesterday all Dangu came here. Olga and I sang the Litany, and '*Jesu wie süss.*' Our visitors seemed very much pleased, and Olga played even better than usual. That dear, dear Chapel! Oh! how many different kinds of memories are bound up with poor Boury! Thoughts of death, marriage, friendship, piety, love of the poor, interesting conversations, and innocent jests. In short, dear Boury is quite after my own heart! I get on admirably with Olga, who is so good and pleasant to live with. Yesterday I exhibited to the whole party the handkerchief I have embroidered for her, and they admired it very much. Emma sends her love. I saw her and her mother on Monday, which gave me pleasure, for I love them both dearly."

EUGENIE TO PAULINE.

"Lumigny, November 9th.

"I cannot tell you what nice and well-written letters I get from Olga, full of sweet pretty little thoughts. She gives me an account of her life, which seems to be well and usefully occupied. She has taken the children's classes again on week-days, and on Sundays she assembles the young women of eighteen and twenty, and reads to them. She speaks of her delight in ornamenting the Chapel with flowers, and says her young days are so happy, that she shall always look back to them as the happiest of her life. She is quite right, for I have known the same kind of happiness, and I can testify that the recollection of it brightens the thoughts of past life. But there are few girls who at her age would like this sort of existence as much as our good little sister; and it touches me to see her, so young and so pretty, having had no great troubles in her life, and yet preferring such simple and holy occupations to the pleasures of the world.

"My Paulette, how much I love you! I feel it more every day, and each one of your letters shows me what a close intimacy there is between us. More so, I think, than has ever been the case with any sisters. Thank God! there has been no change in this respect; marriage, separation, different modes of life, nothing disturbs this strict union. You have been such a good and faithful friend to me, my dear sister, and I hope that He who has watched us walking hand in hand here below, will not separate us in Heaven. When death comes before us in a sad and repulsive form, we should quickly turn our eyes to that glorious Home. It is but a dark passage leading to boundless light. You will understand our poor father's grief. His friend, the Duke of Fitzjames* has died suddenly. He was much in my father's thoughts. He had been to see him and was going again. He feels it very acutely. If we do not all hold ourselves ready it is not for want of warning. How many, both young and old, among those we have known, have vanished! This dear Duke loved us, especially you, as if we were his own children. As he is now, we trust, in a place of hope, let us pray for the repose of his soul."

ALEXANDRINE TO EUGENIE.

"Boury, December 7th.

"My head aches a little with the fatigue of entertaining all the visitors who came this morning. I could not say much to the poor Duchesse de Fitzjames.† Only to look at her made me cry, and I am sure she knows how deeply I feel for her. She tries all the time to keep back her tears, but can never long restrain them; she is most sweet and gentle, occupies herself about others, and even smiles sometimes. But her grief is one of the very greatest, so unforeseen, with so few consolations, and she loved him so devotedly! It will be terrible for her to go back alone to her house in Paris. She went the two nights she was here to night-prayers in the Chapel; those same night-prayers, during which you sang on one occasion the hymn: 'Come, Holy Ghost,' at the

* First aide-de-camp to Charles X.

† Sidonie de Choiseul Gouffier.

poor Duke's request. When she was in the carriage this morning I kissed her hand, and said we should pray for her a great deal. She answered in a voice stifled with tears: '*Pray for him!*' I said that we had done so already, and all of you also. Do pray for him most earnestly."

"Boury, December 8th.

"Césarine* has been here, and very pleasant. She is so obliging and agreeable, with tastes that I like, and talents that I admire. Your father had at first wished that the picture she had made of me for you should be a surprise, but afterwards he forgot this, and spoke of it himself to Mons. de Mun, without enjoining secrecy. I should have rather enjoyed the idea of sending you the parcel without your having the least idea that you would find your old sister's face withinside of it. Everybody says it is like me, and I see in it an expression which pleases me, because it gives the idea of one who is thinking of God, and of some beloved person. Césarine has a most charming talent. She wished to introduce many things into the picture, but I would have my dress and also the table and curtain just as it is.† Fancy her wishing to put a black lace veil on my head! I would not hear of it, and I am afraid she thought me very obstinate. Do you know that that good little goose of sixteen, Helen B——, has married a certain *Tricochet*, all for love, and without a farthing? She was so determined, that she would have run away with him, and the Abbé married them last Saturday just before the old beadle's burial, so that the sound of the wedding fiddles mingled with the passing-bell. This is positively true."

ALEXANDRINE TO PAULINE.

"Boury, December 26th, 1838.

"MY DEAREST—I was waiting for a letter from you before writing. Your letters are far better than mine, but you see I am not good at writing. I always find that to tell everything takes too much time, and if one writes at ever so much length it is not enough, and further explanations are generally necessary. But do not be afraid. I shall not forget any of the little things we like to talk over together. You shall hear everything about

* Césarine de Béarn, Marquise de Caraman. It is to her charming talent that we are indebted not only for Alexandrine's picture, which is mentioned in this letter, but also for the only one we possess of my mother, and another equally like of Olga.

† Both memorials of Albert.

everything when we meet, and it will be as it was the last time, we shall find the days and the nights too short for all we have to say. I do not at all despair of your both being here for Eugénie's confinement. God grant it! The day after to-morrow the Abbé will have been gone a fortnight. I am glad he goes to Rome, but I shall be still more glad when he comes back. Poor dear Mamma has written me a beautiful letter. She thanks me for having been to Communion for her and my brothers, and says: '*She hopes it will be accounted to them as if they had received it themselves.*' She always writes in the kindest manner, praising me very sweetly, and says I am more and more dear to her—I should like the Emperor to see her letters. But *you*, Pauline, must not praise me so falsely. How dare you say that I am the most unselfish person in the world, when I have made even to you so many selfish complaints? And then if you knew how I love to be comfortable and how I hate mud and pain!"

EUGENIE TO PAULINE.

"Lumigny, December 11th, 1838.

"I am spending this Advent season as you may suppose in recommending myself to the Blessed Virgin. Then will come that dear Christmas-time which I have always loved so much. That holy crib that I always think of with such joy! Now indeed more than ever I shall go there in spirit and lay that child in the manger which I present with such ardent love to the Divine Infant Whom it will worship one day itself. And when, five months hence, if God so wills it, that dear infant is born in Mary's own month, may I not hope that the Divine protection asked before its birth will never be withdrawn?"

"Lumigny, Christmas Day, 1838.

"You have heard from Mamma of Marie's* death. My poor Marie! How terrible this blow is! All that time at Lucca and Rome when she was so bright, so happy, comes back to my mind with such tender feelings of affection for her! Death is not sad because of Heaven, but still this vanishing from earth is dreadful. She suffered intensely and with great resignation. No one knows beforehand what strength will be given in the time of trial when it comes through God's will. In sending it, He sends extraordinary graces to bear it.) Marie received all the Last

* Marie Borghese, Vicomtesse de Mortemart.

Sacraments, and her last words gave me the sweet and comforting assurance that she died with trust and hope."

EUGENIE TO PAULINE.

"Lumigny, January 8th, 1839.

"Pauline, I was numbering up the other day in my mind the blessings which God has bestowed upon me. I have had every kind of happiness. First and foremost I was born a Christian and a Catholic; brought up in pious habits and in the knowledge of spiritual interior joys. I have had parents whose sole study has been to make their children happy; sisters who have been beloved friends—a true friend like Alexandrine, and lastly a good husband and a home which make one feel even after the experience of all those previous joys that now for the first time happiness is complete. Well, over and above all this comes the crowning gift, the dearest and most sacred of all ties. After having learnt what it is to be the happiest of daughters, sisters, wives, and friends, I am about to be a mother! Has any one, my own, dear Pauline, ever received so many benefits from God? I feel what an immense weight of gratitude it lays upon me, and what an account I shall have to give in return, and yet when I went over the past year in my mind, I found only much ingratitude to set against this great debt. My eyes filled with tears, and I felt as if for the first time I had ever made a firm resolution. It was that this whole year should be one thanksgiving for the last, and in all my words, thoughts, and actions, give thanks for the benefits I have received. It seems to me that I am now trying really to cure my faults. Alas! you know well what they are! But I have never been so resolved, so in earnest, or so convinced of the necessity of doing what I know I ought. I feel that ingratitude for such a lot as mine would be a fearful sin, and that I shall have to give an account for everything I have received. God tries us by happiness as well as by sorrow, and in neither case must He be forgotten. You will find me, I hope, improved, what you liked in me come out, and what was bad corrected. People do mend, so this may happen even to me.

"My dear sister, here are four pages, for which, were I writing to any one but you, I should have to apologise, but to my earliest and best friend I may say all I feel. To-day, I thought I had nothing to say, and I have filled four pages! Women are born talkers. If our mother Eve had held her tongue, we should be better off than we are."

"Lumigny, January 29th, 1839.

"It seems wonderful. A year ago, my trousseau was being exhibited, and now I am looking at the clothes made ready for my baby. What changes in one year! Who would have foreseen that all this could happen and my inward peace remain undisturbed. I was for a long time afraid it would not be so. It is only since the last two or three months that my heart and my head are in tolerable order. I do not waste time in thinking what I can do for Almighty God, but I try every day to do the small things He requires of me, knowing that efforts to overcome my faults are more pleasing to Him than fasts and hair-shirts. Ah! I do hope I may become good and love Him in return for His goodness! Do you know that a sister of Malibran's has just come out, who has, they say, the same kind of talent? Will she ever equal our poor Malibran, whom every one now forgets? For my part I faithfully say the *De Profundis* for her; does anybody else, I wonder, think of praying for her soul? There is nothing which so much saddens the thought of fame as the oblivion which follows death! I have begun the '*Pickwick Club*.' It kills one sometimes with laughter, but what pathos there is in the story of that miserable actor, with which it opens. The mixture of the pathetic and the horrible gives it an air of truth, and it affected me almost to tears. The idea that there can be real misery of that kind in every theatre, will pursue me whenever I am at the play. To think of the bitter tears which red and white paint may be concealing, would be enough to make one repent of laughing. Only fancy that my father-in-law questioned me the other day about my political opinions. He is extremely surprised that my father's daughter should not be deeply interested in public affairs, and he would be so glad if I would talk politics a little. What am I to do? Will you teach me?"

"Lumigny, March 22nd, 1839.

"While making preparations for the birth of the dear little one, who will soon, we hope, appear, I do not forget that that moment may be the one appointed by God for my departure from this world, and I prepare for that also as much as I can. I have arranged all my letters, for I like everything to be in order, both in my soul and my mind. I have no fears, nor even gloomy thoughts, about that time, but I tell myself that many people do die then, and that though it does not seem probable in my case, I must nevertheless be prepared; and for this end, I now always hear Mass with that intention, and trust that God will grant me a good death. Pray for me to live, if you like, but pray, too, that I may die well."

Eugénie's eldest son was born on the 20th of April, and Alexandrine wrote me the news.

ALEXANDRINE TO PAULINE.

"Paris, April 24th, 1839.

"MY DEAREST SISTER—*Thank God!* These are the first words I must write! You have not had to bear an anxious suspense, but perhaps the news will be a surprise to you. Eugénie came here on Saturday, the 19th, and on Sunday, at five o'clock in the morning, her child—Eugénie's child—was born. The sun had just begun to gild the houses opposite, which I thought was pretty. It was on Sunday, and you will see what the Gospel for the day was:—'*When a woman is in travail, she is sorrowful, but when her child is born, her sorrow is turned into joy.*' Everybody was struck with this. The Bishop of Meaux happened to be here, and baptised the baby. When it was taken to dear Eugénie afterwards, she said: 'Now God may take it back if He will.' Before this, she said to me: 'Ah! I bore my pains very badly. I begged the Blessed Virgin that my sufferings might cease,' and she actually reproached herself for this. Mons. de Mun was at Church at Lumigny when the news came. The Curé gave it out directly after Vespers, and immediately the *Te Deum* was sung. I love this baby more than I ever expected to do, but oh! Pauline, the birth of this little child, which gives me so much joy, and whom I look at and kiss with so much pleasure, makes me bitterly feel my own solitude. I am so useless in both these families. If I had had a child, things would have been different, besides the immense comfort it would have been to myself. Before Eugénie was married she said sometimes: 'If I ever wish to marry and have a child, it is that I might give it to you.' And now, on the contrary, this dear little thing will steal away from me another large part of its mother's heart. It is right, it ought to be so, but it is not the less dreary for me. My dearest, do be indulgent to my complaints."

"April 25th.—Good-morning and good-bye. Eugénie is going on well, thank God! and I am less sad."

EUGENIE TO PAULINE.

"June 5th, 1839.

"MY BEST-LOVED PAULINE—I must only write one word, but it will be with my own hand; it is so long since I have written to you. Before I speak of myself, I must say something about your last letter, and the delightful news it contained. Oh! what it will be to see you, to have you at Brussels, so near us; and where I can so easily go, for many of Adrian's relations live there, and are always asking us to visit them. What happiness it will be, dear Pauline, to put my little child into your arms. It does seem so extraordinary. I can hardly believe he really exists, even while I am looking at him, and kissing him. He is a darling, and I think will be pretty. Farewell, my dear sister, I love you more than ever."

ALEXANDRINE TO PAULINE.

"Paris, June 10th, 1839.

"DEAR PAULINE—I am writing to you while Fernand is singing to the piano something so pretty, that I am more inclined to listen and dream, than to write; but I must tell you that during the last few days, I have felt so strongly the love and goodness of God, that it has filled me with joy. Ah! my dear sister, let us love God, and all those we love in Him alone. This is the way to be happy. Our dear Lord is good thus to increase my faith, just when I am most deprived of the solace of friendship. I took leave of Montal a week ago. He was here when we heard of your appointment to Brussels, and he was charmed, both on his own account, as on ours. My dearest darling, is it possible that you will be here in a few weeks? I need not say how the thought of it gladdens my heart. No; you are right, it may not be difficult to save one's soul, but perfection is another thing. And yet my dear patron Saint, St. Augustine, said: 'Love God, and do what you please.' Is that so terrible? Our Lord teaches us also, that everything is comprised in the love of God and our neighbor. Let us always aim at that, and we shall keep in the right way, and need not repine too much about austerities.

Love is the best teacher, and shows us a straight road, and a pleasant one, too, for what is there sweeter than love? Love fulfils the law."

ALEXANDRINE TO PAULINE.

"Boury, July 17th.

"I have just received your dear letter, in which you say that our story edifies you. Dear friend, how lovingly you dwell on that story, and what pleasant things you say about it. I do thank you for that. You cannot think how much good it does me to know that I am so often in your thoughts; poor me, who care so much about being loved, and who even covet a very high degree of affection. But I think I have not yet mentioned the 29th of June. You know I was here alone, without Eugénie, without your mother, and in bad weather. Nevertheless, in spite of wind and rain, I had the happiness of carrying a quantity of flowers to Albert's grave. But we shall be able to talk about all that when you are here. We expect a letter from you on Saturday, to tell us something about your coming."

Towards the end of July, Eugénie went to Boury, for the first time since her marriage. She spent some happy weeks there, and then left it never to see it again. On her return home she wrote me the following letter:—

EUGENIE TO PAULINE.

"Lumigny, August 7th, 1839.

"I spent a delightful time at Boury. I never cared for it so much, never felt more tender love for our beloved parents, and for our dear brothers and sisters. And how I did enjoy that pleasant kind of life, and the Chapel, now quite finished, and so pretty! You know all the changes that have been made in it; the greatest improvement I think is the tribune. The organ and voices sound so much better from above. But you will soon see it all yourself. The last days I was at Boury, that thought was always in my mind. I wish I could have stayed there till you arrived, but you will soon come here, will you not, my Paulette? It is out of the question that we should be long within reach of each other without meeting. The very thought of seeing you makes my heart beat; I do so long to feel your arms about my neck. Oh! my dear people, make haste to set out and to get here!"

ALEXANDRINE TO PAULINE.

"Boury, October 9th, 1839.

"At this moment, I am alone, my dear; yes, alone with Julian in this large house,* but I do not mind it. I bear these solitary hours better than I used to do. Just after they went away, when I was sitting alone and in the dark, it was rather melancholy. But I did not dwell upon it. I either read, or write our story, and when I am doing that, six hours of complete solitude do not seem to me long enough. These recollections have, thank God! a soothing effect upon me, notwithstanding the suffering mixed up with them, and the days pass away without weariness with God and Albert. I am now writing the account of our early married days, and it engrosses me to such a degree that I quite forget what is going on around me, and live my past life over again. Whatever people may say, I think imagination is a most blessed and most useful quality; it is like a magic mirror. When I look at that old family journal, that we called the 'newspaper,' it touches me to see your and my absent brothers' handwriting, and I say to myself: 'My happiness is shattered, but there still remain dear fragments of it, which I would fain gather round me, and you will always be the dearest and most important of them all to me. I like also sometimes to play on the organ, when I am by myself, but whether I am in my own room, or in the dear Chapel, I always feel glad to be here rather than at Paris, or Dangu. I like the melancholy silence of this place, a thousand times better than the noise of the world. It seems to me even more wonderful than wrong to make amusement the business of life, when from whatever side you view it, life is so sad and full of suffering. Do not suppose I would banish amusements from our earthly existence. By no means—if Albert had lived I should have taken my full share of them, and been just as strict a Catholic as I am now. But I want amusement to be the recreation, and refreshment, not the business of life."

I have now reached the period in which Olga will become more prominent in these memoirs. She was now about the age of eighteen, and it is time to describe her more particularly, or rather to let her describe herself, as the others have done. I open then the little journal where she also used to write down the

* My mother and Olga were gone out on a visit in the neighborhood.

thoughts occurring to her mind, and the little incidents of her peaceful days. It is, no doubt, an imperfect, perhaps a childish record ; but there is about it, I think, a very sweet fragrance of youth and poetry, with a piety which sometimes rises to elevation of thought. That chosen soul expanded and ripened later so fast, that it is well to study her character a little at this time of her life, so that when we find her strong and courageous in the time of trial, it may be borne in mind that our dear little sister was hardly more than a child. The very sight of her poor little journal affects me, for the trembling and uncertain writing reminds me of the continual deprivations against which she struggled so patiently. In another part of this narrative, I spoke of Olga's partial blindness, which, though not externally affecting her eyes, spoiled our enjoyment, often deprived her of sight and made study peculiarly difficult to her. Yet how she delighted in it, and with what perseverance she would wait with a book in her hand, till the moment came when she could see enough to read! In the same way she would sit at the piano, in a part of the room sheltered from the light, playing sometimes for hours together, and making laborious efforts to overcome the difficulties occasioned by her weak sight, without ever uttering a word of complaint, or imagining that her perseverance had any peculiar merit in it. Thus many little daily acts of self-denial simply and constantly practised, prepared the way for those greater virtues which were soon so strikingly offered to our imitation in her brief life. Now I return to that journal, which begins with her serious mood :—

OLGA'S JOURNAL.

"Lumigny, June 25th, 1839.

"Eugénie has read Albert's journal to me. How short and full of suffering has been his earthly life! But the goodness of God softened the bitterness of his pains by immense consolations. He said himself:—'Everything that ends is very short—,' and God has removed him from this sad world to a beautiful land where joy lasts for ever, and where he is waiting for us. Pray, dear Albert, for your very poor little sister. Remember, I am your sister. Think of me, and pray that I may die well, and be one day where you are now."

"Lumigny, August 16th, 1838.

"Poor Madame Collat died this morning. I went to see her with Eugénie after leaving the Church, and gazed sometime on

That grave strewn with roses made me think of Heaven. Later in the day I [illegible] a walk with my father, who talked to me so beautifully [illegible]igion. He has such ardent love of God!"

"October 17th.

"I find I am m[illegible] amused by our quiet evenings here than by the gay parties at Dangu. Quiet enjoyments have a charm which makes me feel really happy. But still I like society, and it amuses me; and after I have led that sort of life for a time, I find it very difficult to settle down again to our usual sober habits. A little while ago, for instance, I thought it would be very disagreeable to spend the winter at Boury, and now I shall make up my mind to it quite well. I have just now quite a passion for study, and I should like to have time to give myself up to it, so that I shall comfort myself if we spend the winter here. But I begin to believe in our going to Naples, and that idea is charming too. I am so changeable! The day before yesterday I should have felt it a real disappointment if the Naples journey had been given up. To-day I almost think I would rather stay here, and to-morrow it will be something else. There is no doubt that travelling is very amusing, and a kind of study; a very interesting one too. But I am not well-informed enough. If I knew more, Italy would be *most* interesting; but it does not much matter, I shall find it very amusing to be at Naples again, and I dare say I can learn something there. If anybody read this, it would seem rather pedantic, but it is nevertheless true that I have a passion for study. Two years ago, or perhaps even a year ago, I wished to study, only to find additional proofs of the truths of religion. Now my desire is less perfect, for I like to know what has taken place in former times. It interests me to hear about people who have lived before me. This wish may pass away, for I am not very constant, and it is likely enough that the pleasures of Naples will make me forget my wish to be learned. '*Sarà quel che sarà.*' The Abbé Gerbet will be there, and will check me if I incline to the wrong side. It will give me great pleasure to see my friends Euphémie and Nathalie* again. Yes, I shall certainly be very glad to go to Naples. There is the second bell, and I have lost all this time! It is very amusing to write down all one's thoughts. I have not often time for it, so when once I begin, I cannot stop."

* Euphémie de Sonnenberg and Nathalie de Narishkin.

"Paris, November 15th, 1839.

"Paris—yes, I have been at *Paris*, since Monday. It is a month since I wrote my journal, and it is always so when I have the most to say. Pauline and Augustus arrived from Lisbon on Sunday last, the 3rd, at dinner-time. My father and mother had been as far as Beauvais to meet them, but did not find them there. While they were gone, I stayed with Alex in the drawing-room, sometimes singing and playing on the piano, to while away the time, but oftener starting up at the least noise, and running from the drawing-room to the house-door and back again, in that excited state of expectation which is full of joy and impatience. Imagine our disappointment when my father and mother came back alone! Then Alexandrine and I established ourselves in the corridor, listening with all our might, and at every moment mistaking the sound of the pouring rain for the jingling of the bells. At last we heard a louder noise. It was really the bells this time. Quick! Father, mother, everybody—here they are! Everybody rushes, but nothing comes of it. There is a profond silence and a general impatience. At last a voice is heard: 'It is a courier. They started from Gisors before he did, and will be here in ten minutes!' Great is the delight of every one, and joyful the waiting and watching. At last, when half an hour had elapsed, the carriage was seen driving up to the door—without any bells jingling though—and we soon have our Pauline in our arms. No end of conversations that evening, and then music. We sang the Spanish and Portuguese songs she had brought for us, and then talked about Naples.

We had now left Lisbon for good, but were not going to remain long in France, for before settling in Brussels, which was our future destination, we were going to spend the winter at Naples with my family. The plan mentioned in Olga's journal was decided upon, and my father, mother, sisters, and Alexandrine were all going to Italy. No one was to remain in France but Eugénie. The prospect of this separation, which was so soon to follow upon my return, rather saddened the few days I spent with her. How would that cloud have darkened had the future been revealed to us! An epoch in our lives had closed with Eugénie's last visit to Boury. She had returned for a few days to the spot where she had spent two happy and busy years, and had once more taken her place for a little while in that family circle, bringing with her her new happiness and increased affection for all its members. Once more had Eugénie prayed in that Chapel, played upon that organ, visited the cemetery, and gone about the village, looking at all those things, and enjoying the thought that I too should soon see them again. Little did she think that it was the *last* time her eyes would rest on those familiar scenes, or still less foresee what members besides herself would be missing when that family party met there again. And when, after a short visit, I left Eugénie at Lumigny, well, happy, and with her beautiful child in her arms, as little did it occur to me what the effect would be upon her of the sudden departure of all those beloved ones who used from time to time to share the solitude of her life. I did not guess how bitterly she would reproach herself for her inability to fill the aching void left by the absence of so many of those she loved; nor, alas! was I aware that she was even then laboring under a disease which aggravated her trouble, and by which it was perhaps also painfully increased. Nothing could be more joyful than our departure for Italy, whence our return was to be so sad. My mother was delighted to get my father away from a northern winter, and to give Olga's youth a little amusement and excitement. Alexandrine was glad to visit once more a country she loved so much, and which was full of the recollections she most liked to dwell upon. Olga, too, was naturally pleased at the prospect of this most charming of all journeys, while I, who had been so long separated from my family, found it delightful to be thus travelling in company with them. One after another, we left Lumigny to meet at Marseilles on the 14th of December, and now I shall leave Olga to take up the thread of the narrative.

OLGA'S JOURNAL.

"Marseilles, December 15th, 1839.

"We are going straight to Naples, without stopping at Rome, where my father will go alone. I am a little sorry for this, but it is not quite decided, and at any rate we shall go there later.

"Yesterday on the road, I felt again afraid of growing ugly. Olga, my dear friend, do you know that it is not at all pretty to think so much about this? What if you should become ugly? You must offer it up to God like any other trial, and perhaps it will keep you from many sins of vanity. Provided you are good, what does it signify about anything else? Oh! yes, I know all that, and I should rather be good and ugly than bad and pretty; but I should like better to be both pretty and good. If I go on getting so fat it will be impossible to be pretty; and this vexes me. If I do not commit sins of vanity, I shall perhaps be impatient and envious instead. For shame! how silly and frivolous I am!"

"17th. On board the steam-boat off Genoa.

"Mamma declares I cannot write here, but I am, however, comfortably settled on the floor in the cabin, and the inkstand on a stool beside me. Oh! what a climate and what a country this is! Yesterday we stayed on deck till near ten o'clock, in the loveliest moonlight evening, singing a number of pretty airs. The weather, the calm sea, the glorious night, were indeed enchanting, and it was the 16th of December! What were our dear ones at Lumigny doing the while? Either freezing, or roasting by the great fire in the drawing-room. We thought of that yesterday, and that perhaps they were asleep by that same fireside, while we were laughing and singing in the open air as if it had been the month of May. My father called us all at five o'clock to see the sun-rise. I went on deck with my sisters. It is so beautiful to watch that magnificent sun rising out of the sea, and on the other side the coast from Nice to Genoa, which I saw for the first time, and which is enchanting. How delightful it must be to live in a country like this, and how much better I should like to be always here than at our melancholy Boury, where I so often longed to see the Mediterranean and these mountains again, and felt stifled in that hole! Poor Boury! I beg your pardon, but I do not think you are pretty. I have had very happy days there, nevertheless, but still I should like to live in this magnificent country. Romantic ideas have also been floating through my mind this morning. I thought it would be pleasant to meet with a good husband in these parts, a good, pious man, who would be fond of me, and who would have a pretty villa on this charming coast, in which I should spend my life. And then I made out for myself a most delightful existence. He was to be rich, that we might do a great deal of good, and live very comfortably.—How foolish any one would think me who read this!—I thought we should make short journeys to Lumigny, Boury, and Paris, and lead a most agreeable life. I am always picturing to myself the future as if it must of course be happy. I am afraid this is enough to bring me ill luck. God's will be done!"

"Genoa, December 18th.

"I am still in extasies about this country. Fancy my sitting here with the window open, and no fire, and that it was much too hot while we were walking, and that I have by me a lovely nosegay of roses, violets, and jonquils, the perfume of which is delicious. It was gathered for me at the Villa Pallavicini, not in a hot-house but in a garden full of flowers. It is really too charming. We are not conscious of winter here. We have seen several Churches, and first the *Annunziata*, which perfectly delights me. It is so long since I saw an Italian Church, and I appreciate them much more now than I used to do. We went also to *San Syro*, which is fine, but I like the *Annunziata* best of all, and we also visited the Cathedral and *San Lorenzo*, and the tomb of St. Catherine of Genoa; the sight of that tomb impressed me very much. It is in the hospital in which St. Catherine lived, and we went through the large, beautiful, airy wards. The actual body of the Saint, which can be seen, is frightful. It is clothed, and covered with jewels. I thought of the vanity of beauty, and that the Saints in Heaven must think how wise they were to despise it, and yet I cannot help feeling that I should be sorry to be ugly! Lastly, they showed us the Saint's room, by the side of which there is now a Chapel. The paintings on the walls were done in her time, and there were also some sentences inscribed which were either spoken or written by her: '*Amor mio, non più peccati! Amor mio, non più mondo! Se una goccia di quello che sente un cuore amante di Dio cadesse nell inferno, i demoni diventerebbero Angeli, perchè dove c'entra un poco di amor di Dio, non vì può essere ne pena ne male.*'*

"While I was there the thought, and almost the wish, to become a nun came into my head. The ****'s would say this was an *inspiration*, and indeed the impression was very strong. Afterwards we went into two or three Churches, when my only prayer was that I might do God's will. Afterwards I thought that I am too self-indulgent, too indolent, too much wanting in fervor, ever to make this great sacrifice. But for some days

* O my loving Lord, no more sins! O my loving Lord, no more world! If a single drop of what a loving heart feels for God was to fall into Hell, the devils would become angels, for where a little love of God exists there can be neither suffering nor evil.

the idea has kept on coming back to me, at any rate, I thought that nuns must be very happy. As I look at the sun and admire the beauty of this enchanting country, it strikes me how I should enjoy these things if I were a nun, for if we are always so delighted with the good or great things done by any creature we love, how great must be the extasy of a nun, when she thinks that God, who is more to her than husband, father, brother, mother, or child, is the Creator of all this magnificent world. Oh! yes, my God, Thou art the author of all goodness and beauty, and I understand that a passionate love of Thee must be the most powerful of all feelings! At Civita Vecchia we took leave of my father and Alexandrine, who went on to Rome, while we accompanied my mother to Naples."

ALEXANDRINE TO EUGENIE.

"Rome, December 21st, 1839.

"MY BELOVED SISTER—Here I am at Rome! I write to tell you so, both on my own account and your dear mother's, who begged me to give you tidings of us as soon as I possibly could. It was the last thing she said to me when I was taking leave of her. She is gone on straight to Naples with Pauline, Albertine and Olga, who was crying bitterly at not going to Rome. Your father, Etienne de Biron, Mons. de Tocqueville,* Mons. de Rivière and I, took the diligence at Civita Vecchia. But as Mons. de Tocqueville forgot his writing-desk, and went back on foot to Civita Vecchia to fetch it, and as the pole of our vehicle broke, we were thirteen hours instead of six on the road to Rome. It was not till two o'clock this morning that we drove by that dear, grand St. Peter's, magnificently lit up by the full moon. It was with the deepest emotion I saw it again, feeling as I do now that *I belong to it.* I went to bed at four o'clock, but slept only for three hours. We found the Abbé Gerbet waiting for us this morning in the sitting room. I went to hear his Mass in the Princess Volkonsky's Chapel. He seemed to me to say Mass with more intense and devout recollection than ever. To-morrow I am to go to Communion at St. Peter's, which is real happiness, and Albert will rejoice to see me revisit St. Peter's in this way. At Genoa, I felt also great joy at being again in an Italian Church, and seeing it full of Franciscans.

* Elder brother of the author of "La Democratie in Amérique."

The same day I went with the others to visit the body of St. Catharine of Genoa. At Leghorn the sight of Dipoggi,* and of the inn where he saw me with Albert, made me cry. And then I had the heart-ache because I could not go on to Pisa. When we went on board again there was much hesitation before your mother could decide on going on straight to Naples, and returning to Rome with Olga for the Holy Week. I think your father will be at Naples about the middle of January. This is a stupid letter, the fact is I feel stupid myself, and I am sure you will understand why. Say a thousand kind things to Adrian, and his father and mother, to whom I shall soon write. How are you? Do get into the habit of mentioning yourself. Pray for me, and may God bless you! From my window I can see our *Casa Margherita!*"

ALEXANDRINE TO EUGENIE.

"Rome, December 31st, 1839.

"MY DEAREST SISTER—I have too much to say to you, too much to say writing from Rome! Thank you for your dear letter, which I only received on Christmas Eve. Yes, I can imagine that you miss me, even in the midst of all your happiness, for however happy we are, the soul will often crave for something more perfect still. Perhaps not even in Heaven will this faculty be lost, but there our desires will be fulfilled as soon as they arise.

"I must begin by saying that Mde. Th——, that charming Hortense we have heard so much about, is here, and yesterday—without any previous introduction—I went to see her. I thought her certainly exceedingly pretty, and she seems a very admirable person, as indeed, I have no doubt she is. She came to Rome unexpectedly, on account of her health. Had she remained in Paris, she would have had to be in bed all the winter. I shall still find her here at Easter. Constance and I spent all Christmas night on foot, going from the magnificent midnight Mass at San Luigi dei Francesi to Santa Maria Maggiore, where there was a very fine procession, the carrying of the Holy Crib, and High Mass at the beautiful Chapel of the Blessed Sacrament. Then, after taking a cup of coffee, but without changing our clothes, we went on to St. Peter's, where the Pope said Mass.

* The French consul.

It touched me so much to look at him, and think I was now his child; and it was with a feeling of great joy that I knelt to receive a blessing from his hand. Then, at the elevation of the Mass said at St. Peter's Tomb, with what rapture I fell again on my knees amongst those poor English and other foreign ladies, who sat down all the time. Ah! if they only knew the intense gladness there is in a Catholic heart, they would perhaps make some efforts to become acquainted with our Faith."

"January 16th.

"My dear, dear sister, to-day I have got your second letter, before I answered the first, and I am vexed also not to have written to your mother-in-law, but I have not had time, for, as Constance says: 'I do not give myself time to breathe.' It would never have entered my head that any one could ask you what it was that absorbed me so much at Rome? Why—the question answers itself. Is not Rome the sanctuary of the whole world? It is true, though, that hitherto it has not been studied, or well known enough in that respect, and I hope the Abbé Gerbet's new book* will exhibit it in its true light. It is on this account, and with the idea that it may be useful to the Church, that he remains here to finish that work. He is very much touched with what you say, and feels as warmly and kindly towards you as ever. Holy friendships of that kind last for ever, and never injure one another. I have made two new friends, my dear Hortense, and a German, Baroness Kimsky, a convert from Protestantism, both very holy women. It is wonderful and usefully humbling to one's pride, to see such people. Both of them really *love* suffering; and one has a spirit of devotion, and the other of charity, which makes me feel as if I ought to sink under the ground. I have seen the Holy Father, and knelt with such pleasure at his feet. He granted me several precious favors, which rejoiced my heart."

After this short stay at Rome, Alexandrine went to Naples, which awakened other and more painful recollections.

ALEXANDRINE TO EUGENIE.

"Naples, February 2nd.

"My Dearest—What do you say to this date, written *by me*—'*Naples!*' How wonderful this life is, and how fortunate that

* *Esquisse de Rome Chrétienne* (Sketch of Christian Rome).

we have a better one to hope for. I came here on Thursday night about eleven o'clock, and the mere passing by the houses at Chiaja, gave me a heavy, bitter feeling of depression. Only think that by the vetturino's mistake, I drovè by our old house, and yours, and thus saw them both again the first thing. Ah! my angel husband! Who but God could have comforted me after losing all my earthly happiness? It is a great comfort to pray in the Churches here; at Naples, where I lived only for a human love; at Naples, where I thought I had everything when I had Albert; at Naples, where I shall never see him again, and where nothing is left me but God. Nothing but God! And this is so often the thought of our earthly unworthiness, as if we had not enough in possessing Him! My room looks into the garden of the Palazzo Acton, where I was married, and beyond it I can see the Vomero. Oh! with what marvelling I looked at all these things, the day after I came. Well, I like to see it all, and I do hope it is God's goodness, and the conviction of my departed angel's bliss and not my own indifference, that makes these recollections sweet to me.

"At Santa-Maria-in-Portico, where I went yesterday, for the sake of its associations, I was thinking that Albert would rather see me there now a Catholic without him, than as I was formerly a Protestant with him; I felt, however, a bitter regret that I had not been a Catholic during our short married life. But I quickly remembered that whatever God does, is well done, so everything must have been for the best. I am not unhappy here, and I like my room. The good Neapolitans look upon me as a fanatic, and on that account leave me in peace, and I am glad to be with all our dear people, and to rest after the fatigue of Rome. You and our beloved angel are both continually in my thoughts, and what would not I give to have you with me! You ask me how I get on here after Rome. Rome has, indeed, quite a different atmosphere; the very one for suffering hearts, because everything there speaks of God, whereas everything here suggests thoughts of earthly happiness. So that when that is all over, it might be sad to live here, for there is no place in the world so well adapted to be the scene of human love and human joys! But how many of those we used to know here, death has carried off! I have still so many things to tell me. I saw Monte Cassino, by the Pope's permission, and went into the monastery. What a situation that is, and what peace reigns on those solitary heights. The monks are admirably good, and have that peaceful, kind look, I so often see in convents. Good-bye. May God make you and yours saints!"

ALEXANDRINE TO COUNT DE MONTALEMBERT.

"Naples, February 3rd, 1840.

"I am at Naples. I cannot tell you what I feel at the sight of all these places. There is not a house at Chiaja, not a spot in the neighborhood that is not hallowed by recollections which can never be effaced from my mind. But my love for going over *everything* that belongs to the past makes me like to be here, and what would be bitter in the contrast between that past and the present is sweetened by the one unfailing consolation, the blessing of being here *as a Catholic*. My room looks into the garden of the Palazzo Acton, where I was married, and a little farther on I see the Vomero. Nothing could suit me better, especially as here I am out of the way of the intolerable noise of the Chiaja. I left Rome a week ago, and saw Monte Cassino on the way. I was enchanted with that old sanctuary, and what a situation it is! What peace and goodness in the faces of those men raised up above the earth, and who both literally and spiritually speaking, look down on the great highways of the world, the hum of which scarcely reaches their ears. And what reverence we feel for those religious brethren and sisters of past ages, whose own history is lost in obscurity, whilst their admirable works still exist! I saw there Don Luigi Tosti, whom I thought very pleasing, and who was enchanted by the gift of your *St. Elisabeth*, and your remembrance of him.

"To crown that pleasant day, I met at the monastery the Abbé Jandel,* who though not yet thirty, has been Superior at the Seminary, and is now going to enter the Dominican Noviciate at Viterbo. He is an excellent man, and I was very glad to have him as a travelling companion. He told me that during the last few months twenty or thirty subjects have offered to join Father Lacordaire."

Eugénie had been very anxious as to the effect which her return to Naples would have on Alexandrine, and when she received her letters written in a spirit of such gentle resignation, it

* Now General of the Dominican Order, or Friars' Preachers.

touched her so much that she expressed this feeling in most enthusiastic terms, as will be seen by the following reply :—

ALEXANDRINE TO EUGENIE.

"Naples, March 8th, 1840.

"My dear sister, one line only in answer to the '*Bull of Canonisation*,' as the Abbé calls it, which you have despatched to me, and to which he listened with the utmost amazement. We can neither of us get over it, and I assure you that his exclamations would have greatly tended to obviate the perils of this *apotheosis*, had I been inclined to take it in earnest. He could only say: 'What has she taken into her head? Why, this passes all belief!' We laughed over it very much, and I will venture to say you have quite forgotten how absurd your praises were. It was a fine specimen of one of your fits of enthusiasm, and all because I had written something from Naples about being resigned to my sorrow. Yet you know that in my worst moments of grief I always wished to see Naples once more. As to the change you think you see in me since your marriage, it is a delusion springing from the fact that you did not then know what it is to love, and to love a husband, so it did not surprise you in the same way as it does now that I can endure to live without Albert. It is true, however, that I now have less of that bad feeling which used to make me suffer at the sight of the happiness of others. This is a great mercy, and perhaps also the result of habit, which is so strong that we can get accustomed even to the loss of happiness. God is infinitely good to me, as He is to all His creatures, and He has given me interests in religion, and a love of Catholicism, which I can only compare to the love I have felt and do feel for Albert, and this is what helps me to bear such a sorrow as mine almost without a murmur. But these pleasures of the soul which I still enjoy, though Albert is gone, do not prevent my having faults, and very deep-rooted ones too; and if, while you were writing that wonderful panegyric, you could have known how bad my temper often is, what unkind feelings I have about other people, and then all my self-indulgence and cowardice, you would perceive that I am as far from a religious vocation as you now seem to think me near it.

"Adrian often surprises one by his ideas upon that subject. Am I to take them as an omen? There is of course nothing impossible with God. The only thing true in your tirade is what you say of the manner in which the Abbé has directed me. I am constantly astonished at his wisdom, even though I have now known him so long."

Whilst Alexandrine's life was thus divided between her past recollections and her eternal hopes, Olga was just at the age when earth seems to hold out the most seductive promises. For the first and only time in her existence she caught a glimpse of the world and its pleasures. It proved a brief one, for short as her life was destined to be, it was doomed to undergo almost as deep and complete a transformation as Alexandrine's. But even during that transient gleam of sunshine which was now gilding her eighteenth year, there are pages in her journal which show how good and serious thoughts were always mingled with the lighter impressions natural to youth.

OLGA'S JOURNAL.

"To-day I have had sorrows and pleasures. Sorrow because my father was displeased at my staying so long at the Narishkins' yesterday evening, and I am so foolish that I sat with him a whole hour wishing to say something about it, and not able to open my lips, and I ended by crying! Mamma said that it made her anxious to see how I always allow myself to be carried away by present pleasures. It is quite true. I let myself be influenced by every impression, without having energy enough to consider the consequences, and to take good resolutions. But *pazienza.* May God make me good and help me to get the better of my faults. I have had to-day one real and great pleasure. Fernand told me that yesterday evening, when he was with E., S., R., and M., a beautiful letter had been read aloud which Father Lacordaire had written some years ago to R. They had joked about it at first, but in the end they all became quite serious, and made good resolutions. This morning I had a note from the N.s, who told me that R. had said his prayers yesterday for the first time since October. This gave me more pleasure than I can express. It seems to me that if everybody were good, I should be better.

"O! my God, by Thy Passion and by Thy Death, grant that these good resolutions may last. Let all these men become good. Bless them all, my God, and Fernand, and grant him the grace to love Thee. Make E. really good, and S. a Catholic, and R. as pious as he used to be. Protect them, help them, strengthen them all. Do, my God, give them grace to keep their resolutions, and let them all have wives who will love them and help them to be good. I shall pray for them to-morrow. I am going early to Church for confession and Communion.

"This evening the Abbé told me to say my prayers, and to drive away all sad thoughts before going to sleep. I will try to do this, and I pray that God may bless me, for I love Him, and will always love Him. May Thy will be done in me, my God! Grant me to become really good, humble, and modest, and give me strength to amend my faults. Lord, Thou knowest I should like to be happy, but this I am sure will not displease Thee. Thou knowest the sort of happiness I desire. But if what I ask is displeasing to Thee, do not hearken to my prayer. Let me *die* rather than offend Thee by mortal sin; this is a prayer I have always made: may I persevere in it to the end. I pray for all those I love. My dear father and mother, brothers and sisters, for Mathilde, Fanny, Euphémie and Nathalie.* Forgive me, O Lord, my many faults. I will not think of them too much, I would rather dwell upon Thy infinite love. I cast myself into Thy arms. O! let me love thee. Let me never love any one more than Thee!"

At that time Olga wrote to Eugénie letters which prove with what confidence she opened her whole heart to her sister; and how well Eugénie deserved and turned to account the confidence reposed in her, the following answer will show:—

EUGENIE TO OLGA.

"February 17th, 1840.

"My dear little Sister—To tell you the truth, I think the feelings you describe are only the momentary effect of your first year in the world, when everything naturally enough strikes, surprises, and excites you. Mistrust yourself, my Olgette; try as much as you can to keep your thoughts under control. When you are in society, amuse yourself with simplicity of heart. You are very young, and when real troubles come, you will be sorry to have unnecessarily saddened that poor little heart of yours at a time when it was inclined to be gay and happy.

* Mathilde, Countess Amédée des Cars; Fanny, Princess de Rospigliosi; Euphémie, Baroness de Reding; Nathalie Narishkin, now Superior of a house of Sisters of Charity in Paris.

What is the ruling idea which disturbs your mind? Is it not a vague anxiety about the future; a restless impatience to know how your lot will be fixed? Try to calm these feelings, and to keep your soul in peace. Put your trust in God. Turn to Him whenever you are in danger of being carried away by the excitements of the world. My dear little sister, one thing above all others I would recommend to you, not because of any past deficiency on your part in respect to the points in question, but in order to warn you never to neglect it. Whatever may be your thoughts, fancies, or feelings, always mention them—never shut them up in your heart. The devil takes easily advantage of these bad fits of reserve. With a mother like ours, and such a sister as Pauline, to both of whom you can say anything, and who sympathise with all your feelings, even whilst they reason with and advise you, it would be almost a sin not to avail yourself of so great a help. These serious observations which I have thought it right to make, have not prevented me from being deeply interested in all that you say in your long letter. Your description of the journey, and of the sights at Genoa, the pretty account of St. Catherine, your sudden notion of becoming a nun, have all amused me, and are quite natural. I can see that then your impressions were of a religious kind, whilst at Naples they have been for the most part worldly; and who knows whether at the bottom of all these fancies, impulses, and dreamings, there is not lying concealed a grand vocation to some great height of sanctity which will prove Madame de Castel to have been in the right? And then when young ladies read your life, they will be delighted to find in so wonderful a saint all their own little frivolous follies and nonsensical fancies, which they will then indulge with the comfortable idea of ending in the same manner!

"I was sure that your friend Nathalie would become charming. I can exactly fancy what she is like, and it must be just the sort of face I admire. If she remembers my existence, give her my love, and to dear Euphémie also. I am glad you have seen such good friends once more. And now my dear little sister, let me give you some more advice. Watch over yourself, mistrust your inclination to indolence. Exert both your body and mind. Force yourself to move about, as I force myself to speak and to laugh, that I may conquer my natural taste for silence. Take long walks, do a great deal during the day, never refuse to go on an errand. Hand a chair to anybody who has none, pick up the handkerchiefs that people may happen to drop, and struggle against absence of mind as you would fight against bad thoughts. Believe me, all this is necessary. These are all real little acts of virtue; they will cost you something, but they must be done. Then another thing—look after Albertine. You must help her a little to grow out of her childishness, for this is really your business. Bestow upon her a little of the interest that you waste on other things. Be to her what Pauline was to me. When she took me in hand I was a rough stone, but she shaped and polished me. The doors of my understanding were closed, but she opened them, and that time of my life has always seemed to me a passage from night to day. Will you not do the same for Albertine? Had she been with me I would have undertaken that task, *con amore*, for Pauline would always have been in my mind. Do not forget to answer me about all this; and tell me how you manage about your dress, and what state your purse is in. Take care not to get into debt. My sweet little sister, I love you with all my heart! God keep you from all harm!"

In the beginning of April, Alexandrine went with my husband and myself to Rome for Holy Week. She wrote at that time to M. de Montalembert the following account of an interesting day spent at the Dominican Convent of La Quercia:—

"Rome, April 27th, 1840.

"MY DEAR FRIEND—On the 14th of April, the young Princess Borghese,* and her husband, Pauline, Augustus, and I, met at Viterbo, and the next day, Palm Sunday, we went early to La Quercia. The bells rang, and the organ played triumphant strains in that beautiful Church. They made us all go into the choir—we three women on one side, and opposite to us, the delegate, Prince Borghese and Augustus. I had knelt down and bowed my head, but when I raised it again, I saw near me two Dominicans prostrate on the ground. It was Brother Lacordaire and Brother Requedat. They soon rose, and listened to the sermon addressed to them by the Priest who, for that day, took the Superior's place. It was an excellent discourse. He spoke of what their future life was to be: one of humility, obedience and mortification. He said they might be ordered into different

* The beautiful and holy Lady Gwendoline Talbot, daughter of Lord Shrewsbury; the first wife of Mark Anthony, Prince Borghese.

countries, and would have to go wherever they were sent. That they must never attribute anything to their own abilities, but nevertheless exert to the utttermost any talents they possessed, and should they be called upon to give up their lives as martyrs for religion, before they had done anything else in this world, nothing could be better. At these words Pauline saw a smile of rapture in M. Requedat's face. Then they both made their profession in the hands of the Superior, who afterwards affectionately embraced them. It was very soon over, and then we were taken to see the miraculous Madonna which is kept in the Oak-tree [whence the name of La Quercia]. Afterwards the two Fathers were sent for, to say a few words to us. Father Lacordaire thanked us for having come, and told Augustus and Pauline that in so doing he considered that we had become partners in his undertaking. It has been, indeed, a great honor to be present at the beginning of this great work, and an important moment to look back to. This evening I went with the Cravens and Madame Thayer to Cardinal Pacca's reception. I was delighted with him. He said you were a very admirable young man."

"April 28th.

"MY DEAR FRIEND—At last I have heard Father Lacordaire preach, and I think it surpassed my expectations, which is not saying a little. Oh, how I do like that fiery zeal, that steely strength of conviction, that eloquence! How I wished, after hearing him, I could *do* something. Some people were displeased with his sermon, but I despise their criticisms. I should so much like to have heard him again. He asked affectionately after you. I have not time to say anything more, though Rome abounds with subjects of interest, as you know. I am, perhaps, going to Russia. Pray for me. Dear Anna,* I love you, pray for me sometimes. God grant we may meet again some time or other in this poor world!"

My mother and Olga were with us at Cardinal Pacca's reception. They had come from Naples, and were going on, the next day, to Goritz, where my mother was to spend two months with her sister the Duchesse de Blacas, who was residing at that time with the exiled royal family. It then consisted of the Count de

* Countess de Montalembert.

Chambord, his sister,* who was not yet married, and the Dauphin and Dauphiness.† During this journey Olga wrote very little in her journal. I shall give, however, some brief extracts from it, partly because reminiscences of royal personages, however slight, are always interesting, and also that I may linger, with a kind of mournful pleasure, over the pages which speak of the father and sisters I was so soon to lose.

Olga was travelling vetturino with my mother and Fernand, and wrote as follows:—

OLGA'S JOURNAL.

"Terni, May 5th, 1840.

"Enchanting country, where I should like always to live! Certainly I have not at this moment the least wish to go back to France. We went into the Church, which is not ugly, indeed rather pretty, but there is not the least bit of marble in it, which is strange here. My mother cried a great deal in that Church; it was only this morning that I was remarking the wonderful sweetness of her temper. My dear, good mother, always so sweet, so kind, so equable, notwithstanding her anxiety about my father;‡ how I felt to love her, and how I hate that shyness which will not let me show it! I am tired of writing. I will go and walk with Fernand, and then go to bed. O! God, bless and protect me, and all those whom I love.

"Foligno, May 6th.

"I have a fit of enthusiasm about Italy; this dear land in which I should like to spend my life. Foolish girl that I am, always spoiling my existence with these castles in the air! To-day we breakfasted at Spoleto, having left Terni at six o'clock. The road was too beautiful. The mountains covered with verdure, and flowers everywhere. Our journey is like a pilgrimage. We prayed in four different Churches to-day, and this evening had Benediction in the Cathedral, which is rather a fine one. After dinner I went out, and then sang with Fernand. Dear kind Fernand, I so much love him! Afterwards we had tea, and I read Father Geramb's work. It is very interesting. I should like to go to Jerusalem. I am tired to death, or I would describe our

* Marie Louise, afterwards Duchess of Parma.

† Marie Therèse, the daughter of Louis XVI., and her husband, the son of Charles X. and father of Count de Chambord.

‡ My father's health gave rise to the greatest anxiety, which she concealed, not to give us pain.

walk. We talked about happiness. I am sure there must be some kind of happiness in this world. How can one have a doubt about it, especially in travelling, in looking as we are now doing on this lovely earth?"

"Tolentino, May 7th.

"A tiresome and tiring journey. The winding road never gets out of the mountains, and at each fresh turning another mountain is seen. A bad dinner at the inn, but the people who kept it were very good-natured. I walked with Mamma and Fernand. We talked of natural and supernatural fears. Fernand said he believed in intermediate beings, and so do I, if he means the Angels. We went to the cathedral, where the body of St. Nicholas of Tolentino is preserved."

"Goritz, May 12th.

"We have arrived. I wrote nothing at Loreto, Ancona, or Trieste. I do not care about the two last, but I had many things to say about Loreto. I have seen my aunt and cousins de Blacas again.* My aunt is very kind, and I love her so much. To-day we went to see the King and Queen.† *O! Madonna mia*, how frightened I was! And yet they were not the least terrible. The King was exceedingly kind, and though the Queen is more formidable, she was just as good-natured. Mademoiselle‡ is charming, and I am sure I shall be very fond of her. We are to dine there this evening. I hope I shall not be so frightened. I want only to be good, and to let God do with me what he pleases. I have been so delighted with all I have seen from Rome to Ancona. This is the country to be happy in!"

"May 14th.

"My aunt has been so kind as to put a piano in our room, so that I have been playing part of the morning. I have not brought any music, but I remembered by heart a duett out of the *Giuramento*, with all the accompaniment, and I sang it with Fernand. I also made out several other accompaniments which I was not a little proud of. To-day there is a soirée at the Palace. Every Thursday and Sunday they are at home to all the society of Goritz. This society looks very respectable, but they are not a very pretty set of people. The Cs. and As. are nearly the only

* The Duc de Blacas had died the preceding spring in the same place where Charles X. had breathed his last. The faithful and devoted servant of fallen majesty lies buried at the feet of his royal master.

† Since the death of Charles X. the title of King is given to the Dauphin.

‡ The Comte de Chambord's sister.

families, but they have branches and sprigs without end. Mademoiselle is really charming, and has been most kind and gracious to me. I am quite captivated with her."

"May 15th.

"I went out driving with Mademoiselle, who came to fetch me in a *frightful* calèche, with Mde. de G., to whom I talked a great deal. Then we walked. Mademoiselle is a most enchanting little princess. I talk a little more now and do not despair of becoming in time quite conversible."

"May 16th.

"To-day to Grafenberg, a sort of little château where King Charles X. died. Mamma walked on before with my aunt, and I was behind with * * * I can venture to assert that I carried on the whole conversation, and am really improving. In the evening we dined with the King * * * The Duchess de Gontaut arrived and took my place next Mademoiselle, which put me out, for I quite worship her."

"May 17th.

"This evening, at the King's, there were more visitors from Goritz, and several pretty women. As we could not work on Sunday, we played at cards. It was *onze-et-demi*, and I lost. Mademoiselle looked very pretty with natural flowers in her hair. At half-past eight, the Queen gets up and dismisses the company, and then sits down again with the select few till nine, when everybody goes away. Mademoiselle told me that she always goes to bed at half-past nine and gets up at six. Nine hours of sleep—that is pretty well. Poor princes! They have not a very gay life of it. In the evening they sit at work at a round table, and Mademoiselle often yawns. She told me how they spent their time when her brother was away, and she was alone with her uncle and aunt and Mde. de G. She said it was *very dull*. Indeed I should think so; it must be worse than Boury, when there is no one there but me to keep up the conversation! Though I am sometimes tired of Boury, and have intensely wished to travel a little, I never was unhappy at home. On the contrary, I had delightful times of tranquillity and peace, which I think cannot be enjoyed unless one leads a regular life, and especially if we are surrounded by a large family, and as charming a one as my own. A monotonous life is by no means a tiresome one. Still one feels the want of some change now and then. My life, such as I plan it, would be delightful!"

"May 23d.

"I drove and walked to-day with Mademoiselle. As we were going to the Strasaldo she gave me a pretty little parasol. I do not think there has ever been—no, not even in a fairy tale—a more charming princess. I stayed with her a long time. She played on the harp and I sang. We got up at five o'clock in the morning to take leave of the Queen. We, that is my Mother, Stanislaus and Olivier, drove to St. Maur, my aunt's country house, with her. It is a charming place; but these walks are always a real cross to me on account of my eyes. I am told not to speak of it to everybody, which I should like to do, as an excuse for my awkwardness, and the blunders I make on these occasions. I cannot say a word, for I do not know what to answer, when I am asked what I think of the views. O! my God, it is indeed a cross, and I trust that it is reckoned as one in Thy sight. I offer it up to Thee, no doubt, but I cannot say it is a welcome one, or that I should not be very glad not to have it."

"May 24th.

"The Queen and Mademoiselle went away this morning for a few days, which vexed me, for I should like to have seen much more of the Princess. I have read over what I wrote yesterday in my journal, and thought it dreadfully silly; and then, unfortunately, it came in Mamma's way, who thought so too. I really will not write any more what comes into my head, for it seems so foolish when I read it again. I will give up castle-building, and leave everything to God, which is not very meritorious, for I wish for nothing—not even what I thought I wished for yesterday. It has thrown cold water on all my schemes to find that Mamma thought them silly. However, *lasciamo fare a Dio.* Imaginative feelings are always very absurd. I will not write any more, and will think as little as possible of those sort of things. Yesterday, however, I wanted very much to go to Milan with Mademoiselle, and began castle-building again."

"May 30th.

"At five o'clock this morning I went with Fernand, Stanislaus, and Olivier to the holy mountain, which is a pilgrimage in the neighborhood. The view from it is beautiful, but, as usual, my pleasure was quite spoilt by my blindness, and also a little by my stupidity. Others would have enlivened these sort of expeditions by their cheerfulness and gaiety, but I always feel that everybody must be bored to death with me. This too, at least in part, proceeds, I think, from my blindness, for if I could see, I should find a great many more topics of conversation; as it is, I rack my mind for a word to say, and do not succeed after all. Then I am vexed and should like to cry, which makes me think that I ought to live always as I do now, in a large, happy family, or in a united and affectionate home, where I am not the only one to carry on the conversation."

"May 31st.

"A general departure. The king started at twelve o'clock with Louis, and we at one for Trieste."

"June 5th, Sulmona.

"A detestable inn. Fernand and I were both quite out of temper, but it is impossible ever to get a single complaint out of Mamma. I was almost provoked with her patience, and kept telling her the most dreadful things about the dirt of the place; notwithstanding which this dear mother only observed that the town was full of curious old remains, and she would go out and see them and learn their history; whilst I, who usually like these things so much, was so angry about our beds and dinner that I could not look at anything."

"Naples, June 6th, 1840.

"With what delight I write the date of this place! What a long journey we have had. We stopped at a dreadful inn where we could not stay to sleep, but travelled on all through the night. Fernand told me that suspicious persons had been seen in the house, and that we might very likely be robbed. We did not tell my mother, but for a long time fear kept me awake. I was getting by heart a speech I intended to make to the brigands, and was determined to show great presence of mind, but nothing came of it. I began to doze involuntarily, and at last gave up struggling to keep awake, and only opened my eyes at Capua, where we had to wait till the gates were unlocked. At nine we arrived at Naples, and were up the stairs and in my father's room before he had heard any noise."

During the time which elapsed between my mother's return and my departure from Naples, Alexandrine wished to revisit with me all the places in the neighborhood in any way connected with the past. We went therefore to Castellamare, Sorrento, to the Vomero, and also to the Villa Trecase, where my family had lived for some time, and the road which led to the house where she had been with her mother; the garden, the terrace, the Church, the very spot near the Floridiana, where Albert had said: "I love you," and the Villa Pietracatella, where she had spent the most enchanting part of her life. But, oh! how different it all looked to us now! As to the other places I have named, neither youth nor love could add anything to their natural beauty, which outstrips imagination itself; but it was not the case in this instance. That particular villa had been chosen at the time Madame d'Alopeus had settled there, purposely to avoid the sea-breezes, and was so situated that it was only by getting up to the roof that the bay and the mountains beyond could be perceived. It was surrounded by a melancholy garden which effectually hid all the view, and little could be seen from it but the unspeakable beauty of the sky, and the graceful outline of a few pines, just opposite to what had been Alexandrine's window. When we saw it again in an uninhabited state, the deserted house looked most dreary, and everything about it was decayed and gone to wreck, like the happiness of which it had once been the scene. "*And this is the place,*" exclaimed Alexandrine, "*where I was so happy! It was actually here that I thought life and this world were too beautiful!*" Ah! how many thoughts this sad pilgrimage suggested to us both. We were still young, and for one of us life seemed already ended, and nothing remained of the happiness dreamt of, and afterwards realized beyond all hope amid these scenes, but a sorrow as great as that happiness, and lasting as life itself. And that life yet promised to be a long one. Alongside of all this sadness, we had, as I must hasten to say, the comfort of the Abbé Gerbet's consoling and strengthening words. He had accompanied us on our pilgrimage, and well did he know how to raise up with a firm and strong hand the bruised and aching soul; how to divest memory of its sharpest thorns, and make it serve as the means to strengthen faith in the unseen, and awaken hope in its undying realities. Blessed through all eternity will be the words which in that hour and at so many other times, fell from his lips into the depths of our hearts! Towards the end of July I left Naples with my husband, and my father went with us to the steamboat, which was just ready to start. They hurried us on board without permitting my father to follow, but as there was afterwards a few minutes' delay, I ran down the ladder before they could prevent me, and embraced him once more. It was for the last time in this world! Having gone on board again, I followed with my eyes the little boat nearing the shore, and stood looking at my beloved father and kissing my hand to him, till the steamer left the harbor, and carried me away from him for ever.

This farewell, now so sorrowfully remembered, is not the only sad recollection of that summer, for we were beginning to feel uneasy at the unsatisfactory accounts of Eugénie's health, though in a great measure comforted by the hope that the birth of her second child would put an end to her ailments. Looking back to it now, that anxiety seems like the little cloud which rises up and spreads over the whole sky, casting a foreboding shadow even upon the pale gleam of sunshine which preceded its coming. When we reached Brussels, I left my husband to arrange everything about our new home, and hurried on myself to Lumigny, where I was expected with more than usual impatience. I was also most anxious to see Eugénie again, and at the first moment I felt nothing but pleasure, for she appeared to me to be quite well. I soon, however, perceived a change which surprised me. For the first time, I saw clouds passing over her soul, and her mind, which was usually so simple and bright, was now full of exaggerated and imaginary troubles. For the first time in my life, in short, I found her out of spirits, and this deeply affected me.

Up to that time, notwithstanding her serious habits of thought, and the deeply religious tone of her mind, and though she was often and willingly silent, nothing could be more foreign to her character than sadness. These words of Lamartine seemed to have been made for her:—

"Sa voix argentine,
Echo limpide et pur de son âme enfantine,
Musique de cette âme où tout semblait chanter,
Egayait jusqu'à l'air qui l'entendait monter!"*

Truly were her voice and her soul joyous, and had continued to be so even when the sorrows she had undergone and shared had at an early age disenchanted life. But now the trial of

* "Her silvery voice,
Pure and transparent echo of her childlike soul,
Music of that soul where everything seemed to sing,
Cheered the very air which heard it ascend."
Lamartine's "Harmonies."

despondency and anguish had come upon my sister, and those who are versed in the history of chosen souls, and who know what spiritual riches lie hidden in suffering and humiliation, will not be surprised at what she had to go through. But I was both pained and astonished at this change, and did everything I could to enliven and rouse her, and especially to reason her out of that excessive and morbid diffidence, which was the only real trouble they had. She tormented herself really and truly about what she called her want of cleverness, liveliness, or talent for conversation, but it would be difficult to imagine how unhappy it made her. At this time of her life the singular and charming modesty for which she had been always remarkable, had become a misfortune, and almost a fault, or, at any rate, a weakness which ill health aggravated and turned into a suffering.

It used to make me cry and laugh at the same time to see my darling Eugénie, who seemed to me so bright, so intelligent, so full of earnest and deep thoughts, and whose natural gaiety was so exuberant that she had been often obliged to check her inclination to view things and people in a ridiculous light, and to restrain the exercise of her talent for mimicry—to see her, I say, reproaching herself with being stupid, tiresome, and useless, and that with a grief and a bitterness which may have aggravated the state of suffering which no doubt was the original cause of this depression.

Whilst I was staying at Lumigny, those of my family whom I had left behind in Italy went from Naples to the Villa Cittadella, near Lucca, the same in which we had spent the summer of 1829. There the following pages of Olga's journal were written. They are curious as a contrast between her thoughts of Eugénie, and Eugénie's opinion of herself.

OLGA'S JOURNAL.

"Lucca, Villa Cittadella, September 9th, 1840.

"We heard this morning from Pauline. Eugénie has not been well, and the excitement of Pauline's arrival did her harm, but, thank God! she is better. Not a word from herself for me to-day, but that is natural, for Pauline was there, and she was ill; but in thinking of the questions she would put to Pauline about us all, I fancied I should be the last she would ask about. I am afraid she does not love me as much as she used sometimes to say she did. I shall never forget the pleasure it gave me. I love her so very much! I am jealous of her loving and of her being obliged to love so many others better than me. Adrian, Pauline, Alexandrine, all come before me, and I love her perhaps as much as all of them put together. I think she is of all people in the world the one I would rather be alone with. I said to Euphémie, who repeated one day some little criticism that had been made upon Eugénie, that if I heard that or anything else said that was like blame of her, I should be ready to fight the person who said it. Though I am so very fond of her, and I have always been fonder of her, I think, than of the others, she frightens me sometimes, and I have not felt quite at my ease with her. When I said just now that she was the person I liked best to be alone with, and I do feel it, because I should wish to have her *quite to myself*, I stopped to consider whether I should really not rather have one of my friends with whom I am quite at my ease, and over whom I have a kind of authority, for those dear girls do exactly what I wish, and like everything that I do. But I think not. I love my friends exceedingly; they are very good, I often think better than I am, but my love for Eugénie is more intense, and it is mixed with great admiration. I should like to be always with her, and for her to guide me about everything as she used to do. She always makes me better. She is like a Saint or a guardian Angel, protecting and advising me, and I would rather live in submission to her, than exercise a kind of authority over my friends. This shows me that admiration and respect are a necessary part of love, and that where there is the highest respect and admiration, there will be the deepest love. This ought to carry me yet further, and lead me to the conclusion that it is a simple and natural thing to love God above all things, as there are no bounds to the respect and admiration due to Him. I love, admire, and reverence Eugénie."

Alexandrine wrote to me from Cittadella on the subject of Eugénie's low spirits, and the kind of trial she was enduring—a letter which seems to me full of Christian wisdom:

"Villa Cittadella, September 20th, 1840.

"I have been thinking very much of your letter about Eugénie. As you say, it is singular that such a trial should have been sent to our beloved sister, though I see in it the Hand of God, Who will not let His chosen souls be exposed to the poison of self-approval. Her beautiful humility will thus be more easily preserved. But it is remarkable that all the great qualities of her soul and mind are apparently less useful where she is, than the trifling qualifications she does not possess would be. I can perfectly well understand her despondency, without of course approving of it. Our poor Eugénie! Her special characteristics are a tender, joyous love of God, and great activity, and now she feels that a little more talent for conversation on general matters, and an aptitude for drawing out others in that way, would be of more value to her than those higher gifts. This is certainly a cross, but it is sweetened by having a husband whom she loves and who loves her, and a charming child. Are not these immense blessings? I know it is natural to wish for more than we possess, even when we own we have more than others. We are intended for the perfection of happiness, and this is why we are never quite satisfied in this life, because happiness is never perfect. What truisms I am writing! But this solitude makes me meditative. (Everything, you see, is judged of by comparison. A king is poor, with what makes another a rich man.) You used to picture to yourself the happiness of having a child like hers; and when that day at Albano you were speaking of this with tears in your eyes, I thought to myself how thoroughly happy I should be if, like you, I had my husband still beside me. And be sure, that even were that wish of yours fulfilled, other things would be wanting, for which you would still be longing. I do not know if you think this a consolation, but it is true. This life is the way of the Cross, and during this last week I have seen many things which make me feel how useful crosses are to the soul, and which I am going to write to that dear, dear sister, for they will do her good."

Alexandrine left Lucca with my father and mother to go to Pisa, and about the same time I left Lumigny to return to Brussels. It was at that time that Alexandrine visited, among other persons and places which old associations endeared to her, the Franciscan Convent and Padre Galligani, and there had that touching interview with Fra Clementino, which she has herself related in her story. Very soon afterwards Alexandrine's stay at Pisa was cut short by a sad event, which is spoken of in Eugénie's next letters.

EUGENIE TO PAULINE.

"Lumigny, November 10th.

"Have you heard the sad, terrible news which has just reached us? Mark Antony's wife* is dead. Ah! what is this life, this world and its happiness? Is it ever possible even to call oneself happy? And is not this daily expectation of the end of everything a living death? Dead! when it was only the other day that you were speaking of her beauty and strength, and telling me how quickly she recovered the birth of her last child, and returned to Rome the very picture of earthly happiness, to enjoy every blessing life can give. And now it is all over! As far as regards herself, it is a well-known fact that, surrounded as she was by riches, she had placed her real treasure in Heaven, and her works will follow her; but that poor young husband, and his four little children—what a house of mourning! I feel quite crushed by this blow. It was a sore throat she died of. Oh! it is almost a misfortune to be happy in this world! It makes one envy those who love nothing, hope for nothing, and whose whole thoughts and heart are set upon another world. I cannot think how we can be at peace for a single hour. How do I know for certain that you are not dead? That Adrian will come back alive from hunting? that I shall ever see Mamma again? Oh! may God teach us to love only Him, and to be always ready to give up life, and to go back to Him! Good-bye. Ah! Pauline, let us live on, but so live as if we were dead. Let us love our dear ones for the sake of their souls only, and that we may see them again in Heaven. This world is far too sad to set one's heart upon."

"November 12th.

"It seems that the Princess was breakfasting with her husband, and was suddenly suffocated, while complaining only of a slight sore throat.† Poor, beautiful young creature! But as you say, if we have faith we ought not to pity her, and though we never have enough faith, still, the little we possess ought to relieve us in this case of all dread of such a sudden death. Everything you say of the Princess leads one to suppose that her constant habits of prayer, and frequent Communion, her con tinual practice of good works, and the holy thoughts habitual to

* The Princess Borghese.
† This was a mistake, but Eugénie's reflections upon it are dear to me, on account of their having proved applicable to her own case.

her mind, must have kept her soul in readiness to die at any moment. I have the strongest belief that God never recalls a soul pleasing to Him in an unprovided state, though it may be a sudden manner. To such a soul as hers, He would certainly grant time for preparation, or if He does not do so, it seems to me a proof that it was fit to go, and that in mercy He spared it the agony and temptations of the last struggle. The thought of this young creature's departed soul is to me full of peace! What radiant happiness she is perhaps enjoying now! Compared with that, her brilliant life on earth appears gloomy indeed."

"Lumigny, January 6th, 1841.

"A letter from Rome, from M. Esbelin, gives us at last all the details of the death of the beautiful young saint. The day after a fête at the Villa Borghese, she caught cold, and complained of a sore throat. Having been very ill all the day, she was a little better in the evening, and the next morning she did not suffer at all. She was quite cheerful, and jested about her health. This was at eight o'clock. At ten the doctors came to examine her throat, and saw, to their horror, that mortification had begun, and that death was inevitable. They broke it to the poor young wife and the unhappy husband, who refused to believe it. At eleven o'clock Père Rozaven was sent for. Quite resigned, and not suffering at all, she took leave of her husband, and died at twelve o'clock without either pain or struggle. Does not this sort of death seem almost impossible to realise? But though there is something terrible about it for the survivors, and also as to the sacrifice the dying one had to make, I cannot but think there is great beauty in the tranquil departure of so pure a soul. It seemed to the bystanders as if they could almost see the Angels carrying her gently to the Feet of God, Whom she had so loved and served. His Presence must have been felt in that last peaceful moment.

"The accounts of the grief of all Rome are not at all exaggerated. Fifty young men drew the funeral car to Santa Maria Maggiore, and the whole way along the road, garlands and flowers were thrown from the windows. It was more like a triumph than a funeral. The people who followed the car blocked up the streets, calling the young Princess by the tenderest names. The general feelings of grief called forth by her death, are a touching homage paid to that young life, so full of good works. When, afterwards, Mark Antony asked the names of the young men who had drawn the car, one of them made this answer: '*Tell him that it was the Romans.*' Since that day, she appears in a thousand different ways to that people so full of faith and poetry; some have seen her taking her flight to Heaven in a white radiant form; and again she comes robed in light, to help and comfort the suffering. Among the people, dreams and apparitions are daily related about the Princess, whom they call *the Angel of Rome.* The streets are full of pictures of her, and verses are sung in her honor; the whole city is bent on erecting a monument to her memory, and a prize is offered to whoever shall produce the best design. In short, nothing can be more touching and remarkable than the sorrow of a whole population for one private person. And it is very honorable to her, for if through their wealth and position the Borgheses are paramount in Rome, it is on account of her good works that she is worshipped as a saint, and it makes one love the Roman people. Good-bye, my dear sister; I love you with my whole heart. Pray for me. I am better than I was last week, but I am often ill. I have a continual pain in my back and between my shoulders, and a very bad one in my side."

"Lumigny, January 30th, 1841.

"Auguste d'Ursel* left us last Wednesday, and I must own to you that I was more out of spirits than ever while he was here. He will tell you so, and he will complain that he did not hear me sing, except in the Chapel. I do not know if he is very fond of music; however, in any case I should like to have given him pleasure, but the day that I was asked to sing for him, I was very unwell. Fernand was not here to sing a duet, I knew nothing I could sing alone, and I felt like the girl in the *Demoiselle à marier*, that I should cry if I opened my lips. I was not greatly pressed, and I felt as if they must have thought me cross, and that you would scold me. I wanted to tell you this, in case that good Auguste tells tales of me. He will not now have the pleasure of astonishing you. Adrian is gone to Paris with him, and I am ashamed of finding it so difficult to get through a week without him. I really am an intolerable goose. Ah! I do hope God will forgive me. I have so many, many times reproached

* Younger brother of the Duc d'Ursel, and first cousin to Adrian.

myself for these fits of despondency, and been so sorry for them, that I hope now really to amend, and to be very different when I get up from this bed, where I shall offer up to God in expiation for my faults, all the pain He may choose to send me."

"Lumigny, February 15th, 1841.

"For three days Adrian and I have been alone together. It is the first time since our marriage that this has been the case, and we reproach ourselves for finding it delightful. I suppose it is natural to like a little variety. Probably if we had spent one or two years in this way we should want to see people here; but as the pleasure of being alone and independent is what we have known least since we were married, we have wished for it at times; and, in short, these four or five days have been charming. To complete our enjoyment, the weather is magnificent; a perfect spring, mild and warm, so that I am writing with the window open. This soft air does my body as much good as our *tête-à-tête* does to my mind, and I feel a calm, a peace, and *well-being* that I have not experienced for a long time."

"February 26th.

"Shall I see you in three weeks? I do not believe it—I do not let myself believe it. I had rather not reckon on so much happiness. You will find *our* child* grown very pretty, and saying more words than he did in September; and there will be another, if God spares me to see it born and alive. How strange that I should have actually two children of my own! Dear, pretty little darling, your letter puts me into foolish spirits, into that state in which one feels inclined to talk a great deal without having anything to say. You will find me, I hope, beginning to sit up, and it will be delightful to have you with me while I am recovering. Good-bye. Give Augustus a kiss for me, and a most affectionate one, for this blessed thought of sending you here was his own idea. How glad I should be to see him again, to show Robert† to him, and to see them become 'a pair of friends.' We four might spend, I can tell you, some *piacevolissimi* days in Paris. Good-bye, you dear, good, very good little people. Adrian is almost as glad as I am at your charming plan. He says *quite* as glad, but that I will not admit; no other

* Eugénie used to like to call her eldest son *our* child. She often said to me, "It seems impossible that what so entirely belongs to me should not belong to you also."

† Eugénie's eldest child.

gladness can come up to mine. His good parents, too, were delighted on learning the news when they came home."

I did go to Lumigny a little while afterwards; but before I speak of the meeting with Eugénie, I must relate what had happened in the meanwhile to Alexandrine. I must be brief, for, alas! melancholy events crowd upon me so sadly at this point of my story, that on many of them I cannot dwell. Alexandrine was, as I have said, at Pisa when the news of the sudden death of the young Princess Borghese reached her; and in the first moment of that terrible catastrophe, those most deeply affected by it very much wished her to go to them at Rome. It seemed to Prince Borghese and his mother that she would be a great comfort to them, and that one who had suffered so much herself would enter into their feelings and soothe their griefs better than any one else. Alexandrine accordingly complied with their request, and remained with them in the Palazzo Borghese until my father and mother went to Rome in February. Their plan then, and Alexandrine's also, was to return to France immediately after Easter, but unforeseen events caused a change in all their arrangements. In the early part of the spring, Alexandrine had gone to the Convent of the Trinità da Monte, to make her retreat, and had been there three days when she received a letter summoning her to the bedside of her eldest brother, Count Alexander d'Alopeus. He had lately been transferred from the legation at the Hague to Turin, and having been attacked with pleurisy, was then lying at the point of death. There was not a moment to be lost if she wished to see him again, and she accordingly left Rome at eleven o'clock that same night for Civita Vecchia. But she had not travelled far when a dreadful storm frightened the horses; her carriage was broken to pieces, and in wind, rain, and darkness she had to make her way on foot to a farm belonging to a Roman nobleman, where she was hospitably entertained while another conveyance was sent for. In spite of delays and of all the incidents of this dreadful journey, she reached Turin in time to see and embrace her brother once more, but could give him no other consolation than her tender care during the remainder of his short and fatal illness. After this new trouble, which was embittered to her by many additional circumstances, Alexandrine had no other thought or desire than to see her mother. The Prince and Princess Lapoukhyn were then on their way to Italy, and Alexandrine met her poor mother at Vienna just as the news of her son's death reached her. As may be imagined, Alexandrine could not think of leaving her again, and after a short stay in Germany they went on to Rome, which my father and mother were on the point of leaving for France. But on account of a change of circumstances at Lumigny and in Paris, this plan was given up.

Eugénie had been safely confined in March of another boy, and a few weeks afterwards I reached Lumigny, hoping to find her entirely recovered. Instead of this, she seemed to me weaker and paler than she ought to have been, and our meeting was a sad one, for it was the first time that a shade of definite fear took the place of those vague anxieties I had hitherto felt. But I would not for a moment entertain the painful thought. I found a thousand good reasons to account for her mental and physical prostration, and I flattered myself with the hope that our stay together in Paris would quite restore her strength. The idea of being there together in the same house and in the spring time was the fulfilment of a long-cherished desire. We looked forward to it as to a holiday and a festival. But these kind of joys were over for us in this world. At Paris she was seriously ill, and during our stay there the terror I had fought against at Lumigny rushed again upon me, and I could only compare it to the tooth of some wild beast eating into my heart. I struggled to overcome it, and the remembrance of that struggle fills me yet with greater anguish than even the thought of the final sorrow that followed. Yet, whenever this terrible fear loosened its hold of my heart, I began to hope again. Eugénie did, indeed, suddenly get better. The doctor decided that she must go to Italy with her husband, and my father and mother then determined to remain in that country. Either the pleasure of this prospect, or one of those changes so frequent in her deceitful malady, wrought such an improvement, that the hope of her recovery became almost a certainty. It was now the middle of May, and as Eugénie was to set out at the beginning of June, I went to stay at Lumigny during the intervening time. Her strength seemed revived, her face had recovered its look of health, and I felt completely reassured; and peaceful and happy indeed were those last days —the last we were ever to spend together. God willed that all fears should pass away from me for a while, and that before losing her for ever, I should once more enjoy, to the full, the blessedness of our perfect friendship. The weather was beautiful, and we spent long hours together in the garden. I particularly remember two conversations in which Eugénie seemed to me to have recovered all her old gaiety, freedom of mind, and sunshine of heart. One of these was among the rose-beds on the right side of the château, where we were talking and making up huge bouquets of roses. The other, as we were sitting on a garden seat at the bottom of the lawn with the two children; one playing on the grass, and the other asleep in its cradle. Eugénie looked at the baby with loving sadness, for she was to leave him behind. They were to go the next day but one, and Robert only was to go with them. The day came, the 16th of June, which was the last, though we knew it not, of our perfect happiness on earth. For the last time we looked into each other's faces, for the last time heard each other's voices, and said to each other our last words. Was it better not to have known it? Ah! yes, there can be no doubt that it was thus mercifully ordained.

At midnight I left her to return to Brussels, and they started the following morning for Italy. I find these words in my journal: "Eugénie and I went to Communion this morning with the intention of gaining a blessing on both our journeys, and that God might soon restore us to one another. This evening, at Benediction, we prayed very earnestly for those who are to start to-morrow, and for those also who remain behind. Once again in my room we prayed together. May God watch over her!"

After Benediction, prayers, and the evening in the drawing-room were over, we went up to her room to talk and pray again, and then parted in quite a different manner than in the preceding September. We were sitting close together, and I said to Eugénie:—"There now, this time we will have no tears. We will not be sorrowful, for this parting is not at all like what have gone before. We are both going away, and are both glad to go where we are going." Then we kissed each other without much sadness, though our tears fell fast in spite of ourselves. Fernand, who was to be my companion, came in to say that it was nearly twelve o'clock, and time to start. Ah! how I remember every moment of that evening! We went to the nursery to kiss the sleeping children, and then returned to the drawing-room, where Mons. and Mde. de Mun were waiting to bid me good-bye. Eugénie led me to the door on the stairs, and was told not to go further on account of the night air. We both stopped, and I gave her my last kiss. Oh! it was a very tender one. It could not, I think, have been more tender had I known what that moment really was for us both. She clasped me in her arms with an intense affection which nothing could have increased, and they were obliged to draw me away. I looked at her once again at the corner of the staircase, and after that I saw her no more. Adrian put me into the carriage, bade me good-bye, and heard me say twice over: "May God bless you both!"

On that night, when I last saw Eugénie, she wore a silk gown with a white scarf. Her hair had been cut off the year before, and was short and curling round her head. There was not then about her a trace of suffering or sickness. The very same day the year after, in the same house, I saw her children in deep mourning for her.

* * * * * *

Eugénie joined my father and mother at the Villa Buonovisi, near Lucca, where she spent the summer and autumn, and there Alexandrine, who was at Florence with her mother, came and spent several weeks with them. M. and Madame Théodore de Bussière also formed part of their circle of friends, and it was soon increased by the arrival of Fernand and his young wife.* During this time, Eugénie's letters sometimes expressed pleasure at the revival of her strength, sometimes a return of that depression of spirits, which had been the first and fatal symptom of her illness. It was only for a short time at Rome, where she arrived towards the end of October, that she found any real relief from it.

EUGENIE TO PAULINE.

"Rome, November 4th, 1841.

"DEAREST SISTER OF MY WHOLE LIFE—It has been wrong of me not to write to you since our arrival here. I will not excuse myself by recounting the troubles of our first days here, but will at once go back to Florence, where I left Alexandrine. How sorry I was to part with her! She is glad to be with her mother, but

* Mlle. Marie Gibert, whom Fernand married after Eugénie's departure.

she would be very lonely in that gay place, if she had not God in her heart, and Angels always about her. She has pretty rooms —three bright little cells, well-furnished and full of flowers, and there she has four hours every day to herself. But it is not very easy for her to go out at the time of Benediction, or to visit the poor. She cried a good deal at parting, and it is sad to be so near her and not with her. But she will come here for Lent, and the Princess and good Prince too. And now I am at Rome, and I cannot say what an hourly satisfaction it is to me. To be here in my present state of mind, with means of seeing, understanding, and appreciating everything in the best way possible, is an enjoyment I never weary of. The Abbé Gerbet has done me so much good! His encouraging words, his kind firmness, have as usual worked wonders on my soul. I feel roused, strengthened, and interested in everything—*younger* than I have done for some time; and I think I am getting out of my torpid state. Oh! I will obey him. I will make everything I see and do here conduce to the increase of peace and joy in God, to freedom and openness of soul. I have seen nothing but St. Peter's as yet, and I was much struck with the truth of what the Abbé Gerbet says in his book* of the sort of *triumphant* feeling this wonderful Church inspires. In Gothic Churches our first impulse is to kneel and bow down in humble prayer and deep contrition, while in St. Peter's, on the contrary, the spontaneous feeling is to open our arms wide with joy, and to look up to Heaven with rapturous enthusiasm. Sin does not seem to crush us there. A consciousness of forgiveness through the triumph of the Resurrection fills the whole soul. Think what it will be to see the Churhes, the catacombs again, &c., with the Abbé, whom these holy places inspire with such wonderful thoughts, and Théodore de Bussière, who finds out a multitude of interesting things with a view to the book he is writing, I think on the Seven Basilicas."

"Rome, November 21st.

"I cannot tell you how much the life I am now leading delights me. Why are you not here, my precious sister, who have shared all my sorrows, complaints, stupidity, and ingratitude to God? Would you could now at least be gladdened by the happy state of my soul. I seem to have come to life again, and I hope

* Esquisse de Rome Chrétienne.

never to sink back into apathy. You would not now be obliged to begin twenty different subjects without being able to interest me in any of them. I am taking to everything again, and like to read, to hear, and to understand. Who knows even if I shall not get to care about politics? Ah! Rome is a blessed city!

"Father de Ravignan, who is here, is going to preach the Lent sermons. Think how I shall enjoy them—I, who have never heard a good sermon in my life. This morning, at the meeting of the Enfants de Mariè, at the Trinità da Monte, he gave us an admirable instruction on devotedness to God and interior peace. Oh! I felt that Divine peace fill my soul when he promised, when he *assured* us that we must possess it because we were of 'good will.' Certainly in this place more than any other it is easy to feel spiritual joy."

"Rome, December 14th, 1841.

"How the time passes! I am perfectly amazed to find it is more than ten days since I wrote to you. I am never for one moment bored, and I enjoy myself more and more at Rome. Ah! my dear friends, why are you not with us? Would you could hear Father de Ravignan's admirable sermons. How beautiful, how wonderful they are! and what acts of faith and love they compel one to make! Remember what a privation it has been to me to be so long deprived of spiritual food, and then fancy what it must be to be here! My soul is refreshed, my feelings on every subject seem to revive, and you know how dull they had grown. May God be blessed and thanked for having allowed me this happiness, and given me this grace. May I profit by it, and above all never again in future fall back into that languid apathy. Those Lent sermons do an immense good, and have brought about a Christian reaction among the pupils of the Academy, to whom they are specially addressed. Many Protestants go to hear them also, and several of them have been much struck. Father de Ravignan addressed them particularly the other day, and with deep feeling deplored their errors, earnestly beseeching them at least to *wish* to know the truth; I cannot but think they must carry away some deep impressions. And indeed they do. E. de G. is quite changed; the influence of Rome acts upon him, and I think he will go away a *practical* Catholic. His wife has a delightful mind, which naturally inclines to everything holy and good. I am in all the excitement of expecting Adrian, who must have set out yesterday.* I wonder if he has actually done so? I wish my good Angel would tell me. It is a real suffering sometimes to be without news. Alex writes to me that she is quite well, and that she sees a good deal of Mlle. de Fauveau, who likes and admires her immensely. Olga is charming, and in great beauty. Robert gets strong, and I am not ill; I cough very little, and I look well. May God and His Angels watch over you! I send you all the blessings of the holy city."

"January 11th, 1842.

"You can judge from my last letter how much good my retreat has done me. On the last day almost *every one* who had attended it went to Communion—young and old, men and women. A more edifying sight could not be seen. Each one of us looks upon Father de Ravignan as a friend. He came to bid us good-bye, and to give us his blessing. Everybody was in tears. Adrian got here on the 31st December, and all my time has since been taken up. This is why I have not written. Then I fell ill again; had more fever and oppression on the chest, and coughed a little more. To-day I am so much better that I am going to a great dinner at the Palazzo Borghese, in honor of the new cardinals. Poor Mamma cannot go. She is suffering from erysipelas, and is obliged to keep her bed. She is not very ill, but her face is much swelled, and she must be careful. I will write again the day after to-morrow, to say how she is. If there is anything you want to know, ask me, for I am often bewildered, and do not know at times what I have said and have not said. You must forgive it, dearest sister. May God grant us soon to meet again. Can we be said to live, and to lead a happy life, when we are separated from half of those we love? This world is what we were told it would be on the day of the first sin. We mourn, we weep, we are ever craving for a change. Oh! after all this suffering Heaven will be very sweet!"

"January 13th.

"Mamma is better, and is up to-day, but we have all the trouble in the world in getting her to take the least care of her health. As for myself, the weather is very damp, and I suffer from it. It is tiresome to have been so much better, and to fall back just when Adrian has come, so that he cannot see and

* He had gone to Lumigny for two months.

enjoy that great improvement which I boasted of in all my letters. However, these are the little clouds that must attend all earthly happiness, for a life without clouds, if any such there be, seems to me a terrible and undesirable thing."

I am now come to a point in my story which I approach with a kind of dread. Shall I pass over it swiftly, or shall I linger on the sorrowful details? I hardly know. God will guide my pen, and then, perhaps, together with the painful and terrible recollections of the past, He will renew in my soul the consoling and strengthening feelings which will facilitate my task.

Eugénie's last letter was dated January 13th. On the 17th, five days afterwards, without any premonitory symptoms, without any increase of his habitual ailments, my father was taken suddenly ill, and in less than four hours he was dead. I have nothing to add to the following letters:—

MADAME DE LA FERRONNAYS TO PAULINE.

"Rome, January 21st, 1842.

"What will become of you, my poor beloved Pauline, and how will you bear the shock which my letter must give you? This anxiety increases my anguish. You will know without my saying it, how I miss you at this dreadful moment, the dread of which has haunted me for nearly forty years. The idea took possession of me as soon as I became his wife: 'What if I were to lose him!' Every day of my life this has been my constant thought. I have never for an hour felt secure, or lost sight of this fear. Nothing but hope and trust in God could keep my mind properly balanced, and I was only comforted by prayer. On my knees I felt at peace, but never for long together. When I saw him well with my own eyes, I was calm, but sometimes, perhaps only in going from one room to another, the anguish returned. My heart was always beating, as if in terror of something, and when the abyss at last opened before me, I had measured its depths too surely not to take in at once its full extent. Without deception, without that thought we so often cling to, that it may be all a dream, I felt the ground failing under me. Oh, how little detachment from the world, or love of God, or desire for Heaven, I had in comparison with him! He was the object of my life, and therefore I clung to earth. Suffering was necessary to wean me from it. God has laid a heavy cross upon me; I shall bear it, I hope, if only He gives me strength."

"January 22nd.

"MY BELOVED CHILD—This is the first day in which there has been nothing to do. The painful duties of the previous ones brought with them their own strength, but to-day everything is over. May God, and the thought of my husband's happiness, fill up this dreadful void! And now shall I be able to give you an account that will make you feel as if you had been with us all this time? It is heart-breaking, but it is better than silence, for it will be speaking of him. A fortnight ago my dearest husband had a little fever; the weather was bad, and snow had fallen, which happens so seldom here, and our invalids both felt it. Eugénie had been very unwell, and anxiety about her had taken up my thoughts. When your father was better I fell ill, and spent that last week in bed, little thinking how it would end. In the mean time, he could not restrain or control his religious zeal. He had visited the Seven Churches alone, and ended by communicating at St. Peter's. And there was I in bed—which so seldom happens—and could not share all this with him! Nor could he bring himself to wait for me. He told me that he would like to go to Communion again on the following Tuesday, the Feast of St. Peter's Chair, but that he did not know if he should be able. He intended, I think, to go to St. Peter's. He indeed communicated with God that day, but it was in Heaven, not on earth.

"On Sunday he was very well, and went to dine with the Dowager Princess Borghese. He conversed nearly all the evening with Théodore [de Bussière] and the Abbé Dupanloup,* and among other things spoke of the love he had felt all his life for the Blessed Virgin. He looked upon it as the thread which had kept him from perishing, and had finally brought him back to God. Théodore told him of a Jew, a real enemy of Our Lord, whose conversion he ardently desires. He is a brother of the Abbé Ratisbonne. This interested your father exceedingly. He talked also about death, and your dearest father said that we must always be ready, for we never knew when the hour would come. Afterwards he spoke lovingly of God, so rightly called

* The Bishop of Orleans, who had thus been with my father, as he had been with Albert, during the last moments of his life.

our *good* God,* he said. When he came home he told me with envy of all the good that Bussière is doing, and said sorrowfully: 'And I do nothing at all!'

"On Monday the weather was magnificent. He went to Mass, and after breakfast it was settled that he should drive with Eugénie, for though much better, I did not venture out. In the evening, however, I was to take Olga and Albertine to a ball at the Austrian ambassador's, and they were getting their dresses ready for it. Our Guardian Angels, and all who watch over us in Heaven must have pitied the poor children. Your father walked with Eugénie and Adrian up and down the beautiful green space which lies between St. John Lateran and Santa Croce di Gierusalemme, greatly enjoying the lovely weather. Once only for a moment he felt his pain at the heart. It went away almost immediately, and he went on gathering flowers with them. He left them in his little carriage, and drove to Sta. Maria Maggiore, where he prayed a long time before the picture of the Blessed Virgin in the Borghese Chapel, which was uncovered that day. He also made the preparation for death on his knees, a daily practice with him, and said more than twenty times the *Memorare* for various intentions. Then he went to the *Sacramentale* for Benediction, and came home pleased with his morning, and refreshed by his walk. 'I will walk every day,' he said; 'I think it will do me good.' He told me what prayers he had said, and also '*that he had made an offering of his life to God, with a perfect readiness to yield it up if He wished to take it; or, if He chose to leave him in this world, to spend it entirely in serving and honoring Him.*' He then began to write at his desk, and I went to my room, where I knelt down to say the prayers I had not been able to say with him in Church. That week in bed had made me rather languid. There was a wretched brazier in the drawing-room, which for several days we had said must not be left there, for it gave us headaches. That evening there was scarcely any fire in it, and we never thought of having it taken away. After dinner your father went to sit beside this brazier, saying that his feet were cold, and then he got up and began to play with Robert. He was quite cheerful, and seemed well. Soon after that he went out of the room, and a moment afterwards they came to tell me that he had an attack of 'his pain.'

* This habitual expression, "le bon Dieu," loses all its force in the translation.—TRANSLATOR.

I ran to him, and found him indeed in great pain, and soon afterwards he was very sick. I sent for the doctor, though I did not feel then any real anxiety. Your sisters were having their hair dressed. Ah! my God! I went to their room, and told them I was sorry to think I could not take them to the ball, *though I was convinced the attack would soon go off.* I regretted, I said, to be obliged to deprive them of this pleasure. His pain did indeed soon subside, he seemed better, and the surgeon, who was to have bled him, was sent away. How strange it is that those who feel most intensely lose their head and power of thinking when the fatal hour comes! We had so often seen him in the same state, and hope, always so strong in these cases, deceived us all. . . .

"My dear child, I cannot finish to-day, for it is almost more now than my strength can bear, but I will do so to-morrow, for I want to tell you everything myself. I must go to Church, for there only I can weep or live. I am also quite astounded at this moment, by the wonderful event that has taken place. The Abbé Gerbet is writing to you to-day, to give you a full account of it; but it must be for ourselves only. Let us lay all these things to heart, and say nothing about them. I am unworthy of so great a mercy. O my God, my God! I can neither think nor speak!"

"January 23rd.

"My Pauline, I will go on talking to you, for it seems to me that it is the only thing that does me a little good. Can you picture to yourself, my precious child, the depths of wretchedness into which I have fallen, and in which I am every day sinking deeper? It seems like Purgatory begun, and Heaven only can set me free. I cannot weep, my sufferings are too deeply seated for tears. Tears imply that one day they will be dried up, but when once the grave has closed over us we do not weep. Our doom is fixed. And then comes the torturing thought that we have not done all we might have done. But how can one guard against the flash of lightning which in one instant does its work? And yet there was time lost, we were stupefied, bewildered. I think now, 'If such and such things had been done ——,' but then the doctor was there, and I who am always timid about trying remedies could never have dared propose anything myself. But to return to what I was telling you when I broke off. Your father's pain ceased, and the surgeon went away without bleeding him, but ten minutes after he was gone, the pain came on again. I ran to the head of the stairs to have the surgeon stopped, and almost at the same instant some one told me that the Abbé Gerbet was come. I went back, and imagine the terror I felt at hearing the words of Absolution which the Abbé was even then giving to your father! 'Ah! my God! my God! is it come to this?'—I inwardly exclaimed, and seized the doctor by the arm: 'Is there then no hope?' He hesitated a moment, and then said, 'NO.' And I heard the Abbé say, 'Put your trust in God;' and your father answered, 'I put my whole trust in Him.' Then the Abbé said, 'Do you repent of every sin of your past life?' 'Yes! yes!' your father replied, with a wonderful earnestness. His eyes shone in a way that I had never seen before. There was a Heavenly expression in them. 'Thank you, thank you!' he said. 'Farewell, my children—my wife, farewell!' Then he seized the Crucifix, (indulgenced for the hour of death) which was hanging by his bedside, and kissed it fervently. Eugénie placed a pillow under his head, and he said: 'Thanks, my child!' with a look that will for ever be to her a blessed recollection. But he began to sink. I spoke to him, and he did not hear me. I entreated him to press my hand, but that dear hand was motionless. The pulse gave one bound, and after that beat no more. . . .

"I saw all this. My eyes looked upon a scene, the bare thought of which used nearly to deprive me of reason; and God gave me at that moment such inconceivable strength, that I can only ascribe it to my poor husband's prayers. I made as thorough an act of submission as I could. It was as if he were holding me in his arms to support me the while. I am so grateful to all my kind friends for having understood that it was only by his side I could gain strength. They left me there, and I was quite calm. Adrian found me on my knees some hours afterwards, holding that dear hand so often clasped in mine. He must have thought me mad when I said, 'I am quite well, I feel so near to him. I think we have never been so closely united as now.'

"This was an immense grace vouchsafed to me at that dreadful moment, when I felt as if the world and everything in it were at an end. I was as it were lifted up with him very near to God, and almost forgot my misery in the thought of his happiness.

Thus passed all that first night. At daybreak I left my beloved one to go and hear Mass in the Church opposite, and went to Communion, as he had intended to do that day—the Feast of St. Peter's Chair. How I went through it I hardly know. In some strange state of abstraction, no doubt, for I could neither pray or weep.

"Very soon I returned to my poor husband's side. I spent the day sitting there, holding his hand and warming it with my own, that it might preserve awhile the semblance of life. And now that that time is gone by, I cannot understand how I had strength to endure it; but God gave it me. All the second night also I remained by him, alone as I thought, but in reality there came friends, and good priests, one after another, to pray; I laid my head near his on the pillow, and still holding him by the hand, I slept a little. Then I awoke and tried to pray, but could scarcely pronounce any intelligible words, I was utterly prostrated. Ah! what a night was that! At five o'clock living friends began to gather round me, and they begged me to go to Eugénie's room and rest a little. O! my God, has it really come to this? The anguish dreamed of for forty years, has it really fallen to my lot? . . . .

"I should have liked to watch and pray without stirring through the whole of the third night, but sometimes fatigue overpowered me, and I sank exhausted into an arm-chair. Father Géramb sat up with me. He came at eleven o'clock, and went away at eight in the morning. At six they forced me to go and rest in Eugénie's room, but I went back in an hour's time, for I could now, less than ever, absent myself from his room, for I felt that the hour was drawing near when I should be deprived of him altogether. To express the agony I went through is impossible, and I could only repeat, over and over again, that I wished to unite it with Our Lord's agony and the Blessed Virgin's sorrow at the foot of the Cross. It was then, my dear child, that God sent me so great, so Divine, a consolation, that for the time being my sufferings seemed almost suspended. As I was kneeling near the coffin, I felt my arm touched, and the Abbé Gerbet, very much agitated, said, 'Bussière would like to tell you something that will give you pleasure, and which has something to do with M. de la Ferronnays.' I got up quickly, and found Théodore in a state of great excitement. You know from the Abbé's letter what he related to me.* A sort of resurrection took place in my heart! It was like a moment of sunshine which did not, however, last long. For a moment it raised me above myself, but I soon sank again. Still this consolation had a real effect upon me. I am none the less alone, and none the less is everything ended for me on earth, but *he is happy.* I can no longer have a doubt of it. As the Abbé Dupanloup said, we may believe he died while making a perfect act of love, which brought him immediately into the Bosom of God. This thought sustained me. The young Jew [Ratisbonne] keeps continually repeating, 'Is it not strange to feel so closely connected with a man one has never seen—whose name even one hardly knew, and after his death?' He wanted to spend the night here in prayer, urging that he should not sufficiently express his gratitude, unless he showed this mark of respect and affection to one to whom he owed everything. But they would not let him stay after ten o'clock. What I heard so sank into my heart that I forgot myself for a while in the thought of that Heavenly Glory now enjoyed by him for whom I had so often and earnestly desired this world's honors. But soon my anguish was renewed, and when the evening drew in, I could not but feel that in a little while everything would be taken from me. They told me that if I liked I could go to one of the tribunes in the Church, but I did not know if I should have strength, or if I should be allowed to do so. I kissed the pall that covered him, and the anguish of that moment was beyond all expression.

"At last the Abbé Gerbet came, and kneeling by me, kissed the coffin also, and said to me, 'Go into the tribune in the Church.' I had given up all hope of being allowed to do this, but getting up I went out, and was present at the office for the dead. Of the *dead*, and for whom? . . . . O! my God, I saw him brought into the Church! . . . . When they took me away, I bent down to the ground as I passed by him, and then got into the carriage. All these things, the very thought of which was like death, did not make me shed a tear. And now I must leave you, my child. Clasp your poor mother in your arms. My dear children, be very happy, that there may still be some little sweetness left in my life."

* The account is given in the Abbé's letter which follows.

THE ABBÉ GERBET TO PAULINE.

"January 22nd, 1842.

"MY DEAR CHILD—In my last letter to Mr. Craven I told you that in the midst of your tears you had also much to give thanks for; but when I bade you lift up your heart to God with praise, because the holy death of a father is a great grace to his children, I did not then know in what a wonderful manner these words were to come true. God has granted to your family, and to you all, one of the most magnificent consolations imaginable—one of those rare, wonderful consolations which it would not enter into our minds to ask. I cannot yet give you all the details in this letter—you will presently see why; but I hasten to send an outline of the facts. You know, dear child, how little I am inclined to believe lightly in miraculous occurrences; the very reverence due to supernatural manifestations, obliges us not to yield an easy credence to facts of this nature. But many other people as well as myself cannot shut their eyes to the real character of the event in question. A Jew belonging to a very rich family of Alsace, was walking about in the Church of Sant' Andrea delle Fratte, during the preparations that were making for your dear father's funeral, when he was suddenly converted, like St. Paul on the way to Damascus, by a miraculous stroke of the Divine power and goodness. He was standing in front of the Chapel Dedicated to the Guardian Angels, when suddenly he had a bright vision of the Blessed Virgin, who made him a sign to go up to the Chapel. Some irresistible force compelled him to obey, and there he fell on his knees—a Christian. His first words on lifting his head, with his face bathed in tears, were, '*That gentleman must have prayed very much for me!*' What wonderful words, my dear child, concerning your dear father, whose body was just going to be brought into the Church! It is not possible to doubt this young man's sincerity. He is very rich, and we cannot feel about him as we should at first sight be inclined to do towards any poor Jew who might become a Christian for the sake of gain. M. Ratisbonne is the son of a Strasburg banker, wealthy, and much respected. He was to have married in the spring a young Jewish cousin, and his conversion will probably break off his marriage. All his temporal interests militate against his conversion, and his Jewish prejudices, together with a general indifference to religious observances, opposed it also. He is a young man of very good manners, clever and gifted with talent for conversation. He is very intimate with Gustave de Bussière, who knew him at college, and kept up the friendship since. He is twenty-eight years old.

"I saw M. Ratisbonne this morning, and gathered these particulars from his own lips. I can hardly tell you how much it makes me think of the conversion of St. Paul. He said, 'I was converted in an instant.' He would like to die for the faith, and indeed, trials will not be wanting him. It was Théodore de Bussière who was led by providential circumstances to accompany him that day to several Churches. The first words he said after receiving that extraordinary grace, were significant enough as to your father's share in his conversion, but there are other circumstances which will be detailed in the full account I shall send you of all that preceded and followed the event.* But I must begin by submitting it to M. Ratisbonne and to Bussière, to make sure of the accuracy of the details. Meanwhile, my dear child, I beg of you not to speak of this to any one except Mr. Craven, for when this sort of thing is mentioned, it should be with the explanations and attestations which establish the facts. O! my God, this has been indeed a magnificent grace, an immense consolation. With these words, my dear child, I take leave of you and your husband. I know all you have felt and will feel."

Eugénie wrote to me the same day, as follows:—

"My Pauline—My beloved sister, I can only write a word or two. I cannot write at length. And it is not grief that thus takes all power from me, but the overwhelming, marvellous consolations which have been showered upon us for the last three days. We have witnessed a miracle of grace, and if we ever had any faith, we must now lift up our voices to praise, bless, and thank God for all He has done for us. Pauline, I say it in sober earnestness, in the full possession of my reason, enlightened by Divine faith, I say it now, three days after my father's death, as I said it on the morrow of the day he died. God has visited us in a miraculous manner, and I adore Him with a deeper worship than ever. I do not feel equal to giving you an account of what

* The Abbé did not accomplish this. The two best accounts are by M. de Bussière and Count Theobald Walsh.

has happened, but you will soon hear all the details of the astonishing things that have taken place around us. O! Pauline, why are you not here to enjoy these blessed consolations? Believe me, I do beg of you—believe me when I say that we ought to be comforted, for we are Christians, my beloved sister. We may indeed weep for our much-loved father, but let us weep as those who have a great hope—nay, more, who possess the *certainty* of a blessedness which the heart of man cannot conceive. Mamma—you know it already—has been like a true Mother of Sorrows at the foot of the Cross, with her heart broken, but tranquil and calm. She is a real miracle of grace.

"Good-bye. We are all well. God is with us, and this house of sorrow is transformed. May you be blessed, and feel these consolations in your heart.

"EUGÉNIE."

I need not say anything of my own grief, or of the feelings of supernatural joy which these letters gave me. Such things can be understood, but hardly expressed in words. I can only say that the very abundance of consolation which attended our affliction, even while it was instilling comfort into my heart, brought with it a kind of apprehension. It seemed as if so extraordinary a grace could only have been granted to give us strength for future suffering. This foreboding was soon verified.

Alexandrine—who had hastened to Rome on hearing of our misfortune—wrote to me: "I have never yet seen so sweet and tranquil a grief; such goodness and simplicity; such evident marks of God's protection. I have always loved and reverenced our Mother, but never so much as now. O, if *my* poor mother could come here! If she could only see and taste the Heavenly beauty of all that I witness."

But notwithstanding these consolations and soothing circumstances, it soon became evident that Eugénie, who had been a little revived by the intensity of her grief and faith, began to lose strength again. Soon the fever returned, and with the prostration which followed it, came back also depression of mind. It was Alexandrine who first gave me to understand how serious the relapse was. My poor mother wished to spare me as much as possible, and was herself willing to be deceived. My anxiety, therefore, became greater than ever, when, instead of the natural tone of her mind, which I had noticed in Eugénie's last letters, I again discerned tokens of that depression which had been throughout, the worst symptom and the greatest trial of her illness. There had been an intermission of this suffering. During the first weeks of her stay in Rome she had felt and appeared like herself again. At the time of my father's death especially, her mind had shaken off the weight of her enfeebled body, and recovered the cheerful energy of past days. But the heights of Calvary were not yet reached.

Ah! Redeemer of men, Thou Thyself a Man, and suffering like poor man, Thy creature—Thou, too, didst know the agony of despondency, weariness, and sorrow; and yet, notwithstanding, didst walk under the burthen of Thy Cross with a firm step, and without a murmur or complaint—but at length being come to the end, Thou, too, before Thy death, didst utter one loud cry for consolation. And so it was with this poor child, who, when crushed with weakness and pain, uttered these lowly words: "*My God, I dare not say, 'She whom Thou lovest is sick,' but I do say, 'She who loves Thee is sick, and craves Thy help!'*"

To me she wrote on the 10th of March:—

"My Dear Sister—Your letters make me sad, because they show the excess of my own spiritual misery. I am ashamed of thinking so much of life, of regretting the happiness of this world, and instead of being, as I used to be, ready to die and leave everything to God's will, to be grieving over pleasures I can no longer share, and even asking God sometimes to give me two more years of health and enjoyment. What will you say to such a cowardly prayer? God withholds His grace from me just now, and I think I have never borne suffering so badly. Farewell, my dear sister. Pray for your poor little dear one, and ask for her the grace to suffer with patience. O! I do wish I could see you! Farewell."

This letter, the last I ever received from her, pierced my heart with a grief almost as keen as the suffering I felt when I heard of her death. "O! my God!" I kept repeating, "O my God! take her if Thou wilt. I do not ask to keep her, but do not let her lose Thee!" I went to St. Gudule, where I earnestly prayed, not that her health might be restored, but that her beloved soul might find light and peace again in a perfect acquiescence with that Divine Will which she had always loved beyond all things; that all regret for earthly things might cease, and then that God would deal with her as He pleased. This prayer was continually on my lips and in my heart during those days of anguish. If I had been with her I should have been spared this cruel suffering; for that letter which almost broke my heart did not really represent the habitual state of her soul. There is a chalice we must all drink of, that natural repugnance to suffer and die, which Eugénie had never hitherto understood, so great had been from childhood her loving habit of looking upon death as the means of going to God. But now she was called upon for a moment to taste its bitterness, and thus to make the full and generous sacrifice of her life. This hard trial was courageously met, and during her last days on earth the impression left on the minds of all those about her was one of perfect serenity, submission to God's will, and of a peace which no depression of mind nor pain of body could affect.

On the 2nd of April, Adrian and Eugénie left Rome, a strange decision of the doctors having compelled them to try the effect of change of air. My poor mother, Olga, Alexandrine, and Mons. and Mde. de Bussière accompanied them to Albano. There she took leave of them for the last time. They lifted her child into the carriage that she might kiss him once more; and Madame de Bussière, who was close to the door of the carriage, heard her murmur: "You will never see your mother again." But she did not break down. She went away with calmness, courage, and even a sort of joy, as if she felt it easier to make the sacrifice of her life when not surrounded by all those she loved, or was anxious perhaps to lavish upon her husband alone such tokens of tenderness which her failing strength enabled her to give. It was settled that in case any unfavorable symptom occurred, her family should instantly be sent for. Eugénie was a little better at Naples, where she stayed till the 5th of April, and on that day embarked for Palermo. Her friend the Marquise de Raigecourt, who was then going with her husband to the East, was in the same vessel, and also the Comte Auguste d'Ursel, and the Vicomte de Gontant. God orders all for the best. Much as I have often envied these friends, I should perhaps not have had courage to take my place by her side, and to see her die; for the blow which was so terrible from a distance might have killed me if I had been there.

They arrived at Palermo on the 6th of April. She was not ill, she seemed even to be better, but her long illness, my father's death, the interior trials she had gone through at Rome, and her last days at Naples, had no doubt exhausted her remaining strength. She was ready to depart, and without any new suffering, without leavetakings, and without further preparation than what she made day by day, this dearest, sweetest sister was taken to her rest by Him Who gave her to me to love on earth, and will give her back to me for all eternity in Heaven.* The following letter brought the terrible news to Rome:

THE MARQUIS DE RAIGECOURT TO THE ABBÉ GERBET.

"Palermo, April 7th, 1842.

"MY DEAR MONSIEUR L'ABBÉ—All is over. This morning, between seven and eight, I was present at the death, or rather the flight to Heaven, of an angel. Poor Adrian came in great agitation and knocked at my door, when I hastened to his wife's bedside. Madame de Raigecourt soon followed. A few moments afterwards Madame de Mun had ceased to breathe, without any effort or struggle, and as gently as she had lived. There was no time to call either priest or doctor; and indeed the latter would have been useless, and the former not necessary, except for the sake of example. For what better preparation for death could there be than such a life and such sufferings, and the whole habit of mind of a person so near perfection? These words of Scripture might well be applied to her: '*Opera illorum sequuntur illos.*' Would you like to know what was the last thing she did at Naples? Just before coming away she made a touching, gentle little exhortation to a person you are interested about, and who is a prey to a moral disease more terrible by far than her bodily one, and then hanging a medal round his neck, she begged him to wear it in remembrance of her and her father. Tell this to Madame de la Ferronnays, for she will know who it is, and it will give her comfort. Ah! how I could kiss the ground on which Madame de la Ferronnays treads! She is a

* In her blotting-paper book was found a letter beginning: "Dear sister of my life," the last words her dear hand ever wrote to me.

martyr, and what a martyrdom it is, and how sweetly, calmly, submissively borne! May she meet this long-foreseen blow with that fortitude which is not derived from any earthly source. May she feel that she must live on for the sake of the children still spared to her. You have again, my dear Monsieur l'Abbé, a sad task to fulfil with regard to this pious and afflicted family. God give you grace and strength to accomplish it! I thought it best to make the event known to you, their guide and comforter, that you might be able to carry to them at the same time as the dreadful news, words of consolation. M. d'Ursel has given up his journey to stay with M. de Mun; which I would gladly have done also, but I am afraid of exposing my wife in her delicate state, to much agitation,* and I have therefore reluctantly decided to continue our voyage.

"MARQUIS DE RAIGECOURT."

"P.S.—Do not let any one suppose there was any imprudence in crossing to Sicily. Mde. de Mun did not suffer from sea-sickness, she was better yesterday evening than I had yet seen her, and nothing gave signs of her approaching end. It was perhaps ordained by God that she should die at a distance from her family, to spare her mother and Mlle. Olga another blow, which might have proved fatal to the latter."

The Abbé Gerbet broke the terrible news to my mother, and then he thought of me; but my mother, regardless of her own sufferings, wished to write to me herself, and that sad day on which those two letters were written, was my own birthday, April the 12th.

MADAME DE LA FERRONNAYS TO PAULINE.

"Rome, April 12th, 1842.

"MY POOR BELOVED PAULINE—We were very wretched before, but now we are still more deeply afflicted. God has chosen to take them both. I knew it would be so. Those who are in Heaven and know its happiness and the misery of this world, cannot but pray for those they love to be removed from it. My well-beloved child, I weep with you and for you, and for myself, and for all those who are left behind. As to her, she is in the midst of

* The Marquise de Raigecourt died one year after Eugénie. It is probable that the terrible emotion she must have gone through at Palermo hastened her end. She was devotedly attached to Eugénie, and her death was the greatest sorrow she had known.

Heavenly joys with her dear father, and Albert, and the four little angels who have waited for us all so long.

"My poor child, do not grieve that you were not there. We were not there either. Our good Angels saw that we should not have strength to receive another last sigh so soon, and they led that beloved one a little apart to carry her gently away. Yes, she is there where she had so long desired to be, where you, my dear daughter, had pictured her to yourself in that 'dream' which I read a week ago with such unspeakable emotion. Ah! my God, when shall we all get there? And now, my precious child, I am in a fever to see you again. I shall not feel to exist until I fold you in my arms. I think I shall set out as soon as Adrian comes. If it were possible I would start to-day. I do so long to fly for refuge to my dear child. My treasure, take care of yourself, look to yourself, think how necessary you are to your poor mother, who sees the tree which sheltered her stripped of its branches. Oh! I suffer when I think of the pain I inflict on you. My thoughts are more taken up with your sorrow than with my own grief. My poor Olga is well; she is calm and brave, and feels how necessary she is to her unhappy mother. For her the shock would certainly have been greater and more overwhelming, if she had seen her sister die. Let us join in prayer, nor leave the foot of the Cross, where God and the Blessed Virgin will help us. My dear Augustus and Pauline, weep with me, and I shall soon be mourning and praying with you. I will never leave you again. I love you both so much, my heart can find no rest but in the thought of you. Oh! that it should be on the 12th of April I should have to inflict on you this blow! There is not a single bright day left for us now."

THE ABBÉ GERBET TO PAULINE.

"It has pleased God, my dear child, once again to call upon you to renew the sacrifice of parting with a dear friend, with the additional pang of not being present at the departure of the beloved one. Alas! we have all had to offer up this aggravated suffering. If no Heavenly vision, such as hallowed your dear father's grave, has honored your sister's remains, the holiness of her life has nevertheless shed a brightness over its closing scene in which, without the shadow of a cloud, we can confidently see that her soul is saved. I should look upon all doubt about her salvation as a temptation dishonorable to the Divine stamp which God so visibly set upon her. On the day before she left Naples she was at confession; and health alone prevented her from going to Communion. She had, however, enjoyed that blessing a short time before, and was always communicating in spirit. Would I could describe to you the piety with which she spent the Holy Week in Rome. I have no doubt she felt as if ascending to Calvary, and as she uttered the words of the Gospel, '*Father, into Thy Hands I commend my spirit,*' her soul must have been so closely united to her crucified Saviour, that death removed her from the Cross only to place her in the Arms of Our Lord, Who has promised to crown His saints.

"My dear child, let us solace our grief with this perfect confidence, or rather *assurance* of her happiness; but pray for her, nevertheless, as if we were not convinced of it, and also for all those she has left behind in this valley of tears. We must strengthen our souls with these words, '*For we have not here a lasting city; but we seek one that is to come.*'* There is no help or comfort but in this thought, which we should meditate upon at the foot of the Cross. God loves you very much, and by means of these severe trials He will make you advance in His love. Your growth in holiness will be the crown you will lay on those beloved graves. This letter is addressed as much to Mr. Craven as to you. He was such a perfect brother to Eugénie, and feels your sorrows to be his own, that neither in my thought nor in my letters can I ever separate you. Now that I can endeavor to comfort you without having also to speak always of new fears, I shall often write, though anything I can say will be of little use, compared with the consolations God Himself will impart to your soul. Our friendship has been sealed by the side of three graves, and as long as I remain in this world I hope to minister to those whose griefs I have shared, and to mourn and pray with them over those tombs, which seem to me like a pledge of God's Presence amongst us."

What I felt on receiving these letters, and during the days and weeks that followed, I will not dwell upon. But personal recol-

* Heb. xiii. 14.

lections make no part of my story, and, alas! the tale of that eventful year is not yet full. In the Marquis de Raigecourt's letter a fear was expressed as to the effect which a sudden blow might produce on Olga's health. And it was true that in the midst of so much sorrow my mother had undergone serious uneasiness on her account, foreboding fresh trials. In consequence of the shock she had experienced on the evening of the 17th of January, and just when Eugénie was beginning to grow worse, Olga had had a long and dangerous illness. She certainly seemed to recover afterwards, but her constitution had received a blow from which it never recovered. When she was summoned to her father's deathbed, she had just been placing a wreath of flowers on her head. When she took it off, she never again wore any earthly ornament. From that moment life was, as it were, over for her; or, indeed, then began a new life, a new path, in which she was to make such rapid strides as soon to deserve that imperishable crown, the flowers of which never fade or die.

OLGA TO PAULINE.

"Rome, April 16th, 1842.

"My beloved Pauline—Though my eyes are very bad, I want to write to you, for Alexandrine has not time to do so, and you must not be a whole day without letters. We do so long to know how you are, and how God has helped you to bear this sudden blow. Poor darling! Would that I could comfort you. Would you were here weeping and praying with us, and sharing the painful sweetness of looking over everything that belonged to that idolized sister, and reading her journals, which are a great source of comfort, for after having had such thoughts, and written such things, and suffered as we know she did, we may surely believe this dear one to be in Heaven, with God Whom she so loved, with Albert, and praying for us all. Ah! my God, how life passes away! This is a comfort, for we must hope that a day will come at last when we too shall be in that dear Heaven. The days indeed seem to fly. The same hour each evening comes back so quickly that I could almost fancy I had never moved, that only five minutes had elapsed since the previous night. It will be three months to-morrow since our Eugénie was weeping over my father's death, and now she has seen him again. We have nothing to do here but to prepare for death, and advance as much as possible in the knowledge of God. Oh, how that dear sister loved Him! A few days before she left Rome and this world, she was speaking to the good Abbé de la Bouillerie* of the passage in the Gospel where Martha says to our Lord: '*He whom Thou lovest is sick.*' Eugénie said that in meditating on those words she never ventured to repeat '*She whom Thou lovest is sick,*' but '*She who loves Thee so much* is sick,' adding with a smile, 'And that is indeed true.' Poor darling sister, if you knew how she was changed, and how thin she had become, but still so pretty! Dear Eugénie! she was so necessary to our happiness; she made our home so pleasant, and was in every way so charming. God has taken her away to wean us from this life, and make us long for the next. We are every moment expecting poor Adrian. What we shall do afterwards God only knows. I must leave off on account of my eyes. May God help us all. I love you most affectionately."

OLGA TO PAULINE.

"Rome, May 10th, 1842.

"MY DARLING PAULINE—How I wish I could see you again! How overwhelmed with grief you are, my poor sister; but it is impossible to last long, and Eugénie will obtain for you a little tranquillity of mind. Why are you not here? I am continually amazed at the peace we enjoy. Even I, who last summer used to shudder and shed tears at the bare thought that she might die, am so calm now that I am sometimes afraid it comes from coldness of heart. But I have had, or rather, God has given me, such good, strengthening thoughts. I have seen that the earthly happiness so much longed for, so much regretted, is scarcely worth the trouble it costs, and that life is at best very short. Pleasure is so mixed with suffering that one can scarcely separate the two; and suffering passes away also, and is often mixed with Heavenly joys. Yes! everything comes to an end. Even during the terrible scene of Adrian's return, I said to myself, 'This will pass away also, and when we shall have been ages in Heaven, with what feelings shall we look back to these short moments of trial?' Why, we shall praise God for having sent them to us, for we shall see that they were the means of teaching us

* Since Bishop of Carcassonne, well known for his admirable labors in Paris in behalf of the Patronage des Enfans.—TRANSLATOR.

something of the worthlessness of this world, and of winning for us the glorious eternal life we shall then be enjoying. God gave me to understand this in my youth; and it is a great grace, if I can only correspond with it. Spring and the fine weather painfully affected my mother the other day, but I felt quite differently. The new life of nature made me think of the new life which has begun for Eugénie. But what a contrast! These leaves and flowers will fade away and die, while she, our Heavenly Flower, has done with all that perishes and passes away. And then—I always come back to that—life is so short! We have only to love God, to do the utmost good we can, save our own souls and help to save those of others, and that will be enough to fill up all our life and heart, and in a happy manner too. But do not go and fancy I am good, because I write these sort of things. It is not I who say them, it is the grace of God speaking in me. I am very miserable, cold, indifferent, and lazy about prayer. Pray a little for me that I may not lose the good impressions I have lately received.

"Good-bye, dear, dear one. I am dreadfully hurried.

"OLGA."

Certainly it was grace that influenced her, but she was faithful in the use of it.

From April the 21st, the day on which I received the news of Eugénie's death till May the 26th, I did not open the journal in which I was in the habit of recording the daily events of my life. I then wrote at Paris, "I have been ill a long time; not able to speak, or scarcely to think;" the very next day God vouchsafed to send me a real consolation. It was Sunday, and Corpus Christi. I went to Mass at the Mother-House of the Sisters of Charity in the Rue du Bac. There for the first time I saw Alphonse Ratisbonne, who had just come from Rome; and the words we exchanged in the convent-garden gave me the first feelings of pleasure and entire resignation that I had known since our sorrows. He was still dressed as a layman, but was about to enter the Society of Jesus. I asked him why he could not become a priest and yet remain with his brother the Abbé; and he replied, that after the extraordinary grace he had received he could not give God "*less than all.*"—This answer struck me very much. He added that there was no earthly tie so strong as that by which he felt himself bound to my father: "I owe him more than life, and I am more his child than even you are," he said. These words, the tone in which he said them, and his own account of the marvellous grace vouchsafed him, which even at a distance had touched me so deeply, did me a great deal of good, and strengthened me for the trial of the next day. I was going to Boury with my husband to receive my mother, who was to arrive there soon after us. In speaking of my first meeting with Alexandrine after Albert's death I said that the recollection of that arrival was sweet and happy compared with those I had to go through there later in life. This will not surprise those who can picture to themselves what it was to wait for my mother in that forlorn and empty house, and to fold her in my arms after all the sorrows which had befallen us. They had left, alas! but too visible traces on her face, and at the first moment I thought her more changed than Olga, who appeared quite restored to health. During that melancholy time at Boury, and our still more melancholy visit to Lumigny, where I went in June, exactly a year after I had taken leave there of Eugénie, we had no fresh anxiety on Olga's account. In a little while I went back to Brussels, where my mother and my sister were to come to us, and for a few weeks it proved a pleasant occupation to me to arrange the rooms they were to occupy in our house. For I need not say that we responded to my poor mother's wish to make her home with us by our own ardent desire to keep her under our roof.

So they came, and Alexandrine soon followed them. Since her brother's death she had only left her mother for the last few days of Eugénie's stay in Rome; and after her death, which produced, as will be seen, a deep and decisive effect upon her soul and her after-life, she returned to Florence, and then accompanied her mother to Germany, taking Albertine with her to the Baths at Ems. From thence she brought her to Brussels, where she herself stayed a few weeks, but afterwards returned to Frankfort, to spend the winter with the Princess Lapoukhyn. There she remained until a new sorrow brought her back to us whose griefs had become her own. Even after all that had passed since we had been together at Naples, this short meeting was a great comfort to me, and then I began to notice the change which I have already mentioned. It seemed like a perfect transformation wrought by the blessed departed spirit with whom she had been so intimately united on earth.

In the autumn of that year we went for some time to Blankenburg, then a desolate and very melancholy place by the sea side, which we chose in preference to Ostend on occount of our deep mourning. It was there, on that dreary beach, on a day which I shall never forget, under a lurid and stormy sky, that I happened to look at Olga, and, struck by the change in her face, felt persuaded that she too was about to die. She, that sweet, young, good sister, who gave me back, at least in part, what I had lost; with whom I no longer felt the difference in age, so much had her mind as well as her soul been matured during the months that had gone by, and who indeed even in childhood had been thoughtful beyond her years—was she too going to die? It was a dreadful conviction, and I tried at first to shake it off, endeavoring to persuade myself that her pallor and the vivid red of her lips, which had so much alarmed me, were merely accidental. But this was that *first* moment of dread, more terrible perhaps than any other, and which I have never forgotten. It was like the terror I had felt at Paris about Eugénie the year before her death. The following day Olga was seized with such a violent pain in the side that my mother, who was obliged to remain at Blankenburg with my youngest sister, asked me to take Olga at once to Brussels to consult a good physician. We went, and Olga laughed about it, and said there was no occasion to be anxious about her. Still, at Bruges, where we stopped for two hours, she had not strength to accompany me to the Church, though she had a great curiosity to see the tombs of Mary of Burgundy and Charles the Bold. I did not like to tell her that she was too ill to go, and was about to take her there, when, just as we were setting out, she sat down again, and begged me to go without her.

When we arrived at Brussels, where my husband had preceded us, we found him waiting for us in the hall. The house was arranged in the English manner, with the dining-room on the ground-floor. We went into it for supper, and during the meal Olga was in such good spirits that I had a little moment of joy. It seemed impossible she could be really very ill. Near the dining-room was a study, into which we went after supper. This room was full of books and old furniture, which with the fire-light and candles gave it such a studious appearance that Olga exclaimed in a great delight: "Oh! this is where I shall establish myself to study! You must put a table for me in this corner for my books, and then you may lend me whatever I may read." After that she went merrily upstairs to the bed-room where she was to suffer so much, and we never again saw her in the library in which she had hoped to spend so many happy hours. Her illness lasted five months, while we watched the fluctuations of that terrible disease which more than any other torments the heart with hopes and fears. These painful alternations were endured with unwearying patience. She speaks, indeed, sometimes in her letters, of the irritability of her nerves, and her fears lest others should have to suffer on that account, but never had any one less reason for such apprehensions. In the first days of her illness she used sometimes to shed tears, but after the beginning of January, when her case had become hopeless, she never gave way to emotion. Her courage and serenity, as well as her tender affection for all those about her went on increasing. In short, it pleased God fully to grant the desires expressed in the following letters to Alexandrine, written at different times of her long illness.

The first was dated November 29th, 1842:

"My beloved Alex, you are a very dear sister to write me such a delightfully affectionate letter. I am not worthy to have sisters like you, my dear ones. God quite spoils His poor child, who shows so much coldness in return for all the tenderness lavished upon her. The happiness I look forward to, if I get to Heaven, is an immense amount of love to God and of all creatures, and a continual ardent enthusiasm. This is pretty much what you would expect, I suppose? It was very wrong of me to be so long without writing, and to let you begin. I might have written long ago, though I lead the life of an invalid, and am not at all well yet.

"I think the doctors do not know what to prescribe for me. I have a pain in my side, and a continual nervous irritability. I cry about the least trifle, and even the care taken of me makes me inwardly cross. No one escapes, not even Mamma and Pauline. They say it is not visible, which astonishes me, for I cry, and there is nothing more difficult to hide than that. I make resolutions to overcome myself, for if I am to be ill a long time, and if I am likely to get worse, that irritability will increase if I do not make some effort to subdue it in the beginning. I well know what it makes others suffer, and it would be dreadful to add to the grief of my dear family at seeing me ill that other grief of not feeling at their ease when they are nursing me, of fearing to annoy me, and of doing what is disagreeable to me. I know this is sometimes the case in illness, and it might happen so with me. This is the *greatest* of all sufferings. Oh! may it at least touch none but me! Alex, pray a little, that I may have strength to overcome myself. If only I could leave off crying. But perhaps God wishes me to accept this weakness as a humiliation, otherwise I suffer very little. I am never bored, I am not out of spirits. Sometimes the wish to be in Paris has troubled me very much, but I have subdued this desire, for we must only wish what is God's will. What a wonderful story that is of Mlle. de Maistre! Thank you for your delightful letter about her. It gave me a thrill, and, oh! how I wish for many such emotions! Will faith be reckoned to us as a virtue, who seem every day to see, as it were, into the next world? Doubts are no longer my spiritual difficulty, but rather the weakness of my love of God, my tepidity, my negligence in prayer, my want of trust in God, or confiding faith and interior joy. I have Mass here, and sometimes go to Communion. That good Father Boone has been exceedingly kind to me, and this is, indeed, true charity. So you are become one of Christ's own poor? How comes it that He deals thus with those who are only wishing for money to do good?* But I suppose He does it that we may renounce ourselves, and pursue self into its last stronghold, by enduring perhaps the greatest of all crosses, that of seeing others suffer without being able to help them. Poor Alex! what will you do now? How is Putbus going on? I am always praying for him. Good-bye. I think I have nothing more to say but that I love you."

Olga's second letter to Alexandrine was written on the 2nd of January, 1843, a few weeks before her death.

"My dear old Sister—I must write you a line to-day. I should have done so yesterday, but I was lazy. I wish you a good, a *holy* new year; that we may all do God's will, may love Him more and more, and that your mother may become a Ca-

* Alexandrine had made some fruitless efforts to invest some money for the benefit of the poor.

tholic, and also your dear brother* and his wife. I have asked Eugénie and Albert to obtain this for me as a new year's gift. I am so sorry they are leaving you. If only you could come here! I am weak, I cough, I have a pain in my side, I am weary and nervous; and though I said I wished you were here, it is perhaps better not, for you might provoke me when those odious moments of nervousness come on, and if even for an instant I seemed to take a dislike to you, it would vex me dreadfully. Dear, darling little sister, pray that I may suffer patiently as long as it is God's will. I have resolved to act exactly as I should do if I knew that I should die of this illness. I try to look forward to death without fear, and to read everything that can make me love God more and more. If only I could pray well, but, alas! . . . . Still I hope that our good God accepts my sufferings as if I offered them up more perfectly. He is so merciful, He asks from us nothing but a good will, and I trust mine is good. I have not faith enough in His goodness, nor trust, nor love. Good-bye. I am tired. The doctor says I shall get well in the spring. Remember me to your mother, and wish her for me all the blessings of the new year."

The year 1843 opened as sadly for us as the preceding one. During the month of January all the symptoms of Olga's disease increased, and the danger which had been apprehended for four months became imminent. One day, in the drawing-room, where she could still come down, and where she spent some hours every day, Olga had been for some time thoughtful, and I was sitting beside her, silently and sadly listening to her rapid breathing, and gazing at her face, which was altering more and more. Suddenly she said to me quietly, "Do you know I think I am very happily situated?" I felt surprised. "Yes," she repeated, "I am very well off; for either I shall get well, or I shall die. If I get well I shall be very glad. I shall enjoy the spring, and the pleasure of getting strong again as I did last year at Rome, and, above all, of going to Paris and seeing my dear Narishkins. If, on the other hand, I die, all this year of sorrow that we have gone through, and my illness, and then the plenary indulgences that I may gain at death, make me hope that I shall go very quickly to Heaven." It affected me so much to hear her speak

* The brother who had been in exile, and had married since his return.

in this way, that I remained speechless. After a moment's reflection she said with the same composure, "After all, if I did get well now, I should have to begin to suffer again some day before I die. So that already having had so much pain, and come so far . . . . . ." Here she broke off, and then added, "Anyhow, I hope that if you saw or were told that I was getting worse, you would not be so foolish as not to tell me so directly." She stopped there, and kissing her forehead, I told her to bless God for the peace He had given her soul.

That blessed peace remained the same throughout the last stage of cruel suffering which then began; when fever, coughing, and increased oppression of breathing deprived her of all rest during the day and of sleep at night. She used often to make verses during those long sleepless nights; lines which, if not always correct, are, to my mind, full of the true spirit of poetry as well as fervent piety. It seemed as if under the pressure of suffering that chosen soul emitted some exquisitely sweet perfume. This is no sudden thought. It was constantly in my mind as I sat by her side, feeling my grief almost swallowed up at times in the emotion and joy of seeing her thus entirely resigned to God, and giving us all so wonderful an example. Olga had prayed not to feel or show irritability, and she obtained that grace, for her meekness and patience increased with each day that brought her nearer to her end. My poor mother had the especial comfort of being more able than any one else to soothe and comfort her. Olga said that she suffered less when her head was resting upon her mother's shoulder than at any other time, and she would remain whole hours in that position, holding her by the hand, and from time to time saying sweet and tender words. As she had intended, she neither read nor wished to have anything read to her, which did not tend to bring her nearer to God; such as prayers or passages from the lives and writings of the Saints; and her memory, which never failed in the least, brought back to her mind all the pious sayings she now applied to herself. Thus she had once read that St. Bernard compared souls to precious stones, which are rough and dull unless they are cut, shaped, and chiselled. One day when she had suffered more than usual, and I kissed her with tears in my eyes saying: "Oh, poor child, how you suffer!" she smiled and said, "What would you have? We must let God cut us into shape." These sort of remarks were always on her lips. Another day she said, "I do not *like* pain, but I can understand that we must suffer. When the head is sick the whole body suffers, and Jesus Christ is our Head." Some weeks afterwards she said to Charles: "Every day I make a bouquet* of my sufferings, and offer it to God for some one or other. I assure you I do not forget you or yours."

Her last days were drawing near. Alexandrine had come to see her once more, and soon afterwards my brothers and their wives. Olga had also earnestly hoped to see her two friends, Catherine and Nathalie Narishkin, whom one of their aunts had promised to bring to Brussels, but she had not that happiness. On the third of February, Father Pilat,† her confessor, proposed to give her Extreme Unction and the Viaticum. She gladly assented, and prepared to receive the last Sacraments not only gratefully but with holy joy. I wrote in my journal: "A holy, solemn and sweet day, like a day of First Communion;" and again, "After a sound and peaceful sleep which followed the administration of the Sacraments, Olga said, 'It is so sweet, on waking, to feel that I am in the same state as on the day of my baptism.' And the same evening she exclaimed: 'Oh, what a happy day this has been! How gratefully I shall remember it if I get well! I am sorry that Eugénie had not this happiness.'" After night prayers, which we always said in her room, she wished us to add the *Te Deum* in thanksgiving for that blessing.

On the 10th of February, the day when that dear soul was to break its bonds,‡ she prepared in the morning to go to Communion as usual, for Mass had been said for a week in the next room, and Communion given to her every day. But the extreme weakness which had followed the sufferings of the last night made her afraid of not being able to communicate. Alexandrine said to her: "You are going to receive Him Who will give you strength." "Yes," Olga humbly replied; "but *how* shall I receive Him?" A little while afterwards I said to her: "My dear little sister, I need not remind you that it is those whom

* Catholics are accustomed to make little acts of different virtues, or to accept the pain, weariness, etc., of sickness during each day, and offer them as flowers are offered on an altar. —TRANSLATOR.

† Superior of the Redemptorists at Brussels.

‡ One of these days, when Olga was asked which she should like best, some tisane or water, she replied: "I should like water best." Then she added: "Jesus Christ on the Cross never said '*I like.*'"

God loves best who suffer as you are doing." "Ah!" she replied, with an angelic expression: "that is the A B C of religion!" She heard Mass, received Communion, and then asked us to read to her in Italian Silvio Pellico's act of love which begins, "*Amo, e sovra il mio cor.*" After that, by her desire, we left her for an hour. At noon we were called in haste. She was in her agony. * * * *

A short and incoherent passage in my journal relates exactly what passed, and on that account I give it in preference to any other description.

"Brussels, February 10th, 1843.

"As soon as the feeling of exhaustion and suffocation began, Olga asked for a priest, and looked anxiously towards the door to see if my brothers were coming. Mr. Slevin,* after some minutes, began the prayers for the agonizing. Olga folded her arms across her breast, and said in a low and fervent voice: '*I believe, I love, I hope, and I repent;*' and then, 'Forgive me . . all of you. God bless you all.' A moment afterwards she said, glancing towards a Madonna by Sasso Ferrato near her bed, 'I leave my Virgin to Adrian.' Then seeing her brothers, she first called Charles, kissed him, and said: 'Do love God, and be very good.' A little while after she addressed the same words to Fernand, with even more earnestness, and gave him some farewell messages for the Narishkins. She kissed Marie† and Emma, to whom she whispered a few words, and then she turned to her maid and said: 'Thank you, Justine.'‡ Afterwards she embraced me, and last of all my mother, for whom she seemed to wish to keep her last kiss. Once more she repeated, '*I believe, I love, I hope, I repent.* I commend my soul into Thy hands!' . . Then came some inarticulate efforts at speech. I could only make out the name of *Eugénie.* It was the last word she uttered. Father Pilat came in haste, and pronounced over her, at this last moment, the great indulgence attached to the scapular. Olga raised her eyes to Heaven. This was her last look, and her last act was to kiss her little Crucifix which was always in her hand, and which she had repeatedly pressed to her lips during that short agony.

"Ah! my God, let that scene always remain present to us!

* An Irish priest then staying in the house.

† Fernand's wife. ‡ The ladies maid who nursed her.

Notwithstanding the fearful alteration in her features, there was a beaming expression in her face. She was gasping for breath, but as one might be at the moment of winning a race, breathless and weary, yet joyful and triumphant, knowing that very soon the toil will be over, and the crown be won.

* * * * * *

"After an hour spent by her side we forced my poor mother to leave the room for some time. We went away with her, and when we returned, the most consoling change had taken place. All trace of sickness had disappeared, and the room had been turned into a Chapel, in the centre of which our angel lay asleep, dressed in white, and surrounded with flowers. She was looking more beautiful than she had ever done in life. We spent the rest of the day peacefully beside her, feeling almost joyful, praying and weeping indeed, but without any of the bitterness of grief. Our blessed sister departed from this world at one o'clock. At two—and what a shock it gave me—I received a note from Nathalie Narishkin, to say that *they were coming to see Olga!* This seemed dreadful at the first moment, but the God of all peace calmed our hearts, and our sister's beloved friends felt as we did the sweetness of praying by that dear and holy body. They could not tear themselves away from the chamber of death, and thus it was that they saw Olga again."

At the time when I wrote the above lines, these friends whom Olga had so earnestly wished to see before she died, and whose conversion to her own faith she had yet more earnestly desired, were both members of the Greek Church. They spent the whole of that first day and also the ensuing night beside her whom they had so dearly loved, praying with my mother, who did now as she had done at Rome when watching by my father's mortal remains. Motionless beside the corpse, for twenty-four hours, she held her child's hand in her own, keeping away from it all that time the dreadful chill of death. Who can tell what passed between those pure and fervent souls in prayer on earth, and the blessed spirit hovering over them? These mysteries are hidden from us; all we do know is, that the future realized beyond all hope the desires Olga had carried up with her to Heaven, and both her friends became Catholics. Nathalie, the youngest and best beloved, was called to the highest lot of all, and a few years afterwards put on the habit of the Sisters of St. Vincent de Paul.

That habit she has now worn for seventeen years, and I fain would speak of the position she holds in that holy army, and the reverence and affection she inspires within and without its ranks, did I not fear to wound the humility of one who may perhaps peruse these pages.

Olga's remains were exposed for three days, during which all our friends at Brussels came to pray with us beside her. Afterwards the body was carried to Boury, and of the three beloved ones for whom we were in mourning at the same time, she alone went to rest beside Albert in the burial-place intended for us all. How vain is all human foresight, both before and beyond the grave.*

The Pope's Nuncio, Monsignor (now Cardinal) Fornari, had been more than once to help us comfort our dear and patient sufferer, and after death to pray by her remains. Among those who sometimes came with him was a man whose name will perhaps create surprise; one at that time, comparatively speaking, unknown, but who has since acquired a formidable renown. I speak of Vincent Gioberti. I cannot revert in thought to that epoch without thinking of him, nor think of him without bearing witness to a fact which, amidst both the adulation and blame lavished upon him, has been too much overlooked. It was religion which at that time imparted so great a splendor to his talents, and during that sad winter, when we saw so much of him, there were brilliant moments in which his vigorous faith made us grasp and embrace invisible truths with a clearness which eloquence alone could not have brought about. We have seen unbelievers after hearing him disturbed in their scepticism, and indifferent Catholics going from our drawing-room to kneel before a priest, and dating their conversion from the day they had met Gioberti. We have seen him turn pale with intense feeling while listening to the account of Ratisbonne's conversion, and shed tears near Olga's lifeless body. And thus it happens that one who has been the subject of so much enthusiasm and so many anathemas, remains connected in our mind with the image of a powerful champion of the truth, of a master in science, of a man capable of the utmost humiliation faith can impose, and accessible to the tenderest emotion which charity can inspire.

* M. de la Ferronnays is buried in the Church of Sant' Andrea delle Fratte, and Eugénie at Lumigny.

Anger and pride afterwards infused their poison into that life, and the light which might have been so bright and pure became darkened. He was punished for forgetting those words: "*Blessed are the meek, for they shall possess the earth.*" May he have obtained pardon from Him Who also said: "*Blessed are they that hunger and thirst after justice, for they shall be filled.*"

Alexandrine did not leave us after Olga's death. The Princess Lapoukhyn went back to the Ukraine, and she herself wished her daughter to resume her place in the sad family-circle from which she had been absent a whole year, and which death so cruelly and rapidly narrowed. Alexandrine therefore remained with my mother and with us for six weeks, and then we all set out together for Paris. Before I left Brussels I received the following letter from M. de Montalembert:

COUNT DE MONTALEMBERT TO PAULINE.

"Madeira, March 4th, 1843.

"MY DEAREST FRIENDS—I dreaded the worst when I left you, but I did not expect that the blow would fall so soon. A letter by the last steamer brought us the news that that lovely and holy Olga is gone to Heaven. All our letters from Paris and Brussels were also full of details, which made us anticipate the approaching end of her sufferings, and in the midst of our grief drew from us tears of very sweet sympathy and admiration. Those touching and wonderful words of hers, when asked what she liked to take: 'Jesus Christ did not say on the Cross, "*I like*,"'* are as a glimpse of Heaven, and lift up even so dull a soul as mine to those glorious regions, where, alas! it is not given me to dwell. And thus even before a whole year has elapsed, she has followed Eugénie! One more angel flown from your own happy home—one more angel from the bright group I knew and loved so dearly in former days. Albert, Eugénie, Olga, and their admirable father. Ah! what a joyful, tender meeting those blessed souls must have had! And what it must be to think that you are overshadowed by their love, transfigured and intensified as it must be in Heaven. This must give you strength and comfort in the midst of your anguish. I really know no one in the world who can look up, as you may do, to Heaven, and see there such friends, such guardians, such forerunners.

* P. 479.

"At the same time, believe me I deeply sympathise with your sufferings under these swift and often-repeated blows, and the ever-recurring comparison between the present and the past, when you possessed *everything at once.* I like to feel—perhaps presumptuously, but indeed with true sympathy for you—that among all your friends there are not many who appreciate as I do all that you have lost. Have you any who loved Albert better, reverenced and admired Eugénie more, or better understood what you all were to one another? It is now eleven years since I first saw you at the Villa Trecase, in the midst of such delightful happiness; and from that time I have looked upon you more and more as my own family. And how fond we were of that dear Olga! I thought her so attractive. Anna and I were always speaking of her since her first appearance in Paris, at a wedding-soirée at Madame de Sourches', where she looked so pretty, so modest, so pleasing. Let me say that I feel this last sorrow of yours in a very special way. And your angelic mother? I hear that she has been heroic, but that is always the case; it is like a second nature to her. There are, and must necessarily be, special and great graces bestowed on a mother who has given back so much to God. In return for those sacrifices, He doubtless gives strength and generosity of soul. Speak to her, I beseech you, of my deep reverence and devoted affection for her. And Alexandrine, is she with you? I look to her as your comforter in these days of mourning, for she is admirably qualified to perform that part, more, I think, than yourself. She has risen above sorrow. We cannot pity her now, but we can always love her, which I do, and I tell her so through you, my poor afflicted friends. So then death has not spared even that good dear house at Brussels, which I was so fond of, and looked upon as a home. How often I enjoyed in thought, future meetings with you all under its roof. It was there I saw Olga in August with, as it then appeared, a long life before her, and in October I saw her again, as it has turned out, for the last time. What are you going to do? Shall we find you in Belgium when we pass through in June? But all this I shall know before you get this letter, for I will not for a moment suppose that neither you nor Augustus have written to us. We are doubting between Algiers, Palermo, and Rome for the winter. All my wishes are for Rome. May you be there, too, my dear good friends. Look upon me always as the particular friend of your sorrows, the friend of all whom you have most loved, and most mourn for."

Adrian de Mun, whom we always considered as a brother, was the only one not with us at Olga's death; but, as I have already said, she did not forget him in that solemn hour, and some of the last words she had spoken were a message to him. A more imperative duty had detained him beside another death-bed. The Marquis de Mun, his father, was now sinking under a disease which had been first brought on by anguish at the loss of his daughter. It might almost be said that his was a nature not intended for suffering, and that his trials had been beyond his strength, if we did not know that God justly and wisely ordains these mysterious dispensations. But there certainly never was a character which seemed less formed for grief and tears. Openness of heart, universal benevolence, the gaiety and grace which belonged to a former generation, joined to a kindness, which is always the greatest beauty a mind can possess, all these delightful qualities shone conspicuously in M. de Mun, and gave others that sense of enjoyment in his society which is like sunshine to the soul.* But dark clouds of sorrow had overcast that bright sunshine, and a heart which could not believe in anything but happiness, was doomed to endless tears! Overflowing with a tenderness almost verging on idolatry for those it loved, it had been forced to part with the object of its dearest affections, and had now lost even the transient gleam of joy which his son's happiness had imparted. By his side his wife's heart was breaking, crushed by the same blows, and in a yet more hopeless manner than his own. Though since his trials M. de Mun had become more pious than in his youth, he was not much influenced by those supernatural feelings which facilitate prayer and lighten the burthen of life. He was also subject to agitation and fear, which might have rendered the approach of death very painful. But on our arrival at Lumigny we found him not only calm and peaceful, but in a state of mind not always granted to a soul in that solemn moment, even when assisted by grace. I was reading one day to our dying friend the chapter of the *Imitation of Christ*, which speaks of the happiness of Heaven. He stopped me, and said: "I have read that often before, but never under-

* "*Le Souvenirs de Madame de Montagu*," which everybody has read, show us M. de Mun in his youth such as I have here described him.

stood it, but now I do, my dear child, and I like you to know it." Then he added, with characteristic simplicity: "You must all be surprised to see me die so bravely, and I did not expect it myself. I believe my dear La Ferronnays has obtained me this grace." These words were a blessed addition to our treasury of consolations. We saw him die with this peaceful courage. To the end his words were all blessings upon his son, or expressions of the most touching affection and gratitude to his wife and friends.

My mother and Alexandrine remained several weeks with Madame de Mun, and afterwards went back together to Boury. Sad as the return was to be, my mother would not yield to the temptation of staying away. She knew, and Alexandrine too, that peace and consolation are not obtained by weakly yielding to our feelings, but by courageously overcoming them. They struggled, therefore, against the painful impression which awaited them in the deserted château, and lived there surrounded by the recollections which filled it, without endeavoring to escape from them; nay, rather finding a sad solace in meeting with reminiscences of the dear departed at every turn.

The following letter from my mother, at this period of her sorrowful earthly journey, contains a touching picture of their life.

MADAME DE LA FERRONNAYS TO PAULINE.

"Boury, September 1st, 1843.

"My Dearly Beloved Daughter—Let me see how long it is since I wrote to you. Looking in my diary, I find it is four days. A long time, indeed! Formerly, one letter was scarcely finished before another was begun. Then there was movement and life around me, but what can I do now to get out of the living tomb in which I seem enclosed? I see nothing, hear nothing, think of nothing, and such is the regularity of our convent-like habits, that I often have not time to write. This regularity acts like a soothing appliance to the sores of my bruised heart, and God knows what sores they are! Three bleeding wounds lately inflicted, and another yet unhealed and quivering still. If the thought of God were not present to us in the midst of all our occupations, if He were not Himself the direct object of most of them, we should see nothing but death on every side of us. But He gives us strength to live; at least I hope so.

"I often pass from one state of mind to another. The other day, as I stood on the entrance steps, I suddenly felt like somebody cast away on a desert island, and I have often that restlessness of mind which makes us wish to be anywhere but where we are. On the whole, however, I would rather stay here than elsewhere, for it seems as if in this place I belonged more entirely to all those dear departed ones; and then there is that beloved Chapel, where I hope they sometimes grieve for me, and feel how much I miss their beautiful hymns and Heavenly voices. My dear Alexandrine practises on the organ, which is so kind of her. I am sure she does it to please me, and so it does, for I cling to everything that is like the past, or that can the least remind me of it. Is this weakness or strength? I cannot tell, but I should be inclined to call it weakness, or perhaps a want of entire resignation. I have not the courage to make a complete sacrifice, and I cling to little things for want of great ones. But I think I may say that the wish to be of some use to those who try to help me, has something to do with it. I feel it gives them a little interest and employment. If I were alone, it would be another thing. Poor Alexandrine practised yesterday on the organ till near midnight, and this morning played some beautiful things. But where are the voices? Ah! nothing can ever bring those back again.

"After breakfast I read with Albertine, and then with Alexandrine. Then Albertine brings me her historical note books. I make her practise, then I go to my own room; afterwards I devote myself to the arranging of my letters,* and then the time flies. But I must hurry over that business, for I have enough to last me a long while. At four o'clock in the afternoon I go to the cemetery, and for a little while to the Chapel; then comes dinner, then a visit to Louise Thiars, or other poor people, and then we meet in the drawing-room, where we are reading aloud the life of St. Francis of Assisi. Then come night prayers, and afterwards tea and bed-time. It is when I am quite alone in my room that I feel nervous tremors, which keep me awake. The sense of solitude becomes so overpowering, that I should perhaps never be able to sleep at all if I did not think those precious ones were still about me, watching over my rest. We

* The whole of her husband's letters to herself were collected and arranged in two thick volumes.

shall, I think, stay as we are, at all events till the 1st of November, and perhaps longer, if the weather is fine.

"My dear child, I like to think that you will have fine weather for your sea-bathing. This time last year we were at Blankenburg. If only the weather had been as it is now! But no, she was ill, and had even then the pain in her side . . . . I constantly feel as if I were for the first time hearing of these calamities. Each time I think of them it is as if a fresh blow were struck on my heart—that poor heart which beats so fast both night and day! It is four o'clock, and they are come in for the letters. I love you with all my heart, my darling, and your hus band, too. I miss you both every minute."

There are souls whom grief embitters or hardens into a cold reserve. This letter is a proof that my mother's strong, gentle character was not of this description. After all her trials she remained exactly what she was before. Their effect upon Alexandrine, and the change wrought in her by the accumulated sorrows of the last two years, and especially by Eugénie's death, remains to be told.

"Excelsior!"

Seven years had now passed since Albert's death. Seven years since Alexandrine had begun that story of their love and their life which had been during all that time her dearest occupation. It was now finished, and the last pages had been written during her sad stay in Brussels. Olga was dying by her side on the day this long work was brought to a conclusion. Towards its close it had revived the most heartrending recollections. And now in the space of one year she had lost first Eugénie, the gentle and perfect companion of her sorrow, who next to Albert had exercised the sweetest and most powerful influence over her life; then my father, whom she loved with a filial affection, and lastly her own brother, whose death grieved her deeply, and the more so, because it was not attended by the consolation which had hallowed the closing scenes of those other deathbeds. In the midst of all these sorrows, which carried away one after another "the fragments of her shattered happiness," she brought to a close, as I have already said, the record of her past joys. It was ended, and from that time forward she would have found it impossible to pursue any similar occupation. It would have given her none of the consolation and pleasure which had made it hitherto delightful. Her character, her mind, her whole life, seemed raised above earthly joys and consolations, and her way of looking at the past underwent also a change. She still thought of Albert, and loved him with the same love; but in a certain sense she ceased to grieve for him. A sudden and clear view of the blessedness of those who mourn seems to have been vouchsafed to her. This was no doubt the earthly reward of her unmurmuring submission to God's will, even during the first days of her grief. Resignation had then been an act of faith, and often a very difficult and painful duty. But at the close of that year marked by so many sorrows and so many graces, she seemed to realize what hitherto she had only believed. I cannot otherwise account for the blessed change which took place in her, and which I would fain ascribe to the blessed influence of those departed souls who had been such gentle and tender friends to her in life!

And thus I found during the sorrowful days we passed together, that Alexandrine had none of those fits of depression which she had such difficulty formerly in overcoming. I had not now to comfort her. She had become herself the comforter of others, and as M. de Montalembert had justly said: "She had now risen higher than grief." Many a time a word from her gave me fresh courage; a word spoken with tears indeed, but with a peaceful serenity which imparted strength. On the day that Olga had received Extreme Unction, notwithstanding the Heavenly peace that had attended that touching scene, I felt quite overcome when I had left her room, and Alexandrine found me weeping bitterly. She did not try to stop my tears, and stood looking at me without speaking. I looked up, and oh! what an expression there was in her face! Of more than fortitude, of more than peace, almost of joy. At last she said: "You weep because our dear Olga is going to Heaven, and now that she has all but left this world you would bring her back! *What happiness then can you promise her on earth?*" These words were the expression of a clear and simple truth. But the manner in which they were spoken and their effect upon me I have never forgotten. She often said things the full force of which it is difficult to convey to those who have not heard them, but I must try as best I can to reproduce the impression they made upon myself.

We have seen Alexandrine at Boury three months after the death of Olga. My mother's letter described them in that desolate château during those melancholy days. Alexandrine seeking to awaken on the organ a feeble plaintive echo of the melodies they both had loved, and my mother striving to give her the pleasure of feeling that she had succeeded in cheering her. This is not perhaps the saddest of the recollections which live in my memory, but it affects me more deeply than any other. Are not love and pity when in unison, the tenderest chords in the heart? That autumn did not elapse without new trials, for the Princess Lapoukhyn, who had returned to the Ukraine, fell dangerously ill at Korsen, and for several days Alexandrine expected to receive the news of her mother's death. She wrote to me then as follows: "I am very little inclined to *write*, Pauline, but I must write to you. Your dear mother has told you everything. She is so kind to me. I love her more than ever. She is such a help, such a comfort to me. Pauline, that cross which I have always apprehended is now drawing near, touching me, perhaps at this very moment laid upon me. My mother's death, and her dying a Protestant, appears so likely, that I have scarcely a hope that it will not happen. To-morrow I shall perhaps know something positive. You pray, do you not, and you get prayers for that beloved mother, that dear, tender mother, so passionately fond of me? Ah! God may have been jealous of my love for her—perhaps I loved her too much! Everything I possess, everything I see around me are gifts from her, often very simple gifts, for to her great regret I would not now let her make me costly presents. What I have suffered during the last week has been a new kind of grief to me. How right I was to say that we did not know what might happen in two months time. Oh! please, please, do not be glad nor sorry again for anything beforehand. Perhaps by this time she is dead, this beloved, beautiful, good, sweet, and poor—*poor* mother of mine! Father de Ravignan tells me he is convinced she will recover; and they all bid me take comfort in the thought that she is in good faith. Alas! these were the consolations that were given me at the time of my brother's death, and now they are again brought forward in my mother's case. Oh! Pauline, never complain of anything unless you see one you love die without being converted, or something of the same kind! In your letter of the day before yesterday, you say of yourself, 'After having gone through everything most afflicting. . . .' O my dear love, believe me there are sadder things than deaths visibly blessed! Oh! what is now going on at Korsen? She suffers so much, and without the powerful aid our faith affords. I have just received your dear affectionate letter. Thanks, my dearest. God is love, and He deals with us mercifully, and never tries us beyond our strength. I have experienced once more how useful trials are, so do not let us be afraid of crosses. Mamma is admirably resigned and good; she writes to me that she is sure this trial has been sent for her salvation and to make her better. What wonderful helps God gives us! I feel able to breathe, and to breathe freely. I was so happy to see Adrian again, who was most affectionate, and Father de Ravignan, who did me unspeakable good. Ah! if only my poor mother could know such help as that. My dear love, my kind friends, pray all of you, and get prayers for me."

One of Alexandrine's prayers was granted, and she soon had the happiness to hear of her mother's recovery, but this anxiety, which had followed upon so many other sorrows, and her very thankfulness, mixed as it was with the pain of an earnest and unfulfilled desire, gave, I imagine, a tangible form to an idea which had hitherto only just crossed her mind. It was the same thought which Alphonse Ratisbonne put into words when he said, "I cannot give God less than *all*." It took possession of Alexandrine, and for the space of a year greatly disturbed her peace. I shall not dwell long upon this part of her life, for I am not thoroughly acquainted with its details. This state of mind, or it may be this spiritual trial, was not of a kind to be spoken of by letter. The very importance of the question in itself would have forbidden it. Alexandrine thought, as she afterwards told me, in explaining her silence on this subject, that "when God sows a seed in a soul, it should be left untouched even as a seed put into the ground, for otherwise neither the one nor the other can bring forth fruit."

The Abbé Gerbet, to whom Alexandrine would naturally have opened her mind in this difficulty, was absent; a circumstance which added another void to the many blanks which the events of that year had created around her. But the merciful

Hand of God was extended over His child. She had lost indeed the holy guide, the incomparable friend who had directed the first steps of her Catholic life, with so much gentleness and authority; who had poured Heavenly balm into her bruised heart, and at the same time revived its latent energy. But another guide was now given her in his stead, who might perhaps have seemed to her severe, if she had known him in the days when earthly regret in some measure withheld her heart from God, but who now exactly met the actual wants of her soul, raised and strengthened as it was by impulses already received. Her first director had taught her to walk, the second helped her to ascend; both were the instruments and messengers of God, but it was given to each of them to correspond with the needs of the hour in which they were sent. In the first Alexandrine found a father and a saint; in the second, an angel.

We have seen and known him, and I am not afraid of being thought exaggerated in using this word by many who have preserved in their hearts and memory the indelible image of Father de Ravignan's look, voice and manner, and who remember the influence he exercised over all within his reach. He was undoubtedly a great and fascinating orator, but it was not his eloquence that won souls. There are ordinary phrases, a thousand times repeated without producing any effect, which, when he uttered them, seemed to be heard for the first time. For instance, I heard him say one day, not in the pulpit, but at a little meeting for charitable purposes, "Life is nothing!" and I can only say that the expression and the tone of voice which accompanied these words were enough to make them a most eloquent sermon upon the misery and vanity of this world. It cannot be wondered at that such teaching as this should have inspired Alexandrine with a thought consonant to her fervor, but which the sequel proved, led her beyond what God required. Nor can it be a matter of reproach that she should have committed the generous mistake of thinking she was called upon to leave all things for Him. But when such a mistake has been made, not through excitement or pride, but from a simple excess of zeal, or love, the error should be humbly recognised, and the ordinary path resumed without hesitation or discouragement. It may happen that an increase of holiness, and a greater facility in overcoming the obstacles of the road, show that in leaving it awhile for a higher path, the soul has suffered no detriment, but on the contrary, has in that circuitous way been brought nearer to its end. This was the case with Alexandrine. After spending some time at the Catechumenate of the Congregation of the *Filles de Sion*, then just founded by Alphonse Ratisbonne, she left it by Father de Ravignan's advice. The trial had been made with his consent, but he would not allow her to pursue it further. She wrote to me on the second of January, 1845 :—

"MY BELOVED SISTER—I write to wish you every best blessing, both for yourself and for every one you love, and to tell you that at this very moment I am returning to our dearest mother, to resume, or rather to learn,* my sweet part of *Ruth*. What do you say to this? God brings us together again, and my joy is very great. I love you all, more even than I thought I did. I am going to give your dear mother a surprise, which will, I hope, make up for the last I gave her."

My mother's joy was indeed very great, though she had made, with her usual courage, a sacrifice which she was soon, alas! called upon to renew in another and severer form. Before Alexandrine went to make trial of the religious life, the fear of not doing everything in God's service within her strength had become a continual anxiety, and she was only freed from this torment when experience had shown her the measure of her strength. It was therefore no doubt as wise to allow her to make the trial as it was prudent to put a stop to it before another step in that path —the highest of all, but to which she was not called—had injured her health, without profiting her soul. She therefore returned to my mother with a simplicity equal to the courage with which she had left her; and, moreover, with a joyful heart, for the anxious feelings which had so long haunted her, were set at rest for ever. A week after her return she wrote to me :—

"Paris, January 14th, 1845.

"MY BELOVED SISTER—How I thank you for your dear letter. You have been so very good about all this. We shall now be more united than ever. At any rate, this is what I feel, and your mother is so delightfully kind to me. I still feel bewildered, as if I had been in a storm, and it was going down by degrees.

* The original, "reprendre ou plutôt apprendre" loses its point in the translation.—TRANSLATOR.

I return quietly, but with rapture, to my parish work. I have found M. Esbelin, who is working harder than ever among our poor; but, Oh! my dear friend, what a favor from God it is to meet with such a man as Father de Ravignan! I cannot write to you very fully just now, for I am like somebody who is awaking from a long dream. I do hope this has been my *best* cross. Oh! darling, let us cast ourselves on Him Who wishes us to be *quite little children*. It is wonderful how He guides all things, and only lays upon us as much as we can carry. Why are we so impatient, and why lose in that way the most *precious* part of our trials? for they end sooner than we expect. My dear, good, lovely sister, you are not without your own troubles, but I shall soon share them with you. How pleasant it will be! I should like to be lodged in some little garret in your house, so as to be under the same roof with you. We always wish for the most perfect things in this imperfect world, which is often a fault, and it makes us unhappy. What does Augustus say about my recent follies? I should certainly have died there by inches. Now my heart and pulse beat naturally again. And you, darling, how are you? Oh! I love you so much, and I will love more than ever! There is nothing else to care for, and it leads to everything else. Good-bye till we meet, my dearest. I think your kindness will rejoice at finding my old self again in this letter, and that you will recognise in it your Alexandrine. You judge me very correctly, my dear sister. God reward you for your affection. Pray for your poor old worldling, who is much more worldly than you are!"

My judgment of Alexandrine was that she liked retirement, but had a natural repugnance to a cloistered life, and that to a certain point freedom of action and independence were as necessary to her spiritual and mental, as to her physical well-being. She became convinced of this after that humble and earnest experiment, which obliged her to retrace her steps, but which did not in the least impede her ultimate progress. On her return to her home, and to what she called her parish duties, she set to work with more zeal and devotedness than ever. She had loved the poor, as she had loved her God, from her childhood; but these two great loves had gone on increasing with her growth in Catholic faith, hope, and charity. And now she gave up to them everything she could give in this world, her thoughts, her time, her means, her health, and in the end, her life.

At that moment, in Paris, an immense development of good works had taken place, inspired by a charity which did not allow any variety of misery or need to go unaided. This movement has been so energetically seconded by thousands of zealous spirits and active workers, that we may almost say that by this time it embraces every kind of suffering in that immense city. Alexandrine joined that great body of volunteers in the cause of charity who follow everywhere in France the regular army arrayed under the banner of St. Vincent de Paul, the father of the poor, and the leader of all who love them. Vincent de Paul, that name beloved by those who seem to love nothing, reverenced by those who seem to reverence nothing, and which cannot be insulted without arousing the indignation even of the ungodly, who join with Christians in crying shame upon the blasphemers of charity. She enrolled herself in these blessed ranks, where women as well as men have their allotted places. Many of her associates are still living, and bear witness to the brave and gentle virtues of their beloved companion. Though up to the end of her life Alexandrine seldom wrote without saying something worthy of being preserved, I shall not have many whole letters of hers to transcribe in future, for her time for letter-writing was over, and I am come to that period of her life which I mentioned at the beginning of her story. It no longer suited Alexandrine to sit for whole hours at her table, lost in sweet or painful thought, gathering up carefully every memorial of the past endeared by joy, love, or sorrow, and inevitably making herself the chief actor in these scenes. She no longer wrote to me or to others in order to converse in an intimate and perhaps somewhat self-indulgent strain. Her letters now became short and concise. She did not revert to the past; she did not dwell on her own feelings; she scarcely spoke at all of herself. Bravely and cheerfully she wrote, and with an ever-increasing tenderness for her friends. Though she was very calm, and now seldom gave way to emotion, she seemed to have a desire to act, to hasten on, to finish what she had to do, as if she felt that time was short, and her earthly course drawing towards its end.

Since the foregoing year our destination had again been changed, and the fluctuations of diplomacy had now brought us to Germany. We lived sometimes in Carlsruhe, but more habitually at Baden, and it was there that I saw Alexandrine for the first time after that trial which she had called "her best cross." She came to spend with us part of the summer of 1845, and during that time I was able myself to judge of the heights to which her soul had been gradually rising, and of the purposes I have just described.

Instead of the "garret" that she had wished to inhabit in our house, we had, of course, prepared a pretty room, which I had been at some pains to arrange for her; but as soon as she took possession of it, I was compelled, to please her, to take everything ornamental out of it. She was only satisfied when the room became again as simple and common-looking as possible, and had lost all appearance of elegance. She laughed, and was surprised herself at the dislike which she now felt for all the little luxuries with which she had formerly taken delight. The strange part of it was, and she always said so, that this was not the result of any effort or sacrifice on her part. She no longer cared for any of the things that she had formerly liked; but at the bottom of this self-denial which cost her so little, there was, however, something besides a mere change in her tastes and habits, something also besides an austere disgust for the superfluities of this world (an austerity which never belonged to her character). There was in it, beyond all, and above all, a love for the poor, which had become so strong, that she wished to deprive herself of everything for their sake, and even in a measure to assimilate her condition to theirs, which is another of the tendencies of love. Though she was only going to spend a few weeks at Baden, she found out a great number of poor, so that her time was almost as fully occupied there as at Paris.

Every morning before Mass, she went out laden with the things she was going to take to them, and in the afternoon she found that more than one visit of the same kind had to be paid, from which she never allowed herself to be deterred either by heat, rain, fatigue, or length of distance. That business once ended, it was her delight to study her favorite books, to mark particular passages, and make extracts from them. We know by this time what sort of books they were. Generally speaking, those only fixed her attention in which God occupied the first, if not the only place. She would sometimes also glance over poems read in other days with Albert, and liked to look out his favorite passages. As to other purely literary works; novels, biographies, or histories, which formed the subject of conversation around her, and at one time would have interested herself, she no longer cared for them in the least. The taste she had once had for these intellectual amusements and luxuries had as completely vanished as her relish for the ornaments and amusements of the world, music only excepted. One day during that summer we found ourselves accidentally at the Hotel d'Angleterre. Those who know Baden are aware that from one of the balconies of this hotel all that takes place on the promenade below can be seen and heard. We were sitting there at the close of the evening, listening to the band playing (and playing admirably) a waltz. Numerous groups were strolling about the walks, or resting under the trees, and seen thus at a distance everything had that joyous appearance which a great assemblage of people in the open air and on a beautiful summer evening is apt to present; indeed, it is one of those outward impressions which awaken in the hearts of the young that exuberant sense of gaiety and life which is not always free from danger. A few years before, Alexandrine would have carefully shunned every sight of the kind, both from the bitter regret it would have been likely to arouse, as well as from a dread of finding herself alive to any kind of worldly enjoyment. Knowing this to have been the case, I asked her on the day I am speaking of, what impression those festive sounds, which reminded me so much of former days, made upon her. She replied, with a quiet smile, that *she did not think of those days any longer*, and she sat on for some time looking sometimes at the promenade, and sometimes at the starry sky, with an expression I occasionally observed in her face, and which made it quite beautiful. As I write now, I see her just as I saw her then, with that look which I find it difficult to describe, and impossible to forget. She continued thus for a moment, then, taking out of her pocket a little book in which she was in the habit of writing any passage which struck her, she said: "Here is something really beautiful, interesting, and important." And she read me the following words in Latin (St. Augustine's, I believe,) "*O! amare. O! ire! O! sibi perire! O! ad Deum pervenire.*" Never can I forget the expression with which she uttered these words, nor the time, the place, or the day when I heard them. But I feel that it is all but impossible to convey to others the effect they made upon me. What has been said, however, may give some idea of the nature of the change which had taken place in her soul; a change which was only the gradual and complete triumph of that great love which, without excluding any one of the lesser loves which flow from it, can alone suffice to fill the heart. Soon after that day Alexandrine left me, and the following passages are extracts from the letters which I received from her.

ALEXANDRINE TO PAULINE.

"I fancy you have already very much got over the first gloomy impression which Germany produced upon you. I expect that you will meet there with a thousand little agreeable adventures, and I think of my Paule travelling about gathering honey as she goes from every little flower. We must allow ourselves to be moved about *like pieces of furniture.* I have tried it myself, and find it rather pleasant. See on this subject what I have copied from St. Francis de Sales: (*'If you are caught in the net of tribulation, do not look at your sorrow, but look at God, and leave all to Him.'*) How much generosity there is in those words: *'Look not at your sorrow;'* and he repeats constantly what your dear father always used to say, *'Lasciamo fare a Dio.'** Oh! Pauline! we should be very happy if we could feel thus. When will you give yourself up unreservedly to God? When will you believe that He who loves us more than we can love ourselves; that He Who counts the very hairs of our head, and without Whose permission the least of those hairs which we despise (however much we idolise ourselves), does not fall; when will you believe that He orders everything for us in the tenderest, most perfect way possible? *'Man moves and God leads him.'* We must, therefore, do all we can, and especially all we ought, and leave the result to God. This is what I am always advised to do, and this is the only means of getting out of that sort of worry which is almost as bad as sin, because *'Non est in commotione Dominus.'*† That text of the Bible was our dear Eugénie's favorite saying.

"I do not practise what I preach, but I have quite decided to come to it by dint of labor, for I am convinced that, as St.

* Let us leave it to God to do. † 3 Kings xix. 11. [Vulgate.]

Francis de Sales says, '*Anxiety of mind is the worst of all evils except sin!*' I shall fight against it to the knife, in whatever shape it comes, whether in consequence of some great blunder, or some great fault, or after a cross. Ah! in this life so full of tears, there is only one kind of happiness possible and intended by God, Who left it behind Him when He ascended into Heaven, and that is peace. Let us not then, deprive ourselves of it by our own folly. Ask God that by His grace I may be victorious in this struggle, and I will ask the same for you. Let us both have the courage to be happy, and accustom ourselves to look at all things, great and small, as directly coming to us from God's Hands. This holy precept is impressed on my mind. Would I had it stamped on my heart, and every action of my life. Peace is so necessary on account of the impossibility of achieving anything good without it, that to establish its dominion in our hearts, we are sometimes told for a while to sacrifice even greater things to obtain it. There is a time for everything. We must allow our souls to ripen by degrees under the rays of that Divine Sun Who requires of us only to bask in His rays. When we give our will, we give everything. Let us give it up to God, and let Him do with us what He will, without thinking any more about ourselves. It is the pleasantest way of reaching the degree of perfection God has in view for us. I have been preaching to myself in a way that I hope will be profitable, and I ought to thank you for having given me the opportunity. My good old darling, as you liked my extracts, and I like this way of communicating my favorite ideas, I am going to copy something else for you, and also to beg you to read immediately, in the Spanish book which I am returning to you, the twenty-sixth chapter of St. Theresa's 'Way of Perfection,' and tell me if it is not charming. And now here is an extract from St. Francis de Sales: 'As our heart expands, or, to speak more accurately, as we allow it to be expanded, that God may empty it as He desires, His mercy is shed abroad in our souls, and his inspirations, which are always more powerful in proportion as we co-operate with them, increase Divine love in us.' Why, therefore, should not our love be as fervent as the love of St. Augustine, St. Francis, St. Catherine, &c.? Oh yes, dearest, we shall be very intimate throughout eternity with Eugénie and with Olga and with many dear friends, and with many new friends also, of whose number we shall neither weary nor be jealous.

"Ah! my Paule, I have heard many encouraging things. Let us, therefore, put away all trouble, and being carried on by the full tide of grace, push forward without dwelling too much on our faults. It is bold of me to say this, but I think I am right. I have read, and read over again, so many peace-giving things, that I begin to know them just a little tiny bit by heart. I heard a magnificent sermon by Father Lacordaire at Saint Roch, on *the two worlds of enjoyment and expiation.* He spoke of the necessity of expiation, either by entering religious life, or in the world by almsgiving, and of the extraordinary folly of those, who from their horror of suffering, wish to prevent their neighbors also from expiating their own and others' sins. At the end of his discourse his countenance became very animated, and in a majestic manner he denounced the people who cast out those who devote themselves voluntarily to expiation for mankind.

"We shall never have trust enough in God's goodness to us, and you know well that '*Chi tutto spera, tutto ottiene.*'* You see that it is only by preaching that I can answer your appeal, which touches me very much, and gratifies both my love and my sisterly pride. But apropos of preaching, the best thing I can do is to tell you some of the things which I have heard from Madame Swetchine. She said the other day that we ought not to find fault with life, that it was very beautiful, more and more beautiful, happy, and interesting. And yet that gentle and pious woman is overwhelmed by mental and physical suffering; disease of the heart and liver, and want of sleep, followed by such weariness as you can hardly imagine. She also said to me: 'I like whatever comes.' And the way in which she explains this, shows that she is indeed 'the drop of water drowned in an ocean of sweets' of which St. Francis de Sales speaks, and this is what makes her see that all that happens and *is*, is for the best. Ah! to feel this is to be in the way of truth.

"What can be more delightful than to be in perfect harmony with everything that proceeds from the Divine source of love and happiness? But our infirmity falls short of our convictions, and we complain, feeling all the time that it is wrong to complain. It is not any particular desire—even were it too ardent

* He who hopes all obtains all.

—but a generally repining spirit, which would be likely to make your prayers less pleasing to God. He does so like us to be always contented. Madame Swetchine says: 'I was *born happy!*' Yet trials have certainly not been wanting to her. You will forgive my repeating all this, for you love me, and I love you; but I assure you that God helps us immensely when we on our side make little efforts to please Him. Oh! dearest sister, would that my letter could give you joy and courage! How much I wish it! You do not know how I love you; you will only know it in Heaven. Here there is not time to love, and yet we do. For my part, I never loved you all so much."

Alexandrine spent the winter of 1846 at Madame de Mun's house, who found the greatest comfort in her society. She often said that the mere sight of her was like a sunbeam to her sad heart. Alexandrine had tried to induce her to adopt her own active life of charity, not because she was doing no good, for she did a great deal in her way, but because she thought Madame de Mun would find in it some of the strength and power of enjoyment she herself had derived from it, and by that means would shake off the moral and physical depression which, together with age and suffering, made every exertion difficult and painful. It was with a melancholy smile that she sometimes complained that Alexandrine seemed to do with delight what she accomplished with great effort, and that once in particular when they went together to the Hospital Beaujon, and she was feeling more sad and depressed than usual, she turned round and was surprised to see Alexandrine with her eyes sparkling, and her whole countenance so full of joy, that any one would have thought she was going to a party of pleasure. It was, however, impossible to feel more deeply for the sorrows of those she visited, and big tears used to roll down her cheeks by the side of those beds she so gladly attended. But her sense of the honor and happiness of ministering to the poor was so intense, that she found in it a true and keen enjoyment equal to anything she had called by that name, at a time when earth seemed to be promising her all she could desire or ask. I remember an instance of this which she mentioned to me as we were coming out of a garret where she used to visit a poor family who in the midst of the most terrible destitution afforded a remarkable example of resignation and pious courage. The husband was a young house-painter, who had fallen from a scaffolding, and was thus rendered lame and infirm for life. His wife was dying of consumption, and their only child of eleven or twelve years of age, instead of being able to assist them, was sickly and an idiot. These poor people were often visited and relieved by Father Lacordaire. He had mentioned them to Alexandrine, who had ever since taken the utmost interest in them. She used often to carry them food, etc., but said that she went chiefly to learn from them lessons of patience under suffering. One day, as she was leaving this wretched abode she happened to hear the sound of music. It was merely a military band passing through the streets, but it seemed in keeping with her inward feeling of joy, and gave her so strange a sensation of happiness that she did not remember to have experienced anything equal to it in her happiest days. That sort of joy in assisting the poor was indeed habitual with her, and it may be remembered that she felt it six years before by the death-bed of the young priest at Ischl. Her wish to help the poor was so ardent, that when success attended her efforts she felt as if it was her place to be grateful to them, and her manner expressed that feeling. This lent a rare and peculiar charm to her charitable ministrations.

Alexandrine joined us at Baden in the course of the following summer, after she had been at Liége for the Jubilee, which she very much enjoyed, in spite of considerable fatigue. She wrote me this note from Liége:—

"After the journey we had to dine with the Bishop, and then came Vespers and the sermons in the evening. I had only four hours' sleep to prepare myself for the fatigue of attending the beautiful services of the next day, for several hours together. But the sermon from the Bishop of Langres (Monseigneur Parisis), would have been enough in itself to repay me for coming to Liége. It was enough to convert every Protestant in the world, and to reduce them to silence without leaving them even the possibility of a '*but.*' Yesterday we heard Father de Ravignan and the Abbé Dupanloup, and I assure you that neither of them suffered by comparison with the other. How I look forward to the pleasant '*far niente*' which awaits me with you at Baden, for I love you more than ever."

Alexandrine passed a part of the summer at Baden. She had the pleasure of meeting there the friend of her early youth—

Madame Wolff, that other Pauline to whom in spite of time and absence she had remained tenderly attached. During those short visits to Germany she enjoyed the society of Count Putbus, who always came to see her, and also that of many of the friends she had known at Berlin. Amongst them was M. de Radowitz, whom she saw at Carlsruhe with very special pleasure. I cannot write that dear and honored name without dwelling for a moment on a remembrance not exactly connected, perhaps, with this narrative, but which I cannot pass over in silence. M. de Radowitz had just lost his only daughter, who died at sixteen, in the full bloom of her youth, intelligence, and beauty. My husband and I had spent the last days and nights of her short and fatal illness with him and by her side. This mutual grief served to confirm the valued friendship which filled so great a place in our lives, and of which I would fain leave a record in these pages.

Some years afterwards, when M. de Radowitz was a member of the Parliament of Frankfort, he was described in an unfriendly spirit, as "the warlike monk," [der kriegerische Mönch], and I have always thought the name had a very applicable and glorious meaning. There certainly was something of the monk in that great man; somewhat of the monk's faith, knowledge, purity of heart and daily life; that long-continued habit of contemplating Divine mysteries with the eye of a Christian, and then boldly diving into the deepest recesses of the human mind. He had also the courage and the energy of a soldier and a love for the art of war, almost equal to his passion for study. This man, who had read everything and forgotten nothing, used to declare that he had no knowledge except of military affairs! He was married to a woman thoroughly worthy of him. This was the great and only happiness of his life, and with the exception of that immense blessing, he suffered from or because of everything he loved. Through Germany, his beloved Fatherland, through the Church, more beloved even than Germany; through his king, for whom his feelings were more those of a friend than a subject —and through his beloved children—for all these were made sources of affliction to him. A year after his daughter's death another was born, and his fatherly heart clung to her with all the passionate fondness which had made him so deeply feel the ruin of his first-cherished hopes; but this unexpected happiness proved only another mysterious trial, for in little more than a year this second child also died. To these bereavements succeeded numberless bitter sorrows, which soon brought him to the rest of his eternal Home.

A letter which he wrote me at the time of that last affliction is worth publication. Those who have known and loved M. de Radowitz will read it with emotion, and his name was famous enough at one time to make anything from his pen generally interesting. It will corroborate what I have said, and furnish an excuse for this digression, the only one I have allowed myself in the course of my narrative. While speaking of a year fraught with the remembrance of this dear friend, I could not resist the desire of paying a tribute to the memory of a man who was great in abilities, great in nobleness of soul, and possessed the excellent gift of making those he associated with better in mind and heart through the influence of his own virtue and genius.

"Berlin, July 5th, 1850.

"MY DEAR FRIEND—I have just received the excellent letter you sent me to Erfurth. I never for an instant doubted that your heart was with us during the sorrowful hours we have lately gone through; but I own that I felt a craving to hear from you the expressions of affection and sympathy in our grief. The loss of a child of fifteen months old would seem perhaps but a light affliction to those who have not known what my life has been during the last few years. But this little girl, which God had given us when we had abandoned all hope of such happiness, had looked to me like a token that life and its joys were not yet ended. Since the death of my daughter Mary, my existence has been in every way shattered. The terrible fall of a Government to which duty and affection bind me alike, seemed to me like the close of a life which I can speak of in Montlosier's words: '*Je ne l'ai point épargnée, mais que je n'ai pû la rendre utile.*'*

"A deep melancholy took possession of me, but that little angel had given me as it were a new life. Think, dear friend, what I felt by the side of her cot as she lay dying! The merciless torrent of political affairs forced me to Berlin, and at the moment when I was almost overwhelmed by the weight of an immense responsibility, a telegram brought me the news that my wife was dying. I signed the last protocol of the conferences before leaving, and then came back to Erfurth, God only knows

* I have not spared it, but failed to make it useful.

in what a state of mind. He did not break the bruised reed, He spared my wife, and may He be for ever blessed for this mercy! This is all I can tell you about ourselves, dear friend; but it is what you wished to hear. It is impossible to say what will become of us, even for the shortest time. My private life is still bound up with my political position, and I must patiently await the time when God will suffer me to retire from a whirlwind which is rather driving me than I directing it. The gladdest day for me will be the one when I shall be at liberty to shut myself up in some quiet place, and live only for my friends, my studies, and above all for that life to come, compared with which all the so-called great affairs of the world are in reality child's play. Let us hear from you, dear friend; there are not four people in the world I love so well as you. RADOWITZ."

It was during her last stay at Baden that Alexandrine spoke to me for the first time of a plan which she carried into effect not long afterwards, and about which we were not at that time quite of the same opinion. She wished to take an apartment in a convent at Paris as a *pied-à-terre*, when my mother was not in town. After she had left me we continued to discuss this subject in our letters, and two months later she wrote the following answer to what I had written on the subject:

"How can you, dearest sister, make any kind of apology for what you say about my poor lodging? Are not our hearts to be always open to each other? Can there be any comfort without this openness? No, and for that reason let me answer what you urge. First that I have admitted and do admit the admirable way in which you accepted my experiment of the religious life, but I wish you would, in a like manner, accept this trifling change which your imagination makes out to be something alarming. In reality I should not be oftener separated from you all than I have frequently been of late; for instance, last winter, which I spent in Paris without your mother. Adrian, who approves of this idea, says that it seems to him a very natural one for a poor unsettled being without a husband or children. The blessing of a religious vocation has not, alas! been granted me, but is not a pious life devoted to good works some kind of vocation? Your mother does not like Paris, and stays there as short a time as possible; is it not fair that I should have a hole, a tiny lodging of some kind, if it was only to store up the things I keep for my little works of charity, but which will leave me quite free to live all the rest of the year with her if I wish it? As to you, my dear old Paule, I would readily wager that I shall see you in that way a great deal oftener than I have lately done. Well, God's will be done in this as in everything else!"

Nothing certainly could seem more natural than this arrangement, or better adapted to the mode of life she had adopted. I am therefore almost inclined to look upon the extreme dislike I felt to it as a foreboding. But the fact was that I really felt afraid (a fear which the event too plainly justified) that when once left to herself, Alexandrine would deprive herself of many things which habit had made necessary to her, and which she had made use of as a matter of course whilst living with her relatives. My mother had the same fears, but, as usual, she abstained from any opposition which might have been influenced by her own wishes, and left Alexandrine quite free to act as she thought best. This new arrangement was not however carried into effect until the following year. Nothing further was said about it at the time I am speaking of, and the winter of 1847, like that of 1846, was spent by Alexandrine at Madame de Mun's home in the Rue de Penthièvre. My mother occupied an apartment under the same roof, and as I was in Paris that year, I saw them both every day.

Alexandrine returned to all her favorite occupations with an ardor beyond her strength, and a generosity beyond her means. To meet the deficiency in her resources, she gradually restricted her own expenditure to the narrowest compass, and deprived herself of everything short of absolute necessaries. One day I happened to look into her wardrobe, and was dismayed at its scantiness. When we any of us made this kind of discovery, she blushed and smiled, made the best excuses she could find in return for our scoldings, and then went on just the same, giving away all she possessed, and finding every day new occasions for these acts of self-spoliation. She had of course long ago sold or given away all her jewels and trinkets, but if she ever happened to find among her things an article of the smallest value, it was immediately disposed of for the benefit of the poor. For instance, one day she took out of its frame a beautiful miniature of Princess Lapoukhyn at the age of twenty, and sold the gold and enamel frame, defending herself by saying that it was the only thing of value she still possessed, and did not in the least enhance the value of her mother's charming likeness. Two black gowns, and a barely sufficient amount of linen, constituted her whole wardrobe, so that she had reduced herself as far as was possible in her position of life, to a state of actual poverty. Her long errands were almost always performed on foot, and at dinner-time she came home often covered with dirt and wet to the skin. One day, when she was visiting some Sisters of Charity in a distant part of Paris, one of them looked at her from head to foot, and then begged an alms for a poor woman much in need of a pair of shoes. Alexandrine instantly produced her purse and gave the required amount, with which the Sister went away, and in a quarter of an hour returned, laughing, and bringing with her a pair of shoes, which she insisted on Madame Albert's putting on instead of those she was wearing, which were certainly in the worst possible condition. On her return from these distant excursions, she usually put on her evening dress and came down to Madame de Mun's drawing-room, where she found my mother, who also had often been engaged in similar charitable duties. During that winter I often joined this little circle, now so thinned by death, and so soon to break up altogether. For one brief moment I would fain pause and look back in thought to that well-remembered room and its long table, at which my mother and Madame de Mun were wont to sit with Eugénie's children playing at their feet; and at the place near the lamp, where Alexandrine was to be seen every evening, with her head bending over her work; her brown hair divided into two long plaits, a way of wearing it which particularly became her, though it was certainly not chosen on that account. She did not however, profess to be free from all thought about her appearance,—on the contrary she was always accusing herself of still caring for admiration,—and when once she heard that somebody who had accidentally spoken to her had said she was pretty, she exclaimed with half-jesting indignation: "I really believe that if I were in my last agony that would please me still!" Very pretty certainly she looked on those evenings, in her simple black dress; always calm and serene, and brightening up whenever the great interests and objects of life were the subjects of conversation. Otherwise she remained silent, occupying herself with her embroidery, or else, taking her little book of extracts, so full of beautiful thoughts, from her pocket,—she read them over and added new ones from her favorite books.

Those coming and going to that drawing-room must have often watched and admired her; and any visitor who, from time to time, said things which coincided with her feelings, or related in her presence any facts interesting to the Church, or consoling to the soul, will never forget the beaming expression of her countenance, as she looked up, and, as it were, thanked them for their words. Ah! those dear visions of the past, it is indeed a blessed faculty which enables us to call them up again! Alexandrine was right when she said that imagination is a beautiful gift, *a magic mirror.*

She occasionally left this home-circle to visit the friends whose affection she had always considered as one of the chief blessings of her life. Foremost of all was Albert's friend, the dear companion of other days. Alexandrine's affection for M. de Montalembert never underwent the slightest change, and his wife was included in that friendship, and in their house she was always welcomed as a sister. Similar recollections attached her also to M. and Madame Rio, and she saw them as often as their frequent absence from Paris allowed. Madame de Gontaut she loved, revered, and looked up to as her pattern in the ways of charity. She also affectionately admired Madame Amédée Thayer, who proved the courageous and devoted friend of her latter days. These and a few other friendships of the same kind sometimes attracted her from home, but only into the most private circles, for nothing but the most strictly chosen society would have suited her mode of dress, or her wishes and tastes.

Time never hung heavy on Alexandrine's hands. After such trials and sufferings, she could say as Madame Swetchine did: "that life was lovely and happy; and ever as it went on, fairer, happier, and more interesting." The melancholy which was natural to her character in youth, and which the radiant happiness that for a moment filled up her life had not been able to overcome—that melancholy which was the sign perhaps of some kind of softness of soul, and which so many deaths, and such floods of tears could naturally have increased—had been completely put down and overcome by the love of God and the poor. One day as I saw her moving about her room which she had made so bare, with an air of the greatest gaiety, we both of us suddenly recalled the terrible days of the past when her grief had been full of gloom, and then she said what was very striking to any one who knew how deep was her unutterable love to the very last. "Yes, that is all true; those were cruel and dreadful days; but now by God's grace, *I mourn for my Albert gaily.*"

In the month of July, 1847, I was with my mother and Alexandrine at Boury. We were all met there for the first time after Albert's death, and there I was to see her for the last time. A few short days we spent together before our parting, which, as far as this world is concerned, was to last for ever. Perhaps—I may say it again—perhaps it was well for me that I knew it not; well for me that I could not foresee I was about to leave Alexandrine for ever; that when I prayed beside my mother in the Chapel, the thought never crossed my mind that that best and dearest happiness of my life was also drawing to a close; and that in leaving Boury, I knew not the deep significance of our last word—ADIEU.

Alexandrine and I talked over her intended change of abode. She had finally made up her mind to spend the time between her return to Paris in November and my mother's arrival there in February at the Convent of St. Thomas of Villanova. I opposed this plan with some warmth, which however I soon repented, and ended by begging her to forgive me, and yielded entirely to her arguments, for I felt it would be wrong to make any effort to withdraw her from Paris and the life she led there, or to deprive her of the happiness she found in it. I have already spoken of that happiness, but the last conversation that we held together impressed my mind in a remarkable manner. It struck me so much at the time that not to forget it I wrote down every word of it, little knowing the comfort I was laying up for myself. I shall make no change in those pages, but simply copy what I find in my journal.

"July 13th, 1847.

"The Eve of my Departure from Boury.

"We went to the cemetery as usual, to pray by the side of our two dear graves. Alexandrine knelt on the stone which covers both Albert's tomb and the resting-place which for the last twelve years had been marked out for her; while I knelt on Olga's grave. It was a warm and lovely evening. When we left the cemetery, we chose the longest way home, and walked slowly back. It was natural that on that beautiful evening, after our visit to the Church-yard, and alone with me, Alexandrine should dwell on the thoughts always uppermost in her mind. For my part, I liked better than anything else to hear her speak of God and her own soul, and lost no opportunity of drawing out her thoughts, for they always did me so much good. As we left a corn-field, and came upon the road leading to the house, I stood still a moment, to look at the sky, where the sun was setting in the midst of so radiant a glory that the whole dreary landscape looked beautiful in its light. I said to Alexandrine, 'I do so like the time of sunset!' 'I do not,' she replied. 'Since my troubles'—an expression she very seldom used—'Since my troubles the sunset has had a mournful effect upon me. It ushers in the night, and I do not like the night time. I like the morning, and the time of spring, for these are what most typify to me the realities of eternal life. Night is the symbol of darkness and sin; evening makes me think that everything draws to an end, and both of these are sad. But the morning and the spring remind me that everything will wake up and be born again. That is what I love.' We walked on, and just as we had passed through the gate, she said: 'Try and throw yourself into the thought, that everything that gives us such pleasure on earth is absolutely nothing but a shadow, and that the reality of it all is in Heaven. After all, is not love the sweetest thing on earth? Is it not, then, easy to believe that to love *Love Itself* must be the perfection of all sweetness? And to love Jesus Christ is nothing else, when we learn to love Him absolutely as we love on earth. I should never have been comforted if I had not learnt that that kind of love really exists and lasts for ever.' We sat down on a bench, still conversing. A little while after Alexandrine got up to gather a spray of the jessamine which clothed the wall. She gave me the spray, and then stood before me with a little sprig of it in her hand, continuing the conversation. I had said to her:—'It is a great blessing that you can love God in that way.' She answered me in words, and with an expression and bearing, which must always remain imprinted on my mind: 'Oh! Pauline! how can I help loving God—how can I help being carried away when I think of Him? How can I even have any merit in it like the merit of faith, when I think of the miracle which He has wrought in my soul, when

I feel that after having so loved and so ardently desired this world's happiness—after having possessed it and lost it, and been drowned in the very depths of despair—my soul is now transformed, and so full of happiness, that all I have ever known or imagined is nothing, absolutely *nothing* in comparison!' Surprised to hear her speak in this way, I said: 'But if life with Albert such as you dreamed, were placed before you, and it were promised you for a length of years——?' She answered without the least hesitation: '*I would not take it back.*'" Such were our last words together, and when I wish to think of her as she was on the day when we were to part for ever, I still see her standing before me near that bench, with her speaking countenance, her eyes upraised, holding that little spray of jessamine in her hand.

The next day I left Boury. Since that day I have many times been there to pray in the cemetery burial ground, but never once have I entered the house again.

The conversation I have just related should of itself have made me feel that the time had come when Alexandrine had nothing further to do on earth but to die. I wondered afterwards that it had not struck me, and that her words had not thrilled through my heart like a farewell. For the happiness which now filled her mind, so far surpassing that other earthly joy which she had renounced for the gift of faith, was but the forerunner of one more perfect, the "*refreshing dew*," as the Abbé Gerbet says, which falls before the coming day, whose brightness even now dawned upon her. But a vain wish mingles with that consoling thought, and desires that the beloved soul which has reached those heights, should be allowed to break its chains without effort, and escape a last conflict which my weakness shrinks from describing. For a moment, indeed, I thought of laying down my pen, and ending this record, while leaving on my readers' minds the bright image of Alexandrine, such as it appeared to me on the eve of our last farewell. But this would not be fulfilling my task, nor would it be doing entire justice to her holy and beloved memory. And then the crowning grace of her life—the sweetest, most powerful, and most encouraging example she has bequeathed to us would remain unrevealed.

My own share in Alexandrine's story is almost at an end. A few extracts from her letters between the time I left Boury and the beginning of her last illness in Paris, and my mother's later on, will conclude the picture of her life and death. Very dear and precious to me are those letters of my mother—for in describing the last days of her beloved adopted daughter, she was describing her own last earthly trial. The measure both of her sorrows and of the grace with which they were met, was filled to the brim beside Alexandrine's dying bed.

ALEXANDRINE TO PAULINE.

"I love you better than ever, dearest Pauline, and it is very sweet to me to feel that you love me. (As we advance in this sorrowful life, our friendships seem to take deeper root, and though some of its blossoms may fall to the ground, the fruit, which is far more precious, remains.) You made me lift up my heart in thanksgiving, for it is indeed true that after all the sorrows and the fears for myself and others, which nearly drove me to despair, nothing can be more wonderful than to find myself happier than I have ever been or hoped to be. And this in spite of a strange liability to depression, anxiety, and spiritual darkness which often affects my soul. When you come to think of it, what an admirable thing a soul is! How easy it is to feel, without entering into explanation, that *one* soul is of more value than the whole material world put together."

"October 20th, 1847.

"If I said I should like to see Gioberti* a Jesuit, I meant it only in the sense of an *atonement*, for God forbid I should be so foolishly and wretchedly narrow-minded as to wish everybody to have the same vocation. On the contrary, I particularly appreciate variety in unity. I say this every day. I wish people to understand that variety is necessary, and that no two leaves are alike. We want fruit-trees and forest-trees, lilies and blades of grass, drops of water and stones. . . . . Yes, indeed I do love happiness and comfort, to say the least of it, as much as you do; but do we ever really enjoy them on earth? Are not these things always in bulb, and never in flower in this world? And the more we do without them here, so much the more we shall enjoy them hereafter."

"Paris, November 6th, 1847.

"DEAR LOVE—I had intended to answer your letter briefly, and to say nothing more on the subject, but the Abbé Debeau-

* It was four years since we had known him at Brussels, and he had just published his book against the Society of Jesus.

vais* (who always inclines to the side of prudence and moderation) has just been saying that in our days it is cowardly not to show our love for the Society of Jesus. This has touched my pride, and you may now expect rather a *fiery* letter. Well, then, I *do* love the Society of Jesus, and I glory in loving it, without any party spirit, for I am ready to admire virtue and goodness wherever they exist. Do you suppose that the love of truth which God has given me burns less brightly in my soul since I have been in the focus of eternal light? Yes, I do love the Society of Jesus, and why? Because the most obscure and narrow-minded Jesuit teaches me to love our Lord Jesus Christ more than Gioberti with all his philosophy;† yet you know I like philosophy, and believe it to be a necessary instrument in the salvation of many souls. . . . . . You tell me that the great cause of animosity lies in this, that the Jesuits are an obstacle to the diffusion of liberal ideas; and this tempts me to exclaim, 'My Lord Jesus Christ, didst Thou say, "*Be ye liberal*," or "*Be ye perfect*"?' But do not imagine from this that I have no love for true liberty, for I love it whenever it is real, but then not so much as perfection. I do not deny that I am biassed on this subject, but by God's infinite grace the bias is towards '*Jesus Christ and Him Crucified*.' May I lean more and more to that side, and lose myself, heart and mind, in the depths of that knowledge, rather than be swayed by any amount of learning, genius, or eloquence, which could in the slightest degree draw me aside. St. Thomas of Aquin and St. Bonaventure knew nothing but '*Jesus Christ and Him Crucified*,' yet whose genius has ever surpassed the former of these great men? Everything is comprised in these few words, and neither of them would ever have ventured to write what Gioberti has written.‡ And do not tell me it is

* The Curé of St. Thomas d'Aquin, in Paris.

† She sent me at the same time this little fable:

"A king had a delicious garden, full of more or less beautiful flowers. One of the noblemen of his Court was always praising this lovely garden, but at the same time declaiming in a strange and violent manner against one variety of flower, and that not the least beautiful in the parterre, and which the king liked exceedingly. The nobleman wanted to root up this flower, and even went so far as to tear up several with his own hands. One day the king said to him: 'I am glad to see that you like my garden so much, but would it not show more love for it if you did not hate those particular flowers so much?'"

‡ I find in another letter the following excellent remarks upon Gioberti:—

"October 10th, 1847.—To return to the great Christian philosopher, Gioberti, and I call him so in no ironical sense, for you know I have always, and still do, look upon him as such. I think I have already told you that I admit the justice of the comparison you draw between him and Pascal. You also know that I am too Italian and too Roman not to understand the interest you both take in him. I also agree with you that ——— is unjust to him, and that you do right to rejoice at the effect he has produced in Germany. But I must remind you that Madame Swetchine was struck at once with the total absence his writings evince of the first the order that he attacks, and not its individual members. What would you feel if some one were to say, 'Those la Ferronnays are an anti-Christian, hypocritical family, always irreligiously disposed, but amongst them there is that good Pauline, and that pious little Albertine, who has such and such good qualities, etc.' I should prefer giving up individuals, not indeed to the good pleasure of their enemies, but so far as their accusations are proved. As to the order, so long as I see none that do more good than the Jesuits, so long as I find no better Confessors, Missionaries, or even Colleges elsewhere, I shall rest contented with their teaching, and satisfied with admiring the Society of Jesus.

"Yesterday I met the Abbé Dupanloup at Mde. de Gontaut's. He so far agrees with you in thinking the Jesuits are as unfortunate in being defended by ——, as in being attacked by Gioberti. But I do wish you could have heard him, and opened wide your ears, both of body and mind. It is time, my beloved sister, it really is time that your bright and clear intellect should no longer be led astray by the charms of genius and eloquence; —Divine rays, indeed, when they emanate from the living Light, but destructive and noxious beams when they diverge from that only true centre. It is well understood between us that all this discussion is not to interfere in the least with our friendship, the sweetest charm of my life. I am going soon to forget the world for a little while, or to look upon it from its Heavenly side. I shall often think of you during my eight days' retreat, and in the sacred Heart of our Lord."

"Paris, November 27th, 1847.

"What will you say to a letter beginning with these words:

'Death—application of the senses.'*

"I cannot help laughing about it in my solitude. It is the fruit of my retreat. Dearest Pauline, you must give yourself before long this spiritual enjoyment. You must allow your soul the benefit of those strong impressions which we would fain

principles of *asceticism*. The same gifts are not, of course, bestowed on all, but poor Gioberti ought to know that he is ignorant of the only really important science, that of the interior life, and it is this ignorance which renders him quite incapable of appreciating the Jesuits. I understand all the struggles of your mind and heart, but the heart is very large. Let us, like our beloved Lord, love everything that is worthy of love."

* While Alexandrine was going through the spiritual exercises, it occurred to her to write out for me the whole of the Meditation on Death, which had never before struck her so much. I was indeed a little surprised at the opening words of her letter, and the fact of her own death following so soon after, gave greater weight to the circumstance in my mind.

never lose, and which always have a ripening effect. Ah! people seek excitement, they will weep at a play over fictitious sorrows, and are affected by some imaginary event infinitely less important than the very least of those political changes which our friend Radowitz so nobly despised. And apropos of that, I admire all the grand ideas you unfold to me; but politics are after all merely that drama in which 'men vex themselves, and God leads them.' I can believe, though I have never seen it, that there may be a magnificent drama of politics, but as to the usual tissue of intrigues which go by that name, Radowitz is right; there will be no result, not even a little smoke. What a long parenthesis! Well, I was saying that as people find so great a charm in the excitement of emotions, they ought to seek it where it is all real, where we soon discover that the invisible world is far more real than the world before our eyes; scenes where we ourselves have a part to play in that *Divina Commedia* which has its own facts and characters—exceeding all that fiction can ever invent. We come out of retreat changed, amazed, and happy. Oh! dearest sister, give yourself this happiness.

"Mademoiselle Aubin, whom you remember at the Roule, and thought so agreeable, said that when she came out of retreat she felt like the Saint who used to ask: 'Do people still go on building houses?' In spite of my wandering mind, the same thing occurred to me when I returned to the noise and business of life. I can quite understand your feelings that nothing detaches you from earth like the *transfiguration of death*. Every one has their particular attraction, and must be left freely to follow it. But how can you say that you do not see the object of a meditation which makes us, as it were, actually *touch* what our bodies will become, when we are all so prone to love those bodies too much, and to think so little of their approaching end? If it only tended to humble us and show us our nothingness, it would still be very useful."

A few days before that last retreat, which proved to have been a special preparation for eternity, Alexandrine had taken possession of her little room in the convent of St. Thomas of Villanova; and at the end of her eight days' solitude she established herself in her new abode, and resumed with ardor all the pursuits to which her whole time was devoted. She had only come to

Paris at that time of the year, and only chose that humble lodging, that the poor might not be deprived of three months of a life she would like to have given up wholly to their service. Alone at Paris, and without any family or social duties to perform, she was able to give full scope to her charitable zeal. At all hours, and in all weathers, she went out on foot; and often returned shivering, wet to the skin, to a room where, to save the expense of fuel, she would not allow a fire to be kept up during her absence. Her food also was very different from the living to which she had been accustomed. It is impossible to say whether she injured her health by this mode of life, or whether, while combating what she looked upon as fatigue, she was not in reality struggling with the symptoms of incipient disease.

One morning at Mass in the convent Chapel, a lady happened to hear her cough, and noticing her pale looks and poor apparel, she went to one of the Sisters, and told her that there was a lady in the Church who was probably too poor to provide herself with necessaries, and that she should be very happy to supply her with milk daily, if she had not the means to purchase it. This kind soul was quite ashamed when the Sister told her the poor lady was Madame Albert de la Ferronnays; but Alexandrine, much amused, laughed exceedingly at the mistake, and did not treat herself better than before.

Thus things went on till the beginning of 1848, in so many ways a sad and memorable year, more so to me than any which had preceded it, with the exception of 1842—the most melancholy of my life. On New Year's Day, my mother being still absent, Alexandrine dined with my eldest brother, and all the members of our family then in Paris. She was flushed and feverish, which made her look well, but a few days afterwards she was obliged to take to her bed. On the 6th of January, in spite of the cold, and though very unwell, she would go to the Chapel to hear Mass and receive Communion. She had to go to bed again immediately afterwards. On the following day, feeling much worse, she sent for Madame Amedée Thayer, and though no one thought her illness dangerous, she earnestly begged to be anointed. This desire no doubt implied a strong conviction on her own part that her sickness was a serious one, but she had another motive for wishing to receive the last sacrament that day. And this was to spare my mother—who was expected the next morning—the emotion of witnessing a scene which must have painfully reminded her of so many previous trials of the same kind. But as it happened, my poor mother had already arrived. With her usual unselfishness, she gave up being with Alexandrine in that solemn moment, and remained praying in the convent Chapel, that she might not know how entirely her affectionate solicitude had failed of its end.

For some days Alexandrine did not apparently get worse, and my mother's letters contain the account of these hopes and fears, which she wrote as follows:

"Alas! my poor child, my own dear child, I think God intends to take her from us. It looks as if He had led her to this house to prepare for eternity. All those who helped to bring her here, have been no doubt the unconscious instruments of His will. *Our Lady of Deliverance*, near whom she was so pleased to come and dwell, will prove, I foresee, the pledge of her own deliverance from this world. It would be impossible to describe the state I am in. *This* fear, Pauline, had never crossed my mind. It may be that a little prudent care might have prevented her illness, but how can I tell that she would have taken those precautions even if I had been by her side? How can I be sure that I should have prevailed on her to do so, or that I should myself have discerned how serious her case was? For some time past she had looked pale and thin. We all urged her to take care of herself, and now and then she pretended to rest, but whenever any pressing case of necessity occurred, she was off that moment, without giving a thought to her health, and always walked such immense distances. And so, my poor Pauline, what can we say? Only that Almighty God sees fit to overwhelm us with trials, and we must submit to His will. He shows me every day more and more how unavailing are my prayers. I feel it acutely, but I have not a word to say against that either."

"February 5th, 1848.

"The dear child is not worse, and though excessively thin, she still looks well. But constant fever and oppression leave us very little hope, and if I have any, it is more in prayer than in physicians. I now see plainly that what induced her to come here, was her love of poverty, and I am sure it was on that account that Father de Ravignan gave his consent. Every day that passionate love of poverty seems to grow upon her, and there can be no doubt that when once left to herself, her life was a series of privations. And yet I reproach myself for having tried to prevent her from coming to this home, and for having looked upon her resolution from a merely human point of view, for it is clear to me now, that God was disposing everything according to His own designs for this dear child; that He placed her where she was preparing for death without knowing it, and that He accepted her intention of leading a life of poverty, detachment, and close union with Himself. What a reward for her; but oh! what grief to us!"

"February 8th.

"We are in constant expectation of the final blow, but it has not fallen yet. Perhaps at this very moment you are receiving the letter in which I gave you some slight hopes, for I myself had began to hope again a little. But she is so weak, that no remedies take effect. Nature does not help us. It is her zeal which has killed her, and this should not have been allowed. Still its certainty does not lessen the holiness and merits of a life God is about to crown. Poor dear, admirable child! she speaks quite simply of her death, and yesterday she said: 'Mother, let us speak openly about it.' Dearest Pauline, I assure you that I thank God that you are away, and that it is impossible for you to come. It is for me a slow martyrdom, and it is difficult to understand how one can live through such anguish. My God, how little we foresee what is in store for us! . . ."

"Paris, February 9th, 1848.

"My poor Dearest Child—It is all over! Albert and Alexandrine are now united for ever. O! my God, my God! what a hard decree is this for us; but yet no doubt a merciful one for her, for it seems evident that she was so ready to go that nothing remained for her but to mount up to Heaven, and when that is the case our prayers and tears avail but little, for God hastens to summon his bright and shining soul to eternal glory. In the midst of all anguish, you were continually in my thoughts. What I was suffering told me what you would suffer, and you know, my poor beloved child, how my broken heart melts with tenderness for you. But I must give you the sad details while I have strength, and it is a comfort to speak of that dear child. I wish I could make her poor mother share all the consolation we derive from the recollection of her holy example. And oh! how my heart aches when I think of her!

"Yesterday Alexandrine was very restless and in great pain, and in the evening she said to Hortense, [Madame A. Thayer,] that she should much like to take a composing draught which Cruveilhier had ordered, but that she was afraid it would vex me because I preferred homeopathy. I hastened to say that I held to nothing but what would give her relief, upon which she took the draught, and it refreshed and calmed her. When I kissed her and wished her good-night, she asked me to make my usual *little sign of the Cross on her forehead*, desiring me to tell you *how much she loved you.* I went into the other room to say my prayers and lie down on the bed, but ready to jump up at the first alarm. Madame Thayer came to me a few minutes afterwards, and said the composing draught had done Alexandrine so much good that she felt quite relieved. 'And so I hope,' she added, 'that the night will be a quiet one.' 'Alas!' I answered with a sort of fright, 'there is often an improvement of this kind before the end.' She assured me that she did not think this was likely; on the contrary, she thought that she might linger yet for several days. With this hope I went to sleep about eleven o'clock. I woke at three in the morning, and heard Madame Thayer's maid go up to her bedside. I sprang up and ran to Alexandrine, when one of the Sisters said she had just been about to call me, because she thought Alexandrine was getting weaker. Sœur Marie then came up, and when she had looked at her, told me she thought the end was very near. It was a great shock even though I had been expecting it. When Alexandrine saw us she said: '*Do you think I am worse?*' The Sister answered: 'Yes.' A moment afterwards Alexandrine said again: '*But what makes you think I am going? I do not feel worse than usual.*' The Sister told her she was getting weaker, but all I could do was to press her hand. She was calm, and though she breathed with difficulty, still she could very well say all she wished. At one moment she thought something they were giving her to moisten her mouth was intended to revive her strength and so prolong her life, and this seemed to distress her. They told her it was not so, and Hortense bade her have no such fears; that she was going to die, and in a few moments would see God. Albertine, Adrian, Charles, and Fernand, had all been quickly summoned and now arrived. The prayers for the agonizing were said. Alexandrine made the responses in a firm and distinct voice, and repeated all the short prayers and ejaculations suggested to her. For one short moment she underwent some kind of sharp agony, and her mind seemed to wander. She thought she had not received the Sacrament; and asked why there were no prayers said. She seemed frightened because she did not see a priest by her side. This was painful, but it lasted only a moment, and was like a last trial. Sœur Marie told her that she must not fear, that God was with her, and that she must put her whole trust in Jesus Christ. She then grew perfectly calm, and said: '*You have done me great good! There is peace again!*' Father de Montezon,* with two other priests, then came in. Father de Montezon gave her the last blessing and the plenary indulgence, and continued to pray beside her. She joined in the prayers, and every time the names of Jesus, Mary, and Joseph were pronounced, she repeated them after him. Even after she seemed to be for some time unconscious she put up her lips to kiss the Crucifix. At half-past eight o'clock she breathed her last. Dear angel, she is gone to be for ever with her Albert, and with all our dear ones in Heaven, and we can weep for nothing but our own loss! . . . .

"My dearest daughter, I scarcely know where I am, or whether I am alive or in a dream. What life will now be to me I cannot think, but I will not trouble myself about that, or even think of it. Comfort yourself, my blessed child, with the thought that she is near you. She said, 'I am sure that I shall be near her; that I shall see you all.' She longed to depart, and the day before yesterday was grieved at thinking that she would not *that night* see God! Everything in her life was specially ordained, and this is another of those moments in which we can only humble ourselves in marvelling worship of God's decrees. That dear child will pray so much for you. She said so several times, and the enclosed letter which she wrote you a few hours before her death, will be your best comfort. You know that she wrote to her mother too, on her deathbed. May God support her and you too, my child! Let us try to live in Heaven with them."

This is Alexandrine's last letter:—

* Father de Ravignan was absent at that time, and in an almost hopeless state of health. He began to recover immediately after Alexandrine's death.

"My most dear Sister and Friend—God, Who orders everything for the best, has surely wisely ordained it that you should not be here. I wished for you most earnestly, but what does it matter? We are not really divided, and I shall soon be where the wonderful communion we all have in God is understood. I hope I shall be able to look down upon you; but pray for me a great deal when I am in Purgatory. It requires such purity to enter Heaven, but still through God's grace I meekly trust in His exceeding mercy. I shall love you more than ever where all is love. Those other precious ones and I shall speak together. But Oh! why do I not speak of what it will be to see God, and the Blessed Virgin, and all Angels and Saints, and to be freed from the many dreadful sorrows of this life of sin! Give my love to Augustus, whom I never separate in my heart from you."

When she had finished these lines, she wished to write to her mother, and devoted to her the last effort of strength:—

"My poor dearest Mamma—I am not better, but I hope nothing will shake your trust in God, which I know is so strong, and which will lead you to truth and love. We shall meet again—we shall never be divided; but that it may be so, you must offer your dear will most truly to God, and follow the one only light which will help you to find that blessed way, whose happiness I feel now more deeply than ever. I entreat of you, as I have so often done before, to ask the Blessed Virgin, the Mother of Mercies, every day to show you the way. You know how I love, how I reverence you, and how much more now I should suffer at the thought of your sufferings, if I did not leave you in the Arms of God, to Whom we can trust all things. Farewell! We shall meet again, as I know, and then it will be where there is no more sorrow, and where we shall possess that infinite happiness of never offending God. I always include the good Prince in all my loving feelings for you."

She had dictated these two letters; but at the end of the one to her mother she traced with her dying hand these words in German:—

"*Liebe süsse Mama!*" [Dear, sweet Mamma].

Such was the last act of her life, and such her last thought on earth.

Alexandrine's story is ended, and there is little more to add; now that the last of the three beloved sisters who form the subjects of this story has breathed her last, it may be thought time to take leave of the readers who have followed me from one dying scene to another. But at the close of a glorious day it is still meet to gaze on its reflected light; and when music dies on the ear, we sometimes strive to catch the last lingering sounds as they float away into space; and therefore blessed and peaceful deaths leave behind them also their bright light and tuneful echoes, which we are loath to lose. Perhaps, then, my readers may be willing to gaze with me yet awhile on the image of the departed Alexandrine, to lend ear to the last accents of her voice, and to accompany her mortal remains to that tomb where long ago her place had been prepared by Albert's side.

MADAME DE LA FERRONNAYS TO PAULINE.

"Paris, February 10th.
"The Anniversary of Olga's Death.

"MY POOR CHILD—You are hearing Mass to-day for our dear Olga, and it is to-morrow that you will hear of our new sorrow, which is such an intense one to me, but which I feel more deeply still on your account. Beloved child! you are always present to my thoughts; but what can your poor old mother do to heal so cruel a wound? God alone can do this, and that dear friend, in the midst of her present happiness, will not forget the sister who mourns her loss with a breaking heart; she will obtain for her the consolation she so much needs. You must not distress yourself about the wish she had expressed to live at the beginning of her illness, and which had surprised you in Alexandrine; it only lasted a short time. During the last ten days, she more than wished, she passionately desired to die.* Every delay was irksome to her. She was continually asking *how long she would last*, and when she was told, 'perhaps a few days,' she used to say, with regret, '*Then I shall not see God to-day!*' Once she said, '*Let Pauline know how very sweet it is to die.*' And another time, turning to me: '*And you, dear mother, do you not also long to see God?*' Yet, coward that I am, I felt afraid that she would carry me off with her into the next world, just as she had tried to take

* On one of those days as Madame de Gontaut was sitting with her, and said something which implied that she was not so dangerously ill as she supposed, Alexandrine exclaimed, "Oh! no, do not say so—let me taste the sweet thought of death!"

me with her into the noviciate of the Daughters of Sion, and to share her retreats, and then to live in this house. I told her I had not courage to call upon death in that way, and that it was enough for me to leave myself in God's Hands, Who would do with me as He would.

"Now I am going to pray beside her *if I can.* To-morrow there will be a service at l'Abbaye au Bois, and then your brothers and Adrian will take her to Boury, with my new sorrow in that sorrowful place. Alexandrine has left everything she had power to leave to two charitable institutions. God bless you, my poor child!"

THE SAME TO THE SAME.

"Paris, February 15th, 1848.

"Alexandrine had asked, as you know, to be buried *like the poor.* To carry out her wishes, we had no hangings placed in the Church, and everything was done as simply as possible. But it was nevertheless crowded with people, for the interest felt about her, and the sorrow for her loss, are universal. After the service the coffin was placed in the carriage which was to take it to Boury. Your brothers and Adrian had the consolation of accompanying it. I stayed behind in the Church, and only went away when everybody else had left it. When they arrived at Boury, where the news of her death had only been announced on the Sunday before, there was a general outpouring of grief and dismay among the poor, at the idea of their dearly-loved saint coming back to them in this way. The whole neighborhood assembled to meet the corpse, and filled the Church on the following day. The coffin rested that night in the Chapel of the château, and the funeral took place the next morning, amidst the most touching manifestations of grief and reverence. The Confraternity would not allow any one but their own members to carry her to the grave, and they laid her themselves by the side of her husband. And so they are once more together, and that empty place is filled up now. I scarcely know if I am awake or dreaming. There is a total loss of everything which had again begun to make up a new life for me. This is, at any rate, what I feel at this moment. It will not be till I see you again, till I hold you in my arms, my dearest child—you, my only life in this world—that I shall begin to feel a little alive again; but the thought of your affliction breaks my heart."

I then received the following letter from the friend most closely connected with the troubled days of Alexandrine's brief happiness, as well as with the serene and holy end of her life.* It describes her as she appeared to him on her death-bed, and this will be the finishing touch to the picture which these pages have sought to produce.

"I am slowly recovering from an illness which was very near being a brain fever, and which kept me from witnessing the last moments of one whom we shall never again see on earth. But before my sickness began, I did see her on what was to be her death-bed, and I shall never, please God, forget the beautiful serenity of her countenance, the evident tokens of God's benediction resting upon her. On Sunday again—I never saw her afterwards—we spoke of you. In all she said there was as much, or even more than usual of the poetic beauty which lent so great a charm to all her expressions of piety or affection; all her own graceful and appropriate ideas, which never failed to exhibit religion under the sweetest and most attractive form. And then that ardent love of the Church, so rare in our days even amongst the most pious; so calculated to kindle love in us, and serve as our example. Ah! may we prove ourselves worthy of that great example God has given us in so gentle and winning a form! And now you are the only surviver of that group of devoted friends whom everybody admired and envied, and whom I looked upon as the perfect ideal of Christian friendship, and happiness on earth. Nobody was more completely identified than myself with the ideas and feelings personified, as it were, by you and your two sisters, and the blow which has fallen upon you strikes me to the depths of my heart. Alexandrine was the last link which connected me with the recollections of my youthful and troubled life in Italy, previous to the beginning of my political career. How can I ever forget what she and Albert were to me at Pisa? Let us always keep up our friendship, for we have passed the age when it is possible to replace by new affections those which death or other causes destroy. Alexandrine is hap-

* On the 9th of February, M. de Montalembert had written in his diary, the following lines:

"She has died happy. It has been a blessed end. She kept constantly repeating: 'I feel perfectly satisfied. I want nothing. Is it possible that this can be death? that it should be so easy to die. Where are those agonies of death I had dreaded so much? Mind you tell Pauline that it is nothing, nothing at all to die in this way. I die happy and joyful. I shall go to Heaven. I shall see Albert again, and Eugénie, and Olga. It will be so delightful!"

py—for ever happy now. I think we may rest on that belief, with a firm and consoling trust. Your old and faithful friend,

"MONTAL."

The year 1848, marked at its outset by Alexandrine's death, witnessed also my mother's departure from this world. But before entering on the subject occupying the few remaining pages of this book, I lift up my heart for one moment to God, and thank Him for all the joys I have known, the tears I have shed, and even for the apparently hard dispensation which ordained that my mother should so soon follow that long train of dear departed souls to the grave—she to whom I have no fear in ascribing all the blessings and consolation which attended the many trials of this record.

We cannot of course penetrate the secrets known only to God, but if we could discern what prayers had obtained such special mercies, there would not be one amongst us who would hesitate to attribute them to the petitions which rose day by day from the tender, and pure, and fervent, and humble heart of our mother. Even while I write these words I seem to hear the voices of the beloved dead confirming my belief that her first joy on entering Heaven was to hear them bless her for their happiness.

The last letter I received from my mother was dated on the 15th of February. The events which followed so close upon that day increased her desire to seek shelter with us in Germany. Baden was not yet invaded by the revolutionary torrent, and when she arrived there with my young sister in the beginning of March, it was with the full intention of settling there and never leaving me again. This hope was realized, but it was a short-lived happiness. I am, however, deeply grateful that those days with her were granted to me, and that in the great affliction which ensued, I enjoyed consolations so often denied me in other sorrows, and so abundantly vouchsafed on this occasion.

On All Souls' day—the 2nd of November, I suddenly awoke in the midst of a sad dream. I got up and hastened to the Church, where Mass was said at seven. It was hung with black on account of the day. I had dreamt that I saw my mother dying, and the sight of the black hangings gave me pain. I mentioned it to her when I came home, with a little emotion and much joy that it had been only a dream. A week afterwards, my mother was ailing, but so slightly that it seemed absurd to be anxious. Still I could not help feeling a little uneasiness, though everybody told me there was no cause for it. She scarcely suffered at all, and went on in this way for four days. But on the 14th of November, the doctor suddenly told us that she was in danger, and an hour afterwards, that the case was hopeless! For her, this seemed indeed a sudden and unexpected summons; for us, a terrible shock.

Sentence was pronounced at seven o'clock in the evening. What followed, is described in some hardly legible pages, written in the midst of my anguish, through a nervous apprehension that grief might affect my memory, and blot out of my mind the blessed words I had heard from her lips. As she was coming out of the bath, leaning upon me, and I was thinking how I could break to her what the doctor had told us, she said: "But I cannot see anything. I think I am going to die. I believe this is death. My God, I give Thee my heart, my soul, my will, and my life!" Oh what joy those words gave me at that terrible moment! I knelt down and begged her to make her little usual sign of the Cross on my forehead.* She did so, both for me and for Albertine, and then for Augustus, and laid her hand on his head. I asked her to forgive me everything I had ever done to vex her. She answered with a smile: "Oh! yes, certainly," and added in a moment, "I assure you that I think of death with great joy; but, my children, why have you not sent for a priest?" We had sent for her confessor, who was a very infirm old man, and the answer had been, that he would call the next day. "To-morrow?" my mother said; "perhaps to-morrow will be too late." We then offered to send for the Curé of the parish, though he did not speak French, and asked her if she wished to receive Extreme Unction immediately. "Yes—yes, certainly," she answered, and a moment afterwards said: "*Your dream is coming to pass.*" While we were waiting for the priest, she explained to me some little matters with regard to her last wishes, and then spoke of the Curé, who knew no language but German, which she could hardly speak at all. "But to be sure," she

* That was the way in which she used always to give us her blessing.

said, "I went to confession a few days ago,* and since then the only thing I have on my conscience is what I said to you the other day about Father de Ravignan." What she alluded to was this: I had been entreating her to take more care of her health, and not to go out fasting before seven o'clock in the morning, when the ground was covered with snow, and added that if Father de Ravignan had been there, he would have said the same thing. She had answered: "I am not so sure of that; those good fathers are sometimes harder upon us than upon nuns!" Ah! such were the words for which my sweet, saintly mother blamed herself; such the only self-reproach which troubled her conscience when about to appear before God!

At nine o'clock the Curé came, and we left her alone with him for a little while, and then returned to be present whilst she received Extreme Unction, which she did with a calmness which no words can describe. Afterwards she seemed better, and inclined to sleep. Nothing indicated the immediate danger which the physician had spoken of. I left the room for a moment, but Albertine hastily called me back. My mother had tried to get up, and fainted. She looked dying then, but after a while she rallied again, and we lifted her into her bed. She fell asleep, and for some hours we could not help indulging hopes. Towards three o'clock she once more tried to stand, and this brought on a sort of convulsion, which frightened us. Augustus was at her feet; I supported her in my arms. With Albertine's assistance we again placed her in bed. As she was sitting upon it before lying down, I noticed in her face the great and solemn change—that change preceding death, which in her case was very beautiful. Her large, soft eyes seemed to be looking beyond this world, and as soon as her head rested upon the pillows, she said to me in a calm, distinct voice: "Give me your father's Crucifix." It was the one he had held in his hands when he was dying. She took it into her hands, and it was then only that she loosed her hold of the little case which contained my father's picture, which she had never been without. At night it was always put under her pillow, and up to the moment I speak of, she had constantly held it in her hand. But now she took the Crucifix, kissed it tenderly, and said, as she had done before: "*My God, I give thee my heart, my soul, my will, and my*

* She used to go to Communion every morning, and had confessed three days before.

life ;" and then repeated Olga's dying words: "*I believe, I love, I hope, I repent.*" She had said to me three years before: "Olga said everything in those four words. I should like to die with those words on my lips." And this she did. I knelt down again by her side, and began the Litany of the Blessed Virgin—my dear mother followed and repeated every word—then she made the sign of the Cross again on our foreheads, and said: "I bless you all, absent and present, elder ones and younger ones." Then taking up the Crucifix, she looked at it with an indescribable expression of love, and exclaimed: "*Soon—Soon!*" Then in the same voice, and with the same expression, she several times repeated: "*My God, I commend my soul into Thy hands. I give Thee my heart, my soul, and my life. I believe, I hope, I love, and I repent.*"

I said aloud a *Pater*, an *Ave*, and a *Memorare*, because she had asked me the day before to say them to obtain for her a happy death. She repeated these prayers after me, and then a *Credo* by herself. I heard her distinctly saying: "*I believe in the resurrection of the body, in the Communion of Saints.*" These two articles of the Creed have always remained fixed in my mind with the very tone of her voice. Ah! my God! After that she dozed a little, and then awoke somewhat troubled, and said: "*O! my God! O! my God!*" as if in pain. We began to pray again, and she became quite calm, and repeated everything after us. While we were saying the Litany of the Blessed Virgin she ceased to speak, but at each answer pressed Augustus by the hand, till she gently fell back into my arms and breathed her last. As long as she could see, her eyes seemed to follow me, and for more than two days her face retained the same expression. All the sweet beauty of her soul and of her life were heightened in death. Dear, beloved, gentle, and holy mother of mine! pray for your children. For those who are now with you. For those you have left behind.

My brothers came a week afterwards to remove the beloved remains to Boury, and there they rest between the tomb of Albert and Alexandrine, and Olga's early grave.

L'ENVOI.

THIS record is ended. There is nothing to add to the joy, the sorrow, the consolation, and the example of those whose story it contains. Let all who have read it with pious interest, now of their great charity beg of God that the writer may have grace to be faithful to the example vouchsafed to her; and if, in concluding, she may add one other petition, it shall be in the words of the opening prayer: "O! my God, grant to those who loved Thee so deeply in life, after death to kindle Thy love in the hearts of men."

THE END.

APPENDIX.

ONE evening, in Venice, (the 4th of April, 1836,) Fernand brought the first portion of the following passages to Alexandrine, who read them with great emotion. At a time when her love was seeking through so much suffering and with such ardor to find its way to faith, truth, and the love of God, it can be easily imagined what an effect these pages produced upon her mind. They will also show how Eugénie's ardent piety must have helped Alexandrine, at this important and sad moment of her life, to rise above this world.

EUGENIE'S NOTE BOOKS, 1835–1836.

"Is this wish to die a presumptuous feeling, my God? Am I then so certain that I should go to Thee? All men's thoughts are known to Thee. It is Thou, my God, who hast placed me in this happy position in which I have no opportunity of doing harm. I do not make a merit of it, for I know very well that if the least temptation should present itself, I should immediately do wrong, for I am wicked, and all the more wicked because Thou givest me moments of such fervent devotion. Yes, it is true, I wish to die because I would see Thee, my God, but it is Thou who givest me that wish. I know this, so there is no presumption in it. O! save me from the danger of thinking myself good. Keep my heart for Thyself, and when I am in the world, where my head is so easily turned, strengthen me by the remembrance of this time of sensible devotion. Strengthen me, because, though I see the dangers of the world, I yet am amused. I lose my head, and my poor heart shuts up, because I have not time to listen to it. Keep me, therefore, O my God, for I am Thy child. Surely I am Thy child. If I am likely to do harm in the world, let me die first. To die is a reward, for to die is to go to Heaven, but if I do what is wrong, I shall have to wait a long time before I get there.

"Come, O, my God! I love Thee so much! The very thought of Thee and of Heaven where I wish to go, enflames my heart. Thou wilt surely let me go there; I only hope not to be afraid at the last moment. Send me other trials, my God, but not that one.

"Death has always been the favorite idea of my life; it has always smiled upon me. Thou wilt not permit that at the last moment that continual idea of going to Thee should forsake me. I have tried to examine myself by imagining myself very ill, dying in a room saddened by disease and suffering.

"Well, I could not find in my heart any feeling of fear. Again, I saw myself surrounded by all the happiness earth can give; about to stand before the Altar, the bride of one I loved and who loved me, and dying before I approached it. And, my God, Thou knowest that the vision of these earthly joys vanished before the better one of going to Thee! I have imagined myself dying suddenly, assassinated, poisoned, everything most miserable, and always the thought 'My God! Take me! My God! let me go to Thee' was uppermost. Nothing has ever been able to make death frightful to me, nothing has made the word 'death' a mournful one. It always sounds to me sweet and bright. It is always united in my mind with those two other beautiful words 'love and hope.' Couldst Thou deny me the joy of dying without fear! O, no, my beloved Heavenly Father! Thou wilt never deny it me, for I am Thy child, and I love Thee, and Thou knowest what Thou hast promised to that Word!

"There is in me a droll mixture of vanity and shyness. I often wish, out of vanity, to talk to people whose opinion I greatly value. I want to show that I can enter into certain ideas and feelings; and then all at once I feel awkward, confused, and as if I should never find words if I attempted to speak, and all my wish to show off disappears. I put on at once a stupid, indifferent manner lest any one should suspect me of having any sense, and should think of speaking to me. This happened to me the other day with the Abbé Martin. I wanted to ask him if it was presumption in me always to think of Heaven when I think of death. From two or three words he said to me, I fancied he did not consider me capable of serious thoughts, and feared to weary me by conversing gravely, and I took it into my head to show him he was mistaken. But as I was about to open my lips, I felt myself blushing and confused, and inwardly said: 'Oh! how much easier it is to be ignorant, or to seem so, at least, and to be taken for a fool. What nonsense it is to condemn myself from time to time to this little punishment in order to satisfy my vanity, and, after all, to display what?' I am quite contented that everybody should think me still more ignorant than I am. 'Blessed are the poor in spirit!' This is better than knowledge, and certainly better than vanity.

"Life is fatiguing, because it is made up of fits and starts. This is wearisome, but consoling when we find ourselves in a bad mood, because we can make sure it will not last, and I can quite understand that God should not allow those happy moments of fervent, burning devotion, in which we seem to care no longer for earth, and think only of Heaven, to last a long time. Those moments are His chiefest graces, and it is only now and then He bestows them. One such instant in a lifetime would call for eternal gratitude, for that sort of happiness is a foretaste of Heaven.

"To return to what I was saying, we pass from one state to another, and now, after the long and happy time of fervor I have had, I feel getting colder. It is disagreeable, and I pray less well. If I was to go out in the world now, I should be losing my head again, as I used to do; not quite so foolishly, however, I hope, for it seems to me that God has established in my heart a solid love of goodness and of Himself, which I do not lose even in my giddiest moments, and this prevents the illusions of amusement from taking entirely possession of me, and helps me to return to God. I keep always speaking to Almighty God, and I believe this to be a good plan, for He always hears. Thus I thanked Him lately for the good mood I was in, because it was all full of Him. Now, that is changing, I say: 'Well, my God, let it be as Thou wilt, but do not quite abandon me. It is precisely in the world that I require Thy Presence, because of its dangers, and that the devil is there, on the watch for my soul. To mix a little bit in the world is not bad for me. It is rather good than otherwise, for it teaches me its little worth, and sends me back to Thee with an increase of love. But then, my God, Thou must only loose Thy hold of me a little, just only enough to try me. Thou must never quite let me go. I will cling to Thee; my God, do not forsake me.'

"Everything we say to God is a prayer, and when the mind cannot apply, a conversation with our Blessed Lord may sometimes supply the place of our ordinary devotions. We must always think of God, if only to think that we do not think of Him enough. We must complain of it to Him, and in His great goodness He will recall our wandering thoughts. For my part I leave everything to His care, and wish nothing but as He wills, for I know that the only thing I cannot desire can never be His will, which is, that I should cease to be His child. When I feel nothing but dryness, I offer up to Him that trial. He then gives me, in return, greater graces than before, and the Devil is outwitted. And now I must go to bed. May God and His holy Angels watch over me!

"Well, I am now fallen into that terrible fit of dryness, which I was so afraid of. My God, Thou seest the state I am in! How badly I pray, with what distractions! with what indifference! It is very terrible, and of all the trials God sends the hardest to endure. It matters little what we suffer, if only we can speak to Him, and pray and feel Him near to us; all then becomes easy. I do not ask, my God, not to have trials—on the contrary, I desire them—I do not want to be too happy; I am frightened when I think I have had as yet nothing but happiness in my life! I am afraid of earthly joys; I always fear they will delay those of Heaven, and that an uninterruptedly happy life can never earn the same reward as one full of sufferings, but Thou hast ordained everything, my God, as is best for us. So there is nothing more to be said. Thou hast made me what I am, and hast ordered my lot so as to make gratitude a familiar word and an easy feeling to me, overwhelmed as I am with blessings. Thy will be done; perhaps Thou art preparing future trials for me, only do not deprive me of the power to pray. I suffer this evening; it is an immense trial not to be able to express my love to Thee, my God, to whom alone I would fain belong. Have mercy on me. Everything seems to fail when my only strength forsakes me. Prayerless days are lifeless days. Give me new life, my God, my God! Oh! to die and be certain that one will never more commit sin, never more offend God. To be for ever delivered from that terrible fear!

"To think that I should offend Thee, my God, whom I love so devotedly! and I do offend Thee a thousand times over; by slight offences, perhaps, but not slight in Thine eyes, when committed by those to whom Thou givest immense happiness in devotion and prayer, by those to whom Thou makest goodness easy and sin hard. O! yes; a slight offence is a crime in me, and my daily, hourly fear is to commit faults. Send me sorrows, sickness, trials, but not the blindness which takes evil for good, not that self-deceit wherewith we make to ourselves a false conscience. That is what I most fear. My God, Thou hast said we cannot serve two masters. My heart is too entirely devoted to Thee to be still with the world, and therefore I am not at peace even in the midst of happiness. It is only at Thy Feet I want to be happy, only in the utterance of Thy adorable Name; and, in fact, that is my only real joy. My heart beats with that joy when I enter a Church. I repeat Thy Divine Name a thousand times, and then the name of Mary, because Thy lips were wont to utter it. Let me die rather than offend Thee. I love Thee, and Thee only, my God."

"BOURY, 1836.

"It is strange how often in the book we are reading a passage meets our eyes which seems to fall in with our frame of mind at the moment. This is always happening to me. This morning, after I had been thinking for a long time that nothing can really make us happy but the love of God on earth, and then death, which takes us to Him, I opened my little 'daily monitor,' and found in it these lines for the day—

'Take my poor heart, and let it be
For ever closed to all but Thee.
Seal Thou my breast, and let it wear
That pledge of love for ever there.'

Yes! my God, I will meditate upon Thee without ceasing. I will muse on the day when I shall at last behold Thee. I will always think of death, that so I may die thinking of Thee. How strange the world is! Nothing seems to worldly people more natural than to be engrossed with the love of a creature, and they cannot understand how the love of God can take possession of a soul. Would that my heart could be laid open, they would see then how true this is. It is sweet, no doubt, to love as much as we can possibly love our dear ones on earth, but nothing can be so sweet as to die and go to God. O, my God, whom I love supremely, what shall I do? Thou hast said 'We cannot serve two masters.' What shall I do, then? I am Thine, and Thou art mine. Vouchsafe, then, to take me to Thyself.

"'1. Out of the depths have I cried unto Thee, O Lord; Lord, hear my voice.

"'2. Let Thine ears be attentive to the voice of my supplication.

"'3. If Thou, O! Lord, wilt mark iniquities; Lord, who shall abide it?

"'4. For with Thee there is merciful forgiveness, and because of Thy law, I have waited for Thee, O Lord.

"'5. My soul hath waited on the Lord, my soul hath hoped in the Lord.

"'6. From the morning watch even until night: let Israel hope in the Lord.

"'7. For with the Lord there is mercy; and with Him is plentiful redemption.

"'8. And He shall redeem Israel from all his iniquities.'

"To think that this is a prayer for the *dead!* each word is one of joy, hope, and trust.

"God condemns only those who *despair*, those who refuse to be saved. He is always ready to forgive. What love there is in each of the words he addresses to us, and how little in our thoughts of Him!" . . . .

"March, 1836.—My God, everything is possible to Thee. I do not complain of the trials Thou sendest in this world, but vouchsafe to hear the prayer which I make with the deepest faith. Accept an exchange of trials. Let Albert recover, and give me his illness. Let me suffer a long time, till I am fit to die, and then let me go to Thee. This will still be a trial for them all, for they will grieve to lose me. It is not therefore a release from suffering that I pray for. What I ask is, for one suffering to be exchanged for another. I know that trials are the only way to Thee. My God, everything is possible with Thee. Remember the Centurion. Remember Jairus's daughter. Remember all them who said to Thee with faith, 'Heal this child,' or 'Heal this man.' See, my God, with what faith I cry, 'O! Lord, heal Albert!' Give me his sickness, let it be terrible, let it be like a fire in my breast, to purify my heart. Let my throat suffer sharply to make up for the faults of vanity I have committed when my voice was admired, and I took pleasure in being listened to. Punish me, O! my

God, for I am full of vanity. I will bless every pain, and then when I shall have been ill a long time, Thou wilt let me die. O! everything, everything to obtain that! To obtain to go to Thee, my God, my only Love! There is no word impossible with Thee. Hear my prayer. The world will be surprised, and it will say it is inexplicable! Albert so weak, and so sickly, recovers; and Eugénie so strong, and so healthy, dies! And I shall say to myself: Cannot God do what He pleases? God has so willed it—this explains it all.

"Is it a foreboding that Thou wilt grant my request which makes me unable to fix my thoughts on any future prospect as regards myself? When marriage is spoken of, an interior voice seems to whisper to me: 'Do not trouble yourself about it. It is of no use.' Is this the voice of my Guardian Angel? Dear Angel, carry up my prayer to God; tell Him that to see Him is my true life; beg Him to let me die that I may live. On one side, O! my God, I picture to myself a happy life, blest by the affection of dearly beloved friends and relatives—in short, the highest possible earthly bliss; on the other, I see a long painful sickness, and at the end of it, Thee, my God, the joy of going to Thee! and I choose the better part. Wilt Thou not say of me as Thou didst of Mary: 'It shall not be taken away from her.'"

"April, 1836.—I know my own weakness, but more than ever I come to Thee. It is no self-deceit, is it, my God, to think I love Thee? Accept my love and the desire I have to belong to Thee in this world, or if I must tread a more difficult path, if I may not be exclusively consecrated to Thy service, then guard and protect the weakest of all Thy weak creatures! My God, I have a longing for Thy Churches, and to hear Thy Name spoken of. I long for Thy love. Give me an immense charity; take and purify my heart, and make it love Thee, and keep it near to Thyself. How can I seclude myself? Let my lips speak, let my hands move for this tiresome word, but let my heart cleave to Thee, and all my outward actions be gentle and patient, as well as that heart which I beseech Thee to sanctify. Preserve it from vanity and pride; make it humble, and teach it to love Thee. O, my God, only grant me this!"

"VENICE, April 5th, 1836.

"What joys there are, my God, for those who love Thee! They find Thee everywhere; Thou never betrayest or forsakest them, and when with one hand Thou dost afflict, with the other Thou givest comfort. Our trials become joys, for when we love we long to suffer. Thy Churches are like homes to me. I draw a deep breath of grateful happiness when I enter them. I love Thee and I love all mankind, but give me a yet more ardent charity. I felt a ray of it fall on my heart this morning, during the ceremony of the blessing of the ships; as I looked at that immense multitude, a tender affection for all those human beings, and for all mankind, seemed to fill my soul. I prayed for them all, and it seemed to me as if I would have willingly suffered and died for each one of them in particular. It is very seldom that I feel, to this degree, a real fraternal affection for the whole human race. It is a grace, for every good thing comes from Thee, my God! Increase in me this feeling, and let me never ascribe my good thoughts to myself. Give me a true humility, and accept the earnest desire I have, never to let pride or vanity swell my heart."

(Here ends the portion of Eugénie's Journal, which Alexandrine saw at Venice. The subsequent pages were copied, at a later period, from various note books, in which she continued to write her thoughts during that year 1836.)

"My God, Thou dost justly call Thyself 'the life,' and say that Thou givest life to those who ask for it. Yesterday, my love was cold. I prayed without feeling; and a lifeless prayer is worse than death, so I sought Thee, that it might live again. This morning, whilst the priest was giving me absolution, it was as if fire had descended into my cold heart. Tears came into my eyes, and I was happy. What must be the love of Angels, the love of Saints, the love of Heaven, since the love I feel, which can be only the mere shadow of a shade of Thy Divine love fills my soul, and burns in my heart during those short moments when Thou vouchsafest to visit me in a way, which, if it were to last, must kill me. I can understand that an excess of love should end life when a person has reached that state where nothing can draw him away from contemplation and adoration. They are too near Thee to remain on earth! They become angels, and die; this has happened to some Saints."

"Venice, April 9th, 1836.

"I cannot help weeping when I think that I shall return to the world, that I shall lose the recollection of this time of holy fervor; that I may be again what I was before, that I may forget my God, and offend Him. O! my Guardian Angel! my beloved Angel! who art beside me at this moment, and who beholdest my tears, present them, I beseech thee, to God, implore Him to accept them, and to send me in return help and strength, and consolation, when I shall be cold, distracted, and in danger of forgetting Him."

"Venice, April 10th, 1836.

"To-morrow we leave Venice! Sad as this time has been to us, I nevertheless feel a sort of regret at leaving this place as if I was parting with some one I loved. This is always the case with me when I have enjoyed anywhere great religious consolations. It seems to me as if by changing my abode my feelings might also change. Alas, this is so often the case with mè that I have reason to apprehend it. I am so easily distracted. Here it seemed to me so easy to love God. Each Church, as I look at it even from a distance, reminds me of happy moments; there is nothing gloomy to those who love God. The heart is too full of hope and trust to admit gloom. And so, in spite of our fears and our grief for Albert, I do not carry away a painful impression of Venice. I never anywhere prayed so ardently for him as here. It seemed to me as if God always heard those prayers, and now I am going. Thanks be to Thee, my God, for all the fervent love, the thoughts of Heaven, the distaste of this world I have been blest with here; do not abandon me, I know too well my own weakness. The least thing will draw me aside from that blessed path which I have been lately treading; perhaps Thou wilt permit this to happen as a punishment for my proud thoughts. Every trial Thou sendest me I will bear, not in my own strength, but in that which Thou wilt give me. Let me always love Thee, and let my heart never attach itself to the world. *I will have nothing to say to it.*"

"April 11th, 1836.

"'Serve the Lord with gladness.'

"O! yes, my God, it is with joy, with rapture that I will love Thee, serve Thee, and strive to please Thee in all things! It gives me such delight to go into a Church. This used not to be the case; a change has come over me. What must I then have been if now that I am still so wicked, so miserable, so little well disposed, I am nevertheless improved? We can do nothing of ourselves, no, not even wish to be good. Thank God, he has given me that wish. O! yes, I am certain I wish to love Him with all the ardor of which a human heart is capable, and then to obtain the grace of a more than human love. Our souls must be inflamed by a love like that of the angels before they can draw near to God.

"My dislike to the world increases. What shall I do if I must live in it? Must I devote to it the time I have learnt to turn to account by consecrating it to God? Must I wean myself from Him?

"Well, I can only wait; whatever is to be my fate, God will pity His poor child, and never forsake her. After having made me see and understand, O Lord, that there is nothing worth living for but Thy divine Self; after inspiring me with the holy ambition of knowing no happiness but in Thee, never wilt Thou permit me to be dazzled by the world, and to forget Thee. If riches, if prosperity are to be my portion, Thou wilt preserve me from pride, and keep alive in my heart the will to forsake everything for thy sake. Everywhere I may love Thee, and if it is not to be with the freedom, the tranquillity, and the attachment of a life consecrated to Thee alone, Thy holy will be done. But, in that case, my God, increase in me the spirit of prayer and of perseverance, for the road will be more difficult.

"Shakespeare says that it is happiness not to be born. O no, that is not true, for we must be born in order to know and to love God. But the real happiness is to die."

"Avignon, April 24th, 1836.

"Alexandrine was saying the other day that those who love Heaven have not a strong feeling of love for their own country! O! how I agree with her! I feel a complete indifference to all earthly places. I would readily leave even all those I have most cared about, if I thought that by changing or going from one place to another I should get nearer to God.

"The home of the soul (*la patrie*) is the place where we live and love and would always be, or, if absent from it, where we pine to go. We can have no real home but in Heaven, or if we must choose one on earth we shall find it in God's Churches, in the places where He is worshipped beneath the Cross which reminds us of His sufferings, and in the hearts which sigh for His love.

"I do not care about this earth. I can hardly fix my eyes upon the loveliness with which Thou hast adorned it. When my attention is called to a fine view, in spite of myself I raise my eyes to the skies, more beautiful than everything else, and I forget to admire the earth. I like to gaze on the sky, to fill and to dazzle my eyes with its radiance. There is no sorrow which the sight of the sky would not soothe; for the only sorrow which I could not get over would be to have displeased Thee, my God, and even then I should look up to Heaven, for there alone could I find pardon. My God, be Thou my dream, my Thought, my only Love, my only Home!"

"Aix, April 26th, 1836.

"Heaven! shall I ever be in Heaven? My God, forgive the loving impatience which makes life so irksome. Is it wrong to wish to die when it is that we may see Thee? It is not that I am afraid of trials or sufferings, nor does it proceed from feelings of despondency. But life when not filled with the thought of Thee, seems to me such a folly. Thou readest my heart. If it is wrong to wish to go to Thee, take from me that wish—take it away, O! my God! all I ask is submission and humility."

"April 27, 1836.

"I am afraid I shall live to be a hundred years old. God will punish my presumptuous wish to die by an interminable life—ninety years of waiting, ninety years of liability to sin. Wilt thou condemn me to that, my God? How much harm I may do during that time! And shall I be fit to die at the end of it? I shall never, I know, deserve to go to Thee, but at least the younger I am when I die, the less shall I have widened, by my sins, the distance between my God and me.

"Purgatory is better than life—we are nearer to God in purgatory than on earth. It purifies us for God."

"Paris, May 14th, 1836.

"O, how beautiful this night has been! I watched (by Albert), I prayed, and fervently, too, till morning. My God, I thank Thee, my God, I bless Thee, for Thy great mercy to me. After a day of sad despondency Thou hast renewed my courage, Thou hast made me feel that Thou wilt never forsake me. Once this night my heart was so full that it seemed ready to burst. And yet all the time I was happy, calm, and satisfied. It is sad to return to this wearisome life after forgetting, for a moment, everything but God. Yes, those words are not too strong. All I have felt this night came from God. I am not afraid of being presumptuous in saying so. It is of Thee, not of myself, I think, in the midst of these consolations. I feel no anxiety, and that perfect peace deepens in me the sense of Thy adorable Presence.

"My God, I love Thee! that was the cry of my soul this night. Did the Angels carry up to the foot of Thy Throne those words which I would fain utter and then die? Yes, I would utter them, if I could, with a vehemence which would kill me. I forgot, last night, everything but God, and felt myself raised above this world. But whenever I returned to Albert, there also I was calm and happy.

"I am just come from Church; I did not hear Mass, and did not open my book, but it did not signify. The sight of those young communicants gave me so many sweet thoughts. I had, as at Venice, a feeling of great charity and real love for all my fellow creatures, but especially for those children so blessed by God to-day. If I could have been told that by suffering or dying for the least of these little ones, I should preserve him from sin, or save him from offending God, I should not have hesitated to do so. The thought of any one *never* offending God makes my heart beat with joy. O! if by dying a thousand times over I could destroy sin in the hearts of all men, God knows I would do it. May He increase and confirm in me this desire, that charity which I so ardently wish to possess. My God! bless these children, bless them with the remembrance of this happy day, in which they have received Thee for the first time. How they hate sin at this moment, what promises they make never to offend Thee! Oh! let these holy thoughts ever dwell in their souls, and preserve them from the only dreadful evil, sin, and make me again, my God, what I was on the day of my First Communion, and my heart as simple and pure as the hearts of these pious little children."

"Paris, May 20th, 1836.

"Yesterday and to-day I have been frivolous. I thought of my dress, I looked at myself in the glass, and though I certainly did not think myself pretty, I did all I could to improve my appearance. In proportion as those foolish ideas passed through my mind, God's grace seems to forsake my soul, and a painful indifference to harden my heart. My vanity gets the better of me on every occasion. Yesterday, M—— said I had a fine voice, which flattered me exceedingly, and, like a fool, I took great pleasure in singing before him. My God, take away from me a voice which is a constant temptation to vanity! I am not pretty enough to care much for compliments about my looks, as I do not, in general, believe them; I am on my guard against their effect, but I cannot help knowing that I have a good voice, and when I sing before peoplè I am aware that they think so. I sometimes quite hate that voice of mine, and wish to lose it, as it is not to be employed for God's service alone. It is a gift of His: I make a bad use of it, and should be glad if He took it away. . . . . . . I feel now that if I was religious, and heard nothing of the world, I should not regret it. But if thrown into the midst of it with all my miseries and my weaknesses, who knows that I shall not give myself up to it with an ardor proportionate to all the hatred I now have for it. Oh! for a convent, a convent! Some place free from temptation, where I could go and assuage this great desire for love and prayer; where I would love only God; serve only God; and, ah! I must not forget it, obey only God! Let me then not murmur, not rebel. Thy will be done, my God! But if I am not unworthy of that blessed peace, grant me this blessing if it must be otherwise. Still I will adore and thank Thee; all that Thou sendest is to be welcomed."

"Paris, May 29th, 1836. Trinity Sunday.

The day on which Alexandrine was received into the Church.

"O! Lord, how to speak of this day, how to thank Thee for its graces, I know not. Thy sweet, dear little lamb has been gathered into the fold. Vouchsafe to cherish and to comfort her, and, in return for her long years of banishment, make her entrance into her true home a most joyful one. Bless her with Thy best gifts, and if, in Thy great love, Thou wilt send her sufferings, give her that boundless love for Thee alone, which will make her bear everything that comes from Thy adorable Hand.

"Angels of God, watch over her—surround her. Let her peace be deep, and her soul serene!"

"Paris, June 18th, 1836.

"I think I have discovered in myself a kind of indifference, which is not very unlike insensibility. I am not sure that to care as little as I do for the things of this world may not, after all, indicate some amount of heartlessness. I have also thought that I have an unsatisfactory sort of fervor that everything with me goes by fits and starts. At one moment I love the world, and I forget God; at another time I give way to an amount or excess of fervor, and while it lasts I should be ready to accuse even Saints of coldness. All this is not real devotion. Shall I never possess a firm and steady piety? I am still so deficient in it. My heart and my mind are both sad to-night. I have thought so much, and about so many opposite things. My head is confused. Have I offended Thee, my God, so much that Thou wilt no longer console me?

"Vouchsafe to make me feel that at the bottom of my soul I love Thee, and then this sadness will be changed into an immense joy. Did I deceive myself when I thought I loved Thee? when I longed for Thy love? And this complete submission of Thy will, which it seems to me I feel, is that a deception also? Is everything in me false? What is it all, my God, and what am I myself?"

"Paris, June 19, 1836.

"I am sent for to sing. I have always an involuntary wish to please. Vanity must certainly be of all the bad tendencies of the human heart the most difficult to eradicate. What a deplorable weakness it is! I have a deceitful mind and a weak heart. What sort of a person must I be then? Well, such as I am, my God, I give myself to Thee, with all my wretched pride and vanity. It is not a costly offering I make Thee, but where shall weakness fly if not there where strength is found—where everything is forgiven, everything purified, and evil turned into good. Men would not tolerate my wretched weaknesses; men are very severe; but God, God looks tenderly on our imperfections if we will only suffer Him to forgive us, for it is only when the obstinacy of our will rejects His pardon, that it is refused; and indeed *refused* is not the word, God never *refuses.* It is we who will not ask. He *never, never* rejects. Oh! how wide, how full of hope, joy, and consolation, is that thought! My God, I bless, adore, and glorify Thy Name! Thou art the joy of my soul!"

The following letter ought not to be omitted in this record.

"*M. de Montalembert's Letter after my Mother's Death.*

"Valenciennes, November 24th, 1848.

"It was just as I was leaving Trélon and my family, to return to the noise and confusion of

Paris and the National Assembly, that I received your dear husband's letter, and the news of your last affliction. Shall I own that even whilst sympathising with your grief, I could not help feeling that holy joy which diffuses itself like some Heavenly perfume in the soul, when we think of the sufferings and death of the righteous. Oh! certainly, I understand your anguish, and I pity you who are condemned to outlive so many holy souls, once your companions in this pilgrimage, but who have now left you behind to mourn their loss and envy their lot. But what immense consolation you must have derived from the sight of your Mother's perfectly Christian end, of which Craven has drawn a picture worthy of the subject. I share your consolation as well as your grief; and in the thoughts that both suggest I find a little strength and courage in the midst of the daily annoyances and even dangers of my present life. The happiness of being a Catholic is never so great and intense as in those moments when we see a Christian soul about to leave this world, and setting the seal to the sublime truths professed through life, by a last effort of virtue, by humility, and resignation. More than any one, almost, you have known this blessing in the midst of the reiterated calamities which have befallen your admirable family. The edifying description your husband has given of that death bed where you received your Mother's last blessing has made me feel as if I had been present there. So soon after Alexandrine! Yes, it is very sad, very heartbreaking for you, but you must bear in mind that they were both of them ripe for Heaven. And how beautiful and desirable Heaven appears in presence of all the meanness, disgrace, and calamities which afflict the world, and our poor country in particular.

"How often, in comparing the present crisis with that of 1830, has your image and that of your family risen before me. It was in 1831 that I was, so to speak, aggregated to your family, and since that time you have been all more or less associated with every event and emotion of my life. But death has been merciless! Albert, Eugénie, your Father, Olga, Alexandrine, and your Mother; all successively carried off within such a short time. And this gloomy year, 1848, marked by two such irreparable losses! What a subject for thought, for regret, and for tears; but also what a motive for us, the unhappy survivors, to remain more closely united than ever. I ardently desire that our friendship may always continue. Thank your husband very affectionately for his admirable letter.

"And now farewell, my dear, good, faithful friend. God bless and comfort you! and may He grant us yet to spend some peaceful days together.

"Your devoted brother and friend,

"M."

After having spent some years in the Society of Jesus, Alphonse Ratisbonne left it in order to follow the original vocation to which he had felt himself called at the time of his conversion to Christianity, but which he had then given up out of a desire to make a more absolute act of self-abnegation. That vocation was to devote himself to the conversion and the education of his brethren the Jews.

The following conversation which I had with him on this subject, in 1856, and which I then wrote down in my journal, may perhaps be interesting.

"Paris, September 21st, 1856.

"Alphonse, or rather Father Marie Ratisbonne, has just returned from the Holy Land. I had not seen him for six years, and should scarcely have known him in consequence of the long beard which he wears like all the priests who have been in the East. But his eyes have still that same expression which always struck me from the time of his conversion.

"We talked for a long time of all that had taken place since we had last met. He belonged then to the Society of Jesus, and has since left it. He spoke to me of this resolution, and of what had brought it about in a simple, touching, and persuasive manner, and with a most affectionate and filial reverence for the great order in which the first ten years of his Christian life were spent. He said he should always feel the happy effects of the training he had received whilst preparing for the priestly and apostolic life, but that subsequently the desire to devote himself to the conversion of the Jews had never ceased to pursue him; that he had, at last, determined to leave the Society, and consecrate his life to his brethren, provided the Holy Father, when informed of his resolution, advised him to carry it out.

"It was therefore, with the highest sanction which a Catholic, whether priest or layman, can obtain, that Alphonse Ratisbonne returned to his original vocation. The congregation and works of our Lady of Sion, which his brother began, and to which they now both devote themselves, has extended immensely, and everything seems to show that God's blessing is upon it, that Alphonse Ratisbonne has found his true vocation, and is now occupying his appointed place in the Church of God.

"He has just returned from Jerusalem, and when he speaks of what he felt in the Holy City, his descriptions differ from those even of the most pious travellers. He is not eloquent: he speaks slowly and simply. He does not seem to attend to the choice of his words, but he succeeds in conveying to others the strength of his own convictions. The expression of his eyes; the sound of his voice; his very silence betrays 'that there is that within which passeth show.'

"The holy and touching desire which fills his mind at this moment is the purchase at Jerusalem of the Terrace of Pilate's palace, the actual scene of the 'Ecce Homo,' which is now in the hands of the Turks. He wishes to establish there a house of his order, so that on the same spot where, eighteen hundred years ago, rose the fearful cry, 'Let his Blood fall on us, and on our children!' there should now arise, day and night, prayers of repentance and expiation from the lips of those very children. May God bless this project, and him who conceived it!"

This plan has now been fully carried out.

www.ingramcontent.com/pod-product-compliance
Lightning Source LLC
LaVergne TN
LVHW021304110826
845150LV00003B/472

* 9 7 8 1 4 2 5 5 5 9 5 0 2 *